FOSTER ON EU LAW

FOSTER ON EU LAW

NIGEL FOSTER

Professor of European Law, Buckingham Law School
Formerly, Jean Monnet Professor of European Law,
Cardiff Law School

OXFORD
UNIVERSITY PRESS

OXFORD

UNIVERSITY PRESS

Great Clarendon Street, Oxford OX2 6DP

Oxford University Press is a department of the University of Oxford.
It furthers the University's objective of excellence in research, scholarship,
and education by publishing worldwide in

Oxford New York

Auckland Cape Town Dar es Salaam Hong Kong Karachi
Kuala Lumpur Madrid Melbourne Mexico City Nairobi
New Delhi Shanghai Taipei Toronto

With offices in

Argentina Austria Brazil Chile Czech Republic France Greece
Guatemala Hungary Italy Japan Poland Portugal Singapore
South Korea Switzerland Thailand Turkey Ukraine Vietnam

Oxford is a registered trade mark of Oxford University Press
in the UK and in certain other countries

Published in the United States
by Oxford University Press Inc., New York

British Library Cataloguing in Publication Data

Data available

Library of Congress Cataloging in Publication Data

Data available

Typeset in Adobe Minion and ITC Stone Sans
by RefineCatch Limited, Bungay, Suffolk
Printed in Great Britain
on acid-free paper by
Ashford Colour Press Ltd, Gosport, Hampshire

ISBN 978–0–19–926842–9

3 5 7 9 10 8 6 4 2

To Lynsey and Alexander

All my life I will remember the seconds you were born and will love you equally as long.

Dad

Preface

The preface is where the author writes why he or she has written the book, and provides embarrassing details of the deprivations suffered by him or her and especially his or her family whilst undergoing the self-imposed purgatory of seemingly endless days and nights putting the words on the screen, driven, nay, possessed by the conception that it is for the better good of mankind that the book is written. Sometimes there is an interruption when the spouse produces some children to kiss/chasten/say hello to/say goodbye to. One just finds time to comment, 'my—don't the children look small today'. The reply: 'no, those are your grandchildren, our children left home during an earlier chapter, would you like to play with the grandchildren?' The answer: 'Umm, perhaps later, I just have to finish this chapter'!

There follows thanks for the almost, if not entirely, unending patience of the publisher's staff and in particular the editor in charge or should I say the two or three or four or five editors who have been overseeing the project or counting the missed deadlines (the writing having taken so long, the earlier editors have had time to produce their own dynasty of potential book purchasers).

So, after that first paragraph, will I do something completely different? Nope: it's tradition, and here is my version of it.

I've taught EC and EU law for over 22 years now (and hey! I studied it before both at undergraduate and postgraduate levels!) and from the beginning, I thought there was a need for a manageable single text course book. In 1983 there were very few on the market and there was no credible one-stop shop, now there are a number, however, I think the original premise holds true. Throughout the years, my colleagues and I have failed to recommend wholeheartedly a single text and instead we have jointly recommended a number of texts. So, to a large extent, this is why I thought the market was still there and indeed growing, for a new mid-range textbook. It is my clear belief, backed up by an awful lot of experience, that students want a single accessible book which covers the course and which can be absorbed easily. Obviously, a few will wish to read much more widely—those who have a real interest—and for them a number of books exist and are excellent. Most students though, simply want to pass the exam as well as they can but with the minimum of effort—and I don't blame them—it's perfectly rational behaviour. Who can blame them when most university managements pursue exactly the same policy for the RAE[1]—concentration of effort on securing the best result in the exercise because the result is more important than the

---

[1] The Research Assessment Exercise.

journey, that is, the end justifies the means even if that means diverting resources from teaching to increase research output. Not in my book! This is a student text-book—pure and simple!

I should mention the numbering policy for the Treaties. For the most part, only the present numbers will be used, except where vital to the point, in which case the old numbers will also be mentioned and this is mainly in respect of case law. The main reason not to mention the old numbers is that it will be increasingly necessary to make reference to the new CT articles numbers when discussing reform, and three sets of numbers is simply too much.

The thanks bit:

Thanks to many staff of Oxford University Press who have participated in the conception and production of this book. Over the long period I have taken in writing it, thanks are due to Jane Kavanagh, Claire Brewer, Angela Griffin, Kate Whetter, and Penelope Woolf. Thanks also to Phil Dines in production, and Clare Weaver in marketing for their work on the book. Most of all though, thanks to Sarah Hyland, who together we have developed an excellent working relationship of the best quality and mutual understanding—thanks Sarah, it has been a real pleasure working with you.

Thanks also go to a number of research assistants who have helped keep me up to date with the fast moving events in EU law: Dafydd Nelson, Emily Cartwright, Julija Konarskaja, and Emmanuelle Bertoli.

But most of all my thanks and love go to my family who have (not always) borne the brunt of my self-imposed isolation with good humour and understanding.

Quite rightly this book is dedicated to my two children, Lynsey and Alexander, whom I love with equal passion.

I have tried to state the law accurately up to January 2006; however, it is always possible that I did not get things entirely correct. For errors and omissions, I am solely responsible. I would be grateful to be advised of any errors discovered and also any general comments in respect of coverage, treatment, or any other aspect of the book.

Nigel Foster
Konstanz Germany
January 2006

Outline Contents

Outline Contents

Detailed Contents

PART I INTRODUCTION TO THE INSTITUTIONAL AND PROCEDURAL LAW OF THE EU

PART II INTRODUCTION TO THE SUBSTANTIVE LAW OF THE EU

Alphabetical Table of Cases

Numerical Table of Cases

Court of First Instance

Opinions of the ECJ

Decisions of the European Commission

National Courts Decisions

Table of EU Primary Legislation

Table of EU Secondary Legislation

Decisions

Abbreviations

AG	Advocate General
CAP	Common Agricultural Policy
CCT	Common Customs Tariff
CFI	Court of First Instance
CFSP	Common Foreign and Security Policy
CHEE	Charge(s) having equivalent effect
CMLR	Common Market Law Reports
COR	Committee of the Regions
COREPER	Committee of Permanent Representatives
CT	Constitutional Treaty
EC	European Community/ies
ECA	European Communities Act 1972
ECB	European Central Bank
ECHR	European Convention on Human Rights
ECJ	European Court of Justice
ECR	European Court Reports
ECSC	European Coal and Steel Community Treaty
ECU	European Currency Unit
EDC	European Defence Community
EEA	European Economic Area
EEC	European Economic Community
EESC	European Economic and Social Committee (formally ECOSOC)
EFTA	European Free Trade Association
EIB	European Investment Bank
EMS	European Monetary System
EMU	Economic and Monetary Union
EP	European Parliament
EPC	European Political Community & European Political Cooperation
ERTA	European Road Transport Agreement
ESCB	European System of Central Banks
ESDP	European Security and Defence Policy
EU	European Union
FCC	Federal Constitutional Court
GATT	General Agreement on Tariffs and Trade
IGC	Inter-Governmental Conference

NATO	North Atlantic Treaty Organization
OJ	Official Journal
OMC	Open Method of Coordination
PJCC	Provision on Police and Judicial Cooperation in Criminal Matters
plc	Public Limited Company
QMV	Qualified Majority Voting
SDA	Sex Discrimination Act
SEA	Single European Act
TCN	Third Country National
TEU	Treaty on European Union (Maastricht Treaty)
ToA	Treaty of Amsterdam
UK	United Kingdom
WEU	Western European Union
WTO	World Trade Organization

PART I

INTRODUCTION TO THE INSTITUTIONAL AND PROCEDURAL LAW OF THE EU

PART I: INTRODUCTION TO THE INSTITUTIONAL AND PROCEDURAL LAW OF THE EU

The first 'half' of this book considers the topics which may well be covered in one or two introductory or first year courses in universities according to how the teaching of EU law is organized in your university. The fashion for this can change over the years but if there are introductory courses in the first year, then Part I will be particularly suitable for them with Part II on the substantive law suitable for the second or final year courses on EU law.

Although the Constitutional Treaty has not been ratified by all member states and entered into force, when EU law will be the reality, I have decided to follow fashion and refer to the law of the European Union as EU law even though the vast bulk of the law considered in university EU law courses is actually EC law stemming from the EC Treaty. However, somewhat optimistically in advance of the CT, EU law it is!

The six chapters in Part I set the scene for the understanding of the substantive law in Part II—without Part I, then very many things in Part II will not make much sense. The chapters look at the historical roots of the European Communities as they developed into the present-day European Union. The chapter considers essentially the rationale for the EU, why it was established, and some of the difficulties along that path to the present day and in particular at the end of the chapter a section on the Constitutional Treaty, progress on which was stalled after the electorates in France and Holland rejected it, although Austria and other countries are seeking to revive it during their presidencies. Having established why it was formed, Chapter 2 considers basically what was formed by looking at the institutions set up to run the Communities which further investigates their powers and duties and interaction with each other. Chapter 2 also introduces the Court of Justice and its role and jurisdiction in adjudicating EC law. Chapter 3 then moves on to consider in more detail how the Union is run by looking particularly at the legal system which binds it all together, the various sources and forms of law which make up that legal system, how those laws are made by the institutions dealt with in Chapter 2 and looking at the end of the chapter at newly emergent alternatives to hard law-making. The very dynamic interrelationship of the institutions in the law-making processes is highlighted.

Chapter 4 investigates the multi-faceted relationship with the member states, including the transfer of power and competences to the Union and thus necessarily involves a discussion of the Constitutional basis of the Union. It considers further the division of competences between the Union and the member states and the ways in which the member states have tried to regulate the division and exercise of competences. The chapter then deals with the supremacy aspect of this relationship from both the point of view of the Union as understood by the Court of Justice and from the point of view of a number of the member states.

Chapters 5 and 6 divide between them the procedural law of the Community by considering the jurisdiction of the European Court of Justice and the system of remedies as provided by the Treaty and significantly developed by the Court of Justice. Thus individual remedies are covered as are the various actions against member states and institutions, the details of which can be seen in the full contents list.

The book then turns to substantive law in Part II, an introduction to which is given at the start of Part II.

Whether EU law is studied in two or more courses or all in one course, it can be observed that many of the cases which appear in Part I are ones which have arisen in an action in one of the substantive law topics. For example, *Van Gend en Loos*, which first established direct effects, is a case concerned with customs duties in the common market, *Von Colson*, establishing indirect effects, arises from a sex discrimination case; and *Factortame*, concerned with nationality discrimination, supremacy, and national procedural rules, is one essentially based on the right of establishment from the free movement of persons. EU law and the book abound with many more examples. Studying both parts together very often reinforces the study and understanding of each other.

1

The History and Constitutional Basis of the European Union

1.1 Introduction

Any study of European Union law and its predecessor, European Community law, must be preceded by the study and understanding of the history and development of the Union. Without it, you will be lost. It will not be possible to understand just why the Union, even if the supposed tidying-up by the Constitutional Treaty of 2004 takes place, is and would remain so complex and so strangely constructed. You will not understand why the law-making procedures and forms of law remain so complex, why there are such concepts as 'direct effects' and 'subsidiarity' and why there is a huge body of further reading on such strange subjects as 'comitology'. In any subject, merely learning the rules does not help you understand the purpose for which they were enacted and the reasons which led to them in the first place. This is even more the case with the European Union. Many of the laws, whilst clearly aimed at specific topics such as ensuring free movement of goods or persons or requiring the equality of treatment of different groups or regulating the recognition of a profession in the member states, are a compromise of different perspectives. In the EU, these perspectives arise from different nations, different cultural understandings, different histories and different social and economic backgrounds and systems, hence the Treaties and laws which have been produced under the Treaties are often achieved only as a compromise of these different elements. On their own, the individual rules may not make a great deal of sense; with an understanding of the history and development, hopefully, they might make a lot more sense.

The following chapter tries to set the context and provide an understanding of the historical basis of the Union before looking in detail at the constitutional base for the Union.

A brief mention will be made here in respect of the terms 'European Union' and 'European Community' as their use can be confusing. The term 'European Union' was brought in by the Treaty on European Union (also known and referred to as the Maastricht Treaty) and describes the extension by the member states into additional policies and areas of cooperation. The EU consists of three pillars comprising the existing Communities (the three original treaties), a common foreign and security policy and, following the reorganization by the Treaty of Amsterdam, a third pillar now called Provisions on Judicial and Police cooperation in Criminal Matters. When or if the Treaty establishing a Constitution for Europe comes into force, all three pillars will be merged and it will be correct to refer only to the European Union. At present, most Community law courses and indeed books, whether called EU law or EC law, are not likely to consider the law of the second and third pillars in any depth, if at all. Most courses will study EC law only, as contained in the EC Treaty, and will not consider the parts of the EU outside of the EC Treaty. Furthermore, and these matters will be considered in depth in the forthcoming chapters, EU law, where it exists, is of a different nature from EC law.

1.2 The Motives for European Integration

Even a cursory glance at European history will reveal what a chaotic, despotic, border changing, bone crunching, blood spilling time we have had over the centuries. The *pièce de résistance* of the series of wars, is of course, World War II when some 55 million souls worldwide, but mostly in Europe, lost their lives! There have been centuries of invasions, occupations, and dictatorial rule in most if not all the countries of Europe at some stage. Of course, since World War II, we don't, gas, maim, butcher, torture, or murder people in the previous biblical proportions as before, but even post-World War II, we have seen some pretty nasty regimes imposing their will against peoples and countries in Europe and further conflicts between European nations and peoples. As a result, since 1945, an estimated further 900,000 people have died in Europe, which is incredible, more so because some of these events are not decades in the past but much more recent. In the 1990s the Balkans wars, especially Croatia and Kosovo, became the latest names to be added to the list of European killing fields.[1] With this firmly in mind, it should come as no surprise that the strong reaction after World War II to this death and destruction was a very important and motivating factor in the moves to create a more peaceful and stable European environment in which countries can develop and prosper without resorting to the obliteration or subjugation of others. It is too easy, in this period of relative peace and stability now, to understate this motive. Of course, there are reasons underlying the violence, and featuring large,

---

[1] For the full catalogue of such events, refer to the chilling *Historical Atlas of the 20th Century: Wars, Massacres and Atrocities of the Twentieth Century*: http://users.erols.com/mwhite28/war–1900.htm.

as Ward clearly sets out in the first two pages of his critical introduction to EU law, is the desire to make Europe one, to homogenize Europe, to unify Europe, and in pursuit of this goal, for one country or ethnic group to impose their culture or religion or government on others. Unfortunately, most of these attempts have not been peaceful nor voluntarily received on the part of the subjects on the receiving end of such unwelcome attention and over the ages, these attempts have affected the majority of the citizens of Europe. Generally the attempts to unite, from the Romans to World War II, have led to wholesale loss of life, even attempted genocide and that ghastly modern euphemism for the same: 'ethnic cleansing'! It is therefore this bleak but simple and understandable backdrop which led to an increased desire to do something to stop the cycle of death and destruction. Whilst there had been ideas and discussions to unite European nations over the centuries, particularly following World War I, it was only after WWII, that these desires and expressions found substantive fruition.

1.3 The Founding of the European Communities

The period following World War II saw a number of moves towards the integration of European nation states. Political and economic cooperation and development between nations was regarded as crucial to replace the economic competition which was viewed as a major factor in the outbreak of wars between European nation states. Some of these moves were taking place within a worldwide effort for greater political cooperation between nation states, the most notable being the establishment of United Nations in 1945 and the Council of Europe in 1949. The Council of Europe must not be confused with the EU institutions, the Council of Ministers and the European Council, despite similarity of name. The most notable achievement of the Council of Europe is the establishment of the European Convention for the Protection of Human Rights Fundamental and its enforcement machinery, notably the European Court of Human Rights, based in Strasbourg.

There were also inherently economically motivated steps towards international cooperation which resulted in the establishment of such organizations as the International Monetary Fund (IMF), the General Agreement on Tariffs and Trade (GATT) and, most notably, the Marshall Plan which funded the establishment of the Organization for European Economic Corporation (OEEC), designed initially to finance the post-war reconstruction of Europe. When we come to the European Communities, which were the forerunners of the European Union we have today, the purposes are not so distinctly discernable. As remains the case today, even before the foundation of the Communities, there was a conflict of opinion between those who wished to see

European integration take the form of a much more involved model, such as a federal model, and those who wished merely to see a purely economic form of integration, such as a free-trade area. The first steps were, predictably, a modest compromise of the political, economic, and social desires of various parties. The scene was set by the address by Winston Churchill at the University of Zürich in September 1946, and his call to build 'a kind of United States of Europe' and in particular, for the time, the brave call for a partnership between France and Germany. However, even within that speech, Churchill and Britain did not envisage a role as a key participant and instead envisaged Britain outside of any general European integration, alongside the USA and Russia observing and assisting a European state to rise from the ashes of the destruction of World War II.

At the time, a further and developing factor, which considerably influenced the desire on the part of the European nations to cooperate, was the deteriorating relations between the former Allied powers. It was not long after the Americans, British, and the Russians had met victoriously in the streets of Berlin in 1945, that the understandings between those countries broke down and they became increasingly suspicious of each other. Winston Churchill described in March 1946 in Fulton Missouri the situation of increasing Soviet influence and control over Eastern Europe, in a phrase that was taken up generally, as a kind of 'iron curtain'[2] which had descended between Western and Eastern Europe. The general situation came to be described as the 'Cold War' and lasted in lesser and greater states of tension until the collapse of Communism in Europe in 1989–90. It became all the more real when the prospect of reuniting the divided eastern and western occupied zones of Germany in the late 1940s disappeared and, instead, the two separated states of West and East Germany were established. With this increased fear of the domination of Europe by the Soviet Union and possible expansion, and Soviet influence and control over the countries of Western Europe, the tension mounted in the late 1940s and throughout the 1950s. At its worst, in the 1960s, the Cold War threatened the nuclear annihilation of the opposing parties. It thus became increasingly important that the countries of Western Europe integrate amongst themselves to form a bulwark against further Soviet expansion. The Cold War was thus a clear and real catalyst for Western European integration.

1.3.1 The Schuman Plan (1950)

The climate was certainly ready for a greater form of integration in Europe and the first direct impetus for the Communities came in the form of the plan proposed in

---

[2] 'From Stettin in the Baltic to Trieste in the Adriatic, an iron curtain has descended across the Continent': http://history1900s.about.com/library/weekly/990824a.htm.

May 1950 by the French Foreign Minister, Robert Schuman, in conjunction with the research and plans of Jean Monnet, a French Government official, to link the French and German Coal and Steel industries. These industries would be taken out of the hands of the nation states and put under the control of a supranational body. This would not only help economic recovery but also remove the disastrous competition between the two states. It was aimed to make future war not only unthinkable but also materially impossible because it put the control over coal and steel production, vital then for the production of armaments and thus the capability of waging war, in the hands of a supranational authority and not the individual member states. The plan was deliberately left open for other European countries to join in its discussions. The UK though, was reluctant to involve itself, even in the negotiations. The plan was readily accepted by Germany under Chancellor Adenauer and Belgium, The Netherlands, and Luxembourg. The Benelux nations who had already moved ahead with their customs union, also saw the benefits to be gained from membership and this form of integration. Italy also considered it to be in its economic interest to join and perhaps more importantly, as a defence against communist takeover. So six nations went ahead to sign the European Coal and Steel Community Treaty (ECSC) in Paris in 1951 and which entered into force on 1 January 1952. This first form of integration was thus both politically and economically motivated. It was also a mix of both intergovernmental and supranational integration, (considered below), as the institutions set up included both the High Authority (to become the European Commission), a supranational body, and the Council of Ministers from the member states. Whilst the Community established did not fulfil the wishes of Monnet who was a federalist, he was appointed the first President of the High Authority and the degree of integration it achieved was, without any doubt, a very important and indispensable first step from which further integration could follow. Indeed, it was assumed by some, the so-called neo-functionalists, that further integration would be inevitable.[3] It was not long before the next proposals for greater integration were put forward.

1.3.2 The Proposed European Defence Community and European Political Community

The Schuman Plan which formed the basis of the ECSC was not the only proposal for integration being discussed and negotiated at the time. Monnet put forward a proposal (the Pleven Plan) for a European Defence Community (EDC) in 1952. In addition, because it was argued to be politically and practically necessary, in support of that, a European Political Community (EPC) was also proposed in 1953, to provide

---

[3] This will be considered at 1.5.1 below.

the overseeing of political control and foreign policy for the EDC. The proposals and the negotiations proved to be complex and drawn out because they were surrounded by other political considerations such as the expansion of communism in South East Asia and fears in respect of the rearmament of West Germany. Both of these proposals, with hindsight, were far too ambitious for the time and thus very premature. They faced opposition from both outside the ECSC, the UK in particular, and within the Community, most notably and fundamentally, France, who after some prevarication failed to ratify the EDC in the National Assembly. Even today the prospect of a common European Army and political union is far too radical; then it was just unrealistic. Since 1955, though, there has been a limited defence arrangement with the Western European Union (WEU) which was established to fill the vacuum of the collapsed EDC. The WEU has now, ironically, been taken under EU auspices by the Treaty of European Union (1992) and works closely with NATO. The Nice Treaty makes formal reference to the WEU in Article 17 and, prompted by the Balkans wars in the 1990s, movement was made towards establishing an effective European Security and Defence Policy (ESDP) which was formally set up in 1999 and led to the establishment, not long afterwards, of the EU Rapid Reaction Force.

1.3.3 Progress Nevertheless

The Constitutional Treaty if it enters into force will establish a framework for a common defence policy whilst confirming the commitments of those EU member states who are members of NATO, to that organization (see Art 1–41).

It might have been thought that the unfortunate failure to agree the EDC would have put paid to any further attempts at European integration and it was without a doubt a blow to the European federalists, however, rather than jeopardize any such attempts, it appeared to strengthen the resolve of some of the original six member states to take matters further. Once again, Jean Monnet was centrally involved. He had resigned as President of the ECSC High Authority in order to promote European integration.[4] Working in particular with the Benelux nations, it was proposed that rather than leave the integration to two industries, the nations should integrate the whole of their economies and following the Messina Intergovernmental Conference in 1955, the Spaak Report (named after the Belgium Prime Minister) was prepared to consider the establishment of a Economic Community and an Atomic Energy Community for energy and the peaceful use of nuclear power. There were also additional external catalysts for such further moves including the Algerian war of independence, the Soviet suppression of the 1956 Hungarian Uprising and the Suez

---

[4] As the founder and leading member of the Action Committee for the United States of Europe.

Canal climb-down,[5] which served to highlight the real politics at play in the world in the 1950s and the precarious position of individual nation states in Europe, who no longer wielded the influence that they did prior to the World War II. All of this assisted in bringing the European Treaty negotiations to a much quicker and successful conclusion. Thus, in 1957, the Treaties of Rome were agreed by the same six nations establishing the European Economic Community (EEC) and the European Atomic Energy Community (EURATOM).

At first, all three Communities each had their own institutions but a shared a Court of Justice. The separate institutions were merged under the Treaty establishing a single Council and a single Commission of the European Communities (the Merger Treaty) in 1965, but which entered into force in 1967, the provisions of which have been incorporated into the present treaties. Due to the range of subject matters and policies covered, the EEC Treaty was the most important. The ECSC Treaty, established for 50 years only, expired in 2002 and the EC Treaty then took over the obligations and responsibilities arising under the ECSC Treaty. These will be further assumed by the Constitutional Treaty if it enters into force.

1.4 The Relationship of the UK with the European Communities

1.4.1 The Early Relationship (to the 1970s)

As noted above, in the late 1940s and early 1950s, the UK was also initially keen to see a united Europe but without its direct participation. It had at the time a historical legacy which involved quite different economic and social ties, including the Empire and Commonwealth and the Atlantic alliance, both of which featured strongly in the recently won World War II. These ties of security and common language are often overlooked but played no small part in the attitude of Britain to European integration in the immediate post-war years. Britain also regarded its status as remaining a world power whose sovereignty and independence could not be compromised by membership of such an organization. As well as the offer being extended to participate in the ECSC negotiations, Britain was also invited to participate in the EEC and EURATOM negotiations. However, it played no significant or indeed useful part and withdrew

---

[5] This was the joint invasion by British and French forces to regain control of the Suez Canal after it had been forcibly nationalized by President Nassar of Egypt. Britain and France were forced to give way in the face of growing world and US pressure.

after minimal participation. Instead, with Austria, Switzerland, and other nations, the UK embarked on what might have seemed a potentially wrecking path of establishing the European Free Trade Association (EFTA) in 1958, which involved no supranational or political aims and was intended merely to set up a free trade area for goods. It was not long, however, before a change of heart and policy took place, in what could be regarded as a tacit admission of error. Within months of the entry into force of the EEC Treaty, the Macmillan *Conservative* Government led the UK application for associate membership and very shortly after that, on 9 August 1961, the UK application for full membership. The reasons for previously not joining had been undermined. Amongst the changes were the demise of the UK's previous world power status, the fact that direct links with most of the world had been weakened by the economic demise of the UK, the Suez climb-down and the continuing conversion of the Empire into a Commonwealth of independent states. Trade patterns were also shifting towards Europe and the Atlantic alliance was less prominent and pointedly so after the disagreement as to how to handle the Suez crisis. More than anything, Britain had observed the much faster economic progress made by the six and this provoked the desire for membership. Whether Britain was ever interested in the entire Community package is not clear. Britain had now, however, to bargain from the outside and its applications both for associate and full membership were steadfastly and consistently rejected by Charles de Gaulle, the French President, as was the 1967 application by the Wilson *Labour* Government. De Gaulle's opposition to the potentially distorting influence of the UK in the Community was clearly expressed at the time.

1.4.2 From Rejection to Acceptance? (1970s to date)

In 1970, following the resignation and withdrawal from politics of de Gaulle in France, the entry application by the Conservative Prime Minister Edward Heath was successful. Thus, the UK joined in 1973, as did Ireland and Denmark, mainly because of their trade dependency with the UK. However, soon afterwards, the UK sought to renegotiate entry terms and held a referendum on membership. The timing of the 1973 entry was in fact unfortunate. Instead of the UK being able to participate equally in the post-war boom and recovery, the world economy and that of Europe had received a severe set back and Britain, along with the rest of the Western world, became the hostage of massive oil price increases. Instead of a period of economic prosperity, the 1970s witnessed high inflation and economic stagnation (sometimes termed 'stagflation'). To aggravate matters still further, the high and arguably inequitable level of the British budget contribution became the focus of attention. It did not take long before disquiet with the terms of entry arose. It seems that we paid too high a price to join the club and that the budget wrangles that both then and in the future were to polarize opinion both in Europe and the UK were inevitable. Given the pattern of trade in the UK which initially favoured imports from Commonwealth non-EEC countries, coupled with having to pay the higher EEC Common Agricultural Policy (CAP) regulated food prices, meant that British contributions were extremely high and simply added to then severe UK domestic economic problems.

To recap for a moment, in the context of the UK entry, the Community was spawned in the aftermath of World War II. For membership, the original states exchanged some sovereignty and monetary contribution for security, the stability of democratic nationhood and economic progress. It is argued, Britain did not need the first two and the third proved illusory in the 1970s and 1980s. Hence, when in 1974, a new Government was elected in the UK, a renegotiation of the terms of entry was started. This was climaxed by the clear cut (over 67 per cent in favour) approval of the British public in the then unprecedented 1975 referendum which not only *post-facto* approved membership but also the renegotiated terms and specifically the revised budget contributions. However, it was only a partial cure for the level of contributions, and this dispute was later reopened by the UK Prime Minister, Margaret Thatcher. Its effect was, however, to cast the UK firmly in the role of the reluctant partner and as a troublemaker in Europe. Viewed politically the UK had decided to cast its lot with the EC, aware that some loss of sovereignty was involved and that a potentially high monetary contribution was required. One side of the bargain was not, as with other member states, the security of nationhood or the stamp of approval and stability of the democratic political system that membership gave. The fact that the UK had won the war and had centuries of stability meant that these were so well secured in the UK that the European Communities could never seriously be considered for these advantages, or to keep the peace, which Britain had secured for itself by victory in the last war, albeit with considerable help. The other side of the bargain, was to share in the spoils of European economic progress. Given the changing circumstances, this proved to be a dubious economic gain. No wonder that there was a feeling by some, that still remains, that membership had sold Britain short.

In the 1980s the first part of the decade was occupied with further wrangles over the British budget contribution and reluctance to reform the Communities which hindered progress on other matters in the Community and did not engender relaxed relations with Britain's partners in the Community. It was surprising that the then Conservative Prime Minister, Mrs Thatcher signed the Single European Act (SEA) which saw the first major reform of the original Treaties, because of the steps contained within it for further integration and some democratization of the Communities. Indeed, it was regarded later as an error by Mrs Thatcher,[6] who was most probably

---

[6] See Ward, op. cit. p. 108.

lured into agreeing to the SEA by the promise of the liberalized trade advantages of the single market, which will be considered below.

The budget contributions were settled again in 1984, only to be questioned again in the 1990s and yet again in 2002, 2004, and 2005. During the negotiations for the second major reform of the Communities and in particular, monetary Union, following which the Treaty of European Union in Maastricht (and also known and referred to as the Maastricht Treaty) was painfully agreed, Britain demonstrated once again just how out of line it was with its other partners. Part of the agreement reached, was that the UK should opt out of the Social Policy Chapter whereas all other member states agreed to this. The Treaty on European Union (TEU) agreed at Maastricht also provided a process and timetable for moving towards economic and monetary union. The UK negotiated another opt-out here in respect of the decision of whether to join the final stage, in which a single currency would be established. Exacerbating the poor relationship with the other European partners was the fact that John Major's *Conservative* Government (1992–7) was so clearly and publicly split on the issue of Europe, that almost any decision which was needed on the Communities was one which was close to impossible to achieve. Hence the idea that any progress could be made by all of the then twelve member states of the Communities was an unrealistic idea. Thankfully, that abysmal state of affairs did not continue beyond 1997. The change of Government in the United Kingdom on the 1 May 1997 also saw an immediate change in the relationship with Europe. Whether this has lasted or will last for any sensible timescale remains to be judged. However in 1997, whilst the delayed negotiations for the TEU were still ongoing, the new Labour Government announced its intention to sign up to the social chapter, which was carried through soon afterwards, and generally to take a more positive participatory role in Europe. The UK opposition to monetary union seemed to have been removed, at least in principle, although nine years on, the uncertainty as to when the UK will actually join, continues.

Finally, the treaty negotiations for the Amsterdam and Nice Treaties, the Convention and IGC for the Constitution for Europe, the expansion to twenty-five states in 2004 and the changing political relationships between the leading EU states (notably France, Germany and the UK) have led to a far more complex Union now than previously. Inevitably in a European Union which now has a membership of twenty-five states, each individual state will have less prominence. However, France, Germany and the UK remain the largest and most economically powerful three states in the Union, each of them can still play a leading role in EU affairs, both positive and negative. The UK's attitude remains somewhat ambivalent, expressing on the one hand to be at the heart of Europe and on the other, showing a reluctance to commit as deeply as other member states, notably with the Euro. The Labour Government has also showed that it has to play a political defence game to resist too much integration in Europe, largely because of a predominantly Eurosceptic British Press and a British public consistently starved of the true facts or any sensible information about the European Union.

It can only be hoped that if there is a UK referendum on the Constitutional Treaty it will provide the UK electorate with an informed opportunity to express their view and may help decide for the next generation on which side of the fence the UK wants to be.

1.5 The Basic Objectives and Nature of the Communities

Whilst the formal aims of the Communities can readily be seen by looking at the preambles to the treaties, there is a deeper underlying debate about the overall goal of the Communities. The stated general aims include the creation of the common market which was to be achieved by abolishing obstacles to the freedom of movement of all the factors of production, namely goods, workers, providers of services, and capital. The Treaty also provided for the abolition of customs duties between the member states and the application of a common customs tariff to imports from third countries. There were to be common policies in the spheres of agriculture and transport and a system ensuring that competition in the common market is not distorted by the activities of cartels or market monopolists. An embryonic social policy and regional policy also appeared. Apart from these formally set out objectives, there has been a debate older than the Communities themselves as to whether there was a grand or master plan for the integration of Europe. Even if it were not originally clear that the 'pooling of resources', as then termed, by a transfer of sovereign powers meant that the Communities took over in certain agreed areas, this was made clear not long afterwards by the European Court of Justice in its landmark decisions in *Van Gend en Loos* and *Costa v ENEL*.[7] The debate has continued as to whether the Communities were supposed to integrate only in the specific areas as originally set out in the ECSC and the then EEC Treaty and arguably confined largely to free trade, or whether something more dynamic was intended. Many terms have been used to describe these developments. It was originally considered that because there was success in certain policies this would automatically lead to a spillover from one area to another to lead to increasing integration. This is termed 'functional integration' or 'neofunctionalism'. Others have described this as creeping federalism. In fact, it was considered that in order for the original policies to work properly there had to be continuing integration, otherwise the whole project would probably first stagnate and then roll backwards to

---

[7] This will be fully explored in Chapter 4.

collapse. Thus, sector by sector integration and the process of European union was regarded as an inexorable process. For example, the setting of common trade tariffs and the establishment of the common market for the free circulation of goods would require and lead to exchange rates being stabilized to ensure that production factors and costs in the member states were broadly equal. This in turn requires monetary union to be established to ensure exchange rates do not drift apart and this requires full economic union to be achieved so that the value of different components of the common currency is not changed by different economic and fiscal policies in different countries. Obviously then the fiscal policies must be integrated and this economic integration would require that the political integration would have to follow in order to provide stable and consistent policy control over the economic conditions applying in the Community. According to this view, federalism, in some form, would thus seem to be the probable outcome of this process. Such an outcome, is a vehemently contested one.

Before discussing this further, a number of other terms which will be used need to be defined. A free trade area involves the removal of all customs and tariffs between members but is usually regulated by the unanimous agreement of all members. A customs union involves a free internal area and a common policy on tariffs of all the member states and third party states. A common market includes the above plus the free movement of all factors of production and an economic union also includes the establishment of a common economic policy and fiscal policy.

1.5.1 Intergovernmentalism, Supranationalism, and Federalism

These terms are employed to describe the form of integration undertaken by the Communities. Intergovernmentalism is the normal way in which international organizations work, whose decisions require unanimity and are rarely enforceable and if so only between the signatory states and not the citizens of those states. Supranationalism describes the fact that the decision-making is made at a new and higher level than that of the member states themselves and that such decisions replace or override national rules. The term 'federalism' itself is a rather flexible term in that it can refer to a fairly wide band of integration models but essentially for the purposes of this discussion would mean that there would also be a form of political integration whereby the member states would transfer sovereign powers to the federation which would control the activities of the members from the centre. There are plenty of examples of states set up on a federal basis in the world, including the USA, Germany, Switzerland, Canada, Australia, Switzerland, and Belgium. Certain local issues are still regulated by the constituent states such as education, culture, and land management but most economic and political power is transferred to the centre including, most notably, defence and trade. Is this the goal of European integration? Only a few persons have argued openly for this degree of integration although some of the founding fathers of the Community, Monnet, Schuman, and Spaak had expected that sector by sector functional integration would lead slowly to ever greater degrees of federalism. It is also arguable that an agenda of federalism has been buried under the euphemism ' "a closer", or "ever closer" Union' and to make the progress to the ultimate destination of the Communities more acceptable these terms have been used in the EEC Treaty (which became the EC Treaty in 1993) and in the TEU. It is though unclear and arguably deliberately so, whether they refer to federalism or something short of that. The original plans put forward by Monnet for the ECSC may have been much more federal in nature and openly so, particularly as the Community was to be governed by a supranational High Authority only, but it was at the insistence of the member states, that the original ECSC was also governed by a Council of Ministers, clearly intergovernmental, and by a parliamentary assembly. This mixed model was followed in both the EURATOM and EEC Treaties. Therefore, while the Communities and some of its institutions do operate on the supranational level, it does not signify an inevitable move to federalism. Only as future developments unravel, will its final destination become clearer.

The Constitutional Treaty which is subject to a reconsideration by the member states across Europe can be seen either as a tidying up exercise of the existing levels of commitment of integration or a further step itself in the direction of a federal Europe. What is clear, is that there should be plenty of discussion of this in the immediate and medium term future as national decisions and referenda across the EU are being held on the Constitutional Treaty. The debate may perhaps elevate to the level of discussing where we think the EU should be in the years to come.[8]

1.5.2 Progress to a Federal Europe?

Despite the failure of the EDC, the European Coal and Steel Community remained successful and was joined in 1957 by the other two communities. EURATOM was not particularly successful, as it was originally designed under the assumption that there would be extreme difficulty is in the energy market but which proved not to be the case as the world energy market stabilized itself considerably in the late 1950s. The EEC proved immediately to be a success under the leadership of the first Commission President, the German Walter Hallstein and it was far more political in outlook, despite the contrary view of de Gaulle, as to how the Communities should be organized and governed. It is particularly noteworthy in view of the failure of the original

---

[8] And pigs may indeed sprout wings and fly!

member states to agree on the EDC and EPC. The success of the EEC seemed to give support to the neofunctionalist view that success in one sector would lead inevitably to success in other sectors and assist the process of European integration. Indeed, the success in the area of the common customs tariff appeared to work as envisaged by the neofunctionalists/federalists and lead to spillover into other areas and in particular to create further pressure for the reform of the Common Agricultural Policy (CAP). This form of functionalism was adopted deliberately by the High Authority and the EEC Commission as the way to achieve further progress with European integration and these bodies put forward a linked package deal of reforms for the Communities. However, such reforms were quickly thwarted by a boycott of the Community institutions by de Gaulle in 1965,[9] and his savage defence of state nationalism. Previous signs of the stance to be adopted by de Gaulle had already been seen by his unilateral veto of British entry to the Communities in 1963, despite the fact that entry negotiations had been ongoing for two years. Since those days and despite periods of stagnation, the Communities have moved on with numerous Treaty revisions and most recently the member states agreement but not ratification of a Constitutional Treaty for Europe. These developments will be considered in the following sections and returned to at the end of the chapter in respect of the Constitutional Treaty.

1.6 The Widening and Deepening of the Communities and Union

This section concerns the parallel developments of the Communities by which they have increased not only in terms of the number of member states and external interfaces with the outside world but also the extent to which the member states have gone in integrating economically, socially, and politically within the Communities and now Union.

   In 1969 a fresh start for the Communities appeared to take place. Whilst in itself it did not lead to massive nor immediate change, it did allow for a new agenda for change to be constructed. As much as anything, it was allowed to happen because of the resignation of de Gaulle as French President and his disappearance from the European political scene. The member states held a summit in the Hague in 1969, to try to get the Communities moving again after the setbacks they had suffered. Notable were the 1963 and 1965 crises caused by de Gaulle, the former being the first of the rejections of UK membership and the latter, the boycott of the European Institutions.

---

[9] This is further considered below in Section 1.6.6.2 and Chapter 2, Section 2.4.3.4.

The Hague Summit set as its goals the completion, widening and deepening of the Communities. Although, the completion of the common market, which should have been fully achieved by 1969, took considerably longer and actually had to wait until 1992, the widening and deepening of the Communities were processes which were always going to be ongoing. The terms, 'widening' and 'deepening', are the ones which were used then and still survive in Community jargon and describe the development of the Communities in two ways.

Widening refers primarily to the process of the expansion of the Communities to include new member states but can also apply to the extension of the Community into new policy areas and in developing new sectors for integration. Deepening refers to the degree of integration which takes place in terms of how integration takes place. By this it is meant the extent to which integration is intergovernmental or supra-national but deepening could also apply to integration in new policy areas because it would consider the extent to which the Communities have encroached into previously exclusively held areas of the member states' competences. So to some extent the terms are overlapping and the same development can be argued to fit into both categories. At a fairly simple level though, they refer in turn to the quantitative and qualitative changes over the years.

1.6.1 The Widening of the Communities

The Paris Intergovernmental Conference of 1972, finally paved the way, following the political demise of de Gaulle in 1969, for the first expansion of the member states which took place in 1973 when the UK, Ireland, and Denmark joined. Were it not for de Gaulle, this would have happened sooner and might have been better for the Community if it had. Norway was also to have joined at this time but a referendum of the Norwegian electorate on the eve of membership resulted in a majority against and Norway failed to become a member, not for the last time!

A second expansion took place in 1981, when Greece joined and a third expansion took place in 1986, after protracted negotiation periods for Spain and Portugal. Whilst none of these three countries were economically in a strong position in relation to the existing member states, and in view of this were regarded by some as unfit for membership, politically their acceptance into the Communities was regarded as cru-cial. This was considered both to support the recently emerged democracies in all of these countries after varying periods of authoritarian or dictatorial right wing rule and to act as a counter force to any possible violent reaction to the left and possible establishment of Governments sympathetic to Moscow. The Cold War still featured prominently in this period of history, hence, entry was facilitated sooner than the economic conditions might have permitted.

A smaller automatic expansion took place in 1990, with the unification of West and East Germany as the first tangible change to result from the fall of the communist regimes in the Soviet Union and Eastern European countries. It woke up the Communities to the possibility of a number of the former Eastern European states seeking membership and prompted a longer term evaluation of the conditions required of aspirant member states. This led to a set of criteria being agreed at the Copenhagen Summit in June 1993, which outlined the bottom line for aspiring new members. The requirements included the need for stable government and institutions guaranteeing democracy, the rule of law, human rights, and the protection of minorities. Economically, applicant states would have to have a functioning market economy and the ability to cope with life in the single market. The applicants would have to accept the *acquis communautaire*[10] in its entirety including the overall political, economic, social, and monetary aims of the Union, no easy task, even for the present member states.

The next and fourth enlargement took place sooner than expected as a result of the changes in Eastern Europe and the economic success facilitated by the Single European Act (SEA), discussed below.

1.6.2 The European Economic Area and the 1995 Expansion

After observing in the late 1980s, the economic benefits of the SEA enjoyed by the member states of the Communities, other European states, most of whom had cooperation or association agreements with the Communities and were members of EFTA, started to make overtures to the Communities for greater cooperation and some for possible membership. Initially, further expansion was not favoured by the Commission of the European Communities as it was thought it would stifle plans for deeper integration of the then existing member states, in particular progress on both the single market and possible further progress to monetary union. Additionally, prior to the collapse of Communism in Europe in the late 1980s, for varying reasons some of the EFTA member states were uncertain about full membership, hence a lesser form of integration was proposed by the European Commission, in which the participants could benefit from the advantages of the single market and the

---

[10] *Acquis communautaire* is the term given to describe the accumulated body of Community law including Treaties, secondary legislation and judicial developments. There was an exhibition in Brussels (2004) which graphically displayed the EU's *acquis communautaire*. It ran to over 80,000 pages and took up approximately 8 metres when stretched out in display cases in the exhibition! Actually, according to the Commission's own figures, at the end of 2002, the number of pages of binding legislation in the OJ was 97,000 pages. See http://europa.eu.int/rapid/pressReleasesAction.do?reference=IP/03/214&format=HTML&aged=1&language=EN&guiLanguage=en.

competition policy but not be involved in the other economic or political aspects of the Communities including decision making in the Communities. This offer was open to all of the then existing members of the EFTA. However, the negotiations for this new form of cooperation were very drawn out and subject to considerable delays during their course. They were also taking place against the backdrop of the collapse of communism in Eastern Europe. One of the consequences of this was that the previous objections or difficulties that might be raised by Eastern Bloc countries and the Soviet Union in particular, that full membership of militarily neutral countries of the Communities, i.e. Austria, Finland, and Sweden, would not be compatible with their status as neutral countries, were significantly undermined if not completely negated. Regardless, in October 1991, the EFTA member states of Austria, Finland, Iceland, Liechtenstein, Norway, Sweden, and Switzerland, signed an agreement with the EEC on the creation of the European Economic Area (EEA). The agreement reached was that the EFTA members were not represented in the Community institutions and would take no part in the decision making processes of the Community. They would be subject to all Community law relating to the single market, as defined by the Court of Justice. However, an additional problem was encountered whilst negotiations were being finalized, shortly before the Treaty was to come into force on 1 January 1993. The Swiss electorate rejected membership of the EEA in a referendum in December 1992, which caused considerable political and legal difficulties because Liechtenstein, with whom Switzerland has a monetary union, had agreed to join. The remaining six EFTA states went on to sign the agreement in March 1993, and it came into force on 1 July 1993. It was soon clear though, that as far as business confidence was concerned, full membership of the EU was the condition which attracted investment and not membership of the EEA. Indeed, both the concept and the consequences of the EEA might not, in any case, have been fully understood by outside interests. Hence, almost before the ink had dried on the signatures to the EEA Treaty, Austria, Finland, Norway, and Sweden applied for full membership of the European Communities. In view of the fact that most of the bargaining had already been done for the EEA, entry terms were easily and rapidly decided and the four applications were quickly accepted. On 1 January 1995, therefore the Community was joined by Austria, Finland and Sweden bringing the number of member states to fifteen. The Norwegian electorate, though, once again chose to reject membership in a referendum held in December 1994 and once again Norway failed to join the Communities. The entry of the three former EFTA members meant that the remaining EFTA states, Iceland, Norway, and Liechtenstein are now the only remaining EFTA members of the EEA, none of which have membership applications pending. Switzerland remains outside both the EC and the EEA. Its application for full membership, lodged in 1992 was also withdrawn following the EEA rejection. A special series of bilateral agreements have been negotiated with Switzerland instead, covering many if not most of the aspects of the EEA.

1.6.3 The 2004 Expansion

The expansion which took place on the 1 May 2004, was the largest in the history of the European Union and ten new states joined comprising: Latvia, Lithuania, Estonia, Poland, Hungary, the Czech Republic, Slovakia, Slovenia, Malta, and Cyprus.

Despite the fact that the negotiations were rather oddly conducted with some states being given priority, then this decision was changed and discussions proceeded on the basis of a 'big bang' of ten new states entering at the same time, the overall time taken to resolve terms of entry was surprisingly quick considering the number of states involved and their differing economic and social circumstances. The haste was fuelled by the political events unfolding in the world, in particular by the break up of the Soviet Union and the bloody fragmentation of Yugoslavia. For reasons which had similarly prompted the rapid entries of Greece, Spain, and Portugal in the 1980s, which were also regarded as premature due to the economic weakness of those countries, the ten new countries were brought into the fold much quicker than the economic conditions alone would have permitted because of the political desire to lock these countries into a Western liberal democratic club of nations. Hence, the Eastern expansion took over the agenda and Commission time. The Accession agreements with all of the member states were concluded and the entry terms settled for the Treaty of Accession which was signed in Athens on 16 April 2003. The ten new member states duly joined on 1 May 2004 with celebrations across Europe, albeit low key in some member states, such as the UK.

1.6.4 Future Widening

The next expansion will see the entry of Romania and Bulgaria (the Acceding countries) after the successful conclusion to the accession negotiations in December 2004, a favourable Commission opinion in February 2005 and the conclusion of the Accession Treaty in April 2005. Entry into force of the Accession Treaty is planned for 1 January 2007, if all twenty-seven states ratify the Treaty in time. At the time of writing and the present malaise in the EU for any further progress, this timetable looks doubtful. Apart from those two countries, at present, there are three countries who are official candidate states, Turkey, Macedonia and Croatia. With regard to Turkey, the Commission recommended on 6 October 2004 that the EU should open entry negotiations with Turkey and in December 2004, the Brussels European Council summit approved this position and set 3 October 2005 as the date for the start of entry negotiations. After the usual eleventh hour bargaining, the Austrian Government withdrew its threatened block on talks commencing and the entry negotiations were indeed started on 3 October 2005. Without doubt, these negotiations will be the most controversial in the history of the Union, mainly because of the recognition of Cyprus, the predominantly Muslim population of Turkey but also in view of the human rights record of Turkey and the fact that quite simply, geographically, most of the Turkish landmass lies in Asia and not in Europe. Its economic situation is also regarded as problematic although, it may be argued that this is exactly what the EU should come to terms with and create a multi-ethnic, multi-cultural, and multi-religious Union.[11]

With regard to Croatia, the Commission has recommended opening entry negotiations with Croatia and the December 2004 Brussels European Council Summit had suggested the date of 15 March 2005 to start negotiations. However, these were postponed temporarily whilst Croatia appeared not to be cooperating with the UN Balkans War Crimes Tribunal in the Hague by not yielding up one of their generals for alleged war crimes. This delay was lifted also on 3 October 2005.[12]

As to other possible members, there are the rest of the Balkan states to consider as potential candidates, as well as the States of the former Soviet Union which border the EU. The former Yugoslav Republic of Macedonia made an application to join in March 2004, and is considered as of 17 December 2005 to be a candidate country.

One or two other countries have previously made applications but have either withdrawn these or put them on hold. Norway has twice concluded entry negotiations only for entry to be rejected by the Norwegian electorate at the eleventh hour both times. At present it has no application pending but the possibility of future membership remains high on the political agenda with recent opinion polls showing a majority of Norwegians in favour of full membership.[13]

The rejection by the Swiss of membership of the European Economic Area (EEA) in 1992 also led to the withdrawal of its application for full membership. Even though Swiss governments have expressed the view that Switzerland will eventually apply for full membership, that aim was severely dented, at least for a few years, by a categorical rejection of the Swiss electorate of EU membership in a private initiative referendum in March 2001 when 77 per cent of those voting said 'no'. There are then presently, no plans for reapplication by Switzerland although significant governmental and other

---

[11] The latest position in this fast-moving topic can be found at: http://europa.eu.int/comm/enlargement/turkey/index.htm. For a balanced view of all challenges of Turkish membership, please see K. Dervis, M. Emerson, D. Gros, and Sinan Ulgen, *The European Transformation of Modern Turkey*, 2004, Centre for European Policy Studies, Brussels.

[12] See http://europa.eu.int/comm/enlargement/croatia/eu_relations.htm. http://europa.eu.int/comm/external_relations/see/news/2004/ip04_507.htm.

[13] See for further details http://europa.eu.int/comm/external_relations/norway/intro/index.htm.

elements consider membership of the EU as necessary and indeed inevitable, if not today, then at some stage in the future.[14]

An exhibition in Brussels in October 2004 presented some, not entirely serious, prophecies for the future including the following: 'In 2010', according to the exhibition, 'the EU will expand to include Albania, Armenia, Belarus, Bosnia and Herzegovina, Georgia, Macedonia, Moldova, Montenegro, Serbia and the Ukraine. Following this, in 2015, the EU will take in Morocco, Algeria, Egypt, Tunisia, Libya, Jordan, Israel, Palestine and change its name from the European Union to simply "The Union"'. Moving from fantasy to reality, the fact that the EU is opening accession negotiations with Turkey invites a final consideration in respect of further widening and enlargement. What is the limit? The answer to this is as much driven by the answer to the questions: What is Europe? Politically? Geographically? We already have two Mediterranean island states which have pushed the geographical border of the European Union further. Cyprus lies closer to the Middle East and is nearer to Asia than Europe and Malta is not much further away from Africa than it is from other parts of Europe. Indeed, there are existing parts of some member states which are clearly beyond any usual definition of Europe. The Canaries (Spain) lie off the west coast of Africa, French Guyana is in south America, the Azores and Madeira (Portugal) are in the middle of the Atlantic, and the French islands of Guadeloupe, Martinique, and Reunion lay in the Caribbean. Greenland was part of the EU until it was granted home rule from Denmark in 1979 and left the EU in 1985.

In fact, there are not many European states left to apply, depending on the definition given to 'Europe'. Only Iceland, Norway, Liechtenstein, the remnants of Yugoslavia, Albania, the smaller states of Andorra, Monaco, and perhaps parts of the former Soviet Union. An application to join by Morocco in 1987 was rejected on the geographical ground that Morocco was in Africa and could not be considered as coming within Europe. There is also, perhaps now the more focused question of whether the present citizens of the EU want a bigger Europe. At the time of writing, there appears to be more reticence than support for further expansion.

1.6.4.1 Accession Preconditions

Regardless of which new state is a candidate, under Article 2 of the TEU, all new states are required to accept and adopt the entire body of Community law, the *acquis communautaire*,[15] as contained in the Treaties, Protocols, Declarations, conventions, and agreements with third countries, secondary legislation, and the judgments of the European Court of Justice. Since the TEU, the criteria for membership has been much

---

[14] See for further details http://europa.eu.int/comm/external_relations/switzerland/intro/index.htm.
[15] See n. 10 above.

more clearly spelled out. Article 49 of the TEU provides that 'Any European State which respects the principles set out in Article 6(1) may apply to become a member of the Union.' These principles are liberty, democracy, respect for human rights, and fundamental freedoms and the rule of law. These Union values were reproduced in Article I-2 of the Constitutional Treaty, if that ever sees the light of day. In addition, potential member states will be required to satisfy a number of criteria which have been revised over the years from those provided at Copenhagen in 1993 and refined with the possible applications of the newly emergent democracies in Eastern Europe in mind, should they have chosen to make applications. The criteria were essentially a refinement of previous practice and have been further refined in subsequent summits meetings since. The 1999 Helsinki European Council Summit added a form of 'good neighbour' requirement for entrant states—that disputes with neighbouring countries be resolved before entry. It might have been a good idea but the most visible case requiring the application of that policy was Cyprus, however the Greek and Turkish parts of the island were not able to resolve fully their differences prior to the entry of Cyprus to the EU on 1 May 2004. Thus, the southern Greek half of the island alone joined the EU after a referendum vote in Cyprus to reunite the island was rejected by the Greek Cypriot electorate but approved by the Turkish side. Potential border disputes existing between Estonia and Latvia and the Russian Federation were also not resolved prior to accession. The Helsinki summit also marked a realization that the Copenhagen criteria could not be strictly applied and that some flexibility had to be exercised. The Laeken European Council Summit in December 2001 also emphasized that membership was dependant on candidate countries ensuring that their judicial institutions were capable of meeting the requirements of EU membership. The applicability of the criteria for deciding whether an eligible candidate can become an admissible one were confirmed at the Copenhagen Summit which took place in December 2002 and in relation to Turkish membership, emphasized its need to meet the political criteria.

1.6.5 The EU and the World: External Relations

The EU has diverse roles to play in the world orders. Not surprisingly, given the more limited original political scope of the Communities, trade relations with the rest of the world featured most prominently but not exclusively. However, because these roles and obligations in the areas of external relations have been spread over the various treaties, an overview has been difficult to obtain. Also the competences to undertake external relations have been granted in different terms under the three original treaties, for example, the ECSC Treaty expressly granted the legal capacity to make external agreements generally in pursuit of the objectives of the Treaty, the EURATOM

(EAEC) Treaty also allowed for general agreements to be concluded, whereas the EC Treaty (Art 281) provided that whilst the European Community had been given legal personality, it was provided with powers to conclude specific types of agreements only, such as commercial agreements under the common customs tariff (Arts 131–3 EC) or the Association Agreements. Article 300 provides an express power to conclude international agreements in areas already clearly within the competences of the EU such as the Common Customs Tariff, agriculture, and fisheries. However, the Council of Ministers must first give the Commission the go-ahead and the EP must finally assent to the agreement. As a result, there is a confusing array of trade agreements, association agreements and development aid agreements with third countries which have been negotiated by the Commission under a mandate from the Council but finally concluded by the Council on the basis of a qualified majority. It will only be with the entry into force of the Constitutional Treaty that the Union competences in its various relations with the rest of the world will be clearer. For the moment, I will simply outline the range of external activities undertaken by the EU.

1.6.5.1 Commercial and Financial Activities

In view of the increasing share of world trade that the Union has, it is no wonder that external relations in this area is very important. Even at the start of the Communities, part of the role envisaged was to contribute to the harmonious development of world trade and the liberalization of international trade. From the start therefore, the Community was given the competence to forge economic ties with the outside world (Art 131). Particularly under the Common Customs Tariff, where it was clear that this could only sensibly be done by the Community as a whole, the Community has slowly assumed the competences to negotiate on behalf of the member state including representing the Communities in the important trade institutions set up in the world and to commit them in the GATT and WTO negotiations. Although the EC or EU itself is not a formal member of either organization, certainly in GATT, it has been recognized as replacing the authority of the formal members, which are the individual member states, to represent and negotiate on behalf of them.[16] Such activity has been challenged in the past but the capacity to enter in international commitments was approved of by the Court of Justice, e.g. in Case 22/70 *Commission v Council* (ERTA) and in Opinion 1/76.[17] However, as far as the WTO is concerned, the Commission and Community suffered a blow when the member states insisted on not permitting the extension of Commission competences into the additional areas covered by the WTO talks concerning Persons or Intellectual Property and thus retaining their

---

[16] For further details see Devuyst (2005) 133–140.
[17] Case 22/70 *Commission v Council* [1971] ECR 263, [1971] CMLR 335 and Opinion 1/76 [1977] ECR 741 and see comments on these cases in Chapter 3.

competences. In consequence, the overall picture of who and how the talks would be conducted became confused. This unsatisfactory position was essentially confirmed by the Court of Justice in its Opinion 1/94. To some extent, this has been corrected by the Treaty of Nice which has allowed for Commission competence relating to trade in services, and intellectual property agreements (see Art 133 (5) EC) but does not allow the Community to conclude agreements which go beyond the internal powers of the Community (Art 133 (6)).

The most important agreements are the EEA, noted above, the association agreements with potential member states (at present Bulgaria and Romania, Turkey, Macedonia, and Croatia), the bilateral agreements with Switzerland and Mediterranean countries, and the preferential Treatment Agreements which have been concluded with Mediterranean Countries and through the Lomé Conventions and now the Cotonou Agreement (2000) with seventy-eight African, Caribbean and Pacific (ACP) countries.

1.6.5.2 Political, Defence, and Security Activities

In stark contrast, perhaps not surprising given the predominantly economic concerns of the original Treaties, stands the weak and divided political relations with the world, seen notably and lamentably during the break up of the former Republic of Yugoslavia and the Gulf wars. The political underdevelopment of the Communities and now Union clearly stand out, although it has to be said that these events have become a catalyst for change and improved political cooperation. The first express move into visible political and foreign policies of the Communities came with the SEA recognition of the existing European Political Cooperation (EPC) which had existed since 1970. It was transferred to the Maastricht Treaty along with a Common Foreign and Security Policy (CFSP) in a separate primarily intergovernmental pillar, which is considered in further detail below.

The Constitutional Treaty proposes to bring these matters back within one Treaty framework and creating a Union Minister of Foreign Affairs (Art I-28 CT) who will be one of the Commission Vice-Presidents to carry out the foreign and security policy as determined by the European Council and Council of Ministers.

1.6.5.3 Immigration and Asylum

The EU has had at best an ambivalent attitude to immigration and asylum. Whilst making the usual noises about the respect of the human rights, its external policy has been to erect the fortress Europe to keep persons out. When the political competence of the Communities was expanded to include foreign relations, immigration was placed in the intergovernmental pillar and only after the Amsterdam Treaty, were these matters brought within the ambit of the European Community albeit still on an intergovernmental basis and where deemed to be connected with law and order and safeguarding of internal security, beyond the jurisdiction of the Court of Justice (Art 68 EC). Further consideration of this topic will be given in the chapter on the Free Movement of Persons.

1.6.5.4 Humanitarian and Development Aid

The EC Treaty now contains a Title on Development Cooperation (Arts 177–81) which empowers the Community to pursue a development policy which helps to sustain economic and social development, integration of developing countries into the world economy and campaign against poverty and also to develop and consolidate democracy, the rule of law, human rights, and fundamental freedoms.

1.6.6 The Deepening of the Communities

This section charts the increasing degree of integration entered into by the member states starting with the original treaties establishing the Communities and following this to the present position of the Constitutional Treaty.

1.6.6.1 The Primary Treaties and Early Amendments

The first and fundamental movement on the path of integration was, of course, the ECSC Treaty, now expired, which was soon followed by the agreement and ratification of the EEC and EURATOM Treaties by the original six member states. It was clear at the time of negotiation that a transfer of power was involved, particularly in the climate of the time and the clear federalist intentions of the main protagonists of the plan, Schuman and Monnet.

The only amendments that were made to the primary Treaties for the first two decades were minor ones brought about first, by the decision to merge the institutions of the three Communities and then the Accession treaties required for the new member states. Prior to the Merger Treaty of 1965, each of the Communities had its own Council and High Authority/Commission, however, the Court of Justice and the Parliamentary Assembly had both been shared by all three Communities from the outset. The merger of the institutions was a practical step to provide common coordination and cut out a duplication of effort and resources. It was nothing more significant than that. The first Accession Treaties for Denmark, Ireland and the United Kingdom dealt specifically with the details of accession of the new member states or merely made the changes to the Treaties considered necessary for it to continue working in the same way as previously but with adjustments to reflect the increase in member states and the composition of the institutions, for example, to Council voting numbers and Commission membership. The fundamental constitutional core of the Communities and how they worked remained untouched until 1986.

1.6.6.2 The 1960s and the Luxembourg Accords

Initially, the Communities were very successful in achieving the aims set out and promoting economic growth in the member states, in contrast, with countries such as the UK. The dismantling of customs duties was achieved by the original six member states before the target date set down in the EEC Treaty. Additionally, Competition Policy was seen to be working and the Common Agricultural Policy was clearly successful in terms of guaranteeing production. It was, however, the subject of criticism because its price support mechanisms led over time to the massive over production and stockpiling of commodities such as butter, sugar, and wine which cost the Community not only a great deal of money to dispose of, but also political ill favour in the world as third world agricultural products had no chance of entering the heavily protected European Community market.

However, following this initial period of success and achievement, any chance of either further expansion or deeper integration was stifled. The brake on such progress was most effectively applied to the Commission and the Communities in 1965, by de Gaulle, the French President by a boycott of the institutions that caused lasting damage for decades. In 1965, the Commission proposed that the Communities move to a system of own resources and that the Council should move to majority voting, which was no more than originally envisaged by the Treaty of Rome. It was further proposed, that the Parliamentary Assembly should have some control over the expenditure of the Communities. These proposals were categorically opposed and vetoed by de Gaulle who, when the other member states were not opposed, adopted a policy of non-attendance of the Community institutions by the French representatives, which became known as the institutions boycott or the 'empty chair' policy. All progress, indeed everything in the Communities simply halted. The compromise agreement to break the deadlock was the infamous Luxembourg Accords, in essence an agreement to disagree. This basically provided that in the case where the member states were not able to agree a proposal and where a vital national interest of any member state was at stake, that member state could finally veto the proposal in Council. There was no definition of a vital interest so member states were left to define a vital interest themselves. Thus, until the political demise of de Gaulle, the planned moves for deeper integration were prevented.

1.6.6.3 Stagnation and 'Eurosclerosis'

The whole unfortunate episode surrounding the Luxembourg Accords resulted in stagnation in the decision-making process for many years to come. It led to the long slow painful period of the Communities which has become known as the period of 'Eurosclerosis' and lasted from 1966 until the early to mid-1980s. The basic problem was the near inability of the member states to reach decisions on Community legislation and widespread dissatisfaction at the slow pace at which the goals of the EEC were being achieved. Whilst a lot of the blame can be laid at the door of French boycott and the Luxembourg Accords, the ability to reach decisions was made much more difficult by the doubling of the member states between 1973 and 1985. Trying to obtain the unanimous agreement of first six, then nine, then ten, and then all twelve members proved at times to be simply impossible. Amongst the main concerns were the time taken by the Community Institutions to make new laws and the amount of work the Council was faced with, partly because particular provisions were presented many times as the Commission made amendments to make them acceptable to all member states. A notorious example exists of a Directive which did nothing more controversial than harmonize the training requirements for Architects[18] but which took the institutions seventeen years to agree and finally enact. Further concerns related to the lack of representative democracy in the decision making process of the Community and the delays experienced by litigants to the Court of Justice. It was clear to everyone that some change had to be brought about. Whilst it was true that some adjustments had been made in the form of amendments to the original treaties, these were of a limited nature. More significantly, but restricted to a specific process, was the increase in powers of the European Parliament in the budgetary process by the Budgetary Treaties of 1970 and 1975. Otherwise, little further progress had been achieved in this period.

1.6.6.4 Revival Attempts

In 1969, following the resignation of de Gaulle and the change of government in West Germany to a Social Democrat led one, a summit of the heads of government was arranged in the Hague expressly to relaunch European integration. The 1969 Hague Summit established the system of European Political Cooperation (EPC) but which was deliberately intergovernmental in nature and sat outside of the formal treaty set up. As such, it can be regarded as another move away from supranationalism and the neofunctionalists' dream of progress on European integration. It was also unfortunate, but the reforms and the relaunching of the Communities envisaged at the Hague were severely disrupted by the world economic situation which grew steadily worse in the early 1970s. The Middle East wars and ensuing oil crises led to very high inflation and stagnation in the world economies and to the unwinding of the first attempt at some sort of monetary union, the EMU, which bound European

---

[18] Directive 85/384 (OJ 1985 L223/15).

currencies in to a flexible relationship with each other and the European Monetary Unit.[19] The year 1973 also saw the entry of three new member states, two of which, the United Kingdom and Denmark, were even then the least federal minded member states in the European Communities. This appears to have remained the case ever since. There were nevertheless further attempts to revive the flagging fortunes of the Communities. A further summit in Paris in 1974 led to the formalization of the previously informal European Council Summit meetings to provide an overriding political guide to the Communities. This, however, tended to strengthen further the intergovernmental hand of control over the Communities rather than provoke deeper integration. The Paris Summit also, for the first time, allowed the Commission a role in the summitry, something pressed for by the new Commission President, Roy Jenkins. The Summit also made the decision that the European Parliament should be directly elected as from 1978, although this could not take place until 1979 due to difficulties in the United Kingdom in preparing the legislation. Finally, the European Monetary System (EMS) was established in 1978, despite the collapse of the previous attempt (the EMU). The EMS proved to be stable and with the establishment of the European Currency Unit (ECU) became the precursor to Monetary Union and the Euro.

These limited successes, however, did little to counter the generally prevailing malaise that hung over the Communities and institutions. This was not helped by the attitude and activities of certain member states. Even when de Gaulle disappeared from the international scene in 1979, the new UK Prime Minister, Mrs Thatcher, appeared immediately to take up the baton of intergovernmentalism and the bolstering of purely national interests. Whilst the UK may well have had a case in arguing for a more equitable budget contribution, and neither Mrs Thatcher nor indeed anyone else has gone as far as de Gaulle in disrupting the work of the Communities, the negotiating style and public pronouncements of Thatcher left much to be desired. These budget wrangles and sheer lack of progress generally in the Community dragged on seemingly endlessly into the mid-1980s. The stagnation and intergovernmentalism not only thwarted any moves to more federalism but also engendered a period of national protectionism which itself was threatening to undermine some of the basic goals of the European Communities already achieved, notably the common market itself, which was simply not being completed as envisaged and, if anything, was becoming more fragmented. It was abundantly clear and understood that reform and indeed radical reform of the Community and institutions was necessary. Numerous reports and studies were conducted by the different Community institutions and

---

[19] This was not a currency like the present day Euro but an accounting unit based on the average of the basket of member currencies.

additionally, many external reports had been commissioned over the years which had all recommended changes. A number of areas where improvements were required had already been identified by those reports in the lifetime of the Communities. Amongst them were: the Vedel Report of 1972 with proposals by the Commission to strengthen the Powers of the European Parliament, the Tindemans Report on 'European Union' 1976, the Report of the Three Wise Men 1979, the Spierenburg Report 1979, the Columbo/Genscher Initiative of 1981, the Stuttgart European Council of 1983 which made a 'Solemn Declaration' that there should be greater European integration towards a European Union. There was also the prescient European Parliament publication 'Draft Treaty of the European Parliament establishing the European Union' of 1984 and finally, the Dooge Committee set up by the Fontainebleau Summit of 1984. The fact that there was so many of these speaks volumes for the effectiveness (i.e. lack!) of them in tackling the deep-rooted problems of European stagnation. However, whilst individually, they did not provide a solution, collectively, all of them, especially the latter ones helped finally establish and develop the climate for the eventual changes brought about by treaty change and in particular by the Single European Act (SEA), which led in turn to the Treaty on European Union (the Maastricht Treaty), the Treaties of Amsterdam and Nice, and the Treaty for a Constitution for Europe. In 1985 enough head of steam had built up for the member states to accept, albeit by some reluctantly, that the necessary changes were ones which could only effectively be undertaken by Treaty revision. It was finally considered necessary that the founding Treaties be substantively amended.

1.6.6.5 The Contrasting Positive Role Played by the Court of Justice

An observation that needs to be made at this stage but will be repeated in Chapters 2 and 3, is that whilst the Community Institutions were busily going nowhere on the path to European integration, the Court of Justice appeared not to be affected by the 'Eurosclerosis' and had from a very early date adopted a very supranational tone in its judgments with the far-reaching decisions on direct effects and supremacy in Case 26/62 *Van Gend en Loos* and Case 6/64 *Costa v ENEL*. These judgments contributed greatly not only in terms of building a separate Community legal system but also enhancing the supranational status of the new European legal order and constitutionality of the Communities.

1.6.7 The First Radical Change: The Single European Act

The Single European Act is the first significant amendment of the primary treaties. It is an important watershed in the historical development of the Communities and is not to be underestimated in its importance although it was at the time, not just by external observers and commentators but also the heads of state and government who signed up to it. It is sometimes difficult to grasp its importance because it is the first of a series of package deal changes to the Treaties which not only add new areas of competence but simultaneously make various institutional changes and policy amendments.

The situation in the middle of the 1980s was that both the stagnation of the Communities and the lack of international competitiveness of Europe in relation to American and Japanese industrial and commercial progress, had been clearly recognized. These concerns were taken up by the new Commission President Jacques Delors who brought a package of reforms to the member states, based on the Dooge Committee report together with a new report prepared by the British Vice-President of the Commission, Lord Cockfield dealing with the measures considered necessary for the completion of the single market. Whilst there remained opposition to any significant institutional changes recommended, especially by the UK, the single market completion was the carrot which brought the Eurosceptic governments on board, particularly the UK and Germany, as the proposals were hailed as a shining example of trade liberalization. Whilst the other member states were undoubtedly also interested in the trade and economic aspects of the reforms proposed, the smaller states in particular had a greater desire to see the institutional reforms recommended. All these matters were put on the agenda for the 1985 Intergovernmental Conference (IGC), itself initially opposed by the UK. The single market reforms were linked to the institutional changes, and I think it is fair to say that the far-reaching political consequences of these were seriously downplayed by the EC Commission. It was also true that the far more radical changes proposed by Parliament a year or so earlier in its draft Constitution had caused a lot more consternation and opposition by the member states. The EP proposals were not ones which could be accepted by the Council at the time, hence the Single European Act proposals, which put the primary focus on market liberalization and were far more modest and were much more acceptable to the member states. Even the title underplays the significance of the matter. An 'Act' suggests somewhat less than a new Treaty. It suggests secondary legislation rather than primary treaty material. So in 1985 the draft Single European Act was put to and debated at the intergovernmental conference. It was agreed by the ten member states in December 1985 and came into force in the EEC in May 1987, after signature and ratification by all twelve states (Portugal and Spain having joined the Communities in January 1986).

The SEA amended the EEC Treaty in several important respects and whilst they were not massive changes in themselves, they proved to be a catalyst to further European integration. Apart from the proposals to complete the internal market, perhaps most importantly, was the change of the legislative process affecting ten Treaty Articles and generally the extension of the Community's competence and concern in new policy areas. The SEA also introduced provisions which made it possible to make changes to the judicial structure in the future by supplementing the Court of Justice with an extension which was regarded as being vital to cope with the significant increases in the number of cases reaching the Court and the increased delay being caused as a result. The decision in 1988, on the establishment of a Court of First Instance of the European Communities (CFI) was the result[20] with the CFI being set up in October 1988.

Before considering in further detail, the changes brought about by the SEA, it needs to be stressed here, generally what was being done by the SEA. It was the first substantive amendment of the original treaties. Although this has happened on a number of occasions since then and thus has the appearance of being something which can easily be done, at the time it was, without any doubt, a significant development. For most, if not all of the states, especially the United Kingdom, signing up to and joining the Communities in the first place was a massive and historic commitment. Changing that original deal was not something to be taken lightly and could even be regarded as being as important as the present Constitutional Treaty—but without the same degree of build up. The very substance of the original treaties was being altered and in order to amend a treaty, another treaty is needed, so despite its name, the SEA is a true amending treaty agreed by the member states. The preamble of the SEA states that it is 'a step towards European Union'.

1.6.7.1 The Internal Market and '1992'

In 1985 the Commission had identified 279 areas in which directives or other provisions were considered necessary to complete the internal market. The SEA set a new date of 31 December 1992 for the completion of the internal common market which originally should have been achieved by 1 January 1970, but which had been delayed by the member states. The year 1992 was simply a priority date set by the Commission by which the catching up should have been done. This programme proved to be a success not only in itself, as the member states did get on with enacting the needed legislation, but also because it gave a clear signal to European business that 'Europe meant business'. By the end of October 1992, 282 Directives had been proposed and drafted and by the end of December 1992 all but eighteen had been adopted by the Council. The system of qualified majority voting in the Council, for matters concerned with the completion of in the internal market which had been brought in by the SEA, was highly instrumental in this success. Company mergers and investment increased dramatically and considerable economic progress was made in these years. It was the promise of economic gains to be made that had convinced the member

---

[20] Decision 88/591 (OJ 1988 L319/1).

states to accept the other proposals agreed in the SEA, and as it turned out, proved by and large to be true, although the exact amount of economic benefit to be gained, might have been forecast on the high side.[21]

1.6.7.2 SEA Institutional and Policy Changes

The SEA also made formal, the existence of the European Council of Heads of State and Government, which was originally established as European Political Cooperation (EPC). The SEA reintroduced and extended qualified majority voting (QMV) in the Council, introduced the cooperation procedure in law-making, which provided the EP with a more than just a consultative role for the first time, paved the way for the Court of First Instance, and increased Commission powers, all of which are further considered in Chapter 2.

The SEA also added economic and social cooperation, under which the European Regional Development Fund was established. This was designed to help redress regional imbalances between various areas of the Communities by financing infra-structure developments. It also set up the Social Fund to finance employment initia-tives and the European Investment Bank, which operates as a commercial bank, lending money to finance projects in whose promotion the Community has an interest.

Further new policy areas were added to the EEC Treaty, including research and technology (Arts 163–73), which set out the framework for the pursuit of research and development cooperation, environmental protection, under Article 174 (1)(1)) and introduced the objective of, and initial measures towards monetary union.

1.6.7.3 Evaluation of the SEA

Whilst the SEA had it critics and was condemned by some parties,[22] its success lay not in what it actually changed, although there was considerable progress with the internal market but its true success lay in its longer term influence in reinvigorating integration. It is certainly the case that it did not represent a radical shift to supra-national or federal integration. In contrast to the original treaties, the member states were the ones constructing the agenda for it and not the federalist visionaries of the immediate post-war period. Also, in view of the preceding fifteen to twenty years which had seen a complete standstill on any such progress, it is not surprising that the

---

[21] Completing the Internal Market: White Paper from the Commission to the European Council (Milan, 28–29 June 1985). COM (85) 310, 14 June 1985 and the later Cecchini Report which forecast the cost of non-Europe to be 200bn Euro, see P. Cecchini et al., *The European Challenge 1992. The Benefits of a Single Market*, Aldershot, Wildwood House 1998.

[22] See Ward, pp. 35–7.

changes introduced by the SEA can be regarded as modest and even disappointing. There is a saying that 'an inch is better than a mile, in the right direction'. To view the limited, mainly intergovernmental changes brought by the SEA as a backward step on the integration road, misses the point somewhat. It represented forward movement at a time of massive political conservatism in Europe and perhaps as important, was the fact that for the first time, the original primary Treaties had been substantively amended. The original legal and constitutional base was shown not to be cast in stone and thus set for all time to come. It could be altered, and not just once but as many times as deemed necessary. The SEA allowed that to happen and, after a 20-year delay it did introduce real majority voting in the Council of Ministers, albeit within limited fields for clear and obvious benefits but it allowed the member states to get comfortable with QMV and thus prepared the ground for the future use of majority voting in other areas.

The success of the SEA and benefit to the Communities was also observed externally at that time as other European states on the outside of the Communities were able to witness the increase in investment from outside Europe into the EC and indeed away from their own countries. They wanted in and initially, plans were made to accommodate them in association agreements with the European Communities and in an extended form of these, the European Economic Area (EEA). It led much quicker than originally envisaged to the further widening of the Communities, noted above.

1.6.7.4 Post SEA

It was realized very soon after the signing of the SEA, that it was only part of the answer and it was advocated, largely by the Commission, that further institutional changes were required. As a result, even before the deadline of 1992 had passed, plans were being put forward by the Commission President, Delors for further treaty reform, especially on economic and monetary union and social policy. A further IGC was planned and was set up to debate the adoption of common monetary and fiscal policies which, according to the plan, were deemed necessary to cement in the gains achieved by the largely successful completion of the single market. This further proposal for integration and again the IGC to debate it, were both opposed by the UK.

However, external political events were moving rapidly in the world. Thatcher was deposed by her own party as Conservative leader and thus UK Prime Minister and along with the 'Iron Lady',[23] the 'Iron Curtain' was also being dismantled, changing the political situation in Europe radically and leading very quickly to German reunification. The planned IGC for 1991 to discuss and provide for greater economic

---

[23] One of the nicknames given to Margaret Thatcher.

integration, was supplemented by a parallel second IGC to consider political reform and to produce proposals for a new constitutional basis for the Communities. It was also considered necessary that political decision making should also be integrated further in order to lock in any decisions reached on monetary union. Otherwise, it was feared, that any gains or decisions reached for monetary and economic union would be lost if the political decisions supporting them could still be taken independently by each member state. This in turn would lead to a drifting apart of the economic conditions in the member states and is a clear example of functionalist integration in action, in that integration in one area demands or inevitably leads to integration in another area in order to prevent the first area from unravelling.

The parallel IGCs commenced work in December 1990, but like the EEA negotiations, they were also subject to delays as a result of the economic problems in Europe, inflation in Germany due to the cost of unification and the considerable political, social, and economic change taking place across Europe.

1.6.8 The Maastricht Treaty on European Union (TEU)

These two IGCs of the early 1990s can be regarded as one effectively, particularly as they resulted in proposals for a single amending treaty. However, the Treaty which was drafted and eventually accepted by the member states, considerably complicated the constitutional base of the Communities and Union. First, because it not only amended the existing treaties and most notably the EEC Treaty, but also because it added another treaty to complement and supplement the existing treaties and to remain in force along side the existing treaties. It also proved to be a huge compromise with its opt outs in some matters for some of the member states. It is also criticized for its the complex three pillar construction established to govern the Communities and the various policies of the union involving a mix of intergovernmental and supranational elements.[24]

The main changes introduced by the Treaty, and chief amongst them were the timetable and convergence criteria to move to a single economy and monetary union, complete with a single currency. It provided more political cooperation, especially in the areas of foreign policy, security, home affairs, and justice (Arts 11–45). The EEC Treaty name was changed to European Community (EC) to represent the changes that had taken place and the huge expansion in the range of topics and policies covered by the treaty. A new overall term, the European Union was introduced under Article 1 under the Treaty of European Union and describes the extension by the member

---

[24] In particular see D. Curtin, 'The Constitutional Structure of the Union: a Europe of Bits and Pieces' (1993) 30 *Common Market Law Review*, 17.

states into additional policies and areas of cooperation. The Union consists of three pillars comprising the existing Communities (the three original treaties), a Common Foreign and Security Policy (CFSP) and Cooperation in the Fields of Justice and Home Affairs (CJHA). The TEU also started a trend which was continued at Amsterdam in the attachment to the treaties of numerous protocols and declarations which help in many cases to define further some provisions of the treaties themselves and outline the reservations of some member states. Justifiably, these have been criticized for making Community and Union law too opaque and too splintered.

Apart from the complexity of the new constitutional base, a large part of the problem facing European governments trying to sell this Treaty at home was that the European public had not been taken on board during the period of negotiation. Whilst there was some lip service paid to the idea of European citizenship and what this meant for the personal right of free movement of Union citizens, which was really only given teeth later by the Court of Justice, the European public had largely been left out of the reform process. There were further minor improvements for the European Parliament (EP) in the law-making process, but the TEU also represented a backward step as far as progress towards deeper integration. The other two pillars, as first established, were intergovernmental in nature with decisions having to be taken unanimously by the member states. Very little had been done to increase the demo-cratic credentials of the Communities, the powers of the Council were left largely untouched and indeed strengthened in respect of the two new pillars.

The Treaty did contain an expression of commitment to the rule of law and democracy but failed to provide for any significant democratic accountability of the European Union and the rule of law itself. The EP had no effective voice in the intergovernmental pillars. There was also an attempt to define the relationship between the Union and the member states by the introduction of the term 'Subsidiarity' which was written in the new Treaty (Art B) and which was further defined in Article 5 of the EC Treaty. However, its true import was vague. It was supposed to delineate the respective powers of the Union and the member states but instead has merely confused them and as such is regarded as somewhat reflective of the ambivalence of the member states at the time.[25]

The TEU was also supposed to redress concerns about the democratic deficit in the Communities by increasing the power of the European Parliament by the intro-duction of the co-decision procedure to a limited number of Treaty articles. Whilst this was an important symbolic step, in reality this amounted to no more than a parliamentary veto and did little to promote real democratic decision-making in the Communities. Furthermore, this had the effect of increasing, once again, the range

---

[25] It is discussed in further detail in Chapter 4. See also Ward, p. 47.

and complexity of law-making procedures in the Community, which are considered in detail in Chapter 3.

The TEU also brought into the Union structure the Schengen Agreement of 1985 on free movement and security measures relating to such free movement in the area of the member states who had signed up to it, not though including the UK, Ireland and Denmark.

The TEU was agreed by the member states in February 1992 and was due to come into force on 1 January 1993, however, the process was thrown into confusion by its rejection by a slim Danish majority in a referendum. As a result, further compromises had to be found in order to appease the Danish electorate. The Edinburgh Summit in December 1992, agreed to allow Denmark various protocols and declarations to opt out of participation in stage III of Economic and Monetary Union, the single currency, and the defence arrangements of Maastricht, whilst not actually changing the Treaty itself.

Even, further delays were experienced because of the economic difficulties in some member states and parliamentary and judicially caused delays in the UK and in Germany in finalizing the Treaty ratification. It finally came into force in November 1993, but this Treaty creation was clearly an unhappy experience which, the European leaders promised was going to be better handled next time. However, there was not long to learn the lessons from Maastricht as the next time was just around the corner. Already in 1992, with the political changes in Europe clear in mind, further expansion had already been contemplated by the existing member states and the Copenhagen Summit laid down criteria that would have to be met by aspiring member states, noted above (1.6.4.1).

Whilst politically, the TEU was also supposed to be an attempt to tidy up the constitutional base of the Communities, the end result was far from this goal. All in all, the revised constitutional base was far too fragmented, with the establishment of a three pillared Union and the numerous protocols and declarations allowing various member state opt-outs and positions. Furthermore, the Union which was established was only an 'ever closer one' and not the federal union originally mooted, which suggested far greater integration than the reality which was agreed by the member states, hence the end product was more intergovernmental cooperation.

The TEU and the aftermath also led to new jargon in the Community political and legal order which were the result of the new complex shape of the Union, the difficulties in getting the Treaty ratified in all member states, and to reflect the frustrations of some member states not being happy about the more reluctant states. Hence the terms: 'European Architecture' to describe the new three pillar structure and 'variable geometry' to describe the way that a central core of states might integrate deeper. This is also described in the term: 'multi-speed Europe'.

1.6.9 **Preparations for the Amsterdam IGC and Treaty**

As a part of the agreement for the TEU and specified in the Treaty itself in Article 48, a timetable was pre-planned for the further revision of the Treaties by providing that another intergovernmental Conference (IGC) be constituted in 1996 with a view to signing another amending treaty in Amsterdam in 1997. At the time it was proposed, the objectives were to reform the institutional structure in preparation for enlargement, to consider the role of the individual in relation to the Union, to revise social policy and to review the intergovernmental pillars, in particular the common foreign and security policy, especially in respect of the rights of the free movement of persons. However, due to the delays in ratifying the Maastricht Treaty, the agenda was increasingly hijacked by new items, foremost being the preparations that would be required for the eastern expansion of the Union. The political landscape of the Union had changed greatly in a very short time. One of the few things that enough member states were agreed upon was the opening up of entry negotiations with the new democracies of Eastern Europe. Hence the focus of attention soon shifted to further institutional reform for the next, and probably, much larger expansion of the Union. The focus thus became narrowly concentrated on the size of the Commission, the European Parliament, QMV and the rotation of the presidency of the Council of Ministers. The negotiations were highly problematic and were also getting bogged down with a dispute over the British BSE beef crisis and ban which was taking place at the time and the blocking tactics of other proposals of the then Conservative UK Government in trying to lift the EC ban. Each member state, it seemed, had its own agenda and prepared to push it to the limit. The UK Government was even seeking to reopen previous treaties, to curb the powers of the Court of Justice and reverse some of decisions not favoured by the UK Government. Hence, in this climate, the IGC dragged on into the middle of 1997. This might have been deliberate, as the UK general election had been set for 1 May 1997 and the Labour Party looked to be in a strong position to win. Labour did win in the UK and there was a new Government, who quickly removed some of the objections that the Conservative party raised in the negotiations along with a promise to opt in to the social policy. As a result, final negotiations were soon wrapped up and the Treaty was concluded in Amsterdam in June 1997. It was signed by all member states at a late night summit in October 1997, and following a slow but less troublesome ratification by all member states, entered into force on 1 May 1999.

1.6.9.1 The Treaty of Amsterdam

Whilst not as dramatic as the changes brought about by the TEU, the Treaty of Amsterdam did introduce some changes. Unfortunately, some of these have further complicated the structure of the Union and the treaties. A clear failure was the lack of significant institutional reform, which had become the main focus for the IGC and supposedly indispensable for future expansion. These had to be postponed to yet another IGC which commenced in Brussels in February 2000.

What could be agreed, following the landslide Labour victory in the UK, was that the Agreement on Social Policy, previously lying outside of the Treaty structure, was accepted by all fifteen member states and therefore a chapter on social policy could be incorporated into the EC Treaty. A new section on employment was introduced which provided as one of the first examples of a more open method of coordination, that the member states can develop cooperative ventures to combat unemployment and, part of the Justice and Home Affairs pillar, concerned with the free movement of persons, was moved within the EC Pillar, with opt-outs for the UK, Ireland, and Denmark. It was also agreed that, the European Union would incorporate the Schengen Agreement on the elimination of all border controls for twelve states, in a new Title IV in the EC Treaty, but not for the UK or Ireland and Denmark who secured more opt-outs in this area. The Court of Justice and the EP were also give a greater role in the JHA pillar, now renamed the Provision on Police and Judicial Cooperation in Criminal Matters (PJCC).

The institutional reforms were far more modest. The proposals to extend QMV in Council were severely restricted by Germany, notably, amongst others. However, the variety of legislative procedures, which were getting vastly out of hand, were slightly reduced and the European Parliament's powers were modestly increased by the moderately extended use of the co-decision procedure. The number of Commissioners was capped at twenty, although subsequent IGCs and enlargement reopened this issue along with other institutional matters, considered in detail below and in Chapter 2.

The various changes were consolidated within both the EC and European Union Treaties and unhelpfully, these were renumbered as a result, something which has done little to promote the clarity of Union law. Even more unfortunately, is that the renumbering, if and when the CT comes into force will not have been for the last time! Regrettably, the Treaty of Amsterdam added even more protocols, thus making even more obscure an overall picture of EU and EC law. The Treaty of Amsterdam, according to some, did very little; others regard it as a needed consolidation of European Political Union, although the tangible benefits and progress are hard to discern. Additionally, the Treaty of Amsterdam seemed to throw a spanner in the works of further integration by the replacement of further supranational integration with the possibility of allowing some member states to cooperate further, without all member states having to do so. It introduced into the EC, Article 11 and into the TEU a section (Arts 43 et seq.) on 'closer cooperation' which allows any number of member states who so wish, to integrate in other areas. This seemed to make the fragmentation of the Communities even more possible and allow for the possibility that the body of

Community law known as the *acquis communautaire*, which applies in all member states in the same way, could be undermined as different combinations of member states go their own way with particular policies. Thus far, this has not been taken advantage of, but it has been further defined and regulated in the Constitutional Treaty (Arts I-44 and III-416–23) but with no minimum number of states required.

The Treaty of Amsterdam, as finally agreed, proved to be far from the solution needed for preparing for enlargement, consolidating the political union, and establishing a firm basis for European governance. It did too little to restore public faith and confidence in the Union. As a result of the fact that Amsterdam failed to resolve the institutional reforms considered essential for the next large enlargement of the EU, there was so much left over which had to be addressed before enlargement could take place, yet another IGC was deemed necessary and was called to deal with the leftovers. This was convened in Nice in 2000.

1.6.10 The Nice Intergovernmental Conference and Treaty

The IGC was convened in February 2000 with the more tightly drawn objectives of institutional change ahead of enlargement. Whilst the preparatory negotiations were relatively short lived, the summit in December 2000 proved to be the most difficult and drawn out thus far. It was finally agreed at 5 o'clock in the morning of 11 December 2000, prompting some of the heads of state to declare at the end that 'such an IGC and Council should not be allowed to happen again'.[26] The member states wrangled mainly over the extension of QMV and voting weights in Council and the conclusions reached were neither conclusive nor satisfactory, despite the various statements of success following the summit. The size of the Commission was also a contentious issue. The QMV discussions were, though, seized on by the member states to defend national positions as rigidly as possible. QMV was extended to twenty-seven more Treaty Articles but not in as many areas as proposed by the Commission because of the various red lines drawn by countries which cumulatively, significantly reduced the extension. The discussions were also drawn out because of the arguments over the combinations of country votes to get a qualified majority or a blocking minority, and even qualifications on a majority were devised defining a minimum number of states and/or a percentage (62 per cent) of population of the EU required. (See the Declaration on the Enlargement of the European Union attached to the Treaty of Nice.) In particular, the big three member states, France, Germany, and the UK were fighting to

---

[26] See the comments in particular by Tony Blair and French President, Jacques Chirac: http://news.bbc.co.uk/1/hi/uk_politics/1065039.stm and http://news.bbc.co.uk/1/hi/not_in_website/syndication/monitoring/media_reports/1065523.stm.

keep their level of influence against the wishes of many of the smaller states and whilst agreement was reached at Nice on the voting formula, it was very much an imperfect one and was soon shown to be the case. The co-decision procedure was extended again for the EP so that the cooperation procedure hardly features at all now as a process, in fact only in six Articles, largely to do with monetary union.[27] The ultimate maximum size of the Commission was also postponed again, but yet another protocol addressing these issues[28] was added to the Treaty, which of course simply detracts even further from the transparency of the rules governing the Union.

The Treaty of Nice was signed by the member states in February 2001, but did not enter into force until 1 February 2003 because of the rejection of it by a single member state once again. This time the Irish electorate decided to show their Euro-sceptic credentials and in June 2002 voted against ratification of the Treaty of Nice, although this was on a very low turnout of the electorate. When the government was returned to power with an increased majority, a second referendum was organized and which resulted in a far more positive endorsement of the Treaty by the Irish electorate (about 63 per cent in favour). At the same time the Irish introduced a second question which asked for approval for future moves on integration to be put to a referendum only if the Irish Parliament consider that the changes are so great as to necessitate an amendment to the Constitution. Ireland will, however, put the Constitutional Treaty to a referendum.

The Nice Treaty was also a Treaty which did not bring about any further radical change to the Union but further defined certain policies previously adopted and made other adjustments, mainly to the institutional provisions of the Treaty in preparation for the 'big bang' expansion of the union with ten additional members.

One policy which was tightened was the 'closer cooperation' provision introduced by the Treaty of Amsterdam which was rather open ended and which enables certain states to proceed to further integration outside of the Treaty (Art 11 EC). Article 43 TEU now requires that this can only take place if a minimum of eight states wish to pursue this cooperation and more importantly, they must adhere to the existing *acquis communautaire*, although the requirement for a minimum of eight states is not retained in the Constitutional Treaty.

Other changes agreed at Nice included: amendments to the organization and oper-ation of the European Courts whereby more cases can be heard in chambers of judges.[29] It was agreed that a Charter of Fundamental Human Rights should be

---

[27] See EC Arts 100, 192, 103, 106, 192, and 300, the latter as an alternative.
[28] Protocol on the Enlargement of the European Union.
[29] These details can be found in the Statute of the Court of Justice which is contained in a Protocol attached to the Treaties.

included within the Union, although the member states did not or could not agree that it should formally be a part of the Treaty or of the Union. As it presently stands, it is not therefore legally binding within the legal order. This does not mean to say that the Union is left with a huge gap in its fundamental rights provision. The union is still committed to the respect of and observation of human rights and fundamental freedoms (Art 6 TEU) and in any case, the Court of Justice has built up a considerable body of case law upholding fundamental rights in the Community legal order. The Constitutional Treaty incorporates that catalogue of human rights as binding law in Part II.

The Nice Treaty also introduced a provision designed to do something about the situation where there was a clear risk of a serious breach by a member state of one of the respected principles of liberty, democracy, respect for human rights and fundamental freedoms, and the rule of law contained in Article 6 TEU. This change was provoked as a result of the lack of anything originally contained within the Treaties to deal with such a situation, when this very prospect looked threatening. At the start of 2000 an Austrian government was formed containing the right wing Freedom Party (FPÖ) party led by Jörg Haider, who has been known over the years for making inflammatory statements. Whether there was a real threat or not, the inclusion of this party in the government of one of the member states of the EU, was not appreciated by the other member states and who took political sanctions against Austria and sent an expert there to assess the situation. None of the moves were sanctioned though by any provision in the Treaties. Now Article 7 TEU provides that a risk of breach can be determined and recommendations to deal with the situation can be agreed by a majority decision, including suspension of voting rights of the member state where a persistent breach has been determined.

The Nice Council summit provided finally, a 'Declaration on the Future of the Union' which was to address a number of issues for the next IGC which was planned for 2003. These were to include a better definition and understanding of subsidiarity, to determine the status of the charter, to simplify the Treaties (which thus finally admitted the complexity of the Treaties as they have accumulated and indeed even added to by the agreements at Nice also). Other issues to be addressed were the use of so many protocols and declarations and how national parliaments feed their legitimacy into the Union? It also provided that a Convention on the Future of Europe be established to draft a 'Constitutional' Treaty for the European Union.

To that end, the Laeken Summit was held in December 2001 to formally set up and prepare the agenda for the Convention. It laid out in a declaration, the goals for making the European Union more democratic, transparent, and efficient. In particular attention would be paid to the governance of the Union, institutional preparations for the forthcoming expansion, the division of competences, and democratic participa-tion in decision-making processes of the Union.[30]

1.6.11 The Drafting of the Constitutional Treaty for Europe

The constitutional convention was set up on March 2002 and was based in Brussels. The work of the Convention, headed by a Praesidium of twelve members, was led by Valerie Giscard D'Estaing, the former French President and consisted of representa-tives of the heads of state and government of the fifteen member states and the thirteen candidate countries, thirty representatives of the nationals parliaments and twenty-six from the candidate countries, sixteen members of the EP, and two mem-bers from the Commission. It was intended to involve the peoples of Europe and be a new and different way of preparing change in comparison with the usual government only IGCs. It was charged with looking at how the EU related to its citizens (and vice versa), how competences should be divided between the Union and the constituent states and, within the union how competences were shared between the institutions. It was also to look at the question of democratic legitimacy. The Convention worked until June 2003 when it wrote up its report and a draft Constitutional Treaty was finalized and presented to the European Council in Greece on 18 July 2003. This was subsequently considered by the IGC which commenced in October 2003 and the draft Constitutional Treaty was presented to the Heads of State and Government Summit in Rome in December 2003.

A great deal of the preparatory work and negotiating for the summit trying to resolve the different points of view had already been completed behind the scenes. However, the final hard decisions were left to the European leaders in Rome. Whilst other things were on the agenda, such as the EU Foreign Minister, removing vetoes in areas such as tax, foreign affairs, and social security matters, the summit really came down to the big argument about the QMV numbers agreed in Nice and if not revisit-ing the actual numbers agreed, the Summit became preoccupied with finding ways to get round the dispute about the disparity between voting figures and populations, with a side argument on the number of Commissioners. The argument narrowly focused on the disparity of the respective Council of Ministers voting figures of twenty-nine for Germany and twenty-seven each for Spain and Poland.[31] Various compromises were suggested to ameliorate this disparity using double majorities of percentages of member states and populations but all failed to find favour with member states and the Summit broke down on this point. The failure was the most

---

[30] See the Presidency conclusions of the Laeken summit: http://ue.eu.int/ueDocs/cms_Data/docs/press Data/en/ec/68827.pdf and the section on the division of competences in Ch. 4.

[31] Council voting and in particular, qualified majority voting are considered in detail in Ch. 2.

public and notable failure in the history of the Union. The recriminations started immediately afterwards and the finger of blame pointed most notably at the large states of Poland, Germany, France, Spain, Italy, and the UK. Ironically, agreement had been reached on every other issue but by not reaching agreement on this last matter and instead walking away and abandoning the attempt to agree, everything in the draft Constitutional Treaty was potentially up for renegotiation and further disagreement in the future.

It is worthwhile reflecting for a moment on what was agreed, which included: Transferring power to the EU on fifteen new policy domains, transferring forty Article bases from unanimity to qualified majority, making the charter of fundamental rights legally binding, giving the EU status of a legal person to negotiate international agreements for all members countries, creating a common EU foreign minister to lead a joint foreign ministry with ambassadors, a fixed president for the Council, and qualified majority for the election of all high positioned officials, commencing the project of a common EU defence, and entitling the next treaty 'Constitution' and the express statement that it should have primacy over the national constitutions. In all, no mean feat but also in December 2003, a failure!

1.6.11.1 The Painful Process to Agreement

After Rome, the presidency of the Council passed to the Irish Government which inherited the unenviable task of trying to rescue the draft Constitution. Initially, the member states were hesitant to return to negotiation of the Constitution and immediately afterwards, suggestions were even being remade for a two-speed Europe of the six most federal European states with the others tagging along behind. Ireland conducted considerable diplomacy and behind the scenes for the most part, progress was being made. In the meantime, ten new member states actually joined on 1 May 2004, on the basis of the Nice Treaty and this event and the once again low turnout in the European Parliament elections in early June 2004 seemed to refocus the attention of the member states on reaching agreement on the Constitution. As the various countries expressed their views in pre-summit press briefings and meetings with the Irish Taiosioch, it became increasing clear that no change to the voting figures would be accepted or possible and that discussion would concentrate on the complex double majority voting mechanism in the Council of Ministers whereby in order for a majority vote to carry, a certain percentage of states must have voted for it representing also a certain percentage of population of the Union. Both percentages were subject to extensive discussion.[32] In the draft Constitution, the thresholds were originally set at 50 per cent (of member states) and 60 per cent (of population) but finally agreed as

---

[32] Further explanation of this complication will be provided in Ch. 2.

72 per cent of member states representing 65 per cent of the EU population. This Constitution was finally signed in October 2004 by the member states in Rome and handed over to each of the member states to ratify it by parliamentary approval or referendum or both according to the constitutional or legal requirements of each state.

1.6.12 The Constitutional Treaty for Europe

The Constitution as agreed cannot enter into force until one clear month after the last national ratification. It will be clear that this process, if it is completed at all, will be far longer than originally envisaged by the CT itself which envisaged 1 November 2006 as the entry into force date (Art. IV-447), because of the rejection of the CT by the electorates of France and Holland (although it must be noted that fourteen member states have already ratified the CT). However, at the time of writing, its future is very uncertain and the process of ratification has been suspended or postponed in some of the member states. It is unclear whether there will be another attempt to present the CT as it stands to the people of France and Holland or whether different approaches or lesser forms of further integration are adopted. In the meantime, the Treaty of Nice and any protocols and declarations on transitional measures remain in force.

There is a contingency plan in a Declaration (No 30) attached to the Constitutional Treaty which provides that in the event that one or more countries, up to 20 per cent of the countries, do not ratify the CT, then all member states can meet in the European Council to decide how they go forward and adopt a political solution. It is unclear whether this will be pursued.[33]

1.6.12.1 The Main Features of the Constitutional Treaty for Europe

Should the CT eventually be ratified, the main features include a change to the institutional architecture of the union and its powers, decision-making procedures and institutions. A legally binding Charter of Fundamental Rights has been included which is much broader than the European Convention on Human Rights and Fundamental Freedoms. There are procedures for adopting and reviewing the Constitution, a new President of the European Council, and a Foreign Minister, a smaller Commission comprising two-thirds of the number of member states. The array of legislative measures was supposed to have been simplified but even a cursory look at Articles I-33–39 reveal this to be far from the case. For the first time there is also an exit clause for member states (Art I-60).

[33] For the latest on the ratification process, please see: http://europa.eu.int/constitution/referendum_en.htm.

A very unfortunate feature of the Constitution is the further renumbering of the Treaty articles. This will mean that familiar fundamental provisions and basic rules will once again be hidden until familiarity with the new numbers is established.

1.7 Future Developments and Conclusions

The two most immediate concerns are ones which continue the themes already identified above, that is, the further widening and deepening of the Union. The further widening of the Union has already been considered in detail above but does represent a serious challenge for the cohesion of the Union, particularly in respect to the attitudes already voiced about possible Turkish membership. The process of further deepening is also continuing with the presently stalled ratification of the Constitutional Treaty, although there have been different views on what the CT actually means for further integration. If the Constitution for Europe is ratified by all the member states and comes into force does this mean we are any nearer a true federal union? Of course, as noted above, there is not a single and fixed view of what a federal state is; there are many, but the question is whether the EU displays enough of the characteristics of a state which is federally organized to be considered one. Or if not now, then just how much more is necessary and to what extent, if any, is the CT a step in this direction?

At present, the EU enjoys the transfer of considerable powers from the member states, its own institutions and law-making powers, an internal market, a division of powers and competences, the supremacy of Community law, its own catalogue of fundamental rights, its own parliament and also some of the more symbolic external trappings of statehood such as a currency, a flag, an anthem and a national day. It has a citizenship[34] but no *demos*, a coherent European population who identify themselves with an embryonic European state.

It has been shown above that the path to European Unity is not straight and wide and far from certain. It is not planned in advance and any plans that are put in place can easily be hijacked by rapidly evolving European and world political events, such as oil prices increases, world economic crises, currency collapses, the collapse of communism in Europe and the terrorist attacks of 11 September 2001. The widening and deepening of the EU, whilst considered under separate headings, are inextricably linked matters. The Union has been deepened in order to cope with forthcoming planned widenings (e.g. the first expansion) or deepenings have prompted subsequent

---

[34] To be explored in Chapter 9.

widenings (as with the SEA prompting the EFTA expansion). Expansion reveals difficulties which have to be addressed at the next opportunity, which has to be an IGC, set up either to discuss measures to deepen the Union or widen it. Whilst the twenty-five member states have been able to decide on the Constitutional Treaty, so far they have not all been able to ratify it, nevertheless, the Union of twenty-five member states and soon to be twenty-seven or twenty-nine or more will play an ever increasingly important role in world affairs, not just economically, but politically as well, and if for no other reason then because of its economic size. It needs to adapt to do this and, internally also, it still needs to address the issues of governance and democracy, not so far properly dealt with. However, European integration was regarded from the beginning as a process and not an end in itself. The CT has been regarded as both an example of further deeper integration because it represents a far more comprehensive ordering of the Union and member states, but also as a brake on further unwelcome integration because of its clearer delineation of competences. It makes matters clearer and sets discernible boundaries on the exercise of union power. It remains an unfolding story and the end is not yet written but quite what the end is, will no doubt also continue to be the subject of considerable debate.

Further reading

Books

BLAIR, A. *The European Union since 1945*, Pearson Longman, Harlow 2005.

DEVUYST, Y. *The European Union Transformed: Community Method and Institutional Evolution from the Schuman Plan to the Constitution for Europe*, Peter Lang, Brussels, 2005.

DOUGLAS-SCOTT, S. *Constitutional Law of the European Union*, Longman, Harlow 2002 (chapter 1).

GEORGE, S. and BACHE, I. *Politics in the European Union*, OUP, Oxford 2001 (especially chapters 1–13, 16, and 29).

HILLION, C. (ed.), *EU Enlargement: A Legal Approach*, Hart Publishing, Oxford 2004.

NICHOLLS, A. 'Britain and the EC: the historical Background' in *The UK and EC Membership,* Bulmer et al., Pinter Press, London 1992.

PINDER, J. *European Community: the Building of a Union*, OUP, Oxford 1991.

RODRIGUEZ-POSE, A. *The European Union: Economy, Society and Polity*, OUP, Oxford 2002.

SZYSZCZAK, E. and CYGAN, A. *Understanding EU Law*, Sweet & Maxwell, London 2005.

WARD, I. *A Critical Introduction to European Law*, 2nd edn., Butterworths, London 2003 (in particular chapters 1, 2 and 7).

Articles

BRADLEY, K. 'Institutional Design in the Treaty of Nice' (2001) 38 *CML Rev*, 1095.

CREMONA, M. 'EU Enlargement: Solidarity and conditionality' (2005) 30 *EL Rev*, 3.

DASHWOOD, A. 'The Constitution of the European Union after Nice: Law-Making Procedures' (2001) 26 *EL Rev*, 215.

EVANS, A. 'UK Devolution and EU Law' 28 *EL Rev*, 475.

HALLSTROM, L. 'Support for European Federalism? An Elite View' (2003) vol. 25 no. 1 *Journal of European Integration*, 51–72.

KOKOTT, J-R. 'The European Convention and its Draft Treaty establishing a Constitution for Europe: Appropriate answers to the Laeken questions?' (2003) vol. 40 no. 6 *Common Market Law Review*, 1315.

MEYRING, B. 'Intergovernmentalism and Supranationalism: Two Stereotypes for a Complex reality' (1997) *EL Rev*, 221.

USHER, J. 'The Reception of General Principles of Community law in the United Kingdom' (2005) 16 *EBLR*, 489.

WOUTERS, J. 'Institutional and Constitutional Challenges for the European Union: Some Reflections in the Light of the Treaty of Nice' (2001) 26 *EL Rev*, 342.

Web site Materials

Enlargement of the EU: http://europa.eu.int/pol/enlarg/index_en.htm

A fascinating website of documents, audio and visual clips relating to the history of European integration hosted by Leiden University http://www.eu-history.leiden univ.nl/index.php3?c=11 including the Churchill speeches on 'iron curtain' and 'a kind of United States of Europe'

Altneuland: The EU Constitution in a Contextual Perspective, Jean Monnet Working Paper 5/04, [http://www.jeanmonnet program.org/papers/04/040501.html] but see generally the working papers at this website: http://www.jeanmonnetprogram.org/papers/

Federal Trust Working Papers 26/03 (P Craig, 'What Constitution does the EU need? The House the Giscard Built: Constitutional Rooms with a View') and 27/03 (M. Dougan, 'The Convention's Draft Constitutional Treaty: A Tidying Up Exercise that needs some Tidying Up of its own?'), available on-line at http://www.fedtrust.co.uk/default.asp?groupid=6

The European Integration online Papers web site: http://eiop.or.at/eiop/

The Federal Trust for education and research: http://www.fedtrust.co.uk/

The Federal Union: http://www.federalunion.org.uk/index.shtml

2

The Union Institutions

2.1 Introduction: The Institutional Framework

The original institutional set-up which was established over fifty years ago, has been, in the best of EU traditions, changed, expanded, and complicated quite considerably since then.

The first Community, the ECSC, now no longer in existence, set the institutional scene by establishing a mix of supranational and intergovernmental institutions, although the original intention of the founding fathers was to have supranational institutions only. The tripartite system of the Council of Ministers, the Commission, (then called the High Authority), and the European Parliament (then called the Assembly) was established at that time and became the institutional foundation which has been added to and refined considerably since then. A notable feature has been the refinements to the law-making processes. Originally, this consisted of a proposal being formulated by the Commission which was simply decided upon by the Council of Ministers. The European Parliament, as the forum to discuss and debate proposals, would deliver an opinion on the proposed legislation and thus also play a limited role within this process. In addition, there is now an overall policy steering body, the European Council and additional consultative bodies (the Economic and Social Committee and the Committee of the Regions) to gather public interest group and regional opinions in order to feed these into the decision-making process. All of these aspects will be considered, commencing with a consideration of each of the institutions in turn.

The original three Communities, as first established, each had their own set of institutions (a Council of Ministers and a Commission) sharing a common Court of Justice and a Parliamentary Assembly. Since 1965, the separate Council and Commission for each Community have been merged and a unitary set of four 'official' institutions was established to serve all three Communities. These have since been expanded to five, as the result of the Maastricht Treaty adding the Court of Auditors to the list of principal institutions and the list is due to be added to once again, if the

Constitutional Treaty comes into force by making the European Council, presently standing outside of the institutional structure, into a principal Union Institution.[1]

Presently though, Article 7 of the EC Treaty states that the tasks entrusted to the Community shall be carried out by: a European Parliament, the Council, the Commission, the Court of Justice, and a Court of Auditors. These institutions serve both the two remaining Communities (EC and EURATOM) and also now as a result of Article 3 of the TEU, the European Union. Article 7 EC requires that each institution shall keep within the limits of the powers conferred on it by the Treaty. Article 7 further states that the Council of Ministers and the Commission shall be assisted by two advisory bodies which play an important role in the representation of interests in the Community law-making processes. These are an Economic and Social Committee (EESC) and a Committee of the Regions (COR) which have been established to act in an advisory capacity (Art 7(2)). These are part of a secondary group of bodies completing the institutional structure and include COREPER, the European Investment Bank (EIB), the European System of Central Banks (ESCB) and a European Central Bank (ECB), the latter three established by the Maastricht Treaty (Art 8 TEU).

The detailed provisions governing the institutions are set out in Part V of the EC Treaty, and each section begins with an article outlining the general functions of the institution in question.

2.2 The Commission

The Commission, fulfils the role of an executive administration for the Union and was given the sole right as the proposer of legislation under the original Treaties. This remains the case and makes the Commission more powerful than just a civil service bureaucracy carrying the will of an elected government. It is not, however, to be confused with a government itself. It is, though, able to formulate policy itself within the parameters of the agreed policy areas contained in the Treaties and make proposals for legislation to realize this, although the real power of initiative is somewhat compromised by the overall policy formulation and guidance provided by the Council of Ministers and the European Council, which if the Constitutional Treaty enters into force, will adopt a much more formal role in the institutional management of the Union. The Commission also has its own powers of decision under Article 211 EC, especially under the competition law policy under Articles 81

---

[1] See Art I-19 CT for the new list and Art I-21 CT in particular for the European Council.

and 82 and is able to exercise powers and enact administrative legislation under powers delegated to it by the Council of Ministers[2] which will be considered in further detail below.

2.2.1 Composition of the Commission

The composition, tasks and functions of the Commission are determined by Articles 211–19 EC.

As the Union itself has increased in membership so has the Commission and whilst it used to be the case that the big states had two commissioners each, it became increasingly clear from the 1995 expansion, which saw an increase to twenty Commissioners, that if the Commission were to become too large it would not assist effective management. On a more practical level, there were simply not enough subject matters for an effective and realistic division of work into twenty or more portfolios and it was agreed during the 2004 accession negotiation discussions that these should be reduced. Realizing this, as with many needed reforms in the Union, has been more difficult than anticipated. The discussions for the Convention on the Future of Europe proposed that the number of Commissioners should not even equal the number of member states. This was, with some reluctance on the part of the member states, accepted by them during the 2004 IGC considering the CT, albeit with a transitional arrangement. As from 1 November 2004, it was agreed that for five years, the Commission will consist of twenty-five members, one from each member state. If the CT comes into force during this period, this arrangement will be confirmed but in line with the plan to move away from each state having a commissioner, the CT provides in Article I-26(6) that the number should reduce to two-thirds the number of member states, as from 2014.

The Commissioners, although nominated representatives of the member states, are required to be completely independent in the performance of their duties and not take or seek instructions from any government or any other body (Art I-26(4) and (7)). Too often they are regarded as each member state's representatives in Brussels but, to counterbalance this view, another view suggests that after a while in Brussels, a Member State's Commissioner has a tendency to go native, in other words to take on a much more Community rather than national perspective on things.

The Commission is assisted by about 25,000 staff, and whilst this sounds a lot, it is asserted by the Union itself that this is fewer than in most medium-sized city councils in Europe. The Commission then is simply not a massive bureaucracy. In the member states, there are hundreds of thousands of civil servants with some single departments

---

[2] Regulated by Decision 199/468 (OJ 1999 L184/23).

employing far more than the entire European Commission.[3] Part of the reason for the much lower numbers in the EU, is that most of the work covered or generated by EU legislation is, in fact, carried out by the national agencies, particularly in respect of the Common Agricultural Policy.

2.2.2 Appointment and Removal

Under present rules, first of all, the Commission President is nominated by qualified majority voting by the heads of State and Government meeting in Council under Article 214 EC and is then subject to approval by the EP. The President nominates and the member states then nominate the other Commissioners and the entire Commission is then subject to the approval of the EP en bloc. This makes the rejection of a single Commissioner designate technically impossible although not practically impossible as was seen in 2004 by the objection of the EP to the Italian nomination because of his genuinely held but incongruous views on homosexuality and the role of women. The Commission President designate Barroso decided not to submit the Commission for approval in fear of a probable rejection of the entire Commission but instead reshuffled the proposed Commission which was then approved by the EP and appointed by the Council. The term of office for all Commissioners is for a renewable period of five years. There are five Vice-Presidents in the Barroso Commission, but the number of Vice-Presidents is no longer specified by the Treaty.

The Commission can be removed by a vote of censure by the EP but only collectively (Art 201) and until the replacement Commission is appointed in its entirety, the old Commission stays in office. The CT will retain this method of mass expulsion. It is therefore somewhat of a blunt instrument if the activities of only one Commissioner are objected to, although there is the procedure under Article 216 EC for the Court of Justice, on an application of the Council or the Commission (but not the EP), to compulsorily retire a Commissioner for serious misconduct or where he or she no longer fulfils the conditions required for the performance of his or her duties. The EP can only act against the whole Commission. Censure was threatened in 1999 following a damning report of an independent Committee of experts appointed by the EP which exposed serious fraud, cronyism, and incompetence on the part of individual Commissioners. Whilst it did not come to a vote of censure, it forced the resignation

---

[3] Following the 2004 expansion of the Union, there will be more, however, no figures have yet been released. To test this assertion, I looked at Cardiff, a medium-sized European city, which has about 20,000 staff working directly for the Council, plus those who work in the Welsh Assembly in Cardiff and in the many independent agencies undertaking Council work, making a total of about 30,000. In the UK, the Office for National Statistics reported in April 2004, an increase to a total of over 523,000 direct government civil servants in the UK: http://www.statistics.gov.uk.

of the entire Santer Commission on 15 March 1999 as the only way to oust the culpable Commissioners. A new Commission was approved by the EP in September 1999 under the presidency of Prodi who required from the individual Commissioners a promise to resign on demand, thus increasing the power of the President within the Commission.

2.2.3 Tasks and Duties

Article 211 imposes the general duty of ensuring the proper functioning and development of the common market. The Commission has a number of main functions:

(a) It must ensure that the provisions of the Treaty and the measures taken by the institution under them are applied. The Commission is described as the guardian or watchdog of the Communities, because it is given the task of prosecuting breaches of the Treaty by member states under Article 226, other institutions under Article 230, and individuals under various provisions of the Treaty and secondary Regulation (for example) 1/2003 in respect of competition policy.

(b) It formulates and proposes policy initiatives by way of recommendations or opinions on matters dealt with in the Treaty, if it expressly so provides or if the Commission considers it necessary. Here the Commission is acting as the initiator of legislation.

(c) The Commission has limited powers of independent decision-making by participation in the shaping of measures taken by the Council of Ministers and by the EP in the manner provided for in the Treaty.

(d) It has powers under the delegated legislation procedure conferred on it by the Council of Ministers for the implementation of the rules laid down by the latter, thus acting as the Executive of the Communities. The Commission also manages the Community's annual budget.

The Commission is regarded as the most federal institution of the EC, due largely to its independence from direct national influences. Its decision-making process, under Article 219 EC, provides that the Commission can decide matters collectively by a majority. All members of the Commission are expected to abide collectively by Commission decisions.

Commission activity is most pronounced in the fields of competition policy and in the management of the Common Agricultural and Common Customs policies because of the high degree of day-to-day decision-making necessary. It is also very much involved in representing the Union in international organizations such as

GATT and the WTO and in concluding international agreements on behalf of the Union such as the association agreements with various countries.[4]

2.3 The Council (of Ministers) of the European Union

Unfortunately the Council of Ministers has undergone a few name changes, presently being called simply 'the Council' in contrast to being previously called 'the Council of Ministers'. Under the CT, it will be called the Council of the Union. Furthermore, unhelpfully, there is also the European Council, considered below, with which it should not be confused. Despite the various changes brought about to the legislative processes by the various Treaty amendments in favour of the EP, the Council remains the main legislative organ of the Communities. Its tasks, composition, and functions are outlined in Articles 202–10 EC. It consists of representative Ministers of the member states depending on the subject matter under discussion. Thus, different configurations of the Council take place with the Foreign Ministers attending the General Council and agriculture or finance ministers, for example attend the specialist Councils. In total, there are nine different council configurations The Council can also be constituted by the Heads of State and Government, for example, for the appointment of the Commission under Article 214 EC.

2.3.1 Functions and Powers

Article 202 imposes on the Council of Ministers the duty of ensuring the coordination of the general economic policies of the member states both internally for the EU and also coordinates its economic policy with the rest of the world. The Treaty confers upon it the power to take decisions and to delegate to the Commission. For the most part, the Council has the final power of decision for the adoption of legislative proposals made by the Commission, except in matters governed by the co-decision procedure which provides the EP with a final right of veto, as outlined under Article 251 of the EC Treaty and considered below in the section on legislative procedures. The Council, along with the EP, is also responsible for the adoption of the annual budget.

2.3.2 The Presidency of the Council

The Council of Ministers is chaired by a Presidency which is held by each of the member states in turn for a period of six months only, as determined by Council

---

[4] Which are considered in Chapter 3.

Decision 95/2, although a new decision on rotation may be taken before the Constitutional Treaty enters into force. Thus ministers or the Head of Government or State chair the Council meetings or summit for a period of six months. The term 'Troika' is used in conjunction with the Council to describe the situation where to provide continuity in policy, the current President and both the previous and succeeding Presidents act in conjunction, particularly in the pursuit of international relations. The Constitutional Treaty provides that the President will be elected by QMV in the European Council and will serve for a period of two and a half years, renewable once.

2.3.3 Role and Voting in the Legislative Procedures

Despite all the institutional reforms over the years, the Council still has the major role in deciding on and enacting secondary legislation. Quite how and with whom it acts to do this, depends on the particular Treaty provision under which legislation is enacted, on other words, the legal base. As was outlined in Chapter 1, in broad terms the political institutional balance has seen a number of movements over the decades, mostly in favour of a power shift from the Council to the EP in the law-making process. However, it is not just the EP which participates with the Council and it may have to consult the Economic and Social Committee, and/or the Committee of the Regions. In considering even its participation with the EP only, there are different forms of law-making so that the Council may just consult the EP or cooperate or co-decide with the EP, as will be explained in detail below.

2.3.3.1 Forms of Voting

There are different forms of decision-making within the Council itself, in other words in what manner it takes decisions or how it votes. Article 205 EC provides that subject to Treaty exceptions, the Council will vote by a simple majority. In fact the exceptions are the rule (or the rule is the exception) and voting is mainly by a qualified majority or by unanimity. If and when the Constitutional Treaty comes into force, we are in a period of transition in that there is still a considerable mix of the voting methods employed, although following the reforms introduced under the Amsterdam and Nice Treaties, the co-decision procedure, requiring qualified majority voting on the part of the Council, has emerged as the most frequently employed method of voting, although it would be usual for the President at least to attempt to gain consensus.[5]

2.3.3.2 Unanimity

Turning to the methods themselves, unanimity is clear, all member states must agree,

---

[5] See http://europa.eu.int/institutions/decision-making/index_en.htm.

which means as from 2004, all twenty-five. This is where the member states can wield a veto, see, for example, Article 13 EC requiring unanimity on the part of the Council to enact measures outlawing different forms of discrimination. The more voting is done on this basis, the less potentially and probably will get done, hence a move to more majority voting is crucial. Member states which abstain do not prevent the others from agreeing a measure unanimously, which is then binding on all twenty-five.

2.3.3.3 Simple Majority Voting

Another form of voting, that of simple majority voting, is extremely rare and is only required for one Article (104) of the EC Treaty.

2.3.3.4 Qualified Majority Voting

In 1965 the Council was due to move from unanimity to qualified majority voting, often shortened to QMV, for certain subject areas of the Treaty. This was objected to by President de Gaulle of France and the ensuing dispute led eventually to a boycott of the institutions by the French members. It was only resolved when a compromise, called the 'Luxembourg Accords' or 'Luxembourg Compromise' was reached.[6] This was essentially an agreement to disagree but provided that, where a member state identified a very important national interest, all the member states should try to reach a unanimous decision, rather than that member be overruled. The six member states could not, however, agree on the consequence of a failure to agree. The conclusion, which was certainly that of the French and generally accepted, was that an objecting member state effectively had a veto over the decision. The legal position of the Accords was uncertain, but despite the provision in the Treaty for majority and qualified majority voting, the Council denied itself for many years this ability. Successive enlargements and the difficulties in reaching a consensus led the Council to realize that it could no longer make progress only using unanimity. Thus, particularly after the Treaty revisions of the SEA and TEU, the Council has moved slowly but significantly to using QMV in more and more areas (twelve occasions with the SEA and thirty with the TEU). So much so, that the continued validity of the Luxembourg Accords had been brought into doubt. The Amsterdam and Nice treaties extended its use in another forty-seven instances. Despite the further considerable move to QMV contained within the CT, if and when it enters into force, unanimous voting will be retained for quite a few matters, particularly when measures may be considered necessary to fulfil certain Community aims but for which express powers have not been foreseen. Unanimity has been retained for the areas of common foreign, security and

---

[6] Considered in Section 1.6.6.2.

defence policies, taxation, social security matters, and appointments to most of the institutions.[7]

Qualified Majority Voting has become the single most important issue in the Council of late. To allow it to be used more often has often involved a lot of horse trading. More use of QMV is necessary because it allows votes to be taken by majorities. The possible alternative, to take decisions by simple majority is not a real alternative because it is not politically acceptable for most member states. Thus the use of QMV enhances both democracy and efficiency in law-making in the EU where otherwise decisions would be extremely difficult to reach in a Council of twenty-five possible vetoes.

2.3.3.5 How QMV Works

Article 205 provides that each member state has a block number of votes crudely in proportion to the size of the population but, instead of a simple majority of states or votes being able to secure a decision, a certain majority of votes has to be achieved from the combination of the blocks of votes of the member states.[8] The qualified majority is now 232 votes (72.27 per cent) from a possible total of 321. Thus, a blocking minority of ninety votes will prevent a proposal from being passed. If voting on a proposal which has been introduced by the Council rather than the Commission, an additional requirement is imposed that a minimum of two-thirds of the member states must have voted in favour.

The actual numbers of votes per state has always been a matter of contention and in particular for the larger states. Prior to the reforms adopted at Nice, at the extreme, Germany, with approximately 81 million population had ten votes in comparison to Luxembourg with a population of about 600,000, which had two votes. This was clearly disproportionate! Prior to the last enlargement, it was noted that with a greater number of states, a blocking minority would be harder to achieve as it required more votes and thus more countries. At the same time, though, it was also noted that as the number of states increased, the relative share of influence of the large states decreased, despite their high share of the population. It is worth noting that four countries: Germany, France, the UK, and Italy have just over 57 per cent of the EU-25 population, therefore if voting were undertaken by simple majority based directly on

---

[7] A full list has been included in the accompanying website.
[8] Germany, France, Italy, United Kingdom 29
Spain, Poland 27
The Netherlands 13
Belgium, Czech Republic, Greece, Hungary, Portugal 12
Austria, Sweden 10
Denmark, Ireland, Lithuania, Slovakia, Finland 7
Cyprus, Estonia, Latvia, Luxembourg, Slovenia 4
TOTAL 321

population, it would mean that the four large states could dictate to the other twenty-one states. Even in the EU of twenty-seven (with Romania and Bulgaria), the big four would still have 53 per cent of the EU-27 population. However, for the reason that such behaviour would not be acceptable to the small and medium size states, various compromises have been made to the voting rules, at first informal and then institutionalized as a part of the present Treaty and retained with revision in the CT. The compromises seek to achieve a balance between facilitating decision-making but nevertheless providing that a sizeable minority of states can block decisions. Hence, the reform of QMV became a hotly contended issue, with the debate first concentrating on the number of votes per member state and then the additional requirements based on the number of states voting and the populations of those states.

To go back to basics for a moment, first though, is the idea that the number of Council votes per country should in some way, even if very crudely, represent the population and thus usually the GDP of the countries, or, if you like the political and economic clout! This is tinged with the fear of domination of Europe by a few large states over the wishes of numerous smaller states. Hence, the votes for each country for a qualified majority were deliberately biased for the protection of smaller states and to ensure more of a consensus view. The Treaty of Nice went some way to address the over-representation of the smaller states, by giving the larger member states a higher proportion of votes. To some extent, the acceptance of this change by all states is argued to have been regarded as fair compensation for the loss of a second Commissioner by the large states. However, it was not accepted without further condition because this change meant that a smaller combination of larger states could outvote the small states, something the smaller member states were not happy with. Hence further compromises had been devised for the Treaty of Nice that for votes on proposals not originating from the Commission, a certain member state threshold must be achieved to pass decisions. Any measure must be supported by at least two-thirds of the member states, but further, if requested by a member, a second threshold is added that the qualified majority represent at least 62 per cent of population of the Union. However, even the with Nice reforms, Luxembourg and Malta, the smallest states with populations of about 600,000 and 390,000 but respectively four and three votes in Council, have voting power far in excess of their populations in comparison with Germany with about 81 million population and twenty-nine votes. In addition, Nice also agreed as some sort of behind closed doors political deal, a disproportionately large number of votes for Poland and Spain which are far higher than warranted by the size of the population. It was speculated that this was to facilitate the reform of the CAP and compensate the loss of benefits for Poland and Spain who would otherwise have been considerable beneficiaries of EU funds. However, as soon as Nice was agreed, it became clear that Germany and other states were not happy with the voting figures. It was agreed, however, not to reopen the agreement reached at Nice which had been, almost literally, a nightmare to achieve.[9] The next opportunity to address this was not far away. This was the European Council Summit to discuss and agree the draft Constitutional Treaty as proposed by the Convention on the Future of Europe. However, it became clear that without changing the actual number of votes, as agreed in Nice, any possibility of addressing the continuing concerns of the imbalance of votes could only be done through further tinkering with the proportions of states required to vote in favour of a proposal or/and the proportion of the population of the EU as a whole which should be required to support a qualified majority vote. This became the argument which led to the very public bust-up and failure to agree in Rome in December 2003. The member states simply could not agree on the further compromises needed to respect the allocation of votes at Nice, which had to take account of the largest states' populations and political clout and to be sensitive to the smaller states' fear of being dominated by a few larger states. It took months of shuttle diplomacy under the Irish Presidency in the first part of 2004 to come up with the necessary compromises. In a nutshell, these new reforms will mean that more states will be outvoted more often.

If and when CT enters into force, QMV will operate as follows. The voting figures remain the same but the support of a specified majority of member states is required, which is determined by Article I-25(1) as 55 per cent. Additionally, though, this percentage must be made up by two-thirds of the member states and 65 per cent of the population of the EU. Furthermore, a blocking minority must include at least four member states, to prevent a small minority of large member states from blocking a proposal. Finally, even where there are not sufficient votes or states to constitute a blocking minority, the Council should enter into a conciliation phase but which must not prejudice time limits for enacting legislation. Although the 55 per cent member state requirement and then the additional minimum of fifteen member states appears to be contradictory in that 55 per cent of twenty-five is 13.75 states but fifteen are still required, the rule was negotiated with an eye to the future expansion of the Union when 55 per cent would represent more states. Having said that, when the EU comprises twenty-seven states or more 55 per cent will always be fifteen or more member states thus making the second requirement of fifteen states rather superfluous but who suggested political compromise was a perfect science?

2.3.4 Council General Law-making Powers

Apart from voting which is specified in particular articles throughout the Treaty, the Council also has general powers to enact legislation. Article 93 empowers the Council

---

[9] See the discussion in Chapter 1, at 1.6.10.

of Ministers, acting unanimously to adopt provisions for the harmonization of legislation concerning turnover taxes, excise duties, and other forms of indirect taxes (VAT) to the extent that such harmonization is necessary to ensure the functioning and establishment of the internal market. Article 94 provides for the approximation of laws not catered for by any of the specific parts of the Treaty and requires unanimity by the Council and Article 95, originally introduced by the SEA, provides that the Council shall act by a qualified majority on a proposal which have as their object the establishment and functioning of the internal market.

Article 308 provides the Council may enact measures to attain the objectives of the Community.

Use of this general power has been used extensively by the Council, particularly for measures not originally sanctioned elsewhere, for example, in 1976 to support the enactment of the Equal Treatment Directive (76/207) which went much further than old Article 119 (now Art 141) concerned narrowly with equal pay matters only. It was used often to enact environment measures before the Treaty was amended to include a title on environment. However, its proposed use to accede to the European Convention on Human Rights (ECHR), was prevented by the Court of Justice which stated that in Opinion 1/96, that it could not be used as the basis for acceding to the ECHR.

The Constitutional Treaty proposes to address this competence creep by more clearly establishing the division of competences (Art I-11–14) and which topic was considered in Chapter 1.

2.3.5 COREPER and the Council Secretariat

The Council is not a permanent body, as noted above, and in all configurations meets only on about ninety occasions per year. Hence then it requires assistance to deal with the workload and to provide preparation for and some continuity between meetings. This help comes in two forms.

First, the Committee of Permanent Representatives (COREPER) was established, consisting of representatives of the member states who may be part of the ambassadorial delegation or other civil servants on secondment. It is now formally established within the Treaty, Article 207 EC. This body was brought in to reduce the workload of the Council, to balance the result of the delegation of decision-making power to the Commission and to sift the Commission proposals. It also oversees and to a lesser extent, controls the numerous Management Committees which were set up to supervise the delegation of power to the Commission and which are considered further below. Article 207(2) also provides for a permanent Council Secretariat to undertake much of the more mundane work of the Council such as organization of and preparation for meetings.

2.4 The European Council

The European Council, which is not yet a formal institution of the Union, arose from the Summit meetings of the Heads of State and Government of the member states who met from time to time to discuss matters outside the formal scope of the Community Treaties and provide impetus for the Community or act in response to international crises. After this informal start, Article 2 SEA placed the European Council on a legal basis and formalized European Political Cooperation in the areas of foreign policy consultation and cooperation and monetary cooperation. These moves have been further formalized and brought into the European Union framework by Article 4 of the Maastricht Treaty, which states that the European Council shall provide the Union with the necessary impetus for its development and shall define the general political guidelines, as such then it enjoys a much broader role than the Council of Ministers which is restricted to matters included in the Treaties. The European Council meets at least twice a year to discuss the progress of the Union and to report to the European Parliament on an annual basis. The President of the Commission and the foreign ministers also attend the European Council summits (Art 4 TEU). Under the Constitutional Treaty, it will be made a full institution and will meet four times a year (Art I-19).

Decision-making by the European Council is strictly by unanimity as it is purely an intergovernmental organization and has leant a distinctly intergovernmental stance at the top of the Union institutional hierarchy. Whilst it has, at times, provided the necessary political impetus and will to achieve very notable goals such as economic union and the Euro, it is feared that trying to achieve the agreement of the now twenty-five heads of State or Government will prove very demanding. The Presidency of the European Council mirrors that of the Council of Ministers but, like its decision-making practise, has been criticized for its lack of efficiency, not least by some of the member states itself. The CT will answer some of these criticisms by electing the European Council President by qualified majority for a period of two and a half years renewable once and providing for qualified majority decision-making by the European Council in some limited circumstances including changes to the configuration of Council meetings (Art I-24) and relating to the appointment of members to Union Institutions: The Commission President proposal and the appointment of The Commission (Art I-27), the appointment of a Union Minister for Union affairs (Art I-28) and the appointment of members of the ECB (Art III-382).

2.5 The European Parliament (EP)

As originally conceived and constituted, the European Parliament (EP) was called the Assembly and consisted of members nominated by and largely from the member states' Parliaments. It was arguably more aptly named at that time because it was not a true legislative body capable of law-making in its own right and the EP consists of only one chamber. However, the term 'Parliament' was used by its members from 1962[10] and with more authority following the direct election of its 518 members for the first time in 1979. The term arguably carries more prestige and attracts greater respect from the public. Consequently, the SEA Article 6 provided legal recognition of the Assembly's decision to call itself the European Parliament, and this is clearly confirmed by Article 189 EC as amended by the TEU. The EP is governed by Articles 189–201 of the EC Treaty and has enjoyed significant incremental increases in its powers and functions with each new amending Treaty.

One of the biggest problems the EP has to contend with, through no fault of its own, are the requirements that it still meet in plenary session in Strasbourg, but also meet in Brussels and have the secretariat based in Luxembourg, whilst its members peddle back and forth from their national constituencies. Its seat was supposed to have been settled a long time ago but none of the countries involved is willing to lose the presence of the EP despite the massive increase in costs this results in and worse, the inefficiency engendered due to the waste of time and resources. A protocol to the Treaty of Amsterdam seems to have settled this vexed question but probably only to the satisfaction of the member states directly involved. The EP is destined to be forever in transit between the plenary sessions in Strasbourg, additional sessions in Brussels, and its secretariat in Luxembourg. This will remain the same in the protocol attached the CT.

2.5.1 Membership and Election

The member states agreed in the Amsterdam Treaty, with an eye on the forthcoming big bang expansion in 2004, to set the number of MEPs to a maximum of 700. As a result, Article 189 was amended, however the figure was revised again for the Nice Treaty with the increased number of 732 members to accommodate new member states. Consequently the number of MEPs per state had to be changed but only after fierce debate because this issue became linked to the change in the member state vote weightings under QMV. Strictly speaking this should not be the case as MEPs are

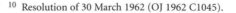

[10] Resolution of 30 March 1962 (OJ 1962 C1045).

elected to serve the electorate in constituencies and are organized into cross-border political groupings rather than member states and that the total number per state should crudely be in proportion to population. However, the broad political deal reached was that the member states who had gained in the QMV numbers lost more MEPs whereas, those member states regarded as losing out under QMV either retained the previous numbers of MEPs or lost proportionately less MEPs compared to other member states. Nice, though has not been the final word and, yet again, in the negotiations for the Constitutional Treaty, the figure has been raised to a maximum of 736 for the twenty-five member states, but with a further agreement that this be increased to 750 from 2009 for a Community of twenty-seven member states. Further possible expansions (Turkey and Croatia) will almost certainly cause this issue to be reopened again.

2.5.1.1 Elections and Political Parties

Article 190(4) requires a common system of election to be set up for the election for the EP. While all member states now, including the UK, have used PR voting systems, this is still not a common one and although the same Thursday into the weekend is used, the actual polling day or days are different in different member states according to election day traditions, e.g. the UK prefers a Thursday whereas other member states have always used a Saturday or Sunday as polling day.

Once elected, MEPs sit in the transnational political groupings, recognized under Article 191 EC, although there is a strong national element and organization within these, particularly as a result of national political party discipline. There are seven distinct groups and a final group for those members not wishing to be aligned to any of the specific groups and which have the following European and UK membership:[11]

 Group of the European People's Party (Christian Democrats) and European Democrats (**PPE-DE**) 268 (twenty-seven in the UK)

 Socialist Group in the European Parliament **PSE** 201 (nineteen in the UK)

 Group of the Alliance of Liberals and Democrats for Europe **ALDE** 88 (twelve in the UK)

---

[11] Full list can be found at http://www.europarl.eu.int/members/expert/groupAndCountry.do?language=en.

 Group of the Greens/European Free Alliance **Verts/ALE** 42 (five in the UK)

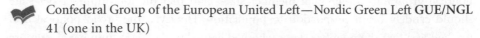 Confederal Group of the European United Left—Nordic Green Left **GUE/NGL** 41 (one in the UK)

iD Independence/Democracy Group **IND/DEM** 36 (ten in the UK)

Union for Europe of the Nations Group **UEN** 27 (none in the UK)

Non-attached Members **NI** 28 (four in the UK)

2.5.2 Functions/Powers

Apart from the obvious function of a Parliament, which is that of a discussion and debate forum, the EP has the following powers and functions:

2.5.2.1 Legislative Powers

Before the SEA was negotiated, as far as legislative participation was concerned, the EP had advisory and consultative powers only. Old Article 137 EEC provided that the Assembly shall 'exercise the advisory and supervisory powers which are conferred on it by this Treaty'. The treaty specified only seventeen instances where the EP had to be consulted before a decision could be adopted by the Council.[12] Its participation in the legislative process was increased by the Conciliation procedure of 1977 and the introduction of the cooperation procedure by the SEA, which is in effect a kind of extended consultation process, noted below. The present authorization for the EP's law-making role is Article 192 EC which empowers the EP to take part in the adoption of Community acts under Articles 251 and 252. The TEU, though, gave the Parliament its most extensive role thus far in the legislative process by introducing the co-decision procedure, which has become the most widely used procedure. It is considered in detail below. This procedure has been extended in line with the extension of QMV in the Council of Ministers. The Constitutional Treaty, if and when it comes into force, will increase its contribution yet again, as far as the number of Treaty articles requiring the co-decision procedure is concerned. However, the EPs legislative role overall remains limited such that the term 'democratic deficit' can arguably still be used to describe the unsatisfactory degree of democratically legitimized participation in the law-making process in the EU by the EP, the only directly elected Union institution.

Finally, the EP has a power of assent, which is a prerequisite for the accession of

---

[12] See, e.g., old Arts 54 and 235 of the EEC Treaty.

new member states or the entry of the Community into international and association agreements (Art 49 TEU and Art 300 EC) and in two other cases, noted below.

2.5.2.2 Control of the Executive

The EP has, through various Treaty amendments, gained powers of appointment and removal of the Commission as well as a general role of the scrutiny of the work of the Commission.

Appointment. Starting with appointment, the Treaty of Amsterdam introduced the requirement that the President of the Commission nominated by the member states is first approved by the EP. Then the whole Commission, as nominated by the member states in conjunction with the President of the Commission, is subject to the approval of the EP (see Art 214 EC). The political strength gained by the EP by this change was demonstrated in 2004, when the proposed new Commission had to be reconstituted because the EP took objection to the proposal of a particular Commissioner. In order to avoid a likely vote not to appoint the entire Commission, Barroso, the proposed Commission President, instead withdrew his proposed team and resubmitted it a couple of weeks later minus the offending person.

Censure/Removal. At least on paper, its most powerful weapon would seem to be its power to censure the Commission, which means in effect to require it to resign from office. Article 201 EC provides that a two-thirds vote of the majority of the members is needed but the Commission is required to resign in its entirety. The censure motion cannot be used against individual Commissioners, which is regarded as unfortunate. For example, in 1999, under the Santer Commission, certain Commissioners were accused of financial improprieties and fraud. A censure motion against the entire Commission failed but following the very critical report of a committee of independent experts set up by the EP and Commission, the entire Commission resigned without a further vote of censure taking place. Whilst the end result was that which was required, that is, that certain commissioners were removed from office, the result is criticized because the particular Commissioners were able to hide behind the collective resignation and not be singled out. Until the new Commissioners are approved, the censured Commissioners remain in office. So far, a motion has been tabled on six occasions but none have been adopted.

Other powers of scrutiny now available to the EP include: The ability to set up a Committee of Inquiry to investigate the alleged contravention or maladministration in the implementation of Community law, formalized in the Treaty structure by the TEU in Article 193 EC, the ability to question, orally or in writing, the Commission under Article 197 and the right to discuss the Commission's annual general reports under Article 200. The EP is also entitled it to request the Commission to submit proposals which the EP considers necessary for the implementation of the EC Treaty (Art 192), although the Commission is not obliged to do anything about such a submission.

2.5.2.3 Budgetary Powers ⅄

From the 1970s the EP had been given budgetary powers in the form of the final say over compulsory and then non-compulsory expenditure. Furthermore, under the Budgetary Treaty of 1975, Parliament was given the power to reject the budget entirely, which it did in 1979 and 1984 (see Art 272 EC). The 1979 rejection was partly in response to the increase in democratic legitimacy which the Parliament gained as a result of being directly elected in that year for the first time. However, rejection is not so drastic as it sounds because if the budget is rejected, the so-called 'one-twelfth rule' comes into operation, which means that until the new budget is approved, the Commission can spend per month up to one-twelfth of the previous year's head of expenditure (Art 273 EC). In order to try to avoid future, nevertheless, disruptive budget rejections, from 1988 various Inter-Institutional Agreements have been agreed by the Institutions[13] to improve the functions on the budgetary procedure and on financial planning. Thus, the EP now discharges the Commission's implementation of the budget on an annual basis, although this has become a more political event and opportunity to hold the Commission to account.

2.5.2.4 Right to Litigate ⤴

Although the EP was not originally named as one of the privileged applicants for the purposes of taking actions under Articles 230 and 232 EC, the Court of Justice held back in the 'Transport' case (*Parliament v Council*, Case 13/83) and in *Parliament v Council* (Case C-70/88, *Chernobyl*), that it is able to bring an action against the other institutions for failure to act under Article 232, and whilst originally, it was held not to have a general right of challenge under Article 230, in the Comitology case (Case 302/87, *European Parliament v Council*), it was held to have the right to take action to protect its own prerogative powers (*European Parliament v Council (Chernobyl)* (see also in this respect, *European Parliament v Council* (Case C-295/80, Students Residence Directive)). Acts which have legally binding consequences of the Parliament can also be challenged under Article 230 (see Case 294/83, *Les Verts v European Parliament and Council v European Parliament* (Case 34/86, Budgetary procedure)). The TEU has also amended Articles 230 and 232 to specify that the acts or omissions of the EP can be challenged under the usual conditions and the Treaty of Nice provided express confirmation in Article 230 that the EP is one of the privileged

---

[13] In the latest version: Agreement of 6 May 1999 (OJ 1999 C172/1).

applicants able itself to challenge acts of the other institutions without any restriction in its *locus standi.*

Finally, other functions and powers of the EP include under Article 194 EC, the right of Community citizens to petition the EP and the right for Community citizens to complain to a Parliamentary Commission, or otherwise known as an Ombudsman set up by the EP, about the maladministration of the Community Institutions, with the exception of the judicial activities of the Community Courts (Art 195 EC). Individuals, legal or natural, may complain either directly or through a MEP, providing the matter has not been subject of legal proceedings. The investigations terminates with the issue of a report to the EP, the institutions concerned and copied to the complainant.

2.6 The European Court of Justice (Court of Justice)

The European Court of Justice, once a single body institution, now comprises the Court of Justice itself with the Court of First Instance and since the Treaty of Nice came into effect on 1 February 2003, the possibility of the creating judicial panels was introduced (Arts 220 and 225 EC), one of which has been created and is considered below. The European Court of Justice is a self-standing independent Community Court and it is not in a hierarchical relationship with the national courts as in a system of appeal. Article 220 EC outlines the general function of the Court of Justice which is to ensure that in the interpretation and application of the Treaty, the law is observed.

2.6.1 Composition and Organization

The Court of Justice presently consists of twenty-five judges and eight Advocates General, nominated and appointed by unanimous agreement by the governments of the member states. This will remain so even if the CT enters into force. The judges must be chosen from persons whose independence is beyond doubt and who possess the qualifications necessary for appointment to the highest judicial office in their own countries or recognized juridical competence which includes academic lawyers, the appointment to the highest courts of which is a tradition in a number of countries, Articles 221–3.

The Court can sit as a full court (with quorum of only fifteen), a grand chamber of thirteen judges to hear cases involving either member states or Community institutions or in chambers of three or five judges, of which there are three chambers of each following the 2004 enlargement.

The TEU introduced an amended Article 221 which reduces the occasions when the court may need to sit in plenary session and which is now when a member state or a Community institution, as a party to an action, requests plenary jurisdiction.

2.6.2 Procedure

The court is faced with a large of number of cases which can arise ad hoc from any of the member states in one of the now twenty official languages acceptable to the Court but the Court operates internally in French as its only working language. The procedure of the Court is governed by a protocol containing the Statute of the Court of Justice and by its Rules of Procedure.[14] As a new international court, its rules were based initially on the rules of procedure of the International Court of Justice in the Hague and reflect generally civilian law procedure with the emphasis on written proceedings rather than oral, as is the case on the UK and other common law systems.

There are essentially four stages to proceedings. Written proceedings followed by investigation and preparatory work on the case, then oral proceedings including the AG's opinion, which can be omitted in certain circumstance, noted below. The final stage is the judgment, which follows deliberation in secret in French. Judgments of the Court of Justice are delivered in a single ruling and Article 2 of the Statute on the Court provides that before taking up judicial office, each judge shall, in open court, take an oath to preserve the secrecy of the Court's deliberations. Arguments in favour of the single opinion of the Court are that it supports the authority of the Community Court and the Community legal system. It helps to build up new a common European law and avoid reliance on the laws of particular states. It also provides for more authoritative decision making for the future. Arguments against are that it often results in terse and cryptic judgments, with little evidence of reasoning, it stifles true legal argument and it may inhibit judges and the development of law. To some extent these criticisms may be countered by the existence and role of Advocates General, which is to assist the Court by giving an opinion, in complete independence and impartiality, on the legal issues of a case which will be examined in depth and to critically review the jurisprudence of the Court on the subject. Although the opinion of the Advocate General is not binding on the Court, it carries weight and adds to the development of Community law. Thus an opinion of the Advocate General acts like a first instance decision subject to an automatic and instant appeal. They can adopt a public view or the parties views but cannot be bound to present any particular view. It is no longer a mandatory requirement that the opinion of the Advocate General be heard before every judgment is given. According to Article 20 of the Statute of the

---

[14] See Foster, *EC Legislation*, 16th edn., pp. 121 and 181.

Court of Justice, the Court may decide in a case which raises no new point of law, after hearing the view of the Advocate General, that the case be determined without a submission from the Advocate General. It was estimated by the Court of Justice that about 30 per cent of the cases in 2004, were not decided with an opinion of an AG.[15]

2.6.2.1 The Form of Judgments

The report is drafted first of all in the language of the case, which is chosen by the parties or the defending Member State from the twenty official languages, following the last expansion. The internal working documents of the court and its deliberations are, however, conducted in French, its working language. The full report, as required by the Rules of Procedure of the Court, comprises of a brief summary of judgment, followed by the report for the hearing drawn up by the Judge Rapporteur containing the facts and procedure, and a summary of the arguments of the parties. The next part of the report contains the opinion of the Advocate General although this does not form an official part of the report. The final part contains both the reasons or grounds for the judgment presented in numbered paragraphs and finally the usually very succinct single ruling of the Court.

2.6.2.2 The Reporting of Cases

There is only one official set of reports of cases emanating from the Court of Justice and the Court of First Instance. These are the European Court Reports which are cited as ECR and preceded by the year of publication. These are published in all of the official languages. These are divided into Part I, containing the judgments of the European Court of Justice, Part II containing the judgments of the Court of First Instance, and ECR-SC containing staff cases which are no longer automatically translated into all of the official languages. However, publication of cases in these reports is severely delayed by two to three years, largely as a result of the translation requirements into the official languages, and alternative reports must be consulted if the full written text is required. The principle alternative which reports cases very soon after judgment, is the series, the Common Market Law Reports, cited as CMLR, which provides reports in English of not only the judgments of the Community courts but also of cases from the national courts of other member states which have considered or applied important points of Community law or which have demonstrated the attitude of the nationals courts to such Community concepts as supremacy or direct effects.

As a further alternative, the Court of Justice produces shorter notes of judgments and opinions in the form of a series entitled 'The proceedings of the Court of Justice

---

[15] Refer to the Annual Report of the Court of Justice, 2004, p. 5: http://europa.eu.int/cj/en/instit/presentationfr/rapport/pei/cj2004.pdf.

and Court of First Instance of the European Communities' but which is now produced only online.[16] Summaries of cases can also be found in the Official Journal and full cases can be found on the internet.[17]

2.6.3 Jurisdiction

Article 220 provides that the Court of Justice and the Court of First Instance, each within its jurisdiction, shall ensure that in the interpretation and application of the Treaty the law is observed. The Court's factual jurisdiction is then determined by Articles 226–43. The Court's geographic jurisdiction is limited by the Treaties to the area of the member states but a judgment of the Court can have consequences and effects outside the geographic area, for example, in *ICI v Commission* (Case 48/69 Dyestuffs) in which the ICI head office, then outside the territory of the Community, was fined through subsidiaries based in the EEC.

In addition the Court has jurisdiction under the EEA Treaty to provide interpretations on disputed rules under the EEA Treaty and under Article 300(6) the other institutions and the member states may obtain the opinion of the Court of Justice on the compatibility of proposed international agreements and Treaties with the EC and EU Treaties.

Finally, the Court's jurisdiction has been extended by the Treaty of Amsterdam and it has been given the power to consider disputes arising between member states under the police and judicial cooperation pillar of the European Union. Member states may also decide whether to accept the Court's jurisdiction to accept preliminary rulings on limited aspects of the decisions and measures taken under that pillar (see Art 35 TEU). This latter jurisdiction will be brought under the Constitutional Treaty, Articles III-269–77, if or when it comes into force.

The Court's jurisdiction can be divided in a number of ways which can be helpful in understanding what the Court of Justice does. One way is to look at the broad types of actions available under Community law and adjudicated by the Court of Justice. This also considers the parties to the actions. Here three main categories can be established. One category includes the actions taken against the member states, then actions concerned with the review of acts of the Community Institutions and a third category consists of preliminary rulings under Article 234 of the Treaty. Certain other aspects of the Court's work, such as interim measures and appeals from the Court of First Instance stand outside of such a division and have to be considered separately. One can also consider the way in which the Court is acting, such as a constitutional court

---

[16] http://europa.eu.int/cj/en/actu/activites/index.htm.
[17] http://europa.eu.int/cj/en/content/juris/index.htm.

when considering the powers of the institutions and member states or the relations between them. It acts as an administrative court in cases of judicial review of acts of the institutions. It acts as an appeal court in hearing cases from the Court of First Instance. It also acts to determine the scale of fines against those offending competition law and also the member states when they breach Community law obligations and as such therefore acts as a kind of administrative criminal law court. Finally, it acts as an advisory court when providing rulings to national courts in response to preliminary ruling references.

The jurisdiction can also be divided into the following two much more commonly found classifications:

(a) direct judicial control whereby the Court interprets a rule and applies it to decide the case itself; and

(b) indirect judicial control whereby the Court interprets and rules on the validity of provisions, not the subject of an action before the Court This jurisdiction is mainly concerned with the rulings on the request of national courts.

2.6.3.1 Direct Actions

Direct actions are also termed the contentious jurisdiction' of the Court under which the Court upholds the lawful exercise of the Community legislative and executive powers in actions against the Community institutions under Articles 230–2, concerning the judicial review of legally binding acts. The Court also upholds compliance of the Community obligations by the member states via Articles 226–8 and conformity with EC law by individuals via various Treaty articles and secondary legislation, for example, Article 83(2)(a) and Regulation 2003/1 concerned with competition policy. Articles 235 and 288(2) confer non-contractual (delictual) jurisdiction and Article 236 gives the Court of Justice jurisdiction over staff cases, now effectively handed over to a Judicial panel with limited appeal rights, considered below. The Court has a preventative judicial control intended to block the conclusion of an envisaged agreement by the Community with a third state or international organization considered incompatible with the EC Treaty under Article 300. It can also be called upon to adjudicate in contractual disputes between Community institutions and contractual partners if called to do so under an arbitration clause in the contract (Art 238). Finally, under Article 241 the Court of Justice hears indirect challenges to Community legislation by individuals in proceedings already taking place before the Court of Justice.

2.6.3.2 Indirect Actions

Indirect judicial control is exercised by the preliminary ruling proceeding of Article

234, whereby references are made from the courts of the member states for judicial rulings by the Court of Justice.

The actions mentioned above will be considered in further detail in Chapters 5 and 6.

2.6.4 Methodology: Interpretation and Precedent

A consideration of the methodology of the work of the Court is helpful in understanding the very pro-integrationist stance, also referred to as the Court's judicial activism, it has often adopted in judgments and how these have helped build a new European legal order.

2.6.4.1 Interpretation

The European Treaties and some of the secondary legislation are framework measures which often require considerable amplification and interpretation. This has given a wide scope to the Court of Justice to engage expansive interpretation of the texts. The Court has taken a very pro-active role at times in European integration, often to the consternation of some of the member states. Notable judgments are those concerned with what are now fundamental decisions of the Court including direct effects, supremacy, and the liability of the member states. In these respects, the cases of *Van Gend en Loos*, *Costa v ENEL*, and *Factortame* (Spanish Fishermen and the UK) would be very good examples. The criticisms of the court's integrationist stance were most strongly voiced during the negotiations for the Treaty of Amsterdam with a UK Government prepared report seeking to curb the activity of the Court of Justice. However, this was not taken any further and in any case, the then Conservative Government was voted out of office before the Amsterdam Treaty negotiations were concluded. Indeed, it can be argued, that if it were not for the lead given by the Court in certain fundamental questions of EC law jurisprudence, the Community legal system would not have obtained the coherency or strength it has today and as a result the Community itself would be less secure. The Court has as a result been highly instrumental in European integration and in interpreting a constitutional basis for the Community and Treaty.[18]

The style of interpretation is described as teleological or far or forward looking, in that the Court tries to determine in the light of the aims and objective of the Treaties and legislation what was intended and what result would assist those goals. The Court

---

[18] For brief but informed discussion on the critique and support of the Court's judicial activism see Ward, pp. 97–101 and Douglas-Scott, pp. 210–23, noted in further reading at the end of the chapter.

of Justice often refers to the spirit of the Treaty, the Community project itself, the preamble and to general provisions of the Treaty, notably Articles 2, 3, 10, and 12 in order to assist it in reaching a particular conclusion. As such then these represent a form of contextual approach taking many things into account in justify a judgment. For example, look at paragraphs 71–5 of the judgment in *Van Gend en Loos* (Case 26/62) in which virtually all of the above justifications are covered in reaching its conclusions that EC law was capable of giving rise to direct effects, despite there being no express words to that end in the Treaty itself.

The Court often refers to the concept of *effet utile*, or the useful effect of Community law which would be undermined if a particular provision was not interpreted in a much more expansive way, more in line with the objectives of the Treaty rather than the actual words used. See, for example, Cases C-6 and 9/90 *Francovich et al v Italy*, in which the establishment of liability on the part of member states could never have been derived from a literal reading of the Treaty or secondary law. These Community methods or interpretation are applied in addition to the usual array of methods of interpretation found in the member states legal systems including the logical, literal, purposive means of interpretation although any strict use of such methods has often been rejected by the Court as unsuitable in the Community context, see, for example, Case 6/60 *Humblet* and Case C-70/88 *Chernobyl* in which direct use of the literal and historical intent methods respectively were rejected.

2.6.4.2 Precedent

While there is no formal system of precedent, the Court of Justice, just like courts in civil law jurisdictions, tries to maintain consistency in its judgments. Past decisions are often cited in Court and do therefore carry some persuasive rather than any formal authority. In particular, whilst all rulings of the Court of Justice are binding within the case itself, certain decisions are regarded as forming a sort of precedent for the national courts. For example, the early decision in *Da Costa* (Cases 28–30/62), that references need not be made to the Court of Justice where the materially identical question had already been answered by the Court of Justice, in that instance, in the recently heard case *Van Gend en Loos*. Furthermore, leading cases in Community law, such as *Van Gend en Loos* and *Costa v ENEL* have acquired a higher more authoritative status than other cases, dealing for example with an interpretation of one of the common custom tariff classifications or some such other mundane item of Community secondary legislation! So much so, that this difference in status has now been more formally recognized by the decision no longer to publish all cases in the official series of courts reports, the ECR. Those from the chambers of three are not to be published, nor are rulings from chambers of five where there has been no opinion of the AG, but that this does not include Article 234 preliminary rulings.[19]

There are instances, though, where the courts uses the terminology of precedent, see, for example, Case *Commission v Assidomän* (Case C-310/97P 1999 ECR I-5363) in which the Court of Justice mentions ratio decidendi at paragraph 54 and both identifies previous precedents and distinguishes past cases relied on by one of the parties (in paras 54–62) and judicial review cases often refer back to the leading Case 25/62 *Plaumann v Commission* (in Case C-263/02 P *Commission* v *Jego-Quere* the *Plaumann* test was held virtually to dictate the result in subsequent cases). Hence, unofficially, the system of case law developed by the Court of Justice increasingly seems to resemble a true case law system relying on precedents to take the law forward to new cases.

2.6.5 The Court of First Instance

The first measure to tackle the growing case load and thus length of proceedings before the Court of Justice was the setting up of a Court of First Instance in 1986 by the SEA and now governed under Article 225 EC. The Court of First Instance commenced operation on 1 September 1989 and has presently twenty-five members, one of which may act as an Advocate General where considered necessary in complex cases. The Court is divided into chambers of three and five judges but can sit in Grand Chamber or full court. More recently, Article 50 of the Statute of the Court of Justice has allowed for a single judge to hear cases in the CFI.

The jurisdiction was initially limited but has been slowly expanded to any area of jurisdiction and from 2004, also includes direct actions for Article 230 annulment applications brought by natural and legal persons but not by the member states or the Union Institutions. It has also been extended to include Article 234 preliminary references unless there is a risk to the unity of Community law, in which case the case should be referred to the Court of Justice by the CFI. Article 225 now allows for future changes of jurisdiction of the CFI to be made by amendment of the Protocol on the Court of Justice rather than by Treaty amendment. The CFI also has jurisdiction to hear appeals from the judicial panels, considered following.

Appeals from the CFI may be made on points of law only to the Court of Justice. Three grounds are given:

(a) lack of competence by the court;

---

[19] They will, however, be available electronically in the language of the case via the Court of Justice web site: http://europa.eu.int/cj/en/index.htm.

(b) breach of procedure; and

(c) the infringement of a Community provision or rule of law by the Court or an error in the interpretation or application of law.

Despite the low numbers of appeals in the early years and optimism that the bringing into operation of the CFI would significantly reduce the backlog and length of proceedings, the continued increase in the numbers of cases being lodged at the CFI and the large numbers of cases which were transferred to it by the Court of Justice, meant that the overall backlog of cases pending judgment before the CFI and the Court of Justice increased still further. However, after years of increasing case loads and growing backlogs, the expansion of the EU and Court of Justice in 2004, which saw a large influx of new judges but, at least at first, few new cases from the new member states, combined with the increased jurisdiction of the CFI, enabled the Court to make inroads into the backlog. In 1998, there were over 1,000 cases pending before the Court of Justice. In 2003, this figure stood at 974 and in 2004, was reduced to 840.[20] With these figures, the length of proceedings which had increased over the years also changed for the better with Article 234 references, direct actions, and appeals all showing reductions in the length of proceedings from 25.5–23.5 months, 24.7–20.2 months, and from 28.7–21.3 months, respectively.

The Constitutional Treaty proposes to rename, quite sensibly in view of the following development, the CFI as the High Court, otherwise the structure and organization of the Union Court system will remain the same.

2.6.6 Judicial Panels

The Treaty of Nice changes to the organization of the Community courts also provided for the establishment of Judicial Panels attached to the CFI to relieve that Court of some of its case law (Art 225a EC). These panels will operate as first instance courts with an appeal to the CFI. The first decision under the new power was taken by the Council of Ministers in November 2004[21] and a European Union Civil Service Tribunal comprising seven judges has been established to hear staff cases with an appeal on law only to the CFI and exceptional review by the Court of Justice. Staff cases were an apparently not inconsiderable load on the Court. The possibility of establishing more panels for specialist subjects remains.

---

[20] For full details see Annual Report of the Court of Justice: http://europa.eu.int/cj/en/instit/presentationfr/rapport/pei/cj2004.pdf p.4.

[21] Decision 2004/752 (OJ 2004 L333/7).

2.7 Other Community Bodies

2.7.1 The Court of Auditors

Whilst this is now a full institution, as promoted by the TEU under Articles 7 and 246–8 EC, it is not one usually covered in any detail in textbooks and therefore will be mentioned here only briefly. The Court of Auditors was established under the 1975 Budgetary Treaty and audits the expenditure of the institutions for legality and sound financial management. It produces an annual report which is forwarded to the EP to debate and provide the Commission a discharge if the expenditure is correct (Art 276 EC). The amended Article 230 now provides that the Court of Auditors can take action to protect its prerogatives.

2.7.2 The Economic and Social Committee (EESC)

This committee, previously also known under the acronym ECOSOC, was introduced to serve in an advisory role to represent various sectional interests and must be consulted for the adoption of certain legislation as determined by the Treaty, although once received its opinion may be ignored by the Council. However, failure to consult would open up the legislation enacted to annulment, by analogy with the EP in Cases 138–9/79 *Roquette and Maizena v Council*. Its members are appointed in a personal capacity along national lines by the Council voting by QMV and are drawn from various sections of society to provide a wide-ranging array of views on legislative proposals. They are also able to give opinions on their own initiative without invitation from the Council, Commission or the EP (Art 262 EC). It is governed by Articles 7 and 257–62 EC.

2.7.3 The Committee of the Regions

A much later Community body, this was established by the TEU and is also an advisory body set up to represent regional and local bodies and to meet the criticisms that the Union fails to recognize regional interests, particularly those of federal states. Usually, only the central or national bodies of federal states were formally represented in the Union institutional set up, i.e. the Council of Ministers, which draws its members from the state governments. The Committee must be consulted for the enactment of certain legislation, see for example, Articles 137, 149, 150, 151, 152, and 157 EC and is governed by Articles 263–5 EC. In the UK membership is drawn from local authorities and the devolved government in Scotland, Wales and Northern Ireland.[22]

Further reading

Books

BROWN, N. and JACOBS, F. *The Court of Justice of the European Communities*, 5th edn., Sweet & Maxwell, London 2000.

DE BURCA, G. and WEILER, J. H. H. *The European Court of Justice*, OUP, Oxford 2001.

DEVUYST, Y. *The European Union Transformed: Community Method and Institutional Evolution from the Schuman Plan to the Constitution for Europe*, Peter Lang, Brussels 2005.

DOUGLAS-SCOTT, S. *Constitutional Law of the European Union*, Longman, Harlow 2002 (chapters 2 and 5).

EDWARDS, G. and SPENCE, D. *The European Commission*, Cartermill International 1997.

SCHERMERS, H. and WAELBROECK, D. *Judicial Protection in the European Communities*, 6th edn., Kluwer, Deventer 2001.

WARD, I. *A Critical Introduction to European Law*, 2nd edn., Butterworths, London 2003.

Articles

DE WITTE, B. 'Anticipating the Institutional Consequences of Expanded Membership of the European Union' [2002] vol. 23 no. 3 *International Political Science Review*, 235–48.

MOBERG, A. 'The Nice Treaty and Voting Rules in the Council' [2002] vol. 40 no. 2 *Journal of Common Market Studies*, 259–82.

TEMPLE LANG, J. 'How much do the Smaller Member States need the European Commission? The Role of the Commission in a Changing Europe' [2002] vol. 39 no. 2 *Common Market Law Review*, 315.

TIMMERMANS, C. The European Union's Judicial System (2004), 41 *CML Rev*, 393.

Web-based Materials

Institutions

The Council of Ministers: http://europa.eu.int/institutions/council/index_en.htm

The Commission: The Commission

The Barroso Commission: http://europa.eu.int/comm/commission_barroso/index_en.htm

The European Parliament: European Parliament

The European Court of Justice: The European Court of Justice

Economic and Social Committee (EESC): http://www.esc.eu.int/index_en.asp

---

[22] Full details of the selection criteria and process for all member states can be found at: http://www.cor.eu.int/en/presentation/members.htm.

Committee of the Regions: http://www.cor.eu.int/en/index.htm

European Commission web site on the Co-decision process: http://europa.eu.int/comm/codecision/index_en.htm including a very good flow chart: http://europa.eu.int/comm/codecision/stepbystep/diagram_en.htm

3

Community Law: Sources, Forms, and Principles

3.1 Introduction

This chapter starts by taking an overall view of the Community legal order, the different forms of Community law and the variety of sources of law contributing to this legal order. In addition and playing an increasingly significant role in the Community legal order, the non-strictly legally binding rules known as 'soft law' are also considered. Following this, the ways or processes by which the binding laws are made are considered and finally, the budgetary process and alternative decision-making and law-making developments are reviewed.

3.2 The Community Legal System

The EC and EU Treaties, as amended, are the principal sources of law for the Union and until a Constitutional Treaty is finally established, the European Community Treaty remains the one we are most concerned with. As will be clear from the opening chapters, the Treaties and Community law are not static bodies of law but are amended from time to time as the member states agree, as can clearly be seen by the changes introduced by the Single European Act (SEA), the Maastricht Treaty (TEU) and more recently by the Treaties of Amsterdam and Nice. In establishing the basic format of the Communities at the time of their founding, legal models were sought on which to build the legal system for the Communities. At that time, there were no member states from common law jurisdictions and it is therefore to be expected that the Community legal system would broadly resemble a civil law system and in particular, follow legal structures found in the French and German legal systems. For example, much of the procedure of the courts is based on French administrative law, as are actions for damages under the second paragraph of Article 288. In turn, looking over the longer term development of Community law, this has been both influenced by the legal structures and principles of law in the member states and in turn Community law has influenced the development of law in the member states.[1]

Thus, the construction of the Community legal order proceeded by the establishment of framework treaties providing broad principles and aims, which reflected the way in which civil law countries approach legislative enactment with codified law. They commence with general abstract principles, such as the Preamble and Articles 2 and 3 of the EC Treaty. Indeed, the EC Treaty also includes something else with which lawyers from civil law countries are quite familiar, and this is a form of good faith clause, included in Article 10 EC, which imposes an obligation on the member states to both positively act to achieve the goals of the Treaty and not to act in any way which would jeopardize those aims.

The rest of the EC Treaty, although putting the broad aims into greater detail, nevertheless provide merely an outline for the areas of law, the member states agreed should be integrated. It provides, for example, the basic legal regime for free movement of goods and workers, competition law, and agriculture. Some sections are more detailed than others and whereas, free movement of goods has required little secondary legislation, competition law and agriculture have been subject to considerable legislative addition. Thus, for the most part, the Treaties require completion by detailed Regulations and Directives. The areas agreed by the member states can and have been added to, for example, environmental and consumer protection by the SEA and new policy areas introduced by the Treaty of European Union, notably economic and monetary union and health and safety and industry policies. Incidentally, all Treaty Article references in this volume are to the EC Treaty, and where appropriate to the predecessor EEC treaty, unless where otherwise stated.

Apart from the secondary legislation needed to put into effect the goals of the various policies, any gaps and ambiguities in the legislation and interpretation of the Treaty and secondary legislation are resolved by the European Court of Justice and as a result a body of case law has slowly arisen, itself relying on a variety of internal and external sources, such as general principles and fundamental rights. These latter sources will also be considered within this chapter.

3.2.1 The Style of the Community Legal System

Before moving on to consider the individual elements of the Community legal system, it is worthwhile considering how the legal system is intended to work. Like the civil

---

[1] For examples, refer to Lord Irvine of Lairg, 'The Influence of Europe on Public Law in the United Kingdom', in B. S. Markesinis (ed.), *The Coming Together of the Common Law and the Civil Law, The Clifford Chance Millennium Lectures*, Hart Publishing, Oxford, 2000, pp. 24–5.

law systems, the Community legal system is a deductive system, therefore the approach adopted to the application of the law is from the general to the particular. This means starting with general principles of the Treaty or Code and becoming increasingly particular, through more specific Treaty articles and secondary legislation and, where necessary or helpful; by the use of case law. Deductive law concerns the application of enacted law in all future situations, to be supplemented by case law, only where necessary. The common law approach, in contrast, is the gradual development and build up of rules of law from the particular situations or cases to establish a general rule. The cases give rise to a general principle of law which is then applied in future cases. This system is known as 'inductive reasoning'.

Where deductive reasoning is applied to resolving legal disputes, the result in a particular case is achieved by working from the general to the particular, that is from the broad framework Treaty rules, which may often include the preamble, Articles 2, 3, 10, and 12, to the relevant provisions of the specific chapter or title of the Treaty, then any secondary legislation on the topic and finally to the relevant case law on the interpretation and application of the Treaty or other legislative provisions. As will be demonstrated in the following chapters, the interpretation techniques of the Court of Justice also follow the approach of taking into account the general aims to help decide in particular cases. The Court will often make reference to the preamble and general provisions of the Treaty to justify a particular decision and applies law in the scope of the Treaty as a whole, in the light of the basic aims and objectives of the Treaty and not just the specific legislation. For example, Article 2 is referred to in Case 7/75, *Mrs and Mrs F. v the Belgian State* concerning social security, Article 3 in Case 6/72, *Europemballage and Continental Can v Commission* and Case 14/83, *Von Colson* which was very strongly argued on the basis of Article 10 EC. A more recent case is Case 22/87, *Francovich*, which was also argued strongly on the basis on Article 10 to establish for the first time under Community law, state liability for the failure of the member state to implement a Directive.

Article 12 EC,[2] the general prohibition of discrimination on the grounds of nationality is also relevant to all areas of Community law and used as a general tool of the Court of Justice to reach just results in particular occasions which might not otherwise have been reached by the application of more specific provisions. For example, it has been used to extend the equality of law requirement in respect of vocational training and fees into more broad stream education, as can be seen in Cases 24/86, *Blaizot*, 263/86, *Humbel*, 39/86, *Lair*, and 293/83 *Gravier*, amongst others.

---

[2] Which was old Art 6 and before that Art 7 EEC, which will be the numbers found in the old case law. Article 12 is also considered in Chapter 10.

3.2.2 The Classification of the Elements of Community Law

Community law can be divided broadly into three main components: institutional law, procedural law, and substantive law.

3.2.2.1 Institutional Law

Institutional law is in essence and sometimes called, the constitutional law of the Community and now the Union. It concerns the structure or constitution of the Communities, the regulation of the main institutions and other bodies of the Community, the sources of Community law, and the special concepts of Community law including supremacy and direct effects. Institutional law also concerns the relationship of the institutions between themselves, the relationship of the Community with the member states and its external relations with other countries and international organizations. The institutions are the bodies responsible for the legislative and budgetary processes and as their relationship alters in time due to Treaty amendment, disputes arise over the boundaries of the powers and duties of the institutions and their relationship to each other, which gives rise to increasing case law. As in other areas of Community law, the role of the Court of Justice has been fundamental to the development of the Community. The Court has been called upon many times to adjudicate inter-institutional disputes and those between institutions and member states. It is becoming increasingly involved as the institutions seek to protect their powers or legally extend them, for example, the Court has been cautiously assisting the EP in pressing for and gaining increased litigation rights to reflect its democratic power in the Community. Generally also, the Court of Justice has been instrumental in the development of the legal system because of this judicial activism, and not without criticism at times. Its pronouncements on the status and effects of the provisions of Community law have resulted in the establishment and development of ground-breaking and now fundamental leading principles of Community law, including direct effects, supremacy, and state liability. The institutional law is an expanding area of Community law as exemplified by the changes wrought by the SEA and the TEU to the EC Treaty, which have expanded the areas of competence and altered the power relationships in the Community by providing the EP with greater legislative power, for example.

3.2.2.2 Procedural Law

This is sometimes referred to as the administrative law of the Community and largely involves judicial review or judicial control in the Community. It is concerned with the various actions that can be taken by the institutions, member states, and natural and legal persons under rules provided by the EC Treaty. These actions then are mainly concerned with the enforcement of rights against the Community institutions, the member states, and individuals. Procedural law covers a range of remedies; indirect actions involving the national courts and direct actions at the level of the Community, both of which will be considered in Chapters 5 and 6.

Procedural law is thus concerned with the details of actions before the Courts, all of which must be based on a specific provision within the Treaties or on a principle of law developed by the Court of Justice. The Court is often at its most restrictive in this area, for example, by restraining the right or ability of individuals to challenge acts of the Community by a fairly strict interpretation of the rights provided in the Treaty Articles. The admissibility barriers that have to be overcome by individuals for actions under Articles 230, 232, and 241 are considerable and will be considered in Chapter 6. Cases referred to the Court of Justice from the national courts are received for the most part much more favourably.

3.2.2.3 Substantive Law

Substantive law involves the legal rules established to carry out the broad policy areas of law agreed under the Community Treaties and can be distinguished from the law relating to the institutions and the procedural law of the Communities. The substantive law is largely secondary law and takes effect predominantly in the member states and not at the Community level, despite its primary base in Treaty articles. The substantive law of the Community is also described as economic law or the law of the economy of the Community and even as European Community private law. However, this is not a particularly meaningful label as the concept of economic law varies from state to state and between political systems. Additionally, this simplistic tag may not explain the attitude of the Community, as expressed by the Court of Justice, to the substantive law of the Community, and suggests it is only concerned with the economic considerations of the Community and not wider concerns which may be relevant. The Community is quite clearly, as demonstrated by the preamble and opening Articles to the EC Treaty, particularly as amended by the Treaties of Amsterdam and Nice, concerned with far more than the setting up of a regulatory framework for limited aspects of the economies dealing only with free trade rules. Examples which reflect purely economic integration or cooperation would be agreements between the EFTA and GATT countries, who only want the economic trade rules. Latterly, far more social concerns and policies are being given voice in the Community legal order and Treaties, see for example the much expanded titles on social policy, education, culture, and public health in the EC Treaty (Arts 136–52). Further evidence can be found in the statements made by the Court of Justice that the Community places social concerns above economic considerations in Case C-324/96 *Deutsche Telekom v Vick*.

There are a large and increasing number of areas of substantive law which now arise from the Community Treaties and subsequent intergovernmental agreements. These have been increased by the SEA and the TEU, Amsterdam and Nice Treaties. The substantive law chapters following, however, will deal with four topics only, all of which were within the original policies of the Community, although to a different extent, social provision being at the time, very limited. Those included are the free movement of goods, free movement of workers and persons, competition law and equality law, which is now a much expanded version of the limited non-discrimination rights which appeared in the original EEC Treaty. The first three, at least, are centrally concerned with the achievement of the economic goals of the Community but it has been the subject of argument as to whether the concerns and thus law in these areas have been promulgated only for economic ends or whether there are other wider social concerns and aims of the Communities. The general question to be asked is whether there was an also an intent for these laws to achieve social aims or whether it is just because these economic laws were seen to impact so strongly on the social level in the member states that this view may now be taken. The Court of Justice has for a long time referred to the support that must be given to the four freedoms of the Community which it regards as fundamental elements or cornerstones of the Community and will do its best to uphold them. It will interpret the Community rules of law generously, i.e. wherever possible it will try to uphold the Community rules in the face of national legislation. The exceptions or derogations allowed the member states in some of the provisions are interpreted narrowly against the member states. The aim is to give the greatest possible effect to Community rights and less scope to member state derogations which if allowed free rein would undermine the aims of the Community. See, for example, a case from the area of the free movement of goods, Case 40/82 *Commission v UK* concerned with a justification by the UK for restricting the import of turkeys into the UK, just before Christmas, on the protection of health grounds.

3.3 The Sources and Forms of Community Law

What should be mentioned again, at the outset of this particular section of the book is the term '*acquis communautaire*' which might or probably will be encountered in EU law studies and was considered also in Chapters 1 and 2. This refers to, or is a way of, describing the whole body of Community law which has been built up over the years and now decades and which comprises all the sources of law considered in this chapter. It is more likely to be heard in connection with the entry of new member states who are now required to accept in total the *acquis communautaire*. This is non-negotiable! It was estimated this amounts now to about 80,000 pages of legal text![3]

3.3.1 The Treaties

The primary source of law in the Communities comes from the Treaties, the most notable of which is the EC Treaty, sometimes referred to as the Treaty of Rome, although, in fact there were two Treaties of Rome. The two other original founding Treaties, the European Coal and Steel Treaty (ECSC), which is no longer in force, and the European Atomic Energy Treaty (EURATOM) have been supplemented considerably by a number of Treaties agreed by the member states. These include the Merger Treaty and the various Acts of Accession providing details for the entry into the Communities of new member states. However, the most important additional treaties are the Single European Act, the Treaty on European Union (the Maastricht Treaty) the Treaty of Amsterdam, and the Treaty of Nice, which have cumulatively amended the original treaties considerably in comparison with the scope of the original Treaties.

All the Treaties of the Communities are drawn up in all the official languages of the Communities, which are equally authentic. Any difficulties which arise from the fact that different meanings may, despite all attempts, arise between languages is usually overcome by the Court of Justice applying the teleological interpretation of the spirit of the provision rather than the letter. A comparison of a number of language version may be necessary in order to discern the true meaning of a particular provision.[4]

The special nature of these Treaties is encapsulated within the concept of direct applicability, which means that on the accession of a member state to the Union, all of the provisions of the Treaties automatically become part of the generally binding law of the member state, which is applicable not only to the member states but also to the citizens of that country. This form of law is also known as 'self executing law', a term previously recognized in International law, to describe the way in which some provisions of law have legal validity in the member states, in that no further action need be taken by a member state to incorporate or transform the treaty into the national legal order once it has ratified the Treaty, although some member states, such as the UK, may need an introductory Act to formally mark the presence of the Treaty, but even

[3] In September 2004 an exhibition in Brussels to demonstrate the EU to visitors, featured an exhibition of the *acquis communautaire* which ran, allegedly when spread out to over 80,000 pages, over 8 metres, see the press release Joint presidency/Commission press announcement 'The image of Europe'. [08–09–2004] I Press releases I General Affairs and External Relations]. It is also defined in an EU web site: http://europa.eu.int/comm/justice_home/glossary/glossary_a_en.htm.

[4] See, for example, Case C-106/89 *Marleasing SA v La Comercial Internacional de Alimentacion SA* and Case C-149/97 *Institute of the Motor Industry v Customs and Excise Commissioners* in which the different language versions of the 6th VAT directive were discussed.

then would not reproduce the text of the Treaty into a national act. It does not rely on the way in which the member state has incorporated it for its validity. The early case of *Van Gend en Loos* (Case 26/62) is confirmation of the deeper impact of this directly applicable Community law because the Court of Justice made it clear that Community law is also the legal concern of individuals and not just the member states.

The Treaties are framework Treaties in that they lay down broad guidelines for the pursuit of certain agreed aims and objectives. They do not provide extensive details for the implementation of these policies, which is left for the most part to secondary legislation of the Community or failing that, to the Court of Justice who will rule on what was intended by the Treaty provision. For example, although the EC Treaty broadly provides that workers should be guaranteed freedom of movement in the Communities, it did not define, nor indeed did any secondary legislation define, what was meant by worker. It was thus up to the Court of Justice to provides definitions of what it considered should be included in the definition of worker in the Community context.

The scope of the Treaties has expanded considerably since the establishment of the EEC in 1957 and now covers wide areas of the economic and social life of the member states including economic and monetary policy, judicial and police cooperation, culture and tourism, humanitarian aid, and foreign policy amongst many others, although not all to the same level of integration and Community control. The Constitutional Treaty, if it comes into force will not actually add to these areas of Union influence with the exception of making the catalogue of human rights a binding part of the Treaty.

3.3.1.1 The Protocols attached to the Treaties

As has been noted in Chapter 1, the two main Treaties have been amended on a number of occasions, often significantly but even with the additional amended Treaties, they do not represent the entirety of primary Community law. Following an unfortunate practise of humble and limited beginnings, each successive intergovernmental conference has added what has now amounted to a complex and vast range of protocols to the EC and TEU Treaties. The 2003 IGC specifically requested the EC Commission's legal service to look at the situation of the protocols. One hundred and twenty-three protocols were identified.[5] Article 311 EC declares these protocols to be an integral part of the Treaty. What this means in practise is unclear but it is generally understood in International law terms that protocols are a lesser form but no less binding version of an International Treaty Agreement. They are used to provide interpretation for articles of Treaties and are often employed to provide agreed

---

[5] http://euobs.com/?aid=13235&rk=1.

regulation of more technical matters. In the Community legal system, they possess Treaty status, although the value of this status has not yet been questioned before the Court of Justice. What is clear is that the Treaty constitutional set up has become increasingly complex. Whilst some steps have been attempted to consolidate them, if anything so far this has tended to make life even more complex—i.e. the renumbering of the EC and TEU Treaties by the Amsterdam Treaty. One of the aims in drafting the Constitutional Treaty was that this matter would be looked at and, as with the Treaties themselves, be considerably simplified. However, all that happened was that the Protocols attached to various Treaties were consolidated and attached as a long list of Protocols to the CT, which may or may not be ratified.

3.3.1.2 Declarations

In addition, attached to each subsequent Treaty is usually a list of declarations of the member states, sometimes by all member states but mainly by just a few or just one member state which makes a unilateral declaration on a particular matter, e.g. the Declaration by Austria and Luxembourg on Credit Institutions which was attached to the Amsterdam Treaty. These Declarations need to be noted because, like the protocols, they may alter our view or perception of the meaning or application of Treaty provision, however, unlike the protocols enjoy no express Treaty status, and are thus very uncertain in EU Law.[6]

3.3.2 Secondary Legislation

In the Communities, secondary legislation arises entirely subject to the authority, higher rank and procedures provided for in the Treaties. Article 249 EC Treaty provides the means by which the Community Institutions are able to enact secondary legislation, which are also a source of law for the UK and other member states and are binding on them. The acts of secondary legislation presently consist of Regulations, Directives, and Decisions, although the Constitutional Treaty envisages a radical shake–up to the forms of secondary legislation, if and when it comes into force.

All Community secondary legislation is published in the Official Journal (OJ) which, as it suggests is the official publication of the Community and is published in two main parts with a supplement. The L Series (Legislation) contains the binding

---

[6] See for an early look at this: A. G. Toth, 'The Legal Status of the Declarations Annexed to the Single European Act', *Common Market Law Review* 23, 1986, p. 803. Without making any clear-cut express statement as to the status, the ECJ held in Case C-192/99, *ex parte Manjit Kaur v Secretary of State for the Home Department* that in order to determine UK nationality it was necessary to refer to the 1982 Declaration attached to the Treaties, thus acknowledging a legal affect of the instrument without though expressly declaring it to be binding on the member states.

legislative acts. The C Series (information and notices) contains a very wide range of documents which are not binding as such and includes notices, draft legislative acts, press releases, job advertisements, and all other non-legally binding publications with the exception of the public procurement notices which are published in the S series supplement. The OJ is officially authentic only in its printed form and can be found in this format in Libraries and Official Documentation centres.[7]

3.3.2.1 Regulations

Regulations are defined in Article 249: 'A regulation shall have general application. It shall be binding in its entirety and directly applicable in all member states.' They are general provisions of legislation applicable to the entire Community, member states, institutions, and individuals, rather than to specific individuals or groups. Regulations are detailed forms of law so that the law in all member states is exactly the same. As far as implementation is concerned, like Treaty provisions, Regulations are directly applicable or self executing. This is the mode of incorporation of law which is generally or universally binding. Regulations become legally valid in the member states without any need for implementation on the date specified or on the 20th day after publication in the OJ (see Art 254). It was held in Case 39/72, *Commission v Italy* that member states cannot subject the Regulation to any implementing measures other than those required by the act itself. There may however be circumstances where the member states are required to provide implementing measures to ensure the effectiveness of the Regulation as in Case 128/78, *Commission v UK* (Re: Tachographs) in which administrative rules had to be implemented concerning the enforcement and sanctions for failure to install tachographs in lorry cabs.

3.3.2.2 Directives

Directives are also defined in Article 249: 'A directive shall be binding as to the result to be achieved, upon each member state to which it is addressed, but shall leave to the national authorities the choice of form and methods.' Directives are binding on whom addressed and can be targeted if desired to specific member states although in practise they are addressed to all member states. Directives set out aims which must be achieved but leave the choice of the form and method of implementation to the member states. This was done to ease the way in which national law could be harmonized in line with Community law and give the members states a wider area of discretion to do this. If, for example a member state considers that the existing national law is already in conformity with the requirements of a new Directive then it need not do

---

[7] Which can be located in most University Libraries but easiest access to it today is inevitably online: http://europa.eu.int/eur-lex/lex/JOIndex.do?ihmlang=en.

anything, apart from the requirement now in most if not all Directives that the member state inform the Commission of measures taken to implement the Directive.

Directives enter into force either on the date specified or 20 days after publication, which is rare (see Art 254 EC). Member states are given a period in which to implement Directives which can range from one year to five or more depending on the complexity of the subject matter and the urgency for the legislation, but two years is usual. Some Directives, especially if consolidating and adding rules to an existing area of Community law may contain more than one entry into force date to take account of the law which should have already been enacted and the new provisions for which the member states is given a further implementation period, see for example, Directive 2000/38[8] in the area of Free Movement of Persons.

Although they are not directly applicable in the sense of being automatic, general in application and give rights without further implementation, Directives have been held to give rise to directly enforceable rights in specific circumstances and if certain criteria are satisfied, for example, where they have not been implemented at all or where they have been incorrectly implemented. This judicial development will be considered below in the section on direct effects.

3.3.2.3 Decisions

Decisions are also defined in Article 249 EC: 'A decision shall be binding in its entirety upon those to whom it is addressed.' Decisions are specific binding and enforceable acts of law which are addressed to member states or to specific individuals, for example, in the area of Competition law determining the agreements between companies to be either in conformity or in conflict with EC competition law rules. They have not generated much in the way of case law to date.

3.3.2.4 Other Acts Producing Binding Legal Effects

Article 249 is not exhaustive of the legally binding acts which can be created by the institutions and the Court of Justice has held that it can review all measures taken by the institutions, whatever their nature and form, which are designed to produce legal effects. Thus such acts need not stem from the specific acts listed in Article 249 and are often termed 'sui generis' meaning literally in a class of its own or unique. Hence then the establishment of another class of binding law in the Community legal order, some examples of which could easily be classified under other headings, especially the contribution of the Court of Justice. See Cases 8–11/66, the *Noordwijks Cement Accord* in which a Commission letter not formally labelled as a Regulation, Directive or Decision could nevertheless be challenged under Article 230, which is the action to

---

[8] (OJ 2004 L158/77).

challenge the validity of binding acts of Community law, because the letter had led to a change in legal status of applicant companies rendering them subject to Competition law liability, where they had been previously immune. See also Case 22/70 *Commission v Council* (ERTA) in which a decision of the member states outside of the Council of Ministers was nevertheless held to be a reviewable act of the Community. Even a press release has been found to have legal effects in Case C-106/96 *UK v Commission* and was consequently annulled for lacking a legal base.

3.3.2.5 Recommendations and Opinions

Whilst, expressly under Article 249, recommendations and opinions do not have any binding force, it was established in Case 322/88 *Grimaldi*, that despite this, national courts are required to take recommendations into account when interpreting national law based on Community law. Recommendations in particular, often provide a gloss on a Regulation or Directive or extend its scope of application. See for example Recommendation 89/49 which extended the scope of application of Directive 89/48 to qualifications obtained by EC nationals but outside the EC.[9]

3.3.2.6 Procedural Requirements

Article 253 of the Treaty requires that the binding acts of institutions shall state the reasons on which they are based and shall refer to any proposals or opinions which were required to be obtained. In practice this means the Treaty base must be cited also. Failure by the institutions to comply with these requirements will give rise to grounds for judicial review and possible annulment of the measure under Article 230. For example, it was held in Case C-325/91 *France v Commission* that there was a requirement to state the Treaty base, without which the measure is void.

Article 254 provides the rules concerning the publication of the various acts. Regulations, Directives, and Decisions adopted under Article 251 must be signed by the Presidents of the EP and the Council and published in the OJ. Directives addressed to all member states must also be published. They become valid on the specified date, in the absence of which on the 20th day following publication. Otherwise Directives and Decisions take affect on the date of notification given in the acts, although these are also published in the Official Journal.

The formal acts of the EU were due for a radical shake up under the CT, mainly into legislative and administrative types of acts. The shake-up is designed to replace the very many different less formal types of acts which have been developed over the years or specifically introduced under the TEU but which in view of the uncertainty surrounding the CT now, no further details will be provided at this stage.

---

[9] Recommendation 89/49 (OJ 1989, L19/24) extending Directive 89/48 (OJ 1989, L19/16).

3.3.2.7 Acts under the Second and Third Pillars of the TEU

Whilst the present Treaties are still in force, which may now be for longer than envisaged due to the referendum rejections of the CT in France and the Netherlands, legislative acts can be enacted also under the other pillars. Under the Common Foreign and Security Policy and the Police and Judicial Cooperation in Criminal Matters pillars of the TEU, the Council, acting intergovernmentally, i.e. unanimously, can adopt 'joint actions', 'common positions', 'framework decisions', 'decisions' or 'Conventions'. Despite Article 35 TEU stating expressly that Framework Decisions were to have no direct effects, the Court of Justice held in Case C-105/03: *Maria Pupino* that they were binding and could nevertheless be applied in national courts to influence the interpretation of national law to read in conformity with the Framework Decision.[10] We will not go into further details in this volume as these forms go beyond the intended scope of this book.[11] Furthermore, the Constitutional Treaty or a different form of reform of the Treaties will more than likely revise the whole area into one hierarchy of acts, which has been a long term goal of the Commission.

3.3.3 International Agreements and Conventions

Within the Treaty itself there are provisions which empower the Council and the Commission to conduct external relations, the agreements of which are binding on both the Community and the member states and as such then form a further true source of Community law. This is possible as the Community has legal personality (it is a legal person capable of entering into formally binding agreements). It is usually represented by the European Commission in negotiations.

The express treaty making powers of the Community can be found in three principal Treaty Articles and the types of agreement which can be concluded, fall into three main types. The first concerns the Community acting alone to conclude agreements with a non-member state or states or with organizations of non-member states, the second concerns mixed agreements by the Community acting with the member states and the third concerns agreements with non-member states concluded by the member states acting alone. According to the Court of Justice, it has proved possible, for the member states without involving the Community directly, to bind the Community in special circumstances.

Article 133 EC provides that Community commercial and trade policy is conducted

---

[10] In this respect then producing indirect effects, considered in detail in Chapter 5.

[11] For further details of the present regime under the second and third pillars of the EU refer to Nanette A. E. M. Neuwahl, A partner with a troubled personality: EU treaty-making in matters of CFSP and JHA after Amsterdam, *EFA Rev*, 1998, 3(2), 177–95.

by the Commission under the authority of the Council. Under this provision, the EU acts as a single actor and the European Commission negotiates trade agreements and represents European interests on behalf of the twenty-five member states. The Council concludes the agreements and can thus bind the member states to agreements from bilateral trade agreements with individual countries and to the multiparty GATT and WTO agreements, although as seen below much of the subject matter of the GATT and WTO agreements falls outside the express and exclusive competence of the Community. However, confirmation that particular provisions of the GATT agreement can be binding on the Community was confirmed by the Court of Justice in Case 21-24/72 *International Fruit*.

Article 310 provides for the conclusion of Association Agreements with non-member states which can be regarded as either a precursor to membership or as an agreement in their own right without any view to future membership of the EU. These can be concluded by the Council with the assent of the EP either, with individual third countries or within more extensive multinational agreements to govern, amongst other things, various aspects of the trade relations between them. The most important agreements are the EEA, noted in Chapter 1, the association agreements with potential member states (at present Bulgaria and Romania, Turkey, Macedonia, and Croatia), the bilateral agreements with Switzerland and Mediterranean countries, and the Preferential Treatment Agreements, which have been concluded with Mediterranean countries and, through the Yaounde and Lomé Conventions and now the Cotonou Agreement (2000) with seventy-eight African, Caribbean, and Pacific (ACP) countries, all of which provide binding rules for the Community.[12] For example, in Case 181/73 *Haegemann v Belgium*, provisions of the Association agreement between the Community and Greece were held to be binding on the member states even though such agreements were not envisaged by Article 249.

Finally and more generally, the Treaty provides under Article 300, a power for the conclusion of international agreements with non-member states in matters covered by areas of the Treaty not specifically catered for by the other two Treaty making power Articles. In furtherance of this, Articles 302–4 require the Commission to maintain appropriate relations with international organizations. According to Article 300(7) such agreements are expressly binding on the Community and member states. In many of these areas, however, the Community must act with the member states because the subject matters of the agreements often straddle matters coming both within Community competence and outside Community competence. These agreements and international agreements entered into by the member states alone can still

---

[12] For a comprehensive review of international agreement entered into by the EU and its member states see: N. Lavranos, *Decisions of International Organizations and European Law*, University of Amsterdam, 2004.

bind the Community, as confirmed in Case 21-4/72 *International Fruit Company*, for example, in which the Court of Justice held that the provisions of GATT concluded by the member states prior to membership of the Community or prior to the assumption of responsibility for the agreement by the Community, bind the Community. The direct effects of these agreements will be considered below under that section.

Under the CT, if and when it enters into force, the Union, rather than just the EC, will have legal personality and this will mean that the EU will have a right to conclude international agreements over a wider range of topics than previously such as UN conferences, international finance and trade conferences and more widely in GATT and WTO. In this case, the EU would not be subject to limitations outlined in Opinion 1/94,[13] which constrained the Commission's ability to negotiate without the member states in the field of services in the WTO. In addition, the new Union Minister for Foreign Affairs will be responsible for negotiating agreements relating to the Common Foreign and Security Policy. However, before this happens the CT must come into force, which is a long way off at the time of writing.

3.3.4 The Court of Justice's Contribution

When the EC was established, the legal system was to be found only in the written medium within the Treaties and what limited secondary legislation there existed at the time. Initially, there seemed to be little room for an additional and non-written source of law. However, because the Treaties are largely framework Treaties, they require substantial supplement. Whilst, much of this is provided by the secondary legislation of the Community, both this secondary legislation and the founding and primary treaties articles may need to be interpreted. There is then much scope for activity on the part of the Court of Justice. Furthermore, as with all legal systems, codified or written law cannot possibly cater for all economic and social developments that can take place and the judges must at times either adapt existing rules to fit the situation or introduce new rules to settle the matter judiciously. The Court of Justice has determined that the Treaty and secondary legislation must be interpreted and applied according to the scheme of the Treaty as a whole and in the light of the broad principles of the preamble and Articles 2, 3, 10, and 12 of the Treaty to achieve the result required for the Community. The resulting case law or jurisprudence has grown from a wide variety of law. It is not restricted in origin to the crude judicial interpretation of words or phrases from Community legislative provisions. Instead, the Court of Justice has cast its net of judicial interpretation much wider and signalled a clear departure from the reliance on Treaties only or indeed on International law, by the

---

[13] ECR [1994] I–5267, referred to in Chapter 1, 1.6.5.1.

development of some of the most fundamental doctrines and principles of Community law. These include direct effects, supremacy, state liability, and the development of general principles of Community law and the application of outside general principles, fundamental rights and procedural rules. This law as developed by the Court of Justice in cases before it, is quite clearly a Community source of law and indeed a highly influential one. In some instances, it has been directly influential in bringing about Treaty changes well before the formal Treaty amendment of such provisions by the member states (see for example Arts 230 and 232 EC and the extension of judicial review rights to the EP). The decisions of the Court of Justice are binding on the member states not just where the court decides strictly on the basis of Community Treaties or secondary law but also where it decides on the basis of legal rules it has observed and used as inspiration from outside of the Community or in order to develop a new Community rule itself. To back up this position, Article 244 of the EC Treaty provides that judgments shall be enforceable.

In developing Community law, the Court has been able to rely on and simultaneously develop general principles and fundamental rights within the legal order which have been used both to assist the Court of Justice in the interpretation and application of Community law and by parties engaging in litigation involving Community law, to assist them in challenging Community law or the actions of Community institutions and additionally, the actions of the members states in the application of Community law. There are three principal Treaty Articles which provide some justification for the Court of Justice in introducing general principles into the Community legal order.

Article 220 is a general guideline set by the Treaty for the functioning of the Court of Justice. It states: 'The Court of Justice and the Court of First Instance, each within its jurisdiction, shall ensure that in the interpretation and application of the Treaty the law is observed.' This is taken to mean the law outside of the Treaty rather than some tautological reference back to the Treaty itself.[14] Article 220 has thus been employed to justify the introduction of very many different general principles of law, most notably human rights, which will be considered further below.

Two further Articles of the Treaty, more specifically, mandate the Court to take account of general principles of law. Article 230 refers to the infringement of any rule of law relating to the application of the Treaty as one of the grounds for an action for the challenge to the validity of Community law and Article 288(2), concerned with damages claims, allows the settlement of claims by the Community on the basis of the general principles of the laws of the member states. Whilst the latter two are specific to

---

[14] See for an early defence of a wider role for Art 220: P. Pescatore, 'Fundamental Rights and Freedom in the system of the European Communities', (1970) A.J.I.L. 343 and the discussion by Douglas-Scott, op. cit., p. 212.

the claims raised under those Treaty Articles they do, however, serve to reinforce the Court of Justice's claim that it can rely on general principles as a source of law in the Community legal order. The sources of general principles are the national legal systems, in particular the constitutions of member states and the many rules of natural justice, often found in a majority of the member states. Others have been developed from the Treaty, which has supplied the basis for a general principle of non-discrimination. This has been built on the principles of non-discrimination on the grounds of nationality and sex and developed into a general principle of equality and non-discrimination.[15]

These additional sources of law are sometimes classified into broad groupings. Whilst this is probably not particularly useful because of the diversity of principles and the degree of overlap, presenting them in this way may, however, aid accessibility. I have therefore divided them into three groups concerned with human or fundamental rights, equality principles and finally, those relating to general procedural rights, however it must be stressed the categories are far from watertight and there is considerable overlap.

3.3.5 Human or Fundamental Rights

Originally, there was no catalogue of rights in the EC Treaty and fundamental rights provision was completely absent from any of the Treaties although some isolated Articles provided rights which either coincided with general principles or helped in the development of general principles of Community law. These are Article 2 (concerned with social protection, the standard of living, and quality of life), Articles 3 and 39 (dealing with the free movement of persons), Articles 12, 34, and 39(2) (concerned with discrimination), Article 43 (social security), and Article 141 (equal pay). Apart from these unconnected Articles there is as yet no specific and binding set of obligations imposed by the Treaty on the Community institutions to guarantee individual rights of citizens. This initial apparent lack of commitment to human rights was in turn reflected in the early decisions of the Court of Justice when faced with arguments or pleas raised by litigants based on basic or human rights. Hence, the early case law of the Court of Justice presents the view of a Community unsympathetic to the fundamental human rights of individuals. See Case 1/58 *Stork v High Authority* and Case 40/64 *Sgarlata v Commission* in which arguments based on individual rights were clearly rejected in favour of upholding Community law. This position can be contrasted with the then six member states' positions regarding human rights. Following World War II, Western European Nations were more than ever ideologically

---

[15] This will be covered in brief below and in further detail in Chapter 10.

committed to the concept of protecting human rights. The German and Italian constitutions were rewritten with very strong commitments to basic rights contained
within a rights catalogue. By 1955 all the original members of the EEC except France
had ratified the European Convention of Human Rights. The Community and Court
was thus morally if not legally obliged to observe fundamental human rights especially those contained in the constitutions of the member states. Thus, the Court of
Justice could not maintain its unsympathetic stance and adopted from the late 1960s,
a new response which was seen clearly in Case 26/69, *Stauder v City of Ulm*. A German
citizen protested that his fundamental right of human dignity, protected by Article 1
of the German *Grundgesetz* (its Basic Law or Constitution) was being infringed by
having his name on the coupon when claiming reduced price butter released by the
Community. The Court of Justice held that the Community did not require his name
but the Community law itself had not prejudiced his fundamental rights which were
'enshrined in the general principles of Community law and protected by the Court'.

After the French Ratification of ECHR in 1974, the Court of Justice referred also to
the ECHR as an example of the member state's commitment to fundamental rights.
Encouragement came also from the Joint Declaration by Community Institutions
on Fundamental Rights, 5 April 1977, which stressed the importance of national
constitutions and the ECHR. Hence, for the first time in Case 44/79, *Hauer v Land
Rheinland-Pfalz*, the Court of Justice considered in some detail a provision (Art 1 of
Protocol 1) of the ECHR to help it decide the case. Although it recognized the right of
property in the case, the exercise of it was subject to overriding Community interests.
Thus, despite recognition of the fundamental rights, cases have usually been resolved
on the basis of either Community law applying or the rights being subject to
limitations mainly of the Community interest.

In a number of cases the Court reaffirmed its statement that fundamental rights
form part of the general principles based on Constitutional traditions of member
states. For example, Case 11/70 *Internationale Handelsgesellschaft* showed the potential
for conflict and ultimate harm to the Community legal order if the Community failed
to uphold human rights provisions. No self-respecting legal system in Europe could
ignore or be seen to be ignoring such ideologically important rights as these and in
that case, the Court of Justice gave a guarantee that members states' constitutions will
not be infringed despite the superiority of Community law because of the commitment of the Community to human rights and the fact that they form part of the
Community legal order. In Case 63/83, *R v Kirk*, a fine imposed on a fishing boat
captain by a UK Court which was based on a national UK Statutory Order was held
to infringe the principle of non-retroactivity because the Order was supposedly
validated by later Community legislation. The Court of Justice held that such an action
violated the principle of non-retroactivity of Criminal Law enshrined in Article 7

ECHR and now a principle of Community law. Non-retroactivity was also confirmed as a principle of Community law in *Kolpinghuis Nijmegan*, considered further below. In Case 222/86, *UNECTEF v Heylens et al.*, the Court of Justice was able to refer to Articles 6 and 13 ECHR to support the right to judicial review and the right to be heard in support of a claim for an additional right, the right to free access to employment. In Case 5/88 *Wachauf*, the Court of Justice extended its support of fundamental rights by holding that the actions of member states in implementing Community measures must also comply with the requirements of human rights provisions.

The Court of Justice continues to refer to the ECHR in support of its judgments. For example, see the recent cases from the area of the free movement of persons including Case C-413/99 *Baumbast*, Case C-459/99 *MRAX* and Case C-109/01 *Akrich*, all of which featured Article 8 ECHR, the right to family life and which are considered further in Chapter 8.

The elevated status given to the ECHR by the Court of Justice has now been reflected in a greater status within the Treaty base. Article 6 of the TEU obliges the European Union to a broad general commitment to respect the articles of the ECHR and those human rights common to the member states as general principles of Community law. Any applicant states wishing to join the European Union are now obligated by Article 49 TEU to have respect for human rights and any member state which seriously and persistently offends human rights may have its rights under the Treaties suspended by the other member states under Article 7 TEU. The court's frequent reference to the ECHR, and general concern for the provision of a clear set of rights, has given rise to years of debate as to whether and if the Community should or could accede to the ECHR. In 1996 the Court of Justice gave Opinion 2/94 that under the treaties at the time, the Union did not have the power to accede. Now that the EU has its own catalogue of rights, in the form of the Fundamental Rights Charter, it might be argued that membership is more acceptable but conversely, with its own catalogue of rights there might be no further need for either the debate or accession to the ECHR. However, this catalogue is not presently binding but it would have constitutional and binding status in the Constitutional Treaty which also sets out the express aim of accession of the ECHR. In the present uncertainty surrounding the CT itself, the fundamental rights provision in the EU also remains in a precarious position. Not until the Constitutional Treaty or something similar comes into effect will the catalogue of rights become a binding catalogue of rights on the Community and member states. Until then, the liberal interpretation of the Court of Justice will continue to have to be relied on and accession to the ECHR may well remain outside the competence of the EU until expressly sanctioned by Treaty Amendment.

3.3.6 Equality and Non-discrimination

The prohibition of discrimination is catered for in the EC Treaty under a number of Articles: Article 12, the non-discrimination Article on the grounds of nationality, Article 141 relating to sex discrimination, Article 34(3) in respect of the Common Agricultural Policy and Article 39(2) for the free movement of workers. It is also a general principle recognized by the Court of Justice. It applies in all areas of Community law, especially to the fundamental freedoms. For example, in Case 75 and 117/82 *Razzouk and Beydoun v Commission*, the Court held that a Commission Decision, which discriminated between men and women in relation to a certain pensions payment, should be annulled as being contrary to the fundamental right of equal treatment of sexes. The principle was applied in Case 114/76 *Bergman v Grows-Farm* (skimmed milk powder), whereby the Court of Justice held that a scheme to force animal feed producers to incorporate skimmed milk powder in animal feed discriminated against non-dairy farmers. It was also applied to religious discrimination in Case 130/75 *Prais v Council*, although on the facts involving a Community competition for a post held on a Jewish religious festival, the Council was held not to have breached the general principle of equality. It was nevertheless held by the Court of Justice that wherever possible Community employees and citizens should have the general principle of non-discrimination in respect of religious freedom upheld in their favour.

The Community has moved further towards the development of a general principle of equality or at least non-discrimination in a range of issues, in an amendment made to the EC Treaty by the Treaty of Amsterdam. Article 13 provides that the Council may take appropriate action to combat discrimination based on sex, racial or ethnic origin, religion or belief, disability, age or sexual orientation and the Commission and Council have now issued Directives under this article.[16]

3.3.7 General Principles of Procedural Law and Natural Justice

A number of principles are closely associated with the administrative law principles found in many of the member states but may also be classified under the rules of natural justice. These can be found in differing forms in the member states legal systems for example, as common law rules in the UK or as a part of the constitution in Germany.[17]

---

[16] See, e.g., Directives 2000/43 (OJ 2000 L180/22) and 2000/78 (OJ 2000 L3030/16) which will be considered further in Chapter 10.

[17] See Arts 101–4 of the *Grundgesetz*.

3.3.7.1 The Right to Judicial Review

A general right to have administrative decisions reviewed by a court exists. The Court of Justice bases its view on the constitutions of the member states and notably on the ECHR, Article 6 dealing with a fair and public hearing and Article 13 ECHR dealing with the provision of an effective judicial remedy. See Case 222/84 *Johnston v The Chief Constable R.U.C.* and Case 222/86 *UNECTEF v Heylens.* In the latter case the Court of Justice had already determined that free access to employment was a fundamental right which should be respected in the Community. It thus becomes essential that there must be a remedy of a judicial nature against any decision of a national authority refusing the benefit of that right. The UNECTEF case established that the duty to give reasons was a general principle to be recognized in the Community legal order.

In Case 17/74 *Transocean Marine Paints Association v Commission,* the principle of the right to a fair hearing (under the Latin maxim: *Audi Alterem Partem*) was introduced by the AG. He argued that in the absence of being allowed to present their view on the condition imposed in a decision, the Commission's Decision would be in breach of a general principle of law, clearly applicable in the UK and other legal systems. This was upheld by the Court.

The Court of Justice held in Case 33 and 59/79 *Kuhner* also that where a person's rights were effected they must be given the opportunity to make their views known and the right to be heard must be upheld as a general principle of good administration.

3.3.7.2 Confidentiality/Legal Privilege

In Case 175/79 *A M & S v Commission,* a company refused to hand over certain documents, during a raid by Commission officials under the rules on competition law, on the grounds that by doing so the principle of legal privilege would be breached. The Court of Justice held the principle was recognized in Community legal order providing it was in relation to or preparation for a client's defence but it must be between a party and an independent lawyer. Supporting and extending this principle are Cases 136/79 *National Panasonic* and T-30/89 *Hilti.* The *Hilti* case decided that the privilege extends also to in-house lawyer's reports of the independent lawyers findings. In Case C-36/92 P *Samenwerkende,* a refusal to hand over documents considered to be confidential was held to be unjustified in the light of the existing protections in Community law under which the Commission is required to notify undertakings of the documents they intend to release to the national authorities and thus give the undertakings the chance to seek judicial review to protect these documents. As such the refusal to supply would be unjustified. In the end, the Court of First

Instance and European Court of Justice must be the arbiters of what is privileged. The principle of professional secrecy does not apply to allow a company to protect documents from the Commission but to ensure that information received by the Commission in an investigation is not disclosed to competitors.[18]

3.3.7.3 Legal Certainty

The basic concept underlying legal certainty incorporates a number of ideas concerned with the boundary between legality and illegality or lawfulness and unlawfulness which should be marked clearly in advance. Additionally, the existence of sanctions or punishment for the breach of the rule or overstepping the boundary should also be reasonably ascertainable, not the exact punishment but at least the type and scope or range of punishment applicable. As such the principle of proportionality is included in this category. Textbook and writers' considerations of Community law differ in their classification of general principles and proportionality may thus be classified as a distinct and separate principle. The different treatment accorded it is not really important. The point is that it is nevertheless recognized as a general principle by the Court of Justice and often quoted in cases to defeat the arguments of the member state or the Commission in justifying action or behaviour which has affected the rights of others, mainly individuals in the Community context. Legal certainty thus includes the underlying concepts of legitimate expectations, protection of vested rights, proportionality, and non-retroactivity. Legal certainty was first acknowledged by the Court of Justice in Case 43/75 *Defrenne v Sabena (No. 2)* and later confirmed in Case 262/88 *Barber v Guardian Royal Exchange* to support the Court's argument that the judgment could not be retroactively effective, although there is an argument to suggest that if a Treaty Article is held to be directly effective, as in the *Sabena* case, it must have been so from the outset of the Community and not from the date of judgment of the Court of Justice.

3.3.7.4 Non-Retroactivity

This principle is seen in it's purest form in Case 63/83 *R v Kent Kirk* and Case 262/88 *Barber* (considered above) and is firmly established as a general principle of Community law. Law should not retroactively impose punishments or be the legal base for punishments, particularly with regard to criminal sanctions or be the basis for a change in legal status or administrative sanctions. Case 80/86, *Public Prosecutor v Kolpinghuis Nijmegan* is also a very good example of the principle being cited by the Court of Justice in defence of the rights of the individual. In this case they were used

---

[18] Refer to Arts 27 and 28 of Regulation 1/2003 (OJ 2003 L1/1) and Cases 209–15 and 218/78 *Dow Benelux, Van Landewyck* and 53/85 *AKZO*)

to protect the Company from being prosecuted by the Dutch authorities on the strength of retroactive Community law validating national law where Holland had failed to implement the Directive correctly into national law.

Civil or non-criminal law retroactivity may also occur when a person's actual rights or expected rights are altered, redefined or totally removed. See, for example, Case 106 and 107/63 *Toepfer v Commission* dealing with the retroactive validation of import licence refusals by the German authorities. The principle of non-retroactivity may take on more subtle forms in civil law application to remove the difficulties created by the alteration or withdrawal of rights by Community legal measures. These cases also involve the next principle in that the plea is very often that the legitimate expectations on the individual have been infringed by the Community measure complained about. Particularly where the Commission is trying to regulate a very difficult market in goods, provided the legitimate expectations of the parties affected have been respected, then a measure which is retroactive in effect may be upheld, see Case 98/78 *Racke v HZA Mainz* concerned with the regulation of the wine market, then producing massive surpluses, the so-called 'wine lake'.

3.3.7.5 Legitimate Expectation or Vested Rights

The legitimate expectations of affected parties must be observed, especially when they predate a Community provision affecting their rights, hence there is some degree of overlap with non-retroactivity. In Case 88/76 *Sugar Export v Commission*, a Regulation was enacted by the Commission on 30 June 1976 which removed the right of Sugar Exporters to cancel licences previously granted when refunds payable on sugar exports, to reduce the over production and surplus of sugar in the Community, dropped in value. 1 July was set as the date of entry into force but the Regulation was not published until 2 July 1976. Sugar Exporters applied for a cancellation on 1 July 1976 but was at first refused by the Commission. The Court interpreted the Regulation as coming into force on 2 July 1976 and held whilst there was no intention of retroactivity, the rights vested in the applicant, applicable as on 1 July 1976, must be protected. The principle was confirmed by the Court of Justice in Case 112/77, *Töpfer v Commission* under similar factual circumstances dealing with the sudden removal of the right to cancel an export licence. In Case 81/72 *Commission v Council* (Staff Salaries), the principle was employed in different circumstances when the Council adopted a three-year experimental period for a system of staff salary payments but changed this after only nine months. Despite the view that Council could not bind itself as such, the Court of Justice held the employees had a reasonable or legitimate expectation that the Council would abide by its decision.

3.3.7.6 Proportionality

The principle of proportionality embodies the concept that the punishment should fit the crime and not go further, or must be reasonable in the circumstances and puts the question to the relevant authority of whether the same result could have been achieved by other methods or means less harmful to the party concerned. So in the Community context, it means that individuals should not be affected by actions beyond that necessary in the public or Community interest and any fines or punishment must be in proportion to the seriousness of the breach. It occurs frequently throughout all areas of Community law and especially to the internal market. It was invoked in Cases 11/70 *Internationale Handelsgesellschaft*, 36/75 *Rutili* and 159/79 *R v Pieck* in respect of the free movement of persons and in Case 178/84 *Commission v Germany* (Beer Purity) in relation to the free movement of goods. A good example is Case 181/84, *R v Intervention Board for Agricultural Produce ex parte Man*, in which a company was required to give a security deposit to the Intervention Board when seeking a licence to export sugar outside the Community. The applicant was late, but only by 4 hours, in completing the relevant paperwork. The Board acting under a Community Regulation, declared the entire deposit of over one and a half million pounds to be forfeit. The Court held that the automatic forfeit of the entire deposit in the event of any failure was too drastic in view of the function of the system of export licences, i.e. it was disproportionate to the aims.

The principle of proportionality has now been given statutory recognition under Article 5 of the EC Treaty to apply to relations between the Union and the member states in ensuring that any action at the Community level must be in proportion to the aims of the Community and not to go beyond those strict aims (see Chapter 4 for further details) Article 5 EC provides 'Any action by the Community shall not go beyond what is necessary to achieve the objectives of the Treaty'.

3.3.7.7 Summary

The category of general principles is already a wide one and potentially capable of great expansion. Indeed, in keeping with a system of law in which case law is regarded as important and can supply legal principles which become general principles to be applied in future cases, other new principles, in addition to those considered above which are the most frequently raised, can arise. Amongst those knocking on the door of more widespread recognition is 'transparency', although the Court of Justice has been equivocal about its status as a possible general principle,[19] its actual status in the legal system has nevertheless been endorsed by statutory intervention, first by a number of decisions but now by Regulation 1049/2001 (OJ 2001 L145/43). This provides a

---

[19] See Case C-58/94, *Netherlands v Council* and Case C-353/99P *Hautala v Council*.

right of access to Community documents. Another example of a potential general principle is 'Good faith' which received support as a general principle of Community law in Case 366/95 *Steff-houlberg Export*, concerned with the recovery of exports refunds which had been found to have been unduly paid. The export company were not responsible for the breach of rules and had acted in good faith. Under national law, and also in view of the time elapsed, the refunds should not be recoverable. The Court of Justice held this to be the position under EC law also.

3.3.8 'Soft Law'

'Soft Law' is a concept which is already recognized in national legal systems and which relates mainly to guidelines and rules of conduct. It has also developed within the Community system and encapsulates various rules of conduct which are not legally binding or enforceable in a court, or where failure to comply with them would not necessarily lead to a certain and specific sanction. Nevertheless, a number of forms of soft law have developed in the EC including a very early example, the Luxembourg accords, which was considered in Chapter 1.

Soft law includes all those rules or guidelines which aid the interpretation or assist in the application of enforceable Community law or which influence political behaviour of the member states and the institutions. There are also forms of soft law which have relevance for legal and natural persons.

Some forms of soft law are more clearly evident in the Community legal system than others, for example, recommendations and opinions which are mentioned in Article 249 and which state quite clearly that they have no binding force, although they can have a form of persuasive authority for the member states in interpreting and applying National law as was noted by the Court of Justice in C-322/88 *Grimaldi v Fonds des Maladies Professionelles*. Another form of soft law are all the general principles and fundamental rights which are not strictly legal binding or directly legally enforceable in the Community legal order, unless where expressly stated by the Court of Justice, but are nevertheless highly persuasive rules by which the Community and its institutions should behave.

There are various forms of communications from the Commission including guidelines in policy areas,[20] Commission notices, especially in the area of Competition policy, e.g. the minor Agreements notice,[21] various procedures and opinions under the second and third pillars and sometimes even press statements have been

---

[20] See, for example, a guideline taken completely at random from the Europa web site: COM (2004) 353(01) Communication from the Commission: Science and Technology, the key to Europe's future—Guidelines for future European Union policy to support research.

[21] Refer to OJ 2001 C 368/13.

held to have a quasi legal status. Whilst not binding, they are nevertheless highly influential on the Court of Justice but it remains the case that there is no clear-cut view of their validity.[22] Whilst soft law may be regarded as extremely helpful and might help grease the axles of the Community law machine by helping it to run more smoothly, it is not without its difficulties, particularly as any rules which are not benign, that is, which alter the legal or factual position of an individual or by their nature dictate behaviour, are for the most part beyond legal question or challenge. As such, they would seem to infringe the general principle of legal certainty and the democratic answerability. See, for example, the difficulties and discussion with regard to the legal validity of comfort letters in competition law.[23] However as a result of the change to the Competition law procedure and notification rules, this long-standing practise has been scrapped, but a new form of non-legally binding Notice has been brought in by Regulation 1/2003 and known as a 'guidance notice' but which should be used in very limited circumstances only.[24] As notification is no longer an automatic requirement, it is hoped that such letters will be a rare event.

Finally, in a move which may also be considered in this context, although the final result may end up in binding legislation, is the Open Method of Coordination (OMC), which was mentioned in Chapter 2 and can be regarded as having some of the features of soft law in that the rules are contrived by methods other than the legislative procedures laid down in Articles 249–52 and are thus beyond the legal redresses provided for in the Treaties but which rules do however result in standard forms of Community law which are then subject to challenge.[25]

3.4 The Participation of the Institutions in the Legislative and Budgetary Processes

The first part of this chapter concerned the various forms of law to be found in the Community legal order, this next section deals with how the binding secondary law of the Community is enacted. These forms of law now constitute the vast bulk of Community law, and their enactment has unfortunately become rather complex over the years, involving principally three institutions but according to the process required, of which there are many, often more of the Union bodies. First though, an

[22] Refer to L. Senden, *Soft Law in European Community Law*, Hart Publishing, Oxford 2004.
[23] In particular Case 99/79 *SA Lancome v ETOS BV* (the perfumes case).
[24] See the Notice 'Informal Guidance relating to novel questions concerning Arts 81 and 82 EC Treaty that arise in individual cases (guidance letters) OJ 2001 C101/78.
[25] See, for example, Directive 97/81 on Part-time Work (OJ 1998, L14/9).

allied issue needs to be addressed in order to provide a complete picture and to explain what determines which particular process should be employed in any given circumstance.

3.4.1 The Legal Base for Legislative Proposals

Articles of the Treaty which empower the EU Institutions to enact further legislation to carry out the policies of that title or chapter provide the key to the legislative procedure which must be used to enact the laws. They either provide details of the procedure themselves (e.g. Article 52 which provides that 'the council shall, on a proposal from the Commission and after consulting the Economic and Social Committee and the European Parliament, issue Directives acting by a qualified majority'.) or refer to another Treaty Article, as in Articles 40, 42, or 44, which refer to the co-decision procedure in Article 251 or Articles 99 and 102 which refer to the coopera-tion in Article 252. These in turn, provide details of the procedure to be used. The original Treaty Article is known then as the legal base which thus determines the participants in the procedure and the level of their participation. Law-making always involves the Commission and Council plus the EP and sometimes, as noted above, the EESC or the Committee of the Regions. The Treaty base is then fundamental to the relative powers and ability of the other institutions to affect the content of Com-munity law. For example, the use of QMV in the Council of Ministers is extremely important to the Commission who stand a greater chance of having proposals accepted by a majority rather than by all members states in Council. Minority or marginal views can thus be ignored rather than taken into account at the draft stages. The legal base is also vital to the level of participation of the EP in the legislative process, i.e. whether it is merely consulted, or cooperates with the Council, both of which procedures give the final say to the Council or whether co-decision is used in which case the EP has more power. For example, measures in support of the single market under Article 95 require majority voting rather than unanimity in the Coun-cil. As indicated, because this makes life easier for the Commission, the Commission tries to exploit this by introducing as much legislation as possible under Article 95, whereas the Council has argued the proposals should have as their legal base other Articles requiring unanimity (i.e. Article 94 concerned directly with approximating legislation for the common market). Looked at from another point of view, a single member state which objects to a particular measure would wish to veto it and would want unanimity voting in Council to have that chance. It would object to the Council deciding to adopt the measure under a legal base requiring QMV. For the most part, the particular Treaty legal base is clear in that the subject matter of the proposal is clearly within the subject matter of a specific Treaty Article and therefore base.

However, the subject matter may straddle different Treaty subject areas and thus lend itself to more than one Treaty base. Hence, there is sufficient ground for differences of opinion as to which is the correct Treaty base to use, and the institutions and member states have often fought over this. In particular, the EP has not refrained from challenging the Council for the use of the incorrect legal base and regularly brings cases before the Court of Justice.

An early example, and one likely to be in materials books, is Case 68/86 *UK v Council* (Hormones) which concerned a Directive banning growth-producing hormones, based on old Article 43 concerned with measures in support of the Common Agricultural Policy, which required a qualified majority only. This was objected to by the UK which argued that it should have been based on the old Article 100—a single market measure which required unanimity. The question raised was whether this was free movement, as argued by UK, thus a single market measure or really to do with agricultural policy, in which case the Treaty Article under that section would be the most appropriate. The Court of Justice held that the CAP Article was the appropriate one as it lent itself more to the subject matter concerned. Similarly, in Case C-155/91 *Commission v Council* (Waste Directive), the Waste Directive 91/156, adopted by the Council under old Article 130s (an environment measure legal base then requiring unanimity), was challenged by the Commission on the basis that old Article 100a concerned with the internal market, requiring majority voting only, should have been used as the legal base. On this occasion, the Court disagreed and held that the protection of the environment, as stated in the Directive, was the real reason and not the free movement of waste. Therefore, the challenge by the Commission was rejected. The issue was not so much the right to move waste around, but the promotion of the most efficient way of dealing with waste to protect the environment by removing any prevention of movement to the most efficient operators or disposers of waste.

A further case concerned the adoption by the Council in June 1993, of a Directive specifying a minimum working week, albeit with the ability of workers to work longer voluntarily. The UK, which was opposed to this, was unable to veto the proposal as it was introduced under the Health and Safety of workers provision under the old Article 118a of EEC Treaty requiring a qualified majority in the Council. In Case C-84/94 *UK v Council*, the UK formally requested the Court of Justice to annul the Directive, arguing that it would have been more appropriate to base the measure on Article 308 (old 235) or 94 (old 100), either of which would have required unanimity on the part of the Council thus allowing the UK the chance to veto the measure before its possible enactment. The Court of Justice was, however, satisfied with the choice of Article 118a.

In Case C-295/90 *European Parliament v Council* (Students residence), Parliament successfully challenged the adoption of Directive 90/366 on the residence of students which the Council adopted under old Article 235 requiring only consultation rather than under old Article 7 (prohibition of discrimination on the grounds of nationality) which would require the cooperation procedure to be used. The Directive was annulled and has been re-enacted as Directive 93/96. The EP had no objection to the rights provided by the measure itself, merely the way it had been enacted which had denied it its full participation.

A final case here to focus on the issues raised above is Case C-300/89 *Commission v Council* (*Re*: Titanium Dioxide Directive). The Council adopted a Directive on the basis of old Article 130s as an environmental measure which then required unanimity in Council and only consultation of the EP, despite the protests of the EP at the time. The Commission argued it should have been adopted using Article 100A as a single market measure, which then required QMV and the cooperation procedure instead. Whilst the Court acknowledged that both could be a valid base, the use of Article 130s instead of Article 100a deprived the EP of its greater role in the legislative process. Even if both were used, as suggested by the Council, it would still have to decide unanimously and be able therefore to overrule any objections of the EP.

What emerges from this case law is that the view of the Court of Justice is essentially that in the interests of the democratic process, law-making, which now involves the EP, demands that where two legal bases are available requiring differing procedures, the one allowing the EP the greater role must be used so as not to deprive the EP and the Community of its democratic right, unless it can be shown the matter is primarily more concerned with a particular Treaty base.

In view of the simplification of the legislative procedures by the Treaties of Amsterdam and Nice and the fact that many more Treaty subject areas have moved under the co-decision procedure in favour of the EP, increasingly there is less room for a dispute as to the correct legal base, therefore less scope for argument and less possibility for court action in the future. Even more matters will be decided by QMV and co-decision under the Constitutional Treaty thus reducing even further the scope for conflict and thus litigation between the institutions and member states, paid for essentially each and every time by the European Taxpayer.

3.5 Law-making Principles and Procedures

A number of factors have influenced, first the establishment of the particular law-making procedures and legal forms in the EC and EU and, secondly their expansion and evolution. These are charted from the relatively straightforward beginnings via a period of numerous and complex forms and procedures to what hopefully will be a considerable rationalization by the Constitutional Treaty, should it or some similar reform enter into force. The issues provoking such change include the democratic deficit of the law-making procedure overall, the expansions in the number of member states, voting arrangements in the Council, and the establishment of the two inter-governmental pillars by the TEU. As a result, there have been numerous Treaty amendments both increasing and complicating the legislative procedures. Whilst the Treaty of Amsterdam made an attempt to rein in the prolixity and complexity of these procedures, it is the plans for reform within the Constitutional Treaty which provide the best chance to rationalize the procedures, but unfortunately not to the extent first proposed, as will become apparent below.

Three institutions are principally involved in law-making. However, it is worth noting that before law-making even commences, the overall policy is decided by the member states during both Treaty negotiation and amendment and on an ongoing basis by the European Council in making recommendations and requesting actions by the main institutions, notably the Council of Ministers but also the Commission.

There are at present four or five law-making procedures in the EU plus the dele-gated legislative power of the Commission. One procedure, although still on paper is no longer used hence my seeming uncertainty 'four or five'. In addition, three of the procedures are now subject to minimal use and one clear leading law-making procedure has emerged.

3.5.1 The Law-making Procedures

All law-making procedures start with the Commission, which puts policy into effect by means of preparing and proposing legislative instruments. The Council and Parliament then dispose of these legislative proposals. i.e. they decide the final shape and enact the legislation. The actual details of each procedure varies according to the way the Council votes and the different forms of participation of the EP. Additionally, for some procedures, other institutions are involved, most notably EESC and the Committee of the Regions. The institutions involved overall and the extent to which they are involved are determined by the Treaty. First of all, Article 249 et seq. provides the details of a number of procedures which are available to enact community legisla-tion. Which particular process is employed depends on the subject matter for which legislation is required and then in turn, the Treaty Article or Articles which govern those matters. i.e. legislation is enacted under a particular procedure prescribed in the legal base, noted above, which is the Treaty Article covering the subject matter of the legislation under consideration. For example, Article 40 which empowers legislation to be enacted for the free movement of workers requires that the co-decision pro-cedure be used (detailed in Art 251). In addition to the procedures themselves, we need to consider why they have become so convoluted and the consequences of this, although it is not necessary to learn the fine details and points of each and every legislative process. This, apart from being tedious, is not very productive, and like many sets of rules, will simply change over time.

3.5.1.1 The Original Consultation Procedure

Originally, a limited number of Treaty Articles (seventeen) provided that the Council was required to consult the EP as to its opinion before coming to a decision on Community secondary law. Under this procedure, the Commission proposes legislation which is deems necessary to fulfil a Community aim, the European Parliament is then consulted and it offers its opinion, and the Council decides on the matter, either by qualified majority vote, but usually unanimously. However, on receipt of the opinion of the EP, the Council could proceed to ignore it and override any view given by the EP. It is to be noted though that in Cases 138–39/79, *Roquette and Maizena v Council*, the Court annulled a Regulation because the Council had failed to consult or obtain the opinion of the EP before it passed the legislation. Furthermore, in Case C-65/93 *European Parliament* v *Council*, it was held that if the Commission proposal had been substantially altered, the EP must be consulted again, and failure to do so will also result in annulment of the measure, which occurred in that case. The Consultation procedure is now restricted to the CAP (Art 37), Article 13, and the non-express powers or additional powers under Article 308.

Under the CT, a revised version of this procedure will be retained for the equivalent of Article 13 EC (Art III-124) only, requiring unanimity on the part of the Council after obtaining the consent (not consultation) of the EP.

3.5.1.2 The Cooperation Procedure

This was introduced under Articles 6 and 7 SEA as the first real expansion of the power of the EP in the law-making process. It did so by establishing a form of first and second reading in a kind of extended consultation process. It also set time limits for the process of legislation in order to try to prevent delays which might have crept in by the institutions prevaricating. It was, however, introduced to certain limited areas only, largely affecting the internal market. Under the TEU, this was re-enacted as Article 252 EC.

In brief, the procedure works as follows: The Commission proposal is sent to the European Parliament for an opinion before being transmitted to the Council, which adopts a common position on the basis of a QMV. Then, rather than proceed immediately to decide on the matter as it would have done under the old consultation procedure, this common position is sent to the EP whereby changes can be suggested within three months. The EP can approve the proposal which can then be adopted by the Council, the EP can do nothing, in which case the Council can adopt the common position by a simple majority vote or the EP can reject the common position. The Council can nevertheless adopt it but only if it does so within three months and by a unanimous vote. Finally, if the EP makes amendments, the Commission must re-examine the proposal and re-submit it to the Council within one month. The Council then has three months to act. It can adopt by a qualified majority, amend by unanimity or do nothing, in which case the proposed measure will lapse. This complex procedure was the subject of much criticism in respect of the time taken to complete it and a significant drawback of the procedure from the point of view of participatory democracy is that the Council retains the final say over legislation regardless of the opinion of the EP. In this respect it is not much better than the consultation procedure, just longer.

Thankfully, the number of Treaty Articles which employ the procedure has been reduced by each successive Treaty amendment. At Amsterdam, the member states agreed to transfer all policy areas under this procedure to the co-decision procedure, with the exception of EMU, thus it is of far less importance, and, following Nice, only five Treaty Articles (Arts 99, 102, 103, 106, and 300), mainly concerned with economic policy, require the use of this procedure. It will disappear entirely if the Constitutional Treaty comes into force.

3.5.1.3 The Co-decision Procedure

Article 249 EC was amended by the TEU to provide that the EP act more extensively with the Council and Commission in the legislative process by the introduction of the co-decision procedure, detailed in Article 251 EC. It is really a variation of the cooperation procedure but with the enhanced participation of the EP to the extent that ultimately, the EP can reject a legislative proposal at a second reading. The EP cannot impose its own will on the content of a legislative proposal, thus parliamentary veto might be a better description of the process.[26] Note that in the procedure, the Council votes mainly by QMV but at times, according to some Treaty Articles and parts of the procedure itself, it must vote unanimously. The following description takes into account the amendments made to the procedure by the Treaty of Amsterdam which ironed out some of the initial teething troubles and delays originally experienced in the operation of the procedure. The description has been marked with reference numbers which relate to Figure 3.1, below.

The main stages of this procedure are that the Commission proposal (1), taking

---

[26] See http://ue.eu.int/uedocs/cmsUpload/code_EN.pdf for a very good Council produced guide to this procedure. See also a good Commission web site on the same: http://europa.eu.int/comm/codecision/index_en.htm.

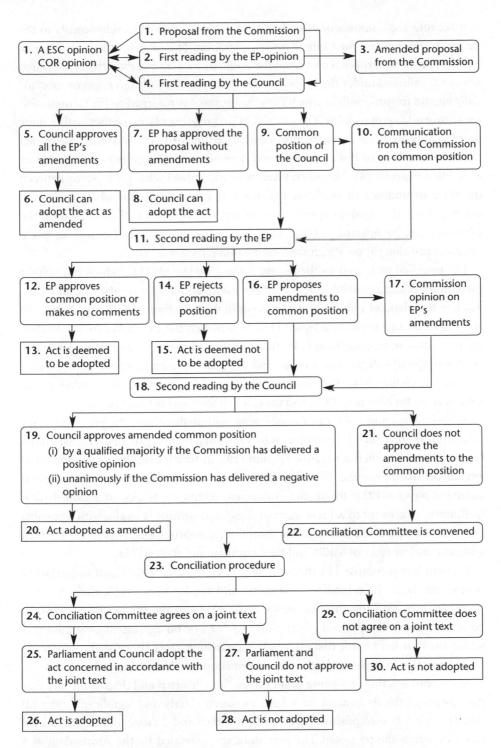

Fig. 3.1 The Co-decision Procedure

Source: Flowchart of the co-decision procedure reproduced with grateful acknowledgment under the general authorization of the European Commission, see http://europa.eu.int/comm/codecision/stepbystep/diagram_en.htm and http://europa.eu.int/geninfo/legal_notices_en.htm

into account the opinions of other bodies (1.A), is forwarded simultaneously to the EP for its opinion and the Council for consideration. The EP can, at first reading (2), either approve the proposal or amend the proposal by a simple majority or, although not strictly allowed under the procedure detailed in Article 251, can reject or substantially amend the proposal, in which case, the proposal is returned to the Commission for an amended proposal (3). The Council, at first reading (4), can either, within three months, approve those amendments by a qualified majority (5), in which case the act can be adopted (6), or if there have been no amendments (7), simply adopt the act by a qualified majority (8). This often involves considerable exchanges of views between the three institutions to reach an agreement at first reading but where successful, disposes with the need to spend time on the rest of the procedure. Instead, the provision can be enacted without further ado. Otherwise, the Council adopts a common position (9) on which the Commission comments (10).

The proposal then goes to the second reading by the EP (11), which can, within three months and a possible one month extension, either approve the common position, or for whatever reason, do nothing within the time limit (12). In which case the act is deemed to have been adopted (13). If, however, the EP rejects, by an absolute majority, the common position (14), the act is deemed not to have been accepted (15), i.e. the proposal will not become law and the procedure ends. The EP though may propose amendments to the common position (16), which are forwarded to the Commission for comment (17), and the Council for a second reading (18).

At second reading (18), the Council may, within three months plus a month's extension, approve the EP amendments by a qualified majority or, unanimously, if the Commission has issued a negative opinion (19), in which case the act is adopted as amended (20). If, on the other hand, the Council does not accept the amended common position (21), the matter is referred, within six weeks, to a Conciliation Committee to attempt to achieve a compromise also within six weeks, with a possible two-week extension (22 and 23). The committee comprises members of the Council with an equal number of MEPS and the Commissioner responsible.

If a joint text is approved by the committee (24), the Council, by qualified majority (unless the Treaty base requires unanimity) and the EP by a simple majority, may adopt the provision together within six weeks (25) and the act is adopted (26). If, however, there is no approval of the joint text (27), or no agreement on a joint text within the time limit in the first place (29), then in both cases, the procedure comes to an end and the act is deemed not to have been adopted (28 and 30).

As you can see, this procedure is not for the faint-hearted and despite the fact that the powers of the Parliament have been increased clearly and significantly, the EP cannot enforce its own positive view over the Council and if they cannot agree, the EP can only wreck the proposal! The procedure was extended by the Amsterdam and

Nice Treaties into many new areas of the Treaty and is now the most often employed legislative procedure in the Treaty. It will be extended again under the CT.[27]

3.5.1.4 The Assent Procedure

The assent procedure was introduced by the SEA and extended under the TEU, so that the EP's assent is required by the Council in respect of membership applications to the EU, the Union's membership of international agreements and organizations and for association agreements with third countries (Article 49 TEU and Articles 310 and 300(3)). In the event of disagreement, the EP has effectively a right of veto. Assent is also employed to confirm serious and persistent breaches by a member state (Art 7 TEU) and in establishing a procedure for the election of MEPs (Art 190 EC).

3.5.1.5 The Conciliation Procedure

The conciliation procedure was introduced by the Joint Declaration of the Council, Commission and Parliament in 1975 for certain types of financial legislation. At the time, the EP had no say over compulsory expenditure in the budget and it was agreed that it should nevertheless be given an opportunity to participate in the decisions concerning substantial compulsory expenditure. The procedure can be enacted by either the EP or the Council and on such proposals, the EP is able to give its opinion, which may, however, be disregarded by the Council. Whilst it may still exist on paper, it no longer features as a legislative process and will not feature under the CT.

3.5.2 Why so many types of Legislative Procedures?

As was noted above, the increase of the decision-making procedures is the product of a number of developments in the EU: the democratic deficit, the various expansions of member states, voting arrangements in the Council for the member states, movement and expansion of the EU into new policy areas, and as a response to the international regulation of pan European or even global problems such as the environment or business regulation. One of the unfortunate consequences of the increase in procedures is that it had led to legal disputes between the member states and institutions and between the institutions themselves, about whether the correct legal procedure and legal base has been used and not, for the most part, concerned with the substance of the final legislative act. Many cases were more concerned with the degree of power wielded by the EP or individual states on the Council. As a result, the procedures have become even further removed from a sensible understanding of the legislative

---

[27] A complete list of the legal bases requiring co-decision can be found at http://europa.eu.int/comm/codecision/procedure/legalbasis_en.htm.

processes by lawyers, yet alone lay persons. The desire to reform the procedures in addition to the desire to reform the type and number of legal instruments, if or when the CT comes into force, will certainly lead to the most comprehensive overhaul of the procedures and instruments in the history of the EU. The legal instruments reform will be considered briefly in Chapter 3. With regard to the procedures, the draft Constitutional Treaty for Europe proposed that the co-decision route become the only procedure, the member states however, insisted on retaining the consultation procedure requiring Council unanimity in a number of areas. Under the agreed CT, the co-decision procedure, renamed the ordinary legislative procedure, will apply to economic and monetary union and will replace consultation for the CAP and be extended to the Common Commercial Tariff, the free movement of TCNs and into the area of Freedom, Security, and Justice, previously under one of the intergovern-mental pillars. The areas retaining consultation and unanimity on the part of the Council are not inconsiderable, and the examples here are not exhaustive. It will still apply to tax, some aspects of social and environmental policy, some bases of Foreign and Security Policy and Justice and Home Affairs issues.[28]

3.6 The Delegation of Powers

Prior to the SEA, the only Article of the Treaty which dealt with delegation was Article 211 which provided: 'In order to ensure the proper functioning and development of the Common Market, the Commission shall exercise the powers conferred on it by the Council for the implementation of the rules laid down by the latter.' In order for day-to-day decision-making to be effective, in most, if not all, democratic systems of government, some form of executive action is required, either to implement or com-plete legislative acts, or be used in respect of detailed, technical issues not requiring the debate or input of the main legislators.

Delegation can be in the form of wide discretionary powers and include legislative as well as administrative forms of secondary legislation. Delegation may, however, be subjected to confirmation or limits or rules laid down by the delegating authority, or the delegating authority may retain the right to rescind the decision. This latter right is usually subject to a time limit by which the delegating authority must act. In the Community legal order, a system of committees was set up to supervise the exercise of delegated power whereby the Council has retained control over the delegated power.

---

[28] A full list of the Articles in the CT retaining the use of the old consultation procedure can be found in the accompanying web site.

Delegation and the management committees have been considered by the Court of Justice as early as 1958. In Case 9/56, *Meroni v High Authority*, the Court of Justice stressed the necessity of preserving the balance of powers in the institutional structure of the Communities as envisaged by the Treaties and which would therefore not allow the delegation of discretionary powers involving policy decisions. In Case 25/70, *Köster*, the delegation of power to the Commission within the management committee procedure was challenged on the ground that the procedure disturbed the institutional balance of Community contrary to the Treaty and undermined the independence of the Commission. The Court observed the management committee could not take decisions itself but merely provided options for implementation and therefore the power balance was not disturbed. Thus, providing the empowering legislation is adopted by the procedures envisaged by the Treaty, the details can be delegated to the Commission. The Court of Justice held further in Case 23/75 *Rey Soda*, that implementing powers under Article 211 must be interpreted widely, especially under the Common Agricultural Policy where actions must often be taken on a day-to-day basis and discretion is necessary to cope with changing circumstances.

The SEA amended Article 202 EC by adding a third indent which provided that 'The Council may impose certain requirements in respect of the exercise of these powers' and further provided the right to reserve to itself implementing powers. Consequent to this, Decision 87/373, known as the 'Comitology Decision' as amended by Council Decision 99/468/EC was adopted to determine principles and rules governing the system of management committees. The Decision provides for three standard Committee types. Advisory Committees, Management Committees which have two procedural variants providing greater powers of decision for the Commission and Regulatory Committees which require positive approval of the decisions by the Committee. The committees consist of representatives of the member states and a non-voting Commission chair.

In Case 16/88, *Commission v Council (Re: Management Committee procedure)* concerning the Commissions power of implementation under Article 274, the Council delegated power to conclude certain contracts to the Commission subject to a management Committee procedure. The Commission argued that implementation under Article 274 concerning budgetary procedure was not subject to management committees. The Court held that as they were also legislative in character, they were validly subject to the management committee procedures.

It is argued that since the formalization of the procedure, too much power has been given to the Committees and is consequently lost from the Commission and European Parliament. The system allows the Council to withdraw delegated powers at any time when decided by the Committee. The EP attempted to challenge the committee management structure in the Comitology Decision (Case 302/87 *European*

Parliament v Council), particularly because the Council failed to state in which circumstances particular procedures would apply, but the challenge failed due to inadmissibility, at that time, of the direct challenge by the EP.

In other specific circumstances, the Commission has further powers of its own under Article 85 competition law exemptions and under Article 86 concerned with state aids.

The CT will attempt to tidy up this area of decision-making under Article I-36 by providing for delegation to the Commission under express terms and conditions and subject to a formal scrutiny by both the EP and the Council.

3.7 Community Financing

As a result of the delay to the introduction of the system of own resources by the objections of the French President de Gaulle in 1965–6, a system of Community own resources and a revised budgetary procedure were not introduced until 1970[29] when Parliament was given the last word on non-compulsory expenditure. This regime was amended by the Budgetary Treaty of 1975.[30]

'Own resources' means that the Community can rely on certain incomes which have been designated Community income. These include agricultural levies, duties received under the Common Customs Tariff, and a percentage on the revenues from Value Added Tax as agreed by the member states and currently set at 1.6 per cent of the rate used for VAT assessment. This system became self sufficient as from 1 January 1980.

The procedure for determining expenditure and the annual budget is governed by Articles 272–3 EC. Two forms of expenditure are categorized: compulsory and non-compulsory. Compulsory expenditure is that automatically arising from or the inevitable consequence of Treaty obligations to third parties. Non-compulsory covers the expenditure required in respect of the institutions and that which is not obliged by the Treaty and largely applies, for example, to the Social and Regional Funds.

3.7.1 The Budgetary Procedure

The Commission proposes the first draft and the maximum increase for non-compulsory expenditure and forwards it to the Council which prepares the draft budget by a qualified majority. The draft is then sent to the EP who can approve it within forty-five days in which case it will be adopted, or the EP can amend the draft in respect of non-compulsory expenditure and modifications can be made by the EP

---

[29] Decision 70/243 JO 1975 L94/19.   [30] OJ 1975 L359/1.

in respect of compulsory expenditure. The draft is then returned to the Council. Ultimately, however, the EP cannot interfere with compulsory expenditure which includes the Common Agricultural Policy and which consumes between 55 and 75 per cent of the total budget. Any such EP amendments or modifications can be rejected by the Council by a qualified majority.

Amendments can, however, be made by a majority to non-compulsory expenditure such as the regional and social funds but these can be modified by the Council by a qualified majority within fifteen days. The draft is returned to the EP which can no longer modify the compulsory expenditure but can modify non-compulsory expend-iture items within fifteen days by a majority and at least three-fifths voting. The EP can then either adopt or reject the budget, as it did in 1979 following the direct elections and again in 1984. In the case of rejection, which has to be for important reasons, the one-twelfth rule automatically applies until the dispute is resolved whereby the Commission is provided with one-twelfth of the previous year's money per month (Art 273(1) EC) and the budget is returned to the Council to be redrafted.

The Constitutional Treaty will increase the say of the EP in the procedure by removing the distinction between compulsory and non-compulsory expenditure and by providing for just one simultaneous reading of the budget by each the Council and the EP with resort to a Conciliation Committee to resolve any differences of opinion. Those items which cannot be resolved can lead to the rejection of the Budget by either the EP or the Council and thus to a new draft budget submission by the Commission (Art III-404 CT).

3.8 The Community Method, OMC, and Governance Issues

There has certainly been considerable discussion about the way in which the Com-munity is governed, not so much perhaps in the standard textbooks, but sufficient for it to be included in this text so that, at least, an understanding of these terms is achieved and a consideration of the main aspects of them provided. Whilst there have been numerous minor changes and additions to the institutional structure, the most important issues remain the same. Essentially, these all relate to how the Communities and now Union should be run. There are also individual topics which re-occur within this overall theme including the relative democratic weakness of the Parliament or lack of any other direct democratic input, the way in which the Council wields its decision making powers and the lack of open government in the EU Institutions. For the most part decision-making remains within the same institutional form of govern-ance, itself changed little since the beginning of the Communities. This is known as the 'Community method' and includes the process of the transfer of power from the member states, the institutional set-up and decision-making in the EU, as described above. The tensions between the intergovernmental and supranational elements of the Communities' form of governance, the limited democratic input and the lack of openness and citizen participation has led to moves to address these concerns by the introduction of alternative methods of policy coordination and governance for the EU. In particular, is the development of the open method of coordination (OMC) which had its roots in the Social dialogue procedure by which Community-wide standards were agreed when the social policy chapter lay outside the Treaty set-up. After consultation and discussion by and between social and other interest groups most directly concerned with the policy, any ensuing agreements which were reached under that policy would be enforceable at the Community level. After the change of UK Government in 1997, the social dialogue method was imported into the EC Treaty under Articles 138–9 EC and extended to a wider social policy field.

The advantage of OMC is that it is regarded as a less painful method of making progress in such areas of shared competence or supporting or coordinating competence of the EC because hard law measures would generally require unanimity by twenty-five member states. Hard law measures are thus difficult to achieve or prove too difficult for some states who might or would veto any legislative proposals in Council in matters of national sensitivity, for example, tax. OMC though has not been widely used and is not without critics. The Community method remains the most preferred and used. Despite the optimism shown for OMC at the Lisbon Summit in 2000, the Convention on the future for Europe and the draft Constitutional Treaty which emerged largely ignored OMC. On the down side, the use of OMC is regarded as a retreat from firm legal commitments to achieve a more social Europe or the downgrading or abandoning of fixed legislative policies on social and employment matters, replacing them instead with the uncertain soft law options of dubious value and validity. OMC may also be seen as undermining the democratic input into the legislative process of the EP, an input which has been so hard fought over so many years and, as a result, it is hard to see a role for the EP without seriously compromising OMC or unnecessarily duplicating effort and input, thus making the democratic involvement process very inefficient. A union of twenty-five member states certainly poses more challenges than when originally, there were just six member states and OMC is regarded as not being very workable, without significant change for an EU of twenty-five or more states.[31]

---

[31] See, D. Hodson and I. Maher, 'The Open-Method as a New Mode of Governance: the Case of Soft Economic Policy Co-Ordination' (2001) 39 *JCMS*, 719, 721–2 and S. De la Rosa, The Open Method of Coordination in the New member states-Perspectives for its use as a Tool of Soft Law (2005) 11 *ELJ*, 618.

3.9 The Institutional Balance: Getting it Right

As outlined, above, there are a number of dynamics taking place in the policy and law-making procedures of the EU. The most notable one remains the balance between the direct democratic legitimacy of the EP in the face of the legislative superiority of the Council. The problem though with increasing the input and power of the EP, whilst it would increase democratic participation, albeit indirectly, might jeopardize the present level of efficiency of the law-making process. Whilst it is far from perfect at the moment, it does seem to have achieved a relatively happy medium of getting most things done. An increase in the power of Parliament to truly rival the Council might have the knock on effect of creating a conflict between the two institutions which results in stalling the law-making processes and if nothing ever gets done, it is hardly a useful democratic input. In other words, too much participation by the EP would lead to a slowing down of the legislative processes. Should efficiency be sacrificed for the sake of democracy? Whereas the question may well be put of the present state of affairs as to whether democracy should be sacrificed for the sake of efficiency?

Under the CT, there is a plan for more involvement of National Parliaments. The Constitutional Treaty proposes that the National Parliaments obtain powers to check that subsidiarity is conformed with (Art I-11), take a view on accession applications, oversee legislative proposals, and be kept informed about policy initiatives in the same way as the EP, especially in the matters covered by the old third pillar dealing with justice affairs. National Parliaments are also to be given a formal view (Art I-42) in any future Treaty amendment proposals. The difficulty with these proposals is that the National Parliaments may then become a rival for power with the EP and may also reduce efficiency in the law-making processes if the views of twenty-five National Parliaments have to be obtained before progress can be made.

Turning to the alternative, OMC also has its alleged advantages of increased participation, openness, and flexibility, but it is also fraught with danger in that decisions made under it may be beyond legal challenge. It also increases the power of the Commission and member states without any reference and probably at the expense of the EP and if expanded, the EESC and the COR.

All these questions may well be revisited in the reflection and revision of the CT currently under way.

Further reading

Books

ALSTON, P. (ed.), *The EU and Human Rights*, OUP, Oxford 1991.

CRAIG, P. and HARLOW, C. (eds.), *Lawmaking in the European Union*, Kluwer, Deventer 1998.

DOUGLAS-SCOTT, S. *Constitutional Law of the European Union*, Longman, Harlow 2002 (chapter 3).

PEERS, S. and WARD A. (eds.), *The EU Charter of Fundamental Rights: Politics, Law and Policy*, Hart Publishing, Oxford 2004.

PRINSSEN, J. M. and SCHRAUWEN, A. (eds.), *Direct Effect. Rethinking a Classic of EC Legal Doctrine*, Europa Law Publishing, Groningen 2002.

SENDEN, L. *Soft Law in European Community Law*, Hart Publishing, Oxford 2004.

Articles

ARNULL, A. 'From Charter to Constitution and beyond: Fundamental Rights in the New European Union' (2003) *Public Law*, 774.

BORRAS, S. and GREVE, B. Special Issue: The Open Method of Co-ordination in the European Union (2004) 11(2) *Journal of European Public Policy*.

DASHWOOD, A. 'The Limits of Community Competence' (1996) 21 *EL Rev*, 211.

DE BÙRCA, G. 'The Constitutional Challenge of New Governance in the European Union' (2003) 28 *European Law Review*, 814–40.

DUVIGNEAU, J. L. 'From advisory opinion 2/94 to the Amsterdam Treaty: human rights protection in the European Union' (1998) *LIEI*, 25(2), 61–91.

HOSLI, M. Coalitions and Power: Effects of Qualified Majority Voting on the Council of the European Union (1996) 34 *JCMS*, 255.

JACOBS, F. 'Human Rights in the EU: The Role of the Court of Justice' (2001) 26 *EL Rev*, 331.

KIRCHHOF, P. 'The Balance of Powers Between National and European Institutions' [1999] vol. 5 no. 3 *European Law Journal*, 225–42.

LENAERTS, K. 'Fundamental Rights in the European Union' (2000) 25 *EL Rev*, 575.

WELLENS, K. C. and BORCHARDT, G. M. 'Soft Law in European Community law' (1989) *ELR*, 267.

Web sites

A web site of the EU on Governance in Europe: http://europa.eu.int/comm/governance/index_en.htm

The Commission Web site on Social Dialogue.   http://europa.eu.int/comm/employment_social/social_dialogue/dialogue_en.htm

The Co-decision procedure: http://europa.eu.int/comm/codecision/index_en.htm

4

The EU Constitutional Arrangement: The EU and its Member States

4.1 Introduction

Whilst it was never entirely clear-cut just what the nature of the Community was when it was first established involving as it did, a mix of intergovernmental and supranational elements, it has developed considerably since then and become a very complex entity. As a result many questions have been raised about the nature of the Union and its relationship with the member states. How democratic is it? Is it moving towards a federal set up of some sorts? Whilst demanding constitutionality of new member states, to what extent does the Union itself conform to the constitutional standards regarded as imperative for modern democracies? To a large extent, these questions were taken on following the Laeken Summit by the Convention on the Future Europe which prepared the Constitutional Treaty agreed by the member states in 2004. This chapter attempts to explore this multifaceted and increasingly intricate relationship between the Union and the member states. It commences with the transfer of sovereign powers and democratic legitimacy of the Union and connected to this, the establishment of constitutionalism within the Union.

The second section will consider the division and control of competences between the Union and the member states and in this context, also the principle of subsidiarity. Both the division of competences and the principle of subsidiarity are political solutions to the very emotive questions about how power is shared between the Union and Community and the member states, subsidiarity being a way of deciding how to determine where the line between Union and member states' competences should be drawn. Even after the division of competences has been decided, which means the right to act and thus enact legislation in certain areas, there remains the question of the status of those acts produced under the Community competence and whether they take priority over national law. Which means of course the issue of supremacy, considered in the final section of this chapter.

4.2 The Transfer of Sovereign Powers

When the European Communities were first set up, as catalogued in Chapter 1, it was done very clearly at the time in full recognition that in order to be able to achieve the goals set for it, the member states had to pool their resources in the new entity, or in other words, they had to transfer some of their sovereign rights to the Communities and their institutions in order for them to do their work. This was later acknowledged quite clearly by the Court of Justice in the seminal *Van Gend en Loos* case but with the proviso that the power transfer or transfer of sovereignty was done only within limited fields and was not a general transfer of power. A general transfer would include the ability to decide its own competences and is often described in the German as *Kompetenz kompetenz*, the ability to redefine competences without reference to any other body. In similar terms is the term 'omnipotence' as employed in the Dicean discussion about Parliamentary Sovereignty in the UK. This was not the case with the transfers of powers by the member states to the Communities and Union.[1] So any power the Community has, is only there by the virtue of the transfer by the member states. However, the Communities and Union are not static entities, they have developed considerably since first being established and the competences have grown hand in hand with the complexity of the Union. Each successive Treaty amendment has transferred further powers to the Union with a corresponding loss of sovereignty in those areas as agreed by the member states. How these powers are divided and employed is considered under the section below on competences. First, as one of the requirements of constitutionality, democracy will be considered.

4.3 Democracy in the Union

4.3.1 The Democratic Credentials of the Union

Whilst Article 6 TUE requires that the Union is founded on democracy, amongst other values, and that under Article 49 TEU any potential new member state needs to comply with this, it is debatable whether the Union itself corresponds to this. As first established, there was certainly very little democratic input. The Assembly, as the EP was first titled, consisted of appointed members and it was only from 1979 that the EP

---

[1] But some movement in this direction may be argued to exist now in the CT (the self-revising ability under Art IV-445).

was directly elected. Despite it now being directly elected, the EP still has a limited role in the law-making processes and legislative power remains largely with the Council of Ministers. Whilst the individual ministers come from nationally elected bodies for the most part, so there is some sort of indirect democracy, they are not directly accountable to the European citizens and can not carry out a national mandate in the Council negotiations. Under QMV they can be outvoted. Furthermore, the European Council plays an increasing role in policy formulation and overall steering of the Union. The unelected Commission still has the right of initiative of legislation and although the EP can ask it to propose law, the EP cannot insist it does so and as was seen in Chapter 2, the EP has fairly limited parliamentary control over the legislature and not much more over the executive. All of these aspects mean that the democratic deficit, which is levelled at the Union, can still be regarded as existing. This has been recognized in the Union and at the Laeken Summit, where the member states called for more democracy. Whether the eventual outcome of the Laeken declaration, which was the CT is the answer to this call is arguable, and if it is not ratified by all member states the CT will not be capable of satisfying any answers. Linked to this desire for more democracy, are the other principles contained within the Laeken Summit declaration for more openness and transparency in the Union.

4.3.2 Transparency and Open Governance

The lack of previous openness and transparency, particularly in the Council of Ministers' decision-making processes, is regarded as one of the reasons for European voter apathy in the EP elections, and is itself symptomatic of the democratic deficit in the Union. This was recognized partially as a result of the Danish initial rejection of the TEU and later with the Irish rejection of the Nice Treaty. Some small steps, though, have been taken to tackle the problem and provide for more open Governance. Specifically, two Decisions[2] were enacted providing access to Commission and Council documents but which allowed the Institutions to subject those rights to their own internal rules. The Court of First Instance and the Court of Justice, were however, able to define ever more expansive individual rights stemming from the decisions. In Case T-194/94 *Carvel*, the right of access was held to be an individually enforceable right. The Swedish journalists Case T-175/95, opened up access to Council documents from the third pillar to public scrutiny. The case, caused the Council to create restrictions to access in its Decision 2000/527.[3] Case C-353/99P *Heidi Hautala v Council*, appeared to establish a right to information in the face of the weakness of the

---

[2] Decision 93/731 OJ 1993 L340/43 and Decision 94/90 OJ 1994 L46/58.
[3] OJ 2000 L212/09.

actual rights contained in the Decisions. However, the member states did agree at Amsterdam to a new Article 255 EC to provide a Treaty right of access to documents, the details of which were to be determined by subsequent legislation. After much wrangling a new Community measure, Regulation 1049/2001[4] was adopted, which although containing various exceptions to access to the documents held by the Council, the Commission and the European Parliament, is a positive step forward in creating a more open form of decision-making in the Union.

4.4 The Constitutional Basis of the Union

4.4.1 The Community and Union Treaties

Within the usual understanding of International law norms, treaties are just agreements between signatory member states. They do nothing other than obligate the states to comply with the terms of the agreement, which are usually limited to distinct subject areas, such as free trade in goods. In contrast, the EC and EU Treaties provide the Communities with certain characteristics which go much further than a simple international agreement. They provide for their own institutional set up, exclusive competences in some areas and their own law-making powers to enable them to enact Regulations, Directives, and Decisions which are binding in the member states. Laws are thus enacted by its own set of institutions including a directly elected European Parliament, thus involving a distinct political input. However, the member states in the Council of Ministers remain in the driving seat as far as dominating the legislative process is concerned. Very significant in this new order is that some of the secondary legislation that can be enacted are self executing laws which are directly applicable in the member states. Furthermore, the voting process for that legislation can be by forms of majority voting, which means that some of the member states can be over-ruled, yet the law still applies and is binding in their states. The Union and member states are required also to uphold the express commitments to the rule of law and fundamental rights. There is a supreme or constitutional court, the European Court of Justice to adjudicate on disputes between the constituent bodies. Furthermore, the agreements reached are not static ones, although there was little change for the first 20 years life of the Communities, the Communities have developed as they have amended and expanded the Treaties and the competences of both the Communities and the internal institutions.

---

[4] OJ 2001 L145/43.

Much of the above is in keeping with expectations of what would normally appear in a constitutional document. Indeed, the status of the Treaties as a constitutional framework was not long in doubt in the view of the Court of Justice which confirmed, in its leading judgments of *Van Gend en Loos* and 6/64 *Costa v ENEL*, that the Community Treaties went beyond the usual intergovernmental treaties and agreements between sovereign states and had created a new legal order.

On the side of caution for a moment, there are also certain attributes of the Communities which do not comply with constitutionalism or statehood. There is no overall competence of the Union to decide its own competence, noted above. The member states remain the ones who decide whether the competences of the Union should be increased. The union has only an incomplete external competence, there is no single body which makes law and represents the Union externally, as would the government of a federal state, and extremely importantly, there is no coherent identity by the people of Europe.[5] So, whilst there are some features of constitutionalism, it is far from perfect. For the moment, after considering the important but sometimes overlooked protocols, the further consideration of how constitutionalism is being developed within the Union will be considered, in particular in respect of the division of competences and subsidiarity.

4.4.1.1 Protocols and Declarations

A particular complication to the body of constitutional law is the addition of numerous Protocols whose status is declared in Article 311 EC to be an integral part of Treaty law. Protocols are an instrument that have been used increasingly in the Community and now Union legal order. They are agreements of the member states which have been reached usually at the same IGCs when substantial Treaty amendments have been agreed but which for varying reasons have not been incorporated into to the main body of the Treaties. They often provide further definition to principles outlined in the Treaties such as the Protocol on Subsidiarity but all too often contain some of the most controversial decisions reached by the member states such as the Protocol on Social Policy which was not agreed by all member states or important decisions on enlargement or the institutions or the relationship of the national parliaments to the Union. Protocols dealt with the opt-outs from various stages of the integration process such as monetary union for the UK or the opt-outs of the Schengen Agreement for the UK, Ireland, and Denmark. There are protocols on what the member states and Community institutions must understand from a Court of Justice judgment, for example in the *Barber* case from 1990[6] which sought to prevent

---

[5] Allied to this, or as argued by some, the root of this, is that there is no single identifiable European people, or *demos* as it is termed.

[6] Which is considered in Chapter 10.

the retroactive effect of an Court of Justice judgment so as to limit the exposure of businesses and the insurance industry to back dated claims for equal pay. Others are of a more technical nature and contain, for example, detailed rules on the European Court of Justice or the European Central Bank.

Each of the Treaty amendments have added Protocols to the body of the constitutional law of the Union, including the Constitutional Treaty for Europe agreed in June 2004. As they are the equivalent and status of Treaty law and amend either directly or impliedly the Treaty provision, then they amend the constitutional base of the Union. This is not very helpful as there are now so many protocols on all sorts of matters that an overall view of the constitutional and legal basis of the Union has become, if not impossible, then extremely difficult to gain. The Constitutional Treaty was supposed to have tidied up the law base of the Community but has done little to this particular area apart from replace all the protocols attached to all the previous Treaties with a new set of Protocols attached to the CT.

4.4.1.2 Insistence of Constitutionality

A further element of a constitution is the requirement to be constitutional itself. Articles 49 and 6 (2) and of the TEU now require the Union itself and present and future member states to respect certain principles including liberty, democracy, human rights and fundamental freedoms, and the rule of law, although it might be argued that the Union itself fails to comply with some of these requirements, notably democracy with its rather weak democratic legitimization through the EP only, as noted above.

In providing on a basic level for the governance of the Communities, the basic Treaties, in the view of the Court of Justice in cases including *Les Verts* case[7] and in its Opinion on the EEA[8] represented the constitutional framework of the Communities. In *Les Verts*, the Court of Justice held that the EC is based 'on the rule of law, inasmuch as neither its member states nor its institutions can avoid a review of the question whether the measures adopted by them are in conformity with the basic constitutional charter, the Treaty'.

As such, then, a constitutional framework already exists without any further need or without actually changing anything, however, the Constitutional Treaty would certainly contain all the elements of constitutionality. All the basic principles and rules are contained in Part I, in typical constitutional manner. These include the outline of competences, the principles of representative and participatory democracy, rules regulating entry, and exit of member states and the range of values in Article 6 TEU.

---

[7] Case 294/83 *Parti Ecologiste 'Les Verts' v EP* [1986] ECR 1339.
[8] Opinion 1/91 (Draft Opinion on the EEA) [1991] ECR I–6079.

Whether, as such, the Constitution makes the EU any more federal or supranational than the previous Treaties is at present an open question.

4.4.2 The Constitutional Treaty

In the run up to the 2004 IGC, which debated the results of the Convention on the Future of Europe and the new forthcoming Treaty, there was a lot of discussion about the meaning of the title given to the results of the work carried out by the Convention and in particular one word within that title. The word which was picked over, discussed, defined, and analysed was 'Constitution' within the overall title then of 'Draft Treaty establishing a Constitution for Europe'. As much attention was given to this word as to the word 'Federal' when the Treaty on European Union was being debated in Maastricht. Both words, it seems, for some parties including certain member states, are highly emotive words because of the political connotations and consequences attached to them. Federal was so emotive it was dropped in favour of the euphemism 'ever closer union' which was accepted and written in to the TEU. The term 'Constitution' in this later debate was also regarded as a highly sensitive word but was, surprisingly, accepted far more readily by the member states. It seems the 'C' word is not as offensive as the 'F' word. At the present stage, the EU may have a Constitution but it cannot be Federal. Why is this? To answer this, we need first of all to try to determine what a Constitution means, then what it means within the surrounding context of the debate on the reform and further progression of European integration?

A constitution is, according to the *Oxford English Dictionary*, 'a body of fundamental principles according to which a State or other organization is governed' and within that fairly simply definition lies some of the difficulty pounced upon by both sides of the argument. As a body of fundamental principles, a constitution sets outs the range of powers, duties, and obligations of the constituent parts of the organization, in other words, the governing or central body and its members. On the one hand, some argued (UK Labour position mid-2003) that a constitution was something enjoyed by as humble an organization as a local allotment association or a local political social club and therefore nothing to be feared. On the other hand, was the view put forward that a constitution is something so closely connected with states and statecraft that in the European context it actually meant the establishment or progress towards the 'dreaded' European Superstate or some sort of acknowledgement at least that the EU was a true state and not simply a collective of sovereign member states. In other words, that the term 'Constitution' in this context could only mean elevating the European Union to some form of statehood and therefore was to be avoided at all costs.

Leaving aside the further consequences of the adoption of this term for the moment, it is clear that the term can apply to a range of organizations and obviously includes states. The questions might then be posed in relation to the European Union whether the EU as an organization, of whatever type, should and does have a constitution? We need first then to consider whether the EU should have a Constitution? If we mean a body of fundamental principles to regulate both the internal and external affairs of the organization, the answer must be 'yes'. It makes sense that an organization, and particularly one so large and so complex as the EU, definitely should have a Constitution.

Secondly, it is a simple question to ask; does the Community and Union have a set of fundamental principles or rules or laws and the answer is again, 'yes', in the form of the treaties as amended and extended. Then the question is begged: Do these amount to a Constitution? This is where we need to look deeper. Presently, these are not termed a 'Constitution' but this does not mean to say that there is not a constitutional order in the EU. The discussion of constitutionalism in the Union, however, is not just about whether there is, or is not something called a 'Constitution' but it is also very much connected to the debates surrounding the governance of the EU and the transfer of power to the Union from the member states. How competence and competences are divided between the member states and the Union and exercised by the institutions of the Union, which in turn, involves discussion of another eurojargon term: 'subsidiarity'.

4.5 The Division of Competences and Subsidiarity

Allied to the topics of the transfer of member states' sovereign powers and the supremacy of Community law, are the issues of competences, the division of them and subsidiarity, a tool by which the most appropriate division of competences can be determined.

Van Gend en Loos clearly showed that the transfer of sovereign powers from and by the member states to the Community was the very empowerment of the Community itself. This transfer provides the competence for the Community to make its own laws, although at the time, as was stated by the Court of Justice, this was in limited fields. The original treaties, and indeed those still applicable, though do not provide a clear-cut expression of the relationship between the law of the European Communities, i.e. the law created under the Treaties by the institutions and the national or domestic laws of the member states. There was no rule to say that in the event of conflict between rules covering the same subject matter, which should take priority. Neither did the original Treaties make any expression as to their own status, i.e. were they constitutional rules or just another international treaty between member states? Whilst the question of supremacy was quickly and clearly settled by the Court of Justice, at least from the Community standpoint, and discussed in the next section, the matter of competence is not so easily dealt with. In order for Community law to be supreme, the Community must possess the competence to act in the first place. If it does not have the competence to act in a certain way or create certain new laws, then by logic such laws cannot take priority over member states national law. This interlinked relationship between supremacy and competence can be observed in Case 22/70 *Commission v Council* (ERTA) (paras. 30–1) and in Opinion 1/94 in which it was held that if the Community has competence, the member states cannot act contrary to it, i.e. this is another way of expressing Community law supremacy.

4.5.1 The Division of Competences

One of the most fundamental elements of a constitutional order is the vertical division of competence or power between the constituent elements of the state and the central organization in question. In the European Union constitutional order, the law-making powers of the Communities and the Union and their ability to take independent action were originally provided by a transfer of sovereign powers from the member states when, either as original member states, they created the Communities, or as later entrants, when they joined the Community. This transfer was expressly acknowledged by the Court of Justice in *Van Gend en Loos* and is essentially the legitimization of Community action but it is to be stressed that this transfer is only within the areas agreed by the member states. On the face of it, any transfer of power and competence should in theory be a clear-cut process whereby any exercise of these powers by the institutions of the Union can only be within the terms granted by the member states and contained in the treaties. In other words there should be nothing done by the Community institutions which is not expressly permitted by the Treaties. This in Community law jargon is called attributed competence. The other side of this particular coin, is that what is attributed to the Community and Union by the member states is consequentially removed from member states' competence. In other words, the member states no longer have competence in the fields transferred.

4.5.1.1 Exclusive and Concurrent Competences

The range of actions of the Community can be seen in Articles 2 and 3 EC which set out in general terms the objectives and activities of the Communities but do not specifically detail any one of them. This is left to specific titles and chapters later in the

Treaty. Where the Treaty specifies an object, it invariably provides a power to achieve that object, for example, the original Articles 48 and 49 of the EEC Treaty (now Arts 39 and 40) set out respectively the objective and power of achieving the free movement of workers in the Community.

If the division of competences and those which were exclusively the Community's were clearly set out, there would be no particular difficulty. Unfortunately, in the beginning, the division of competences were not clearly set out, however, because the initial treaties were much more limited in scope, this was less of a concern. A further unique dynamic of the Communities, in contrast with traditional international organizations, is that the Communities were not intended to be a static one-off creation but to be a long-term and evolving creation. Indeed, as discussed in Chapter 1, the founding intentions were that integration in one area was expected to spread to other areas and powers would be needed to regulate those new areas. In addition, the Community would have to react to events in the world as they unfolded and which affected the Community. Hence then, it was anticipated that the competences of the Communities equally needed to be dynamic and evolving, and not static. This means the EU would also have to be reactive and the competences capable of expansion.

It is necessary, therefore, to consider what the competences were, how they developed in the EU legal order, how the member states considered and reacted to this, and what measures were taken to control the competence creep which was observed.

The Community enjoys exclusive competences in a few areas only, such as, for certain aspects of the common customs duties, commercial policy to third countries (as upheld by the Court of Justice in its Opinion 1/75), and parts of the common fishing policy.

In other areas, i.e. most areas, the dividing line is not so clear and competence is concurrent, also termed 'shared' or 'non-exclusive' competence, between the member states and the Community. Outside those exclusive and concurrent competences are areas of law over which powers have not been transferred to the Union and the member states retain exclusive competence.

It is in this large area of shared competences that the difficulties arise, where it can be unclear whether the Community or the member states enjoy the competence for a particular action. Furthermore, the degree of sharing also alters according to the subject matter, e.g. in areas such as the internal market, as soon as the Community acts under its competence, it assumes exclusive power to act and the member states are then deprived of the power to act in conflict. If the Community chooses not to act, the member states retain the power to act. Thus where it does act, it takes over competence. This is known as pre-emption. A good example can be seen in the area of the free movement of goods which will be considered later in this book. The Court of

Justice held in one of its most famous and leading cases,[9] that only where the Community had not acted, could the member states act independently and even then, if concerned with a general area that was otherwise regulated by the Court of Justice, the member states could act only within prescribed limits. As a result, there can be a genuine grey area between what is sanctioned and what is not, i.e. what is within the Community competence and what is still within the member state competence.

This is a matter which has troubled the Communities time and again, particularly as it became clear from the progressive judgments of the Court of Justice that the Community had indeed taken over from the member states in some areas in which the member states were not sure they had agreed to or indeed had thought that they had not agreed to or considered they had excluded from Community competence. For example, in Case C-262/88 *Barber*, pension payments were held to be pay and therefore within the EC equal pay competence and not therefore a matter of state competence and exclusive regulation, as was previously considered to be the case because of its assumed connection with state pension policy, a matter still within the exclusive competence of the member states, according to Directive 79/7.[10] Hence then, there was a reaction by some of the member states who considered that the Commission and Community were extending their competences by stealth and not the agreement of the member states. The next sections consider how competences could be and were extended and what measures were developed by the member states to control this.

4.5.1.2 Extension of Competences

Under traditional International law understanding, the only way to add any competences to the created international organization is by Treaty amendment. Whilst Treaty amendment has taken place in the EU, it is only one of three ways for the competences of the Communities to be extended.

The first, by Treaty amendment, is deliberate and clear-cut. The fields of Community competence have expanded greatly as a result of the member states assigning additional competences to the Union with successive Treaty changes adding, for example, a chapter on environmental policy to the EC Treaty by the SEA.

The second and third ways are not express and have led to the use of the term 'competence creep' to describe the manner in which the institutions' competences have advanced incrementally. These are by implied and general powers which have been employed by the institutions, notably the Commission but which have often been subject to the review of the Court of Justice, highlighting that this too is a dynamic and evolving area of Community law. The difficulties experienced in this area were in

---

[9] 120/78 *Rewe-Zentral AG v Bundesmonopolverwaltung für Branntwein (Cassis de Dijon)* [1978] ECR 649, [1979] 3 CMLR 494.

[10] Art 7 of the Directive (OJ 1979 L6/24).

fact specifically taken on in the Constitutional convention and the CT, noted below, but which at present lies dormant.

4.5.1.3 Implied Powers

The exercise of implied powers is the second means of competence expansion. This was recognized by the Court of Justice in cases dealing with both internal and external powers of the Commission where, in the absence of express powers in the Treaty, powers are nevertheless required to achieve a community goal, and are thus implied. This development is also referred to as parallelism.

Internal. The Court of Justice supported implied powers in the Community legal order as early as Case 8/55 *Fedechar* and interpreted them expansively in Cases 281, 283–5, 287/85 *Commission v Germany* in which a Treaty Article (then Art 118) which provided for cooperation between member states in a social field, was employed by the Commission to enact a Decision requiring the member states to supply information. When the Decision was challenged, the Court of Justice held that where an Article of the EEC Treaty confers a specific task on the Commission it must be accepted, if that provision is not to be rendered wholly ineffective, that it confers on the Commission necessarily and per se the powers which are indispensable in order to carry out that task.[11] See also the air transport Cases 467–9/98 *Commission v Finland* in which it was confirmed that where the Community has acted in pursuit of exclusive internal powers it possesses, any action by the member states in adopting an international agreement affecting the common Community rules, was an unlawful intrusion on Community competence.

External. It is the context of the mixed agreements that attempts by the Commission to takeover the competences to conduct these negotiations have been resisted or disputed by the member states. As the Treaty does not regulate expressly for such circumstances, disputes have arisen and these disputes in turn have led to the development of implied powers. In Case 22/70 *Commission v Council* (ERTA) the then six member states had negotiated independently a Road Transport agreement which was then adopted by resolution by the Council but subsequently challenged by the Commission because there was a previous Community act regulating this area. The Court of Justice held that the authority of the Community to conclude international agreements arise not only from express conferment but also implied from other Treaty provisions providing express internal competences in the same area. Thus, where the internal powers have been acted upon, the member states are prevented from acting externally in those areas, particularly where such action would impact on the internal

---

[11] See para. 28 of the judgment.

policy. Thus the Community alone is in the position to carry out the contractual obligations towards third countries. In the particular case, because the member states negotiations were the continuance of agreements reached originally before the internal policy was formulated, it was held that the member states within the Council were entitled to act.[12]

Therefore, although Opinion 1/94 was concerned with the competence of the Community or member states with the Community to conclude the GATS and TRIPS elements of the WTO talks, the ECJ held that implied powers only operate between the member states and the Community and not the Commission and the Council.

4.5.1.4 General Powers

The third way by which competences have been stretched are via the general law-making powers which include both specific and general variants. The specific variants are those which grant subsidiary law-making powers to complete goals in specific areas such as Articles 94 and 95 EC, which provide in turn for the approximation of laws affecting the establishment or functioning of the internal market and for measures for the completion of the internal market.

Article 95 provides, as an exception to the powers granted in Article 94, that action can be taken by QMV and not unanimity as required for Article 94, to achieve the objectives of Article 14, the internal market, where powers are not otherwise provided by the Treaty. In other words, action can be taken outside of the express and exclusive grant of powers to the Community by a majority and not by the agreement of all member states.

The general variant is Article 308, the residual law-making power, which provides that where in furtherance of any of the objectives of the Treaty and where no specific power exists, the Community may act by means of the Council acting unanimously after consulting the EP.

As these are general powers, they have led to problems as to just how far they sanction Community activity in the face of member states' activity. However, they have been generously interpreted by the Court of Justice. Article 308 was used as the Treaty base for the original Equal Treatment Directive 76/207 because at the time, the relevant Treaty base (Art 119) only extended as far as equal pay. Article 308 was also used quite extensively to introduce legislation concerned with environmental matters where there was not, at the time, a Treaty Article base available.[13]

A limit to such use was found when the Court of Justice held in its Opinion 2/94 of

---

[12] Case 22/70 ERTA [1971] ECR 63, paras 16–18 and 22 of the judgment and see also Opinion 1/76 Laying up Fund [1977] ECR 741.

[13] For further discussion on Treaty bases, refer to Chapter 3.

1996 that Article 235 (as 308 was then) could not be used to accede to the European Convention on Human Rights because of the profound constitutional impact it would have on the Community and the member states, which was not envisaged nor indeed sanctioned by the Treaty. Furthermore, the use of Article 308 would be improper if a specific Treaty base was shown to exist (see Case 8/73 HZA *Bremerhafen v Massey-Ferguson*) and which should have therefore been used instead. However, these increases in the competences of the Community, without express Treaty sanction, have been increasingly criticized and challenged in general democratic terms. Even if using either Articles 94 or 308 requiring unanimity of all member states in the Council of Ministers, national parliaments are being bypassed and the change is being effected without any formal Treaty amendment process. Hence, there have been challenges to some proposed and completed Community actions by the member states in Council, before the Court of Justice (see Case 242/87 *Council v Commission (Erasmus)*) and by a series of amendments to the Treaties to try to curb this development and drafting the legal bases restrictively so that the Commission cannot use the base for further legislative intervention. See, for example, Article 152(4)(c), which provides for 'incentive measures designed to protect and improve human health, excluding any harmonization of the laws and regulations of the member states'. In other words the Community can take action providing it does not interfere with the existing laws in the member states.

One of the attempts, outside of specific treaty article amendments to try to delineate or make clearer that area of grey and to define the division of competences, is the introduction of the principles of subsidiarity and proportionality. These were designed to address the concerns of the member states about how competence was being exercised, albeit without much clear success so far.

4.5.2 Proportionality

This, apart from being a legal principle in its own right and often employed by individuals in challenges to Community action, is also linked to the subsidiarity principle in Article 5(3) EC concerned with the exercise of powers by the institutions. 'Any action by the Community shall not go beyond what is necessary to achieve the objectives of this Treaty'. It was, for example, raised in Case 84/94 *UK v Council* (Working Time Directive) with the argument that the restrictions imposed on working time were not minimum requirements but excessive. This view was rejected by the ECJ on the grounds that unless there had been a manifest error or misuse of powers, the Council must be allowed to exercise its discretion in law-making involving social policy choices. Proportionality has been considered in more detail as one of the general principles in Chapter 3.

4.5.3 **The Principle of Subsidiarity**

Subsidiarity requires decisions to be taken at the most appropriate level whether that is at the level of the Union or the level of the member states. Thus, the desire to regulate activities within the Community should not insist on action at the Community level when it is not necessary. While there was arguably always the view that legal measures which were taken centrally by the Community institutions should only be taken where necessary and that if not suitable, member states were allowed to regulate matters individually, this understanding did not find formal expression in any Community provision. There are implied examples of its use, such as the discretion given the member states to meet the requirements of a Directive or the principles of mutual recognition and the rule of reason established by the Court of Justice in the *Cassis de Dijon* case,[14] but as originally established, the Communities had no express statement of this principle.

The principle of subsidiarity made its first express appearance in the Community legal order in 1986 when introduced by the Treaty amendments made by the SEA. At that time, however, it was introduced specifically in respect of environmental measures under Article 174 (old 130r)(4) only. Essentially, it provided that the Community should only take action where objectives could be better attained at the Community level than the level of individual member states. It was introduced generally into the Community legal order by the Treaty of European Union. Article 1 of the TEU provides that, decisions are to be taken as closely as possible to the citizen and Article 2 provides that, 'The objectives of the Union shall be achieved . . . while respecting the principle of subsidiary as defined in Article 5 (old 3b) of the Treaty establishing the European Community.'

Article 5 (1) EC makes it clear that there is a limit to what the Communities can do:

The Community shall act within the limits of the powers conferred upon it by this Treaty and the objectives assigned to it therein. In areas which do not fall within its competence, the Community shall take action, in accordance with the principle of subsidiarity, only if and in so far as the objectives of the proposed action cannot be sufficiently achieved by the member states and can therefore, by reason of the scale or effects of the proposed action, be better achieved by the Community. Any action by the Community shall not go beyond what is necessary to achieve the objectives of this Treaty.

The first sentence of the Article is then a statement that the Community cannot act without a specific power to do so.

Article 5 EC also encapsulates the principle of conferral, expressly included in the CT, which provides that the EU can only act to the extent that competences have been

---

[14] The rule of reason and the principle of mutual recognition are discussed in Chapter 7.

conferred on it to do so. The exact meaning of the second two sentences is, however, far from clear, particularly regarding where the line might be drawn between the competence of the Community and the competences of the member states. Thus, the general introduction of these concepts have not proved to be the instant fix desired by the member states, let alone a concept which is readily understandable or indeed translatable into a clear-cut process by which it is decided whether Community action is appropriate and thus lawful within the terms of the concept. It seems to suggest that decision-taking which might be accumulated in the centre, i.e. by the institutions, but which is not actually necessary at this level, should instead be taken by the member states. Decisions, in short, should be taken closer to the people, which is the formulation of the principle contained in the statement made in Article 1 TEU. In support of Article 5 is Article 7 EC, which requires that each institution act within the limits of the power conferred on it.

The difficulties with this principle thus remain as to who decides when to apply it and, whether it has been observed in the decision-making process. If the matter is one within the exclusive competence of the Community, subsidiarity does not apply. The problem is, though, as noted above, exclusivity itself is not a clear-cut term. The practice has arisen now that in order to justify taking the action, the Commission needs to outline why it has competence to take the particular action and does so in the preamble and recitals to proposed legislation.[15]

It may therefore give rise to considerable litigation to determine whether it has been adhered to correctly. Whilst the principle itself was not disturbed by the Treaty of Amsterdam, it did add a Protocol as an attempt to clarify its meaning.[16] Apart from requiring certain action on the part of the Commission to consult before formally proposing legislation and making reports to the European Council, the Council and the EP, it provides that Community action would be appropriate where the transnational aspects cannot be satisfactorily regulated by the member states, where either no action by the Community or member states' action would conflict with the requirements of the Treaty and where the Community actions would render clear benefits over national action. Whether these criteria make it any clearer is itself unclear. Paragraph 3 of the protocol states that the principle is a dynamic concept which can be expanded or restricted or discontinued where circumstances so require. Hence then, it seems that the principle will remain as difficult as ever to tie down

---

[15] See, for example, Directive 2002/14 on employee consultation, recital 17 (Foster, *EC Legislation*, 16th edn., p. 424).

[16] Protocol on the Application of the principles of Subsidiarity and Proportionality (Foster (ed.), *EC Legislation*, 16th edn., p. 116).

4.5.3.1 Challenges for Non-compliance with the Principle

Although non-compliance with the subsidiarity principle would seem to be a ground for annulment under an Article 230 judicial review action before the Court of Justice, in its present form, the principle has received little judicial guidance thus far. This is no surprise given the obscurity of the principle which involves the balancing of economic and political priorities.

In Case C-84/94 *UK v Council* (Working time Directive) and Case C-377/98 *Netherlands v EP and Council* (Biotechnology Directive), arguments raised by the member states in the cases that subsidiarity had not been observed were roundly rejected by the Court of Justice. In *UK v Council* (Working Time Directive), the Court of Justice dismissed this part of the action with little discussion merely to confirm that the Council had a clear power to act on working hours as an issue of health and safety of workers. In other words if it had the competence to act, it could act. However, in Case C-376/98 *Germany v Parliament and Council* (Tobacco Advertising Ban Directive), the harmonizing Directive 98/43 banning most forms of tobacco advertising was enacted under what is now Article 95 EC as an internal market measure. This was challenged by Germany arguing that the measure was more closely allied to a public health measure and thus should have been enacted under the present Article 152 EC which expressly prohibits harmonizing legislation. The Court of Justice held that measures under Article 95 must have primary object of improving conditions for the establishment or functioning of the internal market and that other articles of the Treaty may not be used as a legal basis in order to circumvent the express exclusion of harmonization. It held further that to construe the internal market article as meaning that it vests in the Community legislature a general power to regulate the internal market would be incompatible with the principle embodied in Article 5 EC that the powers of the Community are limited to those specifically conferred upon it. The Court of Justice thus held that as the measure did little to enhance the internal market and annulled it entirely. The judgment is not a clear endorsement that subsidiarity is a clearly justiciable issue, more that it is another confirmation that where an incorrect legal base is used, this provides grounds for the annulment of the measure based on it.[17] The judgment is regarded as a reply to national courts, in particular the German Constitutional court,[18] which might have been minded to take Community law into their own hands, by showing that the Court of Justice is prepared to police incursions into the member states competences by the EU's institutions. Almost inevitably, the Court of Justice will be given further opportunities to come up with clearer and

---

[17] See for further details the section on Legal base in Chapter 3.

[18] This is considered below in this chapter in the section concerned with Community law reception in Germany.

workable definitions of its meaning. It is possible that the principle of subsidiarity will also join the ranks of general principles of Community law, although it is one introduced deliberately by the member states rather than created or introduced by the Court of Justice.

The principle of subsidiarity found expression in Declaration 23 on the Future of the Union attached to the Nice Treaty which required that the division of competences should be considered. This was later backed up by the Laeken Summit which set up the Convention on the Future of Europe and provided that the Convention explore a better division and definition of competence in the EU to make it clearer and more transparent and so that a competence creep can be avoided but that at the same time the progress of the Union would not be stifled. The aims of this review were to reinforce the taking into account and the application of the principle of subsidiarity by the institutions participating in the legislative process, during the drafting and examination phase of the legislative act, to set up an 'early warning system' of a political nature, intended to reinforce the monitoring of compliance with the principle of subsidiarity by national parliaments and to broaden the possibility of referral to the Court of Justice for non-compliance with the principle of subsidiarity. A revised version of subsidiarity was then incorporated into the Constitutional Treaty.

4.5.4 The Constitutional Treaty and the Division of Competences

The concerns about the lack of democratic accountability, lack of transparency, and clear-cut division of competences in the Union and that the Union is taking over far more power from the member states than is desirable or necessary, to some degree, led to the rejection of the CT by the electorates in France and Holland in 2005. This is ironic, in that the rejections and the subsequent shelving of the CT has actually prevented further progress in providing a clearer constitutional Treaty basis for the division of power because the CT contains Articles which were intended to address these very issues—it may be argued not perfectly—but they were along the right lines. Apart from repeating the principle of subsidiarity in Article I-3(5) and Article I-11(1), the CT has also set out, for the first time in the EU, a far clearer division of competences.

Article I-11 provides that the limits of Union competences are governed by the principle of conferral and the use of Union competences is governed by the principles of subsidiarity and proportionality. It goes on to outline that conferral means that the Union shall act within the limits of the competences conferred upon it by the member states in the Constitution to attain the objectives set out in the Constitution and make clear that competences not conferred upon the Union in the Constitution remain with the member states. Furthermore, the principle of subsidiarity was restated in the CT, Article I-11 which, as with the present EU and EC Treaties, also relies on a Protocol for further definition. The CT also provides a procedure whereby the national parliaments can police the use of subsidiarity and address the Commission if they feel it has been breached.

Article I-13 sets out the exclusive competences, for example the customs duties, where the member states are not able to act at all, Article I-14 sets out the areas of concurrent or shared competences, whereby the member states may only act if the EU has not yet acted or has ceased to act and Article I-17 provides competences for the EU to act in support of the member states' own actions only. Part One of the CT provides the overview, the details of these areas are then to be found in Part Three of the CT, which essentially reproduces most of the present EC Treaty.

Until the Constitutional Treaty enters into force, if at all, further clarification of the principle will have to be by way of the Court of Justice.

4.6 The Supremacy of Community Law

The supremacy or priority of Community law can be considered from two perspectives. First, from the point of view of the Community and secondly, the member states, although dealing with this latter aspect in a Union now of twenty-five member states must be by necessity selective. Therefore only a sample of the member states will be chosen concentrating on the older and larger member states. As with the doctrine of direct effects, considered in Chapter 5, it is through the decisions and interpretation of the Court of Justice that the reasons and logic for the supremacy of Community law have been developed.

4.6.1 The View of the Court of Justice

There is no express declaration or specific legal base for the supremacy of Community law in the treaties as they presently stand. It can be argued that some of the Articles of the EC Treaty impliedly require primacy, for example, Article 10 (the fidelity or good faith clause), Article 12 (the general prohibition of discrimination on the grounds of nationality), Article 249 (the direct applicability of Regulations), and Article 292 (the reservation of Community and not national dispute resolution for matters coming within the scope of the Treaties). In the absence of an express statement written into the Treaties,[19] another route was needed to establish this supremacy of Community

---

[19] That is before the CT, Art I-6 which may or may not be ratified and come into force.

law over national law. From the outset, the Communities included their own supreme Court of Justice which is the equivalent of a constitutional court to adjudicate on disputes between the institutions of the Communities and between the member states and the institutions. Without an express statement of priority, the Court of Justice took the lead in providing basic constitutional principles on which the new legal order was based. The Court of Justice's view on supremacy is quite straightforward. In the first pronouncement dealing with this, the Court of Justice held in *Van Gend en Loos*, that the member states had limited their sovereignty, albeit within limited fields as agreed in the Treaty and held that individuals in the Community could uphold rights under Community law in the national courts and in the face of conflicting national law. From its case law, notably Case 26/62 *Van Gend en Loos*, Case 6/64 *Costa v ENEL* and Case 106/77 *Simmenthal*, it is clear that Community law is assumed to be an autonomous legal order which is related to International law and national law but nevertheless distinct from them and thus subject to its own logic in relation to supremacy over the law of the member states. It was not long though before this supremacy over national law was stated expressly by the Court of Justice in the *Costa v ENEL* case in 1964.

The *Van Gend en Loos* case, already considered in Chapter 3 as the leading case in the development of the doctrine of direct effects, substantially prepared the ground for the Court of Justice to build its argument for supremacy of Community law. The case affirmed the Court's jurisdiction in interpreting Community legal provisions, the object of which is to ensure uniform interpretation in the member states. The case established direct effect of Community law in the national legal orders. The Court of Justice held that 'the Community constitutes a new legal order of International law for the benefit of which the States have limited their sovereign rights, albeit in limited fields, and the subjects of which comprise not only member states but also their nationals'. Further elaboration of the new legal order in *Van Gend en Loos* was given in Case 6/64 *Flaminio Costa v ENEL*. This case primarily concerned the payment of an electricity bill of a very low value (then approximately £1.00). In 1962 the Italian Government passed an act to nationalize the electricity industry and the newly nationalized industry sent out bills to recover debts previously outstanding. Mr Costa claimed the action was in conflict with Article 37 (now 31) of the EEC Treaty concerned with State monopolies and refused to pay his bill. The case however also raised the wider issue of whether a national court should refer to the Court of Justice if it considers Community law may be applicable or, in the view of the Italian Government, simply apply the subsequent national law.

In addressing this question, the Court of Justice again stressed the autonomous legal order of Community law:

By contrast with ordinary international treaties the EEC Treaty has created its own legal system which became an integral part of the legal systems of the member states and which their courts are bound to apply. By creating a Community of unlimited duration, having its own institutions, its own personality, its own legal capacity, and more particularly real powers stemming from a limitation of sovereignty or a transfer of powers from the states to the Community the member states have limited their sovereign rights and have created a body of law to bind their nationals and themselves.

The Court also established that Community law takes priority over all conflicting provisions of national law whether passed before or after the Community measure in question:

The integration into the laws of each Member State of provisions which derive from the Community, and more generally, the terms and spirit of the Treaty, make it impossible for the states, as a corollary, to accord precedence to a unilateral and subsequent measure over a legal system accepted by them on the basis of reciprocity. Such a measure cannot therefore be inconsistent with that legal system.

As additional justifications, the Court of Justice also invoked the use of some of the general provisions of the Treaty: old Article 5 (now 10) (the requirement to ensure the attainment of the objectives of the Treaty) old Article 7 (EEC) (now 12), the prohibition of discrimination, both of which would be breached if subsequent national legislation was to have precedence; and old Article 189 (now 249), regarding the binding and direct application of Regulations, which would be meaningless if subsequent national legislation could prevail. The Court summed up its position:

It follows . . . that the law stemming from the treaty, an independent source of law, could not because of its special and original nature, be overridden by domestic legal provisions, however framed, without being deprived of its character as Community law and without the legal basis of the Community itself being called into question.

Therefore, the conclusion must be that Community law must be supreme over subsequent national law.

In Case 106/77 *Simmenthal*, the Court of Justice ruled that:

A national court which is called upon, within the limits of its jurisdiction, to apply provisions of Community law, is under a duty to give full effect to those provisions, if necessary of its own motion to set aside any conflicting provisions of national legislation, even if adopted subsequently.

The Court of Justice ruled that directly effective provisions of Community law preclude the valid adoption of new legislative measures to the extent that they would be incompatible with Community provisions. Any inconsistent national legislation recognized by national legislatures as having legal effect would deny the effectiveness of the obligations undertaken by the member state and imperil the existence of the Community. This case is considered further below in respect of constitutional practice.

Therefore the voluntary limitation of sovereignty and the need for an effective and uniform Community law requires supremacy. To give effect to subsequent national law over and above the Community legal system which member states have accepted would be inconsistent.

In the *Factortame (No. 2) Case* (221/89), the Court of Justice, building on the principle laid down in *Simmenthal* that a provision of EC law must be implemented as effectively as possible, held that a national court must suspend national legislation that may be incompatible with EC law until a final determination on its compatibility has been made. Thus, national rules which prevented a national court from issuing an interim injunction suspending the application of a national statute during a dispute whilst considering the existence of alleged rights under Community law, must be set aside. It was later held in Case C-221/89 that the UK law did in fact breach Community law.

Finally, in this context it is worth mentioning the consequence of a member state not giving primacy to Community law when it should have done, in that liability on the part of the state will be incurred. This principle was first established by the Court of Justice in *Francovich* and later confirmed in *Factortame III* and other cases.[20]

So far the national legislation considered has been so called 'ordinary' national legislation, that is municipal law and the Court of Justice has maintained a consistent position on supremacy, including the supremacy of secondary Community law over 'ordinary' national legislation. What about provisions of a member state's Constitution? It is in this respect that the most serious conflicts between the views of the national judiciaries and the Court of Justice have arisen.

4.6.2 Supremacy and Member State Constitutional Law

The Court of Justice's view in respect of national constitutional law differs little from that in respect of 'ordinary' national law and can be seen in Case 11/70, *Internationale Handelgesellschaft*. This case concerned the claim that Community levies were contrary to the German constitution (Arts 2.1 and 14 *Grundgesetz*) and thus, as far as the national court was concerned, inapplicable. On referral to the Court of Justice, it held that national courts do not possess the power to review Community law. The important question arising from the case was whether the Court of Justice was in a position to declare supremacy over national constitutional law and so in effect review that law. In doing so, it would effectively, deny the ability of national courts to overcome the fact that there is a clear distinction or separation of the national and Community law

---

[20] Discussed in Chapter 5.

legal systems otherwise known as the autonomy of jurisdictions, but nevertheless do so itself. In other words, national courts could not question the supremacy of Community law but the Court of Justice would be able to determine that national constitutional law was not in conformity with Community law, something clearly of great concern to national supreme courts.

The second case arises from a conflict between the Italian constitution and Community law. In Italy, the constitutional practice existed that the power to disregard or declare invalid a provision of national law was the sole right of the Italian Constitutional Court. In Case 106/77 *Simmenthal*, a lower court was faced with inconsistency between a Community law provision and a national provision. The national court was aware that a reference to the Italian constitutional court would have the effect of subrogating Community law to national legal practice, inconsistent with existent Community case law on the matter, as was evident from the earlier Case 6/64 *Costa v ENEL*. However, disregarding the national law was contrary to Italian constitutional requirements. The Italian magistrate referred to both courts but asked the Court of Justice whether subsequent national measures which conflict with Community must be disregarded without waiting until those measures are set aside by legislative or other constitutional means. The Court of Justice first declared that the doctrine of direct effects of Community legislation was not dependant on any national constitutional provisions but a source of rights in themselves. Therefore national courts must give full effect to those rights including a refusal to apply conflicting national legislation. The Court of Justice also ruled that directly effective provisions of Community law also preclude the valid adoption of new legislative measures to the extent that they would be incompatible with Community provisions. The national court should disregard the inconsistent national law. The Court established that if there were no violation of Community fundamental rights, the Community measures were acceptable and there should be no reference to national constitutions to test their validity. It held:

The law stemming from the treaty, an independent source of law, cannot because of its very nature be overridden by rules of national law, however framed, without being deprived of its character as Community law. Therefore the validity of a Community measure or its effect within a Member State cannot be affected by allegations that it runs counter to either fundamental rights as formulated by the Constitution of that State or the principles of a national constitutional structure.

The Court of Justice has not been so expressly forthright since *Simmenthal*. The conclusion following this case is that any inconsistent national legislation recognized by national legislatures as having legal effect would, in the Court's view, deny the effectiveness of the obligations undertaken by the member states and in particular, the good faith clause, Article 10 EC and thus imperil the very foundations of the

Community. In its widest interpretation, the judgment holds that: 'Inconsistent national measures of any sort which are introduced by member states are effectively invalid from their adoption.'

The stance taken by the Court of Justice is in sharp contrast to the initial stance by some of the member states' courts. Indeed, the *IH* case produced a head-on clash between the Court of Justice and the German Federal Constitutional Court and German Constitution, which will be further reviewed from the German perspective below.

Case C-213/89 *Factortame (No 1)* is further another confirmation that national constitutional practises or rules, in this case the doctrine of parliamentary sovereignty in the UK, must not be allowed to stand in the way of a Community law right. It was previously the position in the UK under the doctrine of parliamentary sovereignty that the courts had no power to set aside or not apply an Act of Parliament. The Court of Justice held[21] that even the Community law rule was still in dispute, the national procedure should be changed so as not to possibly interfere with the full effectiveness of the Community law right. This case is also a witness to Community law incursion into national procedure, which will be taken up further in Chapter 5. The Court of Justice is therefore clear that Community law is supreme over all types of national law. The above cases are just the leading cases on supremacy, those which expressly declare Community law primacy. Many other cases imply Community law supremacy, for example, all cases which declare direct effects presuppose a supremacy. If Community law is not supreme over national law, especially subsequent law, than direct effects would be denied. Conversely if direct effects were denied where they fulfil the criteria, supremacy is therefore also denied because national law would be seen to prevail.

In summary, the Community view on supremacy is that because of its unique nature, Community law denies the member states the right to resolve conflicts of law by reference to their own rules or constitutional provisions. Community law obtains it's supremacy because of the transfer of state power and sovereignty to the Community by the member states in those areas agreed. The member states have provided the Community with legislative powers to enable it to perform it's tasks. There would be no point in such a transfer of power if the member states could annul or suspend the effect of Community law by later national law or provisions of the constitutions. If that were allowed to be the case, the existence of the Community legal order and the Community itself would be called into question. A precondition of the existence and functioning of the Community is the uniform and consistent application of Community law in all the member states. It can only achieve such an effect if it takes

---

[21] See paras. 17–23 of the judgment.

precedence over national law. Therefore, the legal and logical consequences of this is the fact that any provision of national law, regardless of its date of enactment or rank, which conflicts with Community law must be invalid.

If, and when the Constitutional Treaty comes into force, supremacy of EU law over national law will be expressly stated (Art I-6), although without expressly stating that it will be supreme over the member states' constitutions. As such, even with this express statement of supremacy, there will remain room for argument, particularly as will be seen below, from some of the member states' constitutional courts.

4.7 Community Law in the Member States

With twenty-five member states now, it would occupy far too much space to look at the reception of Community law in all of them, therefore only a sample of states has been chosen and headlining those is an extended look at the United Kingdom. Before this is undertaken, it needs to be considered how International law, as the Community Treaties and Community law were first thought to be, is received into the national legal systems.

4.7.1 Theories of Incorporation of International Law: Monism and Dualism

The method of incorporation of International law into the member states' legal systems and Community law is determined initially by the particular outlook a state has in respect of the validity of such law. There are two prevailing theories of the incorporation of external law into national legal systems which are applicable in the context of the initial incorporation of the Community Treaties into the member state legal systems. These theories are monism and dualism.

Monism basically assumes that International law and national law form part of a single system or hierarchy of laws, therefore the acceptance of International law would not require formal incorporation by legislative transformation but after Treaty agreement and assent or ratification, it would be self-executing. In other words, it would be directly applicable within the state. So, all that is required by such a state to achieve this is the assent to, or ratification of an international Treaty. It does not, however, determine where on the single hierarchy, the International law should be placed and this leaves open difficulties of whether in individual states, it takes priority over all law or just over municipal/ordinary national law and not constitutional law. France is a good example of a monist state and will be considered below.

Dualism, on the other hand, regards International law and national law as fundamentally different systems of law which exist along side each other. In order to overcome the barrier existing between the two systems, legislation is required to transform rules of International law into the national legal system before it can have any binding effect within the state in such circumstances. It is for the member states to determine where the International law is then placed within the national hierarchy of laws. The United Kingdom is the most obvious example of a dualist state and is the state which will be considered first in looking at the reception of Community law into the member states.

4.8 Community Law in the UK

The United Kingdom was not one of the original and founding member states of the Communities. It had a number of difficulties to overcome in order to accommodate the duties of membership of the EEC in 1973. It had to accept all the previous Community legislation passed, not only the Treaties but the Regulations, Directives but also the judicial legal developments of this established new legal order. This is known in Community jargon as the acceptance of the *acquis communautaire.*[22] It had on the other hand, time to adjust for this. Being a later entrant state, the UK could see in advance the legal and constitutional problems which would arise as a result of membership. They could see the judicial developments of direct effects and the supremacy of EC law and take account of them before entry. So there were no excuses to say 'but we didn't know!' The particular difficulties faced by the UK legal system in accommodating EC membership and EC law were that of the largely unwritten constitution, the dualist approach to International law and the doctrine of Parliamentary Sovereignty.

4.8.1 The 'Unwritten' Constitution

The UK does not have a single codified constitutional document, instead the UK Constitution is made up by a number of written and unwritten elements. Furthermore, there is no concept or form of entrenchment of particular parts of either the Constitution itself or of any of the special or other parts of the Constitution which are regarded as particularly important including Acts of Parliament, all of which can be removed by simple repeal by the same or any future Parliament. This has the

---

[22] A concept which has also been considered in Chapters 1 and 3.

consequence that even if a particular political action or legal action is so important and envisaged as very long term if not permanent, it is very difficult, if not impossible, under UK constitutional law to entrench this. Hence then, it is impossible to alter the UK constitution with any certainty. Thus, any transfer of power to the Communities under traditional constitutional thinking could not be regarded as permanent and could always be reversed by a subsequent Act of Parliament.

4.8.2 The Dualist Approach to International Law

International Treaties are a prerogative of the Crown as represented by the Government in Parliament in the UK and the courts have no jurisdiction in respect of the validity of such treaties, although they can form persuasive arguments for the interpretation of national law. In order to apply expressly in the UK legal order, a provision of an international Treaty must first have been enacted by the UK Parliament as an act of national legislation. It has to be converted into domestic law before it can have any binding effect within the UK. This particular approach to International law provoked the question of how to convert the original three EC Treaties into national law without transforming every provision into an Act of Parliament, which would have been contrary to the Treaty. Furthermore, it was necessary to ensure that the Treaties or any of their provisions were not simply overruled by the implied repeal of subsequent acts of Parliament. As it stood, the dualist approach, if followed would not have recognized the unequivocal supremacy of Community law.

4.8.3 The Doctrine of Parliamentary Supremacy

Formally, UK Parliamentary Sovereignty means that there are no legal limitations on the UK Parliament and it has the right to make or unmake any law whatsoever. Further, no person or body is recognized as having a right to override or set aside the legislation of parliament. The doctrine also implies that as such as it is impossible to bind future parliaments. Subsequent Acts can either expressly or impliedly override a prior Act. There is no constitutional role for UK courts, which therefore cannot review the validity of Acts passed by parliament. The courts must enforce and apply Acts of Parliament equally and without question.[23]

One of the problems in considering this doctrine of parliamentary sovereignty is the nature of the concept itself. It is not a rigid constitutional enactment and is really just a constitutional convention which was built up over centuries and refined by eminent jurists to the position stated by Dicey in the latter half of the nineteenth

---

[23] See the UK case of *BRB v Picken* [1974] AC/765.

century. As a convention it is subject to the erosion of time to reflect the changing circumstances in which it must be employed. Even Dicey conceded this was not an absolute convention and there were political, if not legal limits to it. The fact that there has been considerable comment and publicity about the attack on parliamentary sovereignty as a consequence of Community membership misconceives the status of this particular parliamentary convention. However, further consideration here is beyond the scope of this volume.[24] It posed, however, a distinct problem for the UK and until relatively recently also for the courts in considering whether in a situation of conflict, Community law or a national statute should take priority.

4.8.4 UK Entry and the European Communities Act (ECA) 1972

The European Communities Act 1972 was the Act of Parliament which facilitated UK entry into the Communities. Both entry to the EC and Community law implementation in the UK initially focuses on how the 1972 EC Act observes and takes account of such well-established Community law concepts as direct effect and supremacy and the difficulties noted above in respect of dualism and sovereignty. In contrast to the earlier practice of incorporation of international Treaties, the EC Act did not reproduce the whole of the Treaties or subsequent secondary legislation as Acts of Parliament. If this was done, the words of any future Act which conflicted with Community law obligations could override the prior Treaty. Instead, the Community Treaties were adopted by a simple assent. Section 1 of the ACT future proofs the Act by allowing for subsequent EC and EU Treaties to be regarded in the same way as the original Treaties. The Act thus impliedly recognizes the unique new legal system and is regarded now as a special form of UK legislation.[25]

Section 2 (1) recognizes the legal validity and direct applicability of Community Treaties and Regulations already in existence in the Community legal order and provides that all such future Community legal provisions shall also be recognized as such. It also recognizes the doctrine of direct effect. It provides:

All such rights powers, liabilities, obligations and restrictions from time to time created or arising under the Treaties, and all such remedies and procedures from time to time provided for by or under the Treaties, as in accordance with the Treaties are without further enactment to be given legal effect or used in the United Kingdom shall be recognized and available in law, and be enforced, allowed and followed accordingly.

---

[24] For a full consideration of this topic refer to T. Allen, 'The Limits of Parliamentary Sovereignty' (1986) *Public Law*, 614–29, J. D. B. Mitchell, 'What happened to the Constitution on 1 January 1973?' (1980) *Cambrian Law Review*, 69, H. W. R. Wade, 'Sovereignty and the European Communities' (1972), 88 *LQR* 1, H. W. R. Wade, 'What has Happened to the Sovereignty of Parliament?' (1991) 107 *Law Quarterly Review*, 1–4.

[25] See now the High Court judgment in *Thoburn v Sunderland City Council* [2002] 1 CMLR 50 considered below.

It is somewhat convoluted but the subsection recognizes the doctrine of direct effect and allows for future developments by the Court of Justice. This is termed in the Act as 'enforceable Community right . . . and similar expressions'. Thus, those rights or duties which are, as a matter of Community law, directly applicable or effective are to be given legal effect in the UK.

Section 2 (2) allows for the implementation of other Community obligations which are not automatically applicable in the UK, via forms of UK secondary legislation such as Orders in Council or Statutory Instruments. The power that the executive has to make secondary legislation is subject to the limits in Schedule 2 of the Act, in respect of the imposing or creation of taxation, the introduction of retrospective legislation, sub-delegation, and the introduction of new criminal offences with more than a two-year period of imprisonment as penalty or a higher value limit of more than level 5 on the fine scale or £100 per day.[26]

Section 2 (4) is the subsection which recognizes the supremacy of Community law and therefore also concerns sovereignty.

Any such provision and any enactment passed or to be passed (that refers to any secondary legislation and act of Parliament which has been passed previously or may be passed in the future) shall be construed and have effect subject to the foregoing provisions of this section.

That is a reference to the entire Section and in particular 2(1), and means that any future act of Parliament must be construed in such a way as to give effect to the enforceable Community rights in existence. This is achieved by denying effectiveness to any national legislation passed later which is in conflict and this is in turn controlled by directions to the courts concerned with the application or construction of legislation. The courts are required to interpret any future act to be consistent with Community law or in effect, to be subordinate where inconsistency arises. This view was clearly confirmed by the House of Lords in *Factortame* when it held that 2(4) should be understood as if 'a section were incorporated into the Merchant Shipping Act which enacted that the provisions with regard to the registration of British fishing vessels were to be "without prejudice to the directly enforceable Community rights of national of any member states of the EC"'.[27]

Section 3(1) then instructs the courts to refer questions on the interpretation and hence the supremacy of Community law to the Court of Justice if the UK courts cannot solve the problem themselves by reference to previous Court of Justice rulings. This follows the *Costa v ENEL* ruling and is backed up by 3(2) which requires the courts to judicially follow decisions of the Court of Justice on any question of

---

[26] As at present, but these figures are revised periodically.
[27] *R v Secretary of State for Transport, ex parte Factortame and others (No. 1)* [1990] 2 AC 85 at 140.

Community law. This would include direct effects and supremacy although it does not expressly say so.

It is suggested then that the combination of s. 2(1) and s. 2(4) with the control of s. 3(1) and (2) achieve the essential requirements of the recognition of direct effects and the supremacy of Community law for past and future UK legislation.

4.8.4.1 The ECA and Parliamentary Sovereignty

The view of how the ECA has affected parliamentary sovereignty is determined by what the Act actually achieves. There are two main positions in respect of this. Either s. 2(4) acts as a rule of construction or it attempts a form of entrenchment whereby it modifies the doctrine of parliamentary sovereignty. As a rule of construction it commands the courts to interpret national law to comply with Community law. The earlier decisions on Community law by courts in England and Wales considered that this should apply only where the national legislation is reasonably capable of such construction, see for example, the cases of *Macarthy's v Smith and Garland*,[28] considered below. However, this view is being modified because it is regarded as too restrictive a view of what is achieved by the EC Act, see *Factortame*, below. The alternative of limited entrenchment means that it allows the courts to directly apply Community law over national law regardless of the actual words. This enables the courts to ignore any implied repeal or unintentional inconsistency of future acts of Parliament and thus arguably modifies the doctrine of parliamentary sovereignty in that one parliament has been seen to bind a future one. Express inconsistency remains a problem even under this interpretation. However, how Community law is received in the member states is often and ultimately dependant on the national judiciary as well as national Parliaments, therefore a consideration of its reception in the courts is vital.

4.8.5 Judicial Reception of Community Law in the UK

Where there is a conflict between an earlier UK law with later Community law, there is no difficulty, the doctrines of Parliamentary supremacy and the supremacy of Community law will produce the same result, as for example in Case 83/78 *Pigs Marketing Board (Northern Ireland) v Redmond* from 1979 in which the Community Agricultural Policy rule on the organization of the market was seen to prevail over national law.

The difficulty arises when there is a conflict between a later UK law and an earlier Community law provision. In such a case, are the words within the ECA to be taken as

---

[28] *Macarthy's v Smith* [1979] 3 All ER 325 at 329.

a rule of interpretation or a question of entrenchment which effectively involves the modification of doctrine of Parliamentary supremacy by ss. 2(4) and 3 of the European Communities Act?

The most important of the earlier cases is *Macarthy's v Smith and Garland*, concerning a clash between the Equal Treatment Act s. 6 and the EC Treaty, Article 119 (now 141) in which the Court of Appeal clearly held: 'It is important now to declare and it must be made plain. The provisions of Article 119 take priority over anything in our English Statute on Equal Pay which is inconsistent with Article 119. That priority is given by our own law, by the ECA 1972 itself. Community law is now part of our law and whenever there is any inconsistency Community law has priority.' However, Lord Denning, in an *obiter* passage, thought that with regard to an express or intentional repudiation of the Treaty by Parliament or expressly acting inconsistently, the Courts would be bound to follow the express and clear intent of Parliament to repudiate the Treaty or a section of it by the subsequent Act. That not being the case, though, Community law takes priority according to the Court of Appeal. This case has survived the years and even the subsequent cases of the House of Lords concerned with the relationship between Community and National law have not removed it from our consideration because, even though Denning's words are merely *obiter*, they remain the only clear statement by a superior court about what might happen in the event of an express statement by Parliament of the intention to conflict with Community law.

In *Garland v BREL*, the first important statement from the House of Lords, Mrs Garland had complained that the practice of allowing the families of male ex-employees of BREL concessionary rail travel facilities after retirement but not families of female ex-employees was discriminatory. Under s. 6 (4) of the Sex Discrimination Act 1975, provisions in relation to retirement were exempted from the rules on sex discrimination and Mrs Garland's claim failed initially. Previous UK case law[29] had determined that s. 6(4) Sex Discrimination Act 1975 be given a wide interpretation so as to discount anything to do with or connected to retirement therefore discrimination in such circumstance was lawful. Article 141 (old 119 EEC) and Directive 76/207, however, made no such exception regarding retirement, therefore UK and Community law were regarded by the House of Lords as inconsistent. The House of Lords asked the Court of Justice to give a ruling on the interpretation of Article 141 (old 119) to determine if it covered conditions in retirement. The Court of Justice held it did so. Upon return to the House of Lords they considered themselves bound in view of the Court of Justice ruling and ECA 1972 to interpret the Sex Discrimination Act 1975 in such a way as not to be inconsistent with the UK obligations under

---

[29] One of which is *Roberts v Cleveland Area Health Authority* [1979] 2 All ER 1163, [1979] ICR 558.

Community law. Whilst the House of Lords stated the case was no occasion to pronounce on any further effects of the ECA they nevertheless did state *obiter* that UK courts should interpret UK law to be consistent no matter how wide a departure from the prima facie meaning it was. The case therefore very much follows the line that s. 2(4) allows courts to construe subsequent statutes quite widely in order to give consistency to Community law, clearly therefore a rule of construction.

In *Duke v GEC Reliance*, brought at roughly the same time as the *Marshall* case, Mrs Duke was required to retire at 60, earlier than men who could retire at 65. Section 6(4) of Sex Discrimination Act 1975 was applied to render the discrimination lawful. The House considered the *Marshall* ruling in which the Equal Treatment Directive was held to apply to retirement itself and to have direct effects but because this concerned a private sector employer, the House of Lords rightly concluded that the Directive itself could not be enforced against individuals, i.e. it had no horizontal direct effects. Therefore a head on clash between the Community law Directive and a UK Statute took place with the Directive being later in time. The post accession statute was inconsistent with a subsequent community obligation, and thus too late for any intention of Parliament to comply with the Directive to be contained within the provisions of the national law. Consequently, the House of Lords held there was no enforceable Community right to which the provisions of the English Sex Discrimination Act would be required to give way by virtue of s. 2(4) of the European Communities Act and that s. 2(4) cannot apply to construe a UK Statute to enforce Community directives against individuals. In the view of the House of Lords in the case, it could only apply to directly applicable Community law. The House of Lords held s. 2(4) refers to s. 2(1) which only refers to directly effective Community law or directly applicable law, therefore it was not appropriate. Mrs Duke was defeated by the House of Lords as was the view of s. 2(4) even as a rule of construction. This case has not been followed by the House of Lords in later cases.

Pickstone v Freemans plc involved a generous interpretation of the 1983 UK Regulations, which amended the Equal Pay Act 1970, to read consistently with Community law obligations. This was largely based on the intention of Parliament in passing the Regulations to ensure national law complied with the Community Directive but also in line with Court of Justice rulings. Section 2(4) was used to justify the Court's interpretation of national law but only in so far as it was reasonably possible. *Duke* was then distinguished on the basis that the Sex Discrimination Act 1975 was not intended to give effect to the later Community law or capable of doing so. In the case law so far, the intent of the UK Parliament as contained within the later statutes appears to have been held in higher regard by the courts for the interpretation of Community law rights rather than the intent of Parliament as expressed in the ECA 1972, that Community law takes priority.

The case of *Litster v Forth Dry Dock & Engineering Co. Ltd.* concerned the rights of employees on the transfer of the undertaking of a business. A number of employees were claiming unfair dismissal after a ship repairing company was transferred between owners. The relevant law is 'The Transfer of Undertakings (Protection of Employment) Regulations' which purported to implement the obligations contained in the EEC Council Directive 77/187 but the national Regulations were considered to be somewhat ambiguous. The Directive could not give rise to direct effects because it involved an attempt to enforce it against a private employer. The House of Lords could not therefore achieve a satisfactory result in keeping with the European Directive and the case law of the Court of Justice by a literal attempt, therefore it concluded that it must use the Community legislation to construe the later UK legislation contrary to its literal meaning and imply additional words to achieve consistency with the purpose of the Directive. Here s. 2(4) is clearly being used as a rule of construction and quite a generous one.

The *R v Secretary of State for Transport ex p. Factortame Ltd* case is a particularly important statement of the view of the House of Lords to the supremacy of Community law. You may find the series of litigation in the *Factortame* cases very confusing, particularly since the case numbers are not always used consistently. To try and clarify the matter, the facts and procedure of the case are as follows. The United Kingdom wanted to protect the British fishing quotas under the European quota system and passed the Merchant Shipping Act in 1988 aimed at stopping the practice of quota hopping by Spanish owned vessels registered in the UK by requiring that a minimum percentage of the directors of a company owning fishing vessels registered in the UK be British nationals. The company and vessel owners sought an interim injunction against the crown not to apply a disputed national regulation issued under that Act. This was granted in the main action on merits by the Queen's Bench divisional court which decided, rather slowly, to refer the substantive issue to the Court of Justice, and this case was given the Court of Justice docket number C-221/89. This is *Factortame No. 2*. The Crown appealed against the injunction, raising a procedural point and a second line of cases commenced which was appealed up to the House of Lords, who also made a reference the Court of Justice but this time on the procedural matter. The procedural action was, however, subject to a much faster appeal process so that it was received earlier by the Court of Justice than the substantive law case and was given the docket number C-213/89, hence it is *Factortame (1)*. Upon the return of the procedural aspect from the Court of Justice which essentially held that the national court should grant interim relief, the House of Lords held if a national rule precludes the national court from granting an interim relief, so that there was the chance that the court could determined whether there is a conflict between national law and Community law without irreparable harm being done, the national court must set aside that rule. If the injunction against the crown were not granted, the Spanish fishing companies would most probably go out of business whilst waiting for the Court of Justice to decide the substantive issues and for that to be returned to the QBD and decided, a process that actually took 2 years and 7 months. Although the substantive point of Community law in relation to the UK law had not been decided at that stage, the House of Lords nevertheless considered that if Community law rights are to be found to be directly enforceable in favour of the appellants, those rights will prevail over the inconsistent national legislation, even if later. *Obiter* it was held 'This (s. 2(4)) has precisely the same effect as if a section were incorporated into the national statute . . . which in terms enacted that the provisions . . . (of an Act) . . . were to be without prejudice to the directly enforceable Community rights of nationals of any member state of the EEC.' Lord Bridge commented on the view that the earlier decisions in favour of Community law were an attack on parliamentary sovereignty:

> If the supremacy within the European Community of Community law over the National law of member states was not always inherent in the EEC Treaty it was certainly well established in the jurisprudence of the Court of Justice long before the United Kingdom joined the Community. Thus, whatever limitation of its sovereignty Parliament accepted when it enacted the European Communities Act 1972 was entirely voluntary. Under the terms of the Act of 1972 it has always been clear that it was the duty of a United Kingdom court, when delivering final judgment, to override any rule of National law found to be in conflict with any directly enforceable rule of Community law. Thus, there is nothing in any way novel in according supremacy to rules of Community law in those areas to which they apply and to insist that, in the protection of rights under Community law, national courts must not be inhibited by rules of national law from granting interim relief in appropriate cases is no more than a logical recognition of that supremacy.

Factortame (2) dealing with the substantive matter was decided in the High Court as predicted, in favour of Community law.

As a result of this case, the view of s. 2(4) ECA is that it is a direct rule to give priority rather than a rule of construction which requires there to be national law to construe. It would also seem to suggest that as far as the House of Lords is now concerned entry to the Communities and s. 2(4) of the ECA has led to the modification of the doctrine of Parliamentary Sovereignty and that Community law in the areas agreed by Treaty is supreme over national law. Whether this overrides the dictum in *Macarthy's v Smith* is open to question. It remains open for Parliament to expressly repeal the Act or pass legislation expressly in breach of Community law obligations. Politically, however, this is extremely unlikely.

The series of *Factortame* cases is extremely important for a number of reasons in Community law, in particular from the point of view of supremacy over national law and constitutional doctrine and should be most carefully studied. The *Factortame* case returned to the High Court (*Factortame No. 3*) on whether damages would be payable. It was held that the legislative failure of the UK Government would give rise to liability providing damage and cause were established. This was appealed to the Court of Appeal who confirmed the decision of the High Court and finally in October 1999, the House of Lords held that the Government had manifestly and gravely disregarded the limits on its discretion and that the breach of Community law was sufficiently serious to entitle the applicants to damages for losses directly caused by the breach. Subsequently, the House of Lords confirmed in case C-9/91 *R v Secretary of State for Employment ex p EOC*, the conclusion reached in *Factortame* and held that in judicial review proceedings, UK courts could declare an Act of Parliament to be incompatible with EC law, although this does not extend to being able to annul the UK Act of Parliament nor indeed command a Government to repeal the act or compel or command a minister to change the law.

So whilst judicially in the UK, Community law supremacy appears to be an accepted and settled matter, this does not prevent cases reaching the courts on this topic. The most prominent of late are the *Metric Martyrs* cases[30] in which an argument was raised that a later UK Act, the 1985 Weights and Measures Act had impliedly repealed the 1972 AC Act and that UK law should then take precedence over EC law. The High Court rejected this view making the comment that the 1972 Act had acquired a 'constitutional quality' which prevented implied repeal. The case appears to confirm the view that there has been a kind of entrenchment introduced which does amend our view of parliamentary sovereignty in the UK.

The conclusion for the UK, is that it has clearly and unambiguously accepted the supremacy of EC law even over UK Acts of Parliament and over constitutional practise. Whether this is four square on the basis of the logic of Community law as provided by the Court of Justice and not by reference to the UK ECA 1972 remains unclear. The case law points to both conclusions, however, the UK seems to have gone further than some of the other member states.

4.9 Reception of Community Law in Other Member States

A majority of member states have not experienced any problems so far, although there is always room judicially for this position to change. Whilst it would be beyond this particular volume to conduct a tour of all the member states, it would be enlightening

---

[30] See above n. 25 at paras 60–7. Case note by Boyron, [2002] vol. 27 no. 6 *EL Rev*, 771–9.

to have just a brief look at some other countries, especially some of the member states who were later entrants, in order to see if there is a theme emerging as regards reception of EC law and particularly with regards to the attitude to the supremacy of Community law and in particular over national constitutional law.

4.9.1 Belgium

In Belgium the constitution was amended under Article 25a to allow for the transfer of powers to institutions governed by International law. However, because Belgium was a dualist country, later laws would prevail over earlier including international treaties if simply converted into national law. Furthermore, as in the UK, the courts in Belgium have no role in respect of judging the validity of international agreements, however, they accepted Community law supremacy in its own right as if it were a monist country and not by dependence on a Belgium Statute. See *Minister for Economic Affairs v S.A. Fromagerie 'Le Ski'*, in which it was held that in the case of conflict between national law and the directly effective law of an international Treaty, the latter would prevail, even if earlier in time. Its position since that early case has not changed.

4.9.2 Germany

4.9.2.1 The German Constitution (*Grundgesetz*)

In Germany, in contrast, difficulties were experienced, especially in respect of the relationship between fundamental rights provision in the German constitution (*Grundgesetz*) and in the Community legal order. Traditionally, Germany adopted the dualist approach to the reception of International law whereby some form of transformation or adoption of international law was necessary in order for it to have any direct application in the state. There had to be a process of incorporation by statute and once incorporated, a law would simply rank as with other *Gesetze* (Acts of the German parliament). If a later law was in conflict with an earlier law, the later law would prevail. Articles 24 and 25 of the *Grundgesetz* provided for the peaceful cooperation of the German state with international organizations. Article 24 *Grundgesetz* allows for membership of international organizations and a transfer of powers to them and was used to establish membership of the European Communities. Although Article 25 declares general rules of public International law to be an integral part of federal law and to take precedence over national law it is silent as to the effect of International law on German constitutional law. More recently, in order to cater specifically for further European integration, particularly into new areas as proposed in the Maastricht Treaty, and to take account of the increasing concern about possible infringements of the *Grundgesetz,* a new Article 23 *Grundgesetz* was added and amendments were made to other key provisions. Article 23 provides that sovereign powers can be transferred to the European Union provided the transfer has the approval of both houses of the German Parliament, the *Bundestag* and *Bundesrat.* Joint approval was also required for the ratification of the European Union Treaty and is further required for any future changes affecting the contents of the *Grundgesetz.*

4.9.2.2 The Reaction of the German Courts

Previously, German courts had been divided as to the effect of Community primary law and secondary law and at times, courts had refused to make a reference in cases of doubt or non-acceptance, thus denying the parties to the case the chance to see whether EEC law would have affected the outcome of the case. The most important court in Germany is the Federal Constitutional Court (FCC) because of its constitutional position in the German State.

In the *Internationale Handelsgesellschaft* case, known in Germany as '*Solange I*', the Constitutional Court held that as long as the recognition of human rights in the EEC had not progressed as far as those provided for by the *Grundgesetz,* German courts retained the right to refer questions on the constitutionality of secondary Community law to the FCC with the possible result that Community law might be ignored if it did not have sufficient regard for basic rights. This position has been modified with the later rulings by the FCC. In the *Wünsche Handelsgesellschaft* decision, known as '*Solange II*', the FCC has accepted that Community recognition and safeguards of fundamental rights through the case law of the Court of Justice are now sufficient and of a comparable nature to those provided for by the *Grundgesetz.* Thus, as long as EC law ensures the effective provision of fundamental rights the FCC will not review Community law in the light of the rights provisions of the Constitution. The Court also stated that it would not be prepared to accept constitutional complaints against Community law from lower courts on this basis. It is argued that a reservation of supremacy is still inherent in the ruling. The basis for the decision is not however the inherent supremacy of Community law, but the fact that Article 24 of the *Grundgesetz* allowed a transfer of powers to the Community and the subsequent accession act obliges the German courts to accept the supremacy of Community law. The decision by the FCC in *Solange II* also held that the Court of Justice was a statutory court within the meaning of Article 101 *Grundgesetz* and individuals have the right to have access to statutory courts. This effectively means that German Courts can no longer refuse to make references in last instance to the Court of Justice, as had happened in the case of *Kloppenburg,*[31] a case in which the Federal Tax Court had denied the direct

---

[31] Bundesfinanzhof 25 April 1985, NJW 1988, 1459, [1988] 3 *CMLR* 1.

effects of Directives and refused a reference to the Court of Justice. The Federal
Constitutional Court held in *Re: VAT Exemption*,[32] the follow up to the *Kloppenburg*
case, and in the separate case of *Re: Patented Feedstuffs*,[33] that German courts which
are courts of last instance in terms of Article 234 of the EC Treaty, would be in breach
of the German Constitution if they failed to refer to the Court of Justice when
necessary. The earlier judgment of the Federal Tax Court was consequently annulled.
Therefore, German Courts of last instance are obliged to make a reference where a
dispute as to interpretation or application of Community law exists. Applications to
the FCC to question the constitutionality of Community legislation have now been
declared to be inadmissible because the Court considered that such acts are not acts of
German public authorities within the scope of the *Grundgesetz* and cannot thus be
complained of to the FCC.[34] Following these cases there would seem to be no procedural difficulty in getting Community rights at least considered in the proper forum
in Germany. Any court which refuses either to follow a previous ruling of the Court
of Justice or which refuse to make an Article 234 ruling may be subject to the review
of the FCC for a breach of Article 101(1) of the *Grundgesetz*.

The German Accession Act to the Treaty on European Union was passed by the
German Parliament in December 1992. However, as a result of considerable criticism
that there had been no real debate on the Maastricht Treaty of European Union in
Germany and that a referendum had not been held to test public opinion on further
integration, constitutional complaints were made to the FCC. In its judgment in
Brunner et al v the Federal Republic of Germany, the FCC considered the changes to the
Constitution, the constitutionality of the TEU, and generally the relationship between
the EC and the German Constitution. Whilst it held that the transfer of powers were
compatible with the principles of the *Grundgesetz*, future extensive transfers could not
be made without the approval of the German Parliament and that the FCC would
reserve to itself a right to review the compatibility of EC law fundamental rights
provisions and the range of rights exercised by the EC with the German Constitution,
thus appearing to backtrack on its previous judgments.

After the Maastricht judgment, the relationship between Court of Justice and the
FCC remains unclear. Even though the FCC claims that fundamental rights will be
protected and upheld by a relationship of cooperation between both courts, it does
not clearly explain how this protection will work in practice. It seems that the FCC has

---

[32] NJW 1988, 2173, [1989] 1 *CMLR* 113.   [33] NJW 1988, 1456, [1989] 2 *CMLR* 902
[34] See BVerfGE 58, 1, 27, known as the 'Eurocontrol I' decision, and the Judgment of 12 May 1990,
NJW 1990, 974 concerning the enactment of the Cigarette Packet Warnings Directive (OJ 1989 C 124/5). For
further details see BVerfG 12 May 1989, NJW 974, Nicolaysen in 24 *EuR* (1989) 215–25 and Roth 28 *CML Rev*
(1991) 137–82 at 144.

accepted the standard of basic rights protection provided by Court of Justice but reserves a right to review EC-acts that would evidently infringe basic rights under the *Grundgesetz*, if the Court of Justice does not offer protection. So far this has been a theoretical case. The lengthy series of cases originating from Germany challenging the Community Banana regime preference of ACP states and not the traditional South American countries supplying Germany and which became known as the 'banana battle' certainly raised the issue again but did not culminate in a decision defining when exactly the FCC is willing to use its reserved power to review EC Acts. In 1993 an EC Regulation[35] on the banana market which was aimed at benefiting bananas imported from the ACP countries, placed quotas and duties on the import of other bananas, mainly those from Latin American countries (and referred to as *Dollarbananen*). Consequently it was subject to a number of challenges and in Cases C-465–6/93 *Atlanta Fruchthandelsgesellschaft I & II*, the Federal Tax Court initially upheld German law on the grounds of basic rights violations over the Community rules, however the basis for challenging the Regulation was dismissed by the Court of Justice. Subsequently, the *Banana Market Regulations* case[36] came before the FCC to consider the possible breach of the *Grundgesetz*, by an import company in Germany. The company had for several years imported about 100,000 tonnes of these bananas per annum, but was allowed a quota of only 150 tonnes to be imported under a preferential duty for 1994 according to the new regulation. Special circumstances in favour of the company had not been taken into account. The company challenged the quota and implicitly the Regulation before the Administrative Court (VG) in *Frankfurt/a.M.* asking for interim measures. Together with other importers in a similar situation they claimed a breach of their basic rights to carry commercial activity, right to property and to exercise a profession (Art 12, 14 GG), as the new quota was about to ruin their business. The Administrative court referred the EC Regulation to the FCC according to Article 100 I GG in order to decide on its compatibility with basic rights under the *Grundgesetz*. According to the *Solange II* decision such a submission would be inadmissible as long as the Community legal order provides a sufficient protection of basic rights, which has generally been accepted. However, in this case the Frankfurt Administrative Court argued that recent case law of the Court of Justice showed a less effective protection of individual's basic rights, especially when weighing individual rights against Community measures of the Common Agricultural Policy. It was noted that the Court of Justice had already upheld the validity of the EC Regulation on bananas in a previous case, when Germany had challenged it because of alleged violations of WTO law and basic rights.[37] After having granted the interim

---

[35] Regulation 404/93 OJ 1993 L47/1.

[36] *Bananenmarktverordnung* of 7 June 2000 BVerfG–2 BvL 1/97.

[37] Case C-280/93 *Germany v Council* [1994] ECR I–4973.

measures to avert the company's financial ruin[38] the FCC finally decided that the complaint of the main procedure was inadmissible. It held that the plaintiff had failed to show a decline of the standard of protection of basic rights in Court of Justice case law. It also pointed out subsequent amendments to the Regulation as well as the Court of Justice's decision of 1996[39] requiring the Commission to provide for transitory hardship clauses and that several parts of the Regulation which had contradicted WTO law had to be partly revised. After a more conciliatory judgment by the Court of Justice in Cases C-364–5/95 *T. Port GmbH & Co v Hauptzollamt Hamburg-Jonas*, the FCC had also toned down its language and held that as in previous cases it was satisfied that the level of human rights protection in the EU was sufficient so as not to engage the need for review by the FCC itself and hence a further challenge before it to the EC Regulation was rejected as inadmissible.[40]

The cases appear to show the Court of Justice as well as the FCC prefer an exchange of views through their decisions rather than open confrontation. Whether the FCC at some point will admit a constitutional complaint due to a decline in the Court of Justice's protection of basic rights remains even more doubtful after this decision.[41]

Turning to the highest German court in civil and criminal matters, the German Supreme Court ruling (*Bundesgerichtshof*) accepted the principle of state liability on the part of the German state for a legislative breach of Community law in Case C-46/93 *Brasserie du Pêcheur v Federal Republic of Germany*. However, the Court held that the breach, which was the prohibition of the use of additives in brewing beer contrary to EC free movement of goods rules, had not been sufficiently serious enough to impose liability.

4.9.3 Italy

In Italy the position both constitutionally and judicially was and is very similar to Germany whereby both had new constitutions set up after World War II with strong provision for fundamental rights. Both states allowed a transfer of power to international organizations but were silent as to effect on constitutional law. Article 11 of the Italian constitution provides for the limitation of national sovereignty in favour of international arrangements to secure peace and justice between nations.

As in Germany, the focus in Italy is on its Constitutional Court. Given that two of the leading Community cases on supremacy, *Costa v ENEL* and *Simmenthal* arose

---

[38] *BVerfG* EuZW 1995, 126.

[39] Case C-68/95 *T. Port GmbH & Co. v Bundesanstalt für Landwirtschaft* [1996] ECR I–6065.

[40] As noted by the *BVerfG*, 2 BvL 1/97, para. 68.

[41] For further discussion see also H.-W. Arndt, *Europarecht*, 4th edn., Heidelberg 1999, 77–80; T. Oppermann, *Europarecht*, 2nd edn. 1999, 571–3, T. Stein, '*Bananen—Split?*', *EuZW*, 1998, 261 seq.

from Italy, it should certainly have been clear to the Italian Constitutional Court, what was expected of it. Again there has been a mixed reaction, also along the lines of the German Constitutional Court.

Despite a previous less enthusiastic response to Community law in the case of *Frontini v Ministero delle Finanze*, in *Granital v Administrazione delle Finanze*,[42] the supremacy of Community law was accepted both on the basis of an interpretation of Article 11 of the Italian Constitution, allowing for the limitation of sovereignty in favour of international organizations, and by reason of the case law of the Court of Justice. The case did however make the reservation that Italian law should only be cast aside where directly applicable Community law exists—similar, in effect, to the judgment of the House of Lords in the *Duke* case. A later decision in *Fragd v Administrazione delle Finanze*,[43] suggests the Italian Constitutional Court is still prepared to review Community law in the light of the fundamental rights provision in the Italian Constitution if Community law was regarded as not respecting these rights. Thus far, this remains the situation in Italy with the possibility for outright rejection of Community law supremacy.

4.9.4 France

The system of French Courts are divided into two hierarchies with their own appeal Courts and final appeal and in addition, the Constitutional court (*Conseil Constitutionnel*). They have had however, significantly different attitudes to EC law, despite the fact both are subject to Article 55 of the French Constitution which is monist and gives International law a rank above municipal law but is silent as to the effect on the Constitution. This is the point that has led to discrepancies between hierarchies.

4.9.4.1 The French Courts of Ordinary Jurisdiction

The Courts of ordinary jurisdiction have felt no hesitation in making Article 234 references to the Court of Justice and giving supremacy to Community law on the basis of Article 55 of the Constitution. The French Supreme Court of Ordinary Jurisdiction, *le Cour de Cassation* has in fact gone further and found for the supremacy of Community without direct reference to Article 55 of the Constitution and more on the basis of the inherent supremacy and direct effects of Community law itself as in the *Café Vabre* case[44] in which Article 90 (old 95) EEC was held to prevail

---

[42] *Granital SpA v Amministrazione delle Finanze* Judgment of 8 June 1984 [1984] 1 Giui It 1521, noted by Gaja (1984) 21 *CML Rev*, 756–72.

[43] *Fragd v Amministrazione delle Finanze* [1985] ECR 1605, noted by Gaja (1990) 27 *CML Rev*, 93.

[44] *Café Vabre* [1975] 2 *CMLR*, 336, noted in 16 *CML Rev*, 367.

over a subsequent national statute. These rulings have been consistently followed by the lower courts and reference to either Article 55 of the Constitution or even the above decisions is rarely made, for example, *Garage Dehus Sarl v Bouche Distribution.*

4.9.4.2 French Administrative Courts

These courts deal with complaints by citizens against any acts of the State administration. The Supreme Administrative Court, the *Conseil D'Etat* has from time to time completely denied the supremacy of Community law or the need to make reference to the Court of Justice relying heavily on the French principle of law, *Acte Clair.* This states that where a provision of law is clear, there is no need to refer to a higher court but simply to apply it. The leading case is *Minister of the Interior v Cohn-Bendit,*[45] in which Daniel Cohn-Bendit (Danny the Red) was deported from France in 1968 and in 1975 requested re-entry but was refused. He claimed the refusal was contrary to Directive 64/221, previously declared directly effective by the Court of Justice in the *Van Duyn* case. The *Conseil D'Etat* held individuals could not directly rely on Directives to challenge an administrative Act and declined to follow previous Court of Justice rulings or make a reference itself. The judgment in the *Cohn-Bendit* case has been followed by the same court and lower courts. More recently, however, two cases have demonstrated a much more cooperative attitude on the part of the French administrative courts. These are first, *Nicolo,* in which the *Conseil d'Etat* reviewed the supremacy of International law including EEC Treaty Articles and held the latter to take precedence over subsequent national law, largely on the basis of Article 55 of the Constitution. The submissions of the Government Commissioner were instructive in his use and observation of the decisions from the courts of other member states and their acceptance of Community law supremacy. Secondly, in *Boisdet,* incompatible national law was declared invalid in the face of a Community Regulation. In doing so the *Conseil d'Etat* followed the case law of the Court of Justice. The recent cases of *Rothmans & Philip Morris Tobacco* and *Arizona Tobacco* have decided that not only are EC Directives to be given priority over national law, even where the directive pre-dated the French statute, but also that an award of damages against the French authorities can be made where damage is suffered as a consequence of non-compliance with EC law, clearly following the lead of the Court of Justice in the *Francovich* case.

Previously receiving no direct mention in the French Constitution, the European Community is now referred to in a new Article 88. This was introduced as a result of the *Conseil Constitutionnel* ruling that the move into new policy areas under the Maastricht

---

[45] *Minister of the Interior v Cohn-Bendit,* Decision of the Conseil d'Etat, 22 December 1979, 8 *Dalloz* 1979, see also [1980] 1 *CMLR,* 543.

Treaty would be incompatible with the Constitution. It too, as with Article 55, the original validation of Community membership and Community law within the French legal order, still however, requires reciprocity. This means that in order for any international Treaty and also now the European Union and Community treaties to be upheld and complied with in France, they must be upheld reciprocally by the other party or parties. Failure to comply by another party under the customary International law understanding of this principle, would mean that France is itself no longer obliged to comply with the Treaty or the part of it not complied with. Clearly in a Union of twenty-five states, this is not very practical and more likely to engender chaos. In any event, reciprocity was expressly excluded as a defence to a breach of Community law in Cases 90–1/63 *Commission v Belgium and Luxembourg* and C-146/89 *Commission v UK* (Fishing limits).[46] However, despite the change to the Constitution and the rules more sympathetic to the supremacy of Community law, cases taking a less cooperative position are still being decided by the *Conseil d'Etat*. In *Compagnie Generale des Eaux*, the Court once again confirmed its earlier position of denying the direct effect of directives when in conflict with a national administrative act.

4.9.5 Austria

The only noteworthy statement in respect of the Austrian courts' attitude to Community law was heard in Case C-224/97 *Ciola v Land Vorarlberg*. The Austrian court's position that Community law should only be followed if such rights have been definitively established by the national court, was rejected by the Court of Justice. Although the Austrian court acknowledged the primacy of Community law but because the facts of the case had pre-dated Austrian accession, the National court took the view that under such circumstances the national law could continue to prevail. The Court of Justice did not agree.[47]

4.9.6 Denmark

In line with the rather eurosceptic view of a good part of the electorate of Denmark, its supreme court has also taken a less positive view of supremacy. The Danish accession acts were challenged in *Carlsen et al v Prime Minister Rasmussen* as providing too much power to the EC institutions and going beyond the transfer of powers authorized by the Danish Constitution, s. 20. The Danish Supreme Court held that ratification of the Maastricht Treat did not violate the Danish Constitution and the at

---

[46] See also section 6.2.2.5 concerned with defences to Commission enforcement actions in Chapter 6.

[47] See for the general position of Austria and EU membership, N. Foster, *Austrian Legal System and Laws*, Cavendish Press London, 2004, chapter 7.

the transfer of powers under s. 20 was wide enough for the EU to act including its perceived need to act under the general residual power of Article 308. However, two provisos were laid down. That power to adopt measures contrary to the constitution cannot be delegated to international organizations and that the national courts retain the power to review Community law in this light and to hold it inapplicable in the event of conflict. Essentially, the same reservations as expressed by the German Federal Constitutional Court.

4.9.7 Finland

Finland and its courts, equipped with a new constitution in 1995 complete with a new fundamental rights catalogue, appear largely to have taken Community law fully onboard and accorded it priority where needed, largely by the interpretation of national law. Although it has been noted that no cases of serious potential conflict have yet arisen but that if one were to arise it would be as a result of the Finnish individual rights protection, thus no different to other member states.[48]

4.9.8 Hungary

The Hungarian Constitutional Court[49] has struck down a national law which was though required by a Commission Regulation on the grounds that it had retroactive effects. The reasoning of the Court reveals that this was considered to be an entirely domestic issue and not therefore a challenge to Community law. There is as yet no further evidence of the Hungarian courts' attitude to EU law supremacy.

4.9.9 Ireland

The Irish constitution has been amended to allow for EC and EU membership (Art 29 (4)). The Irish courts have the power to strike down national laws which are repugnant to the Constitution but it is not stated whether this applies to Community law (Art 15(4.2)) however, the Constitution provides that nothing in the Constitution can disturb the primacy of Community law (Art 29(4.10)) putting it effectively beyond judicial review.

A case which struck at the heart of the religious and moral underpinning of the Constitution caused some difficulty. In Case C-159/90 *Society for the Protection of the Unborn Children Ireland Ltd v Grogan*, in which advertising information about

---

[48] See the comprehensive survey by Tuomas Ojanen, 'The Impact of EU Membership on Finnish Constitutional Law' (2004) 10 *European Public Law*, 531.

[49] The Court's web site is at: http://www.mkab.hu/en/enmain.htm, Judgment 17/2004 AB.

abortion services in another member state was challenged on the grounds of the illegality of abortions in Ireland. The Irish Supreme Court held the that the advertising could be prohibited. The Court of Justice when confronted with the argument that the provision of information was a service within the meaning of Article 49 of the EC Treaty, held that it was not an economic activity and thus outside EC law thus removing the chance of the head on clash with the Irish Constitution. As a result though, Protocol 17 was attached to the TEU which provides that:

Nothing in the Treaty on European Union, or in the Treaties establishing the European Communities, or in the Treaties or Acts modifying or supplementing those Treaties, shall affect the application in Ireland of Article 40.3.3. of the Constitution of Ireland.

More significant is the *Crotty v An Taoiseach* case which concerned a direct challenge to Ireland signing up to the SEA. Following its consideration of what the Irish Constitution actually permitted, the Irish Supreme Court held that the constitutional provision would not cover any further transfers of sovereignty and thus use of that power by the Community unless approved of in a Constitutional amendment. Thus every new EU Treaty including therefore the CT, which introduces significant changes, must be approved by an amendment to the Irish Constitution and that must be done following approval in a referendum.

4.9.10 Poland

In Poland, one of the most recent new states, a challenge had been made to Polish accession to the EU as being contrary to the Polish Constitution. Whilst the Polish Constitutional Court ruled that accession was in line with the Constitution, the judgment revealed some deep-seated resistance to the automatic acceptance of Community law supremacy. It was prepared to accept sympathetic interpretations of Polish law but not to the extent that a contrary result was reached, particularly in the area of the individual rights and freedoms protection contained in the Constitution. In other words, when it comes to a clash involving rights protected by the Polish Constitution, Polish law and not Community law would prevail. This judgment is certainly in line and probably goes further than the German *Brunner* judgment, noted above.[50]

---

[50] A summary of the judgment is available at http://www.trybunal.gov.pl/eng/summaries/documents/K_18_04_GB.pdf and in particular refer to paras 14 and 15 of the reasoning. See also the case comment Krystyna Kowalik-Bańczyk, 'Should We Polish It Up? The Polish Constitutional Tribunal and the Idea of Supremacy of EU Law' (2005) 6 *German Law Journal*, 1355.

For an overall view of the legal preparation for Polish EU membership see: Adam Lazowski, *Adaptation of the Polish legal system to European Union law: Selected aspects*, Sussex European Institute working paper No. 45, http://www.sussex.ac.uk/sei/documents/wp45.pdf. Generally the Constitutional Court can be viewed at: http://www.trybunal.gov.pl/eng/.

4.9.11 Spain

The Spanish Constitutional Court was faced head on with the question of the supremacy of Community law when asked by the Spanish Government to provide an opinion on the compatibility of aspects of the CT with the Spanish Constitution. In particular, Article I-6, that Union law shall take priority over national law was raised along with questions about the legal basis (Art 93 Spanish Constitution) of the accession and provision for fundamental rights protection. The case in fact preceded the Spanish Referendum on membership and the judgment is very much in line with the German *Brunner* case in that whilst accession and the CT was held to be acceptable under the Spanish Constitution without further amendment, the Spanish Constitutional Court reserved the right to judge Community law in the light of its own constitutional protection of rights.[51]

4.10 Summary on Reception: Sufficient Evidence of an Emerging Trend?

The tentative conclusion is that a consensus appears to be emerging from the national and constitutional courts that Community law supremacy is accepted only in so far as it does not infringe the individual rights' protection of the national constitutions, in which case the constitutional courts will exercise their reserved rights over national constitutions to uphold them over inconsistent Community law. Only a few states appear to be accepting Community law unconditionally, such as Belgium and the UK, which may be because their constitutions are more flexible, at least from the view of the judges. Whether it will ever come to a direct rejection of Community law supremacy by a national court is debatable. Perhaps more important is that such a direct rejection is probably avoidable if the Court of Justice is allowed to diffuse any possible conflict before the case reaches a constitutional court, if the question of conflict is referred to the Court of Justice via the Article 234 preliminary ruling procedure first. This procedure is considered in the next chapter. In view of the number of constitutional courts which appear to be reserving a power of review, this is something the member states, the Union, and the Court of Justice needs to be taking seriously, perhaps in (another?) Protocol dealing with judicial cooperation?

---

[51] For a full discussion of Tribunal Constitucional Opinion 1/2004 refer to Fernando Castillo de la Torre, Tribunal Constitucional (Spanish Constitutional Court), Opinion 1/2004 of 13 December 2004, on the Treaty establishing a Constitution for Europe (2005) 42 *CML Rev*, 1169–202.

Further reading

Books

HIX, S. *The Political System of the European Union*, 2nd edn., Macmillan, Basingstoke 2005.

LENAERTS, K. and VAN NUFFEL, P. *Constitutional Law of the European Union*, 2nd edn., Sweet & Maxwell, London 2004.

MAURER, A. and WESSELS, W. (eds.), *National Parliaments on their Ways to Europe: Losers or Latecomers?*, Nomos Verlaggesellschaft, Baden-Baden 2001.

Articles

ALBI, A. and VAN ELSUWEGE, P. 'The EU Constitution, National Constitutions and Sovereignty: An Assessment of a European Constitutional Order' (2004) 29 *EL Rev*, 741.

BECK, G. 'The Problem of Kompetenz-Kompetenz: A Conflict between Right and Right in which there is no Praetor' (2005) 30 *EL Rev*, 42.

CRAIG, P. 'Sovereignty of the United Kingdom Parliament after Factortame' (1991) 9 *YEL*, 221–55.

CRAIG, P. 'Directives: direct effect, indirect effect and the construction of national legislation' (1997) 22 *EL Rev*, 519–38.

CRAIG, P. 'Constitutions, Constitutionalism and the European Union' (2001) 7 *ELJ*, 125.

CYGAN, A. 'Democracy and accountability in the European Union—the view from the House of Commons' (2003), 66 *MLR*, 384.

DASHWOOD, A. 'The Relationship between the Member States and the European Union/European Community' (2004) 41 *CML Rev*, 355–81.

EMILIOU, N. 'Subsidiarity: An Effective Barrier against "the Enterprises of Ambition"?' (1992) 17 *EL Rev*, 383.

FOSTER, N. 'The German Constitution and EC Membership', *Public Law*, Autumn 1994, 392–408.

GAJA, G. 'New Developments in a Continuing Story: The Relationship between EC Law and Italian Law' (1990) 27 *CML Rev*, 83.

HARTLEY, T. 'The Constitutional Foundations of the European Union' (2001), 117 *LQR*, 225.

HØEGH, K. 'The Danish Maastricht Judgment' (1999) 24 *EL Rev*, 80.

HOFFMEISTER, F. 'German Bundesverfassungsgericht: Alcan Decision of 17 February 2000; Constitutional review of EC Regulation on bananas, Decision of 7 June 2000' (2001) 38 *CML Rev*, 791.

HOGAN, G. 'The Nice Treaty and the Irish Constitution' (2001) 7 *EPL*, 565.

HOUSE OF LORDS, European Union Committee, 14th Report of Session 2004–5.

KALEDA, S. 'Immediate Effect of Community law in the New Member States: Is there a place for a Consistent Doctrine?' (2004) 10 *ELJ*, 102.

KUMM, M. 'The Jurisprudence of Constitutional Conflict: Constitutional Supremacy in Europe before and after the Constitutional Treaty' (2005) 11 *ELJ*, 262–307.

MANIN, P. 'The Nicolo Case of the Conseil d'Etat: French Constitutional Law and the Supreme Administrative Court's Acceptance of the Primacy of Community law over Subsequent National Statute Law' (1991) 28 *CML Rev*, 499.

Mouthan, F. 'Amending the amended Constitution' (1998) 23 *EL Rev*, 592.

Oliver, P. 'The French Constitution and the Treaty of Maastricht' (1994) 43 *ICLQ*, 1.

Regan, E. 'What the Constitutional Treaty means: for the Irish Constitution 2005', The Institute of European Affairs, Dublin.

Roseren, P. 'The Application of Community law by French Courts from 1982 to 1993' (1994) 31 *CML Rev*, 315.

Schmid, C. 'All Bark and No Bite: Notes on the Federal Constitutional Court's "Banana Decision" ' [2001] 7 *ELJ*, 95.

Weatherill, S. 'Competence Creep and Competence Control' (2005) 24 *YEL*, 1.

Weatherill, S. 'Better competence monitoring' (2005) 30 *EL Rev*, 23–41.

Usher, J. L. 'The Reception of General Principles of Community Law in the United Kingdom' (2005) *EBLR*, 489.

Strengthening national parliamentary scrutiny of the EU—the Constitution's subsidiarity early warning mechanism, 14 April 2005, Published by the Authority of the House of Lords, London: The Stationery Office Limited, HL Paper 101.

Web based materials

Conveu-30, A collection of seminar papers on Competencies and Balance of Interests from 'Governing Together in the New Europe' given at a Conference at Robinson College, University of Cambridge, 12–13 April 2003, http://www.swp-berlin.org/projekte/projekt.php?page=8&id=43. In particular refer to: Julie Smith/Camilla Soar, Division of Competences in the European Union.

5

Enforcement and Remedies in Community Law Article 234

5.1 Introduction

This chapter brings together a number of related matters for consideration. They are all linked to the preliminary ruling procedure under Article 234 which was the vehicle by which the leading principles and remedies in Community law were developed by the Court of Justice. In particular, it led to the development of the means by which Community law could be enforced by individuals via the national courts rather than by the Commission or other institutions or member states in direct actions before the Court of Justice, which will be considered in Chapter 6. Article 234 thus facilitated the establishment of a system of so-called 'dual vigilance' for the enforcement of Community law. The individual remedies developed include direct effects, indirect effects and state liability as the most important. The system of remedies has developed so extensively that it has also made inroads into national procedural law as a reaction to the impact that those rules can have on the equal application of Community law rights across the member states. These aspects will be considered at the end of this chapter, which will commence first with an introduction to Article 234, followed by a consideration of the range of individual remedies developed and then a more detailed look at how the Article 234 procedure works.

5.2 An Introduction to Article 234

The preliminary ruling procedure, which is also referred to as the Article 234 reference, provides the link or bridge between the national legal systems and the Community legal system. Under Article 234, the courts of the member states can seek a ruling from the Court of Justice on the interpretation of all forms of Community law including international treaties and recommendations and on the validity of Community secondary legislation.

The main task of the Court of Justice is therefore to interpret and rule on the validity of Community law so that a national court can reach a conclusion on a case involving Community law. The national courts' role in the process is to determine the facts of a case, ask a question of the Court of Justices when one arises and later to apply the ruling to the facts of the case. The Court of Justice should not concern itself with the application of the ruling it has made or advise the national court how to apply the ruling. It is to be noted, that within the national courts, it is the right of the national court to decide whether to refer a question and not an individual right of appeal.

Article 234 EC has as its purpose the uniform interpretation and application of Community law in all the member states and contributes to legal certainty by ensuring that EC means the same thing in each and every member state, even more important now with a Union of twenty-five member states. It was designed to work with the cooperation of national courts by providing the means whereby national courts would not give their own interpretations to Community law or decide themselves on its validity. The intended relationship was of equality and cooperation, rather than hierarchy or an appeal system, therefore the Court of Justice should only provide guidelines and not direct the national courts. It provides for the sharing of jurisdiction over Community law between the Court of Justice and the national courts.

Article 234 was the instrument which allowed the Court of Justice to develop the doctrines of direct effects and supremacy, vital for the development of the system of remedies under Community law which have been so helpful to individuals, for example, in getting round the restrictions placed on them by the strict locus standi requirements of the direct actions or where the Commission has been slow in ensuring the member states comply with their obligations. Having created such doctrines the Court receives numerable questions specifically asking whether a particular provision has direct effects.

Under the TEU, Article 35 the Court of Justice is also empowered to give preliminary rulings under the police and criminal justice pillar, provided that the member state concerned has conceded to this jurisdiction.

The details of the Article 234 procedure will be considered after the looking at the remedies established by the Court of Justice, commencing first with direct effect and its distinction from direct applicability, which was encountered first in Chapter 3.

5.3 Direct Applicability and Direct Effects

5.3.1 Definitions and the Distinction Between Directly Applicable and Direct Effects

These two elements of the Community legal system and the distinction between them are fundamental to the study and understanding of the nature of Community law. The doctrine of direct effects is a judicial development of the Court of Justice. It is connected and very often confused with direct applicability, however there are fundamental differences between the two concepts. Directs effects plays a central role in the Community legal order because of its link with the application and enforcement of Community law in the courts of the national legal systems and is therefore very much related with the supremacy of Community law. Unfortunately, the terminology of the Court of Justice and many of the national courts has not always been consistent. This has added greatly to the difficulty in understanding these concepts. Very often the courts do not use the term 'direct effects' but describe a provision of Community law as directly applicable but in the sense that the provision gives rise to rights enforceable by individuals before the national courts. Thankfully, such confusing use of terms is less frequent these days. Direct effects was sometimes considered to be a sub-concept of direct applicability or that direct applicability was a prerequisite for direct effects. The Court of Justice has spoken of Regulations which are directly applicable but which by their very nature can have direct effect in Case 131/79 *Santillo*, which suggests this is automatically the case. In Case 9/70 *Grad*, the Court of Justice stated that the ability of an individual to invoke a Decision before a national court leads to the same result as would be achieved by a directly applicable provision of a Regulation, again as if to suggest the concepts are the same. Hence the confusion and the need for clarification.[1]

5.3.2 Direct Applicability

Direct applicability, a term previously recognized in International law, should be used to describe the way in which some provisions of Community have legal validity in the member states. It is therefore a mode of incorporation of law which is generally or universally binding. The term 'self executing' is also often used to describe such law, in

---

[1] Of the earliest articles on the subject, those which I consider to be clear and succinct are: L. Brinkhorst in a case note on the Grad and SACE decisions in (1971) 8 *CML Rev*, 380–92, Winter, 'Direct Applicability and Direct Effect; Two Distinct and Different Concepts in Community law' (1972) 9 *CML Rev*, 425, and A. Easson, 'The Direct Effect of EEC Directives' (1979) 28 *ICLQ*, 319–53.

that the legal provision itself establishes its validity in the host state. In the EC, 'directly applicable' is specifically mentioned in Article 249 in relation to Regulations which shall have general application and are directly applicable. The member states are obliged not to transform Community Regulations into national legislation, except where necessary under the Regulation: see Cases 39/72 *Commission v Italy* (slaughtered cows) and 128/78 *Commission v UK* (tachographs). It applies also in respect of Treaty Articles as these also satisfy the criteria of directly applicable law by their automatic validity in the member states following the ratification of the Treaty. The Treaty Articles themselves are not actually transformed into national law and they are generally binding in that they also obligate individuals and not just the member states.

5.3.3 Direct Effects

Direct effects is the term given to judicial enforcement of rights arising from provisions of Community law which can be upheld in favour of individuals in the courts of the members states. Providing certain criteria, considered following, are satisfied, a Community law provision will give rise to a right which is enforceable by individuals in the national courts. Whereas directly applicability applies only to Regulations and Treaty articles, direct effects have been declared by the Court of Justice in a series of cases in respect of Treaty Articles, Regulations, Directives, Decisions, and provisions of international agreements to which the Community is a signatory.

5.3.3.1 Treaty Articles

The first and leading case in which this doctrine was established is Case 26/62 *Van Gend en Loos*, which concerned the imposition of a customs tariff by the Dutch authorities allegedly contrary to Community law, old EC Treaty Article 12 (now 25), which provided:

member states shall refrain from introducing between themselves any new customs duties on imports or exports or any charges having equivalent effect, and from increasing those which they already apply in their trade with each other.

The defendant customs authority argued that as the Treaty Article was addressed to the member state, it could not be enforced by individuals against the state. In support of this view, the Belgian, German, and Dutch Governments and even the Advocate General argued that the correct way to enforce the Treaty obligation was by formal action by the Commission (under Art 226 (old Art 169)) or by another member State but not by individuals. The Court of Justice rejected this view and held that the Community had been endowed with sovereign rights, the exercise of which affects not only member states but also their citizens and that Community law was capable of conferring rights on individuals which become part of their legal heritage and enforceable by them before the national courts. It held that the provision (old Art 12), was suited by its nature to produce direct effects. To be capable of direct effects which are enforceable in the national courts, a Treaty provision must satisfy the criteria established by the Court of Justice. It must:

(a) clear and precise;

(b) unconditional (e.g. as to time limits);

(c) not require implementing measures to be taken by member states or Community institutions;

(d) not leave discretion to member states or Community institutions.

The Court of Justice thus not only enabled private parties to defend their rights arising in Community law in the face of inconsistent or contrary national law, but also to added to the system of enforcement of Community law by empowering individuals to take action which would result in enforcement in situations where a member state had failed to comply with Community law and where the Commission had not taken any action. This is regarded as particularly helpful as private individuals have clear reasons of self interest to bring actions and because there are so many of them who may be affected by Community law, the vigilance of Community law is much more widespread and effective.

Case 48/65 *Alfons Lütticke GmbH v Hauptzollamt Saarlouis* is an early demonstration of the difference between Articles of the Treaty which could give rise to direct effects and those which could not. The case declared that old Article 95 (now 90) satisfied the criteria so as to give rise to direct effects but that Article 97 did not.[2] Old Article 95 provided 'No Member State shall impose, directly or indirectly . . . any internal taxation of any kind . . .' and old Article 97 provided: 'member states . . . may, in the case of internal taxation . . ., establish average rates . . .'. The Court of Justice ruled Article 95 had created direct effects but that since member states had a discretion to decide whether to levy an average rate of tax, Article 97 did not produce direct effects.

Since these early cases, direct effects have been found to arise from many Treaty Articles,[3] which often obligate not just organs of the state as in a vertical relationship but other individuals, in particular in the Community context, employers. It was confirmed by the Court of Justice that employers are obligated to comply with the requirements of a Treaty Article and other individuals may enforce corresponding

---

[2] Art 97 has been repealed by the Treaty of Amsterdam.

[3] L. Collins provided a list of those Treaty Articles which had been considered by the Court of Justice for direct effects in *European Community Law in the United Kingdom*, 4th edn., Butterworths, London, 1990, 122–6.

rights directly against the obligated party who has failed to comply with Community law. The first case to confirm this was Case 43/75 *Defrenne v Sabena* (No. 2) in which the rights of an air hostess for equal pay guaranteed under Article 141 (old 119 EEC) were upheld against the employing airline Sabena who were in breach of the obligation. This ability to enforce rights against other individual legal entities is termed 'horizontal direct effects' as it applies between two individuals.

Article 12 EC, a very general a non-discrimination clause imposed on the member states was found to be capable of horizontal direct effects in Case 36/74 *Walrave and Koch*, but Article 10, the good faith clause imposing a general obligation on the member states to act in conformity and not against Community interests was held in Case 44/84 *Hurd v Jones* not to give rise to direct effects, although this Article subsequently has been highly influential in assisting the Court of Justice in developing other means of enforcing Community law.

Provisions of the accession Treaties have also been held to give rise to direct effects. See, for example, Case C-113/89 *Rush Portuguesa v Office National d'Immigration*, which detailed the rights of non-Community workers were entitled to whilst working outside their EC country of immigration, in another host member state.

5.3.3.2 Regulations

While Regulations are clearly directly applicable by reason of Article 249 (old 189) and can therefore also obligate other individuals, they are not necessarily directly effective. The question of whether they can also give rise to direct effects also depends on whether they satisfy the same criteria as for Treaty Articles as laid down in the *Van Gend en Loos* case. The leading case for Regulations is Case 93/71 of *Leonesio v Italian Ministry of Agriculture*, in which Italian farmers were able to enforce a Regulation against the Italian state providing for compensation payments which had been subject to delays by the Italian authorities. The Court of Justice held that the Regulation should not be subject to delays and was immediately enforceable in the national courts.

5.3.3.3 Directives

Directives have caused particular problems for the Court of Justice. At first they were thought, as a general rule, not to be precise enough to give rise to direct effects because they were not directly applicable and only obligated the member states to achieve an end result. Arguably, because they often provide a wide margin of discretion, they were considered incapable by their very nature of ever fulfilling the *Van Gend en Loos* criteria. However, Case 9/70 *Grad*, discussed below, considered and allowed for the possibility that direct effects could arise from other non-directly applicable forms of Community law outside Treaty Articles and Regulations and Case

41/74 *Van Duyn v the Home Office* confirmed that Directives could give rise to direct effects, provided they also satisfy the same criteria. The provisions of the Directive would have to contain a clear and precise obligation, which they can and often do. In this case, Article 3 of Directive 64/221 was held to give rise to rights directly enforceable against the state before the national courts by Miss Van Duyn.

A further aspect of directives which might have caused difficulty was that Directives usually allow the member states, time to implement them, two years being fairly common, which was considered in Case 148/78 *Publico Ministero v Ratti*. This concerned the prosecution of Mr Ratti by the Italian Authorities for breaches of national law concerning product labelling. Although, Mr Ratti had complied with two Community product labelling Directives, the expiry period for implementation of one of the two Directives had not expired. The Court of Justice held he could rely on the one for which the time period had expired provided it satisfied the requirements of clarity and precision etc., but not the Directive whose implementation period had not expired.

Case 51/76 *Verbond* concerned the situation to where a Directive had been implemented but that the implementation was not faithful to the requirements of the Directive. The Court of Justice held that to deny the rights of individuals in such circumstances, would be to weaken the effectiveness of Community obligations and that as a result, individuals helped to ensure that member states kept within the realms of the discretion granted.

For a considerable time, the question of whether Directives could be held to give rise to horizontal direct effects and thus be enforceable against other individuals received no answer from the Court of Justice. At the time, arguments against horizontal effects were that Directives did not have to be published and this would have offended against legal certainty. Furthermore, Directives are addressed and obligate member states and not individuals and therefore the latter should not be obligated by them. Furthermore, by making them enforceable potentially against everyone, it would blur the distinction between them and Regulations because they would resemble directly applicable law, something not intended under the scheme of the EC Treaty. Arguments for horizontal direct effects of Directives are that Community law should be equally actionable against the state and other individuals to ensure uniform consistency throughout the Community and to avoid giving rise to two categories of rights and Treaty Articles are also addressed to member states but can nevertheless obligate individuals. Directives, whilst not initially compulsorily publishable, invariably were published and indeed now must be published (see Art 254 EC). The Court of Justice finally decided this issue in Case 152/84, *Marshall v Southampton Area Health Authority* that Directives could only be enforced against the state or arms of the state and not against individuals, although the case itself concerned vertical direct effects as the Health Authority was held to be a part of the state. The decision, however, led to a whole host of problems because of the distinction which was created between the ability to enforce rights against private as opposed to public employers. The result of this decision is that the scope of the concept of public service as opposed to a private body became crucial as can be seen from the later UK case of *Duke v Reliance* which, on similar facts to *Marshall*, Mrs Duke lost her claim for compensation for being forced to retire earlier than men. Two further decisions in Case 222/84, *Johnston v RUC* and Case C-188/89, *Foster v British Gas* showed that although the concept was wide enough to include national law enforcement agencies and nationalized industries and included any form of state control or authority, a distinction between public and private sector rights nevertheless remains, which is considered in further detail below.

Case 8/81 *Becker* confirmed the restriction of the direct effects of Directives to the vertical axis but highlighted the further benefits of direct effects for the Community legal order in that directly effective Community law also operates in a wider sense as a standard by which national law is in effect considered by the Court of Justice to see if it meets the standard of EC law, rather than simply providing a narrower individual right only. Whilst the Court of Justice has no formal right to review the compatibility of national law, direct effects does allow it to state that there is an incompatibility on the part of the national law with the directly effective standard contained in the Community law. The *Becker* case thus prepares the ground for the establishment of the indirect effects, considered below.

5.3.3.4 Decisions

In Case 9/70, *Grad v Finanzamt Traunstein*, the Court held that it would be contrary to the binding nature of Community law if the provisions of a Decision could not be invoked by individuals. They must also satisfy the criteria and can only be enforced against those obligated. In *Grad*, a Decision addressed to the German state concerned with the harmonization of tax regimes was held to give rise to effects which could be enforced by an individual affected by it.

5.3.3.5 International Agreements

Although there is no statement in the EU or EC Treaties that international agreements entered into by the Community or by the member states within the Community, can give rise to direct effects, the Court of Justice has held that they may also give rise to direct effects providing they satisfy the criteria previously established. Agreements such as association agreements between the Community and a single state or even a number of states lend themselves more easily to producing direct effects due to the more limited nature and scope of the agreements than is the case with the more complex multilateral agreements whose subject matter may well go beyond the jurisdictional scope of the Treaties. For example, provisions of the EEC—Portugal

Association, parts of EEC—Morocco Agreement and provisions of the Yaounde Convention Agreement were held to be directly effective respectively in Case 104/81 *Kupferberg*, Case 87/75 *Bresciani*, and Case C-18/90 *Kziber*. In contrast, provisions of more complex agreements such as the GATT which are mixed agreements involving both the competences of the Community and the member states, have not shown themselves to the Court of Justice to be so amenable to direct effects. In Case 21-24/72 *International Fruit*, the Court of Justice held that the provisions in question were not directly effective because they were held to be too flexible and too easily subject to change by political negotiation rather than clearly applicable in a strict and reasonably foreseeable way by the courts. More recently, in line with the transition from GATT to the WTO, the Court of Justice has appeared to soften its stance and expressed the possibility in Case C-280/93 *Germany v Commission* that the GATT provisions may have direct effects but only where the Community intended to implement a particular GATT provision or expressly referred to it in a Community Act as, for example, in Case 70/87 *Fediol*, in which a reference in a Community Regulation to a commercial practice identified in GATT would allow the Court to interpret the Community act according to the GATT rule. It was, however, emphasized by the Court of Justice in Case C-149/96 *Portugal v Council* that the WTO rules do not give rise to direct effects. The Court of Justice did not wish to tie the hands of the Community by confirming binding rules of law for the Community when those same rules are not considered to be rigidly binding by other parties. The WTO and GATT regimes are not based on binding and immediately enforceable reciprocal rules, but rules, the breach of which, lead first to further negotiation.

5.3.4 Overcoming the Lack of Horizontal Direct Effect for Directives

5.3.4.1 Extending the Definition of 'The State'

One way to get over the unfortunate results of the *Marshall* ruling, which led to differences in treatment between state and private employees, is by expanding the concept of public sector to include more employers and thus more individuals capable of being able to enforce their rights vertically in the national courts through direct effects. In Case C-188/89 *Foster v British Gas*, the House of Lords referred to the Court of Justice the critical question of what was meant by 'state authority'. In *Marshall*, the Health authority was clearly regarded as a part of the state. *Foster v British Gas* involved at that time a nationalized but independently run organization. It was later privatized. The Court of Justice held that emanations of the state against whom direct effects were available were those bodies which provided a public service under the control of the state and which for that purpose were granted special powers.

Direct effects are then available against such bodies. However, although the case showed that the concept was wide enough to include nationalized industries and includes any form of state control or authority, a distinction nevertheless remains between public, however widely framed, and private employers. So, it may be concluded that expanding the scope of what is meant by an 'emanation of the state' will broaden the concept and protect more people, but this still does not get to the heart of the matter. It still allows a variation as between public and private employees and because there are inevitably different situations in each of the member states as regards the public and private sector, there will also be a difference in the rights of individuals between the member states. Thus, because of this distinction, a different result can occur in each member state where national concepts of what is within the control of the state may differ. The difficulties and limits to this approach are demonstrated in the UK case of *Doughty v Rolls Royce plc*, in which the Court of Appeal considered that the nationalized Rolls Royce was not a public body for the purposes of the claim to direct effects in the case, because it was not providing a public service and was not subject to special powers. Whilst the result in the *Rolls Royce* case is almost certainly correct, it can be seen that privatization of once nationalized companies might also affect the rights of individuals. If decided today, *Foster v British Gas* would probably have a different outcome. In a more recent case concerned with the concept of the state, Case C-157/02 *Rieser Internationale Transporte GmbH v Autobahnen- und Schnellstraßen Finanzierungs AG*, the Court of Justice held:

When contracts are concluded with road users, the provisions of a directive capable of having direct effect may be relied upon against a legal person governed by private law where the State has entrusted to that legal person the task of levying tolls for the use of public road networks and where it has direct or indirect control of that legal person.

So private companies undertaking a public duty come within the scope of the *Foster* ruling. There remains, however, no uniformity and indeed no certainty as to the application of Community law between public and private employers within member states and between member states. Certain individuals are thus denied rights that employees in the public sector can enforce in the face of non-compliance by member states. The result of this decision is that the scope of the concept of public service as opposed to a private body remains a crucial but sometimes artificial distinction.

5.3.4.2 Indirect Effects

To some extent Case 8/81 *Becker*, noted above, and its acknowledgement of a wider concept of direct effect as a standard by which national law is in effect reviewed by the Court of Justice, had already pointed EC law in the direction it was about to follow in the next development. Case 14/83 *Von Colson* provided a solution where national law was not in tune with Community law and direct effects were not available. The ruling offers an alternative for individuals defeated by the lack of horizontal direct effects. The case concerned Article 6 of the Equal Treatment Directive (76/207) and a claim against a public employer for the lack of adequate compensation when discriminated against. At the same time, Case 79/83 *Harz v Tradex* was also heard by the Court of Justice which involved a similar claim against a private employer. Rather than highlight the unfortunate results of the lack of horizontal direct effects of Directives against the private but not the public employer, the Court of Justice concentrated on Article 10 EC (old 5) which requires member states to comply with Community obligations. The Court held that this requirement applies to all authorities of member states including the courts which are obliged therefore to interpret national law in such a way as to ensure the obligations of a Directive are obeyed, regardless of whether the national law was based on any particular Directive. The effectiveness of this depends on the willingness or ability of the member states' courts to interpret national law, if it exists, to achieve the correct result.

However, the Court of Justice held in Case 80/86, *Public Prosecutor v Kolpinghuis Nijmegen BF* that the principle could not be applied by a member state to support the retroactive prosecution of a Dutch firm for stocking adulterated mineral water in breach of a Community Directive, which implementation period had expired but which had not been implemented by Holland. The decision is consistent with *Marshall* in that Directives cannot impose obligations on individuals. Thus, the sympathetic interpretation of Community law Directives required by *Von Colson* could not be used in breach of the general principles of legal certainty and non-retroactivity. The lack of national law to interpret, however, has caused problems in furthering the principle enunciated in *Von Colson*. The next case required a further sleight of hand from the Court to achieve a just result which was consistent with its decision in *Marshall*. Case C-106/89 *Marleasing* concerned Directive 68/151 which had not been implemented in Spain but which would have determined the outcome of the case. The Spanish courts wanted to know whether the Directive could nevertheless be directly upheld against an individual by another individual. Whilst the Court of Justice reaffirmed that Directives do not give rise to effects between individuals, it also stressed it was up to the courts to achieve the result required by the Directive by the interpretation of national law whether the national law post-dated or pre-dated the Directive. The national law relevant, the Spanish Civil Code, pre-dated the Directive but had to be interpreted in a way clearly not covered by it to conform with the later unimplemented Directive. Such retroactive interpretation will cause severe difficulties where there is a clear conflict between the national law and the Community Directive as was the case in the UK House of Lords case of *Duke v GEC Reliance* systems in which the House of Lords refused to interpret pre-existing UK law in the light of the later equal treatment Directive, in spite of the decision in *Marshall*. This difficulty was high-lighted at the Community level before the Court of Justice in Case C-334/92 *Wagner Miret* which also involved Spanish legislation pre-dating a Community Directive but which involved head-on incompatibility. The Court of Justice this time acknowledged the unsuitability of the *Von Colson* sympathetic interpretation in all cases and in Case C-168/95 *Criminal Proceedings against Luciano Arcaro*, the Court of Justice acknowl-edged that the limits of the *Von Colson* principle would be overreached if there was a retroactive interpretation of national law in the light of the Directive which would have determined the criminal liability of an individual, confirming the limitation recognized in the *Kolpinghuis* case. Finally in this respect, despite the opinion of the AG in Case C-91/92 *Faccini Dori* that horizontal direct effects of Directives should be recognized, the Court of Justice declined to follow this advice. It reasoned that whilst there was a case for vertical direct effects to stop states' relying on their own wrongs, recognition of horizontal direct effects would blur the distinction between Regula-tions and Directives contrary to the Treaty. Instead, as it did also in Case C-334/93 *Wagner Miret*, the Court of Justice expressed the view that if member states are unable to construe national law to read in conformity, which is a distinct possibility as a result either of the court being incapable or unwilling to do so, it must be assumed that member states nevertheless intend to comply with its Community law obliga-tions. Thus, if there is a breach, member states must compensate any loss incurred as a result of that breach according to the principles established in *Francovich*, considered below. In other words, the failure to succeed under *Von Colson* failure should not be the end of the litigation line under EC law and indeed, unfairly extinguish all remedies available to individuals because of the state's failure to comply with Community law.

5.3.4.3 Incidental' Horizontal Direct Effect

Although the opinion of the AG in Case C-91/92 *Faccini Dori* that horizontal direct effects of directives should be recognized by the Court of Justice was rejected, the Court has nevertheless given judgment in a few cases now which appear to allow horizontal direct effects. The cases involve a directive which has influenced the out-come of cases involving private parties, but in an incidental rather than a direct way and without imposing a strict obligation on any of the individual parties. The Direct-ives are pleaded not to exert rights directly but to overcome what would otherwise be the application of incompatible national law in a way detrimental to one of their interests. These cases also support and are supported by the wider view of direct effects put forward in Case 8/81 *Becker*, as a means by which national law is in effect reviewed by the Court of Justice to see if it meets the standard of EC law, rather than providing an individual right to assert a Community law based right against another party. The case law is at the moment limited.

In Case C-441/93 *Panagis Pafitis v TKE*, shareholders of a bank who were denied a meeting to protest over an increase in capital, as required under EC but not national law, were able to question the national law on the basis of the Directive. As a consequence, the new shareholders were prevented from relying on the national law which was out of line with Community law. Whilst this clearly affected their rights, it was not a case of a direct application of a directive against them by other individuals.

In the leading case in this line Case C-194/94 *CIA Security International SA v Signalson SA and Securitel SPRL*,[4] it was claimed that CIA had breached the national technical standard for alarm systems. CIA pleaded the inapplicability of the national standard because of the failure of the state to notify it to the Commission as required by the Directive 83/189. The Court of Justice accepted this argument, which meant that CIA could in effect rely on the Directive to remove an obligation to meet the national standard which would otherwise have been imposed under national law. The Directive relied on imposed no obligation on the other party, therefore there is no question of horizontal direct effects of a directive. It is true that the other party, who had alleged that CIA had not met the standard, was affected in that their allegation was legally unfounded and that they lost the action as a result, however, the national standard could only be rendered lawful by the state complying with the Directive, thus it remained the state's obligation to ensure its law was in compliance with Community law and not an individual. It has been noted that following this case, the number of notifications of technical standards by the member states increased significantly, thus supporting the free movement of goods regime.[5]

Case C-129/94 *Criminal Proceedings against Bernáldez* is a little more difficult to reconcile. It concerns an unimplemented Directive imposing an obligation on insurance companies to compensate third party victims who suffer damage at the hands of drink drivers, not previously a legal requirement in Spanish law. The Court of Justice held that the unimplemented Directive should be applied to support a claim made for compensation, seemingly, imposing an obligation not contained in Spanish law but under the Directive, on an individual, namely, the Insurance Company.

The next case does not follow the trend set by the first ones for good policy grounds. In Case C-226/97 *Lemmens* lemmens was prosecuted for drink driving, the evidence having been obtained by use of a breath analysis machine whose standards had not been notified to the Commission as required under Directive 83/189. Lemmens sought to argue the inadmissibility of that evidence for his conviction based on the failure of the state to notify the standard and thus, in line with the *CIA* case that a

---

[4] More extensive details of this case can be found in C. Barnard, *The Substantive Law of the EU*, OUP, Oxford, 2004, 122–7.

[5] See ibid., 126.

party need not have to rely on a national standard which has not been notified, his prosecution should not stand. However, the Court of Justice held that whilst the failure to notify the standard may have hindered the marketing of such machines, it did not render unlawful the use of the product and could not therefore aid the defendant in his claim, i.e. it did not affect trade between member states, which was the main purpose of the Directive.

In Case C-443/98 *Unilever Italia SpA v Central Foods SpA*, the principle established in the earlier cases was extended to contractual relations between two individual parties. The Italian state had adopted a food standard contrary to the Community standards Directive and Unilever's supply of olive oil, which did not comply with the Italian standard, was rejected by the purchaser, Central Foods. In an action for payment, Unilever questioned the Italian legislation. The Court of Justice held that the Italian law should not apply and that the case was no different in principle to the *CIA* case above and did not create horizontal direct effects. No obligation had been placed on an individual, merely that unnotified national standards could not apply, regardless of the possible consequence on the contractual relations and liability between the two parties.

Trying to rationalize these cases is not easy. The Court of Justice makes it clear that they are not establishing the horizontal direct effect of Directives. For the most part, the cases are mainly narrowly restricted to the application of Directive 83/189 and its replacement Directive 98/34, requiring the notification of technical standards, although as the case law has revealed, this is not the only Directive involved. More to the point, is that the technical standards Directive essentially involves the relationship between the member states and the Commission and not, as with most other directives, the relations between individuals and the state or between individuals. The following analysis may therefore represent the position reached. Directives are being interpreted to determine the validity of national law in an action which may either affect the legal position of a private party to the action or between private parties in a dispute and that any such incidental effect only applies to prevent reliance on national law which does not conform with Community law. Hence the term or view that the effect as far as the private parties is concerned is incidental only. The real or underlying purpose of the Court's willingness to uphold the provisions of the Directive or regarded from the other side, not to allow the application of non-conforming national law, is merely then to enforce the public law obligations of the state rather than affect the contractual relations between parties. Viewed another way in estoppel terms, parties may rely on the Directive as a shield to estop another party from relying on national law which would otherwise harm their interests. They are not using it as a sword to attack the other party. And viewed in yet a third way, it could be said that both incidental effects and indirect effects are both part of the broader view of direct effects in Case 8/81 *Becker* that the national laws should not be allowed to apply where not in compliance with Community law.

The cases also serve to highlight the fact that legal difficulties between individuals can be caused by the failure of a member state to comply with a Community law Directive. In such circumstances, where a failure adversely and directly affects an individual, there has already been a judicial remedy provided by the Court of Justice which holds the state liable in damages to compensate the individual for any loss sustained. This is considered next.

5.4 State Liability: The Principle in *Francovich*

State liability is the term given to the action first raised and accepted by the Court of Justice in Cases C-6 and 9/90 *Francovich* which allows an action by an individual against a member state when the member state has failed to comply with Community law obligations and which has resulted in damage or loss to the individual. The *Francovich* case has provided an alternative, therefore, to both Commission actions against member states to enforce Community law and the difficulties generated by the lack of horizontal direct effects of Directives, or indeed the entire absence of direct effects where the Community law provision fails to satisfy the *Van Gend en Loos* criteria. Instead, the state is held liable for its failure which results in damage to an individual. The *Francovich* case concerned a claim by Italian nationals against the State for a guaranteed redundancy payment granted by Directive 80/987, which had not been implemented by Italy, or alternatively for damages incurred as a result of the state failing to implement the Directive in time. Francovich and other workers were made redundant when the company employing them became insolvent. The company itself had made no payments and as a result of the insolvency, no action was possible against the company. The Court of Justice had held already, following Article 226 proceedings in Case 22/87 *Commission v Italy*, that Italy had breached its obligations by its failure to implement the Directive, however this could not help Francovich and his co-workers. The Court of Justice held the Directive was not capable of direct effects because of the discretion granted the member states as to the result to be achieved, in particular which authority was to be responsible for setting up a compensation agency and, part of the problem for the national court in the first place, there was no national law to interpret in conformity with the Directive. Instead, relying heavily on the fundamental doctrines of Community law of direct effects and supremacy as outlined in *Van Gend en Loos*, *Costa v ENEL*, *Simmenthal* and *Factortame* cases, the Court determined that the duty of the member states to ensure the full application and enforcement under Articles 10 and 249, if breached, would give rise to liability. The Court rejected the defence that the liability of the state was only a matter for the national laws. It held that the protection of individuals would be weakened if they could not claim damages for loss caused by a member states failure to comply. It considered therefore that the principle was inherent in the scheme of the Treaty that member states should make good any damage caused to individuals which was the consequence of a breach of Community law. The Court held though that the claim required the Directive to contain an individual right, which could be determined by the provisions of the Directive itself and that there must be a link between the breach and the damage caused. The decision in *Francovich* provides individuals with a remedy which stems not from the provision of Community law but from the breach by the member state of the general obligations in Articles 10 and 249 to comply with Community law. Hence, the case adds a remedy for individuals to fill the gap left where Community provisions have not been implemented by member states or are held not to be directly effective or because Directives are only effective on the vertical and not horizontal axis. Damages are consequently to be assessed in accordance with national procedural rules, subject however, to overriding Community principles which will be considered in the final section of this chapter. The ruling has been described by Bebr as the ultimate consequence of *Van Gend en Loos*.[6] The 1994 judgment in *Faccini Dori v Recreb Srl* (C-91/92) confirmed the Court's continued opposition to horizontal direct effects and whilst stressing the need for national courts to interpret national law wherever possible to comply with Directives, but pointed out that in circumstances where the states had caused damage caused by non-implementation of Community law, the state would be subject to a liability to compensate any loss in line with the principle established in the *Francovich* case.

Since those cases, the Court of Justice has had the opportunity to develop the law, starting with joined cases *Brasserie du Pêcheur v Federal Republic of Germany* (C-46/93) and *Factortame (3) v UK* (C-48/93). *Factortame* concerned the breach of a Treaty Article rather than the failure to comply with a Directive but this was held by the Court of Justice to be no bar to incurring liability. The result of this case law is that the principle of state liability is applicable to all domestic acts and omissions, legislative, executive and judicial which are in breach of Community law, directly effective or not and in principle by all three arms of state. There was however, a new focus on the seriousness of the breach. *Factortame (3)* introduced the revised criteria that if the state was facing choices comparable to the institutions when law-making, which essentially involves conducting a balancing act of many interests, the seriousness of breach also must be analogous to that applied to the EC institutions for damage caused

---

[6] G. Bebr, 'Case note on *Francovich*' (1992) 29 *CML Rev*, 557.

unlawfully by legislative acts under Art 288 (2). This is known as the '*Shöppenstedt* formula' (after Case 5/71 *Zuckerfabrik Shöppenstedt*). In order for liability to arise on the part of the member state, there must have been a sufficiently serious breach of a superior rule of law designed for the protection of individuals. This is the standard applied to damage caused by a legislative act rather than from administrative action. As such, it is a higher standard because, according to the Court of Justice, the creation of legislative acts involve choices of economic policy and are thus far more difficult to achieve. The sufficiently serious requirement was further elaborated by the Court of Justice in the case. It suggested this would be satisfied where a member state had manifestly and gravely disregarded the limits of its discretion. The factors that should be taken into account by the national court assessing this are: the clarity and precision of the rule breached; the measure of discretion; whether the infringement and damage was intentional or involuntary; whether the error in law was excusable or inexcusable; whether there was any contribution to the problem by the Community institutions and whether any incompatible national law was being maintained. The cases also confirmed that liability can occur without having to establish a breach by the member state following an Article 226 action by the Commission, however, in cases where the infringement is not yet clear, this could be problematic. If proven, damages arise from the date of the infringement and not the date of proving the infringement, unlike the Article 228 penalty we shall see in the next chapter.

Both at the Community level and at the state level, further case law has been provoked which help determine how serious a breach is required for member states to incur liability. At the Community level, it has proved to be extremely difficult to succeed in damages against the Community institutions.[7] The Court of Justice has taken a similar approach in Case C-392/93, *R v HM Treasury ex parte British Telecom PLC*. In this case the UK government successfully argued that its incorrect implementation of a Directive was due to a misunderstanding of what the Directive required. The Court of Justice agreed that the Directive was capable of more than one interpretation and thus no liability arose. Likewise in Case C-319/96 *Brinkmann*, the incorrect application of a tax classification by Denmark, which although financially damaging to a company, was not deemed sufficiently serious to incur liability because it was a mistake in the interpretation of the Directive which was made also by other states. These cases comply with the analysis at the Community level, in that where there is discretion on the part of the member state in deciding exactly what action is necessary to implement the Community law obligation or where there is an excusable error in interpretation, then the standard of fault for liability will be

---

[7] According to the AG in the *Factortame* case up to 1995, only eight awards had been made, [1996] ECR 1029 at 1101.

raised. In line with this view, where the obligation is much clearer and the breach much more obvious, then liability will be easier to impose as in cases *Francovich* and *Factortame*, noted above and C-5/94 *Hedley Lomas*, C-178/94 *Dillenkofer*, and C-140/97 *Rechberger* in which liability was established basically on the grounds of straightforward infringements of Community law. Case C-352/98P *Bergaderm* indicates an approach of the Court of Justice to align the rules on liability for member states and the Community Institutions so that it may be easier in future for individuals to obtain compensation from Community institutions for mere infringements which have not involved a great deal of discretion on the part of the institution.[8]

In cases where liability does arise, the determination of the degree of the seriousness of the breach and thus whether and the level of damages to be awarded, remain questions of national procedural law providing that remedies are not excessively difficult to obtain in the national legal systems and that damages, where applicable, are an adequate remedy. For further details on the impact on national procedural law of EC law rights, see below.

Whilst previous case law under *Francovich* has indicated that the Court of Justice holds the view that state liability is applicable to all branches of government, there was some reticence that this might apply to the judicial branch given the respect for the independence of the judiciary accorded in Western democracies.[9] However, in Case C-224/01 *Gerhard Köbler v Republic of Austria*, the Court of Justice held that the State may also, potentially at least, be liable for the breaches of Community law by the national courts provided they were manifest and sufficiently serious. It was held, however, in the particular case that the breach complained of was not serious enough despite the opinion of AG Leger that the error of Community law made by the Austria Administrative court was not an excusable error. The case does open the door for incorrect application or interpretation of Community law by a superior national court to lead to state liability in the future.

5.5 Article 234: The Preliminary Ruling Procedure in Operation

As was outlined in the introduction, Article 234 is the preliminary reference procedure by which the courts of the member states can refer questions to the Court of Justice on matters of Community law. A number of details of this procedure need to

---

[8] This will be considered further in Chapter 6, damages actions under Art 288.
[9] See H. Toner, 'Thinking the Unthinkable? State Liability for Judicial Acts' (1997) 17 *YEL*, 165.

be considered to gain a true picture of how this works including: The questions that may or may not be referred; the timing of a question; whether there is discretion or an obligation on any of the national courts to refer and the effects of a ruling by the Court of Justice on both the Community legal order and the national legal order. First of all this section will commence with the issue of which national bodies can make references which will be accepted by the Court of Justice.

5.5.1 Which Law Adjudicating Bodies can Refer?

The Court of Justice has accepted references from a varied number of bodies which are not courts in the strict sense but which nevertheless decide legal issues based on Community law including administrative tribunals, arbitration panels, and insurance officers. The determination of what is an acceptable court or tribunal is a question for the Court of Justice and is not dependant on national concepts. Certain criteria have now been established by which it may reasonably be determined whether a particular body may refer to the Court of Justice for guidance under Article 234. For example, it was clear from *Van Gend en Loos* that not only judicial but administrative tribunals were acceptable. Whilst the majority of fora in the member states deciding legal matters pose no problem, it is the peripheries of the formal legal system and those bodies which lie either partially or entirely outside of the state legal system which raise the question of whether they are suitable for the purposes of Article 234. The following cases have helped define the scope of acceptable bodies.

In Case 61/65 *Vaassen*, a reference was received from the arbitration tribunal of a private Mine Employees' Social Security Fund. The Court of Justice held that because the power to nominate members, give approval to both the panel itself and rules changes were in the hands of a Government minister and the fact that the panel was a permanent body operating under national law and rules of procedure, qualified it as a court or tribunal in the eyes of Community law. Case 246/80 *Broekmeulen v HRC* concerns a reference made by the Appeal Committee of the Dutch Medical Professions Organization. This was held by Court of Justice to be acceptable because it was approved and had the assistance and considerable involvement of the Dutch Public Authorities, its decisions were arrived at after full legal procedure, the decisions affected the right to work under Community law, they were final and there was no appeal to Dutch Courts. However, in the next cases jurisdiction was refused. In Case 138/80 *Borker*, a reference from the Paris Bar Association Council on the right of a French Lawyer to appear as of right before German courts was refused on the ground that there was no lawsuit in progress and the Bar Council was not therefore acting as a court or tribunal called upon to give judgment in proceedings intended to lead to a decision of a judicial nature. In Case 102/81 *Nordsee v Nordstern*, a reference from a privately appointed arbitration body was refused despite the fact that the Arbitrator's decision based on law, including Community law, was binding. The Court of Justice held because there was no involvement of national authorities in the process there was not a sufficiently close link to national organization of legal remedies and thus the arbitrator could not be regarded as a court or tribunal for Article 234. Jurisdiction was also refused in Case C-24/92 *Corbiau v Administration des Contributions* because a reference had been made from the office of the Director of Taxation, a body which acted in both an administrative and judicial capacity and thus lacked sufficient independence to be regarded as a court or tribunal for the purposes of Article 234.

Case C-54/96 *Dorsch* is particularly instructive as the Court of Justice took an opportunity to spell out the criteria to be taken into account in deciding whether the body is an acceptable one, including: Whether the body is established by law; whether it is permanent; whether its jurisdiction is compulsory; whether its procedure is *inter partes*, i.e. between two parties; whether it applies rules of law, and whether it is independent.

In view of this case law, it would seem that it is not critical to acceptance if the body is private or there is not an appeal from its decision. A strong indicator is the level of involvement by national authorities. Whether all of these criteria will be strictly applied in all cases in the future is uncertain because the lack of an appeal in a case may lead to instances where the national body itself has to interpret Community law without guidance if the Court of Justice is unwilling to accept jurisdiction, something which must be less than desirable from a Community point of view.

5.5.2 The Question Referred: Relevance and Admissibility

This section covers a number of connected issues all relating to whether the question raised by the member state body is one which is either relevant or not, or an admissible question as far as the Court of Justice is concerned. To a degree, the response to some of the questions sent to the Court of Justice by member state courts has varied according to the increasing case load of the Court of Justice. Where relevant and admissible, the content and form of the question must also be decided and this will also be considered.

Article 234 itself contains little of guidance except to provide that if the member state court or tribunal considers that a decision on a question of Community law is necessary to enable it to give judgment, it may request a ruling from the Court of Justice. The relationship or partnership which is supposed to hallmark this procedure, requires that once requested, a ruling be given by the Court of Justice to complete the Community side of the procedure. Unfortunately, this is not always as clear-cut in practise and questions arise as to who decides whether a preliminary ruling is necessary; the parties to the case, the national court or the Court of Justice. According to the letter of the Article 234 procedure, it is for the national court to decide to refer a question. The drafters of the Treaty did not envisage this system as providing an individual remedy, however it is often regarded as the initiative of one of the parties to request that a reference be made, but the national court is not obliged to refer.

This analysis continues to be the stated view of the Court of Justice as provided in Case C-236/02 *J. Slob v Productschap Zuivel*, in which the Court held 'It should be stated at the outset that it is for the national court alone to determine the subject matter of the questions which it wishes to refer to the Court. The Court cannot, at the request of one party to the main proceedings, examine questions which have not been submitted to it by the national court.'

The initial approach of the Court of Justice is described as come one–come all and it was happy to correct improperly framed references and accept them. In Case 16/65 *Schwarze v EVGF*, a court requested a ruling on the interpretation of Community law and the validity of national law in conflict. The Court of Justice concluded that Court was concerned more with the validity of a Community act and was therefore able to answer. It has consistently refused to rule on the validity of national laws, however it has often reformatted such a question in order to give an answer to the underlying reason for the reference, which is whether the Community law conflicts with the national law and should take priority. Turning to further case law, the first of which should by now be familiar, according to the Court of Justice in Case 26/62 *Van Gend en Loos*, the finding by a national court that it needs to refer is not to be questioned by the Court of Justice. This position was confirmed in Case 6/64 *Costa v ENEL*, in which the Court of Justice held that it is a decision of the national court alone to judge whether a decision on the question is necessary for it to give judgment. Furthermore, in Case 106/77 *Simmenthal*, the Court of Justice has declared it was unable to review the facts of the case presented to it in the case, i.e. it will not go behind the national decision. However, as the number of cases and backlog increased in the 1980s and 1990s,[10]

[10] Preliminary rulings before the Court of Justice:

Year	Number
1961	1
1965	7
1969	17
1973	61
1977	84
1981	108
1985	139
1989	139
1993	204
1998	264
2004	249

Taken from: http://europa.eu.int/cj/en/instit/presentationfr/rapport/stat/st04cr.pdf.

the Court of Justice was seen to be less willing to accept all references and has from time to time declined to give a ruling on questions referred to it on the grounds that no real question arises or that such references are an abuse or misuse of Article 234. This is not to say it has operated a crude quota to cut down references, because the number of cases that were regarded as irrelevant or inadmissible is minimal.[11]

5.5.2.1 Lack of Relevance, Clarity, or Basic Information

In Case 93/78 *Mattheus*, a disputed contract's continuation was determinable by the entry of Spain, Portugal, and Greece to the Community. When a reference was made to help resolve the disputed contract, the Court of Justice held as this was a matter to be determined by the member states and the potential new states, it refused jurisdiction. The question raised must one that is justiciable before the courts. The Court of Justice has also held that facts and issues must be sufficiently clearly defined in Case C-320/90 *Telemarsicabruzzo SpA*. In Case C-83/91 *Meilicke v ADV/OGA*, the Court of Justice held that the questions raised, could not be answered by reference to the limited information provided in the file, in which case the Court would be exceeding its jurisdiction in answering what was really a hypothetical question.

A formal ground for refusing a judgment is provided following a change to the Rules of Procedure (Art 104(3)) in 1991, whereby the Court of Justice was given the authority to dispose of a case where the question is manifestly identical to one already answered but only, however, if the Court consults and circulates the observations of all parties first. This is so procedurally cumbersome, the course of action is rarely employed. The Court has, however, issued guidelines in 1996, updated in 2005,[12] to the national courts to help them to decide whether a reference should be made. The Court's view is that it is up to the member states' courts to determine if they need a ruling and that the Court of Justice should answer such questions, however formed. References, generally though should be clear and succinct but sufficiently complete to give the Court of Justice a clear understanding of the factual and legal context of the main proceedings. National courts should explain why an interpretation is necessary in their view to enable them to give judgment. After another change to the rules of Procedure, the Court may now, after hearing from the AG, seek clarification from the referring court if the question or issue is unclear (Art 104(5)).

---

[11] Judge David Edward, in the 1999 paper cited in further reading below, estimated that twenty-seven cases only had been rejected since the *Foglia* case in 1980 in the nine years up to 1999, p. 5.

[12] An updated version of which can be found at OJ 2005 C143/1 and http://europa.eu.int/cj/en/instit/txtdocfr/autrestxts/txt8.pdf. The guidelines were introduced into the UK rules of Procedure '*Practice Direction for the Court of Appeal*,' 14 January 1999 and Civil Procedure Rules, Part LXVIII: http://www.dca.gov.uk/civil/procrules_fin/contents/parts/part68.htm.

5.5.2.2 No Genuine Dispute or an Abuse of the Procedure

The two *Foglia v Novello* cases are of special importance. Case 104/79 *Foglia v Novello (No. 1)* concerned a contract for wine between a French buyer Novello and Italian supplier Foglia. Clauses stipulated the buyer and the carrier (Danzas) should not be responsible for French import duties which were contrary to Community law. These were, however, charged on the French border and subsequently reimbursed by Foglia. Foglia sought to recover from Mrs Novello who denied responsibility to pay them on the basis that they were illegally charged by the French Authorities. The Italian judge made a reference to the Court of Justice asking whether the French tax was compatible with the Treaty. The Court of Justice rejected the reference on the grounds that there was no genuine dispute between the parties and that the action had simply been concocted to challenge French legislation. The Court of Justice considered this to be an abuse of the Article 234 procedure, particularly as there were remedies available to dispute the tax before the French courts. However, not satisfied by this, the Italian judge made a further reference, *Foglia v Novello (No. 2)*, in which he specifically pointed out that the previous case marked a radical change in the attitude of the Court of Justice to a national court's decision to refer. He requested the Court of Justice to give guidelines on the respective powers and functions of the Court of Justice and the referring court. The Court of Justice held that its role was not to give abstract or advisory opinions under Article 234 but to contribute to actual decisions and that although discretion is given to the national courts, the limits of that discretion are determinable only by reference to Community law.

Whilst *Foglia* may be regarded as a rarity, it is not alone as is witnessed by Case C-318/00 *Barcardi-Martini v Newcastle United* in which a French law prohibiting the advertising of alcohol was at the centre of a dispute between Newcastle United and the advertisers whose products have been advertised at the home game of Newcastle but unlawfully broadcast in France. The Court of Justice dismissed the reference after seeking clarification from the English High Court as to why Community law would have a bearing of the case in which another member state law was in question but where English law was applicable to the case. The Court of Justice concluded that it did not have sufficient material to make a ruling. A refusal of jurisdiction on the grounds of it being an abuse of the procedure took place also in Case C-188/92 *TWD Textilwerke*. A Commission decision addressed to Germany was not challenged within the two-month time limit under Article 230 but instead via the national court. The Court of Justice held this to be an abuse of the procedure for not acting within the time limit, despite the consequence that this seems to go against the promotion of Article 234 as a vehicle for realizing individual rights in the face of the continued strict application of *locus standi* requirements under Article 230, considered in the next chapter.

5.5.2.3 References Nevertheless Accepted

The decision in *Foglia v Novello* has been cited as authority to the Court of Justice in subsequent cases. In Case 46/80 *Vinal v Orbat*, which involved Italian law in Italy, the government claimed the case was not admissible because it was just an excuse to challenge national law under Article 234. The Court of Justice though accepted the reference. In Case 14/86 *Pretore di Salo v X*, there were no actual proceedings between two parties (i.e. not *inter partes*), something regarded previously as one of the criteria needed to be classed as a court for the purposes of Article 234. The case involved investigative proceedings only of an Italian Magistrate to determine whether a criminal offence might have been committed by a person or persons unknown in the case where a river had been found seriously polluted. Nevertheless, when a question of a possible breach of Community law was referred to the Court of Justice by the Magistrate, it was held to be admissible. The Court of Justice held it was up to the national court to decide if a reference was necessary to help it. In Cases C-297/88 and C-197/89 *Dzodzi v Belgium* and C-28/95 *Leur-Bloem*, the Court of Justice has given rulings in what were essentially purely internal matters involving the application of free movement of persons rules to nationals undertaking no cross-border movement, where the national decision was based on Community law. The Court of Justice considered that if it did not do so, Community law might be interpreted differently in the member states applying it in an internal situation, therefore for the sake of uniformity, the reference was accepted.

5.5.2.4 The Question Referred: Overall View

Although these cases, and others like them,[13] would appear to be contradictory, the case of *Foglia v Novello* must be viewed on its own merits that the Court of Justice did not wish to encourage national courts to challenge the validity of laws of other members states, especially when there existed the possibility of proceedings in the French courts to challenge the French law and from which an Article 234 reference could be launched if deemed necessary by the French judge. Otherwise, the Court of Justice may decline to take a case under Article 234 in a number of situations: Where the question referred is hypothetical; where it is not relevant to the substance of the dispute; where the question is not sufficiently clear for any meaningful legal response; and where the facts are insufficiently clear for the application of the legal rules.

The cooperation between national courts and the Court of Justice still exists, but the Court of Justice no longer simply accepts anything put before it. It has begun to exercise more positive control over its own jurisdiction in the manner similar

---

[13] Reference to Douglas-Scott, 234–342 or to the Tridimas article cited in further reading.

to superior national courts. This approach is reflected in the case law arising from Article 234(2) and (3), considered below.

5.5.3 A Discretion or Obligation to Refer?

Whether there is a discretion or obligation to refer a question, once raised, depends first on which sentence of Article 234 applies. Article 234(2) states that any court may refer if they consider it necessary to reach a decision in the case whereas Article 234(3) states that courts against whose decision there is no judicial remedy, shall bring the matter before the Court of Justice.

5.5.4 The Discretion of Lower Courts

Courts not falling within Article 234(3) are not obliged to refer but have a wide discretion to refer at any stage of the proceedings and in any sort of proceedings, see Cases 13/61 *De Geus v Bosch* and 28–30/62 *Da Costa en Schaake*. Part of the reasoning for this rule is that an aggrieved party can appeal to a higher court if necessary. In Cases 146 and 166/73 *Rheinmühlen-Düsseldorf*, the Court of Justice made it quite clear that any national court which considers that a ruling on Community law will help it decide an issue has the discretion to decide regardless of any national rules of precedent or referral. This was confirmed by the Court in Case C-312/93 *Peterbroeck Van Campenhout v Belgium*, in which the Court of Justice held that a national procedural rule, which prevented a national court from raising a matter of EC law of its own motion, concerning the compatibility of a national law with EC law, was itself contrary to Community law and that national courts must set aside rules of national law preventing the Article 234 procedure from being followed. Case C-213/89 *Factortame (No. 1)* also confirms this point that national law rules of any status must not prevent Community law from applying.[14]

5.5.5 The Timing of the Reference

In principle, national courts can refer at any stage of the proceedings and in any sort of proceedings, as has already been noted in Cases 13/61 *De Geus*, 93/78 *Mattheus v Doego* and 14/86 *Pretore di Salo*. In Cases 36/80 and 76/80 *Irish Creamery Milk Suppliers*, it advised that the optimum time would be when facts have been established and any questions involving national law only had been settled. The Court of Justice has

---

[14] The inroads that the Art 234 procedure has had on national procedural law will be considered further in Section 5.6 below.

also provided extra-judicial guidelines about when a reference should be made if considered necessary. The 2005 revision of the 1996 guidelines point 18, also recommends that the facts and legal context should be established and both parties views heard before the reference is sent. None of which impinges on the ultimate discretion of national courts provided by Article 234, who can decide when to refer and which criteria are necessary to decide this question.

5.5.6 Courts of Last Instance

In this category, an initial problem exists in deciding which courts are courts of last instance for the purpose of Article 234(3). The case law of the Court of Justice suggests that the relevant court for Article 234(3) is the highest court for the case rather than the highest court in the member state. In Case 6/64 *Costa v ENEL* there was no right of appeal from the Italian Magistrates Court because the sum of money involved was so small. The Court of Justice held that national courts against whose decisions there is no judicial remedy must refer a question of Community law to the Court of Justice. In most instances this is an adequate answer and Article 234(3) should apply to those proceedings which deny an appeal or judicial review and thus become last instance. However, the situation in member states may not be so easy to determine, for instance, in the UK, it is possible and has happened that the Court of Appeal and the House of Lords Appeal Committee can refuse leave to appeal in a case which has been decided by the Court of Appeal. This has the result that the lower of the two courts then becomes the court of last instance and results in a denial of the consideration of Community law to an applicant because the case itself has closed and cannot then be referred. This happened in *Magnavision v General Optical Council (No. 2)* whereby the issue of Community law was raised in the first case under this name but was neither considered nor referred, nor was an appeal to the House of Lords allowed. The applicant then applied to the High Court stating that the previous refusal meant the High Court became the court of last instance for the purposes of Article 234. This application was also refused on the grounds that the case had been closed and the High Court also refused to refer this question to Court of Justice, thus denying a consideration of Community law points. The same situation occurred where the Court of Appeal and the House of Lords refused leave to appeal in the case of *Chiron Corporation v Murex Diagnostics Ltd. (No. 8)* which meant that the Court of Appeal became the last instance court. Once again it was too late for a reference to be lodged because the case had been decided and appeals are only considered once the case has finished, a point expressly acknowledged by the House of Lords Appeal Committee in the case. The Court of Justice had also recognized this problem in the Swedish Case 99/00 Criminal proceedings against *Lyckeskog* and had suggested that in such circumstances, the supreme court considering the appeal should consider whether a reference was necessary. In order to both overcome the unfortunate earlier UK position and to take account of the *Lyckeskog* case, a change of the UK appeal procedure was deemed necessary and put into place.[15]

5.5.7 Avoiding the Obligation to Refer: The Development of Precedent and 'Acte Clair'

Whilst Article 234(3) provides the general rule that final courts must refer, over the years, the increase in cases being referred has been seen to have led to a more invasive consideration by the Court of Justice as to the appropriateness of a reference and, in two cases, spanning a period of twenty years, the Court of Justice has outlined the circumstances in which it is not necessary to make a reference. This has arguably created a form of precedent into the Community legal order and may have introduced changes to the relationship between the national courts and the Court of Justice. The Court of Justice has held that it is no longer necessary to make a reference where the provision in question has already been interpreted by Court of Justice or the correct application is so obvious as to leave no scope for any reasonable doubt. Thus, no question of Community law arises to be decided.

5.5.7.1 There is a Previous Ruling on the Point

Case 28-32/62 *Da Costa* raised the same question as had previously been asked in the *Van Gend en Loos* case. The Court of Justice referred to its previous judgment in *Van Gend en Loos* as the basis for deciding the issue and advised that such a situation might, if the national court wished, excuse the obligation to refer. See also now the Rules of Procedure of the Court, Article 104(3), which confirms the position stated in *Da Costa*.

5.5.7.2 The Answer is Obvious (Acte Clair)

The judgment by the Court of Justice in Case 283/81 *CILFIT* expanded the decision of *Da Costa*. In *CILFIT*, the Italian Supreme Court asked the Court of Justice directly in what circumstances it need not refer. The Court of Justice replied that in addition to the reason given in *Da Costa*, a Court might not refer if the correct application, but not interpretation, may be so obvious as to leave no scope for any reasonable doubt

---

[15] The House of Lords Appeal Committee made a recommendation which was adopted as an exception to the rule that no reason be given for the refusal to grant leave to appeal. In cases in which it is contended Community law may have a bearing, the Appeal Committee will give the reason why it considers the matter comes within the reasons of the *CILFIT* case and thus obviate the need for a reference. If a reference is considered necessary, the House of Lords will make one before deciding whether an appeal can be made. See the Practice Directions in Civil Appeals, 34, January 2006: http://www.publications.parliament.uk/pa/ld199697/ldinfo/ld08judg/bluebook/bluebk-1.htm#34.

that the question raised will be solved. This has been argued by many writers[16] to have positively introduced into the Community legal system, the French law doctrine of *acte clair* by which the national court need not make a reference if they consider the answer to the question on Community law obvious. Whilst to a degree this is true, it is not an entirely accurate representation of the judgment. The judgment in *CILFIT* is more restrictive than a straightforward application of *acte clair*. The Court of Justice qualified it by stating that the national court must be convinced that the matter is equally obvious to courts of other member states, that it is sure language differences will not result in inconsistent decisions in member states and that Community law must be applied in light of the application of it as a whole with regard to the objectives of the Community. These criteria would be extremely difficult to fulfil if properly followed, especially now in a Union of twenty-five member states but were arguably provided so as to maintain an appearance of the bridge of equality between Community and national legal systems. The 1996 guidelines, as revised to 2005, point 12, are clear in describing the court's policy as *acte clair*, although the required restrictive interpretation of it remains.

5.5.7.3 Questions of Validity

A question of the validity of secondary Community law must be referred to the Court of Justice. In Case 314/85 *Firma Foto-Frost v Hauptzollamt Lübeck-Ost*, the Court of Justice held national courts could not decide for themselves that Community law provisions were invalid. If this question was raised and an answer not possible from previous judgments then national courts were obliged to refer the question to the Court of Justice. If an appeal is still possible under national rules, this could still be done as an alternative. This point has been written into the Court of Justice guidelines, points 15–17. However, in Case 66/80 *ICC*, which involved the questioning of a Community provision already held to be declared invalid by the Court of Justice in a previous case, the Court of Justice makes it patently clear that, although such a judgment is addressed primarily to the court which requests the original ruling, it can and should be relied on by other national courts before which the matter arises, thus obviating a need to refer the same question again.

5.5.7.4 Use of *Acte Clair* by the National Courts

To some extent the fears that *acte clair* will be abused by national courts has been realized in some cases which have come to light. In *R v London Boroughs' Transport*

---

[16] See, amongst many: C. Barnard and E. Sharpston, 'The Changing Face of Article 177 References' (1997) 34 *CML Rev*, 1113, D. O'Keeffe, 'Is the Spirit of Article 177 under Attack?' (1998) *EL Rev*, 509, H. Rasmussen, 'The European Court's *Acte Clair* Strategy in *CILFIT*' (1984) 9 *EL Rev*, 242.

Committee decided in 1992, the House of Lords refused to refer a question to the Court of Justice claiming the EC Law was obvious but which on the facts appeared arguable. In 1998, a Greek court, the Council of State, itself interpreted EC law (Art 126(1)) in the case of *Katsarou v Greek State*[17] against the interests of an applicant seeking mutual recognition of qualifications as *acte clair* and thus as far as the Greek court was concerned removing any obligation to refer. These cases appear to result in injustice to the litigants affected. This denial of rights may be the price to be paid now for having a more flexible arrangement under Article 234, an aspect which is considered at the end of this section. In Case C-62/00 *Marks & Spencer Plc*, the Court of Appeal in the UK considered that individuals could only rely on the direct effect of sufficiently precise and unconditional Community law provisions if, and in so far as, the provision had not been properly implemented in national law, so that if a Directive had been properly implemented, as in the present case, it could not be relied on in that way. However, the Court of Justice held that it would be inconsistent with the legal order of the Community if individuals were able to rely on a Directive which had been incorrectly implemented but not to be able to rely on it where the national authorities applied the implementing legislation in a way which was incompatible with the Directive.

Even an attempt to obtain a remedy where a reference was denied has thus far, not been successful. In Austria, in Case C-224/01 *Köbler*, the Austrian Supreme Administrative Court had decided a point of Community law itself claiming it to be clear after withdrawing a reference to the Court of Justice seeking a ruling on the same point. The applicant in the case then sought damages from the Austrian State for the loss he had suffered as a result of the decision in the first case which he claimed to be contrary to Community law. On a reference in the second case, the Court of Justice held that the Community law at point was not clear and that the Austrian Court was not entitled to take the view that the matter was clear. However the Austrian Court's infringement for the purposes of the state liability action was not sufficiently serious for the Court of Justice and Köbler lost his claim, although making it clear that a state could be held liable for an incorrect judgment where the breach was sufficiently serious. The Court of Justice did, however, state that the Austrian Court, from which there was no appeal, should have made a reference and should have applied it. Generally the Court of Justice held that courts of last instance must make references in order to prevent rights conferred on individual by Community law being infringed. As such the judgment may represent a refinement of the *acte clair* principle in the Community legal order by removing its availability to courts of last instance. Confirmation of this is needed though from the Court of Justice before this can be stated with certainty.

---

[17] Judgment 3457/1998 of 25 September 1998, *Armenopoulus* 1999, 125, as cited in Tridimas below.

5.5.8 The Effect of an Article 234 Ruling

5.5.8.1 The Effect on the Court of Justice

In strict terms, in the absence of system of binding precedent in the Community legal order, a ruling by the Court of Justice is binding and effective in that case only and there is no further binding effect on the Court of Justice. However, although it is not restrained by any doctrine of precedent, the Court of Justice tends to follow previous decisions to maintain consistency and will cite previous judgments or parts of a judgment as a basis for a current decision. For example, see the cases relating to the definition of the term worker in the chapter on free movement of persons. In this way a development and build up of legal principles as in common law countries does take place. In other circumstances, the Court has been known to overrule previous decisions without much commotion when it feels that the situation warrants it. See under the Article 288 actions for damages section, Case 25/62 *Plaumann* and the later overruling Case 4/69 *Lütticke* which decided that an Article 288 action could be mounted as an independent action and not only if preceded by Article 230 action to annul. The *Plaumann* case was later confirmed as good precedent in Cases C-50/00 *UPA* and C-263/02P *Commission v Jego-Quere*.

5.5.8.2 The Effect on the National Courts

An Article 234 ruling is a mandatory judgment and not an advisory opinion and, as held in Case 69/85 *Wünsche*, fully binding on the national court. A ruling of the Court of Justice is then to be treated in each member state according to how its own system of law regards authoritative judgments. As far as the UK is concerned, national courts are bound under Treaty obligations to apply the ruling received from the Court of Justice to the facts of the case and where that court is the House of Lords, the ruling is consequentially binding on all lower courts, see Case 12/81 *Garland v BREL*.

The revised 1996 guidelines provide that the Court of Justice wishes to see that its judgment has been applied in the national proceedings and to that end, be sent a copy of the national court's final decision.

From the UK, there is now an exceptional case where the national court judge refused to apply the ruling of the Court of Justice because he considered the Court of Justice to have gone beyond its jurisdiction in making findings of fact in a case concerned with trademark infringement of football merchandise. However, Case C-206/01 *Arsenal FC v Matthew Reed* was overruled on appeal by the Court of Appeal and the ruling of the Court of Justice was applied without question.[18]

---

[18] See A. Arnull, '*Arsenal Football Club plc v Matthew Reed*', Case Note (2003) 40 *CML Rev*, 753–69 and G. Davies, 'Of rules and referees: *Arsenal Football Club Plc v Matthew Reed*' Case Note (2003) 28 *EL Rev*, 408–17.

There have been times where the Court of Justice, by analogy with Article 231 which provides the power to determine which effects of a regulation may be regarded as definitive, has limited the temporal effect of a judgment, especially when the result of a judgment would have given rise to previously unforeseen extensive and probably harmful economic consequences. For example, in Cases 43/75 *Defrenne (No. 2)* and C-262/88 *Barber*, the judgments were held not to be retroactive but only effective from the date of judgment or for claims already commenced, because they would unexpectedly have imposed on employers potentially substantial pay outs for numerous backdated claims based on the rulings.[19]

On validity, as noted above, the Court of Justice held in Case 66/80 *ICC*, that although a declaration of invalidity was directly addressed to the referring court only, it was sufficient reason for another court to regard the declaration as generally binding, however, the discretion to refer remains.

5.5.9 The Evolution of Article 234 References

Article 234 has allowed the Court of Justice to develop a system of remedies including direct effects, indirect effects, and state liability, which can be secured in the member states' courts so that future cases need not be referred to the Court of Justice. The increase in cases and increasing case backlog is argued to have led to a change in attitude on the part of the Court of Justice and it is now less willing to accept all references without question. It has, in a limited number of cases, provided the national courts with the grounds for not making a reference when, under a strict reading of the Treaty, a reference would be required. As a result of the development of this system of remedies and judicial devices to avoid references, a form of precedent (the *Da Costa* case) means that a Court of Justice ruling now has a far more general importance than just for the parties in a single case and appears to have placed the Court of Justice at the apex of the systems of nationals courts. Inevitably, this also appears to have changed the nature of relationship from a symbiotic or horizontal one more to a vertical or hierarchical relationship, although some might describe the original understanding of a relationship of equals and cooperation as somewhat illusory.[20] These developments have then given rise to what is described as a form of conscious or deliberate sectoral delegation of responsibility[21] over Community law to the national courts, who then also become enforcers of Community law in their own right in cases where there exists a Court of Justice precedent to rely on. Hence, a more

---

[19] Both of these rulings will be considered in further detail in Chapter 10.
[20] See, amongst others, Douglas-Scott, 249–52, and the articles cited in further reading.
[21] See Craig and de Bùrca, *EU Law*, chapter 11, section 8, pp. 18–21.

hierarchical relationship than was ever intended by the drafters of the Treaty or the member states, has ensued. This view is supported by the change to the Court's Rules of Procedure (104(3)) which allows the Court of Justice to return cases with a reasoned order where a question is identical to a question on which the Court has already ruled, where the answer to such a question may be clearly deduced from existing case law or where the answer to the question is not open to reasonable doubt. It send a clear signal to the national courts that they too could have reached the same conclusion, thus strengthening further the evolution of the Article 234 procedure. Whilst a part of this evolution, the *acte clair* development though has caused some concern especially when it is abused by member state courts which results in injustice to individuals who are denied their Community law rights, although the *Köbler* case discussed above appears to narrow the scope for the application of the doctrine to courts other than last instance courts.

5.5.10 Reforms and Future

In the context of the growing numbers of references, many reforms have been considered and changes suggested. Apart from those most recently made (including the above case law changes) which include the expansion of the CFI jurisdiction to include Article 234 references and the ability to set up judicial panels, further suggestions for reform include:

(i)   limiting the national courts able to make a reference by removing the right of first instance courts to refer;

(ii) only allowing novel or complex cases, i.e. those involving new questions of law;

(iii) permitting national courts to make suggestions as to the answer;

(iv) permitting national courts to decide themselves subject to an appeal to the Court of Justice;

(v)   setting up regional Community Courts, again with an appeal to the Court of Justice.

The latter two represent a much more radical shake up of the system and seem very unlikely in the short to medium term, especially in the light of the fact that the drafting of the CT provided a clear opportunity to change things radically, which it did not do. The CT whilst retaining the main features and wording of Article 234 in Article III-369, makes subtle changes only to the wording and provides, in a recognition that Article 234 cases do also affect criminal law actions, that the Court of Justice will act with the minimum of delay in such references. Otherwise all things remain equal according to the situation after the Treaty of Nice.

5.5.11 Interim Measures within an Article 234 Reference

Interim measures may also be highly relevant to Community law questions which are the subject of a reference to the Court of Justice particularly as a reference may take upwards of 18 months and more likely 2–3 years at the time of writing. In that time, the lack of relief may lead to great damage and in many cases insolvency of the companies involved. The clearest leading case on this is C-213/89 *Factortame* in which the Court of Justice held that regardless of national rules on whether interim relief should be granted, if rights under Community law were at stake pending a ruling on a reference on the substantive question, interim relief should be granted. Cases C-143/88 and 92/89 *Zuckerfabrik Süderdithmarschen AG* involved the possibility of granting interim relief in a preliminary ruling on the validity of a Community law provision. The Court of Justice took the opportunity to provide guidelines for the national courts along the lines of those developed already by the Court of Justice under its Article 243 jurisdiction in direct actions.[22] It held that relief should only be granted provided there was sufficient evidence before the court that serious doubts existed about the validity of the Community law in question, the case was urgent and relief was necessary to avoid serious and irreparable damage. Interim relief grant was extended to positive, rather than just suspensory, measures in Case C-465/93 *Atlanta Fruchthandelsgesellschaft*, which concerned whether a licence to import bananas be granted whilst awaiting the ruling on whether a Community Act regulating the banana market was valid. The Court of Justice held that national courts could do this provided they did so in the light of existing Community case law, the Community interest in the matter and the consequences for the Community regime and the affect on all interested parties. Hence then a common rule has been established which is nevertheless subject to national legal procedure but only to the extent that the Community law right is not endangered, which topic is considered in further detail in the section following.

5.6 National Procedural Law and the System of Remedies

It has already been mentioned that the development of individual remedies as established and developed by the Court of Justice has added a second system of vigilance to the existing direct enforcement of Community law by the Community institutions and member states. Inevitably, though, because direct and indirect effects, incidental

---

[22] Which will be dealt with in Chapter 6 under Art 226 actions.

effect and state liability are individual remedies which are pursued before the national courts, their overall effectiveness is dependant on national rules of procedural law which are per se, outside of the jurisdiction and direct influence of the Community and Court of Justice. These rules can affect and interfere with the realization of Community rights at the national level, and in comparison between member states this situation can be complicated by different rules on standing or time limits or burden of proof or because certain remedies are just not recognized in some member states.

However, because procedural rules were not within the scope or competence of any of the Treaties, they were originally considered to be within the reserved and exclusive competences of the member states. This idea is wrapped up within the term 'National Procedural Autonomy'.

5.6.1 The Principle of National Procedural Autonomy

In the absence of harmonized rules on procedure, rights conferred by Community law must be exercised before national courts in accordance with the traditions laid down by national procedural rules which, in strict terms, are autonomous from the Community legal system. To what extent, though should they be respected where they interfere with Community law rights? Whilst there are general arguments for and against, including that the rule of law and legal certainty would be undermined if entirely respected or that differences in remedies would arise between member states which may distort the uniformity of Community law and the realization of the internal market. On the other hand, it is arguably better to leave the provision of remedies to those who know their own systems best. The position of the Court of Justice up to the 1980s was one which essentially respected national procedural rules subject though to certain guidelines as developed through its case law. In Case 33/76 *Rewe-Zentralfinanz* Court of Justice held that national courts were entitled to apply national procedural limits provided national rules are no less favourable for Community law rights as for domestic situations or make the community right impossible to realize. In Case 45/76 *Comet*, the Court of Justice held that it was up to each member state to determine the procedural conditions governing those actions but that such conditions cannot be less favourable than those relating to similar actions of a domestic nature and should ensure the protection of the rights which citizens have from the direct effect of Community law. Thus where a Community law right is involved, national procedural law must not deprive a litigant of their rights under Community law so that the general principle of Article 12, that there be no discrimination of the grounds of nationality, is not breached. From the first cases and other early case law, stem the principles of practical impossibility and equivalence, the latter holds that Community law rights should be treated in the same way as national rights. It was already seen in relation to cases in respect of supremacy such as Case 6/64 *Costa v ENEL*, that the Court of Justice will not allow national rules to stand in the way of a reference to the Court of Justice or the supremacy of Community law and, as was also seen in the *Simmenthal* and *Factortame (No. 2)* cases, it is not just national substantive laws which must give way to Community law but also any national rules of procedure, including constitutional rules which might get in the way of the effective application of a Community law right, regardless of the origin of these rules. However, it was clearly stated by the Court of Justice in Case 158/80 *Rewe v Hauptzollamt Kiel*, that no new remedies were intended to be created in the national courts to ensure the observance of Community law over and above that already existing in national law, but it became clear that in some cases further intervention was necessary. The alternative, which would require the agreement of the member states to harmonize national procedural rules or replace them with Common Community rules is neither politically acceptable, as member states do not wish to hand over control of their legal systems or practically possible, due to the very different and nationally idiosyncratic legal systems in existence.

5.6.2 Intervention by the Court of Justice

Whilst, the principle of equivalence would ensure the non-discriminatory application of national rules, this does not go far enough to remedy the situation in all cases. National remedies must however, also provide an effective remedy. Any rule which actually prevents individuals on relying on a Community law right would be incompatible with the principle of effectiveness.

In Case 14/83 *Von Colson*, discussed above in relation to indirect effects, the compensation offered by the national court for the discrimination suffered was the payment of the rail fare home. This was held not to be a dissuasive and adequate remedy. The remedy, according to the Court, must guarantee real and effective judicial protection and must have a real deterrent effect. Case C-213/89 *Factortame* highlighted just how radical the solution had to be to ensure the protection of Community law rights in the national courts including in the case the right to interim relief against the UK crown, something which was not constitutionally possible previously. Case C-208/90 *Emmott* concerned a national three-month time limit in which to bring benefits claims which ran from the date the claim arose, from the relevant legislation, in this case the entry into force date of a Community Directive. However, it was not clear due to the faulty transposition of a Community Directive that the applicant's claim was valid and the claim was rejected in any event as being out of time. The Court of Justice held that whilst reasonable time limits are acceptable in respect of a claim based originally in Community law, time can only run from the date the direct-ive is implemented properly and the applicants rights are clear. In Case C-271/91 *Marshall II*, the award for compensation suffered by Ms Marshall for discrimination was set at a statutory ceiling, which was much lower than the real loss of earnings suffered. The Court of Justice held that unlawful dismissal based on a Community right should be subject to full compensation including interest, despite the interpret-ation of the Court of Appeal that damage could not include interest.

In a much more interventionist mode, EC law has also required national courts to provide specific and new forms of remedy most notably in Case C-6/90 *Francovich* and the establishment of the right to damages from the state where liable, as discussed fully above.

Thus national rules are respected to the extent that it does not prohibit with a Community law right, but where they prevent a Community law right from being realized or applied in some way, then the national procedural law must give way. This period of judicial activism and creativeness on the part of the Court of Justice, par-ticularly the *Emmott* case which took things surprisingly far, gave way to a less intru-sive period as generally the Court was reacting to being criticized for its overtly judicial activism.

5.6.3 A More Balanced Approach

A more balanced approach was shown by the Court of Justice in Case C-339/91 *Steenhorst-Neerings* involving the retroactive limitation of a claim to benefits to one year under Dutch law which was held to be acceptable to the Court of Justice. This apparent step back from *Emmott*, means that reasonable time limits are acceptable even though these can vary from state to state. However, *Steenhorst-Neerings* was distinguished from the rule in *Emmott*, which applied after the three-month deadline expired to prevent bringing an action at all because the state itself had contributed to the failure of the applicant to comply with the strict time limit by advising a wait and see attitude to another case also questioning similar rights to equal treatment in payments. The rule in *Steenhorst-Neerings*, in contrast, permitted a claim, but limited the retrospective payments under it, to one year. In Case C-188/95 *Fantask*, the Court of Justice gave general grounds for accepting time limits which could result in differ-ences between the member states. It held that national time limits would continue to apply even in situations where the directive had not been properly implemented into national law for reasons of legal certainty and to protect the taxpayer and authorities. The case itself concerned a five-year limitation period for the recovery of debts, held to be acceptable.

Two similar cases though concerned more closely with procedure were decided differently. Both concerned a variation of a national procedural rule which states that it is up to the parties to introduce legal arguments and not the court. However, if Community law, which may be relevant, is not introduced, then a party may suffer as a result. In these circumstances, it was argued the national court must either introduce the EC law itself or at least make a reference to the Court of Justice, thus infringing the national rule. Questions were referred as to the whether indeed the national procedural law must give way. In Case C-312/93 *Peterbroeck van Campenhout*, the Court of Justice held that national procedural laws should not prevent references being made but this was seemingly contradicted by Cases C-430 and 431/93 *Van Schijndel* in which a similar procedural rule which prevented a reference taking place was upheld as acceptable because the rule applied also in similar domestic circumstances and was there to ensure legal certainty and clarity. Somewhat unhelpfully in *Van Schijndel*, the Court of Justice held that each rule of procedural law and thus each case has to be judged on its merits taking into account the rights of defence, legal certainty, and the role of the national procedure before determining whether it renders the application of Community law impossible or excessively difficult. This would only seem to provoke further references to the Court of Justice each time a slightly new procedural law is brought into question.

In Case C-326/96 *Levez v Jennings*, the Court of Justice considered a UK procedural law which limited the period of claim for damages in sex discrimination cases to a period not exceeding two years running backward from the date of commencement of proceedings. The Court of Justice acknowledged that, in the absence of a Community regime on the matter, it was for member states to determine procedural rules governing Community law rights providing they are equivalent to similar domestic actions and were effective. A limit of two years was not criticized. However, Ms Levez had been misinformed or deliberately misled by the employer as to the higher earnings of a male predecessor and had only learnt the truth on leaving her job. Under such circumstances the Court of Justice held that, if applied, the rule would serve to deprive an employee from effective enforcement of Community law because it would be almost impossible to obtain arrears of remuneration and enable employers to avoid paying damages by deceit. In such circumstances the rule would be manifestly incompatible with principles of EC law. Whilst following the *Emmott* case, each case requires a clear demonstration that the particular facts of the case will lead to a particular unjust result. This is not though consequentially very useful to help determine further cases.

5.6.4 The Extension of *Francovich*

Apart from the development of the *Francovich* remedy noted above, two cases here serve to highlight its further effect on the national legal systems. Case C-453/99

Courage Ltd v Crehan involved a dispute between two private parties involving a claim that a breach of competition law Article 81 EC by another private party caused loss to the applicant. Building on the foundation cases of *Van Gend en Loos*, *Costa v ENEL*, and *Francovich*, the Court of Justice reasoned that the extension of the principle of state liability was required by the new legal order and for the effective protection of rights which would be undermined if it were not open to any individual to claim damages for loss caused to him by a contract or by conduct liable to restrict or distort competition. *Francovich* liability therefore has been extended to determine liability between private parties where one has caused loss to the other by a breach of Community law. Finally, Case C-224/01 *Köbler*, noted above already, extends the possibility that state liability applies also to breaches of Community law rights by the judiciary, in case the state would have to compensate.

5.6.5 Conclusions

National procedural autonomy is still protected under the Community legal order and is still the general rule, but the Court of Justice has intruded into the area by developing the demands for effectiveness and equivalence or by providing new remedies in the member states with the aim of ensuring a balance between the objective to protect the national procedural autonomy and at the same time to protect the effectiveness of EC law. Until there is an agreement by all member states to try to harmonize procedural law, a very difficult task at best, the ad hoc case law development we have witnessed is not likely to change. Indeed, the only change in this respect found in the Constitutional Treaty is quite small. Article I-29 provides as a general statement that member states must provide remedies sufficient to ensure effective legal protection in the fields covered by Union law.

Further reading

Books

Douglas-Scott, S. *Constitutional Law of the European Union*, Longman, Harlow 2002, chapter 9.

Articles

Barnard, C. and Sharpston, E. 'The changing face of Article 177 references' (1997) 34 *CML Rev*, 1113–71.

Bebr, G. 'Casenote on *Francovich*' (1992) 29 *CML Rev*, 557.

Biondi, A. 'The ECJ and certain national procedural limitations: not such a tough relationship' (1999) 36 *CML Rev*, 1271.

Brinkhorst, L. 'Case note on the Grad and SACE decisions' (1971) 8 *CML Rev*, 380–92.

CRAIG, P. 'Directives, Direct, Indirect effect and the Construction of National Legislation' (1997) 22 *EL Rev*, 519.

EASSON, A. 'The Direct Effect of EEC Directives' (1979) 28 *ICLQ*, 319–53.

EDWARDS, D. 'The Preliminary Reference Procedure: Constraints and Remedies', A paper delivered at the CCBE/College of Europe Colloquium Bruges, 19–20 November 1999: Revising the European Union's Judicial System, Assessing the possible solutions, Revising the Preliminary Ruling Mechanism.

EILSMANSBERGER, T. 'The relationship between Rights and Remedies in EC Law: in Search of the Missing Link' (2004) 41 *CML Rev*, 1199.

ELEFTHERIADIS, P. 'The direct effect of Community law: conceptual issues' (1996) 16 *YEL*, 205–21.

KAKOURIS, C. 'Do the Member States Possess Judicial Procedural Autonomy?' (1998) 34 *CML Rev*, 1389.

LEFEVRE, S. 'The Interpretation of Community law by the Court of Justice in Areas of National Competence' (2004) 29 *EL Rev*, 501.

O'KEEFFE, D. 'Is the spirit of Article 177 under attack? Preliminary references and admissibility' (1998) 23 *EL Rev*, 509–36.

TIMMERMANS, C. 'The European Union's Judicial System' (2004) 41 *CML Rev*, 393–405.

TRIDIMAS, T. 'Black, White and Shades of Grey: Horizontality of Directives Revisited' (2002) 21 *YEL*, 327.

TRIDIMAS, T. 'Knocking on Heaven's Door: Fragmentation and Defiance in the Preliminary Reference Procedure' (2003) 40 *CML Rev*, 9.

SCHERMERS, H. 'No direct effect for Directives' (1997) *EPL*, 3(4) 527–40.

STEINER, J. 'From Direct Effects to Francovich: Shifting Means of Enforcement of Community law' (1993) 18 *EL Rev*, 3.

6

The Direct Jurisdiction of the Court of Justice

6.1 Introduction

This chapter considers the actions which are commenced before the Court of Justice itself, the most important of which are the actions to enforce Community law against the member states and actions against the Community institutions. It includes actions by the Commission and other member states against a member state (Arts 226–8), judicial review of acts of the institutions (Art 230), the action against the institutions for a failure to act (Art 232), and actions for damages (Arts 235 and 288). Interim measures under Article 243 will also be considered but staff actions under Article 236 will not. Finally, actions arising from the Commission enforcement of Community competition law against individuals will also be considered briefly.

6.2 Actions against Member States

Direct actions against the member states to ensure compliance with Community law were the first part of the system of dual vigilance enforcement of Community law noted in Chapter 5. They were provided from the outset in the EEC Treaty but are not regarded as being particularly efficient, although improvements have been made. Breaches of member states' obligation to comply with Community law, which is imposed generally by Article 10 EC, are officially established by the Court of Justice following a procedural action against the state. Article 226 is the Treaty basis for Commission action against member states for failures to fulfil obligations under the Treaty. The Commission is acting under its duty as the guardian of the Treaties to ensure that the Treaty and other Community measures are complied with (Art 211). In addition, Article 227 provides for actions by one member state against another member state. Furthermore, in support of both these actions, Article 228 imposes an obligation on member states to comply with judgments of the Court of Justice. This was revised by the TEU and now provides a system of penalties which can be imposed on member states. This will be considered towards the end of this section.

6.2.1 Enforcement Actions by the Commission

In contrast to other international organizations, the European Union has a much more effective control mechanism under Article 226 to ensure compliance with its own laws by member states.

Article 226 provides:

If the Commission considers that a Member State has failed to fulfil an obligation under this Treaty, it shall deliver a reasoned opinion on the matter after giving the State concerned the opportunity to submit its observations. If the State concerned does not comply with the opinion within the period laid down by the Commission, the latter may bring the matter before the Court of Justice.

In addition to the action under Article 226, there are further actions which the Commission can take against the member state in respect of specific subject matters. These are: Article 88(2) in respect of infringements of state aids provisions, Article 95 (4) in respect of derogations from the internal market and Articles 296–8 in respect of emergency security measures, none of which though will be covered in any further detail in this volume.

6.2.1.1 The Breach Actionable

Article 226 is silent as to what constitutes a breach of a duty. The Court of Justice has determined that a breach can not only be constituted by an act of a member state but also the failure to act by a member state. A failure to act is most often observed in the form that a member state has failed to implement community legislation, mainly Directives, or remove national legislation which is now in conflict or inconsistent with Community legislation or has implemented the Directive incorrectly either deliberately or inadvertently or incompletely or considerably delayed. Apart from the general good faith clause under Article 10 and the Article 12 duty not to discriminate on grounds of nationality, there are more specific duties under the various chapters of the Treaty and the very detailed duties imposed by secondary legislation. Thus, breaches may arise from the Treaties, secondary legislation, international agreements, decisions of the Court of Justice and general principles. There are numerous examples of breaches by a member state to be found in the chapters of this book.

Failure to remove inconsistent legislation constitutes a breach even if the authorities no longer apply the national legislation and apply the Community rules in preference. For example, in Case 167/73 *Commission v France*, provisions of the

French Maritime Code restricted the numbers of foreign workers on French vessels but the French pleaded that the national law was not being applied. The Court of Justice held that this law, even if it is not being applied might influence the behaviour of people who rely on the law being applied and thus its non-repeal would create uncertainty. Also as noted below in Case C-265/95 *Commission v France*, doing nothing or little to prevent other persons from restricting the movement of goods when action could and should have been taken will also constitute a breach an obligation.

6.2.1.2 Identifying and Reporting Breaches

A possible breach can come to light by the Commission's own investigations or from the failure of the member states to notify how they have implemented EC law as they are required to do so now under secondary legislation. Breaches can be reported by other member states, the EP or concerned or affected individual citizens or companies. Note that with regard to the latter, they are unable to force the Commission to do anything about a complaint which has been lodged. See Case 247/87 *Star Fruit Company v Commission*, also discussed below. The Article 226 action was not intended to be an individual remedy so whilst complaints might have been welcomed by the Commission, that was as far as their interest in the matter formally extended. The Commission was thus neither under an obligation to act on the complaint or even inform the complaining individual of what, if anything was being done. Although the formal position of an individual in the matter has not changed, the Commission publicizes its progress much more widely than before by issuing notices in the Official Journal.

6.2.1.3 Defendants in an Article 226 Action

A breach of Community law can arise from any part of a state and is not restricted to purely governmental action or inaction. For example, in Case 77/69 *Commission v Belgium* (the Belgium Wood Case), the Government pleaded it should not be held responsible for the negligence of the Belgium Parliament which being out of session was not able to implement a Community Directive in time. The Court of Justice held that 'Obligations arise whatever the agency of the state whose action or inaction is the cause of the failure to fulfil its obligation even in the case of a constitutionally independent institution.' Thus actions of the legislature, the executive, local, and regional authorities are included. It could include breaches by the judiciary in a member state for rendering an incorrect decision although no such action has ever commenced. In Case C-129/00 *Commission v Italy*, the failure to repeal a law which was interpreted by the Italian courts in such a way as to make a Community law right excessively difficult to realize was held by the Court of Justice to be a breach on the part of the Italian state and in C-265/95 *Commission v France* (Spanish Strawberries), the actions by individuals in disrupting fruit and vegetable imports, against which the French authorities effectively did nothing, rendered the state in breach of Community law.

6.2.2 Article 226 Procedure

Article 226 requires certain informal and formal stages to be completed before the matter can be brought to the Court of Justice.

6.2.2.1 The Informal or Administrative Stage

The first part of Article 226 states: 'If the Commission considers that a Member State has failed to fulfil an obligation under this treaty, it shall deliver a reasoned opinion on the matter.' This means the Commission must have reached a conclusion that the member state is probably in breach of an obligation before it can commence an action before the Court. Having formed a view during the pre-procedural investigations and discussions with member state officials in what are described as the 'package meetings' that a state has breached its obligations, the Commission will inform the state by letter and give the state the opportunity to answer the allegation or correct its action or inaction before the formal procedure of Article 226 begins. In view of the discretion which the Commission enjoys, there is no obligation on it to take action. Individuals, who complain or who are concerned have been held by the Court of Justice not to be able to force the Commission to take action, see 48/65 *Lütticke v Commission* or Case 246/81 *Bethell v Commission*. In Case 247/87 *Star Fruit Company v Commission*, the Court of Justice held that the Commission was not bound to commence the proceedings under Article 226 but has a discretion which excludes the right for individuals to require that institution to adopt a specific position.

Each year the Commission prepares a report on the application of Community law which provides statistics for the number of cases being investigated and numbers for each of the stages of Article 226 actions.[1] The informal part of the procedure consists of two distinct phases.

6.2.2.2 Letters of Formal Notice

Not every suspicion of infringement by the Commission will result in the initial formal letter of notice being sent to the member state. In a report by the European Parliament in 1982 it was estimated that only one in a 1,000 cases suspected by the Commission resulted in a Court action. Whilst at this stage the process is informal, it is nevertheless absolutely necessary as a prerequisite for the formal process should the

---

[1] The latest can be found at: http://europa.eu.int/eur-lex/lex/LexUriServ/site/en/com/2004/com2004_0839en01.pdf.

member state fail to take action or correct the alleged breach. The initial letter has been held to be essential for the commencement of proceedings before the Court in Case 274/83 *Commission v Italy*. In 1985, the Commission sent out 503 formal letters (1,016 in 1995 and 1,552 in 2003) stating its point of view. Generally about half of the instances in which a formal notice has been issued, are settled at that stage, although this figure varies from year to year.

6.2.2.3 The Reasoned Opinion

Following the reply from the member state to the formal notice or after the time given by the Commission for an answer, which is usually two months, and during which no reply has been received, the Commission will deliver a reasoned opinion which records the reasons for the failure of the member state. This is delivered to the member state and also provides a further time limit within which the member state is required to bring the alleged infringement to an end. Many of the original complaints are settled informally during this stage and the resulting number of reasoned opinions in 1985 was 233 (192 in 1995 and 533 in 2003). In Case 39/72 *Commission v Italy* (Slaughtered Cows) the Court of Justice has determined that if the state should fail to comply with the reasoned opinion of the Commission within a reasonable time, or as stipulated by the Commission (normally two months), the Commission then has the right, which is still discretionary, to bring the matter before the Court of Justice, further specifying its grounds for action. In terms of the total number of cases each year, about 90 per cent will have been solved by the end of this stage and about 10 per cent only of the original cases will be referred to the Court of Justice. In 1985, 107 cases were brought, 72 in 1995 and 215 in 2003.

6.2.2.4 The Judicial Stage

The final stage of the procedure is action before the Court of Justice and its judgment which is merely declaratory. Only about 5 per cent of cases reach final judgment. After the judgment, the state is required to take the necessary measures to comply. In 1985, twenty-three cases were removed from the Courts register prior to judgment, the member states having complied with Community obligations, thus judgments rendered by the Court in 1985 were only 26, 72 in 1995, and 86 judgments in 2003.

The Court of Justice can proceed to judgment even if the member state has complied with the Commission's reasoned opinion but did so outside of the time limit set. In Case C-240/86 *Commission v Greece*, the Court held that the Commission action remained admissible despite compliance and that the Court of Justice was still entitled to establish the breach, which can be important for the Commission in establishing exactly what the law is or for setting a precedent to control other member state behaviour or as in Case 22/87 *Commission v Italy*, the breach declared by the

Court of Justice was the basis for imposing liability on the state in Cases C-6 and 9/90 *Francovich.*

At the moment there is about a two-year delay in the Court hearing enforcement actions but if the matter is very important, the Court is able to speed up the case. Where such a delay would cause severe difficulties it is possible for the Commission to request and the Court to order interim measures, considered below.

6.2.2.5 Defences Raised by the Member States

The member states have raised various defences, often acceptable in International law but without success in the Community legal order, to justify their non-compliance with obligations. Of the more common are: Force Majeure or overriding necessity in Case 77/69 *Commission v Belgium* (the Belgium Wood Case) and Case 101/84 *Commission v Italy*, Community measures being the cause of political or economic difficulties raised by the UK in Case 128/78 *Commission v UK* (Tachographs) and Italy in Case 7/61 *Commission v Italy* and reciprocity, by which the member state claimed in Cases 90–91/63 *Commission v Belgium and Luxembourg* that because the Council has failed to act, or in Case 232/78 *Commission v France*, that other member states have not complied with their obligations, the member state challenged is justified in not complying. Likewise, arguments that a conflicting national law is not in fact applied or that the administrative practice is in compliance as in Case 167/73 *Commission v France* also fail. About the only defence that will work, given the robust dismissal by the Court of Justice of virtually all other defences raised, is that the Commission got it wrong on the facts, i.e. there was no breach.

6.2.2.6 Suspensory Orders and Interim Measures

One of the criticisms of the Article 226 procedure was and remains the length of time it takes to get to a judgment. This is about two years in terms of the formal judicial stage of proceedings but which does not take account of the informal stage which can extend the whole process by years. During this time a member state's breach can cause considerable economic hardship and damage to individuals affected by it. In order to overcome these, the Court of Justice may order a contested act to be suspended under Article 242 or in any case before it, the Court may proscribe necessary interim measures under Article 243 EC Treaty, both of which have been ordered occasionally in Article 226 actions. A case for the requested measure must specifically be made, interim measures must be requested prior to final judgment and applied only in urgent circumstances. Interim measures are not in any strict sense a direct sanction but they can nevertheless have the effect of rectifying the alleged breach until it has been determined by the Court of Justice whether the conflicting national legislation should be removed. In Case 53/77 *Commission v UK* (Pig Producers), the UK was ordered to halt subsidies to pig producers until the Court could decide whether the scheme was compatible with the rules of the Common Market. The Court has ordered Belgium under Article 243 to allow access on equal terms to other non-Belgian Community nationals to vocational training in Belgian Universities when non-Belgians were asked to pay enrolment fees, Case 293/85 *Commission v Belgium* (University Fees). It also made an interim order in Case 61/77R, *Commission v Ireland* (Irish Fisheries) for Ireland to cease certain fishing measures which the Commission claimed were contrary to Community fishing rules. In all three cases the member states complied immediately. In Case C-195/90 *Commission v Germany*, the Court ordered that a special Road tax for Lorries be suspended pending the outcome of the Commission Article 226 action against Germany. In response, Germany had requested a security undertaking from the Commission, in case the Commission's application was not upheld but this was judged not to be required by the Court of Justice. In the *Factortame* litigation, Case 246/89R *Commission v the UK*, the Commission requested and was granted the suspension of the alleged incompatible UK laws which were causing and would have caused further considerable economic damage to the Spanish fishermen in the UK.

6.2.2.7 The Application and Effect of Judgments

Other international tribunals are unable to enforce their judgments against miscreant member states, for example, the International Court of Justice at the Hague or the European Court of Human Rights in Strasbourg. The best that can really be achieved is the issue and discussion of a report on the failure or breach, whilst waiting for political pressure to bear on the state concerned. In the EU legal order, the initial judgment of the Court of Justice is only declaratory and carries no specific sanctions. This actually stands in contrast with its greater powers of suspension at the interim stage, noted above. The member states are nevertheless placed under a further obligation under Treaty Article 228 to comply with the judgment by taking the necessary measures. If they do not do this, a further action may lie against them by the Commission under Article 226 for a further breach, but this time of Article 228. This has taken place a number of times. The leading instance of this is Case 48/71 *Commission v Italy* (second Art Treasures Case). The Commission discerned that because Italy had not complied with the Court's judgment in the first Art Treasures Case (7/68), judgment should be given that Italy had also failed in its obligation under Article 228. Despite the fact that Italy complied with the original decision prior to judgment, the Court held that Italy had also failed to comply with Article 228. This unsatisfactory situation without ultimate sanction to encourage compliance can allow matters to drag on, as in cases against France for the same infringement which spanned 20 years.[2] These and other cases prompted the member states to reform Article 226.

The Treaty on European Union amended Article 228 to enable the Court of Justice to fine member states for breaches of Community law. The Commission must give a further reasoned opinion on the continued failure and state a time limit for compliance, which if the member state fails to meet will allow the Court to levy the fine. Article 229 provides that the penalties will be determined by Regulations to be adopted by the Council and a penalty calculation system was established by the Commission[3] whereby it will state what penalty, if any, it considers appropriate. The basic penalty is fixed at €500 per day times factors reflecting the gravity and duration of non-compliance and the financial situation of the member state. The penalty can be levied in the form of a lump sum or periodic payment. The penalty will apply from the date of judgment in the action and not from the date of original non-compliance, hence member states have the chance to minimize the penalty. Three cases to the date of writing have resulted in fines being imposed: Case C-387/97 *Commission v Greece* and Case C-278/01 *Commission v Spain* in which the Court of Justice held that the form of the Commission penalty request does not bind the Court which can decide the appropriate type and amount of penalty according to the circumstances. The case against Spain involved the quality of bathing water which was assessed only annually therefore the Court considered a daily penalty not appropriate and instead imposed an annual penalty based on the percentage of beaches not meeting the Directive's standards. In Case C-304/02 *Commission v France* both a lump sum and periodic fine was imposed.

The CT does little to change the procedure under the present Article 226 except to remove the need for the second reasoned opinion under Article 228 when seeking a penalty fine (Art III-362), presumably on the basis that the failure to comply is self-evident.

6.2.3 Actions brought by other Member States

Article 227 is the basis for an action by one member state against another, when one member state considers another to have breached an obligation under Community law. As Article 292 obligates the member states not to pursue other methods of dispute resolution other than that provided by the Treaty, member states are thus obliged to use Article 227 to resolve differences under Community law, although this is not always observed to the letter of the law. It must be noted though that the use of Article 227 by the member states has been minimal. The preference is almost

---

[2] See Case 163/73 *Commission v France* and Case C-334/94 *Commission v France*.
[3] Commission Memoranda OJ 1996 C242/6 and OJ 1997 C63/2.

exclusively to request the Commission to take action under Article 226. The member states have full locus standi in relation to Article 227 which procedure is set out below.

6.2.3.1 Complaining State Refers the Matter to the Commission

Before an action can take place the member state must bring the matter before the Commission.

6.2.3.2 The Commission Issues a Reasoned Opinion

The Commission will ask both states to submit their observations and then deliver a reasoned opinion on the matter. The Commission seeks to bring about a solution before Court action is necessary and may even intervene to take over the action as it did in Case 232/78 *Commission v France*, which commenced as an action by Ireland against France or in Case 1/00 *Commission v France* which was commenced by the UK under Article 227, concerning the French measures which continued after the Commission UK beef export ban had been lifted.

6.2.3.3 Complaining State may then Refer the Matter to the Court of Justice

If a settlement or solution is not reached at this stage and three months has elapsed or if the Commission fails to submit an opinion by three months of being informed of the matter, the member state can take the matter before the Court. Judgment has been reached, up to the date of writing, in only two Article 227 actions; in Case 141/78 *France v UK* in which France successfully challenged the UK's unilateral fishery con-servation measures. The second case brought to judgment under Article 227 is Case C-388/95 *Belgium v Spain* in which Belgium failed in its action to challenge the use of the *Rioja* designation as an impediment to the free movement of goods.

These two rare cases aside, member states usually prefer to ask the Commission to bring actions under Article 226 as an alternative because this is a less politically obvious and contentious manner in which to secure compliance of Community law in the interests of the members state concerned.

Furthermore, under Article 239 member states may agree to refer any dispute relating to the subject matter of the Treaty to the Court of Justice for adjudication, which appears never to have been employed.

6.3 Alternative Actions to Secure Member States' Compliance

Whilst these have been considered in the previous chapter, it is appropriate to mention such actions again here as they are equally, if not a lot more, effective in ensuring compliance with Community law obligations by member states. They include actions where individuals point to the breach of a Community obligation or duty by a member state as a defence against prosecution by that member state or where they seek to challenge national rules which operate against their interest. The doctrine of direct effects thus additionally placed the policing of Community law in the hands of private individuals, who often have more reason and thus more incentive to bring actions than the Commission officials. Individuals may benefit as well as helping to bring about the compliance with Article 226 actions, as exampled by Case 152/78 *Commission v France* (Advertising of Alcoholic Beverages). It was held that a French ban on advertising foreign spirits was discriminatory and contrary to Community law. France failed to remove its legislation and prosecuted an importer for advertising. Waterkeyn the advertiser referred to the previous judgment as a defence. In the follow up Cases 314–316/81 *Procureur de la Republique v Waterkeyn*, it was held that individuals could rely on such past judgments as a defence to protect their rights. In addition, there are possibilities for individuals to sue a state for loss caused by a breach of EC law, previously established in an Article 226 action against the member states, under the state liability principle established first in the case of *Francovich*. This will also play a strong part in encouraging member states to comply with Community law obligations if they find themselves having to pay out significant damages in an increasing number of cases.

The next procedures considered in this chapter are those taken directly against the institutions of the Community and commence with the action to annul acts of the institutions under Article 230.

6.4 Actions to Annul Community Acts

Article 230 is the action to annul binding acts of the Community which are defective in some way. It was held in Case 294/83 *Parti Ecologiste Les Verts v EP* that the EC is a Community based on the rule of law inasmuch as neither its member states nor its institutions can avoid a review of the question whether the measures adopted by them are in conformity with the basic constitutional charter, the Treaty. To this end,

Article 230 EC provides for actions to be brought before the Court of Justice to allow it to review the validity of acts of the Community. If found to be in invalid, the Court of Justice has the sole right to declare those acts void. This action helps to ensure that the Community institutions comply with all requirements of Community law when they take action. This section will consider the two main aspects of this action which are admissibility and the merits or substance of the action. After these technical elements have been covered, we will also consider the suggestions for the reform of Article 230, largely raised due to its apparent strictness and alternatives to it, concluding with that contained in the CT. First, the complex question of admissibility will be addressed.

6.4.1 Admissibility

The issue of the admissibility of Article 230 actions includes the questions of which institutions are subject to review, which acts can be reviewed, the time limit for challenging acts and the applicants who can bring an action. All of these will be considered in turn, but the latter aspect presents the greatest barrier to applicants in practice and understandably demands most emphasis in case law and thus also textbooks. One of the problems in getting to grips with this topic is the wide choice of relevant cases, many of which stand in apparent contradiction with others. An attempt to reconcile these cases can be frustrating because the decisions of the Court of Justice are very often policy driven to achieve a just result in cases which merit it and in all others cases to discourage applications by individuals challenging general legislation. Thus it is hard if not impossible at times to see clear reasoning and development.

6.4.1.1 The Institutions whose Acts are Reviewable

Article 230 as originally constituted, stated that the acts of the Commission and Council are subject to review but case law extended this to acts of the European Parliament. Over a series of cases, the Court of Justice justified this on the basis that as the EP's powers grew, it should be responsible for acts which create legally binding effects in respect of third parties and these should therefore be open to review. See Case 230/81 *Luxembourg v EP* in respect of the choice of the EP's seat, Case 294/83 *Parti Ecologiste Les Verts v EP* in respect of a challenge to the apportionment of election campaign funds and Case 34/86 *Council v European Parliament* (Budgetary Procedure) with regard to budgetary decision of the President of the EP. The development is thus very much allied to the democratic deficit debate and as the EP's role increased in making law, i.e. its rights, so correspondingly has its duties thus there should be a right to challenge decisions of the EP. Article 230 as now amended by the Maastricht Treaty provides:

The Court of Justice shall review the legality of acts adopted jointly by the European Parliament and the Council, of acts of the Council, of the Commission and the ECB, other than recommendations and opinions, and of acts of the European Parliament intended to produce legally binding effects vis-à-vis third parties.

The Court of Justice has held that to be subject to a challenge an institution must be empowered under the Treaty to enact binding measures, therefore this does not include for example, COREPER, see Case C-24/94 *Commission v Council*.

6.4.1.2 Reviewable Acts

In formal terms, the jurisdiction of the Court under Article 230 applies to the legally binding acts of the institutions which are given in Article 249 as Regulations, Directives and Decisions and does not therefore include recommendations or opinions or indeed anything else. However, the term 'Act' and the definition of what constitutes an Act or a Decision has been given a very wide interpretation by the ECJ so as to bring many other forms of acts within the review of Article 230 which would not, on the face of it, be admissible. The reason for such an extension is that these create binding legal effects or affect the legal status of third parties. For example, it was held in the Case 8–11/66 *Noordwijks Cement Accord* that other acts may be subject to review and that the test to apply to a particular act is whether it has binding legal effects or changes the legal position of the applicant. The case involved a letter which changed the immunity from prosecution of certain companies. Further, in Case 22/70 *Commission v Council* (ERTA) it was held that Article 249 is not exhaustive and special acts such as the minuted discussions of the Council, for the European Road Transport Agreement, could also be challenged. As already mentioned, Case 294/83 *Parti Ecologiste Les Verts v European Parliament* and the TEU extended the list of reviewable acts to those of the EP where they give rise to legally binding effects on the position of third parties. However, in Case 7/61 *Commission v Italy* it was held that the reasoned opinion given by the Commission under the Article 226 proceedings did not constitute an act which can be subject of review under Article 230. Similarly in Case 48/65 *Lütticke v Commission*, the applicants had requested the Commission to take action against the German Federal Republic regarding a breach of Community law but the Commission refused. Lütticke applied under Article 230 to annul the decision not to act but it was held that the refusal to act was not a legally binding act and therefore not reviewable.

There have been now over the years, various forms of communication which are not formally binding legislation but have nevertheless been held by the Court of Justice to have legal effects and thus be subject to review under Article 230. The textbooks abound with examples. I shall provide only two here. In Case C-57/95 *French Republic v Commission*, the Court of Justice ruled on a French action to annul a

Commission 'Communication' which it was argued imposed new obligations on the member states. It held, that the Communication challenged, which was published in the OJ 'C' series and was not a legislative act envisaged by Article 249, was a measure which could be the subject of an annulment action. The content of communication was considered and the Court of Justice thought the communication had 'imperative wording' and whose content was the same subject matter as a withdrawn draft direct- ive. Hence, it held that the Communication constituted an act intended to have legal effects on its own, distinct from the Treaty provisions and an action to annul it could be upheld. In Case C-106/96 *UK v Commission*, the Council had decided not to support 'Poverty 4', a programme to combat poverty and social exclusion but the Commission decided nevertheless to fund a number of projects amounting to an expenditure of ECU 6 million and issued a press release to advertise this. If the last case looked a bit like sharp practise, this one looks even more deliberate and helps us understand why the Commission is criticized in some quarters. The Court of Justice held that the Commission lacked the competence to commit the expenditure and the decision was annulled. However, in view of the fact that much of the expenditure had already taken place, the Court decided in the interests of legal certainty to exercise the discretion given to it under Article 231 and rule in favour of the payments made or promised.

Hence then a wide array of measures can be subject to review dependant on the legal effects they produce or their nature and not just the three formal Acts listed in Article 249.

6.4.1.3 Time Limits

Article 230(3) provides that the applicant has two months from the publication of the measure or from the date of notification, or in the absence of publication or notification, from the date it came to the notice of the applicant, regardless of the status of the applicant. The time limit for challenging a Regulation has been deter- mined to run from fifteen days following publication, see Article 81 of the Rules of Procedure of the Court of Justice.

The time limits have been held by the Court of First Instance not to apply where there are such serious defects in the measure that it is to be regarded as non-existent (see T-79/89 *BASF v Commission*).

6.4.1.4 Who May Apply: *Locus Standi*

The question of who may apply relates to what is known as the *locus standi* of applicants. *Locus standi* means literally, the place of standing. It relates to the recogni- tion of a legal interest in a matter which produces the right to mount a legal challenge against a legal provision. No standing means no right to challenge, hence this is absolutely crucial to an applicant's chances. There are now three categories of applicants: Privileged; semi-privileged; and non-privileged.

The privileged applicants are named by Article 230 as the member states, the Council and the Commission and following the Treaty of Nice, the EP, who have the right to attack any act.

The semi-privileged applicants is a category first established in case law for the EP by the Court of Justice but extended to the European Central Bank and, following its elevation to a full Community Institution named in Article 7 EC, the Treaty of Amsterdam added the Court of Auditors, who have the right to challenge acts of the Council and Commission but only for the purpose of protecting their prerogatives. The term 'protection of prerogatives' is one which was essentially developed in case law and means 'where their interests are clearly affected'. See, for example, Case 138/79 *Maizena (Roquette Freres) v Council* as confirmed in Case C-70/88 *EP v Council* (Chernobyl) and more recently in Case C-295/90 *EP v Council* (Students Residence Directive) in which the challenge to the legal base used by the Council was successful. This limited right of challenge is now confirmed in Article 230. The original *locus standi* reflected the original much lesser and limited law-making and participatory role of the EP in the Community.

All other persons are non-privileged applicants, who must satisfy certain conditions before their right of access to the Court of First Instance will be recognized.

6.4.2 Admissibility for Non-privileged Applicants

Article 230(4) provides three situations where non-privileged applicants can bring actions for judicial review. It provides:

Any natural or legal person may, under the same conditions, institute proceedings against a decision addressed to that person or against a decision which, although in the form of a regulation or a decision addressed to another person, is of direct and individual concern to the former.

6.4.2.1 Decisions addressed to the Applicant

Where the applicant is directly addressed they will have automatic standing and this is most likely to occur in specific circumstances where, for example, the applicant has been the subject of a Decision of the Commission under the competition rules of Articles 81 and 82 and Regulation 1/2003 (see cases in Chapter 8). For the purposes of the addressee mounting a challenge, there is no barrier to admissibility providing the time limit has been observed.

6.4.2.2 Decisions in the form of a Regulation

This becomes the first part of two part test, showing that the Regulation is really a Decision and then it has to be shown that it is of direct and individual concern to the applicant, although it is rarely dealt with in this clear progression by the Court in the case law. The application can fail at any or all of these hurdles and if 'individual' is considered first and found to be wanting, the other two considerations become irrelevant.

6.4.2.3 A Decision addressed to 'Another Person'

'Another person' has been held in Case 25/62 *Plaumann v Commission* to include Decisions addressed to the member states and not just other individuals, in which case they too have to be shown to be of direct and individual concern to the applicant.

6.4.3 Challenging a Regulation

6.4.3.1 The General Rule

The starting point or general rule is that an individual cannot challenge a Regulation because true Regulations are directly and generally applicable. They are so-called normative acts which apply to everyone in the Community (in theory—not everybody of course is necessarily interested in the regulation of some of the finer aspects of the CAP such as the organization of lupins!). In view of Article 249, this general rule makes sense. This higher status of Regulations has been recognized in the CT and designated as 'legislative acts' to demonstrate that really Regulations are to be regarded and protected as 'primary law', which because of its general applicability should not be so easily contested by anyone affected by it. This issue will be considered in further detail below.

In Case 17/62 *Fruit and Vegetable Confederation v Commission* it was held:

The essential characteristics of a decision arise from the limitation of the persons to whom it is addressed, whereas a regulation, being essentially of a legislative nature, is applicable, not to a limited number of persons, defined and identifiable, but to categories of persons viewed abstractly and in their entirety.

Therefore it is the nature and content of a provision that is the determining factor and not the form or label it is given.

In Case 6/68 *Zuckerfabrik Watenstedt v Council*, the Court of Justice held:

A measure does not lose its character as a normative act because the factual situation to which it applies makes it possible to identify, more or less accurately, the persons affected. A regulation applies to objectively determined situations and produces legal effects with regard to categories of persons defined in a general and abstract manner.

In other words, being able to see clearly whom a Regulation specifically affects does not actually deprive it of its general character, which means we have to find some different or unusual characteristic in order for an applicant to stand out and be able to challenge it. Case 789/79 *Calpak* is also often cited as support for the general rule in similar language as used in *Zuckerfabrik Watenstedt* above.

There are a number of reasons why this general rule does not apply. A lot of the case law considered under these exceptions are also ones helping us understand the term 'individual concern' which must also be determined, so that often the same case and facts are cited as satisfying, or not, both legal points. Also as noted above, 'individual' may well be considered first as it was in the leading Case 25/62 *Plaumann*.

6.4.3.2 The Exceptions

The closed group category. The closed group enables the identity of the natural or legal persons affected to be fixed and thus ascertainable. In Case 41–44/70 *International Fruit Company v Commission*, a group of Fruit Importers were held entitled to challenge a Regulation where the identity of the natural of legal persons affected was already known and thus fixed and identifiable. Apple importers had applied in advance for import licences and the decision to issue a limited quantity of licences was made on the basis of applications previously received, therefore finite and known. The Regulation was a response to the individuals. No new persons could be added at the time of challenge or thereafter to the list of applicants. Hence then the application was held to be admissible as the Regulation was thus the equivalent of a bundle of Decisions each addressed to an applicant. See also Case C-152/88 *Sofrimport v Commission* concerning a Regulation restricting the import of Chilean apples which was adopted whilst some apples were in transit and of which the Commission was specifically notified to take into account when the ban was enacted. Sofrimport were thus part of a closed group of companies with goods in transit when the Regulation was adopted and which could not be added to. They were thus individually concerned and the application was held to be admissible without a real discussion of whether the Regulation was a disguised Decision. Similar thinking was also employed in considering individual concern below and there is a fair degree of overlap within these issues. Case 62/70 *Bock* and Cases 106 and 107/63 *Töpfer* are also often cited in support of this point.

Where the applicant is named in the regulation. Alternatively where the applicant is named in the Regulation, as in Case 139/80 *Maizena v Council* (aka Roquette Frères), the action will be held to be of direct and individual concern. The Court of Justice held that despite being a measure of general application, certain individuals may challenge Regulations as if they were Decisions, especially when one of the Articles of the Regulation specifically referred to the applicant companies. Cases in this category very often satisfy the next two categories where, as a result of a complaint made by a company about the activities of another company which appear to breach competition or anti-dumping rules, the applicant is named in the regulation or which complaint leads to the enactment of a Regulation as a response to that complaint, the applicant will obtain standing in respect of that Regulation.

Where the applicant has played a part in the issue of legislation. A number of cases considered in the next category are often concerned with alleged breaches of competition law by other companies or the dumping of goods on the Community market. The applicants are the ones who have made a complaint to the Commission which provoked the Commission to take action and issue a Regulation seeking to correct the situation. The applicant is thus the individual concerned and able to challenge the Regulation as in Case 264/82 *Timex* or in Case C-358/89 *Extramet*, where the applicant was involved in the preliminary investigations by the Commission.

Anti-Dumping Regulations (seen as hybrid Regulations/decisions). In the particular area of anti-dumping measures, where as a result of an investigation of individual importers a general Regulation is issued to catch all imports, applicants have been more successful than normal because the Regulations are regarded as hybrid Regulation decisions. In the Case 264/82 *Timex v Commission*, the Timex company had complained about dumping which led to an anti-dumping Regulation which was nevertheless held to be of direct and individual concern to Timex. See also Case C-358/89 *Extramet Industrie v Council* in which the Court had accepted the special circumstances which were that the company was the largest import and end user of Calcium from China and the Soviet Union and the only other supplier was a competitor. A ban on Calcium import would have affected it severely. The company was also involved in the Commission investigations. As such the Court was able to recognize its standing. Given the factors in *Extramet*, it would have qualified under the other categories above also.

Direct and individual concern. Once it has been demonstrated that the Regulation was really a decision, the applicant is still required to satisfy the tests of direct and individual concern, however, individual concern can also be regarded in its own right as one of the exceptions in this category because logically if individual concern is proved and the case concerns a Regulation, a normative or general legal instrument, the conclusion must be that it must be a decision as far as the applicant is concerned as the enquiry is the same for both tests. The *Extramet* case, above, would fit into this argument as does Case C-309/89 *Codorniu v Council* (Spanish Wine Producers) involving a Regulation limiting the use of the term 'Cremant'. Despite the Court of

Justice confirming that the Regulation was a legislative measure applying to traders in general, it could still be of individual concern to one of them. Codorniu had distinguished themselves by the ownership of a trademark for the term Cremant from the year 1924, which the Community had tried to reserve for French and Luxembourg producers. Codorniu were able to challenge a Regulation which prevented their use of a registered trade mark 'Gran Cremant di Cordorniu' as this fact isolated them from other wine producers who had not registered this term and were similarly restricted from using the name. Hence it was a Regulation for some or most but it was a decision for *Cordoniu.*

6.4.4 Direct and Individual Concern

Decisions addressed to other people or decisions in the form of regulations are only challengeable if they concern the applicant directly and individually.

6.4.4.1 Direct Concern

With direct concern, the general rule is that if a member state is granted discretion to act under the provision than the provision cannot by its nature give rise to direct concern. This was certainly the initial view taken by the Court of Justice in Case 25/62 *Plaumann and* Case 69/69 *Alcan.* Also a good example, Case 62/70 *Bock v Commission* (Chinese Mushrooms) involved the authorization for a member state to restrict imports, i.e. it had the discretion. An application was made by Bock to import Chinese mushrooms but been refused by Germany on 11 September and only authorized by the Commission on 15 September. Hence the Decision was a retroactive measure in direct response to the application from Bock who was therefore held to be directly concerned. The discretion to act was already waived.

This trend was continued in Case 11/82 *Piraiki-Patraiki v Commission* in which the French authorities applied for and were authorized to impose quotas on yarn imports from Greece. In considering an application to review this decision, the Court of Justice held that where interested parties could be identified with certainty or a high degree of probability, direct concern would be satisfied, despite the theoretical discretion on the part of the member state. In other words, the country applied for permission to restrict imports and the Commission had granted it, so whilst in theory the country had the discretion to restrict import or not, in reality, it had already exercised and thus extinguished that discretion.

6.4.4.2 Individual Concern

Individual concern has been very hard to demonstrate and has often been tested by the Court of Justice first or at the same time as direct concern to decide admissibility, as in the leading and still very much valid judgment of Case 25/62 *Plaumann v Commission*. A Decision was addressed to the German Government refusing permission to reduce duties on clementines, which was challenged by Plaumann. The test decided for individual concern was whether the decision affects the applicant by virtue of the fact that he is member of the abstractly defined class addressed by the rule, for example, because he is a importer of clementines, or does it affect him because of attributes peculiar to him which differentiate him from all other persons? Plaumann was held to be one of a class of importers and not therefore individually concerned. The reasoning is that any one could become an importer. In a much more extreme version of this, Case 231/82 *Spijker Kwasten B.V. v Commission*, an import ban was imposed on Chinese brushes. Spijker Kwasten was the only importer in Holland and although had previously requested a licence, it was held that the company could not be individually concerned as the Decision restricting imports was valid for the forward period of the next six months therefore it was possible that others could apply for licences in that period, hence no individual concern.

In Case 106-7/63 *Töpfer v Commission*, it was held that in order to establish individual concern, an applicant must be affected alone or as a member of a fixed and closed class. Töpfer was so identified because the company had applied for a licence prior to a retroactive Commission Decision which empowered the refusal of licences and was therefore identifiable. Similarly, in Case 62/70 *Bock v Commission* the company was individually concerned because of applications made by Bock to import Chinese Mushrooms were refused by Germany on 11 September but the required authorization by the Commission was only passed on 15 September. Hence the Decision was a retroactive measure in direct response to the application from Bock who was held to have a vested legal interest and therefore individually concerned.

From the category of anti-dumping cases, the application for review in Case 26/76 *Metro-SB-Grossmarkte v Commission* was held to be admissible because Metro had a legitimate interest in the Decision aimed at another person. Metro had made a complaint under the Competition Law Regulation and had thus played a part which led to the Decision. Other successful cases include Case C-152/88 *Sofrimport v Commission* concerning a Decision taken to restrict the import of Chilean apples whilst some were in transit and of which the Commission was specifically notified to take into account and Case C-389/89 *Cordoniu v Commission* in which the company had clearly distinguished itself as individually concerned. These latter two cases were also considered under the section dealing with disguised decisions and re-enforce the point made above that demonstrating individual concern serves two tests, *locus standi* and showing a Regulation to be a Decision.

6.4.5 Interests Groups and Party Actions

By their very nature, non-individual applications might expect not to have standing because it would be expected that by definition the application cannot be of individual concern. However, trade associations applications have been recognized in Case T-447–9/93 *AITEC v Commission* where it represented the individual interests of some or all of its members. But in Case T-585/93 *Greenpeace v Commission*, the plea that all individuals with an environmental interest and not just an economic interest in the consequences of a decision should be collectively able to be represented by a group failed. The CFI rejected this view, which was confirmed on appeal in Case C-321/95P by the Court of Justice, that the decision had affected individuals only in an abstract and general fashion and the applicants representing them were thus similarly affected and similarly without standing.

6.4.6 Merits or Grounds for Annulment

Once admissibility has been established the grounds or substantive merits must be proved. These are laid down in Article 230(2) and can often overlap in individual cases.

6.4.6.1 Lack of Competence or Authority

The lack of competence on the part of a institution to adopt a particular measure is really the equivalent of *ultra vires*, i.e. beyond the power to act and concerns the requirement that all measures must have the appropriate legal authority. Article 7 requires each institution to act within the limits of power conferred on it. Case 9/56 *Meroni v High Authority* concerned the successful challenge to decisions taken by the High Authority to whom at the time no delegated decision making powers had been granted. There is a fair degree of overlap with the fourth category—misuse of power. Further examples of this ground include Case C-327/91 *France v Commission*, whereby the Commission exceeded its competence when it concluded an international agreement with the USA because Article 300 EC required it to be concluded by the Council. Case C-57/95 *French Republic v Commission*, involves a French action to annul a Commission 'Communication'. The Court of Justice held that the Commission had no such power to adopt an act imposing new obligations on the member states which was not inherent in the Treaty, thus the Commission lacked competence and the Act was annulled. The most important and clearest of these cases now is probably Case C-378/98 *Germany v EP and Council* (Tobacco Advertising) in which a Directive banning Tobacco Advertising was introduced under a Treaty Article concerned with the completion of the internal market and which was held not to authorize the enactment of legislation concerned primarily with public health. The Directive was annulled.

6.4.6.2 Infringement of an Essential Procedural Requirement

Specific requirements are laid down by Article 253 that all Community secondary law must give reasons and refer to any proposals and opinions made in respect of the provisions. The Court of Justice has held that insufficient or vague or inconsistent reasoning would constitute a breach of this ground. It was held in Case 24/62 *Germany v Commission* (Wine Tariff Quotas) that reasons must contain sufficient details of the facts and figures on which they are based. In Case 139/80 *Roquette and Maizena v Council*, the Council failed to consult the EP as required under Article 43(2). It had asked for an opinion but did not wait long enough for the answer before going ahead with the Regulation, which was subsequently annulled. In Case C-325/91 *France v Commission* it was held that there was a requirement to state the Treaty base, the failure to observe this leading to the annulment of the measure and finally, in Case 17/74 *Transocean Marine Paint Association v Commission*, a measure which is not notified will deprive an applicant the right to protest and to have their views made known or represented to the relevant institution and is thus susceptible to annulment under Article 230.

6.4.6.3 Infringement of the Treaty or any rule relating to its application

This is the most frequently argued ground because it is capable of embracing all errors of Community law, including breaches of general principles or human rights such as non-discrimination, proportionality, legitimate expectation, and right to a fair hearing. In the following cases, the Court of Justice recognized the general principles pleaded. Case 101/76 *KSH v Intervention Board* considered the principle of equality, Case 17/74 *Transocean* was concerned with the right to be heard and Case 112/77 *Töpfer* concerned legitimate expectation and legal certainty. Case C-325/91 *France v Commission* would also be applicable here for infringing a Treaty requirement, which was the requirement to state the Treaty base.

6.4.6.4 Misuse of Power by a Community Institution

The basis of this ground concerns the use of power for the wrong purpose as in the very early Case 8/55 *Federation Charbonniere v High Authority* which held in respect of Article 33 ECSC that the substance of the power must be related to the end result and Case 105/75 *Giuffrida v Council* concerning the appointment of a Community official. This category comes very close to the first one, in that the use of power as the basis of unauthorized action is the equivalent of having no lawful basis for the action undertaken or acting beyond power.

6.4.7 The Effect of a Successful Action and Annulment

Article 231 provides that if the action is well founded, the Court of Justice shall declare the act concerned to be void. Article 231(2) provides that in the case of a Regulation, the Court shall, if it considers this necessary, state which of the parts of a Regulation can be considered as definitive and can sever parts where possible. This means that the Court can specify those parts of the measure which will be annulled and those which may remain in force. In Case C-106/96 *UK v Commission* (Poverty 4), considered above, the Court of Justice held that the Commission lacked the competence to commit the expenditure and the decision in the guise of an advertisement was annulled. However, in view of the fact that much of the expenditure had already taken place, the Court of Justice decided in the interests of legal certainty to exercise the discretion given to it under Article 231 and rule in favour of the payments made or promised.

Article 233 provides that where an act has been declared void, the institutions are obliged to take the necessary measures to comply with the judgment of the Court of Justice. The Court may only annul the act referred to it or dismiss the action but cannot order an institution to pay a sum of money, i.e. fine them.

6.4.8 A Restrictive Approach

The reasons for the difficulties in demonstrating *locus standi* have been subject to much debate and policy factors feature large in this discussion. For example, is there a floodgate policy whereby *locus standi* requirements have been interpreted particularly restrictively by the Court of Justice to reduce the number of cases coming before it and the CFI? Litigants face lengthening delays to justice, thus keeping the number of cases down will help reduce delay. Another argument is the suggestion that there is a desire to promote the Court of Justice more as a supreme Court of the member states and not one directly accessible as a first instance Court for individuals, as was considered in Chapter 5. In this case, it is argued that the national courts are best placed to defend individuals' interests and that if required cases for annulment should be referred by the national courts under Article 234. To some extent both these arguments have been answered by the establishment of the Court of First Instance primarily to handle these cases and which elevates the Court of Justice into the role of an appeal court in relation to these categories of cases. Other arguments revolve around discussions about balancing the interests of the Community and individuals. The decision making procedure in the Community is a much more complex procedure and often the result of compromise which makes legislation more difficult to enact. The inevitable economic choices of the Community are bound to affect individuals and sometimes in an adverse way but they must be allowed to be made otherwise the ability of the Community and Commission to operate would be undermined. Individuals actions should not hinder the institutions ability to operate. Comparisons with the member states may be made, that such challenges nationally are also subject to equally tight *locus standi* requirements under the constitutional traditions of the member states which often restrict individual challenges to general legislative measures.

In those areas, by contrast, in which individuals find it easier to achieve standing such as competition law, state aids and anti-dumping measures, it may be argued that the very often closer involvement of particular individuals makes the difference. The applicants are likely to be the ones involved in the process by informing the Commission of certain situations or can be seen clearly to be affected by the measures complained about. This then sets them apart from the many other challenges, arising most frequently against legislative decisions made under the Common Agricultural Policy. Furthermore, there are those cases which arise from the application of retroactive legislation where the applicants are seen clearly as belonging to a fixed and identifiable group and which would suffer an injustice if not allowed standing. In other words, the system works well when it needs to.

However, arguments for a more liberalized test were most clearly made by Advocate General Jacobs in Case C-50/00 *Union des Pequeños Agricultores (UPA) v Council*, influenced by the adoption of a, as yet, non-binding charter of fundamental rights into the EC legal order under which individuals are entitled to expect an effective judicial remedy. It was argued that the Article 230 restrictive *locus standi* test leads to a possible denial of justice under the current system because the law for individuals is complex and unpredictable. Introducing a less strict test would fit in with a general tendency to extend the scope of judicial protection in response to the growth of powers of the Community. Hence then the suggestion that applicants should be regarded as individually concerned where, by reason of his/her particular circumstances, the measure has, or is liable to have, a substantial adverse effect on his interests.

The CFI followed AG Jacob's test in Case T-177/01 *Jego-Quere v Commission* in which it held that to give rise to standing, the measure must affect the applicant's legal position in a manner which is both definite and immediate, by restricting his or her rights or imposing obligations on him or her. The Court of Justice, however, in Case 50/00 *UPA* did not adopt Jacob's test or approve the new test provided by the CFI, upholding the status quo for *locus standi* and making clear that the test established in Case 25/62 *Plaumann* remains valid and applicable. Furthermore, it stated in the appeal Case C-263/02 P *Commission v Jego-Quere*, that any revision to the standing rules was not for the Court to do, but for the member states in the context of a Treaty amendment. Thus it overturned the CFI decision, which it held had erred in law.

In Case C-167/02 *Willi Rothley and Others v European Parliament*, a plea for standing based on the right to judicial protection was dismissed by the Court of Justice which stated that protection is still available through an Article 234 reference raising a question of the validity of Community law, although, as was noted in Chapter 5 and below, there is no guarantee that such a reference will either be made by the national court nor accepted by the Court of Justice. The overall picture remains that of a continuing restrictive *locus standi* for applicants under Article 230 although indirect alternatives are available to individuals, albeit with mixed success, which are considered next.

6.4.9 Alternatives to Article 230

6.4.9.1 A Reference under Article 234

The first alternative as noted above, is a reference from a national court to the Court of Justice for a preliminary ruling on the validity of acts of the institutions which is a question that must be referred, see Case 314/85 *Firma Foto-Frost v Hauptzollamt Lübeck-Ost*. In general terms, actions under Article 234 avoid the strict time limits of Article 230 and are instead subject to the national time limits. For example, the challenge to the Commission Regulations in Case 101/76 *KSH* had failed when raised directly before the Court of Justice but was successful when made within an Article 234 reference in Cases 103 and 145/77 before the UK courts. However, Article 234 cannot be used simply to get round the time limits of Article 230 and in Case C-188/92 TWD *Textilwerke Deggendorf GmbH v Germany*, the Court of Justice held that the time limits in Article 230 apply equally to national court proceedings and Article 234 rulings on invalidity and references will be barred if the applicant would undoubtedly have had standing under Article 230 but failed to take advantage of it within the time limit.

There are further difficulties or requirements facing individuals wishing to raise a question of validity via Article 234. There needs to be an element of national law to be able to raise a matter before the national courts. The use of Article 234 as an alternative has been heavily criticized by AG Jacobs in Case 50/00 *UPA*, who argued that that justice would be better served if access to the Court of Justice under Article 230 were made easier to individuals. An Article 234 reference also increases the time involved in getting an answer by about two years and may lead to contrived cases being concocted in the national courts in order to challenge Community legislation. Finally, the national court retains the discretion whether to refer or not and may not consider a reference necessary. Hence then Article 234 as an alternative is a very uncertain and unpredictable one.

6.4.9.2 The Plea of Illegality—Article 241

If there are other proceedings taking place before the Court of Justice, a party can raise an issue of illegality of a Community Regulation but only indirectly or incidentally and not as an independent cause of action. Thus, Article 241 is not simply a second chance to get around the strict time or *locus standi* limits of Article 230, it is designed to overcome the strict *locus standi* requirements for private parties in cases that would otherwise be unjust.

Although Article 241 appears to be restricted to Regulations, the Court of Justice has held in Case 92/78 *Simmenthal v Commission* that the action would also cover acts which produce similar effects but were not in the form of a Regulation on the grounds that individuals should be given the chance to have reviewed implementing decisions which are of direct and individual concern, thus echoing the *locus standi* requirements under Article 230.

The grounds in the action are the same as Article 230. The effects are a declaration of inapplicability of the general act contested and an annulment of the individual decision due to illegality. It is considered in further detail below.

6.4.9.3 Action for Damages under Articles 235 and 288(2)

The action under Article 230 only annuls the act and does not provide compensation for a damaged but successful applicant, therefore damages must be pursued under Article 288 as a follow on action. However, the Article 288 action is a separate and autonomous action and not dependant on an earlier Article 230 or Article 234 action, see Case 4/69 *Lütticke v Commission*. Therefore it could be commenced without pursuing an Article 230 action first and the legality of a measure alleged to have injured the plaintiff may be put in question indirectly under Article 241, noted above. Article 288 will be also considered in detail below.

6.4.10 The Constitutional Treaty

The Constitutional Treaty does two things which, if it enters into force, has a bearing on this topic. First under Article I-29, it provides that 'member states shall provide rights of appeal sufficient to ensure effective legal protection in the fields covered by Union law' which reinforces the argument that the Court of Justice should not be a court of direct access but that matters be filtered first by the national courts. Secondly, the new Article III-365 CT provides that:

Any natural or legal person may institute proceedings . . . against an act addressed to that person or which is of direct and individual concern to him or her, and against a regulatory act which is of direct concern to him or her and does not entail implementing measures.

This relaxes the requirement in respect of regulatory acts not requiring implementing measures, by which it is assumed, administrative acts in the new reorganization of Community legal instruments under Articles I-33–I-37. Thus it makes no change to the challenge to what are now known as Regulations which are general legislative acts.

6.5 Action for Failure to Act (Article 232)

Article 232 concerns actions against the EP, the Council or the Commission for a failure to act and constitutes an attempt to compel the institution or institutions concerned to take action. The unlawfulness of the institution is the failure to act in violation of a Treaty duty, which clearly presupposes that there was a duty imposed on the institution to act in the first place. It complements an Article 230 action and can be pleaded at the same time. In Case 15/70 *Chevalley v Commission*, the Court of Justice held it was not necessary to state which action was the subject of the application. There are a number of similar features between the two articles, but they were designed to cover different situations: Article 230; illegal action and Article 232; illegal inaction. Both provisions, however, have as their objective the ending of a situation of illegality. Both actions are also similar in respect of the institutions which may be challenged, originally only the Commission and the Council but the TEU formally extended the right of challenge under Article 232 to the EP and the ECB within its field of competence. Actions are heard at first instance by the CFI.

6.5.1 Admissibility and *Locus Standi*

6.5.1.1 Privileged Applicants

The Community institutions and member states have, under Article 232(1) a privileged right of action which is not subject to restrictions on admissibility, and although not express, it was implicit that the EP is a privileged applicant, as confirmed by Case 13/83 *EP v Council* (Transport Policy) in which it was established that the privileged applicants can request actions requiring general legislative acts as well as decisions without having to show any special interest. The ECB was given the right to take action by the TEU in areas falling within its field of competence.

6.5.1.2 Non-privileged Applicants

Individuals on the other hand have a restricted right of *locus standi* under Article 232

(3) and more so than under Article 230 because there is no equivalent of directly and individually concerned:

Any natural or legal person may, under the conditions laid down in the preceding paragraphs, complain to the Court of Justice that an institution of the Community has failed to address that person any act other that a recommendation or an opinion.

It was established by case law that to challenge under Article 232, an individual must have been legally entitled to make a claim for action as a potential addressee, see Case 246/81 *Lord Bethell v EC Commission*, involving a complaint of a failure to act on price fixing by the airlines. In the case though, any potential act would be addressed to the airlines and not Lord Bethell. This strict view on the *locus standi* requirements has been tempered by the Court of Justice in subsequent cases and now the requirements are analogous to the direct and individual concern of Article 230 (see Case C-68/95 *T. Port v Bundesanstalt für Landeswirtschaft und Ernährung*) in that a potential act would have concerned an individual in the same way.

6.5.2 Acts Subject to an Article 232 Action

In many cases, the Court of Justice has rejected applications by individuals for measures of general legislative content, see Case 15/70 *Chevalley v Commission* and Case 42/71 *Nordgetreide v Commission*, in which it was held that applications are restricted to decisions. Regulations cannot be requested because by their nature they are not capable of being addressed to specific individuals only. There must be an obligation under the Treaty to adopt a reviewable act which is enforceable on the part of the institution. A demand for an opinion is not admissible (Case 15/70 *Chevally v Commission*). Case 13/83 *EP v Council* (Transport Policy) holds though that the acts requested need not be spelt out in detail but must be sufficiently identified.

6.5.3 Procedural Requirements

6.5.3.1 The Invitation to Act

There is a preliminary procedural step which must be taken before court action can ensue. Article 232 (2) provides 'The action shall be admissible only if the institution concerned has first been called upon to act.' The applicant must request the institution to take a specific action as legally required and advise that failure to do so will result in a court action under Article 232. The invitation to act need not follow any precise form to qualify for the purposes of Article 232. Only if the institution fails to define its position within the two-month period can the matter be brought before the Court. The application to the Court of Justice must be made within a further two-month period from the end of the initial two-month period. If the institution complies with the request to act as in Case 302/87 *EP v Council* (Comitology), the Court of Justice will not allow the action to proceed.

6.5.3.2 Definition of Position

This requirement has been seen to defeat most actions because where the institution has explained its refusal to act, i.e. defined its position, the action is inadmissible. In Case 48/65 *Lütticke v Commission*, the applicants had requested the Commission to take action against the German Federal Republic regarding a breach of Community law. The Commission was of the opinion that there had been no breach so therefore refused to take action but also notified the applicant of this. The Court of Justice declared the application inadmissible on the grounds that the notification of the refusal was a definition of position. In Case 8/71 *Deutscher Komponistenverband (German Composers Group) v Commission*, a complaint that a decision taken by the Commission was wrong does not allow an applicant to proceed under Article 232 on the basis that the right decision was not taken by Commission, i.e. it had failed to act in the right way. In Case 125/78 *Gema v Commission*, a competition law complaint was made to the Commission under Regulation 17 (now replaced by Regulation 2003/1) about Radio Luxembourg. When the Commission failed to take any action, GEMA attempted an Article 232 action against the Commission. It was held that the letter from the Commission to GEMA stating its decision not to take action was a sufficient definition of position to defeat GEMA's action. Until Case 13/83 *European Parliament v Council* (Transport Policy), a declaration by an institution of its unwillingness to act was regarded by some as constituting a sufficient definition of position for the purposes of the Court of Justice. However, the Court in the Transport case stated that 'In the absence of taking a formal act, the institution called upon to define its position must do more than reply stating its current position which in effect neither denies or admits the alleged failure nor reveals the attitude of the defendant institution to the demanded measures.'

6.5.3.3 The Substantive Action

In the Transport Policy case (above) the EP had complained that the Council had failed in its Treaty obligations under Articles 3, 61, 74, 75, and 84 (now 3, 51, 70, 71, and 80) to introduce a common policy for transport, lay down a framework for this policy and act on sixteen specific proposals of the Commission. The Court of Justice held with regard to the first claim that because the Treaty requirements were so vague there could not be said to exist sufficiently specific obligations as to amount to a failure to act despite the fact that even as such the obligations should have been completed long ago. The Court held that the obligation of Article 61 (now 51) of the Treaty could be identified with sufficient precision as to constitute a failure on the part of the Council to lay down a framework. The second claim of failure to act on sixteen proposals of the Commission was only successful in respect of the proposals in respect of the freedom to provide services. The other measures were within the greater margin of discretion left to the Council by the Treaty.

6.5.3.4 Results of a Declaration of a Failure to Act

The institution is required under Article 233(1) to take the necessary measures to comply with the judgment of the Court of Justice, within a reasonable time. A continued failure to act would of course be actionable under Article 232. As with Articles 226 and 228 actions continued intransigence by an institution is insurmountable but politically unlikely. Article 233 states it is without prejudice to any action for damages under Article 288, the action which is considered next.

6.6 Non-contractual Liability of the EC (Article 288(2))

While the EC Treaty specifically refers contractual liability disputes to the jurisdiction of national courts, Article 235 confers jurisdiction over disputes relating to claims for non-contractual liability damages under Article 288 of the Treaty to the Court of Justice. Article 288(2) requires the Community to make good damage caused by the institutions or servants in the performance of their duties in accordance with the general principles common to the laws of the member states. The term 'non-contractual' is employed to take account of the different legal traditions and to ensure the Community is responsible for all its actions outside of contractual liability. Non-contractual liability thus covers the civil wrongs caused by the legislative and administrative activities of the Community, whether created by the institutions or the servants.

6.6.1 Admissibility/*Locus Standi*

In contrast to Articles 230 and 232 there is not a restrictive *locus standi* imposed on individuals by either Article 235 or 288(2).

6.6.2 Time Limit

There is a five-year limitation period on actions which commences from the occurrence of the event causing the damage (Case 5/71 *Schöppenstedt v Council*) or if not discovered until later, from when the event causing the damage is discovered (Case 145/83 *Adams v Commission*).

6.6.3 The Defendants

In an action against the Community, the appropriate institution should be named as defendant. This can be the Commission or the Council or both who jointly legislate in many areas of Community law, as confirmed by the Court of Justice in Case 63–69/72 *Werhahn v Commission* and indeed now, in view of the greater powers of the EP, also the EP itself, either alone or in connection with the Council of Ministers. Member states would only be sued where they are responsible for the implementation of Community measures and have exceeded the discretion they were given. If there is no discretion on their part, the Commission would be the proper defendant, Case 175/84 *Krohn v Commission*.

6.6.4 An Autonomous or Independent Action

The action for damages has been held by the Court of Justice to be an autonomous form of action having its own particular purpose to fulfil within the Treaty system of remedies, and subject to conditions on its use dictated by its specific nature. In Case 4/69 *Lütticke*, damage had been suffered as a result of the Commission failing to act against Germany. The Commission argued that the action under Article 288 was an attempt to circumvent the *locus standi* requirements of a previous unsuccessful Article 232 action. The Court of Justice rejected this argument and declared that 'the action for damages provided by Articles 235 and 288(2) was established by the Treaty as an independent form of action and whose object was to compensate a party for damage sustained and not to secure the annulment of an illegal measure'. Further, in Case 5/71 *Zuckerfabrik Schöppenstedt v Council*, in an action for damages arising from a Regulation, the Council had argued that the action should be ruled inadmissible because to allow it would frustrate the system of judicial remedies provided by the Treaty by allowing a challenge to a Regulation not allowable under Article 230, i.e. those applications ruled out as a result of a lack of *locus standi* or outside of the short time limit. This was firmly rejected by the Court of Justice. Therefore little difficulty faces applicants in respect of admissibility, the problem lies in proving an act of the Community caused damage and was a sufficiently serious breach.

6.6.5 The Requirements of Liability

Under the EC Treaty, the liability of the Community is to be determined in accordance with the general principles common to the laws of the member states. When the Court of Justice looks to national laws for guidance and general principles, as in other instances of this practise, is not required to accept the lowest common denominator but makes a comparative review and selects principles of law appropriate to the situation. Therefore a body of Community law is being built up in this area. From the case law, requirements have been identified to establish liability for the purpose of Article 288(2) that the Community is liable either (i) for damage caused by one of its institutions or (ii) for damage caused by its servants in the performance of their duties. There must be a wrongful act or omission on the part of the Community which has breached a duty, the applicant must have suffered damage and there must be a causal link between the act or omission and the damage.

6.6.6 The Standard of Liability and Fault

Liability can be imposed for not only administrative acts or omissions but also to legislative acts such as Regulations, Directives, or Decisions. Liability can thus be incurred as a result of failures of administration, the negligence of employees of the institutions in the performance of their duties but not extending to personal faults of employees, and the adoption of invalid legal acts. The act or omission of the Community must be shown to be wrongful, however the degree of wrongfulness or fault varies depending on whether the wrong was committed was the result of an administrative act, an act of one the employees or resulted from a legislative act.

6.6.6.1 Administrative Acts

While a requirement of fault is not express from the Treaty, case law indicates it is necessary for the establishment of liability for damage caused by administrative Acts. In Case 14/60 *Meroni*, the Court of Justice ruled that the liability is based on fault in that there must be negligence in the administration or construction of a scheme of regulation for Ferrous Scrap before there can be liability when the scheme malfunctions. The Court of Justice held that the mere existence of errors in the administration of the scheme is not in itself evidence of a wrongful act or omission, since they might be caused by the fact that the problems tackled by the scheme are difficult to resolve. In Cases 19, 20, 25, and 30/69 *Richez Parise*, the Commission had supplied wrong information to its staff about pensions rights. This information was based on an incorrect interpretation of the rules concerning rights they could claim on the termination of their service. The Court of Justice held that only in exceptional circumstances would an incorrect interpretation constitute a wrongful act. However, in this case the Commission was at fault by failing promptly to remedy the error of interpretation as soon as it became obvious that their interpretation was erroneous. Therefore their failure to issue a correction within a reasonable time was of such nature as to render the Commission liable.

There is a notorious case in Community law concerning the liability of the Community institutions in respect of acts of its servants.[4] Case 145/83 *Stanley Adams v Commission* concerned the liability of the Community for a breach of the duty of care owed to its informants in the sphere of competition law. Adams claimed a breach of confidence of information by releasing documents by which Hoffman la Roche could identify Adams as the person blowing the whistle when they were investigated and fined under competition law. Article 287 EC imposes a duty on members of staff of institutions not to disclose information covered by professional secrecy. It was held that the Commission remained under a duty not to reveal its source even when Adams left his employment. Hoffmann la Roche discovered his identity and the Swiss Public Prosecutor was informed. Adams was tried in his absence and convicted of industrial espionage, which is a criminal offence in Switzerland. The Commission was aware of the risk that Adams would be identified by handing over documents and failed to tell Adams of the threats to prosecute the informant. On return to Switzerland Adams was arrested and jailed. His wife who was suffering from depression committed suicide when informed about a possible 20-year jail sentence for her husband. The Commission was held liable to make good the damage resulting from the discovery of the applicant's identity but Adams had been held to have contributory negligence by not informing Commission he could be identified from documents and failing to ask Commission to keep him informed of progress. The *Adams* case is an illustration of the rules relating to duty, vicarious liability, causation and contributory negligence.

6.6.6.2 Liability for Employees

The possibility of vicarious liability for employees was raised in Case 9/69 *Sayag v Leduc*, in which Mr Sayag was employed by EURATOM and whilst showing guests of the Community round in his own car was involved in an accident in which his passengers were injured. It was held the Commission was not liable because it was not an official act of the Community, 'the Community is only liable for those acts of its servants which, by virtue of an internal and direct relationship, are the necessary extension of the tasks entrusted to the institutions of the Community'. There was also

---

[4] There has even been a film on this: *A Song For Europe/A Crime of Honour*, 1985, directed by John Goldschmidt.

the possible policy reason that the person's own insurance would in any event cover the damage. The scope of liability was thus limited to activities of institutions or the performance of institutional tasks.

6.6.6.3 Liability for Legislative Acts

The principle that there can be liability on the part of the institutions for damage resulting from the adoption of legislative acts was confirmed in Case 5/71 *Schöppenstedt v Council* but the Court of Justice has laid down a strict test, which has been repeated often. In the case, the plaintiffs claimed that a Regulation breached the principle of non-discrimination in Article 34(2) (old 40)(3). 'The community does not incur liability on account of a legislative measure which involves choices of economic policy unless a sufficiently flagrant violation of a superior rule of law for the protection of the individual has occurred.' In *Schöppenstedt*, it was held discrimination was a superior rule of law but that it had not been breached.

The reasoning for the strict test is very similar to the strict requirements for *locus standi* for Article 230 in that the high degree of discretion that the institutions need to carry out the economic tasks they must carry out, necessarily affects many persons, hence then the imposition of a higher burden when choices of economic policy are involved. Therefore it is not just unlawful conduct that will attract liability, but it is the degree of unlawful conduct required under the formula developed by the Court of Justice. All types of legislative act can be subject to an action under Article 288(2).

The formula can be divided into two parts although in some treatments it is divided into three parts as follows:

(a) a violation or breach of superior rule of law (which can be linked with the next part)

(b) the rule must exist for the protection of natural or legal persons and

(c) the violation must have been sufficiently serious.

The rules of law covered. The rules of law include specific legal rules contained in legislation, fundamental rights and general principles. The principles of proportionality, legal certainty, equality/discrimination, and legitimate expectation seem most often to be raised.[5]

The Treaty article in *Schöppenstedt* was regarded as a superior rule of law. Article 34 (2) provides that the CAP and measures taken under it 'shall exclude any discrimination between producers or consumers within the Community' In Case 64/76 *Dumortier Freres v Commission* (Gritz and Quellmehl), the ending of a subsidy was held to be

---

[5] All of these are discussed in Chapter 3.

a breach because it was retained on starch which was is direct competition (see also Case 83/76 *HNL* and Cases 103 and 145/77 *KSH v Council and Commission* (Royal Scholten Holdings)) which are also often cited in respect of the same rule of law.

The protection of the individual. The protection of the individual which includes either natural and legal persons has been interpreted to include the protection of classes of persons also as with the importers in Case 5, 7, 13, and 24/66 *Kampfmeyer.* In Case 74/74 *CNTA v Commission,* involving the general principle of legitimate expectation, the Commission was held liable to pay compensation for losses incurred as a result of a Regulation which abolished with immediate effect and without warning the application of compensatory amounts, as a serious breach of the principle of legitimate expectation, which was designed to provide individual protections.

The breach must be sufficiently serious. This is required because it is a challenge to a economic policy choice of the Community involving exercise of wide discretion. So whilst a breach of an important rule of law which is hierarchically superior to more general rules of law is required, a mere breach is not sufficient to trigger liability. A sufficiently flagrant or serious breach is required. In Cases 83/76 *HNL v Commission,* a Regulation requiring cattlefood manufacturers to use more expensive skimmed milk than cheaper soya in their foods (to use up the 'milk lake') was held to be invalid and declared null and void because it offended the principles of proportionality and discrimination (Art 34(2) (old 40(3)). However, whilst in the Article 288 action, the breach was acknowledged, it was held not to be a sufficiently serious or flagrant breach. Almost inevitably in the regulation of the CAP and particular food products a legislative decision by the Commission to allow or restrict the production will affect, often adversely, the economic position of individual farmers. To permit them to succeed in an actions for damages each time would completely undermine any attempt to control the market. The Commission and Community would be rendered useless. In *HNL* the Court held 'The legislative authority . . . cannot always be hindered in making its decisions by the prospect of applications for damages whenever it has occasion to adopt legislative measures in the public interest which may adversely affect the interests of individuals.' Thus liability is incurred only where there has been a manifest and grave disregard of the limits on the exercise of their powers. This was itself later interpreted in Cases 103 and 145/77 *KSH v Council and Commission* as conduct verging on the arbitrary.

Preliminary rulings in Cases 117/76 and 16/77 *Rucksdeschel* and Case 124/76 and 20/77 *Moulins de Pont a Mousson* (Maize, Gritz, and Quellmehl cases) had held that Regulations providing higher production refunds for Maize Starch than Maize Gritz were incompatible with Article 34(2) and thus invalid. New lower refunds had been set for Maize Gritz and the companies claimed damages. The question was had the

Council of Ministers manifestly and gravely disregarded the limits of power? Thus in the cases known collectively as the 'Maize, Gritz, and Quellmehl cases',[6] the ECJ held that the Council had manifestly and gravely disregarded the limits of power because:

1. Article 34(2) (old 40(3)) was important protection of individuals.

2. Only a small defined and closed group of commercial applicants were affected.

3. The damage must be over and above economic risks normal in business.

4. The equality of treatment ended without sufficient justification.

5. The Council ignored a Commission proposal.

The *Quellmehl* cases had the same result with regard to a discriminatory treatment by the Commission of Maize Starch and Quellmehl, both products used in the baking industry. In both cases, damages plus interest were awarded.

Another product specific series of cases dealt with the production of isoglucose, an artificial sweetener which competed with sugar. It was heavily penalized by a Regulation later annulled but the consequence was that the producers had already suffered massive losses including some producers going out of business. Their claims for losses failed as the breaches were not 'verging on the arbitrary'! Factors which influence the Court of Justice in its determination of whether the breach is sufficiently serious is the effect of the breach and the manner or nature of the breach. The effect of measure relates to its scope, the number of people affected and the damage caused. Other important factors are whether there is a higher Community public interest involved and the numbers involved. Previously it was considered that only a small defined and closed group of applicants could successfully pursue a claim (see Case 152/88 *Sofrimport*) and if large numbers were involved this would defeat a claim but in Cases C-104/89 and 37/90 *Mulder v Council*, the Court of Justice suggested that a large group of applicants need not be fatal to a claim. The presence of a large group of claimants did not defeat a claim although a serious breach still had to be demonstrated and that there was no higher public interest of the Community involved.

6.6.7 The Damage

Having established the existence of an act or omission attributable to the Community, damage to the applicant must be proved. Damage can be purely economic as in Cases 5, 7, 13, and 24/66 *Kampfmeyer* involving a cancellation fee and loss of profits but this

---

[6] *The Maize Gritz and Quellmehl cases* (64 and 113/76, 239/78, 25, 27, and 28/79 *Dumortier Frères v Council*, 241, 242, 245–50/78 *DGV v Commission and Council* [1979] ECR 3017, Case 238/78 *Ireks Arkady v Commission and Council* [1979] ECR 2955, 261 and 262/78 *Interquell v Commission and Council* [1979] ECR 3045).

must be specified and not speculative, or damage can take the form of be moral damage 110/63 *Willame v Commission*. In Case 74/74 *CNTA*, compensation for the losses caused by a sudden change to export refunds contrary to the legitimate expectations of the company was upheld although in the case itself, currency fluctuations meant that no actual loss was recorded.

It has been held that the damage must be over and above the risk of damage normal in business (see Case 64/76 *Dumortier Frères v Council*). In Case C-152/88 *Sofrimport v EC Commission* concerned with Chilean apples in transit, import licences were suspended whilst the cargo was on the high seas. The applicants in *Sofrimport* were successful in obtaining damages because of the complete failure of the Commission to take into account the interests of the applicants when they were required to do so and which therefore amounted to a sufficiently serious breach of legitimate expectation. The damage went beyond the limits of economic risk inherent in business.

6.6.8 The Causal Connection

Lastly, it must be shown that the act of the Community caused the damage. There must be a sufficiently direct connection between the act and the injury. The damages must be ascertainable, Cases 5, 7, 13, and 24/66 *Kampffmeyer*. In Cases 64, 113/76 *Dumortier Frères v the Council* (*Gritz and Quellmehl*) it was held there was no need to make good every harmful consequence especially where remote. Damage must be a sufficiently direct consequence of the unlawful conduct of the institution concerned. In Case 169/73 *Compagnie Continentale Française* it was held that the causal link was only established if the misleading information given would have caused an error in the mind of a reasonable person. In Case 132/77 *Sugar Export*, it was held that the chain of causation may be broken by independent act of third party.

In summary, the damage must be certain, specific, proven, and quantifiable and it may cover imminent foreseeable damage, and lost profits Cases 5, 7, 13–24/66 *Kampffmeyer*

6.6.9 Concurrent Liability/Choice of Court

For the most part the application of Community legislative measures, especially in the agricultural sector, are actually administered and thus dependant on the national intervention agencies who make payments and receive payments. However, if a claim is based on a Community act that was wrongful, the question of whether a national court or the Court of Justice arises. Where claim involves return of sums unlawfully paid to national authorities, compensation must be sought from the national authorities before the national courts followed if necessary by a reference under the Article 234 procedure (Cases 5, 7, 13, and 24/66 *Kampffmeyer*). It is only really the conduct of the institutions or servants that would require application to the Court of Justice or where the claims are for unliquidated damages, that is, those involving loss of profits suffered as a result of illegal Community action, Case 74/74 *CNTA*. See also the Case 175/84 *Krohn v Commission*.

6.7 The Plea of Illegality (Article 241)

This action provides a right to plead the illegality of a Community Regulation in different circumstances from the direct challenge of Article 230.

Article 241 reads:

Notwithstanding the expiry of the period laid down in the fifth paragraph of Article 230, any party may, in proceedings in which a Regulation adopted jointly by the European Parliament and the Council, or a Regulation of the Council, of the Commission, or of the ECB is at issue, plead the grounds specified in the second paragraph of Article 230, in order to invoke before the Court of Justice the inapplicability of that Regulation.

Article 241 is not an independent or direct cause of action to the Court of Justice, as confirmed in Case 33/80 *Renato Albini v Council and Commission* and Cases 31 and 33/62 *Wöhrmann v Commission*. The Court of Justice held that Article 241 was only available in proceedings already brought before the Court of Justice under some other action and only as an incidental or indirect action. For example, it may be that during the course of an Article 230 challenge to a Decision, it comes to light that another EU act, such as a Regulation, which was the legal base for the Decision, was for some reason unlawful but which was beyond challenge itself due to the time limit or a lack of *locus standi* under Article 230, as considered above. This would provide the grounds under which Article 241 might apply. It cannot be used in Article 288 actions, considered above nor in Article 226 actions against member states.[7]

6.7.1 *Locus Standi*

The Article 241 action is available to any party including it is argued, but without clear authority from the Court of Justice, the member states. However, it is more likely to benefit individuals who for good reason are unable to comply with the *locus standi* and time limit requirements of Article 230. However, it is not designed or intended to provide a backdoor for those who have simply failed to meet the requirements

---

[7] See Case 70/72, *Commission v Federal Republic of Germany*.

of Article 230. In Case 156/77 *Commission v Belgium*, a Community Decision was challenged directly before the Court of Justice, however the Court refused the application because Belgium had allowed its right under Article 230 to expire. Article 241 is designed more for those who either have no rights under Article 230 or were unable to meet the *locus standi* requirements, but who nevertheless are affected by the illegality of a Community Regulation. For example, in Case 216/82 *University of Hamburg v Hauptzollamt Hamburg* the University was able to challenge a Decision addressed to the German Government indirectly before the national court because it was directly and individually concerned by it but because the decision was not published, it was unable to challenge it under Article 230.

6.7.2 Acts which can be Reviewed

Article 241 refers to Regulations only, which can be challenged only if they form the legal basis of the subject matter of the direct action, as in Case 9/56 *Meroni v High Authority*. Article 241 does not envisage the challenge of Decisions or other forms of binding act. However, in Case 92/78 *Simmenthal v Commission*, a Decision was challenged which was based generally on prior Regulations and Notices. The Regulations could not be challenged directly under Article 230 because of the restrictive *locus standi* requirements, but could be challenged indirectly via Article 241. The Court held that it was not the form of the act which is important but the substance, therefore other acts which were normative in effect should be regarded as a Regulation for the purposes of Article 241 and could be challenged under Article 241, thus applying to Notices and Decisions where in substance they have the effect of general or normative acts.

Addressees of an individual act such as a Decision cannot challenge it indirectly in the Court of Justice because they should have done so directly under Article 230 within the time limits. To allow otherwise would render the time limit meaningless as confirmed in Case 156/77 *Commission v Belgium*.

6.7.3 Grounds of Review

The substantive grounds of the action are those listed for Article 230. Case 92/78 *Simmenthal* succeeded on its merits that the general measure had been used for purposes other than which it was intended, i.e. proper purpose.

6.7.4 Effect of a Successful Challenge

The result of such an action is that the Regulation in declared inapplicable in that case and not generally void, see Case 9/56 *Meroni v High Authority*. Any acts based on this voidable Regulation however will be void and withdrawn. Also in practice, the Regulation will not be applied in subsequent cases as is the consequence in Article 234 references, for example, refer to Case 66/80 *ICC*.[8]

6.8 Actions Against Natural or Legal Persons

This category represents the third set of direct actions, this time against legal and natural individuals but is only relevant in certain limited circumstances. The Treaty permits action by the Commission against legal and natural persons to ensure that they comply with Community law. Mainly under the competition rules, the Commission is provided with the possibility of taking a Decision that companies have breached the competition rules and is empowered to fine them, against which there is an appeal to the Court of First Instance with the possibility of a further appeal to the European Court of Justice. Article 229 provides the ECJ with unlimited jurisdiction to review such penalties as may be imposed by the Commission under Community law provisions. The power of the Commission to impose fines is provided by Regulation 1/2003 and under the merger Regulation 139/2004. Note the potential size of the fines. In Case T-51/89 *Tetra Pak Rausing SA v Commission* the company was fined 75 million ECU, which was upheld by the Court of Justice in Case C-333/94-P *Tetra Pak Rausing SA v Commission* and in Commission Decision 98/273, Volkswagen were fined 102 Million ECU which was about £67,000,000 but which was reduced before the Court of First instance to 90 Million ECU in Case T-62/98.

Further reading

Books

HARTLEY, T. *The Foundations of European Community law*, 5th edn., Clarendon Press, Oxford 2003, chapters 10–13 and 15–17.

DOUGLAS-SCOTT, S. *Constitutional Law of the European Union*, Longman, Harlow 2002, chapters 10–12.

Articles

ALBORS-LLORENS, A. 'The Standing of Private Parties to Challenge Community Measures: Has the European Court Missed the Boat?' (2003) 62 *Cambridge Law Journal*, 72–92.

---

[8] Refer though for full details, if needed, to the article by Sinaniotis in further reading.

ARNULL, A. 'Private Applicants and the Action for Annulment since Cororniu' (2001) 38 *CML Rev*, 7.

COOKE, J. 'Locus standi of private parties under Article 173(4)' (1997) 6 *IJEL*, 4–23.

CORTES MARTIN, J. M. 'Ubi ius, ibi remedium?—Locus standi of private applicants under Article 230(4) EC at a European constitutional crossroads' (2004) 11 *Maastricht Journal of European and Comparative Law*, 233–61.

CYGAN, A. 'Protecting the interests of civil society in Community decision-making—the limits of Article 230 EC' (2003) 52 *ICLQ*, 995–1012.

HEDEMANN-ROBINSON, M. 'Article 173 EC, general community measures and locus standi for private persons: still a cause for individual concern?' (1996) 2 *EPL*, 127–56.

HILSON, C. 'The role of discretion in EC law on non-contractual liability' (2005) 42 *CML Rev*, 677–95.

IBA'NEZ, A. J. G. 'Exceptions to Article 226: Alternative Administrative Procedures and the Pursuit of Member States' (2000) 6 *ELJ*, 148.

MASTROIANNI, R. 'The enforcement procedure under Article 169 of the EC Treaty and the powers of the European Commission: quis custodiet custodes?' (1995) 1 *EPL*, 535–9.

RASMUSSON, H. 'Why is Article 173 interpreted against Private Plaintiffs' (1980) 2 *EL Rev*, 112.

RAWLINGS, R. 'Engaged Elites Citizen and Institutional Attitudes in Commission Enforcement' (2000) 6 *ELJ*, 4.

SINANIOTIS, D. 'The Plea of Illegality in EC Law' (2001) 7 *EPL*, 103.

TRIDIMAS, T. 'Liability for Breach of Community law: growing up and mellowing down?' (2001) 38 *CML Rev*, 301.

USHER, J. 'Direct and Individual Concern—an Effective Remedy or a Conventional Solution' (2003) 28 *EL Rev*, 575.

WARD, A. 'Locus standi under Article 230(4) of the EC Treaty: crafting a coherent test for a "wobbly polity"' (2003, 22 *YEL*, 45–77.

Web site

Concerned with monitoring the application of Community law in the member states which includes access to the Annual Reports.

http://europa.eu.int/comm/secretariat_general/sgb/droit_com/index_en.htm

PART II

INTRODUCTION TO THE SUBSTANTIVE LAW OF THE EU

PART II: **INTRODUCTION TO THE SUBSTANTIVE LAW OF THE EU**

As was indicated in the introduction to Part I, Part II of this book, concerned with the substantive law of the EU, is predicated on the study and understanding of the topics covered by Part I of this book. Although it would not be impossible to study the substantive law without it, it would make it more difficult. The subjects chosen for Part II are those most commonly found in EU/EC law courses, covering probably about 95 per cent of all such courses. Since substantive law topic choice is no longer dictated by the Law Society and Bar Council as they appear no longer to have a specific requirement, this gave me a free choice of topics to include. Whilst even previously the Law Society and the Bar Council required that an introduction to the internal market and free movement of goods was to be studied only, most courses understandably included that topic. In addition, most university courses consider the free movement of persons, and now citizenship and many courses also include discrimination law, though some restrict this to discrimination on the grounds of sex. The coverage of competition law is much more varied as it is often taught in specialist courses at undergraduate and postgraduate levels and hence omitted from general courses on EU law or it is introduced only briefly; however, it needs a lot of lectures to do it justice. Nevertheless I thought it useful to include competition law in this book. So the subjects included are the internal market and the free movement of goods, competition law, free movement of persons, and citizenship and equality law but dealing mainly with sex discrimination law. These substantive law topics have been covered in four chapters only, which although is not the most common practice, has the advantage in my view of dealing with all relevant material in one place, thus avoiding sometimes unnecessary division and repetition of material.

In turning to the content of the chapters themselves, the 'freedoms' are clearly part of the wider aims of the Community as expressed in the Treaty preamble, Articles 2 and 3 which seek to 'establish economic and social integration amongst the member states, progression towards which is achieved by the forging of common policies and the establishment of the free movement of certain factors'. By freeing the basic factors of production it is hoped that economic development or expansion will be promoted throughout the Community. The four fundamental factors are the freedom of movement of goods, persons, services, and capital, the latter not being covered in this text. Competition law and social policy, including sex discrimination, fall outside of the four freedoms but are discussed in this text. Competition was, along with Agriculture, a policy of the Community, whereas sex discrimination is included as a part of social law.

There is often an overlap of areas of substantive law which is both inevitable and necessary in the context of the internal market. The fundamental freedoms that must be observed by the member states could never be effective without the ability to ensure that private firms are not able to erect their own barriers to trade by cartels. Hence competition rules are essential to ensure the effectiveness of the laws on the free movement of goods and vice versa. Additionally, the prohibition of discrimination also imposes itself in the other areas of substantive law where appropriate, e.g. within the free movement of persons and free movement of goods. As was also indicated in Chapter 3, the Court of Justice has for a long time referred to the support that must be given to the four freedoms of the Community which it regards as fundamental elements or cornerstones of the Community and will do its best to uphold them. It will interpret the Community rules of law generously, i.e. wherever possible it will try to uphold the Community rules in the face of national legislation. The exceptions or derogations allowed the member states in some of the provisions are interpreted narrowly against the member states. The aim is to give the greatest possible effect to Community rights and less scope to member state derogations which, if allowed free rein, would undermine the aims of the Community.

Whether EU law is studied in two or more courses or all in one course, it can be observed that many of the cases which appear in Part I are ones which have arisen in an action in one of the substantive law topics. For example, *Van Gend, en Loos* which first established direct effects, is a case concerned with customs duties in the common market; *Von Colson*, establishing indirect effects arises from a sex discrimination case; and *Factortame*, concerned with nationality discrimination, supremacy, and national procedural rules, is one essentially based on the right of establishment from the free movement of persons. EU law and the book abound with many more examples. Studying both parts together very often reinforces the study and understanding of each other.

7

The Free Movement of Goods

7.1 Introduction

The free movement of goods is, with the Coal and Steel Community, the foundation and very core of the European Community and Union today. It is very much concerned with the economic ideals of the Community to create a single trading block in which all factors of production and particularly goods, flow freely. The free movement of goods is essential to the creating and running of the customs union and the common market and provides the infrastructure for the rest of the Community. Amongst the prime reasons for establishing the European Economic Community and the very concept of a common European market was to create a trading and producing block capable of competing with the American and the then strongly emerging Japanese economy. The benefits of achieving economic integration and a large internal market allow companies to realize growth and to specialize which in turns allows them to compete on the world economic stage. This, it is argued, creates a dynamic, competitive market for the benefit of producers, consumers and the member states. The broader underlying advantages are more than just economic, and indeed as was dealt with in Chapter 1, one of the original main aims of integration was to make the member states interconnected and interdependent and thus less likely to go to war with each other. However, creating and maintaining the Common Market has proved to be much more difficult than first envisaged in view of the member states' attempts to protect their own national producers and industries.

At this early stage, the significance of a complementary Competition law policy should be stressed as it is vital to the successful running of the internal market. The establishment or foundation of the EU is premised on the desire to promote integration and create a single unified market. A competition policy within the overall Treaty regime prevents companies from setting up their own rules and obstacles to trade to replace the national rules and obstacles the Community is trying to abolish. The two go hand in hand, you can't have one without ensuring you have the other. To have prevented the member states on the one hand from restricting the movement of goods just to allow private companies to do it by their agreements and practices, would defeat the objectives of the first policy and, vice versa, to prevent companies from artificially dividing the markets but to allow the member states to do so would undermine a competition policy. Hence there is a need for both and competition law will be the subject of Chapter 8.

7.2 Legislative Provisions

7.2.1 Treaty Articles

The preamble of the EC Treaty has proved instrumental in the Court's rulings in reaching decisions on cases involving the free movement of goods as have Articles 2 and 3, Article 10 (old 5) (the fidelity clause) and Article 12 (old 6) (the prohibition of discrimination on grounds of nationality).

There are four main groups of provisions in the EC Treaty connected with the free movement of goods:

(i)   customs duties and charges having equivalent effect (Arts 23–5);

(ii)   the Common Customs Tariff (Arts 26–7);

(iii)   the use of national taxation systems to discriminate against goods imported from other member states (Art 90); and

(iv)   quantitative restrictions or measures having an equivalent effect on imports and exports (Arts 28–30).

In this chapter in particular, it is worth taking a careful note about the Treaty of Amsterdam article number changes which have made life difficult in this area of law because old Article 30 which provides one of the basic prohibitions in this area became Article 28 and the old Article 36 concerned with derogations became Article 30 (the old Article number for the prohibition). More frequently than for other chapters, both numbers will be provided where confusion would otherwise arise.

As one of the cornerstones and one of the fundamental freedoms of the Community, the free movement of goods has been stoutly defended by the Court of Justice as will be seen in the case law considered later in the chapter. Its objectives are set out in Article 2 EC.

The Community shall have as its task, by establishing a Common market and an economic and monetary union and by implementing common policies or activities referred to in Articles 3 and 4,

Article 3 (a) to (c) provides for the prohibition of customs duties and quantitative restrictions and measures having equivalent effect, a common commercial policy and for an internal market with the free movement of goods.

Article 4 sets a goal, the adoption of an economic policy based on the close coordination of member states' economic policies and on the internal market.

The internal market is then defined in Article 14 (2) EC as 'an area without internal frontiers in which the free movement of goods, persons, services and capital is ensured in accordance with the provisions of this Treaty.

Therefore the aim is to achieve the circulation of goods without customs, duties, charges or other financial or other restrictions; to promote unlimited trade and to remove from the member states the control over export and import matters. The Community is to be solely responsible for the latter.

7.2.2 Secondary Legislation

There is very little secondary legislation of direct importance in this area of Community law but Directive 70/50 will be considered below as will two more recent enactments: Decision 3052/95 and Directive 98/34.

There is, however, a copious amount of case law to consider.

7.3 Progress Towards the Treaty Goals

Whilst the goals of integration have been outlined, progression towards them is not of course an overnight thing and has to be achieved over a series of moves. Various stages in economic integration have been generally recognized which in crude terms are as follows:

7.3.1 A Free Trade Area

This involves the removal of customs duties between member states, however the members of a free trade area decide themselves their external policies and any duties payable by third party countries wishing to export goods to those countries. It is this latter aspect which is regarded as not very useful because third countries may target the country with the lowest external duties. Any goods entering will compete with internal goods of the union and thus certification of origin is often required which is difficult and expensive to administer.

7.3.2 A Customs Union

The next stage is a customs union which builds on the above by creating a common external tariff, presenting a common position to the outside world. The same duties are imposed on goods entering the customs union regardless of where they are imported from. Once imported, the goods circulate freely as union goods throughout the union.

7.3.3 A Common Market

The Common market is the next stage which adds to the above, the free movement of the factors of production (goods, persons, and capital) and a competition policy.

7.3.4 An Economic Union

Almost finally, an economic union would be all of the above plus the harmonization or unification of economic, monetary, and fiscal policies including the creation of a common currency controlled by a central authority. The final step would then be full political union in a confederation or federal state.

7.3.5 Which Stage has the EU Reached?

Whilst its goals are clear, as outlined above, just how far has the EU progressed? Articles 14 and 24 make it clear that a customs Union should be established which includes a common, or otherwise referred to by two other synonymous terms: A single or internal market. The EU certainly has a customs union with a Common Customs Tariff which is exclusively regulated by the Commission. The degree to which a true common market has been achieved is more doubtful given the considerable case law still arising which is evidence of the sheer number of obstacles still in the way of the unified market. However, twelve countries, which now represents less than half of the member states, have gone further and established an economic and monetary union with a European central bank and a single currency.

7.3.5.1 Developments to Date

The initial means by which the goals of the Community were to be achieved commenced with an attempt at total harmonization. In line with the original views, outlined in Chapter 1, that success or harmonization in one area would lead to 'spill-over' to related areas (e.g. workers' rights), it was considered that progress would be steady, however for various reasons, legislative stagnation set in relatively swiftly. Amongst those reasons, the French boycott and subsequent Luxembourg accords, the late 1960s economic downturn, the oil crises and world economic recession and the increase in the number of member states all possessing a veto over legislation not in their national interest all featured to slow progress. Consider, as a classic example, the Architects Harmonization Directive which took eighteen years to enact. Whilst, to a large and necessary extent this was countered by judicial innovation in, for example, Case 26/62 *Van Gend en Loos* and the creation of the doctrine of direct effects and other leading cases which demonstrated that the Court of Justice was to interpret the Treaty in a purposive approach and not the actual words used as in Case 2/74 *Reyners*. However, the member states remained reluctant to carry the common market project forward themselves.

From the late 1970s, these problems were acknowledged and when the new Commission President Delors took office, there was sufficient support from commerce and industry and the member states for the single market project. This led to the Commission White Paper *Completing the Internal Market*[1] which was endorsed by European Council in 1985. It set out 300 legislative measures needed to 'complete the single market and '1992' was set as target date. This also marked a shift in approach in that whilst national rules would be harmonized where needed, other means of achieving the goals were emerging including a shift to new broadly construed technical harmonization and moves towards mutual recognition, spurred on by the Court of Justice decision in Case 120/78 *Cassis de Dijon*. The SEA provided the needed institutional and legal reforms to facilitate the meeting of the targets set by the '1992' project (e.g. 95 and QMV). In addition, other policies started to be put into place which were regarded as necessary to support the single market as a result of the realization that the single market could not be achieved in isolation, so an environmental policy was introduced along with, for example, an economic and social cohesion policy.

The single market was given a particular boost by the Treaty of Maastricht (TEU) which established Economic and Monetary Union, although not for all of the then fifteen member states. This nevertheless led to the expansion of other Community competences in order to complement the internal market, the latter being regarded as incorporating more than economic concerns and more of an ongoing and dynamic project, rather than one with a definable end. It might be argued that this demonstrates a return to functional integration or creeping federalism, noted in Chapter 1, in that the desire to move to economic and monetary union led to the establishment at the Community level of other policies which were regarded as vital to economic and monetary union

---

[1] OJ 1985 COM(85) 310 final.

7.4 Integration Methods

The integration of what were a number of separate national markets was and is to be achieved by two main integration strategies, namely, positive and negative integration. Negative integration is the removal of existing impediments to free movement such as striking down national rules and practices which obstruct or prevent achievement of the internal market and positive integration is achieved by the modification of existing national laws and institutions either by harmonization or the creation of new laws.

7.4.1 Negative Integration

This is the outlawing of national rules and practices which obstruct the fundamental free movement regimes. In the EU legal order, this form of integration is found in the statutory attempt to ensure the free movement of goods under Articles 25–31, workers under Articles 39–42, the provision of services and establishment under Articles 43–55, and capital under Articles 61–9. In the area of goods, Article 28 provides that 'Quantitative restriction on imports and all measures having equivalent effect shall be prohibited between member states.' However, there are statutory exceptions to the total prohibition for specific agreed reasons under Article 30 EC which provides that Article 28 shall not preclude prohibitions or restrictions which are justified on certain grounds contained within an exhaustive list in the article, which will be considered next.

Negative integration represents a deregulatory approach, an attempt to reduce regulation rather than increase regulation in order to remove obstructive laws and practices so that free movement can be achieved. Negative integration has been vastly assisted by the judicial development of direct effects and the other forms of individual enforcement which help police the member states and highlight member states laws and actions which do not conform with the free movement provisions. The leading Case 26/62 *Van Gend en Loos* could not be beaten as a better example. The provision of Article 12 EC, the general rule prohibiting discrimination is also vitally important in this area because prior to the establishment of the common market, free movement of goods could be restricted solely on the basis of the country from which the goods came.

7.4.1.1 The Prohibition of Discrimination

Article 12 EC provides 'Within the scope of application of this Treaty, and without prejudice to any special provisions contained therein, any discrimination on the grounds of nationality shall be prohibited.' Thus the nationality of goods or persons within this internal market should not play a role again. In the history of Europe this is an incredible concept which is perhaps not appreciated today by most of the readers of this book. Previously (and this applies still to those outside the EU) discrimination of different persons, i.e. all those outside a single state, solely on the basis of nationality was perfectly lawful but worse still perfectly acceptable! Now, for many, its seems astonishing that would treat people and goods differently just because of where they come from! But if they come from outside the EU, this is still acceptable, take an example very close to home. In the UK, the state universities charge non-EU and EU students vastly different tuition fees, although the education is the same, purely on the basis of where they come from! Within the EU though the new internal market regime means this is no longer possible or acceptable.

Discrimination can appear in the form of direct discrimination, which is usually clear and easy to spot by a difference in treatment or different rules being applied to imports than to domestic products. It is not restricted to intentional discrimination but also unintentional discrimination if the effect of a rule is nevertheless to discriminate against imports. The prohibition of discrimination in the EU legal order though also includes indirect discrimination and thus catches restrictions which on the face of it do not apply a nationality criteria, although the effects are as if that was the case. Indirect discrimination has now been given statutory definition in the community legal order. 'Indirect discrimination: Where an apparently neutral provision, criterion or practice would put persons of one class at a particular disadvantage compared with persons of the other class, unless that provision, criterion, or practice is objectively justified by a legitimate aim, and the means of achieving that aim are appropriate and necessary.'[2] Indirect discrimination can, however, be objectively justified. The best case to demonstrate this in the area of goods is Case 120/78 *Cassis de Dijon*, which will be considered below in detail, but the criteria which must be met by the objective justification are very clearly set out in a case from the free movement of persons. In Case C-55/94 *Gebhard*, the Court of Justice held that restrictions albeit applying to both national and non-nationals must be applied in a non-discriminatory manner; must be justified by imperative requirements in the general interest; must be suitable for securing the attainment of the objective which they pursue; and they must not go beyond what is necessary in order to attain it.

More recent developments in case law have gone beyond the need to show discrimination and it has been held that any measures which do not discriminate but nevertheless make life more difficult for exporters or importers may also be caught by

---

[2] See Directives 2000/43 (OJ 2000 L180/22), 2000/78 (OJ 2000 L303/16), and 76/207 as amended (OJ 1976 L39/40).

the free movement of goods prohibitions. These will be considered in further detail towards the end of this chapter.

7.4.2 Positive Integration

Positive integration involves the introduction of new laws or viewed in another light marks a return to regulation as a means to ensure that there is an equal playing field for imported and domestically produced goods by the introduction of new Community wide laws or by the setting up of new institutions to provide European wide regulation and control: e.g. European Central Bank and the single currency. It also includes the harmonization or approximation of national legislation by replacing multiple and divergent national rules or where relevant, the absence of national law, with a single EU rule which advances free trade. However, in seeking to establish common rules, the EU has been anxious to avoid agreeing on the lowest common denominator but instead to achieve a common rule which protects other important interests, essentially social interests and which thus avoids in the Community jargon, the 'race to the bottom' like the American Delaware corporation legislation.[3]

In the EU, harmonization is achieved by legislative intervention empowered by specific Treaty bases, for example for the free movement of workers (Arts 40 and 41 EC) and also by the provision of the general legal bases, Articles 94, 95, and 308 EC, which we have already seen in Chapter 4 in the section on competences. There are however limits to the scope and thus use of the general legal bases and therefore to harmonization itself as was seen in case C-376/98 *Germany v Parliament and Council* (Tobacco Advertising Ban Directive). Harmonization, therefore, is not without its problems.

7.4.3 Methods of Harmonization

There are different forms of harmonization that can be undertaken.

7.4.3.1 Total or Complete Harmonization

This is also known as 'exhaustive' harmonization whereby one rule is enacted for the whole Community and which precludes the member states from legislating in the same area so that each member state cannot raise an additional standard which would serve to exclude imports. For example, see Directives 70/156 and 76/756 on car

---

[3] The American state with the most lax company registration and regulation laws, which thus attracts many companies to register in that state and thus get away with lower standards for workers and minority shareholders, amongst others.

headlights which were considered in Case 60/86 *Commission v UK* (Dim-dip Headlights). The Directives covered all car lighting but did not address the dim-dip facility which the UK had previously required for both imports and domestically produced cars. Following the enactment of the Directives, the UK could not impose this on cars made in other EU countries which did not provide this facility. This form of harmonization requires that the standards and thus product must be exactly the same with no regional variations. It is criticized largely because of the images it produces of the euro-sausage or the euro-banana and that Brussels wants to harmonize everything in the EU, hence the view that it is best used in cases where there is compelling evidence for safety reasons that a single common rule is needed.

7.4.3.2 Optional Harmonization

This incorporates the idea that producers need only follow the provisions of a directive where they intend to trade the goods across an EU member state frontier. If they do not intend to export, they can still choose to follow the Directive but it is not regarded as very satisfactory and can lead to two differing standards in each member state. It does not account of the fact that those products may subsequently be imported and traded in other member states and would not then meet the appropriate standard. Also in the home state there would be products on the market meeting both home and EU standards thus leading to possible confusion amongst consumers. Thus it is no surprise that it has not been resorted to very often.

7.4.3.3 Minimum Harmonization

As it suggests, this is the establishment of a minimum standard but does not mean that the member states cannot go further and insist of higher domestic standards. The latter would not apply though to imported goods. For example, Directive 89/622, now replaced, concerns tar and nicotine labelling which was considered in Case C-11/92 *R v Secretary of State for Health, ex parte Gallaher Ltd and others* in which the Court of Justice held that the member states can retain or adopt much higher standards than the minimum standards provided in the Community legislation. In Case C-84/94 *UK v Council* (Working Time), the Court has advised that minimum standards does not mean minimal standards as in necessarily adopting the lowest common denominator. The Community minimum may be set at a fairly high level and member states remain free in any case, then to set higher standards domestically.

7.4.3.4 The New Approach Directives

The new approach directives are those so-called following a change of approach by the Commission to harmonization by which Directives were aimed very broadly at a whole industry and which provided general principles rather than detailed rules. They rely very much on the technical standards being set by private bodies, i.e. those industrial bodies, especially research and standards institutes, who are in the know and are more appropriate in devising the appropriate technical standards, especially for consumer products and safety standards.

7.4.4 Alternatives to Legislative Harmonization

Rather than harmonize, which can be a very long winded process, an alternative led by a judicial development is that of 'mutual recognition' of standards. This principle was one of two established by the Court and made prominent in the landmark case of *Cassis de Dijon* (Case 120/78 *Rewe-Zentrale AG v Bundesmonopolverwaltung für Branntwein*), which will be considered in full below. This decision essentially holds that if a product is lawfully produced in one state meeting the safety and health standards of that state, then states into which the product is imported should accept those standards and thus the products as equivalent of domestic standards and products. They should not then ban their import for not complying with different domestic standards. Following this case, the Commission picked up the ruling as a crucial tool in completing the internal market by insisting, for example, on 'Mutual recognition clauses' in national product regulations whereby a state would be required in setting its own standard for a product, to include a mutual recognition clause that it would accept other national standards. In Case C-184/96 *Commission* v *France* (Foie Gras) the Court held France at fault for not including such a clause, which has now become a standard requirement as a result.

7.5 The Establishment of the Internal Market

7.5.1 The CCP and CCT

The 'common market' which is a customs union provides not only for the elimination of duties regarding goods originating in other member states, but also regarding goods originating in third countries which are in free circulation in the common market and on which customs duties have been paid. The external duties are fixed by the Community for goods imported from outside of the Community and a single set of common tariffs is adopted in trade relations with the outside world. The Common Customs Tariff (CCT) which is also referred to as the common external tariff, imposes a single tariff for all imports and is set by the Commission. Once a product has been imported into the EU it is then in free circulation and further tariffs cannot be imposed on the product, Article 24 (old 10) EC. This aspect is now within the entire competence of the Community and is ever more tied up with world developments on customs duties, most notable GATT (General Agreement on Tariffs and Trade) and the WTO (World Trade Organization).[4]

7.5.2 The Prohibition of Customs Duties

These sections concern not just customs duties in the strict sense which are a hindrance to free trade but also any financial barriers which have an equivalent affect, however named. Necessarily, we must also consider aspects of member states' tax regimes as these may be a disguised way of imposing additional financial burdens on imported products thus making them less or even un-competitive. Therefore the Treaty also includes provisions (Art 90) to deal with these but the Treaty articles concerned with customs duties will be considered first. Note, that the provisions on goods and tax are mutually exclusive sets of provisions even though often dealing with the same factual situation, an aspect which will be considered more fully below.

Articles 23 and 25 (old 9, 12, 13, and 16) EC are aimed at the abolition of customs duties and charges having equivalent effect and at prohibiting the introduction of any such measures.

Article 23 (old 9) states that the Community shall be based on a customs union, with a common customs tariff, involving the prohibition of all customs duties on imports and charges having equivalent effect. This provision covers 'all trade in goods', with goods being defined by the Court of Justice in Case 7/68 *Commission v Italy* (Art Treasures case) as 'products which can be valued in money and which are capable, as such, of forming the subject of commercial transactions'. The definition was extended in Case 45/87 *Commission v Ireland* (Dundalk Water Supply) to include the provision of goods within a contract for the provision of services.

Article 25 prohibits customs duties or charges having equivalent effect and applies both to imports and exports. It also specifically mentions that it applies to customs duties of a fiscal nature. It was held to be directly effective in the leading Case 26/62 *Van Gend en Loos*. Whilst, it is relatively easy to recognize a customs duty which is usually designated as such and is a clear duty applied at the border, it is less easy to identify 'a charge having an equivalent effect' thus a considerable body of case law has arisen trying to define this. The total prohibition of customs duties per se means that cases of such an obvious breach rarely arise, hence then the concentration on charges

---

[4] The general aspects of external relations are considered in Chapter 1. See also see Barnard pp. 30–4 and Chapter 9.

having equivalent effect, often abbreviated as CHEEs and pronounced, as it looks, like something one has with crackers!

7.5.3 A Charge Having Equivalent Effect (CHEE)

In Cases 2 & 3/62 *Commission v Luxembourg* (the gingerbread case), the Court of Justice held that:

a duty, whatever it is called, and whatever its mode of application, may be considered a charge having equivalent effect to a customs duty, provided that it meets the following three criteria: (a) it must imposed unilaterally at the time of importation or subsequently; (b) it must be imposed specifically upon a product imported from a member state to the exclusion of a similar national product; and (c) it must result in an alteration of price and thus have the same effect as a customs duty on the free movement of products.

In certain circumstances a charge may be acceptable, if it is a service rendered for the benefit of the importer, if it is specifically required by Community law or if it is part of a system of internal taxation. These criteria are all subject to further refinement by the Court of Justice. In Case 24/68 *Commission v Italy* (Statistical Levy case), a small (10 lira) levy which was imposed on imports and exports for the purpose of financing statistical surveys was held to breach Community law. Whilst there was no discrimination between imports and exports, the Court of Justice stressed that the purpose of using the concepts of customs duties and charges having equivalent effect was to avoid the imposition of any pecuniary charge on goods circulating within the Community by virtue of the fact that they cross a frontier. The Court stressed that any charge must be considered in the context of the achievement of one of the fundamental objectives of the EC Treaty and in modification of its stance in *Commission v Luxembourg* case, the Court offered the following definition of charge having equivalent effect to include: 'any pecuniary charge, however small and whatever its designation and mode of application, which is imposed unilaterally on domestic or foreign goods by virtue of the fact that they cross a frontier.'

Such a charge is a CHEE even if it is not imposed for the benefit of the member state concerned, even if it is not discriminatory or protective in effect, and even if the product on which it is imposed is not in competition with any domestic product. In this case the levy was found to hamper the interpenetration of goods which the EEC Treaty aimed to secure and thus had an effect equivalent to a customs duty. It was further held that the levy could not be regarded as the consideration for a specific benefit actually conferred, because the advantages of the survey were so general and difficult to assess.

Claims by member states that charges for services rendered, such as for health inspections, and warehousing fees during clearance of customs formalities have been carefully considered by the Court of Justice.

7.5.3.1 Charges for Services Rendered

In Case 132/82 *Commission v Belgium* (Customs Warehouses) the Court of Justice considered the questions of whether a charge having equivalent effect may be permitted as a consideration for services rendered. The Belgian authorities allowed customs formalities for goods originating in or in free circulation in another member state to be completed either at the frontier or within the country. When the goods were presented for customs clearance at special stores of public warehouses, a fee fixed and levied by the municipal authorities was payable. This fee was payable in consideration of the use by the importers of the premises made available to them to store their goods pending clearance through customs. The state did not receive the money. The only role played by the state was to fix the maximum fee payable. The Court of Justice held that when payment of storage charges is demanded solely in connection with the completion of customs formalities it cannot be regarded as consideration for services actually rendered to the importer.

In Cases 2 and 3/69 *Sociaal Fonds voor de Diamantarbeiders*, a levy on import which was used to go towards a social fund for workers in the diamond industry and not used in any protectionary way over national products was held nevertheless to be a charge regardless of the purpose. The effect of the charge is that imported goods become less competitive.

In Case 340/87 *Commission v Italian Republic* (Customs Posts) Italian legislation required importers who presented themselves at Italian customs outside normal Italian opening hours (6 hours per day) to pay a fee. Article 5 of Directive 83/643 required customs offices at frontier posts to open for normal business hours of a least 10 hours per day Monday to Friday. Therefore, in order to comply with the Directive, Italian customs officials would have to work 4 hours overtime and Italian law sought to impose a charge during that 4-hour period. The Italian government maintained that this was a charge for a service rendered which was commensurate to the value of the service. The Court said that it had already held on several occasions that a charge imposed on goods by reason of the fact that they cross a frontier might not be a charge having equivalent effect to a customs duty provided it constituted a benefit specifically or individually conferred on the economic operator concerned, of an amount proportional to that service. In this case the Court of Justice held the charge constituted a breach of the Treaty.

In Case 170/88 *Ford of Spain v the Spanish State*, a claim that a charge levied by the Spanish customs for granting customs clearance at the Ford factory was a charge for services rendered and not a charge having equivalent effect to a customs duty was rejected. The charge was calculated at a rate of 0.165 per cent of the declared value of the goods. The Court of Justice held that even if the contested charge were in fact remuneration for a service rendered to the importer, the amount charged could not be regarded as proportionate to the service. The Spanish government's argument that in some cases the charge would be less than the cost of carrying out the inspections only served to confirm this argument. A charge calculated on the basis of the value of the goods could not correspond to the costs incurred by the customs authorities.

7.5.3.2 Justified Charges

There are circumstances when charges may be justified distinct criteria applying. In Case 87/75 *Bresciani*, the Court of Justice held that veterinary checks and charges performed as a service are acceptable but in that particular case they were not as they were in the public interest at large and not in the interest of each importer. This was followed up in Case 18/87 *Commission v Germany* (Animal Inspection Fees) in which the Court of Justice held that a charge may escape classification as a CHEE. In this case, fees for inspections carried out under the requirements of Council Directive 81/389 were held to be acceptable. According to the Court of Justice they satisfied the criteria that (i) the fees constituted a payment for a service, not exceeding the cost of the actual inspections in respect of which they are charged; (ii) the inspections in question were mandatory and uniform for all the products in question in the Community; (iii) the inspections were provided for by Community law in the interests of the Community; and (iv) the inspections promoted the free movement of goods in particular, by neutralizing the obstacles which may result from unilateral inspection measures adopted under Article 30 of the EC Treaty. The fees in the case were charged by some of the German Länder on the importation of live animals from other member states and their purpose was to cover the cost of health inspections carried out under Council Directive 81/389. The charges in this case satisfied the conditions and were justified. Case C-111/89 *Netherlands v Bakker Hillegom* extended the criteria to include the requirements of international conventions.

If the charge does relate to a system of internal dues applied systematically and in accordance with the same criteria to domestic products and imported products alike and is therefore a genuine, non-discriminatory tax, it falls to be classified under Article 90 and not under Article 25. In Case 90/79 *Commission* v *France* (Reprographic Machines) a levy was charged on all copy machines in order to compensate authors for the breaches of copyright which often occur by the use of such machines. Whilst very few copy machines were manufactured in France and the tax looked like disguised discrimination, it was held to be a genuine non-discriminatory tax. This case highlights the often subtle difference between what is a charge and what is a genuine tax, a distinction which will be considered next.

7.5.4 The Distinction between Internal Taxation and Charges Having Equivalent Effect

If a charge imposed by a member state on imported goods is a measure of internal taxation which is non-discriminatory, then it cannot be a charge having equivalent effect, and cannot be caught by Articles 23–5. It is governed by Article 90 instead of the rules on the free movement and member states have not been slow to realize the potential of Article 90 as a way of justifying a financial charge on imported goods. Whilst the customs duties and charges having equivalent effect mentioned in Articles 23–5 must be abolished, tax measures are allowed because as a general principle, Article 90 allows each member state to establish the system of taxation which it considers most suitable. However, Article 90 prohibits tax from discriminating against imports in the organization or application of an internal system of taxation and was regarded as crucial to complement the free movement provisions where taxation policy was being employed by a state to circumvent the customs rules by the imposition of discriminatory internal taxes. Article 90 EC thus represents an early intervention into the member states' tax regimes, which is likely to be more intrusive in future. Article 25 also now specifically prohibits customs charges of a fiscal nature.

The difference between a charge and a tax is crucial. A charge which is defined by the ECJ as an internal tax to which Article 90 applies, cannot be at the same time be a charge having equivalent effect to a customs duty and therefore be subject to Articles 23–5. In Case 78/96 *Steinlike und Weinlig v Germany* the Court of Justice held that 'Financial charges within a general system of internal taxation applying systematically to domestic and imported products according to the same criteria are not to be considered charges having equivalent effect.' It may be one thing or the other, but cannot be both. They are mutually exclusive categories. There is now a considerable body of case law of the Court of Justice on the distinction between an internal tax (to which Art 90 might apply) and a charge having equivalent effect to a customs duty (which might be prohibited by Arts 23 and 25). In Case 20/76 *Schöttle & Söhne v Finanzamt Freuenstadt*, the Court of Justice held that the purpose of Article 90 (old 95) is to remove disguised restrictions on the free movement of goods which may result from the tax provisions of a member state. It was held that a German tax on transportation of goods for more than a certain distance levied, in this case on a lorry load of gravel, was an indirect tax on the gravel itself.

Case 132/78 *Denkavit v French State* also concerned this distinction. It arose out of a charge on the importation of meat products which was the equivalent of a similar charge imposed on the slaughter of meat in French slaughterhouses.[5] The Court of

---

[5] This is the language used by the Court that the meat is slaughtered but you might spot the inconsistency that it is not meat but animals which are slaughtered; one cannot slaughter meat, it's already dead! See Para. 4.

Justice noted that a charge could escape classification as a charge having equivalent effect to a customs duty only if it related to a general system of internal dues applied systematically and in accordance with the same criteria to domestic products and imported products alike. In paragraph 8 of its judgment, the Court further emphasized that in order to relate to a system of internal taxation, the charge to which an imported product is subject must:

1. be imposed at the same rate on the same product;
2. be imposed at the same marketing stage; and
3. the chargeable event giving rise to the duty must be the same for both products.

It is therefore not sufficient that the objective of the charge imposed on imports is to compensate for similar charges imposed on domestic products at a production or marketing stage prior to that at which the imported products are taxed. The Court held that it was bound to regard the charge in this case as a charge having equivalent effect because

(a) it was charged on imported goods by virtue of the fact that they had crossed a frontier;
(b) the tax was imposed at a different stage of production and on the basis of a different 'chargeable event';
(c) no account was taken of fiscal charges which had been imposed on the products in the member state of origin; and
(d) to find otherwise would render the prohibition on charges having equivalent effect to customs duties empty and meaningless.

Finally, in Case 77/76 *Fratelli Cucchi*, the Court of Justice confirmed the mutually exclusive nature of the charges and internal taxation regimes but stressed that because it is often difficult to tell the difference both 25 and 90 should be invoked together before the Court and the Court of Justice asked to determine which should apply.

7.6 The Prohibition of Discriminatory Taxation

Article 90(1) provides that no member state shall impose directly or indirectly on the products of other member states any internal taxation of any kind in excess of that imposed directly or indirectly on similar domestic products. This prohibits discrimination in favour of the domestic products.

Article 90(2) further provides that no member state shall impose on the products of other member states any internal taxation of such a nature as to afford indirect protection to other products. Article 90 was held to be directly effective and an indispensable foundation of the common market in Case 57/65 *Lütticke v Hauptzollamt Saarlouis.*

Taxation was defined in Case 90/79 *Commission v France* (Reprographic Machines) as a general system of internal dues applied systematically to categories of products in accordance with objective criteria irrespective of the origin of the products. However, internal taxes can never be imposed solely by virtue of the fact that the goods cross a frontier. The reason for their imposition must be that domestic products are subject to taxation and that for competition reasons, imported goods should be subject to the same tax.

7.6.1 Direct and Indirect Taxation

Article 90 seeks to outlaw both directly discriminatory taxation and indirect discrimination in tax regimes. Direct discrimination is where imports and domestic products are deliberately treated differently and is thus automatically unlawful and cannot be justified, whereas, indirect discrimination on the face of it, imposes the same rule both domestic and imported products, but the result is that the import is in fact, disadvantaged. Indirect discrimination may be objectively justified. In Case 28/76 *Molkerei-Zentrale Westfalen v Haupzollamt Paderborn* the Court of Justice ruled that the words 'directly or indirectly' were to be construed broadly and embraced all taxation which was actually and specifically imposed on the domestic product at earlier stages of the manufacturing and marketing process. It is also capable of including taxes on raw materials and to the assessment of the tax. In Case 20/76 *Schöttle & Söhne v Finanzamt Freuenstadt* it was held that a German tax on transportation of goods for more than 50 km, levied in this case on a lorry load of gravel, was an indirect tax on the gravel itself.

7.6.2 'Similar' or 'Other Products'

The criteria for determining whether there is discrimination differs according to whether the case is brought under Article 90(1); concerned with similar products or Article 90(2); dealing with other products. The latter serves to cover imported products that may be different but are nevertheless in competition with the domestic products. In the case of Article 90(1), the taxation on the imported product must not be higher than the tax on the similar domestic product, in which case the rule of non-discrimination has been complied with. Whereas in the case of Article 90(2), the taxation on the imported product must not have a protectionist effect.

To avoid discrimination taking place in breach of Article 90(1) not only must the rates of tax on the imported product and the domestic product be the same (prima facie non-discrimination) but also the basis of imposition of the taxes must not be such that differences between imported and domestic goods may result from it. The rates of tax, the basis of assessment and the rules for levying and collecting it must all be non-discriminatory. In the case of Article 90(2), to be caught by the prohibition on discrimination it has to be proved that the taxation has a protectionist effect. At the root of this difference is the fact that direct comparisons are possible under Article 90(1) whereas under Article 90(2) they are not. So, even where the level of taxation is the same, a delay in the collection in favour of domestic goods was held to be discriminatory and a breach of Article 90. In Case 55/79 *Commission v Ireland* (Excise Payments) under Irish law, producers of beer, wine, and spirits enjoyed an extension of 4–6 weeks of the period for the payment of excise duties, whereas taxes on imported beers wines and spirits had to be paid immediately on importation or on delivery from the bonded warehouse.

In Case 112/84 *Michel Humblot v Directeur des Services Fiscaux*, the French authorities imposed a higher tax on cars with a higher horsepower rating, none of which were manufactured in France and the tax applied in practice only to imported cars. The Court of Justice recognises that a tax which appears to discriminate against a category of imported goods, because no goods in that category are produced domestically, will not necessarily always be in breach of Article 90. However, it held that because many of the imported cars thus taxed would still be in competition with cars produced in France taxed at the lower rate, the tax was nevertheless in breach of Article 90. In contrast is Case C-132/88 *Commission v Greece* (Taxation of Motor Cars) in which a Greek tax on both new and second-hand cars, whether produced in Greece or imported from outside rose steeply in respect of cars above 1800cc cylinder capacity. The cars affected were all imported as no cars above 1600cc were produced in Greece. The Court held that this measure would only be indirectly discriminatory if it were shown that the taxation had the effect of discouraging Greeks from purchasing foreign cars. On the face of it, the tax was motivated by other considerations and there was no protective effect.

Even where there may even be benefits for the imported goods, a difference in the way in which a tax is levied may be held to breach Article 90. In Case C-213/96 *Outokumpu Oy*, a flat rate tax on imported electricity from Sweden was held to infringe Article 90 because the tax rate on domestic electricity was calculated according to the product which was used for its manufacture for environmental reasons. The fact that only in limited circumstances would the rate of imported tax be higher was immaterial to the Court of Justice. The ease of administration in setting up a general system and that it was extremely difficult to determine precisely the method of production of imported electricity were not accepted as grounds justifying the system adopted.

7.6.2.1 Similar Products

Article 90(1) requires that if there is a difference in the way similar products are taxed, the levels of tax have to be equalized. First of all, in determining what constitutes 'similar products' whilst obviously including same products, the Commission and Court need to take in to account the composition, physical characteristics and method of production of the product, as well as considering whether they both meet the same consumer needs. For example in Case 243/84 *John Walker Ltd v Ministeriet for Skatter og Afgifter*, the question 'whether whisky was similar to fruit wine' was posed. Whilst it was clear that both were alcoholic drinks the Court of Justice held that the two drinks were not similar since they exhibited manifestly different characteristics. The wine was fruit based and relied on natural fermentation whereas the Scotch whisky was a cereal based drink produced by distillation. There were also significant differences in the alcohol volume.

In Case 184/85 *Commission v Italy* (Italian Fruit) the similarity between bananas on the one hand and peaches and pears on the other was considered and according to the Court of Justice, they were not similar. The Court referred to the organoleptic (which essentially means sensory) characteristics and the water content which were different and which meant they were suited for different markets.

7.6.2.2 Other Products

As far as Article 90(2) is concerned, for a tax to be caught by the prohibition on discrimination it has to be proved that the taxation has a protectionist effect to the detriments of imported goods which may be in competition with the other domestic good. The main question focuses on whether the products can be substituted by each other. Probably the most important case on Article 90(2) is Case 170/78 *Commission v UK* (Wine Excise Duties No. 2), in which the Court of Justice held that the fact that the UK imposed a higher duty imposed on table wines than on beer was held to give indirect protection to beer (a domestic product) over light table wines (a predominantly imported product) and contravened Article 90(2). The UK government had argued that wine and beer could not be regarded as competing beverages, since beer was widely consumed in public houses, and wine was generally only drunk on special occasions and pointed out the difference in the alcoholic volume. The Court took the view that it was necessary not only to examine the present state of the market, but whether the two products were potentially in competition. Given that the case was over twenty-five years ago, that was a pretty shrewd judgment as they are probably far more in competition with each other now than then. The Court of Justice decided that such a relationship existed on the basis of volume, price and alcoholic strength and mentioned the thirst quenching qualities of both products even where UK beer was then about 3 per cent alcohol and the lightest wines 8–9 per cent.

After such a finding, the member state may abolish discrimination either by lowering the tax on imported goods or by raising the tax on domestic products, or may use a combination of both to remove the discrimination or protection.

7.7 Quantitative Restrictions and Measures Having Equivalent Effect

This section considers the non-financial barriers to the free movement of goods contained within the phrase quantitative restrictions and measures having equivalent effect. Restrictions or obstacles to free movement are caused mainly by divergent national laws regulating products and trade rather than the very crude or obvious and clearly prohibited import or export bans. As was discussed above, harmonization of all products was neither practical nor desirable, therefore the founding fathers adopted a means of negative integration to tackle the obstacles to free movement caused by these divergent national laws, which were often very different, in each member state. So this becomes the focus of attention in this area of free movement. Quantitative restrictions are straightforward, either a ban or quota. It is the extent to which member states can insist that imported products comply with national standards in the face of the attempt to create a genuinely unified single market, that cause the real difficulties.

The development of the rules on the free movement of goods reflects the general approach to the fundamental freedoms in that the Court of Justice has interpreted the principle of free movement as liberally as it can to promote free movement and the derogations allowed the member states as restrictively or narrowly as possible. See Case 8/74 *Dassonville* as a good example of this approach.

7.7.1 The General Scope of the Treaty Prohibition

Article 28 (old 30) lays down a general prohibition on quantitative restrictions and measures having equivalent effect and Article 29 extends that prohibition to exports. Article 30 provides:

The provisions of Articles 28 and 29 shall not preclude prohibitions or restrictions on imports, exports or goods in transit justified on the grounds of:

public morality, public policy or public security;
the protection of health and life of humans, animals or plants;
the protection of national treasures possessing artistic, historic or archaeological value;
or the protection of industrial and commercial property.

The application of these exceptions is subject to the limitation in the second sentence of Article 30, that they may not be used as a means of arbitrary discrimination or a disguised restriction on trade between member states.

Both Articles 28 and 29 have been found to be directly effective, but only vertically against measures taken by the state, see respectively Cases 74/76 *Ianelli and Volpi SpA v Meroni* and 83/78 *Pigs Marketing Board v Redmond*. However, state measures has been interpreted fairly liberally to include both public, semi-public and even private bodies in certain circumstances where there has been a fair degree of state involvement or financing which then taints an otherwise private body with aspects of statehood to include actions taken by those bodies. For example, in Cases 266 and 267/87 *R v Pharmaceutical Society of Great Britain, ex parte Association of Pharmaceutical Importers*, the activities of the Association which regulates the conduct and sets standards for chemists and pharmacists, was included.

Also in Case 249/81 *Commission v Ireland* (Buy Irish) a buy Irish campaign was administered by the Irish Goods Council, a registered private company, however because the Irish Government largely sponsored the campaign to buy Irish products, appointed the management committee and set the broad outlines of the campaign, Article 28 was held to apply. In Case 222/82 *Apple and Pear Development Council v Lewis*, a government sponsored development council was under a duty not to run an advertising campaign to encourage purchase of domestic fruit at the expense of imported products. In this way, it may be argued the extension of the scope of Article 28 is analogous to Case C-188/89 *Foster v British Gas* when considering an emanation of the state for the purposes of direct effects of Directives, as noted above in chapter five. However, strictly considered the actions of private parties are outside the direct application of Articles 28–30.

The concept of 'Measures' includes not only legally binding acts, but also practices 'capable of influencing the conduct of traders and consumers' see Case 249/81 *Commission v Ireland* (Buy Irish) and may include state inaction in the face of private individuals' actions which obstruct the free movement of goods: i.e. where the state did not take effective action to stop the protests which prevented Spanish produce entering France, see Case 265/95 *Commission v France* (French Farmers/Spanish Strawberries). This case is to be contrasted with Case C-112/00 *Schmidberger* in which the protest which blocked the Brenner motorway pass was held to be acceptable and not a breach by the Austrian state for not preventing it. Distinguished on length of protest because it was a single one off event which was not repeated and was a lawful protest unlike the repeated illegal sabotages of imported goods which took place in the *Commission v France* case. The term 'measures' has also been interpreted to include administrative practices, if they have a certain degree of consistency and generality as was held by the Court of Justice in Case 21/84 *Commission v France* (Franking Machines). The preamble to Directive 70/50[6] supports this generous view of measures or rules by including non-legally binding administrative practices.

The following issues will be considered in turn: the meaning of quantitative restrictions and equivalent measures; the derogations of Article 30 (old 36) and the particular problems of measures which apply both to imports and domestic goods.

7.7.2 The Meaning of Quantitative Restrictions

A quantitative restriction is a measure restricting the import or export of a given product by amount or by value. In Case 2/73 *Geddo v Ente Nationale Risi*, the Court of Justice held that a prohibition on quantitative restrictions covers measures which amount to a total or partial restraint of imports, exports or goods in transit. The most obvious examples of quantitative restrictions on imports and exports are complete bans on imports or by subjecting imports to quotas restricting the import or export by either quantity or value. These are clearly in contravention of Article 28 and thus prohibited. It was held by the Court of Justice in Case 34/79 *R v Henn and Darby* to cover measures capable of limiting imports to a finite quantity, including zero, and include import bans. Case 231/78 *Commission v UK* (Import of Potatoes) and Case 232/78 of *Commission v France* (Import of Lamb) are straightforward examples of total bans which are prohibited. A quantitative restriction also includes subjecting the import of goods to the condition of obtaining an import licence. In Case 124/81 *Commission v UK* (Imports of UHT Milk) the failure to obtain an import licence meant that milk could not be imported even though the requirement was a formality and licences were issued on demand. The Court of Justice held that import licences or other similar procedures, even if a pure formality, are precluded by Article 28.

7.7.3 Measures Having Equivalent Effect

The concept of measures having equivalent effect has been defined by secondary legislation (Directive 70/50) and by the jurisprudence of the Court of Justice. The Directive which was introduced to provide guidelines at the time when the common market was being established, continues to provide guidance as to what measures may

---

[6] OJ Sp. Edn. 1970 I L13/29.

be considered a breach of the prohibition under Article 28 (old 30). Whilst it appears not to have been formally repealed and thus still in force and indeed to be found under legislation in force section of EUR-LEX the EC legislation site, its Treaty base was removed by the Treaty of Amsterdam amendments. However, it defines measures having equivalent effect on imports as including distinctly applicable measures, that is those which apply to imports but not domestically produced goods, and which (Article 2):

make imports, or the disposal at any marketing stage of imported products, subject to a condition, other than a formality, which is required in respect of imported products only. They also include any measures which subject imported products or their disposal to a condition which differs from that required for domestic products and which is more difficult to satisfy.

Equally, it covers, in particular, measures which favour domestic products or grant them a preference, other than an aid, to which conditions may or may not be attached. Basically therefore any measure which makes import or export unnecessarily difficult and thus discriminates between the two, would clearly fall within the definition.

It also covers under Article 3 national marketing rules which on their face are non-discriminatory or 'indistinctly applicable', which deal in particular, with size, shape, weight, composition, presentation, identification, or putting up and which are equally applicable to domestic and imported products, where the restrictive effect of such measures on the free movement of goods exceeds the effects intrinsic to trade rules. We will return to this aspect later.

Further help in understanding this concept comes from the Court of Justice and the starting point is Case 8/74 In *Procureur du Roi v Dassonville* in which the term 'measures having equivalent effect' was held to include 'all trading rules enacted by a Member State which are capable of hindering, directly or indirectly, actually or potentially, intra-community trade'. The case concerned criminal proceedings in Belgium against a trader who imported Scotch whisky in free circulation in France into Belgium without being in possession of a certificate of origin from the British customs authorities, thus infringing Belgian customs rules. The Court of Justice held that:

the requirement by a Member State of a certificate of authority, which is less easily obtainable by importers of an authentic product, put into free circulation in a regular manner in another Member State, than by importers of the same product coming directly from the country of origin, constitutes a measure having equivalent effect.

The Court added that in the absence of a Community system to guarantee a product's origin, a member state may take reasonable measures for the protection of consumers in the area of designation of origin of products without necessarily infringing Article 28. However, this is subject to the further qualification that whether or not such measures were authorized by the terms of Article 30 (old 36), they could not constitute an arbitrary discrimination or a disguised restriction on trade between member states.

The scope of the prohibition thus defined is extremely wide and means virtually any measure which hinders imports or exports in any way could be caught.

7.7.4 The Scope of the Prohibition

7.7.4.1 National Promotional Campaigns

Measures which do not have clear visible direct effect on imports may still be caught by the prohibition in Article 28. In Case 249/81 *Commission v Ireland* (Buy Irish), the Court of Justice held that the activities of a company which was government controlled and financed and carried out a government policy of promoting the sale of national products by means of an advertising campaign and promoted the use of a 'home produced' symbol constituted a measure having equivalent effect. It was held not necessary for the government to have taken any compulsory measures and simply by encouraging the purchase of domestic products through a campaigning body was sufficient to count as a measure having equivalent affect. The emphasis is therefore on those rules which are capable of having an effect rather than those rules actually having an effect. In Case 222/82 *Apple and Pear Development Council v Lewis*, the ruling in the Buy Irish case was qualified to hold that a member state could establish a Development Council for fruit production which was composed of members appointed by the Minister responsible and financed only by the growers themselves, as long as the activities consisted of compiling statistics, promotion and undertaking of research and giving technical advice rather than trying to get consumers to purchase only home produced fruit and not imports.

7.7.4.2 Discriminatory National Marketing Rules

National marketing rules often impose restrictions on the production, packaging or distribution of goods which as a consequence infringe Article 28. For example, in Case 113/80 *Commission v Ireland* (Metal Objects/Origin) the requirement to stamp the origin of goods as either Irish or foreign was held to breach the rule. In Case 261/81 *Rau v De Smedt*, the Belgium national rule which required margarine to be packed in cubes and in no other form such as tubs or rectangular blocks was held to be in breach of Article 28. In Cases 266 and 267/87 *R v Pharmaceutical Society of Great Britain*, the rule of the Pharmaceutical Society prohibiting dispensing pharmacists from substituting for the product named on a doctor's prescription, any other with identical therapeutical effect except under certain exceptional conditions was capable of coming within the operation of Article 28. In the case it was capable of being justified on the grounds of the protection of public health.

7.7.4.3 Exports

In Case C-47/90 *Delhaize v Promalvin*, a ban on the export of wine in bulk was held to breach Article 29 which states that quantitative restriction on exports, and all measures having equivalent effect, shall be prohibited between member states. There was no evidence to support the contention that bottling was necessary at the source of production, especially where the wine was transported in bulk internally.

7.8 The Derogations of Article 30

Article 30 provides exceptions to the general prohibition of Article 28. It states that Articles 28 and 29 shall not apply to prohibitions on imports, exports or goods in transit which are justified on any of the following four sets of grounds: (a) public morality, public policy or public security; (b) the protection of health and life of humans animals or plants;(c) the protection of national treasures possessing artistic, historic or archaeological value; or (d) the protection of industrial and commercial property. The application of these exceptions is subject to the limitation, set out in the second sentence of Article 30 (old 36), that they may not be used as a means of arbitrary discrimination or a disguised restriction on trade between member states.

7.8.1 General Purpose and Scope

Article 30 provides the member states with a set and exhaustive list, in other words, it cannot be added to, which allow the member states to restrict the free movement of goods for certain specific reasons only. In Case 72/83 *Campus Oil v Ministry for Industry and Energy*, the Court of Justice held that the purpose of Article 36 was not to reserve certain matters to the exclusive jurisdiction of the member states but instead allows national legislation to derogate from the principle of the free movement of goods to the extent to which this is and remains justified in order to achieve the objectives set out in the Article. In Case 113/80 *Commission v Ireland* (Metal Objects), it was held that because the derogations were exceptions to a fundamental principle, namely the free movement of goods, they were to be construed narrowly and could not, for example, be used for economic reasons as was done by Italy in Case 7/61 *Commission v Italian Republic* (Pigmeat Imports) in order to protect its own pig industry which was suffering economic difficulties.

7.8.2 Public Morality

Case 34/79 *R v Henn & Darby* concerned a ban on the importation of pornographic magazines, despite the fact that similar magazines were lawfully available for purchase in the UK. The Court of Justice ruled that a prohibition which might be stricter than the laws applicable internally, was not designed to discriminate in favour of the domestic product and so was acceptable under the public morality clause of Article 30. It was up to member states to determine the requirements of public morality in their own state, who have therefore, a margin of discretion in this area. This was, however, qualified in Case 121/85 *Conegate v HM Customs and Excise*, the infamous case concerned with the importation of 'blow-up dolls'. It was held that member states did not have complete freedom to exclude such material when similar products could be manufactured lawfully in the UK. The Court held a member state might not rely on the ground of public morality to prohibit the importation of goods from other member states when its legislation contained no prohibition on the manufacture or marketing of such goods in its own territory. The prohibition was therefore a disguised restriction on trade and a means of arbitrary discrimination, and as such contrary to the second sentence of Article 30.

7.8.3 Public Policy

The leading case in this category is Case 7/78 *R v Thompson et al.* which concerned the ban on the unlawful importation into the UK of Krugerrands and a ban on the export of coins, some of which were no longer legal tender, and some of which were. The English coins which were no longer legal tender were held to be goods within the meaning of Article 28, however, it was held that the right to mint coinage was a fundamental interest of the state and a therefore a state which prohibits the destruction of coinage, even when they are no longer legal tender and imposes an export ban to prevent their destruction abroad, will be justified under Article 30 on grounds of public policy.

Other attempts by member states to invoke this exception have failed. See, for example, those cases dealing with lack of effective action by states to curb illegal protests in which the states have claimed that the threat to public order prevented them from intervening to ensure the free movement of goods. The court has not accepted the invocation of Article 30 to justify the lack of action.[7]

---

[7] Case 231/83 *Cullet v Centre Leclerc Toulouse* and Case C-265/95 *Commission v France* (Spanish Strawberries).

7.8.4 **Public Security**

The leading case to deal with security is Case 238/82 *Campus Oil* concerning Irish rules requiring importers of petroleum products to purchase a certain proportion of their requirements from an Irish state-owned refinery at prices fixed by the Minister. The Court of Justice held that the maintenance of essential oil supplies was covered by the public security exception, however any measures taken are subject to the principle of proportionality, considered below.

7.8.5 **The Protection of the Health or Life of Humans or Animals**

This is a frequently argued ground for import restrictions and virtually every sort of good, especially foodstuffs, has been subjected to restrictions on health grounds most of which have been held by the Court of Justice not to conform with Article 30. Whilst in Case 322/01 *Deutscher Apothekerverband* the Court of Justice held that 'the health and life of humans rank foremost among the assets or interests' protected by Article 30 EC, the Court has been extremely vigilant in exposing the disguised restrictions of member states. For example, in Case 124/81 *Commission v UK* (UHT Milk), the systematic checking and opening of sealed UHT cartons of milk for health checks which rendered the contents unusable and thus increased cost to the importer amounted to import restrictions. The Court of Justice held that the health of consumers would be adequately protected by the necessary controls being carried out in the country of production to meet all the reasonable requirements of the country of import. Similarly in Case 42/82 *Commission v France* (Italian Table Wines) systematic checks on three-quarters of each consignment of Italian wine, which was held up at the French border for long periods, sometimes months, was held not to be justified by Article 30. Whilst the Court of Justice acknowledged the right of the member states to carry out checks, they noted that the frequency of analysis of Italian wine was considerably higher than the occasional checks carried out on French wine transported within France. The Court of Justice held that the French authorities had no right to carry out systematic checks, and, in the absence of any reasonable suspicion on the basis of specific evidence in a given case, they ought to have confined themselves to random checks.

A series of cases has now been considered by the Court concerned with import bans on the grounds of protecting public health as a result of the content of food products and mainly concerning food additives. The Court of Justice has held in these cases that in the absence of any Community regulation of the manufacture and marketing of products, the member states are free to regulate this matter as long as they do not infringe the Community provisions on the free movement of goods. In those cases which are concerned with an import ban raised on the grounds of protecting the health of the population from harmful additives, the view of the Court of Justice is based on whether the additives were either permitted in another product or were allowed in another member state or with regard to the results of international scientific research, in particular the work of the World Health Organization, and to eating habits in the country of importation. If the additive does not constitute a danger to public health, a ban would be a breach of Article 28 and not justified under Article 30. Additionally bans would be contrary to the principle of proportionality where there was no accessible procedure by which traders were able to request that the use of specific additives be permitted. Cases include the ban on the import of beer, Case 178/84 *Commission v Germany* (Beer Purity), a ban on the import of sausages containing certain non-meat ingredients, Case 274/87 *Commission v Germany* (Sausage Purity Law) and a ban on the import of low fat cheese, Case 210/89 *Commission v Italy*. However a ban would not infringe Article 28 where additives are also not permitted in domestic products and where there is a system to allow the addition of additives to the list of permitted additives, see Cases 95 and 293/89 *Commission v Italy and Greece*. States must make out, on the basis of latest scientific data, that a real risk to health exists. However, the Court recognizes 'that such an assessment of the risk could reveal that scientific uncertainty persists as regards the existence or extent of real risks to human health'. In such circumstances, it must be accepted that a member state may, in accordance with the precautionary principle, take protective measures without having to wait until the existence and gravity of those risks are fully demonstrated as stated by the Court of Justice in Case C-192/01 *Commission v Denmark* and a number of similar cases. Finally, in this category, which remains a live issue is Case C-358/95 *Tommaso Morellato v Unita Sanitaria Locale* which concerns the import of frozen bread which contravened national statutory limits by having a moisture content exceeding 34 per cent, an ash content of less than 1.40 per cent and containing bran, contrary to national standards. France was unable to demonstrate a threat to public health and it was easy for the Court of Justice to reach the conclusion that the national law constituted a quantitative restriction contrary to Article 28 and was not saved by Article 30.

An area where the public health proviso in Article 30 is of great importance is in the importation of pharmaceutical products where there are often vast price differences between the retail prices of drugs in different member states. Case 215/87 *Schumacher v Hauptzollamt Frankfurt*, concerned the ban on import of medicinal products purchased in France for personal use. The medicines in question were available in Germany without prescription, but at four times the price charged in France. The Court of Justice held that national rules or practices which have or are likely to have a restrictive effect on importation of pharmaceutical products are compatible with the Treaty only in so far as they are necessary for the protection of health and human life. In this case the purchase of the goods in a pharmacy of another member state in effect gives a guarantee equivalent to that resulting from the sale of the product in a pharmacy in the member state into which it is imported. The Court ruled that the rule prohibiting the importation of the goods in this case contravened Article 28 and was not protected by Article 30.

7.8.6 Artistic Heritage

It was held in Case 7/68 *Commission v Italy* (Art Treasures) that this ground does not justify an tax being levied on the export of art treasures which was held to breach Article 25.

7.8.7 The Protection of Artistic or Commercial Property

This is to be read along side of Article 295 which provides that this Treaty shall in no way prejudice the rules in member states governing the system of property ownership. This justification has been held by the Court of Justice not to extend to prevent parallel imports of products lawfully marketed in another member state. Only the specific subject matter can be protected by Article 30 when the rights have not already been exhausted by being put into circulation in the European Community, see Cases 15 and 16/74 *Centrafarm* cases. Such a restriction of the free movement of goods would defeat the aims of the Treaty and could not be justified under Article 30, see Case 78/70 *Deutsche Grammophon Gesellschaft v Metro Grossmarkt*. As most undergraduate courses on EC would not go into any further detail on this topic as a part of free movement of goods, neither shall this book.

7.8.8 Article 30 Second Sentence and Proportionality

The second sentence of Article 30 provides that such prohibitions or restrictions shall not, however, constitute a means of arbitrary discrimination or a disguised restriction on trade between member states and any measure must in any case be proportionate. In Case 42/82 *Commission v France* (Italian Table Wines) the systematic checking of every consignment and subjecting inspections to very long delays of weeks and even months was held to be disproportionate. Similarly, in Case 124/81 *Commission v UK* (UHT Milk), the requirement of an import licence was held to be a disguised restriction despite being issued automatically.

7.8.9 **Decision 3052/95**[8]

In an attempt to better regulate the introduction by member states of measures which derogate from the free movement of goods, this decision was adopted which requires the member states to inform the Commission about any measures which ban the import of goods or refuse goods to be admitted to the market or requires modification of goods for the market or withdraws goods from the market. The Commission then informs the other member states and may decide to seek further details or take action if it concludes the measures actually breach Article 28. So far it has not been very successful and further details will not be provided here.

7.9 **Equally Applicable Measures (Indistinctly Applicable Measures)**

Measures which apply only to imports or exports are called distinctly applicable measures, but it is to be noted that Article 28 prohibits not only national rules that overtly discriminate against imported products, subject to the possibility of justification under Article 30, it may also be used to challenge national rules which on their face make no distinction between domestic and imported goods. Article 3 of Directive 70/50 provides that measures which are equally applicable to domestic and imported goods will only breach Article 28 where the restrictive effect on the free movement of goods exceeds the effects necessary for the trade rules, i.e. they would be disproportionate to the aim and would thus tend to protect domestic products at the expense of the imports:

This Directive also covers measures governing the marketing of products which deal, in particular, with shape, size, weight, composition, presentation, identification or putting up and which are equally applicable to domestic and imported products, where the restrictive effect of such measures on the free movement of goods exceeds the effects intrinsic to trade rules. This is the case, in particular, where the restrictive effects on the free movement of goods are out of proportion to their purpose; and the same objective can be attained by other means which are less of a hindrance to trade.

Those measures which apply to both imports and domestic goods are termed equally or indistinctly applicable.

The wide definition of this in *Dassonville* made no allowance for some measures

---

[8] Decision 3052/95 on exchange of information about national measures derogating from the principle of free movement of goods (OJ 1995 L321/1).

introduced by member states which applied to both imports and domestic products and might be justified on particular grounds, such as the environment but the judgment was actually qualified by the statement that

in the absence of a community system guaranteeing for consumers the authenticity of a product's designation of origin, if a Member State takes reasonable measures to prevent unfair practices in this connection, Article 28 may not be contravened. It is, however subject to the condition that the means of proof required should not act as a hindrance to trade between member states and should, in consequence, be accessible to all Community nationals.

Thus, the *Dassonville* case hints at the possibility that the member states could restrict imports for a good reason and marks the foundation of the so-called rule of reason and was developed further in a landmark decision in Community law which seemed to address the difficulties with indistinctly applicable measures introduced by member states for arguably sound reasons. This is Case 120/78 *Rewe-Zentral AG v Bundesmonopolverwaltung fur Branntwein* better known as *Cassis de Dijon.*

7.9.1 The *Cassis de Dijon* Case

The *Cassis de Dijon* case concerns a prohibition on the marketing in the Federal Republic of Germany of spirits with less than a 25 per cent alcohol content which included Crème de Cassis de Dijon (a blackcurrant alcoholic liqueur), containing only 15–20 per cent alcohol. The ban applied to all low alcohol liqueurs regardless of origin and did not distinguish between national and foreign drinks. The arguments made by Germany for the ban were that lower alcohol liqueurs would lead to alcohol tolerance thus leading to health problems in the future, the lower alcohol also provided a price advantage for the imported products which was unfair and would force down alcohol rates of drinks and thus quality contrary to usual manufacture. However, the actual result was the effective ban, albeit indirect, of French imports. The Court of Justice made a number of statements of importance in its judgment. It held that there was no valid reason why, provided they have been lawfully produced and marketed in one of the member states, alcoholic beverages should not be introduced without restriction into any other member state. As was seen in an earlier case, notably *Commission v UK* (UHT milk) this is a restatement of the principle of equivalence.

The Court of Justice also held that obstacles to the free movement of goods resulting from disparities in the national laws on the marketing of products must be accepted as far as these provisions are necessary to satisfy certain mandatory requirements, considered further below. The judgment was a way of getting around too strict an application of the rule developed in the earlier *Dassonville* case. Therefore, equally applicable measures which hinder trade may be acceptable if they are in pursuit of a reasonable special interest the member state has the right to protect, however they must still be subject to the principle of proportionality and must neither be an arbitrary discrimination nor a disguised restriction on trade. The latter two terms repeat those provided in Article 30. The judgment in *Cassis de Dijon* makes it clear that Article 28 also covers indirect discrimination by reference to the term 'obstacles to movement within the Community resulting from disparities between national laws relating to the marketing of the products in question'. In other words where a national rule has a different effect, although on the face of it applying equally to both imported and domestic products, it may also be caught by Article 28. The case is regarded as a very important tool for the Commission in creating the internal market by the simple rule that goods lawfully manufactured and sold in one member state should be able to move freely throughout the EC and indeed the Commission later issued a practice note based on its interpretation of what the *Cassis de Dijon* case meant.[9]

Examples of the types of mandatory measures, i.e. the national rules which may be raised by the member states referred to by the Court of Justice in *Cassis de Dijon* were 'the effectiveness of fiscal supervision, the protection of public health, the fairness of consumer transactions and the defence of the consumer'. They are not exhaustive and have been added to by the Court of Justice in subsequent cases. In Case 302/86 *Commission v Denmark* (Disposable Beer Cans) environmental grounds were raised, cultural interests in *Cinetheque SA v Federation Nationale des Cinemas Francais*, concerning the sale of video recordings, environmental protection and conservation of the resources of the sea were held to be interests worthy of protection in *Minister of Justice v Kramer*, laws for the protection of workers, *Union Depart. des Syndicats CGT de l'Aisne v Sidef Conforama* and *Criminal Proceedings against Marchandise*, maintenance of the diversity of the press (C-368/95 *Vereinigte Familiapress*) and the protection of fundamental rights freedom of speech and protest (C-112/00 *Schmidberger*).

7.9.2 The Application of the Rule of Reason: The Requirements in Detail

Once it has been established that the interest comes within the rule of reason the criteria of the rule of reason must be satisfied.

7.9.2.1 There Must be no Community System Covering the Interest in Question

In other words, EU legislation must not have occupied the field, there must be no

---

[9] Communication from the Commission concerning the consequences of the judgments by the Court of Justice on 20 February 1979 in Cases 120/78 ('*Cassis de Dijon*') OJ 1980 C256/2.

harmonizing legislation. In Case 16/83 *Criminal Proceedings against Karl Prantl,* a German law provided that only certain quality wines from Franken and Baden could be marketed in the bottle known as Bocksbeutel. Anyone marketing any other wine in the Bocksbeutel committed an offence. The defendant in the main action was charged with selling quantities of Italian red wine in bottles of this type. In fact red wine produced in the Italian Tyrol had been produced in bottles of this type for at least a century, as have Portuguese Wines. There was in place, though, a partial system of Community rules governing the types of wines which might be marketed in specific types of bottle but these had not yet been concluded to rule out national competences in respect of the bottle in question in the case at hand. Thus, it was held that until Community rules are implemented, the rules adopted by the member states could be maintained so long as they did not contravene Articles 28–30. The Court held that the rules in question did in fact contravene Article 28 and were not saved by Article 30.

7.9.2.2 The Measure Must be Indistinctly Applicable

The measure must apply without difference on the face of it to both imports and domestic products, otherwise it cannot be considered under the rule of reason and must be considered narrowly under Articles 28 and 30 only. Case 113/80 *Commission v Ireland* (Metal Objects) confirms the strict view of Article 30. Irish legislation required souvenirs of Ireland which were not domestically produced to bear the designation 'Foreign'. The Commission considered the restrictions contravened Article 28 and Article 2(3)(f) of Directive 70/50 because they were measures which had the effect of lowering the value of an imported product by causing a reduction in its value or an increase in its costs. The Irish government argued that the measures were justified on grounds of consumer protection and therefore fell within the scope of the public policy derogation in Article 30. The Court of Justice held that since Article 30 constitutes a derogation from the basic rule that all obstacles to the free movement of goods between member states are to be eliminated, Article 30 must be construed narrowly. Since neither the protection of consumers nor the fairness of transactions were included amongst the exceptions set out in Article 30 it was held that they cannot be relied on in connection with that Article. The Court then considered whether the measures might be justified as necessary to meet mandatory requirements, however, the rules were not measures which applied to domestic and imported products without distinction. They applied only to imported products and were therefore discriminatory in nature, with the result that the measures were not covered by the decision in *Cassis de Dijon* which applies only to provisions that regulate both imported products and domestic products. The rules were therefore in breach of Article 28.

7.9.2.3 The Measure Must Neither be an Arbitrary Discrimination Nor a Disguised Restriction on Trade

For an example of this, see Case 124/81 *Commission v UK* (UHT Milk) in which the requirement of an import licence was held to be a disguised restriction despite being issued automatically.

7.9.2.4 The Measure Must Meet the Requirements of Proportionality

In Case 113/80 *Commission v Ireland* (Irish Metal Objects), the Court took the view that the interests of consumers and fair trading would have been adequately protected if it were left to domestic manufacturers to take appropriate steps such as affixing, if they so wished, their mark of origin to their own products or packaging. The requirement to stamp foreign was not reasonable.

In Case 261/81 *Walter Rau Lebensmittelwerke v De Smedt*, Belgian legislation prohibiting the marketing of margarine which did not conform to a particular shape. This rule had a clear protective effect and was an obstacle to marketing to importers. The Belgian government argued that the measure was necessary for consumer protection. The Court of Justice ruled that if a member state has a choice between various measures to attain the same objective, it should choose the measure which least restricts the free movement of goods. In this case consumers might have been protected and informed that the product was margarine by other measures which would have constituted less of an interference with free movement of goods, such as labelling. Therefore the rules contravened Article 28. In Case 16/83 *Prantl*, the Court of Justice held that the sale of a product may not be prohibited when a labelling requirement will adequately protect the consumer, so as not to confuse the particular wine in the wine bottle sold.

The various food additives and constituents cases considered above under the Article 30 derogations are also subject to this line of argument that adequate labelling will protect consumers rather than a ban, which would be disproportionate. See Case 174/84 *Commission v Germany* concerning the Beer Purity Law, above, which provided that only malted barley, hops, yeast, and water may be used in the manufacture of beer, and further that only drinks complying with those provisions could be marketed under the designation beer. A further law prohibited importation of beers containing additives unless the additives were specifically authorized. The Court of Justice held that whilst it was legitimate to seek to enable consumers who attribute special qualities to beer manufactured from particular raw materials to make their choice in an informed way, that could be done by labelling. The prohibition went beyond what was necessary for the protection of German consumers, since such protection could quite easily be ensured by compulsory affixing of labels informing consumers about the nature of the product sold.

7.9.3 Legislative Interventions

In order to try to regulate the free movement of goods more effectively and more comprehensively and to avoid some of the difficulties of relying on piecemeal litigation to challenged measures introduced from time to time by the member states, the Commission introduced Directive 83/189, now updated and consolidated by Directive 98/34.[10] These required member states to notify technical standards of products before being adopted so that the Commission could consider whether they created barriers to the free movement of goods. Whilst it was not intended to create rights for individuals and merely provide a channel of communication between the member states and the Commission, the Directives have nevertheless been instrumental in some cases between individuals, see the section on incidental horizontal effects in Chapter 5. These cases have prompted significant use and notifications under the Directive and have probably helped in preventing some national measures which would have created barriers. Further discussion in a book of this nature though is probably not warranted but it nevertheless useful to know of its existence.

7.9.4 Summary of *Cassis de Dijon*

We can take the view of the rule of reason in the *Cassis de Dijon* case that it either classifies measures as falling outside the scope of Article 28 in the first place or that it justifies measures which would otherwise have breached Article 28 as a result of the fact that the mandatory requirements provide further derogations to Article 28. The case of *Cassis de Dijon* certainly allowed member states to maintain some rules which protected an interest but it was often unclear as to whether the national mandatory requirement fell outside or would be in breach of Article 28 except for the fact it was a interest worthy of protection and thus justified (provided all other criteria were satisfied). As a consequence, in some cases there has been a blurring of the distinction between distinctly and indistinctly measures. Normally the route taken would be to decide if the measures are distinctly or indistinctly applicable and decide if they have breached Article 28. Then if distinctly applicable, whether any of the derogations of Article 30 apply or if indistinctly applicable, whether any of the mandatory requirements or an Article 30 derogation applies. Occasionally though as in Case C-67/97 *Bluhme* or Case C-2/90 *Commission v Belgium* (Walloon Waste), the Court of Justice has extended the mandatory requirements to a situation concerned essentially with a distinctly applicable rule permitting one local good only to the exclusion of all others.

[10] OJ 1998 L204/37.

This point was effectively ignored by the Court of Justice in both of the cases above in the interests of environmental protection. However, for the most part the distinction remains. To this must be added a consideration of the difference between equal burden and dual burden rules which was provoked by the *Cassis de Dijon* development. The problem being that whilst dual burden rules could be isolated and easily regarded as being in breach of Article 28, equal burden rules were often left to the national courts to decide whether the national interest (the mandatory requirement) was one which was worthy of protection and thus satisfying the requirements of the *Cassis de Dijon* case, often with different outcomes.

7.9.5 Equal Burden/Dual Burden

An indistinctly applicable rule is one which applies, at least on the face of it, to imported and domestic products alike, it is the same rule in play and therefore the face value conclusion is that the rule imposes an equal burden on both products. However, this is not the conclusion if one takes into account the fact that the importer may have already satisfied a rule applied in the state of export and where the imported product has to comply with two sets of product requirements in order to be marketed lawfully in the state of import: Those operated by the state of origin and those of the state of importation. In this situation the imported product is placed under an additional burden. For example, in Case 261/81 *Walter Rau* (Margarine), noted above, a separate production line would have to be set up for the Belgium market and more if other countries adopted similar requirements, maybe round for Luxembourg and so on, which would not be economically viable for the manufacturer. Hence the conclusion is that it is unfair that two sets of rules must be complied with the consequence that the additional or dual burden rule is caught by Article 28 unless justified by either Article 30 or the rule of reason mandatory requirements.

Equal burden rules in contrast should not have been considered as even coming within Article 28 because by definition the burden of the rules in question in the state of import falls equally on home and domestic products, the imported product suffers no discrimination or disadvantage. Unfortunately, the Court of Justice appeared in some cases to extend the scope of Article 28 to cover the equal burden rules which did apply fairly to both imported and domestic products to national measures which were neither directly nor indirectly discriminatory and where the same requirement applied to both without adding an additional burden on the imports. For example, Cases 60–61/84 *Cinetheque* concerned the prohibition on hire or sale of videos of films within first year of release in order to protect the film industry from production through to the cinemas. The rule applied equally to domestic and imported videos. The Court of Justice held nevertheless that the rule was a measure having equivalent effect because it did restrict the overall import of videos as indeed it equally restricted sales of domestic produced videos although these were less in number. However, it could be justified for a specific reason, which in the case was the addition of 'the protection of artistic works' to the list of mandatory requirements of *Cassis*. Otherwise it would have breached Article 28. However, the damage was done. The *Cassis* case was beneficial to both free movement of goods and in supporting national diversity by allowing regional variations under the mutual equivalence rule. Further, under the rule of reason and mandatory requirements rule, member state interests covered by national rules would be recognized. However, if those equal burden rules were also potentially in breach of Article 28 then, as happened, all sorts of national rules were seized on by traders to attack virtually any nationally imposed restriction on trade practices or commercial freedom which restricted in any way the level of imports. Particularly, it was seized upon by traders who had been caught infringing the national rules who claimed that their right to import goods and sell them had been infringed. Many of the national laws were concerned with sales and marketing rules and actually had no impact on the access of imported goods to the national market. Increasingly, however, national laws were questioned, not on the basis that they hindered imports only but they affected the volume of trade regardless of origin as in Case 61/84 *Cinetheque*, above.

The Sunday trading case law serves as a good example of the confusion that can arise as it was assumed that the national laws did affect Community trade and were in breach of Article 28 unless justified. However, as was demonstrated in these cases, the interest worth protecting could vary. The previous ban which used to exist in the UK, prohibited the trading of very many goods on a Sunday and was not discriminatory but applied to imported and domestic goods alike. However, traders claimed it breached Article 28 because by reducing the volume of sales, it reduced volume of imports and thus it was a measure having equivalent effect. The grounds stated by the member state to justify the law were not contained in Article 30 but arguably within the mandatory requirements of *Cassis*. The case law from the UK in respect of this question has not been particularly helpful, partly as a result of the Court of Justice deciding that national courts must determine for themselves whether the reason for a rule was justified under the rule of reason. However, the ban on Sunday trading concerned both the idea of 'keeping Sunday special' and the protection of workers and as a result led to contradictory decisions depending on whether the UK courts took into account the protection of workers, which would appear to justify a ban on Sunday trading, and the attempt to keep Sunday special which appears not to justify a ban. See Cases 145/88 *Torfaen BC v B & Q plc* and *B & Q Ltd v Shrewsbury BC* [1990] 3 CMLR 535. Before a further UK case reached the Court of Justice, two decisions had been reached by the Court of Justice in Case C-312/89 *Conforama* and Case C-332/89

Criminal Proceedings against Merchandise which were more instructive from the Community law point of view. In a request for preliminary rulings from French and Belgian courts, the Court of Justice held that national restrictions on the opening of shops on Sundays (The French Code de Travail provides for a mandatory day's rest on Sundays whilst the Belgian Loi sur le Travail prohibits the employing of retail shop workers after noon on a Sunday) were not in breach of Community law. It was considered that this area was a matter for the regulation of each individual member state and thus the measures were held not designed to control patterns of trade between member states nor were they applied so as to discriminate against goods from other member states. So when another reference on Sunday trading was referred from the UK, the Court of Justice held in Case C169/91 *Stoke City Council v B & Q plc* that the UK's restrictions on Sunday trading do not conflict with Community law. It held such rules reflected 'choices relating to particular national or regional socio-cultural characteristics'. The member states have the discretion to make such choices. However, this series of cases did raise the question of whether the Court of Justice had gone too far in upholding the sanctity of free movement over national rules by finding that all obstacles to free movement and not merely those concerned with discrimination and protectionism were in breach of Article 28 unless justified. Hence then the next development.

7.10 *Keck and Mithouard*: Certain Selling Arrangements

Faced with many similar arguments by traders against national rules, when presented with a suitable occasion the Court of Justice was able to redefine its position. Cases C-267–68/91 *Keck and Mithouard* concerned the French prohibition of goods at a loss, which was argued to be a restriction of sales contrary to Article 28. The Court of Justice stated that:

In view of the increasing tendency of traders to invoke Article (now 28) of the Treaty as a means of challenging any rules whose effect is to limit their commercial freedom even where such rules are not aimed at products from other member states, the Court considers it necessary to re-examine and clarify its case law on this matter.

The Court considered that traders had been using Community law to try to challenge laws which were not aimed at restricting imports but restricted the sales of all goods, domestic and imported. The Court then stated it considered that selling or marketing arrangements did not come within the concept outlined in *Dassonville* or Article 28. The Court of Justice held that:

Contrary to what has previously been decided, the application to products from other member states of national provisions restricting or prohibiting certain selling arrangements is not such as to hinder directly or indirectly, actually or potentially, trade between member states within the meaning of the *Dassonville* judgment provided that those provisions apply to all affected traders operating within the national territory and provided that they affect in the same manner, in law and in fact, the marketing of domestic products and of those from other member states.

Looked at in another way, an impediment to trade is acceptable where the rule in question is merely a selling arrangement which impedes both the trade in domestic and imported products equally. It was an attempt to remove many national rules which were introduced for reasons other than those which were intended to be a restriction on imports. So, providing national rules do not impede access to markets but merely regulates them without any form of discrimination, either in law and in fact, they will be acceptable and will not fall within Article 28. However, there are problems with the *Keck* judgment because it did not provide an instant clarification of the law, most notably the question of what are 'selling arrangements'? The scope of this expression was explored in subsequent cases.

7.10.1 Post-*Keck* Case Law

Selling arrangements are broadly defined as rules relating to the market circumstances in which the goods are sold. Selling arrangements are usually equal burden rules which now fall outside of the scope of application of Article 28. Selling arrangements are therefore measures dealing with where, when, how, and by whom goods may be sold. For example, Cases C-401 and 402/92, *Tankstation 't Heustke* involved Dutch laws about the opening times of shops at petrol outlets, product advertising rules in Case C-292/92 *Hunermund* and Belgian laws prohibiting offering products for sale at a loss of profit in Case C-63/94 *Belgapom*, and Case C-391/92 *Commission v Greece* which prohibited sale of any processed milk for babies other than in pharmacies. In all of these cases, the Court of Justice found the rules were acceptable under the Article 28.

It would have seemed that post *Keck*, provided a rule was classified as a selling arrangement, it fell outside of Article 28, however if the rule was shown to create a requirement to physically alter the imported product, it would breach Article 28 unless justified. For example, in Case C-470/93 *Mars*, a national law was challenged which prohibited the selling of Mars Bars which had been labelled as providing an extra 10 per cent. The Court of Justice held that as the law concerned the product presentation, labelling, and packaging and was thus a physical requirement and which if upheld meant that it imposed a dual burden. It was therefore held to be a breach of

Article 28. See also Case C-368/95 *Vereinigte Familiapress Zeitungsverlags v Bauer Verlag* which considered the difference between a selling arrangement and physical requirement. An Austrian law prohibiting the offering of free gifts linked to the sale of goods, was the basis for an Austrian publishers action against a German magazine containing a prize crossword puzzle. The Court of Justice repeated its position established since *Keck* that certain national rules would not breach Article 28 unless imposing additional requirements and that the Austrian rules would constitute a hindrance to free movement if the content of the magazine had to be altered for the Austrian Market. However, maintaining the diversity of the press was the legitimate public interest objective given by the authorities and accepted by the Court of Justice.

Unfortunately, the next twist in the case law was the recognition that some selling arrangements, although equal burden and not relating to physical characteristics, nevertheless had an effect which disadvantaged imports by hindering market access or which seemed to favour domestic products, in particular, those in respect of advertising and sales promotion rules.

7.10.2 Market Access or Discrimination or Both?

In the post-*Keck* case law, cases have considered whether Article 28 has been breached because market access has been hindered in some way or that a selling arrangement, which although equal burden, is nevertheless discriminatory in some way. In Case C-412/93 *Leclerc Siplec* AG Jacobs argued that the test should be to consider if there was an impediment to market access and that Article 28 should catch measures which directly and substantially impede access to the market. This was seen previously in free movement of persons area of law in Case C-415/93 *Union Royale Belge des Sociétés de Football Association v Bosman* in which it was held that non-discriminatory rules which prevented football player transfers and which prevented market access should be outlawed.

This was taken up in Cases C-34–36/95 *Konsumenten-ombudsmannen v De Agostini* in which TV advertising directed at children under 12 was prohibited. The measure was considered to be a selling arrangement which applied without discrimination, thus equal burden. However, it was held that would seem to have a greater impact on products from other member states because of the difficulties faced in trying to get access to the market, advertising being the only effective form of promotion. If the national court found that the impact of the prohibition was different it would therefore breach Article 28 unless justified by Article 30 or the mandatory requirements under *Cassis*.

In the subsequent Case C-405/98 *Gourmet International*, a ban on alcohol advertising was challenged under the same argument that it had a greater impact on imported products trying to gain access to the Swedish market because without advertising consumers would only be familiar with domestic products. Thus it was held that the measure would be caught by Article 28 EC Treaty if it prevents access to the market by products from another state, or impede access any more than they impede access of domestic products.

In Case C-254/98 *Heimdienst*, a non-discriminatory Austrian law which applied to all operators trading in the national territory (Austrian and other EU) required goods sold on the doorstep to come from a locally established premises. It was held to be a selling arrangement but one which impeded access to the market of the member state of importation for products from other member states more than it impeded access for domestic products. It is the differential manner in which it affects domestic and other member state products. Thus selling arrangements which either in law or in fact discriminate against non-national providers and thus impede or hinder market access will not escape Article 28 but might still might be justified.

This test of differential impact, i.e. affecting imports more than domestic products, focuses both on market access and that fact that the effective result is discriminatory.

7.11 Overall Summary

We start with a perfectly sound rule (Art 28) which seeks to ensure that there are no restrictions on the free movement of goods. To this we add a further statutory rule (Art 30) which provides exceptions to the first rule because it is recognized that there are genuine circumstances where restrictions and different treatment are justified. So far, so good. Then there are statutory guidelines (Directive 70/50) and case law which help to determine how the rule applies and the circumstances which breach the rule or come within the exceptions. Additionally, there is a focus on the concepts of distinctly applicable measures which can only be justified by Article 30, which is easy to see, and indistinctly applicable measures, which starts to become complex and requires us to be aware of the very important case of *Cassis de Dijon*. The indistinctly applicable measures are presumed to come within and thus breach Article 28 unless justified by Article 30 or a further set of justifications introduced by *Cassis* and subsequent cases (the mandatory requirements). It is worth noting that Article 30 applies to both direct and indirect discrimination but has an exhaustive list of exceptions whereas *Cassis de Dijon* applies to indirect discrimination only but potentially there is a much wider range of exceptions. Thus certain national rules or laws could escape the prohibition of Article 28, but strict criteria were laid down so that member states would not be able to exploit this new possibility (the second sentence require-ment of Art 30 and proportionality).

Then, because it started to happen that every single national rule which applied to goods might be considered to come with the ambit of the *Cassis de Dijon* case, there is another important case (*Keck*). This seeks to lay down another rule or gloss on the original rules to say that certain types of law applicable to the marketing of goods (selling arrangements) should not even be considered as coming within the original rule! (that is if you can remember it . . . Art 28!) and there is further case law now to provide further clarifications of what was meant in *Keck*. Indistinctly applicable sell-ing arrangements are thus presumed outside of Article 28 unless they introduce discrimination or prevent market access by adversely affecting imports more than domestic products (see *Heimdienst*) but these can be justified by Article 30 or *Cassis* (*Familiapress*).

Further reading

Books

BARNARD, C. *The Substantive Law of the EU: The Four Freedoms*, OUP, Oxford 2004, chapters 1–7.

DAVIES, G. *European Union Internal Market Law*, 2nd edn., Cavendish Publishing, London 2003, chapters 1–3.

WEILER, J. H. H. 'The Constitution of the Common Market Place: Text and Context in the Evolution of the Free movement of Goods' in Craig and de Bùrca (eds.) *The Evolution of EU Law*, OUP, Oxford 1999, chapter 21.

Articles

BARNARD, C. 'Fitting the Remaining Pieces into the Goods and Persons Jigsaw?' (2001) 26 *EL Rev*, 35.

CONNOR, T. 'Accentuating the Positive: the "Selling Arrangement", the first Decade, and Beyond' (2005) 54 *ICLQ*, 127.

DAVIES, G. 'Can selling arrangements be harmonised?' (2005) 30 *EL Rev*, 371–85.

KACZOROWSKA, A. 'Gourmet Can Have His *Keck* and Eat It!' (2004) *European Law Journal*, 479.

OLIVER, P. 'Some further reflections on the scope of Articles 28–30 (ex 30–36) EC' (1999) 36 *CML Rev*, 783.

SHUIBHNE, N. 'The Free Movement of Goods and Article 28: An Evolving Framework' (2002) 27 *EL Rev*, 408.

WEATHERILL, S. 'After Keck, Some thoughts on how to clarify the Clarification' (1996) 33 *CML Rev*, 885.

WEATHERILL, S. 'Recent case law concerning the free movement of goods: mapping the frontiers of market deregulation' (1999) 36 *CML Rev*, 51–85.

Web sites

Mutual recognition http://europa.eu.int/comm/internal_market/en/goods/mutrec.htm

Guide to the Concept and Practical

Application of Arts 28–30 EC published by the EU Commission, DG Internal Market, January 2001 http://europa.eu.int/comm/ enterprise/regulation/goods/docs/art2830/ guideart2830_en.pdf

8

Competition Law

8.1 Introduction

Competition law applies to regulate the activities of mainly commercial undertakings to curb the excesses of the free market or to remedy situations which in an unregulated free market would be harmful to some parties or the system of competition itself. The idea of competition lies at the heart of the capitalist system and at the heart of Community Economic law. It conjures up images of the free market—a free market economy with minimal state intervention. It suggests the efficiency of the actors in the market place determining what should be made where and for what price and, more to the point, free from state planning or state production. 'If, as the metaphor goes, a market economy is governed by an invisible hand, competition is surely the brass knuckles by which it enforces its decisions.'[1]

It is often commented that competition is desirable for many reasons. Competition is supposed to ensure efficiency by giving the greatest awards to the keenest in the market place. This efficiency is meant to provide a benefit to all in that it improves living standards, it creates employment, and allows the consumer to benefit from a competitive market. Competition is therefore seen as a healthy and desirable state of affairs by economists particularly of the right wing who would point to the obvious failure of the planned uncompetitive economies of the communist world which were unable to provide the gains in the standard of living achieved in the West. Thus if competition is good, then more competition is surely better. It is therefore desirable to increase the scale over which competition can be achieved, i.e. create a larger and freer market. The internal market of the European Community must therefore be a good thing for the industry and economy of the member states. European-wide competition should stimulate the entire economy of the Community for both the domestic and world markets.

---

[1] **US v Syufy Case** No. 89–15475 United States Court of Appeals for the Ninth Circuit. Case reproduced at: http://notabug.com/kozinski/syufy.

However unfettered competition does not maintain the status quo, left unregulated it is ultimately self destructive. The most efficient undertakings will finally drive other competition out of business leaving a monopoly which can then exploit the market to the detriment of consumers and the economy generally. So, in order to retain fair competition, some form of intervention on the part of a state is required. To continue to reap the benefits of competition, given that perfect competition is well nigh impossible, a state between perfect competition and oligopoly or monopoly must be maintained. For this certain criteria must be fulfilled. There must be no discrimination between buyers and sellers and producers. This is actually a requirement of the Common Agricultural Policy of the EC, see Article 34(2) EC. There should be a supply of homogeneous commodities, i.e. the same or at least very similar products must be available and thus in competition with each other. There should be a large number of buyers and sellers. Where there are a limited number (known as a 'oligopoly') or only one or two ('monopoly' or 'duopoly') the market can be severely affected or influenced by these companies. There should be close and free contact between buyers and sellers in all parts of the market, i.e. no artificial obstacles to trade, by tariffs or geography etc. Without the above, the market distorts or becomes imperfect with the upper hand being achieved by one side or the other, today this is usually the producer or seller rather than the consumer or buyer.

8.2 Competition Law Relevance to the EU

Competition law regulation was regarded as a necessary and essential element in the building of the Community and Union. A view confirmed by Court of Justice in Case C-126/97 *Eco Swiss China Time Ltd*. Apart from the above general reasons, the EU needed an integrated competition policy to complement and to ensure the maintenance of the common market—the whole establishment or foundation of the EU is premised on the desire to promote integration and create a single unified market. One of the wider aims of the internal market is to establish and maintain European-wide competition to stimulate the entire economy of the Community for both the domestic and world markets. A competition policy within the overall Treaty regime prevents Companies from setting up their own rules and obstacles to trade to replace the national rules and obstacles the Community is trying to abolish. The two go hand in hand, you cannot have one without ensuring you have the other. To have prevented the member states on the one hand from restricting the movement of goods just to allow private companies to do it by their agreements and practices would defeat the objectives of the first policy and, vice versa, to prevent companies from artificially dividing the markets but to allow the member states to do so would undermine a competition policy. It is worth noting that some multinational companies are in a better position to divide the market than states. They have the same or greater turnover than the Gross or National Domestic Product of some states. Without regulation, it would be the companies and not the member state who took the decisions on trade flows. In order to retain fair competition in the Community, some form of intervention on the part of Community is therefore required.

8.2.1 Basic Outline of EC Competition Policy

The broad policy objective was to maintain and encourage competition for the benefit of the Community and its citizens, to achieve an open and unified market and the integration of the Community, to encourage economic activity amongst small and medium size enterprise and to maximize efficiency by allowing the free flow of goods and resources.

Much of the basis of Community competition policy has been borrowed from the American experience of the concentration in too few hands of power over the market place and also to some extent post-war German concern with the large firms and cartels which obtained not only too much economic power but consequently undemocratic political power also in the Weimar Republic and in Hitler's Germany.

Thus in the period following World War II, German attitudes to competition were adopted in Europe. Attitudes were also influenced by the desire to protect emerging and expanding industries and companies and to encourage the rebirth of European industry after the devastation of World War II.

The Community is distinctly interventionist and increasingly so in order to outlaw abuses of industry to the detriment of consumers and the market. However too much intervention hinders growth and results in inefficient small-scale production which cannot benefit from the economies of scale. Therefore the Community must tread a middle path. Thus, one of the fundamental positions of the competition law to be established was that there should be no barriers against the entry to the market of new companies and industries so that there would be fairness and equality amongst businesses. It was also considered vital to promote European business to compete with American and Japanese capital and business ventures (arguably now Chinese and Indian). So the competition policy and rules chosen should also promote the integration of European business, especially small and medium size business but at the same time it must be ensured that companies do not become too competitive or over concentrate and are then able to eliminate competition, thereby starting to dominate a market, or to cooperate in such a way as to act as one unit in the Community to the detriment of consumers and smaller firms. In the EU, regulatory action has been focused more on the larger players in the market rather than the small and medium business enterprises.

One of the problems with community competition policy is in respect of the multiple objectives which exist. If they are complimentary then there is no conflict but if they are in fact different—objectives which require different approaches to achieve them—some difficulties, not least at the legal level, will be experienced.

The overall policy is underpinned by conflicting ideologies of why or even of how it is to be achieved. On the one hand a market-oriented approach defines the problems of competition as barriers to free trade which must be removed. This approach presupposes there is formal equality of all of individuals (undertakings) in the market and the Commission is merely interested in the regulation of the market per se and not on the part of any particular interest. This leads to difficulties in satisfying all objectives, especially in the area of merger policy. On the other hand the 'structural approach' concerns changes to the market structure because the inequality of the actors has been recognized. Therefore the Commission is entitled to regulate and structure the market in order to achieve the goals set by the inclusion of competition policy in the Community, which can lead to difficulties in rationalizing all the decisions. Thus, it is argued you can easily achieve single objectives such as a competition policy which has the simple aims of preventing distortion in the market. The actual prevention of this may not be simple but the goal is unambiguous and not confused or subject to conflicting priorities. Or, you can have an industry policy to encourage small and medium size EU firms, or a customs policy to discourage external imports or rules to ensure the free movement of goods. However, when all of these various policies are pursued within one supposed clear objective called competition policy it will lead to difficulties because there is a need to regulate all of them with an eye on the others. In some quarters this is seen as one of the steps on the way to political unity, i.e. functionalism or the interrelatedness of everything. Furthermore, the particular aims pursued can change from time to time. Sometimes, the structural approach has the upper hand and is criticized because it is regarded as applying more overtly political rather than economic motives, in that it gives too much encouragement to the small and medium size business and is too heavy on the large-scale industry which is the only one capable of competing on the world markets with the American and Japanese industries. Then at other times there seems to be more concentration on larger companies or on consumer protection. Thus, the Commission may be interpreting the competition rules to meet changing objectives as politically required, e.g. to make the rules lighter to promote certain industries so that they can compete worldwide, or tighter to discourage entry by others, or to take account of state imposed distortions as with the French Tobacco industry, or to protect certain agricultural products vital for the CAP. Worker protection and environmental considerations may also play their part. The point of all of this is that if you are not aware that this is happening and only seek to learn the rules you will have difficulty in rationalizing rules between cases when rationality does not exist or has been undermined by conflicting policy objectives. Hence my approach is not to present all the rules in competition policy but just to demonstrate the most important in the context of the leading cases.

8.2.2 The Broad Legislative Outline

EC competition rules are generally designed to intervene to prevent agreements which fix prices or conditions or the supply of products, to prohibit agreements which carve up territories and to prevent abuses of market power which have the effect of removing real competition and controlling mergers which would also remove competition. As with the free movement of goods, the rules cover all items capable of forming the subject of commercial transactions.

The aims are set out in the Preamble and Articles 2–4 of the EC Treaty.

The Preamble of the EC Treaty refers to the 'removal of existing obstacles calls for concerted action in order to guarantee steady expansion, balanced trade and fair competition'.

Article 2 refers to 'establishing a Common Market and an economic and monetary union and by implementing the common policies . . . referred to in Articles 3 and 4, to promote . . . a harmonious and balanced development of economic activities'. Article 3(1)(g) of the EC Treaty lists among the activities of the Community 'a system ensuring that competition in the internal market is not distorted'.

Article 10 has also been pleaded with Article 3(1)(g) and Article 81 (old 85) as a general principle of law supporting the argument that competition law also applies in respect of the member states and not just undertakings so that they are prohibited from encouraging or requiring acts or conduct by companies which may distort competition in the Community.

The broad aims are then expanded in three sets of rules: One relating to the activities of legal persons, i.e. the business undertakings; one relating to anti-dumping measures; and finally, one relating to the activities of the member states. The rules concerned with the private undertakings are subdivided in two provisions: Article 81 for agreements between cartels involving more than one entity and the other, Article 82, concerned with dominant positions, dealing predominantly with one entity but also applicable to one of more undertakings. The rules are designed to prevent a number of abuses, which will be considered in detail later.

This chapter will consider the competition rules of Articles 81 and 82 (old 85 and 86) and the relationship between these two articles. It will also be concerned with the mergers policy of the Community and briefly with the procedural law of competition law and merger law.

8.2.3 Application and Interpretation

The Commission is given the task under Article 85 (ex 89) EC and Regulation 1/2003 to ensure that competition in the Community is not distorted. The application of the rules by the Commission and the interpretation of the rules of the Court of Justice has not been done in isolation by looking at the provision alone but has been applied in the light of the objectives of competition policy the rules are applied in the light of the general objective of the Treaty. In Case 6 and 7/73, *Commercial Solvents v Commission*, the Court of Justice held: 'The prohibitions in Articles 85 and 86 (now 81 and 82) must be interpreted and applied in the light of Article 3(f) (now 3(g)) of the Treaty which provides that the activities of the Community shall include the institution of a system ensuring that competition is not distorted, and Article 2 of the Treaty which gives the Community the task of promoting "throughout the Community harmonious development of economic activities" '. Case 26/76, *Metro v Saba (No. 1)*, is a also good example, whereby the Commission, in pursuit of a goal, also relied on Article 2 EEC to justify particular decisions reached. The agreements in the case were deemed to satisfy competition rules because they helped to maintain employment. This latter case serves as an example of where the Commission, in carrying out its tasks in relation to competition law, is also required to balance this policy with other policies such as regional development or concern for unemployment and which may cause it to modify its position on the behaviour of companies. The general economic climate also influences the Commission, particularly in respect of merger policy, in that in times of poor economic growth, the Commission may treat mergers as being more acceptable because of the efficiency gains to be achieved and the greater ability the emerging company will have in the world market.

8.3 Article 81 (old 85)

Article 81 EC deals with restrictive practices. It sets out the prohibitions and details of the consequences of the failure to observe the prohibition. Finally it provides a framework by which exemptions from the prohibitions can be obtained. Article 81(1) EC prohibits agreements between undertakings, decisions by associations of under-takings, and concerted practices which may affect trade between the member states, and which have as their object or effect the prevention, restriction or distortion of competition within the common market. Article 81(2) provides that any agreements or decisions prohibited pursuant to Article 81 shall be automatically void. Article 81(3) concerns the exemptions to the basic rules. Article 81 has been subject to some considerable definition in the jurisprudence of the Court and was held to be capable of producing direct effects in Case 127/73 *BRT v SABAM*.

This section will consider in turn the basic definitions, in particular it will consider what is meant by three key terms: 'Undertakings', the 'object or effect', and 'affect on trade'.

8.3.1 Article 81(1) Definitions

8.3.1.1 'Undertakings'

The term 'undertakings' has been interpreted to include both natural and legal persons as independent or complementary economic actors. According to the Commission in *Polypropylene Cartel Community v ICI*[2] this includes any entity engaged in economic or commercial activities. Any form of business undertaking is included: Artists, *Unitel* an opera singer (Decision 78/516), *A.O.I.P. v Beyrard*, an inventor ([1976] 1 CMLR D14), and groups of companies in *Re Kodak* ([1970] CMLR D 19).

8.3.1.2 'Agreements'

The term 'agreements' is not limited to written and legally enforceable agreements only and it is not the form of the agreement that is important from the Commission's point of view but its effect on competition. Therefore a broad interpretation is given to the term: Agreement, decision, and concerted practice and includes non-binding agreements, as in for example the *Polypropylene Decision*, noted above.

The terms apply to both horizontal (where the parties are at the same level of the economic process) and vertical agreements (where the parties are at different levels of the economic process), as is illustrated by the rulings of the Court of Justice in Cases 56 and 58/64 *Consten & Grundig v Commission*, and Case 56/65 *Societe Technique Miniere v Maschinenbau Ulm* (the STM case). Gentlemen's agreements consisting of an oral or tacit agreement with nothing committed to writing are thus included in this definition, see Case 28/77 *Tepea v Commission*.

8.3.1.3 'Decisions by Associations of Undertakings'

Decisions by associations of undertakings has been held to include a trade associations

---

[2] Commission Decision [1988] 4 CMLR 347.

held liable for behaviour by its members in *AROW v BNIC*,[3] whereby the Bureau National Interprofessionel de Cognac was fined because it had fixed a minimum distribution price for cognac, arguing that this was necessary to guarantee quality. The Commission decided that, given all the other quality control measures which existed in the cognac industry, this argument could not be sustained.

Non-binding recommendations made by trade associations may also amount to decisions as held in Case 8/72 *Vereeniging van Cementhandelaren v Commission* (Cement Association case) and Case 96/82 *IAZ International Belgium NV v Commission*. In the latter, an association of water supply undertakings recommended its members not to connect dishwashers machines to the mains system unless they had a label supplied by Belgian association of dishwasher manufacturers indicating that they complied with relevant Belgian standards. The Court of Justice upheld the Commission's view that this recommendation, despite the fact that it was not binding, could restrict competition since its effect was to discriminate against appliances produced in other member states.

8.3.1.4 'Concerted Practices'

The term 'concerted practice' is potentially very broad. An important example of a 'concerted practice' is found in Cases 48, 49, and 51–57/69 *ICI v Commission* (Aniline Dyes). The Company, ICI was the first among a number of undertakings, accounting for 85 per cent of the market, to raise prices. The companies all said that the price coordination was simply a reflection of parallel behaviour in an oligopolistic market, where each producer followed the price leader, very often seen for example, with petrol prices. The Court of Justice held that this was a concerted practice arising out of coordination which becomes apparent from the behaviour of the participants, and which was designed to replace the risk of competition and the hazards of competitors spontaneous reactions by cooperation constituting a concerted practice. This case is also a precedent for the extra-territorial application of the competition rules, with the Head Office of ICI being in the UK, at the time of the facts of the case, outside the EEC, nevertheless, it was fined for activities which affected trade within the then EEC.

In Cases 40–8, 50, 43, 56, 11, and 113–14/73 *Suiker Unie (Sugar Union) v Commission*, the Community's main sugar producers had made deliveries in Holland only with the assent of the producers in that country, so as to weaken considerably the competitive pressure which unrestricted sugar imports would have engendered. They said they had not agreed to any plan to that effect, and hence there was no concerted practice. The Court of Justice held that there was no need for an actual plan and a concerted practice included 'Any direct or indirect contact between such operators,

---

[3] OJ 1982 L379/1, [1983] 2 CMLR 240.

the object or effect of which is either to influence the conduct on the market of an actual or potential competitor or to disclose to such a competitor the course of conduct which they themselves have decided to adopt or contemplate adopting on the market.'

A concerted practice is present when it enables the firms concerned to set positions which they have secured to the detriment of free movement of goods in the common market and the freedom of consumers to choose their suppliers. Each trader must independently decide on the policy he proposes to follow on the common market. This requirement does not deny traders the right to adapt their conduct to the way their competitors are behaving or are likely to behave but it does rule out any direct or indirect contact where the object or effect is to influence the conduct of an existing or potential market competitor or to reveal to him market policy decisions or intentions.

However, in Cases C-89, 104, 114, 116–17/85, and C-125–29/85, *Ahlström Oy et al v Commission* (Woodpulp Cartel cases), the Court of Justice held that the burden be placed on the Commission to prove a concerted practice by establishing 'firm, precise and consistent body of evidence' that a concerted practice existed. Parallel price increases would not satisfy this unless there was no other plausible explanation for them. Agreements which were taken by the parties within their trade association to fix recommended prices was not upheld as restricting competition contrary to Article 81(1). Here the price increases could be explained by the fact that there was an oligopolistic market in which prices set by the limited number of producers in the market would tend to follow each other closely without there being any understanding or agreement.

Even unilateral conduct on the part of a manufacturer has been deemed by the Court of Justice to be capable of amounting to an agreement or a concerted practice. In Case 25–6/84 *Ford v Commission*, until May 1982, Ford of Germany supplied to its German dealers a quantity of right hand drive cars for sale in the Federal Republic. Since the Spring of 1981 there had been a great increase in demand for right hand drive cars because German prices were considerably lower than those in Britain. Ford of Germany became concerned about the effects of this on the position of Ford Britain and notified the German dealers that, as from 1 May 1982, it would no longer accept their orders for right hand drive cars, and all such cars would have to be purchased in Britain. The Commission decided that the dealer agreement and the termination of deliveries contravened Article 81(1). Ford argued that the cessation of deliveries was a unilateral act not caught by Article 81(1). The Court rejected this argument (para [21]) stating that 'such a decision forms part of the contractual relations between the undertaking and its dealers. Indeed, admission to the Ford dealer network implies acceptance by the contracting parties of the policy pursued by Ford with regard to the models to be delivered to the German market'. The instruction was held to form part of the contractual relations between the undertaking and its dealers and hence then the restriction was held to be a breach of Article 81.

8.3.2 The Object or Effect of Restricting Competition

An agreement or practice is prohibited if it has either the object or effect of restricting competition.

8.3.2.1 Object

Even if, as a result of a consideration of the terms of the agreement, it is clear that the object is to restrict competition, it is still necessary to consider the economic effects of the agreement to determine whether it is caught by Article 81(1), as it may fall within the *de minimis* doctrine, considered below, or it may have no effect on trade between the member states, see Case 56/65 *STM*.

8.3.2.2 Effect

If it is not established that the object of the agreement or practice is to restrict or distort competition, it is necessary for the Commission to undertake an examination of the effect of the agreement on the market. In Case 23/67 *Brasserie de Haecht v Wilkin*, the Court of Justice said that the agreement, decision, or concerted practice had to be examined in the context of the market in which it operated and in the context of the effects surrounding its implementation. This entails scrutiny of the relevant product market and the relevant geographical market, the impact of national laws upon competition, the existence of intellectual property rights and the level of competition on the rest of the market and the behaviour of other competitors.

The Commission therefore has to pay close attention to the definition of the market for the purposes of competition law. As a result of the case law of the Court of Justice, the Commission has now presented its methodology in a 'Notice on the Definition of the Relevant Market'.[4]

8.3.3 Types of Prohibited Agreements

Article 81(1) lists as particular examples of such agreements, which have as their object, the restriction of competition. The non-exhaustive list includes:

(a) directly or indirectly fix purchase or selling prices or any other unfair trading conditions. (These are most often seen in the form of minimum price-fixing arrangements, see for example, Case 8/72 the *Cement Association* or the

---

[4] OJ 1997 C372/5 [1988] 4 CMLR 177.

Decision in *Hennessy/Henkel* [1981] 1 CMLR 601, in which minimum and maximum prices were laid down, which breached Article 81. Other trading conditions includes things like requiring distributors or retailers to provide suitable premises, or displays or training or minimum stocks or holding certain promotions. In return the retailer may be guaranteed a specific protected area. In Case 26/76 *Metro*, it was held that such systems would not breach Article 81 provided that selection of dealers was done objectively. In Case 161/84 *Pronuptia v Schillgalis*, even a requirement that 80 per cent of wedding dresses were purchased from Pronuptia was held to be acceptable in order to protect the know-how and reputation of the franchisor.)

(b) limit or control production, markets, technical development, or investment; most often seen in market sharing agreements (see for example, market partitioning in Case 56 and 58/64 *Consten and Grundig* and *Quinine Cartel*);

(c) share markets or sources of supply (see also *Consten and Grundig*) above;

(d) apply dissimilar conditions to equivalent transactions with other trading parties, thereby placing them at a competitive disadvantage (see for example, Case 26/76 *Metro v Commission* where a difference in prices could be justified by objective factors such as volume of purchases or transport costs); and

(e) make the conclusion of contracts subject to the acceptance by the other parties of supplementary obligations, which, by their nature or according to commercial usage, have no connection with the subject of such contracts. An example of the last of the conditions listed would be the imposition by a producer on a distributor of an export ban (see the *Henessy/Henkel* Decision in which a clause prohibiting the sale of competing products was held to be acceptable but not a clause prohibiting the sale of any other product).

8.3.4 Which May Affect Trade between Member States

To be caught by the provisions of Article 85, the practice complained of must be capable of effecting Community trade if an agreement or similar is to be caught in breach of Article 81. Trade is given a wide definition and encompasses the production and distribution of goods, trade in agricultural produce, the services sector (including banking insurance and professional services), and even opera singers have been held to be involved in trade.

In Case 56 and 58/64 *Consten and Grundig*, the Court of Justice stated that this phrase is intended to set the boundary between the areas covered by Community law and the law of the member states. It held that the question to be asked is whether, it is probable in law or fact that the agreement in question may have an influence, direct or indirect, actual or potential, on the pattern of trade between member states to hinder the attainment of a single market.

The case was concerned with exclusive territorial sales licences which served to encourage the volume of trade. Consten Grundig had granted a distributor a sole representation agreement for the whole of France, Saar, and Corsica. The distributor undertook not to sell similar articles liable to compete with the goods of the contract and not to deliver, either directly or indirectly, for or to other countries from the contract territory. An analogous prohibition was imposed on concessionaires from other territories. The result was to grant absolute territorial protection, and to insulate the French market against parallel imports. The result in this case was it actually promoted trade. The Court of Justice held that the fact that an agreement encourages an increase, even a large one, in the volume of trade between states is not sufficient to exclude the possibility that the agreement may affect trade between member states. Although this may seem strange, the requirement that the agreement must affect inter-state trade goes to the jurisdiction of Community law. The contract between Grundig and Consten, on the one hand by preventing undertakings other than Consten from importing Grundig products into France, and on the other by prohibiting Consten from re-exporting those products to other countries of the Common Market, indisputably adversely affected the flow of trade between the member states. These limitations on the freedom of trade were enough to satisfy the requirement in question.

In Case 56/65, the *STM* case, in similar terms to that seen in the free movement of goods chapter, the Court of Justice provided the basic test that if the agreement may have an influence, direct or indirect, actual or potential, it would satisfy this requirement.

In Case 23/67 *Brasserie de Haecht SA v Wilkin and Wilkin*, the brewery had entered into a contract whereby they had furnished the Wilkins cafe and had granted several loans. The agreement stipulated that the Wilkins were obliged to obtain all their supplies of liquor, beer, and soft drinks for the cafe and for their own personal use exclusively from the de Haecht brewery. They had purchased supplies of liquor from other undertakings and the brewery had sought to rescind the contract and claim repayment of the loans, return of the furniture, and damages. The Tribunal de Commerce asked the Court of Justice whether to judge the agreement on its own or in the light of all such agreements? The Court ruled that indeed the 'economic and legal context' had to be taken into account, such as in this case the fact that the arrangement tying the cafe proprietors to receiving their beer and other drink supplies from one brewery was one which was extensively used, and the extensive use of such contracts would adversely affect competition in the Community at large. The Court further ruled that in order to satisfy the 'capable of affecting trade between member states' requirement:

it must be possible for the agreement, decision or practice, viewed objectively to appear to be capable of having some influence, direct or indirect on trade between member states, partition the market, and hampering the economic interpenetration sought by the Treaty. When this point is considered the agreement, decision or practice cannot therefore be isolated from the others of which it is one.

Therefore if it forms a series of agreements, a single contract should not just be considered on its own.

In Case 8/72 *Vereniging van Cementhandelaren v Commission*, the members of a Dutch cement dealers association argued that since the cartel was purely national in its activities, limited to the territory of the Netherlands, it could not be caught by Article 81(1). The Court of Justice upheld the Commission decision declaring that an agreement extending over the whole of the territory of a Member State by its very nature has the effect of reinforcing the compartmentalization of markets on a national basis. Therefore, one country on its own can be used to establish an effect on trade between member states.

8.3.5 Exemptions from Article 81(1)

Apart from the justification considered below under Article 81(3), certain agreements have been deemed by the Court of Justice and Commission not to fall within the category of a 'restriction of competition'. These judicial exemptions from the application of Article 81 are also referred to as coming within a type of 'rule of reason' in competition law.

8.3.5.1 Objective Necessity

There are cases where the restrictions are objectively necessary for the performance of a particular type of contract as in franchising agreements. See Case 161/84 *Pronuptia de Paris v Schillgalis*, in which the Court of Justice held that the compatibility of distribution franchise agreements with Article 81(1) depended on the clauses contained in the agreements and on the economic context in which they are included.

Clauses which are indispensable to prevent the know how and assistance provided by the franchisor from benefiting competitors and clauses which implement the control necessary for the preservation of the identity and reputation of the organization represented in the trade mark, do not constitute restrictions on competition within the meaning of Article 81(1). The fact that the franchisor has communicated suggested prices to the franchisee does not constitute a restriction on competition, on condition that there has not been a concerted practice between the franchises with a view to effective application of those prices. However, clauses which fix prices or which effect a partitioning of markets between franchisor and franchisee or between franchises and are capable of affecting trade between member states, constitute restrictions on competition contrary to Article 81(1). Very many of these franchise agreements including Pronuptia's were granted individual exemption under Article 81(3) before the modernization in 2004 of this area of competition law. In addition, Commission Regulation 4087/88 on the application of Article 85(3) to categories of franchise agreements was enacted, but is no longer in force.

8.3.5.2 High Commercial Risks

The Court of Justice has held that where the commercial risk undertaken by a distributor, licensee, or franchise is so great, some exclusivity must be conferred on him to induce him into the market. Case 55/65 *STM v Maschinenbau* is an example of this. In this case the French Company La Societe Technique Miniere purchased thirty-seven earth levelling machines, and were given exclusive sales rights for the territory of France. The agreement with the producers, Maschinenbau Ulm stipulated that they could only sell other goods to compete with these levelling machines with the consent of Maschinenbau Ulm. The agreement left STM entitled to export the machines. The Court of Justice held that in order to assess the effect of the agreement on competition, examination should take place of the severity of the clause granting the exclusive right; the nature and quantity of the products which are the subject matter of the agreement; the position of the grantor and the concessionaire on the market for the products in question; the number of parties to the agreements; and the possibilities left for other commercial currents upon the same products by means of re-exports and parallel imports. The Court of Justice held that due to the high cost of the product and specialized nature, the agreements would not offend Article 81.

8.3.5.3 Quality Control

Cases involving selective distribution systems such as in Case 26/76 *Metro v Commission* to ensure the quality of sales and service, to benefit the consumer in terms of safety of electrical goods and to maintain employment in an important industry would not breach Article 81.

8.3.5.4 The *De Minimis* Doctrine

The doctrine of *de minimis* means some agreements which affect competition may nevertheless not be caught by Article 81 because they do not have an appreciable affect on intra-Community trade. It was first formulated in Case 5/69 *Volk v Vervaecke*, where Volk granted an exclusive dealership to Verwaecke for washing machines in the Belgian and Luxembourg market. Verwaecke undertook to place a monthly order for eighty appliances, and Volk undertook to protect Verwaecke's sales territory against parallel imports. There was a dispute as to agreement and the Court of Justice held that an agreement falls outside the scope of Article 81(1) when it has only an insignificant effect on the market, taking into account the weak position which the parties concerned have on the market of the product in question. Consequently an exclusive dealing agreement, even with absolute territorial protection may, having regard to the weak position of the persons concerned on the market in question in the area covered by the absolute protection, escape the prohibition, i.e. it represented too small an effect to significantly affect competition and thus does not fall within Article 81(1). From a strict reading of the article, this does not support it, i.e. other motives underpin the policy of the Commission and the judgment of the court, for example not to suppress small and medium size businesses from expanding or only restricting small business when predatory.

In 2001 the Commission provided an updated 'Notice on Agreements of Minor Importance which do not appreciably restrict competition'[5] setting out the criteria which will be used in determining whether a practice may affect trade between member states. The basic criteria are that the undertakings have less than a 10 per cent market share in the Community as a whole. In line with a general concern which has arisen and has been responded to by the Commission about vertical agreements, the threshold for vertical agreements has been raised to 15 per cent of market share. It is 10 per cent for horizontal agreements. Market share below this remove agreements from the scope of Article 81, unless they are serious or intended breaches of the competition rules or they fix prices. Even above these thresholds, small and medium size enterprise agreements will be considered leniently by the Commission. Although such notices are not binding in law and certainly cannot amend the Treaty provisions, they are a clear indication that providing an agreement falls within the exception allowed, the Commission will not take action under the competition rules. The general concern about the rigidity of the present application of the rules to vertical agreements (see *Consten and Grundig*).

The same pressures also led to the enactment of the block exemptions, which are discussed below.

8.4 Article 81(2) Consequence of a Breach

Article 81(2) provides that 'Any agreements or decisions prohibited pursuant to this article shall be automatically void' In Case 56/65 *STM v Maschinenbau Ulm*, the Court of Justice held that this provision only applies to those parts of the agreement affected

---

[5] OJ 2001 C368/13 which replaces the previous 1997 notice (OJ 1997 C372/13).

by the prohibition in Article 81(1) or to the agreement as a whole if those parts are not severable from the agreement itself.

8.5 Article 81(3) Exemptions

Article 81(3) provides that in certain circumstances Article 81(1) will not apply to an agreement and concerted practice:

which contributes to improving the production or distribution of goods or to promoting technical or economic progress, while allowing consumers a fair share of the resulting benefit, and which does not:

- (a) impose on the undertakings concerned restrictions which are not indispensable to the attainment of these objectives;
- (b) afford such undertakings the possibility of eliminating competition in respect of a substantial part of the products in question.

8.5.1 Individual Notification

Previously and for most of the life of the Communities, it was the case that the first and main way to obtain an exemption, parties to an agreement must have made an individual notification to the Commission. Failure to notify meant that the agreement would have been void and the parties would have been liable to fines. Once notified, the Commission considered whether the agreement could have been exempted and issued an official decision which could be challenged under Article 230 before the Court of First Instance. However, because the Commission simply could not investigate and come to a decision on all the applications made, it dealt with them very often by the so-called comfort letter, considered below. This led though to the revision of this procedure which was contained in a new enforcement of Competition law regulation (Regulation 1/2003[6]) which came into force 1 May 2004 and which abolished the individual notification. This was done to remove the drain on resources that this procedure was for the Commission and coincided when ten new member states joined in 2004 which would have imposed even greater demands on the Commission. The decision making was handed over to the national competition law authorities and facilitated this by making Article 81(3) directly effective so that any disputes can be adjudicated in the national courts. Essentially, the private parties will decide if their agreement

---

[6] OJ 2003 L1/1.

falls within the legal exceptions (rather than the previous exemptions) in Article 81 which decision can then be challenged and defended in the national courts. To assist parties in this, the Commission has issued Guidelines on the application of Article 81(3) of the Treaty.[7] Novel and uncertain cases may still find their way to the Commission for a decision in a procedure under Article 10 of Regulation 1/2003.[8]

8.5.2 Negative Clearance and Comfort Letters

Also prompted by the strain on the time and resources of the Commission, as an alternative to taking every individual application for exemption through to a decision, the Commission frequently settled cases informally by way of a so-called comfort letter. A comfort letter is simply a notification to the parties that, in the Commission's opinion, the agreement does not infringe Article 81(1) or that it qualifies for exemption. The Commission then closes the file after sending the comfort letter. These comfort letters do not bind the national courts or produce legal effects in national law or Community law. This was made clear in a series of cases involving perfume manufacturers, Cases 253/78 and 1–3/79 *Guerlain SA, Rochas SA, Lanvin SA and Nina Ricci SA*. Obviously a statement of this nature from the Commission would be of persuasive authority, but a national court would not necessarily be bound by it. In an action by French shops who were unable to get supplies from Lancome and Guerlain, the Court of Justice rejected the view that the comfort letters provided a defence to such actions against the refusal to supply. This too has now been replaced by the system of assuming that the agreement constitutes a legal exception by the parties, subject to a possible challenge in the national courts and reference to the CFI where relevant, thus comfort letters will no longer be needed or issued.

Whilst to some extent, of historical interest only, there remain a lot of previous agreements still subject to comfort letters or provisional validity. This was considered in Case C-39/96 *Koninklijke Vereeniging ter Bevordering van de Belangen des Boekhandels v Free Record Shop BV*, Free Record Shop Holding NV and concerns competition agreements which were concluded prior to Regulation 17 and notified to the Commission prior to the deadline of 1 November 1962. Normally such agreements would carry provisional validity until the Commission had either given positive clearance or had taken a negative decision holding them to be contrary to EC law.

---

[7] OJ 2004 C101/97.

[8] There are guidelines: Notice on informal guidance relating to novel questions concerning Arts 81 and 82 of the EC Treaty that arise in individual cases (Guidance letters) OJ 2004 C101/78.

Many agreements, similar to this one about the retail price maintenance for books, have continued in this legal limbo ever since. The Commission is simply unable to investigate all of them and many are left without interference. The agreement in question, however, had been challenged as contrary to Article 81 EC by a shop selling below the imposed retail price. Having lain dormant for so long, questions about the continued validity were raised by the national court. The Court of Justice held that until the Commission decides one way or the other the agreement remains provisionally valid even if it has been amended but only in so far as the amendments render the agreement less restrictive. More restrictive amendments would end the validity unless these were severable from the original agreement.

From May 2004, individual companies must decide whether an agreement complies with the four conditions specified in Article 81(3) and if they conclude they do, there is no need to take any further action or to notify the Commission or national competition authorities. However, in case of doubt a new procedure, not too dissimilar to the negative clearance and comfort letter of old, has been introduced, noted above, by which guidance on grey area agreement can be sought from the Commission. The Commission may issue this guidance in a 'guidance letter' but only if the situation is genuinely novel and not coming within any previous case law of decision of block exemptions, considered next.

8.5.3 Block Exemptions

In order to avoid unnecessary work for all involved, companies and the Commission, it was decided that certain categories of common or typical types of commercial agreements, which were considered not to infringe free and fair competition could be exempted from the prohibition in Article 81(2) by virtue of a block exemption, sometimes within certain industries or areas. In such cases there was no need to apply for individual notification. In particular, vertical agreements were considered as more beneficial than harmful to competition in that they often increase investment in the specialization and knowledge of certain products which is of benefit to the ultimate consumers of the products.

The block exemptions set out types of restrictions or provisions which do not infringe Article 81 (1) or would be exempted. The following are now the main block exemptions.

Regulation 2790/1999 (OJ 1999 L336/21) on vertical agreements and concerted practices.
Regulation 2658/2000 (OJ 2000 L304/3) on specialization agreements.
Regulation 2659/2000 (OJ 2000 L304/7) on research and development agreements.
Regulation 1400/2002 (OJ 2002 L203/30) on distribution agreements in respect of motor vehicles.
Regulation 772/2004 (OJ 2004 L123/18) on Technology Transfer Agreements.

There are a number of guides now published by the Commission which help clarify the block exemptions.[9]

The pattern of these block exemptions is to provide examples of agreements and clauses that are permitted, those which are expressly forbidden, and those which depending on the actual details contained within may or may not offend competition law. The first category means that there is no need to take any action or inform the Commission. Agreements of clauses coming within the second category render the entire agreement in breach of Article 81 and liable to fine and the third type under the previous regime required notification and clearance from the Commission and are those which would now probably fall to be considered as to whether they come within the new concept of the legal exception.

Most of the Regulations listed above are replacements for previous Regulations which were revised in the light of practical application and in response to criticisms made by the various industries and companies affected. The new Regulations now focus more on market share and market power in relation to the particular agreements rather than the agreement themselves. For example, for companies with less than a 30 per cent market share, Regulation 2790/1999 removes the need to make an assessment as to whether their agreements fall within the competition law rules thus further reducing the bureaucratic workload on the part of companies and the Commission. In what is now, with the various exemptions in place, a rare case, *JCB* were found to infringe Article 81 by its restrictive distribution agreement and not be exempted by Regulation 2790/1999 because its market share was between 40 and 45 per cent, see Case T-67/01 *JCB v Commission*.

8.6 Article 82 and the Abuse of a Dominant Position

Article 82 applies where individual organizations have a near monopoly position or share an oligopolistic market with a small number of other companies and take unfair advantage of this position to the detriment of the market, other companies, and the end consumers. Article 82 proscribes 'Any abuse by one or more undertakings of a dominant position within the common market or in a substantial part of it shall be prohibited as incompatible with the common market in so far as it may affect trade

---

[9] See, for examples, Guidelines on Vertical Restraints OJ 2000 C291/1, Guidelines on the applicability of Art 81 to Horizontal Agreements OJ 2001 C3/2, and Guidelines on the application of Art 81 of the EC Treaty to technology transfer Agreements OJ 2004 C101/2.

between member states.' Article 86 then goes on to give specific examples of such abuse, considered later.

8.6.1 Definition of Undertakings

The understanding of the term 'undertaking' rather than just concerning an individual company has been extended. The Court of First Instance confirmed in Cases T-68, 77–8/89 *Re: Italian Flat Glass* that Article 82 could apply to activities of more than one undertaking where the companies together could constitute a dominant position. Furthermore, oligopolies (a small number of competing companies in a particular market) may also find their activities being considered under the Merger Regulation, considered in the text below.

8.6.2 Article 82 Requirements

For Article 82 to be applicable there must be domination of the common market or a substantial part of it. This requires a definition of the relevant market by reference to both the product and the geographical area. The necessary requirements are finding that a dominant position exists within a relevant market, and that there has been abuse of the dominant market which has affected trade between member states. The leading and best case for many of the points and issues arising from Article 82 is Case 27/76 *United Brands v Commission* which will be referred to frequently in the following sections.

8.6.2.1 A Dominant Position

The *United Brands* case arose out of a complaint by a number of banana importers about the activities of United Brands Co. Some of the facts of this case are as follows: (they might put you off bananas!) bananas are picked and transported whilst green. They only begin to ripen after they have been gassed, which usually takes place when they reach the country in which they are to be sold. UBC grew, shipped and distributed bananas requiring its distributors/ripeners not to sell on bananas whilst still green (the green banana clause). It charged distributors in different member states different prices, sometimes by as much as 138 per cent without objective justification. UBC had also refused to supply a Danish company with Chiquita bananas because they had advertised another brand. As a result of these activities (and others), the Commission considered United Brands to have infringed Article 82 and imposed a fine of 1 million Units of account (the forerunner of the ECU and Euro). UBC sought the annulment of the decision and fine before the Court of Justice.

The issues for the Court of Justice were: the proof of dominance in the market and the abuse of this which affected trade. It defined a dominant position as:

a position of economic strength enjoyed by an undertaking which enables it to hinder the maintenance of effective competition on the relevant market by allowing it to behave to an appreciable extent independently of its competitors and customers and ultimately of consumers.

This takes us immediately on to the next points, the definition of the product and the geographical area. These are important questions as the definition is very often crucial to determining whether dominance exists.

8.6.2.2 The Relevant Product Market

The test for the relevant product market concerns itself with the interchangeability of the products or product substitution. A number of factors can influence this. For example:

(a) Cross elasticity, i.e. if the price of one product rises, will consumers change to another, for example lager for beer, frozen vegetables for fresh vegetables, margarine for butter, artificial sweeteners for sugar. This can change over time according to fashion.

(b) Physical characteristics which are similar. These are factors which may mean a product is not unique and is capable of being replaced by something else or not!

The Commission has published a Notice on the Definition of the Relevant Market (OJ 1997 C372/5) which provides a summary of the case law and Commission methodology for determining the relevant markets.

What was the product marketing the *UBC* case? UBC said the product market was fruit! The Commission said bananas!, clearly a difference. UBC controlled 40–45 per cent of the banana market, but argued that bananas were only a small part of a larger market in fresh fruit, and that although they might occupy a dominant position in the banana market, they did not occupy a dominant position in the fruit market. Which market was pertinent?

The Commission argued and the Court considered the special characteristics of the banana (sounds like a joke) and stated the relevant product market turned on whether the banana could be 'singled out by such special features distinguishing it from other fruits that it is only to a limited extent interchangeable with them and is only exposed to their competition in a way that is hardly perceptible'.

It then identified a number of characteristics of the banana which would help determine whether the banana had a market of its own.

(a) its physical appearance, chemical composition, taste, shape, softness, vitamin content;

(b) the fact that it is functional easy, hygienic, convenient, has high nutritional value, and is easily digestible; and

(c) the fact that it is economic, in that the constant level of production maintained throughout the year lends itself to advance planning of sales.

All that in a banana!

The Commission and Court actually went further and identified a special sub-market of the old, young, and infirm who rely on bananas. You might ask why and you might also come to the conclusion that the common characteristic might be the absence of teeth! The Court of Justice held 'a very large number of consumers being in constant need for bananas are not noticeably or even appreciably enticed away from the consumption of this product by the arrival of other fruit on the market'. Therefore other fruits were not substitutable and the relevant product market for the Court was the banana market.

In Case 6/72 *Europemballage and Continental Can v Commission*, the Court of Justice stressed the crucial importance of defining the relevant product market, and because the Commission had failed to define the product market properly the decision was quashed. The Commission had said that the companies had a dominant position in the market for cans for meat, cans for fish, and metal tops. It did not explain why these markets were separate from each other, nor from the general market in cans and containers. The Court of Justice held it necessary to identify the 'characteristics of the products in question by virtue of which they are particularly apt to satisfy an inelastic need and are only to a limited extent interchangeable with other products'.

In Cases 6 and 7/73 *ICI Commercial Solvents v Commission*, ICI were found to have a dominant market in one possible product raw material used for the manufacture of drugs. Although others were available the Court held the difficulty of substitution was a deciding factor in determining a dominance. The concept of non-interchangeability is an important test which is applied by the Commission in identifying the relevant product market, see for example, Case 85/76 *Hoffman la Roche*. The same product may in fact be classified into different markets, e.g. in Case 322/81 *Michelin v Commission*, replacement tyres were held by the Court of Justice to constitute a different market than the same tyres when supplied to the car production factories.

8.6.2.3 The Relevant Geographical Market

In *United Brands* the Court of Justice held that this required consideration of the opportunities for competition 'with reference to a clearly defined geographical area in which the product is marketed and where the conditions are sufficiently homogeneous for the effect of the economic power of the undertaking concerned to be able to be evaluated'—in other words it should be plain to see how the competition is affected.

A substantial part of the Community is required but whatever market is demonstrated, it must be drawn to show market dominance. In a narrowly drawn geographical market a firm which operates on a comparatively localized basis might possess adequate market power to occupy a dominant position, but if the market is too narrowly drawn, it will not be sufficiently large to be a substantial part of the common market. This latter problem should be seen in the context of the decision in case *Suiker Unie* whereby the Court of Justice held that dominance of the sugar market in Belgium and Luxembourg, then only about 10–15 per cent of the Community, was dominance of a substantial part of the common market. In Case T-83/91 *Tetra-Pak v Commission* the geographic market was defined as the whole Community.

In *UBC*, the area was agreed to be six (from the then nine states) hence a substantial part in which trading conditions were similar.

8.6.2.4 Market Share and Dominance

After determining what the relative markets are for both product and territory, the market share must be considered. Whilst this is an important consideration for determining dominance, it is not definitive. In Case 85/76, *Hoffman la Roche* had market shares of 70–80 per cent in some drugs, in Case 6/72 *Continental Can* had 70–80 per cent share of the can market in Germany, in Case 6 and 7/73 *ICI* had a virtual monopoly of the raw material and in *Suiker Unie v Commission*, the Sugar Union had 85 per cent of the Belgium production.

United Brands had only 40–45 per cent share of the banana market but the share of the nearest competition becomes relevant. In this case, the next company had only about 16 per cent of the market. Other factors were also critical in the *United Brands* case such as their control of production and shipping of bananas. Other factors were also critical in the *United Brands* case such as their control of production, shipping and dock facilities of bananas which made market entry for any new companies considered entering the market very costly and thus difficult. It also ensured the ability of UBC to act independently of other banana producers and distributors. In *UBC* dominance was therefore satisfied.

The Commission suggested in its 10th Report on Competition Policy that in the case of a highly fragmented market, a share of 20–40 per cent might constitute dominance and in Case T-219/99 *Virgin/British Airways* the CFI upheld the Commission's finding that the 39.7 per cent share that British Airways have of total airline sales in the UK was sufficient to establish dominance. Very important in this decision was the share of the nearest rival, Virgin which was just 5.5 per cent.

Dominance, or in the case near total domination (also called super-dominance) in one market, in the particular example, for drinks containers, may be enough to lead to abuse in an associated markets for containers, even though dominance in that associated market has not been demonstrated or exists, where the products, manufacturers and consumers were largely the same in both markets, see Case 333/94P *Tetra Pak International v Commission (No. 2)*.

In *Continental Can* the Court of Justice held that the acquisition of a position of dominance through takeover or merger might amount to an abuse of a dominant market position.

Collective or joint dominance has also now been established where two or more companies act sufficiently closely as to present themselves on a particular market as a collective entity although legally independent as held first in case C-395 and 396/96P *Compagnie Maritime Belge SA v Commission*. Article 82 does allow for joint dominance in the phrase 'one or more undertakings'. For Article 82, rather than the companies reaching an agreement that would breach Article 81, it is the fact that the combined market share of the companies involved established dominance. Joint dominance is also considered under merger control, below.

8.6.2.5 The Abuse of the Dominant Position

Dominance on its own is not a problem, it must be abused to breach Article 82. Article 82 provides four categories of example abuses, dealing essentially with unfairness, prejudice, discrimination, and unnecessary conditions. These categories though are not exhaustive and other forms of abuse can be found. The four categories along with cases which fit within those categories follow with a more detailed look at two cases thereafter:

(a) directly or indirectly imposing unfair purchase or selling prices or unfair trading conditions: e.g. unfair low prices, loss leaders or unfair high prices as in *United Brands, Hoffmann-La Roche*, or *Tetra-pak*;

(b) limiting production, markets or technical development to the prejudice of consumers: e.g. restrictions on exports in the *Sugar* cases; restrictions on resale in *United Brands*; refusal to supply which might eliminate competitors in *Commercial solvents*;

(c) applying dissimilar conditions to equivalent transactions with other trading parties, thereby placing them at a competitive disadvantage as in: *United Brands*; and

(d) making the conclusion of contracts subject to acceptance by the other parties of supplementary obligations which, by their nature, or according to commercial usage, have no connection with the subject of such contracts, for example, the Green Banana Clause in the *United Brands* case or tying in clauses in *Hoffman-La Roche.*

In the *UBC* case the company had been found to have infringed Article 82 in that it had required its distributors not to sell bananas whilst still green (the green banana clause) and had charged distributors in different member states different prices, sometimes by as much as 138 per cent without objective justification. UBC had also refused to supply a Danish company with Chiquita bananas because they had advertised another brand. In the *Continental Can* case, the Court of Justice held 'Abuse may therefore occur if an undertaking in a dominant position strengthens such a position . . . that the degree of dominance reached subsequently fetters competition.'

Case 7/97 *Oscar Bronner GmbH & Co KG v Mediaprint Zeitungs- und Zeitschriften-verlag GmbH & Co* helps define, perhaps in a more positive way, the boundaries of what may be regarded as the abuse of a dominant position, in that this was not found to be the legal position from the facts. A media undertaking holding a clear dominant position (46.8 per cent circulation) in one market was not obliged to allow access to a home delivery scheme, the only one in the market, to a smaller rival newspaper who could not economically set up their own scheme. There was, in other words, no breach of Article 82 although there was a dominant position in the market. The case stresses that the exploitation of the advantages achieved by reaching a dominant position does not necessarily amount to unlawful abuse.

8.6.2.6 May Affect Trade Between Member States

The effect on trade is virtually taken as read under Article 82 if abuse has been found.

The principles developed in Article 81 cases also apply here. In Case 6 and 7/73 *Commercial Solvents*, ICI claimed that the company to which they had refused to supply raw materials sold 90 per cent of its production of a tuberculosis drug made from those materials outside the EC and in particular in the developing countries. The applicants therefore argued that the abuse of the dominant position would not come within the ambit of the prohibition in Article 82, because it did not have an effect on trade between member states. The Court held that the expression could not be interpreted so as to limit the sphere of application of the prohibition to industrial and commercial activities supplying the member states. By prohibiting the abuse of a dominant position within the market insofar as it may affect trade between member states, Article 82 therefore covers abuse which may directly prejudice consumers as well as abuse which indirectly prejudices them by impairing the effective competitive structure. The Commission must consider all the consequences of the conduct complained of without distinguishing between production intended for sale within the market and that intended for export. When an undertaking in a dominant position within the common market abuses its position so that a competitor within the Common Market is likely to be eliminated, the area of trade is unimportant, once it has been established that this will have repercussions on the competitive structure within the Common Market. In *UBC*, the higher prices and the various restrictions were the equivalent of a prohibition on exports and held to have an appreciable effect on trade between member states.

8.7 The Relationship Between Articles 81 and 82

Articles 81 and 82 are not mutually exclusive categories and both may be considered as applicable to the same set of facts, where, for example, dominant companies then abuse their strength by forcing unfair and restrictive agreements on their customers, see Case 85/76 *Hoffman-La Roche*. Case 6/72 *Europemballage Corp. and Continental Can* concerned an attempt by the Commission to use Article 82 to tackle a merger which, in its view, resulted in anti-competitive behaviour, however, the Commission had failed to establish the relevant markets in a case in which a merger had created dominance but the Commission had failed to established an abuse of a dominant position. The Court's views in the case were however instructive in respect of the relationship of Articles 81 and 82 and the restrictive approach to the problem adopted by the Commission, that by refusing to consider the use of Article 81 as well for mergers it had handicapped itself. The Court of Justice held (for 85 read 81 and for 86 read 82)

Articles 85 and 86 seek to achieve the same aim on different levels, viz. the maintenance of effective competition within the Common Market. The restraint of competition which is prohibited if it is the result of behaviour falling under Article 85, cannot be permissible by the fact that such behaviour succeeds under the influence of a dominant undertaking and results in the merger of the undertakings concerned. In the absence of explicit provisions one cannot assume that the Treaty, which prohibits in Article 85 certain decisions of ordinary associations of undertakings restricting competition without eliminating it, permits in Article 86 that undertakings after merging into an organic unit, should reach such a dominant position that any serious chance of competition is practically rendered impossible. Such diverse legal treatment would make a breach in the entire competition law which could jeopardize the proper functioning of the Common Market.

In other words merger cannot alleviate the application of Article 81 or 82 to concerted actions of companies. The Court further held (old) Articles 85 and 86 cannot be interpreted in such a way that they contradict each other, because they serve to achieve the same aim.

This was the first attempt to use the Treaty provision to tackle the assault on competition resulting from mergers. The Commission then realized that a new approach was required to tackle the problems of concentrations and after some delay, a *Mergers Regulation* (4064/89) was enacted, considered below

The Court further held that (old) Articles 85 and 86 cannot be interpreted in such a way that they contradict each other, because they serve to achieve the same aim.

The difficulties in dealing with the realities of complex commercial cross holding was highlighted by Case 142 and 156/84 *BAT and Reynolds v Commission*. In this case the Court had to determine whether the Commission decision that the acquisition of a minority holding in a competing company was not an infringement of Articles 81 and 82. Two applicant, competitive companies objected to this decision. The original companies remained independent after the agreement, therefore Article 81, which the Court of Justice considered could apply to mergers, was considered first. The Court of Justice upheld the Commission decision that no anti-competitive object or effect had been established and there was no control, thus there was no case under Article 82 either. However, although an acquisition itself might not restrict competition, it may influence conduct to restrict or distort competition. The case is an example of need to consider both in such complex situations.

The Court of Justice has though held that an agreement within the meaning of Article 81(1) between legally separate undertakings may nevertheless result in undertakings being so linked that they become and act as a collective entity as far as their competitors and customers are concerned. As such then it can lead to a position of collective dominance which is then capable of being abused. See Case C-395 and 396P/96 *Compagnie Maritime Belge Transports*. However, in a later case, the Court of Justice considered that the Mergers Regulation is more suitable to situations of collective dominance than Article 82. See Cases C-68/94 *France v Commission* and C-30/95 *Société Commerciale des Potasses et de l'Azote (SCPA) v Commission* and comments below in the mergers section.

Therefore some circumstances need to be considered in the light of both Articles 81 and 82 and the Mergers Regulation.

8.8 The Enforcement of Community Competition Law

This Commission was given extensive independent enforcement powers quite early in the life of the Communities under Council Regulation 17 which was the first Regulation to be enacted implementing Articles 81 and 82 of the Treaty. This has now been, almost entirely, replaced with Regulation 1/2003 which contains similar enforcement rights.

8.8.1 **Council Regulation 1/2003**

Regulation 1/2003 empowers the Commission to carry out its function of ensuring that the provisions of the EC Treaty are applied, to address undertakings, decisions and recommendations for the purpose of bringing to an end infringements of Articles 81–2 and to enforce these by way of fines and periodic payments. It sets out the powers and duties of the Commission in the conduct of investigations of competition law abuses, which can be prompted by individuals and companies, the member states or on the Commission's own initiative.

The main details of the Regulation follow however, whilst this new Regulation has replaced Regulation 17, much of the case law arising from the previous Regulation 17 remains relevant particularly with the rights of parties to be heard and present their view of matters and therefore still need to be considered here as analogous authorities for the new Articles in Regulation 1/2003.

Regulation 1/2003, Articles 1–16 are mainly concerned with the respective powers of the Commission and national authorities, interim measures, cooperation between the Commission and national authorities, and with the procedure of the declarations by the Commission that the agreement either infringes the Treaty articles or is exempt from the Treaty provisions.

Articles 17–21 concern the powers of the Commission in conducting investigations, Articles 23–8, concerned with sanctions available to the Commission in the case of infringements which have been established by it and the rights of the parties under investigation. Articles 17–18 are concerned with requests for information. It generally empowers the Commission to request information to assist its investigations from both the authorities of the member states and from the undertakings. The owners of undertakings or their representatives are obliged to supply the information requested. If this is not forthcoming the Commission can adopt a formal decision requiring the information to be supplied (Art 18(3)). Penalties may then be imposed for non-compliance with the terms of the Decision.

Article 20 empowers the Commission to undertake all necessary investigations including the right of its officials to examine books, take copies of records and books, ask for oral explanations, and enter the premises of undertakings, including now extended powers under Article 21 to search the homes of directors, managers, and other members of staff where there is a reasonable suspicion that records relevant to the investigation are stored there. This can be undertaken without the consent of the undertaking involved providing it is specifically authorized in advance by the Commission, see Case 136/79 *National Panasonic*. Alternatively, a formal Decision may be adopted for a mandatory investigation. There is no need to approach the company in advance and the Commission should not be subjected to a delay before the investigation can take place. The investigations authorized under this provision include the infamous 'Dawn Raids' on the premises of companies under investigation. In Decision 80/334 *Fabbrica Pisana*, it was established that, a duty of the company existed to assist the Commission to find documents. In Cases 46/87 and 227/88 *Hoechst*, the authority to raid was challenged on the ground that it lacked precision but the Court of Justice held that it was acceptable providing the Commission indicated clearly its suspicions rather than have to supply full information, however, force cannot be used by Commission officials to gain entry and examine documents, but assistance to gain entry must be obtained via the national authorities, Case 85/87 *Dow v Commission* and Case 374/87 *Orkem v Commission*. In the latter case, it was held by the Court of Justice that the power to compel the production of information does not extend to requiring the company to admit breaches of the competition rules and thus incriminate itself. In effect a company can be obstructive but may suffer the penalty of fines being imposed on it under Article 23. This can be up to 1 per cent of the previous year's turnover, where a company has misled the Commission, see Cases 40–48/73 *Sugar Union*. Article 23(1) covers a number of situations of not supply information or supplying false, misleading or incomplete information, books, or records.

Previously largely established by case law but now contained within the Regulation, Articles 27 and 28, are details concerning the conduct of hearings, the rights of individuals and companies in those hearings and rights of confidentiality, and professional secrecy. The type of documents which are subject to legal privilege and professional secrecy have been the subject of case law. Legal privilege is recognized and covers correspondence between the company and an independent lawyer, see Case 155/79 *AM & S*. In-house lawyers do not enjoy such privilege, so it depends on the nature of the correspondence. Case T-30/89 *Hilti* decided that the privilege extends to in-house lawyers reports of the independent lawyers findings. In the Case C-36/92P *Samenwerkende*, a refusal to hand over documents considered to be confidential was held to be unjustified in the light of the existing protections in Community law under which the Commission is required to notify undertakings of the documents they intend to release to the national authorities and thus give the undertakings the chance to seek judicial review to protect these documents. As such then refusal to supply would be unjustified. In the end, the Court of First Instance and European Court of Justice must be the arbiters of what is privileged.

The principle of professional secrecy does not apply to allow a company to protect documents from the Commission but to ensure that information received by the Commission in an investigation is not disclosed to competitors, refer to Articles 27 and 28 and Cases 209–15 and 218/78 *Dow Benelux & Van Landewyck* and Case 53/85 *AKZO*.

For a substantive breach of Articles 81 or 82, Article 23 provides the Commission with the right to fine an undertaking not exceeding 10 per cent of the total turnover of the preceding business year, which, given the huge turnover of some multinational companies, the fines can be substantial. In Case T-51/89 *Tetra Pak Rausing SA v Commission* the company was fined 75 million ECU, which was upheld by the Court of Justice in Case C-333/94-P *Tetra Pak Rausing SA v Commission* and in *Commission* Decision 98/273 and case, Volkswagen were fined 102 Million ECU which was about £67,000,000 but which was reduced before the Court of First instance to 90 Million ECU in Case T-62/98. This was topped in 2003 when the Commission fined a number of companies who had been operating a Vitamin cartel a total of €855.22 million in Decision 2003/2, with *Hoffman-La Roche* in that case fined €462 million. The last record is that set in March 2004 when *Microsoft* was fined €497 million.[10]

8.8.2 Leniency Notice

To encourage informant companies, a policy of leniency in fining was partly formalized in a system of so-called leniency notices, whereby companies which cooperated with the Commission in cartel investigations could have their fines drastically reduced, up to a 100 per cent reduction if they are the first company in a cartel to provide information to either launch an investigation into a previously undetected cartel or information to secure a prosecution in an ongoing investigation which lacked evidence. There is now a revised leniency notice covering this area.[11]

8.8.3 Judicial Review of Enforcement

All decisions taken by the Commission under Regulation 1/2003 are subject to review by the Court of First Instance under Article 230 EC with the possibility of a further appeal to the European Court of Justice. Article 229 provides the Court of Justice with unlimited jurisdiction to review such penalties as may be imposed by the Commission under Community law provisions.

8.8.4 Private Enforcement

As with other areas of Community law, enforcement of the Community rules can also take place by individuals before the national courts via the vehicle of direct effects. This is particularly important now, as was noted above, the new Regulation 1/2003

---

[10] Case COMP/C–3/37.792 Microsoft.
[11] Commission notice on immunity from fines and reduction of fines in cartel cases OJ 2002 C45/3.

made Article 81(3), concerned with exemptions, directly effective, which was previously not the case. If the other areas of Community law are anything to go by, this will greatly complement the Commission's power to enforce competition law, which because of its stretched resources is rather limited, by the vigilance of thousands of individuals who may be affected by anti-competitive practices.

A single leading case so far has started to explore this development. Case C-453/99 *Courage v Crehan*, concerns a pub tenant to an agreement which tied him in into buying beer from a particular brewery, Courage plc. He claimed this was in breach of Article 81 and claimed damages. As a party thus also tainted by the agreement, the UK court was minded to dismiss the claim but nevertheless made a reference to the Court of Justice under Article 234 EC. The Court of Justice, in looking back at the importance in securing enforcement rights for individuals and the effectiveness of Community law (*Van Gend en Loos* and *Francovich*)[12] held that the competition law rules were fundamental rules in the EC, and if the agreement was in breach of Article 81 and not able to be exempted, it was void and could not be relied on by anyone, including a party to the agreement. Then, also in line with case developments in other areas, the Court held that in order to ensure the effectiveness of Community law, the procedural rules of the member states should not deprive individuals of rights in the absence of a Community regime. That matter was ultimately up to the member states' courts, but there should be no absolute bar to an action where the contract was held to breach Article 81. Hence then *Courage v Crehan* can rely on a breach of Article 81 and should not be barred from seeking damages for any loss incurred as a result but national law can exclude a claim where the party him or herself in also responsible for the agreement in breach. The party in this case did win damages and there is no doubt that this case and many others will assist Commission enforcement of competition law significantly.

8.9 Conflict of Community and National Law

In theory, the division should be easy, one or more companies activities will only come within EC competition law jurisdiction if they also affect trade between member states, otherwise it will be up to the member states' competition authorities to prosecute the breach. However, the question of the resolution of potential conflicts between EC and national competition law and the problem of double jeopardy was initially addressed in Case 14/68 *Walt Wilhelm v Bundeskartellamt*. The Federal Cartel Authority in Germany and the Commission had instituted proceedings against

---

[12] See the details in Chapter 5.

Walt Wilhelm for breach of competition rules. Walt Wilhelm submitted that the Bundeskartellamt could not maintain proceedings for an offence which was at the same time the object of investigation by the Commission. The Court of Justice ruled that conflicts between Community law and national law in the matter of cartels must be resolved by applying the principle that Community law takes precedence. This was subsequently confirmed in Case 13/77 *GB-INNO-BM*, which considered a clash between Belgium law and EC competition law in which the Court of Justice held that the member states had a duty not to adopt or retain any national measures which might deprive, in the case, Article 82 of its effectiveness. In order to clarify the procedure and assist national courts in considering cases which involve issues of EC competition law the Commission had issued a Notice to National Courts on the Application of Articles 81 and 82 (1993 OJ C39/5) setting out the procedure which should be followed. The notice also indicates that national courts should take notice of 'comfort letters' although they remain non-binding. However, Regulation 1/2003 has now taken over the field in this area now to govern the relationship between the national courts and the Commission. It provides under Article 16 that if a Decision has been reached by the Commission on a competition law matter, the national authorities and courts can no longer reach their own conclusion which conflicts with that decided by the Commission or even that in the process of being decided by the Commission. Which means in practise they must wait for the Commission conclusion before taking any action. Article 15 allows for a cross flow of information between the Commission and national competition authorities to assist both in investigations.

Regulation 1/2003 though has made other changes which affect the relationship. By scrapping, at least on the face of it, the individual notifications procedure and by making Article 81 directly effective, the legal exceptions to Article 81 can be the subject matter of national court adjudication. However, the bottom line is that any decision reached on them cannot run contrary to established or pending Community law and Commission Decisions dealing with the same matter. The national courts must apply Community law where relevant.

8.10 Community Merger Control

It is in the area of mergers and acquisitions, or as termed in the Community, concentrations, that the relationship of Articles 81 and 82 with each other previously came under closest scrutiny. Originally the Commission was of the view that Article 81 would not apply to concentrations. Thus, if competition was restricted or distorted by a concentration of companies, Article 82 was the appropriate measure with which to tackle it. This policy was pursued by the Commission in Case 6/72 *Continental Can* whereby the Commission tried to remedy an abuse of a dominant position which had been achieved by takeovers and substantial holdings in European companies by an American company. It was the first attempt at merger control by the Commission. It was not successful, mainly because the Commission failed to establish the relevant markets, rather than a failure to show abuses by the concentration. The Court of Justice's views in the case were however instructive in respect of the relationship of Articles 81 and 82 and the restrictive approach to the problem adopted by the Commission, that by refusing to consider the use of Article 81 as well for mergers it had handicapped itself. (See above 8.7 Case 6/72 *Europemballage Corp. and Contintental Can* and the Court of Justice's view on the aims of Articles 81 and 82.)

The Court further held Articles 81 and 82 (old 85 and 86) cannot be interpreted in such a way that they contradict each other, because they serve to achieve the same aim.

In Case T-51/89 *Tetra-Pak v Commission*, Tetra-pak were found to be in breach of Article 82 following the acquisition of another company which held an exclusive licence to manufacture sterilized milk cartons. Whilst the acquisition itself did not offend Article 82, the consequent dominant position which was immediately abused did.

The difficulties in dealing with the realities of complex commercial cross holding was highlighted by Cases 142 and 156/84 *BAT and Reynolds v Commission*. The Court of Justice had to determine whether the Commission decision that the acquisition of a minority holding in a competing company was not an infringement of Articles 81 and 82. Two applicants, competitive companies, objected to this. The original companies remained independent after the agreement, therefore Article 81, which the Court of Justice considered could apply to mergers, was considered first. The Court of Justice upheld the Commission decision that no anti-competitive object or effect had been established and there was no control, thus there was no case under Article 82 either. However, although an acquisition itself might not restrict competition, it may influence conduct to restrict or distort competition. The case is an example of need to consider both in such complex situations.

8.10.1 The Mergers Regulation (4064/89)

It was following the *Continental Can* case that the Commission realized that a new approach was required to tackle the problems of mergers, otherwise known as 'concentrations'. The Commission put forward a proposal for a regulation on merger control, but it was sixteen years later, on 21 December 1989, that the Council adopted Council Regulation 4064/89 on the control of concentrations between undertakings.

Under it, the Commission jurisdiction under Articles 81 and 82 (old 85 and 86) and Regulation 17 was repealed in respect of concentrations. The first mergers Regulation has now been replaced by the new Mergers Regulation 139/04 which now provides the legal foundation of Community policy control of mergers and acquisitions. The Mergers Regulation 139/04 establishes a division between large mergers with a European dimension, over which the Commission will exercise supervision, and smaller mergers which will fall under the jurisdiction of national authorities. The concept of a concentration was set out in a Commission Notice (OJ 1998 C66/2).

Article 1 states that the regulation applies to mergers and takeovers with a Community dimension, applies where there is a worldwide turnover of more than €5,000 million and an aggregate Community wide turnover of each of at least two of the undertakings of more than €250 million. A Community dimension may nevertheless pertain, if:

(a) the combined aggregate worldwide turnover of all the undertakings is more than €2,500 million;

(b) in each of at least three member states, the combined aggregate turnover of all the undertakings is more than €100 million;

(c) in each of at least three member states, the aggregate turnover of each of at least two of the undertakings concerned is more than €25 million; and

(d) the aggregate Community-wide turnover of each of at least two of the undertakings concerned is more than €100 million.

However, if each of the undertakings concerned achieves more than two-thirds of its aggregate Community wide turnover within one and the same member state, a concentration will fall outside the scope of the Regulation, and the merger will be subject to national rather than Community control.

Article 2 provides the power of review to determine whether mergers are compatible with the common market. The creation or strengthening of such a position will be declared incompatible with the common market where it would significantly impede effective competition in the common market as a whole or in a substantial part of it. In making this appraisal, the Commission is required to take into account the following matters: the need to preserve and develop effective competition within the common market (similar to the general requirement imposed by Treaty 3(g) EC, the structure of all the markets concerned (product and geographic markets), the actual or potential competition from undertakings located within or without the European Community, and which includes the market position and economic and financial power of the undertakings concerned, suppliers and users access to supplies or markets, legal barriers to entry into the market, supply and demand trends for the relevant goods and services, the interests of intermediate and ultimate consumers and the development of technical and economic progress provided that it is to consumers' advantage and does not form an obstacle to competition.

The last requirements are similar to the exemptions under Article 81(3) EC.

Where a merger is found by the Commission not to impede effective competition, it will be declared compatible with the common market, Article 2(2). The member states however retain the right in such circumstances to veto mergers in particularly sensitive areas of their economies, providing this is compatible with the general requirements of Community law. Article 2(3) then declares that where a merger is found by the Commission impede effective competition, it will be declared in a Decision incompatible with the common market.

Article 3 defines a concentration to include mergers, acquisitions of direct or indirect control of undertakings by persons already controlling at least one undertaking, partial mergers, and merger-like joint ventures. However, it excludes from the scope of the Regulation, coordination of market behaviour of firms which remain independent of each other. Such coordination, if adverse to competition in the common market, would fall within the scope of either Article 81 or Article 82 as in Cases 142 and 156/84 *BAT and Reynolds v Commission*. However, a more recent case would seem to contradict this view. In joined Cases C-68/94 *France v Commission* and C-30/95 *Societe Commerciale des Potasses et de l'Azote (SCPA) v Commission*, the Court of Justice determined that the merger Regulation may apply also to collective dominance. The case concerned a proposal that potash companies in Germany be concentrated, thus creating a de facto monopoly in the German market and a dominant position with the French Company SCPA in the Community market. To obtain Commission approval, the parties agreed to certain conditions relating to cooperation between the dominant firms and the distribution of products in the markets identified. France objected to the Commission decision before the Court of Justice and SCPA, before the CFI. As they both concerned the same decision, the CFI declined jurisdiction and the whole matter was referred to the Court of Justice. The decision is important because it is the first time the Court has clearly stated the Merger Regulation to be applicable to collective dominance, despite the lack of express words to that effect in the Regulation and the doubts of the member states when the Regulation was enacted that it would apply to oligopolies. The Court of Justice, on the other hand, thought that there was nothing in the regulation to exclude its application. That collective dominance was not sufficiently established by the Commission in the case itself does nothing to upset this.

The effect of the Regulation is described as one-stop-shopping in that only one authority, Commission or national authority need take action depending on the area of dominance. It provides for the operation of a so-called principle of exclusivity whereby all decisions on Community wide mergers are taken by the Commission, member states having undertaken not to apply their national competition rules to such cases Article 21(1) and (2), although there is provision for referral to national authorities in certain cases.

8.10.2 Enforcement of Regulation 139/04

Article 4(1) requires the notification of a concentration with a Community dimension within one week after the conclusion of the agreement, the announcement of the public bid, or the acquisition of a controlling interest, whichever of these shall occur first. Fines for a failure to notify can be imposed up to a maximum of €50,000 (Art 14(1)).

Article 7(1) provides that a concentration with a Community dimension shall not be put into effect before notification or in the three weeks following notification. The validity of transactions in securities on stock exchanges is not affected, Article 7(5).

Under Article 10(1) the decision to open proceedings referred to in Article 6 must be taken within one month of the day following receipt of the notification. Article 6 provides that the Commission is under a duty to examine all notifications as soon as they are received, and to notify its decision to the undertakings concerned and the national authorities without delay. If the Commission considers that the proposed concentration falls outside the scope of the regulation, it must record that finding by way of a decision. Where it finds that the proposed concentration has a Community dimension, but does not raise serious doubts as to its compatibility with the common market, it must decide not to oppose it and must declare it compatible with the common market. Where the concentration both falls within the scope of the regulation and raises serious doubts as to its compatibility with the common market, the Commission must decide to issue proceedings.

Article 10(3) requires that a decision that a concentration is incompatible with the common market must be taken within four months of the decision to open proceedings. During this period the parties to the proposed concentration will be free to propose changes to their merger in order to avoid a negative decision.

Where the Commission has found a proposed concentration to be incompatible with the common market, it may require the separation of the undertakings brought together, or the cessation of joint control, or any other action that may be appropriate to restore the conditions of effective competition, Article 8(5). So far, the Regulations have been sparsely used to prevent mergers, most of which have been cleared. An exception was the proposed merger of *Aerospatiale, Alenia and de Havilland (M053)*[13]

---

[13] [1992] 4 CMLR M2.

which was prohibited under the Regulation for the reason that the merger would have had an unacceptable impact on customer choice and the balance of competition in the EU. Following this first blocking by the Commission, another seven mergers have been blocked.

A Commission Decision which was made to block a merger was overturned by the CFI in Case T342/99 *Airtours plc v Commission* when Airtours wished to take over First Choice in the UK. The reason given by the CFI was that the Commission had failed to establish clearly that a position of collective dominance would have been reached following the merger.

Article 13 confers the power to undertake 'all necessary investigations' on the Commission, including the power for officials to examine and take copies of or extracts from books and other business records, to ask for oral explanations on the spot, and to enter any premises, land, or means of transport of the undertakings concerned.

The Regulation also allows for the imposition of fines and periodic payments for failure to notify, for supplying incorrect or misleading information, and for obstructing an investigation by Commission officials, Articles 14 and 15. Where the parties intentionally or negligently fail to comply with an order to suspend the concentration or disregard a decision to stop a merger or undo a merger, the Commission may impose a fine of up to 10 per cent of the aggregate annual turnover of the undertakings, Article 14(2).

Further reading

Books

BISHOP, S. and WALKER, M. *Economics of E.C. Competition Law*, Sweet & Maxwell, London 1999.

CAHILL, D. *The Modernisation of EU Competition Law Enforcement in the European Union*, CUP, Cambridge 2004.

COOK, J. and KERSE, C. *EC Merger Control*, 2nd edn., Sweet & Maxwell, London 1996.

FURSE, M. *Competition Law of the EC and UK*, 4th edn., OUP, Oxford 2004.

JONES, A. and SUFRIN, B. *EC Competition Law*, OUP, Oxford 2001.

GOYDER, D. *EC Competition Law*, 4th edn., OUP, Oxford 2003.

KORAH, V. *An Introductory Guide to EC Competition Law and Practice*, 7th edn., Hart Publishing, Oxford 2000.

Articles

ART, J.-Y. and VAN LIEDEKERKE, D. 'Developments in EC competition law in 1996: an overview' (1997) 34 *CML Rev*, 895–956.

LEVITT, M. 'Access to the File: The Commission's Administrative Procedures under Articles 85 and 86' (1997) 34 *CML Rev*, 1413.

SLOT, P. J. 'A View from the mountain: 40

years of developments in EC competition law' (2004) 41 *CML Rev*, 443.

REICH, N. 'The Courage Doctrine: Encouraging or Discouraging Compensation for Antitrust injuries?' (2005) 42 *CML Rev*, 35.

TURNBULL, S. 'Barriers to Entry, Article 86 EC and the Abuse of a Dominant Position: An Economic Critique of European Community Competition Law' (1996) *ECLR*, 96.

VENIT, J. 'Brave new world: The modernization and decentralization of enforcement under Articles 81 and 82 of the EC Treaty' (2003) 40 *CML Rev*, 545–80.

VICKERS, J. 'Merger policy in Europe: retrospect and prospect' (2004) 25 *European Competition Law Review*, 455–63.

VOGELAAR, F. 'European competition law revisited: the "great overhaul" of 2004 analysed' (2005) 32 *Legal IEI*, 105–9.

WINCKLER, A. and HANSEN, M. 'Collective Dominance under the EC Merger Control Regulation' (1993) 30 *CML Rev*, 787.

Web site

Commission Competition Policy web site: http://europa.eu.int/comm/competition/index_en.html

9

The Free Movement of Persons and European Union Citizenship

9.1 Introduction

Before European citizenship was introduced as a Community law concept and was provided with teeth, Community law was concerned with the free movement of economically active persons only. However, it was not long in the life of the Communities that the Court of Justice started to expand our understanding of the range of persons who could take advantage of the Treaty provisions and the first phase of secondary legislation was enacted which provided rights for non-economically active members of a worker's family. Originally, free movement of persons concerned the direct freedom of movement for workers and self-employed persons only, the latter establishing themselves or providing services in a host member state. In this book, free movement is dealt with in a single chapter, in contrast to many textbooks, hopefully, providing a much clearer overview of the development of the area of law rather than artificially dividing the material. Also, in contrast to most other books on the free movement of persons, workers, establishment, and services will be dealt with together. The reasons for this are that increasingly case law and in particular the new case law concerned with citizenship applies without distinction across all of three of these categories and new secondary law, considered below, has brought much of the secondary legislation in line for all three. It therefore seems of less merit trying to maintain an increasingly irrelevant distinction. However, the economically active remain the starting point for this chapter.

Whilst the original treaty articles on free movement of person have altered little since 1957, their scope and our understanding of it have developed considerably since then. It is not just the original personal scope of the legislation that has been expanded by both additional statutory law and judicial interpretation, it is also the consequences for the Community and national legal regimes that are much greater than that which may have been anticipated by the member states. Free movement of persons is now a much wider concept and has become inextricably linked with the concept of European citizenship, therefore this chapter will also consider those persons who are able to move and reside in other member states under the general rights of movement provided by the Treaty and secondary legislation, notably now through the citizen provisions Articles 17 and 18 EC, considered in detail at the end of the chapter. As ever in considering a legal regime, we need to start with the basics for each of these categories, and these are the EC Treaty provisions, followed by any pertinent secondary legislation and the now extensive case law of the Court of Justice. A particular feature of this area of law are the extensive rights which apply to the family members of EU citizens who take advantage of rights of free movement, by virtue of the so called derived rights. Finally, integrated into these aspects are the new provisions of secondary legislation[1] which has both consolidated the existing secondary legislation and has introduced amended and new rules relating to those taking advantage of free movement rights and which will be considered where appropriate in the text of this chapter.

However, before looking at any of these particular provisions, it is useful to try to discover the original reasons and intentions behind free movement of persons. Was free movement as originally conceived, just a necessary appendage to the free movement of goods and capital in order to complete the freedom of the factors of production for economic or capitalist development? In other words, without providing for the free movement of persons, the development of economic activities and the balanced expansion and accelerated raising of the standard of living referred to in the preamble of the Treaty would not be realizable unless capital could also take advantage of freely movable labour without border restrictions. Hence the argument that the rights were provided merely or deliberately to help create the 'Common Market' in the same way as the free movement of goods. By ensuring the free movement of workers across the member countries of the common market, capital (i.e. employers operating productive facilities) can easily import labour when required, which in turn ensures that economic conditions in all member states of the market are broadly similar and thus competition is not distorted by labour shortages and higher labour costs in some parts of the market.

What is clear is that the free movement of persons section is firmly anchored in the economic part of the treaty, concerned with a basic definition of the internal market and outlined in Article 14, and not within the social policy section much further on in the Treaty. Whilst there have always been claims that the rights were also imbued with a social quality and concern for individual rights, it is really only since the extensive development of the rights by both statutory supplement and generous interpretation

---

[1] In particular Directive 2004/38 of the European Parliament and of the Council of 29 April 2004 on the right of citizens of the Union and their family members to move and reside freely within the territory of the member states [OJ 2004 L158/77] which entered into force on 30 April 2006.

by the Court of Justice that this argument takes on credibility. A review of both the literature of the time and more recent articles and books will reveal that there has been and remains support for both points of view. The truth, probably lies somewhere in between in that whilst it was originally restricted to the pursuit of those engaged in an economic activity in another member state and that the rights were perceived as a form of support for the common market and economic progress in the Community, a view also acknowledged by the Commission in its early documentation,[2] the rights as developed have undoubtedly become a clear part of the social policy of the EC, as evidenced by the growing tendency in textbooks to treat the subject as a part of social policy. This transition of treatment may also have been encouraged by the way in which the free movement provisions were actually used in society. By this I mean, that the evidence of migration in Europe does not show large scale movement by Western Europeans of the original six member states with the exception of Italians moving to Germany.[3] Whilst large numbers of workers were imported into some countries, notably West Germany, France, and the UK to feed growing industrial capacity in the 1950s and 1960s, this was mainly from non-European countries. For the most part movement within Europe was small scale, not large-scale movement from employment black spots in Europe to other parts of the EC.

Furthermore, it is now clear that the movement of large numbers of persons is no longer an economically efficient or sensible option for capital. It is far more effective and cheaper to set up new factories where labour is cheaper rather than labour to move to capital. The examples of China and India could not be clearer. This view was actually formed rather quickly by both capital and the European Commission and that regardless of the original intentions, free movement rights were not being used as originally intended as an instrument of encouraging economic progress but were really being used as individual social rights by member state nationals.[4] By the time that the first legislative expansion of the rights had been carried out, the view was

---

[2] 'Even if initially the free movement of persons was mainly an economic matter, concerning only workers, the concept has gradually expanded to allow any citizen of the Union to move and stay freely within the member states': available at http://europa.eu.int/comm/archives/abc/cit2_en.htm.

[3] Most employment migration was from outside of the EC member states. See inter alia Ken Foster, 'The Free Movement of Workers', in *The Law of the Common Market* 170, 179–80, B. A. Wortley ed., 1974.

[4] 'In a Recommendation and Opinion of July 1962, 1962 J.O. (2118), the Commission argued that this freedom was not concerned with traditional notions of emigration and immigration. These notions assumed that individuals migrated because they were unable to secure satisfactory living standards in their own countries. The Community, however, sought to ensure uniformly high living standards throughout its territory. The problems of depressed areas of high unemployment should be remedied through investments in those areas rather than through emigration. In effect capital should be moved to the unemployed rather than vice versa. . . . Consequently, in the context of the Community the traditional motive for migration would cease to exist . . .' 'Therefore, the freedom of movement in Community law represented a considerable expansion of personal freedom', Andrew Evans, 'European Citizenship' (1982), 45 *MLR* 497, 499.

clearly that such rights were dual in purpose and effect. Another reason for the fact that the original provisions did little to facilitate free movement of persons is not that the rights themselves were toothless, more that until 1961 member states could maintain a priority for national workers, and then up to 1965, member states needed only to accept other member state workers if no nationals had applied for the vacancy within three weeks and, after 1965, member states could insist that potential host workers first notify employment authorities. Finally, member states could rely on escape clauses in Regulation 15/61[5] and Regulation 38/64[6] up to the end of the transition period (1968) which allowed them to suspend Treaty provisions in favour of nationals where national or local interests required it.

Putting into effect the right of free movement for the self-employed also proved to be slow and much more difficult than the simple Treaty expression of the rights would suggest. The attempts by the Commission to harmonize the various professions proved to be very arduous and time consuming and it was not until the intervention of the Court of Justice in leading cases that much more rapid and expansive progress took place, as considered below.

So, instead of becoming a tool for economic development, the use of the free movement provisions by individuals has established it more as a social right. In support of the view that social concerns predominate, the Court of Justice has adopted a very liberal approach for the interpretation of the free movement of workers provisions, both the Treaty principles and the further extensions of these principles in the secondary legislation, e.g. the widely construed concept of worker. In contrast, the exceptions to the rights granted to the member states are interpreted strictly, e.g., see the case law on Article 39(4), the public service proviso, below.

Whilst, the view now might be generally that the rights are as much if not more social, there are some cases along the way which cause us to take a reality check. For example in Case C-159/90 *Grogan*, the economic rights to move to receive services abroad took priority over the legislative provisions of the member state which were the product of deep ethical and moral considerations of the sanctity of life. In the *Grogan* case it was the right to travel to receive abortion services which took priority despite the fact that the national constitution prohibited abortion.

---

[5] J.O. 1961, 1073.   [6] J.O. 1964, 965.

9.2 The Legal Framework—Primary and Secondary Legislation

9.2.1 Treaty Provisions

Referring to the goals of Article 2, Article 3 provides that 'For the purposes set out in Article 2, the activities of the Community shall include, as provided in this Treaty and in accordance with the timetable set out therein:

(c) an internal market characterized by the abolition, as between member states, of obstacles to the free movement of goods, persons, services and capital.

Article 14 (ex 7a) provides in paragraph 2 that 'The internal market shall comprise an area without internal frontiers in which the free movement of goods, persons, services and capital is ensured in accordance with the provisions of this Treaty.'

The following Treaty articles outline the basic requirements to facilitate the free movement of the economically active: Articles 39–42 (old 48–51) for workers, Articles 43–48 (old 52–8) for those wishing to establish and Articles 49–55 (old 59–66) for those wishing to provide services.

For workers, Article 39(1) provides that freedom of movement for workers shall be secured within the Community and in the second paragraph that such freedom of movement shall entail the abolition of any discrimination based on nationality between workers of the member states as regards employment, remuneration, and other conditions of work and employment.

Article 39 (old 48) was held to be horizontally directly effective in Case 167/73 *Commission v France Re French Merchant Seamen* and later horizontal direct effects implied in Case 36/74 *Walrave and Koch* concerned with a private body but established under public law but definitively established in Case C-281/98 *Angonese v Cassa di Risparmio di Bolzano SpA*.

Article 39(3) described in broad outlines, the rights of workers but subjects those rights to the limitations on grounds of public policy, public security or public health, amplified now in the new Directive 2004/38, considered below. The rights as listed are:

(a) to accept offers of employment actually made;

(b) to move freely within the territory of member states for this purpose;

(c) to stay in the member state for the purpose of employment in accordance with the provisions governing the employment of nationals of that state laid down by law, regulation of administrative action;

(d) to remain in the territory of a member state after having been employed in that state and governed by Regulation 1251/70.

Article 39(4) provides that 'The provisions of this Article shall not apply to employment in the public service.'

For establishment, Article 43 (old 52) provides that the freedom of establishment shall include the right to take up and pursue activities as self-employed persons and to set up and manage undertakings, in particular companies or firms.

And finally, for the provision of services, Article 49 (old 59) provides that 'restrictions on freedom to provide services within the Community shall be prohibited in respect of nationals of member states who are established in a State of the Community other than that of the person for whom the services are intended.'

9.2.2 The Basic Right of No Discrimination

The most basic or fundamental right in free movement is that there shall be no discrimination on the grounds of nationality. Article 12 EC (old 6), which prohibits discrimination on the grounds of nationality, has also been highly influential in the development of this area of law by allowing the Court of Justice to outlaw various discriminatory rules and practices by member states and organizations, which were not a clear and direct breach of the provisions on workers, establishment, or services but which nevertheless discriminated against non-nationals. It has been applied, inter alia, for workers in Case 59/85 *Netherlands v Reed*, for services in Case 2/74 *Reyners v Belgium*, and for establishment in Case 246/89 *Commission v U.K.* (Nationality of Fishermen) all of which cases are considered in the text below.

The Court of Justice has often stressed that the concept of discrimination not only covers direct discrimination in which different rules apply to nationals and non-nationals but also covers covert discrimination or indirect which leads to the prejudicial treatment of non-nationals. Rules which seem to apply fairly to both but which have an indirect discriminatory effect on non-nationals. The measure may, however, be objectively justified on other grounds. Furthermore, the prohibition of national rules has also been expanded to catch not just those involving discrimination but all those rules which hinder market access.

Indirect discrimination was demonstrated Case 33/88 *Alluè and Coonan v University of Venice*. The applicants, after five years of employment as foreign language lecturers, were informed that they could not be retained under a 1980 Italian Decree which limited the duration of employment of foreign language lecturers. Not all the foreign language lecturers were non-national, some 25 per cent were nationals, therefore there was no dissimilar treatment, i.e. no overt discrimination. Although the rule applied regardless of the nationality it nevertheless mainly affected the nationals of other member states who made up 75 per cent of such language teachers. It was held by the Court of Justice to be discriminatory where such limitations do not exist in respect of other workers. The rules may also be objectively justified if there is a legitimate aim compatible with the Treaty, the measure is justified by pressing reasons of public interest and the measure is proportionate.[7]

In the same way as will be seen for services and establishment below in Section 9.3.1.3, there has been an attack on national rules which although applying to both home professionals and those establishing in the host country, are regarded as inappropriate for host professionals because they hinder access to movement. Case 415/93 *Bosman* concerns football transfer fee rules which certainly restricted transfers but applied to both national and cross-border transfers, hence there was no discrimination and nationality was not a factor. The Court of Justice held they were nevertheless an obstacle to movement. The *Bosman* ruling was applied to a similarly restrictive German handball rule in Case C-438/00 *Kolpak*, which limited the number of foreign players to two in each squad and which was found to be discriminatory by the Court of Justice and not justified on sporting grounds. It clearly limited the chances of non-Germans of entering the market. Thus for persons, the prohibition of harmful rules goes beyond discrimination to cover rules which impede market access.

9.3 The Personal and Material Scope of the Basic Rights

This section determines who may benefit from the rules provided. The personal scope is determined both by the nationality and coming within the definition of those persons granted the right to move freely by legislation. The material scope of the rights have been determined largely by secondary legislation and concerns the actual rights provided, considered in Section 9.4.

9.3.1 Personal Scope

Two basic definitions have to be established: Nationality and whether the person concerned is a worker or self-employed by establishing or providing services; or otherwise entitled to remain in the member state. In other words, this definition determines which persons can take up the rights provided by the legislation.

9.3.1.1 Nationality

For workers and the self-employed, the right to move freely and obtain other benefits,

---

[7] For a more detailed discussion of objective justification the text following the *Cassis de Dijon* case in Chapter 7 (free movement of goods).

especially those rights which can be taken up by members of the worker's family, is initially dependant on being defined a national of one of the member states. Article 39 secures freedom for workers of the member states. Establishment under Article 43 and services under Article 49 refers to the right of nationals of the member states to either establish or provides services in the other member states. As establishment also includes legal persons in the form of companies predominantly, companies which are registered in one of the member states are also included within the personal scope of the rights.

The actual determination of member state nationality is a matter for each of the member states as expressly stated in Declaration No. 2 on Nationality attached to the Treaty on European Union which provides that nationality shall be settled solely by reference to the National law of the member state concerned. This position was upheld in the Case C-192/99 *Manjit Kaur* in which the Court of Justice held that it is for each member state to lay down the conditions for the acquisition and loss of nationality. It is not, however, necessary for the members of a worker's family to be member state nationals to obtain benefits as will be seen in the secondary legislation and case law considered below.

9.3.1.2 Community Status as a Worker or Self-employed

The second part of the personal scope of the law is that in order for a person to benefit personally or for their family to benefit from rights arising under Articles 39–55 and law made thereunder, the person needs to be classified as a worker or self-employed person. The definition of these concepts, as indicated in the heading, is a matter for Community law and not for each of the national legal systems to determine. Turning first to the term 'worker', there is no definition of the term in the EC Treaty, but the Court of Justice has held that the term must have a Community meaning, and cannot be the subject of differing interpretations by the courts of the member states. In Case 75/63 *Hoekstra v BBDA*, the Court of Justice declared the reason for this view: 'If the definition of this term were a matter for the competence of the national courts, it would be possible for every member state to modify the term worker and so to eliminate at will the protection afforded by the EEC Treaty to certain categories of person.' In the case itself, the Court of Justice gave this limited definition 'A worker is any employed person, irrespective of whether he is wage earning or salaried, blue collar or white collar, an executive or unskilled labourer' but has, in subsequent cases, gone on to expand the definition in a series of cases to include part-time workers, work seekers, and under certain circumstances, those undertaking a period or course of study.

Part-time work. Case 53/81 *Levin v Minister of Justice* concerned the value of work that a person needs to do before they can be classed as a worker. The woman plaintiff was a British citizen working in Holland as a chambermaid for 20 hours per week and whose earnings were below the subsistence level in the Netherlands. The Dutch government argued that because she was a part-time worker earning below the government set subsistence level, she was not a 'favoured EEC citizen' and could not benefit from the provisions of EEC law guaranteeing freedom of movement of workers. The Court of Justice held that these considerations were irrelevant to her status as a worker, and declared that whether she was a full or part-time worker, she was entitled to the status of worker provided that the work was genuine and effective and not so infinitesimal as to be disregarded. The Court of Justice ruled that work will only be disregarded if it is so minimal that it does not constitute economic activity at all. The essential defining characteristic of work is that it is activity of an economic nature.

In 139/85 *Kempf v Minister of Justice*, a German national worked as a part-time flute teacher for twelve lessons per week only. His limited income was topped up to the Dutch minimum income level with supplementary benefit under the Unemployment Benefit Act. He too was refused a residence permit on the grounds that he was not a 'favoured EEC citizen'. The Court of Justice ruled that if a person is in effective and genuine part-time employment he may not be excluded from the sphere of application of the rules on freedom of movement of workers merely because the remuneration he derives from it is below the minimum level of subsistence set by national law. In this regard it is irrelevant whether the supplementary means of subsistence are derived from property, from the income of another member of his family (as in *Levin*), or from public funds of the member state of residence (as in *Kempf*). The Dutch court had found that the work was genuine and effective.

The Court of Justice has held in Case C-357/89 *Raulin v Netherlands Ministry of Education and Science* that in considering whether work is genuine and effective, the national court should take account of all the occupational activities of the person in the host state only and the duration of the activities. This appears to be a decision which hands back the discretion to the member states to define who is a worker at the very margins of those possibly coming within the term. The case concerned a French national who worked for 60 hours in total as a waitress in Holland but who whilst doing so, was granted the status of worker.[8]

In Case 66/85 *Lawrie-Blum v Land Baden-Württemburg*, the Court of Justice considered the compatibility of German rules restricting access to a preparatory service stage which was necessary to become a teacher. It laid down three essential characteristics to establish an employment relationship. The provision of some sort of service, being directed by another person, i.e. not self-employed and in return for

---

[8] See also the similar Case C-413/01 *Ninni-Orasche* involving two and a half months work in three years would qualify according to the ECJ but again it was up to the national authorities to decide as in *Raulin*.

remuneration. This was applied in Case 196/87 *Steymann v Staatssecretaris van Justitie* whereby work in Bagwhan Religious Community's commercial activities for which remuneration paid in form of pocket money and meeting of material needs. Some limits to the definition appear to have been found in Case 344/87 *Bettray v Staatssecretaris Van Justitie*. The Court of Justice held that a national of a member state employed in another member state under a social employment scheme involving therapeutic work as part of drug rehabilitation merely as a means of retraining or reintegration, cannot be regarded as a worker for the purposes of Community law. The activities could not be carried out as real and genuine economic activities. Here the position was artificially created with Government money and not therefore genuine. Although carried out under supervision and remunerated, the court (in contrast to its position in *Levin*) looked at purpose and found that Bettray was not a worker. However, this decision might not hold good any longer in view of the decision in Case C-456/02 *Trojani*, which is one of the cases also considered under citizenship below in Section 9.9.4. *Trojani* had secured accommodation in a Salvation Army hostel, where in return for board and lodging and some pocket money he undertook various jobs for about 30 hours a week as part of a personal socio-occupational reintegration programme, thus straddling both previous cases in terms of fact. He applied for social assistance, which was refused. The Court of Justice held that he had a direct right of residence under Article 18 and where such EU citizens are in possession of a residence permit, they are thus entitled, according to Article 12 EC, to social assistance on the same basis as nationals, thus no real decision was taken on his actual status which was left to the national court to decide, and which will be discussed below although it can be argued that under citizenship rights it is of lesser importance now.

The term 'worker' is however wider than just referring to those in employment and in certain circumstances also applies to those who are seeking work and those who having lost one job involuntarily, are capable of taking another.

Work seekers. Having established in the *Hoekstra* case that certain rights were retained by the worker loosing a job including the status of worker,[9] the proposal for Directive 68/360[10] was discussed in Council which promoted a Community myth that the period sanctioned by the minutes of the Directive was three months. This was the period during which EC nationals made unemployed could claim unemployment benefit whilst seeking work under Regulation 1408/71, Article 69. It was then argued before the Court of Justice to be the time after which a member state could deport a person who had not found work. Two cases follow which have considered these matters.

---

[9] And confirmed in the later Case C-43/99 *Leclere and Deaconescu*.
[10] Now repealed and replaced by Directive 2004/38.

In Case 316/85 *Marie-Christine Lebon*, the Court of Justice held that those in search of work are not entitled to receive workers benefits (in this case a social security support payment). Miss Lebon no longer lived with her parents who were ex-workers, therefore she did not qualify for benefits as a dependent of a worker. She then asked if she qualified for workers' benefits if she was looking or intended to look for work. The Court of Justice held that the benefits provided by legislation on free movement were only for those in actual employment and not for those who migrate in search or work and have not found it. She could temporarily be classified as a worker but not for the purposes of benefits, although a later Case C-138/02 *Collins*, noted briefly below in the next section, has cast doubt on that part of the judgment. Case C-292/89 *Antonissen* clarifies how long the temporary status entitles a person remain to look for work. The UK wished to deport Antonissen, who had been convicted of possession and intent to supply cocaine and asked the Court of Justice whether they could. UK legislation gave EC citizens six months in which to find employment. Antonissen was in the country for over three years without work before his imprisonment. The Court of Justice held that, statements recorded in minutes regarding the acceptable time for the pursuit of work before deportation would not be allowable, have no legal significance and cannot be used to interpret the relevant legislative provisions. A member state may deport an EC migrant worker subject to an appeal if he has not found employment after a period of six months which is to be taken as a guideline only, unless there is evidence which indicates that he or she is continuing to seek employment and that there are genuine chances of being engaged, language which is repeated in new Directive 2004/38, Article 14. Therefore after the expiry of a reasonable period, depending on the circumstances, persons may no longer be afforded the status and benefits of worker under Community law and may lawfully be deported by the member state. The Court of Justice based this right on the Treaty itself and not Directive 68/360.

Worker training, education, and benefits. A further extension to the scope of the concept of worker took place in favour of those no longer in employment, but who were employed previously but are now engaged in some form of study. This category was rather limited but its boundaries may now have been considerably extended by the respect shown by the Court of Justice now to the concept of citizenship, considered below.

The leading case is Case 39/86 *Lair v Universität Hannover*, in which a French national employed in West Germany was refused a grant by the university for a maintenance award and training fees because she had not worked in the country continually for at least five years and therefore whilst at university was not a worker. It was stated in the case that the period at university would lead to a vocational qualification and that the time at University represented a break in employment only. The Court of Justice held since there was no fixed legislative definition of worker, there was nothing to say that the definition must always depend on a continuing employment relationship. Certain rights have been guaranteed to workers after employment has finished, e.g. the right to stay and social security rights. This could also apply to university training providing there was a link or continuity between the previous work and university. In which case, the university support could be considered one of the social rights coming within Regulation 1612/68. The status of worker was therefore retained if a link exists between the previous occupation and the studies in question.

In contrast, in Case 197/86 *Brown v Secretary of State for Scotland*, the Scottish education department refused Brown a grant for university. He had worked for eight months in the UK prior to and as a precursor to university and gained the status of worker. The Court of Justice held that, whilst university training is to be regarded as mainly vocational it was only covered by Article 12 (old 6) EC generally outlawing discrimination. This covers tuition fees but not the maintenance grant, therefore a person who enters employment for eight months and who did so as a precursor or requisite to attend university did not retain the status of worker for the purposes of claiming a grant. Whether this would be decided in the same way again if presented now, bears close inspection in the light of the *Grzelczyk* case, below.

Returning to Case C-357–89 *Raulin*, the Court of Justice held that the 60 hours work had enabled her to claim the protection of Article 39 (48) EC, despite its very temporary nature, however, a migrant worker who then left that employment to begin a course of full-time study unconnected with the previous occupational activities did not retain the status as a worker, a finding upheld by the Dutch court. Raulin, however, did have a right of residence in the host state for the duration of the course of study, regardless of whether or not the host state had issued a residence permit.

Thus, definitions of what constitutes vocational training and the link to work are crucial for the determination of the status of a worker and the consequent benefits and rights, as is the number of weeks or hours worked. However, in Case C-184/99, *Grzelczyk*, a French national who studied and worked on a part-time basis to help support himself for three years in Belgium applied at the beginning of his fourth and final year of study to the CPAS for payment of the *minimex*, a non-contributory minimum subsistence allowance. The CPAS granted Mr. Grzelczyk the *minimex* but then later denied this on the basis that he was not Belgian, hence clear discrimination on the grounds of nationality. This case did not consider whether he enjoyed the status as a worker. The Court of Justice emphasized the new citizenship provisions and new competences, albeit limited, in education allowed it to hold that Articles 12 and 17 preclude discrimination as regards the grant of a non-contributory social benefit to union citizens where they are lawfully resident. Hence it would seem that under these or similar circumstances a link to previous work seems no longer required.

In Case C-138/02 *Collins*, the Court of Justice held that once citizenship had been established then even work seekers could claim certain benefits, in contrast to *Lebon* above, but some benefits could be restricted on objective grounds, such as the habitual residence requirement for a job seekers allowance, which depended on the existence of a genuine link between the work seeker and the state.

Case C-256/01 *Allonby*, concerned the re-employment of former college lecturers in the same establishment but under a self-employed scheme paid by a private independent company. Effectively, the definition of the term worker was also extended to cover self-employed persons. In considering the new relationship, the Court of Justice held 'The formal classification of a self-employed person under national law does not change the fact that a person must be classified as a worker within the meaning of that article if his independence is merely notional.'

9.3.1.3 The Scope of Establishment and the Provision of Services

The self-employed are granted rights under the Treaty to move to another member state to establish either permanently or on a long-term basis (Arts 43–8) or to provide services temporarily (Arts 49–55). The definitions for the personal scope of establishment and for the provision of services are much more straightforward than for workers as the primary Treaty Articles have laid down the basic concepts, which have not then been subject to an expansive interpretation by the Court of Justice. Article 43 deals with rights of freedom of establishment as the right to enter another member state and stay on a long-term or permanent basis, to take up and pursue activities as a self-employed person and to set up and manage undertakings. This includes legal as well as natural persons. A basic definition has been given in Case C-221/89 *Factortame* 'the actual pursuit of an economic activity through a fixed establishment in another member state for an indefinite period'.

Services under Article 49 envisages a temporary state of affairs and appearance, if at all, in the host state would only be for a limited period to provide specific services. There would be no permanent personal or professional presence in the host state or a necessity to reside. The concept of services is defined by Article 50 (old 60)(1) as those 'provided for remuneration, in so far as they are not governed by provisions relating to freedom of movement of goods, capital and persons', in particular, Article 50(d) specifically includes activities of industrial and commercial characters and those of craftsmen and the professions. The provision of services is potentially a much wider category and can be associated with the areas of banking, finance, insurance, and legal services and now with modern technology, telephone, broadcasting, and internet services will become big services areas, notably without the need to move from the host state to provide services in other member states. See, for example, Case C-384/93 *Alpine Investments* concerned with cross frontier telephone sales calling. The scope of the term services has been held by the Court of Justice to include the recipients of services, considered below and even arguably to include prostitution in Case C-268/99 *Jany et al.*

Originally these were regarded as, if not absolutely distinguishable, certainly clearly distinct concepts with no overlap. At times, the distinction between services and establishment can be difficult to ascertain.

In Case 205/84 *Commission v Germany* (Insurance Services), the provision of insurance included the setting up of offices on a long-term basis and staffed by nationals of the host state was considered by the Court of Justice as establishment even though the legal entity (owner/principal) remained in the home state. This ruling is very important as the application of home rules may be stricter for establishment because it appears to be based on achieving complete equality of treatment. The provision of services under Article 50, on the other hand, whilst allowing for the same conditions to be imposed by the host state, has developed on the basis that not all home rules have been found by the Court of Justice to be suitable or acceptable to those providing services. The distinction therefore between establishment and services is important. The Court of Justice has now advised that the provision of services may even justify the setting up of infrastructure in the host state. In Case C-55/94 *Gebhard v Milan Bar Council*, the Court of Justice characterized 'establishment' as the right of a community national to participate on a stable and continuous basis in the economic life of a member state other than his or her own and 'services' by the temporary, precarious and discontinuous nature of the services. The Court held:

> The temporary nature of the activities in question has to be determined in the light, not only of the duration of the provision of the service, but also of its regularity, periodicity or continuity. The fact that the provision of services is temporary does not mean that the provider of services within the meaning of the Treaty may not equip himself with some form of infrastructure in the host member state (including an office, chambers or consulting rooms) in so far as such infrastructure is necessary for the purposes of performing the services in question.

In this case, the setting up of chambers in Italy by a German lawyer on a long-term basis, although still practising in Stuttgart, was held to be establishment.

9.3.1.4 Establishment of Companies

Whilst the study of company law is not usually an intense study in EC law courses, a brief note should be included on the leading cases in this area which have had general implications for establishment.

Article 43 specifically refers to the right to 'manage undertakings, in particular companies and firms within the meaning of the second paragraph of Article 48'. Article 48 in turn provides that those coming within the scope of Article 43 are those formed in accordance with the law of a member state and have their registered office, central administration, or principal place of business within the Community and which includes companies or firms constituted under civil or commercial law.

In Case C-212/97 *Centros Ltd*, two Danish directors registered a company in the UK and requested registration of a branch office in Denmark but which was refused on the grounds that it was an attempt to circumvent the Danish company capital requirements, particularly as there was the intention only to trade in Denmark and not in the UK. Denmark required a much higher minimum paid up capital than the UK. Upon reference to the Court of Justice, it held that the case came within the scope of Article 43 EC and that any concerns that creditors would be at risk had already been catered for in national and Community law. Article 43 conveyed the right to set up companies in one member states and trade via a branch in other member states, subject to the regulation in the host state providing any such regulation satisfy the following requirements, observed elsewhere in free movement law. Any regulation must be non-discriminatory; justified by imperative requirement in the general interest; and be proportionate. The Court of Justice held the complete ban by Denmark did not fulfil those conditions.

In Case C-208/00 *Überseering*, a Dutch registered company was transferred to Germany but was denied legal capacity in Germany by a German court. This was argued to breach the freedom of establishment in Article 43 EC. The Court of Justice agreed with this view. Both cases have been criticized for allowing companies to be registered in the state with the least restrictive requirements and thus introducing a lowest common denominator into EC company law, resembling the Delaware clause from the United States, Delaware being the state with the most lax regulation. The judgments are thus a strong support for the free choice of company registration and free movement.

9.4 The Material Scope of the Rights

Apart from the basic rights being provided by the central Treaty Articles of 39, 43, and 49, the material rights of free movement have largely been provided in secondary law.

9.4.1 Secondary Legislation: Introduction

Each of the free movement sections has its own Treaty base to empower the enactment of secondary legislation in pursuit of the Treaty objectives. Consequently for workers under Article 40 and the self-employed under Treaty Articles 53 (now repealed), 47, and 52 (now 57 and 63), the Commission was empowered to issue of Directives to obtain the general objectives set out in the Treaty. In 1961, a General Programme was set up and a number of specific instances of secondary legislation were enacted.

To a large extent, the rights provided deal with relatively mundane things such as paperwork in support of exit and entry rights and which only infrequently result in important new case law. Furthermore, the Court of Justice has been able to derive very extensive rights from the EC primary legislation, and in particular Article 12 EC, noted above. Finally, the secondary law has undergone radical transformation and therefore the focus or our attention will turn to the new provisions.

The rights for workers, outlined in Article 39 (old 48) of the Treaty were amplified and supplemented most importantly by three measures. Directive 64/221; Regulation 1612/68; and Directive 68/360[11] which were enacted both to facilitate the original rights provided and secondly to provide genuinely new rights, particularly when it came to members of the member state national's family. Prior to these, in 1961 and 1964, Regulations 15/61[12] and 38/64[13] were adopted, although subsequently replaced by Regulation 1612/68. It is stated in the recitals, that freedom of movement constitutes a fundamental right of workers and at the same time one of the means which help to satisfy the requirements of the economies of the member states and afford workers the opportunity to improve their living and working conditions, thus promoting upward social mobility.

(i)   Regulation 1612/68 provides for equality of access to employment for all community nationals, equality of treatment in employment rights and housing rights, the right of a worker to be joined by his family, and the right for his children to be educated on the same terms as the children of nationals of the member state concerned. Articles 10 and 11 have been repealed and replaced by Directive 2004/38.

(ii)   Directive 64/221 governed the coordination of member states implementation of restrictions on freedom of movement of workers based on public policy, public security, or public health and imposes some limitations on the

---

[11] Respectively; OJ Sp. Edn. 1964, L850/64, p. 117, OJ Sp. Edn. 1968, L257/2, p. 475 and OJ Sp. Edn. 1968, L257/13, p. 485 and now replaced or amended by Directive 2004/38.

[12] J.O. 1961, 1073.

[13] J.O. 1964, 965.

use of these powers by the member state governments. It has now been repealed and replaced by Directive 2004/38.

(iii) Directive 68/360 related to the right of workers to leave one member state and enter the territory of another and prescribes the entry formalities which it is permissible for member states to impose, in particular the rules regarding the issue and withdrawal of residence permits. It has now been repealed and replaced by Directive 2004/38.

(These Directives are mentioned here because you will come across these in much literature and case law, however, in the text below the new Directive and Article numbers have been inserted.)

(iv) Regulation 1251/70 deals with rights of residence after retirement or incapacity of workers.

For the self-employed legislative intervention was employed to facilitate entry and procedural rights in a similar manner to workers and initiate a programme of harmonization of the various professions on a one-by-one basis by means of one or more directives for each profession. These are too numerous for a book of this nature, thus only the general directives will be considered.

(v)   For the self-employed, Directives 73/148 and 75/34 are the equivalents of Directives 68/360 and 1251/70 and they too have been repealed and replaced by Directive 2004/38.

(vi) Directive 2004/38 is now the main and most important provision of secondary legislation for the free movement of Union Citizens and as noted has replaced most of the previous secondary legislation. It covers both workers and the self-employed and both generally revises the law and encapsulates much of the case law of the Court of Justice which has often advanced legal rights prior to statutory change. (Indeed, even some of the new provisions following have to some extent already been achieved by the case law mentioned in this chapter.)

The directive clarifies who should be regarded a member of the family or person otherwise provided with rights derived from an economically active EU citizen. It also establishes permanent rights of residence for citizens after a certain period and restricts the member states' right to refuse entry on the grounds of public policy. The new directive will certainly consolidate the law in this area and clarify some of the existing rights. Whilst the right of permanent residence appears new, in reality it merely reflects the existing situation for many union citizens and families who have chosen to live in another member state.

It will not be easy to fit these new provisions into both existing university courses and textbooks but it is now the true state of the law and therefore its provisions will be considered where appropriate in the sections of text following, along with, when considered useful, the previous provisions applicable.

9.4.2 Rights of Entry, Residence, and Exit

The rights to enter, move freely, seek, and take up employment are governed by a combination of Article 39(3), Regulation 1612/68 Articles 1–5, and Directive 2004/38 Articles 4–14, although much of the case law is based on the now repealed Directive 68/360 Articles 1–6 and 8.

Articles 1 and 2 of Regulation 1612/68 provide the right to take up employment in the host state under the same conditions as nationals without discrimination.

Regulation 1612/68 Article 3(1) permits imposition on non-nationals of conditions relating to linguistic ability required by nature of the post to be filled. This is illustrated and interpreted by the Case 379/87 *Groener v Minister for Education* in which the Court of Justice upheld an Irish requirement that teachers in Ireland should be proficient in Irish as a part of a public policy to maintain and promote the Irish Language and culture. Any requirement though, must be proportionate.

Directive 2004/38 provides the rules to regulate the conditions by which workers can leave one member state and enter the territory of another. It prescribes the entry formalities which it is permissible for member states to impose, in particular, the rules regarding the issue and withdrawal of residence permits. Cases arising under the previous Directive sought to remove the unnecessary restrictions on free movement.

Article 4 provides that exit states are obliged to allow nationals and their family with a valid passport to leave with an exit visa or other formality. The exit state is obliged to issue a passport or ID card.

Article 5 states that entrance states cannot demand an entry visa or equivalent documents from EC nationals. They can, however, require a passport or valid identity card and visas from non-Union members of the family.

In Case C-68/89 *Commission v Netherlands* (Entry Requirements), the Court of Justice held generally in respect of 68/360 that the requirements under the Directive for documentation does not give the member state the right to further questioning regarding the purpose and duration of stay, once the correct papers have been shown. Whilst this is reasonable in theory, in practise it is not so likely in today's more security conscious climate. In Case C-344/95 *Commission v Belgium*, a delay in issuing documents, the limited duration of residence permits and payments demanded in excess of that comparable for national identity cards were all measures held by the Court of Justice to breach Directive 68/360.

Article 6 permits the right to enter, travel, and reside in a host member state for a period of up to three months by an EU citizen and his or her family is not restricted to the economically active but to any EU citizen without any other conditions other than the requirement to hold valid identity and/or visa documentation, the latter covered by Articles 5 and 6. The financial self-sufficiency requirements in the previous general free movement directives are not repeated for the period up to three months but the right to reside for a period of more than three months is made conditional on being engaged in a gainful activity, being self-employed or, even, as a recipient of services or being self-sufficient with comprehensive sickness insurance cover.

As well as residence permits for family members, a registration certificate can be demanded which must be granted to any worker who produces a passport and certificate of proof of employment. Members of the workers family must also be afforded a registration certificate on production of a passport and relationship or proof of dependence. In Case C-459/99 *MRAX*, the Court of Justice considered that it was disproportionate and, therefore, prohibited to send back a third country national married to a national of a member state not in possession of a valid visa where he is able to prove his identity and conjugal ties and there is no evidence to establish that he represents a risk to the requirements of public policy, public security or public health. The new Directive in reflecting previous case law provides that the failure to comply with the registration requirement may render the person concerned liable to proportionate and non-discriminatory administrative sanctions only. For example, in Case 159/79 *R v Pieck*, Mr. Pieck, a Dutch national, re-entered the UK after his original six-month entry permit had expired and he had failed to renew it. The authorities sought to deport him. The Court of Justice held that a failure to obtain a permit could only result in penalties for minor offences. In Case 118/75 *Watson v Belman*, Miss Watson, a UK national, was acting as an 'au pair' whilst staying in Italy with Mr. Belman. Both had failed to report this to the national authorities as required and faced imprisonment and fines under National law. In addition Miss Watson was to be deported. The Italian Magistrate asked the Court of Justice if the punishments were compatible with EC law. The Court of Justice held that the use of internal rules, i.e. the requirement to report, was acceptable but the penalty must be in proportion to the offence/damage caused, i.e. a small fine. Therefore any decision to deport would be contrary to the Treaty. In line with previous case law, Article 25 provides that the registration certificate and residence permit are not preconditions for residence, but merely evidence of the entitlement to enter and reside, i.e. not the right itself but merely the proof of it. Administrative rules requiring registration are acceptable, as is an appropriate sanction for their breach but not deportation which would be regarded as disproportionate.

Previously, Article 6 of Directive 68/360 provided that the permits must be valid for the whole territory of the member state and valid for at least five years with automatic renewal. These requirements are reproduced in Articles 22 and 11 of the new directive. It was confirmed in Case 36/75 *Rutili v Minister of Interior*, that an administrative prohibition restricting movement to parts of France, where justified could only be for the entire territory of the member state. Although as held in Case C-100/01 *Olazbal*, when it comes to criminal measures being taken to restrict movement, this would be acceptable providing the action was justified, the seriousness of the crime would otherwise lead to a complete banishment and nationals would be subject to similar punitive measures. Article 15 states that the expiry of the documentation does not constitute grounds for expulsion.

Temporary involuntary unemployment does not remove the employed or self-employed status (Art 14). Whilst the period is not specified, previous case law (Case C-292/89 *Antonissen*) suggest that six months would be the limit, after which the favoured status would then be lost. Whether then the host member state would be entitled to deport the citizen concerned is doubtful in view of the case law considered below in this chapter, unless there were serious grounds for deportation other than involuntary unemployment.[14]

9.4.3 Procedural Safeguards

Before considering the substantive grounds which member states may invoke in order to either refuse entry in the first place or to justify deportation, which are considered under Section 9.6.1 below, it makes sense first to consider any procedural rights which persons may have who are faced with such decisions. If immediate deportation can be prevented, then there is more time to consider the substantive grounds given. Directive 64/221 provided a number of procedural rights which are now contained in Article 31 of Directive 2004/38 and which further support free movement by providing for non-discriminatory rights of appeal, rights to remain to hear the appeal result, to be given reasons for deportation and judicial review of decisions.

There is a right to remain in the member state pending a decision either to grant or refuse a residence permit, save in emergency situations. Article 30 provides that the grounds for deportation must be precisely and comprehensively stated. The concerned person has a right to be informed of the grounds of refusal or deportation unless security is at stake.

The above rights were comprehensively summed up in Cases 115–116/81 *Adoui and Cornauille v Belgian State* in which two French ladies euphemistically described by the Court of Justice as waitresses had their residence permits withdrawn by

---

[14] A UK Employment Appeal Tribunal held though in *Giangregorio* that voluntary unemployment would remove the continued right to a residence permit and thus arguably permit deportation, but it is that the Court of Justice would agree with this view.

the Belgium authorities on the grounds that their personal conduct justified the invocation of the public policy proviso. The conduct as described by the court: 'Displaying themselves in windows in scant dress and being able to be alone with clients.' Basically Belgium was trying to clamp down on the number of French prostitutes settling in Belgium. A reference was made to the Court of Justice, which held that, the public policy proviso does not allow expulsion where similar conduct by nationals does not incur penalty or repressive measures. However, it does not require illegality to be invoked. It was noted that Belgium prostitutes were tolerated and not prosecuted. The Court of Justice held the reasons must be sufficiently detailed to allow a migrant to defend their interests and drafted in such a way and language as to enable the person to comprehend the content or effect.

Article 30(3) provides the right to be notified of any decision to expel or the refusal of a permit and should also state the minimum period given to leave the country which cannot be less than one month in any circumstance. Article 31 provides that there should also be a system for appeal against decisions on their merits as well as legality. Previously Case C-175/94 *Gallagher* considered the body hearing the appeal. Gallagher, who had been convicted of the possession of rifles for unlawful purposes in Ireland, had been deported from the UK. In questioning this decision, he was interviewed in Ireland before the case was heard by the Home Secretary. He challenged these bodies as not being independent. The Court of Justice held however, that it was a matter for the national courts to decide whether the body hearing an appeal was independent but that the directive did not specify how it should be appointed. It should however, be genuinely independent.

In Case 98/79 *Pecastaing v Belgium State*, a French prostitute was asked by the Belgium authorities to leave on grounds of personal conduct. She claimed under Directive 64/221 Articles 8 and 9 she should be able to stay in the country whilst the decision was being reviewed, which could be up to three years during the course of an Article 234 reference. The Court of Justice held that even under Article 234 the right of appeal is not to be diluted and only in cases of emergency should automatic expulsion take place, however the urgency could only finally be determined by the member states. Articles 8 and 9 do not grant rights to remain in the host state pending hearing as long as the person can get a fair hearing and full facilities even whilst out of the country (see now Art 30 of Directive 2004/38).

9.4.4 The Rights Provided by Regulation 1612/68 and Directive 2004/38

Of all of the examples of the earlier legislation, Regulation 1612/68 has certainly proved to be the most supportive of free movement in particular in the way that

Article 7 of the Regulation has been interpreted by the Court of Justice. The Regulation details access to employment and rights for workers and more importantly, as far as an extension of the rights is concerned, introduced the rights of free movement for members of the workers' family, supposedly taken for granted in respect of the original Treaty Articles. Whilst economically active persons received confirmation that their rights extended to matters such as tax and social advantages, vocational training, trade union membership, and housing rights and benefits under Articles 7–9, the most significant provisions introduced by the first expansion of the rights was to the members of the family of the EC worker of the self-employed person moving. This was made even more significant by the fact that these additional rights of free movement and to take up employment or to take up education or vocational training applied also to non-EC member state family members, i.e. to third country nationals (TCNs). It is only in respect of the extension of the rights to family member that Regulation 1612/68 has been altered with Articles 10 and 11 being repealed and replaced and extended by Articles 2 and 3 of the new Directive. These will be considered in context below.

Article 5 of the Regulation obliges member states to give the same assistance to other EC nationals as their own when seeking employment, i.e. by the various national employment agencies.

Regulation 1612/68, Article 7(1) reflecting Article 12 of the EC Treaty, prohibits discrimination against workers on grounds of nationality and specifically mentions terms and conditions of employment, dismissal, and where relevant, reinstatement.

It has been decided that when a worker commences a job in another country, the same as that previously undertaken in the home state, this previous service may count for advantages in the host state. The Court of Justice held that to ignore this is to discriminate contrary to Article 7(1). In Case C-187/96 *Commission v Greece*, the Court of Justice held that a Greek administrative Regulation and practise which did not take into account periods of employment in the public service of other member state when determining seniority increments and salary grading breached Article 39 (old 48) EC and Article 7(1) of 1612/68, i.e. service elsewhere counts.

Article 7(2), which is proving to be a provision with extremely wide scope, refers specifically to equality in social and tax advantages which also apply to the family of worker. Family is open to wide interpretation, as are the benefits under Article 7(2).

In Case 32/75 *Fiorini a.k.a. Christini v SNCF*, a reduced fare entitlement was claimed by the widow of an Italian SNCF worker. Widows of French workers were allowed such a family entitlement but it was denied to the Italian. The SNCF claimed that since it was not express in the contract of employment it was not available to foreign workers. The Court of Justice was asked if this was the kind of social advantage envisaged by Article 7 and it held that Article 7 applies to all advantages, not just those limited to a contract of employment. It therefore applies to the family of an EC worker in the same way as for nationals.

In Case 94/84 *ONE v Deak*, an unemployed Hungarian national living with his mother, an Italian national working in Belgium, was refused special unemployment benefits for non-nationals on the basis that no agreement for such benefits existed between Belgium and Hungary. The Court of Justice held that special unemployment benefits were a social advantage within the meaning of Article 7 and that Deak, regardless of nationality, could derive rights as the descendant of a worker, otherwise a worker might be hindered from moving if the descendants were discriminated against, thus causing financial difficulty.

In Case 137/84 *Mutsch*, a Luxembourg national living in a German-speaking commune in Belgium was denied the use of German before a court, a right granted to the Belgium German minority. The Court of Justice held that right was a social advantage under Article 7(2) despite there being no link to a contract of employment. Article 7(2) has even been interpreted to include a grant to cover funeral expenses in Case C-237/94 *O'Flynn*.

It is of course debatable whether these social advantages do in fact figure highly in a worker's original decision to move to another member state to take up or find work bearing in mind the facts of these cases, i.e. the dependents have mostly followed on afterwards. The Court of Justice, however, seems not to be taking any chances that this may be a factor to ignore and that the law is now as it has developed.

Article 7(3) provides for the same rights and access to vocational training, see for example the *Lair* case considered previously. Article 7(3) appears however to be less expansive that Article 7(2) which equally applies to education as a social advantage, see for example Case C-3/90 *Bernini*.

Article 9 provides that workers shall enjoy all the rights and benefits accorded to national workers in matters of housing including ownership and access to local authority housing lists.

Article 10 has been replaced and the extended by Directive 2004/38 which provides that the rights enjoyed by the Union national under the directive also apply to family members which are defined generously in Article 2 as spouses, registered partners, descendants, and ascendants. Article 2 has provided that the status of partners will be equated with that of spouses in those member states which recognize such a registered or attestable stable relationship and thus brings statute law in line with the case law of the Court of Justice in the *Reed* and *Diatta* cases considered below. Article 2(c) considerably widens the definition of the family in providing that members of the family include the direct descendants and ascendants of the spouse and partner also. Article 3 also provide rights of entry and residence for any other family members not within the definitions in Article 2 who, in the country from which they have come, are dependants or members of the household of the Union citizen having the primary right of residence or where there are serious health or humanitarian grounds for doing so.

Members of the family can be any nationality and includes those under 21 and adult children over 21 where they are dependent on the worker. Dependency was defined in Case 316/85 *Lebon* as a factual situation of support provided by the worker. By way of example, in Case 261/83 *Castelli v ONPTS*, the Italian mother of a retired Italian worker in Belgium claimed an old age pension. Mrs. Castelli had never worked herself in Belgium, therefore her claim was based on her status as a member of her son's family. The Belgian authorities refused to pay on the grounds that she was not Belgian and they did not have a reciprocal agreement with Italy. The Court of Justice held Mrs. Castelli was entitled to install herself with her son under Article 10 of Regulation 1612/68. She was also entitled to remain after her son's retirement and had a right to the pension under Article 7.

In a judgment concerned with both Articles 7 and 10 of the Regulation, but which has now been partly overtaken by the new Directive, the Court of Justice was required to consider whether the term 'spouse' included cohabitees in Case 59/85 *Netherlands v Reed*. Miss Reed applied for a residence permit in Holland claiming her right to remain was based on her cohabitation with a UK national working in the Netherlands. The Dutch Government refused to recognize this. The Court of Justice was aware that provisions of National laws regarding cohabitees legal rights could be quite varied. It was unable to overcome the clear intention of Article 10 which referred to a relationship based on marriage. The court referred instead to the social advantages guaranteed under Article 7 of the Regulation as being capable of including the companionship of a cohabitee which could contribute to integration in the host country. The Court of Justice held that where such relationships amongst nationals are accorded legal advantages under National law, these could not be denied to nationals of other member states without being discriminatory and thus breaching Articles 7 and 48 (now 12 and 39) of the Treaty. This is a somewhat convoluted decision but it does provide justice to free movement in the case. The cohabitee does not have rights in their own right but the companionship of a cohabitee is merely regarded as one of the advantages to which workers are entitled. Hence then the case merely supports the well-established right in EC law not to be discriminated on the grounds of nationality. Of course, in some countries cohabitees are not afforded the same rights as married couples. The reasoning of the Court has been carried over into Article 2 of the new Directive in respect of same sex partner rights. Where National law supports this, EC law will demand that other Community nationals are equally treated and where National law does not support such right, EC law cannot impose them on member states. The UK, does, of course, now formally recognize same sex partnerships. The *Reed* case remains important for its wide interpretation of Article 7(2).

The rights of a spouse have been held not to be dependent on residence with the entitled worker. In Case 267/83 *Diatta v Land Berlin*, Mrs. Diatta, a Senegalese citizen, was married to a Frenchman living and working in Berlin. She obtained work in Berlin shortly after which the couple separated to live apart. Upon application to extend her residence permit, the German authorities refused on the ground that she was no longer a member of the family for the purposes of Regulation 1612/68. The Court of Justice ruled that the rights under 1612/68 were not dependent on the requirements as to how or where members of the family lived. Therefore, a permanent common family dwelling cannot be implied as a condition of the rights granted under Regulation 1612/68. In Case C-413/99 *Baumbast*, the Court of Justice had confirmed that divorce will bring to an end the spousal relationship for the purposes of free movement rights and thus the right to remain in the host state. However, under the new Directive Article 13, in certain circumstances this will not affect the right to remain in the host state. These are where the spouse is a national of another member state or if not, where the marriage or relationship has lasted at least three years including one year in the host state or, and reflecting the *Baumbast* case, where the person is a carer of the Union citizen's children.

In reviewing a case which has the appearance of a marriage of convenience, the Court of Justice has held in Case C-109/01 *Akrich*, that Article 10 of the Regulation and now by analogy the new Directive, applies to third country nationals only if they are lawfully resident in a member state before they can move to another one and is not applicable where a marriage of convenience has been arranged to circumvent a member state's immigration laws.

Article 23 of Directive 2004/38 entitles the family members of an entitled union citizen to take up any activity as an employed person to include any activity or profession providing the appropriate qualifications and formalities are observed. For example, in Case 131/85 *Emir Gül v Regierungspräsident Düsseldorf*, the Court of Justice held that this right includes the right of such concerned persons to access to employment also under the same conditions as nationals of the host state. This was also affirmed in the case of *Diatta v Land Berlin* in favour of Mrs. Diatta.

9.4.5 Education and Carer Rights

Article 12 of Regulation 1612/68 provides that the children of a national of a member state shall be admitted to the general educational, apprenticeship, and vocational training courses under the same conditions as nationals. Case 9/74 *Casagrande* had already extended the right under Article 12 to include not just access to educational facilities but equality of measures intended to facilitate educational attendance and in Case C-7/94 *Gaal*, the Court of Justice extended the right under Article 12 to an independent and over 21-year-old child of a migrant worker who had been employed in another member state. Gaal was the Belgian son of an EC worker in Germany who had since died. Gaal was attending university and applied for a grant to undertake an eight-month period in the UK but this was refused on grounds that he was over 21 and was not dependant hence he was denied, as no longer being applicable, his rights as a descendant of an EC worker. The Court of Justice held he still fell within the personal scope of Article 12 of the Regulation as the definition of a child was not subject to the same definition as in Articles 10 and 11. Article 12 extends to all forms of education including university education and must include older children no longer dependant on their parents. The case was, however, decided on the basis that the child must have lived at some time with a parent who was an EC worker and thus derived his rights in this manner.

Two cases heard together has extended the Court's view of the effect of Articles 12 to provide rights for carers of Union citizen children who are receiving education. In Case C-413/99 *Baumbast and R v Home Secretary*, the non-EU national mothers who would otherwise have been deported if the Court had not held that the children had the right to be cared for where the original basis of their right to stay in the UK had disappeared, one through divorce and the other because there was no longer a Community national working in the UK or indeed any member state. It is probable that such a convoluted decision is no longer necessary under new rights provided by the new directive considered below. The protection of carers was taken even further in Case C-200/02 *Chen* where the child in question, a Community national born to two Chinese nationals who had not even moved from one member state to another and was below school age was the reason why the Chinese nationals gained a right to remain in the UK. It too will be considered in further detail below.

9.4.6 Right to Remain

Article 39(3)(d) provides the right to remain after retirement or incapacity and applies also to members of the family even if workers dies, and to whom Article 7(2) of Regulation 1612/68 continues to apply. Once provided by Regulations 1251/70 and Directive 75/34, the right to remain is now governed and has been expanded by Directive 2004/38 to include permanent residence rights. Article 12 provides that the Union citizen's death or departure from the host member state shall not affect the right of residence of his/her family members who are nationals of a member state and also to non-member state family members who were living with the Union citizen for at least one year before his or her death. Any children retain the right to attend educational establishments also. Article 13 provides that divorce, annulment of marriage, or termination of the partnership or relationship shall not affect the right of residence of a Union citizen's family members who are nationals of a member state and also those who are not nationals of a member state. The latter category is subject to the requirement that the marriage or partnership has lasted at least three years, one being in the host state or where the spouse or partner has custody of family children or is warranted by particularly difficult circumstances. The rights to remain under Articles 12 and 13 are further dependant on the persons considered not being a burden on host state (Art 14).

Article 16 provides that Union citizens who have resided legally for a continuous period of five years in the host member state shall have the right of permanent residence there and that continuity of residence shall not be affected by temporary absences not exceeding a total of six months a year or by longer absences not exceeding twelve months at a time for important reasons such as compulsory military service, serious illness, pregnancy and childbirth, study or vocational training, or a work assignment in another member state or a third country. Paragraph 1 shall apply also to family members who are not nationals of a member state and have resided with the Union citizen in the host member state for five years. Furthermore, Article 17 provides that this period may be reduced in cases of the death or injury of the union national. In respect of family members who are not nationals of a member state Article 18 provides that they shall acquire the right of permanent residence after residing legally for a continuous period of five years in the host member state.

9.5 The Realization of Free Movement of the Self-employed

The basic Treaty rights providing for free movement of the self-employed are subject to national rules including rules, regulations, and conditions of the various professional organizations and bodies (Arts 43 and 50 EC (old 52 and 60)). These in fact were very often the biggest impediments to the free movements and it was first considered by the Commission that these could be removed by harmonization only. Furthermore, both main Treaty articles (Arts 43 and 49 (old 52 and 59)) envisaged that the basic freedoms provided would be fleshed out by the enactment of secondary legislation issued under Articles 44 and 52 (old 54 and 63).

The initial approach of the Commission therefore was the harmonization of rules by the adoption of a general programme of Directives to abolish the restrictions on free movement, and the mutual recognition of qualifications in all sorts of trades and professions on a occupation by occupation basis. This, however, was only achieved painfully slowly by the enactment of a number, about forty, of sectoral directives and this attempt to harmonize the conditions of the various professions proved extremely difficult and time consuming. For example it took eighteen years for the architects Directive[15] alone to be agreed upon and finally enacted. This approach also encouraged the view throughout the Community that the only way in which these rights could be promoted and relied on was if Directives were enacted to establish them and not directly from the Treaty. Thus little progress was made, and even prior to the issue of some Directives considered essential in the process, case law had developed the law considerably.

9.5.1 The Intervention of the Court of Justice

Whilst the Commission was attempting to realize the free movement of establishment and services by negotiation with all the interested national bodies and the harmonization of the various nationals rules governing the professions, legal disputes were starting to reach the Court of Justice which were concerned with self-employed persons who were facing severe restrictions in trying to practise their professions in another country. Two leading cases, in particular, had a considerable impact on the thinking and approach of the Commission in trying to achieve free movement in these areas. They had highlighted the slow progress and denial of the most basic rights of free movement. The cases, in which Articles 52 and 59 (new 43 and 49) were held to create direct effects by the Court of Justice, were decided in favour of the applicants, in the absence of the assumed completing secondary legislation, largely on the basis of the general prohibition of discrimination, Article 12 EC.

Concerned with establishment, Case 2/74 *Reyners v Belgian State* involved the attempt by a suitably qualified Dutchman get access to the Belgium bar but who was refused on the grounds of nationality. The Dutch Government argued that Article 52 (then) was not directly effective because it was incomplete without the issue of Directives required by Article 52 (then). The Court of Justice held that the prohibition of discrimination under Article 52 (now 43) was directly effective and declared that nationality could be no barrier to appropriately qualified lawyers entering a country to practise. The Directives were simply to facilitate free movement and not to establish it, which had already been done by the Treaty by end of the initial transition period of the Communities (1969).

In Case 33/74 *Van Binsbergen*, it was not nationality that was the problem but a residence requirement. The case concerned a professionally qualified Dutchman,

---

[15] Directive 85/384 OJ 1985 L223/15.

resident in Belgium who was refused audience rights before the Dutch courts. The Court of Justice held Article 59 (now 49) was directly effective and was not conditional on the issue of subsequent Directive in respect of the specific professions, nor on a residence requirement in Holland.

These decisions meant that the Court of Justice had opened the way for the basic Treaty rights to establish and provide services in a host state, could be realized without discrimination or the imposition of unnecessary requirements on the basis of the direct effects of the Treaty Articles themselves and without having to wait for the enactment of directives for each and every profession. Other cases soon followed which fleshed out even further the rights available under the Treaty. As with workers, free movement cases tackled the various ways in which national or professionals rules restricted free movement either by direct or indirect discrimination and rules which were non-discriminatory but nevertheless prevented access.

Case 71/76 *Thieffry v Paris Bar Council* backs up the *Reyners* and *Van Binsbergen* cases. In *Thieffry*, the applicant was refused access to the Paris Bar despite having obtained a Belgian diploma in law, recognized by the University of Paris as the equivalent of a French diploma, and having sat and passed the French Certificate for the Profession of Advocate. The Court of Justice held that the relevant national authorities should apply any laws or practices which allow for the securing of freedom of establishment in accordance with the EEC policy although no Directives may have been enacted in that particular area. Therefore, where the competent authorities have recognized a foreign diploma as equivalent to a domestic qualification, recognition of that diploma may not be refused in an individual case solely because it is not a diploma of the Host State.

Moving beyond clear-cut discrimination in Case 205/84 *Commission v Germany* (Insurance Services) Germany had required the providers of insurance to be resident on German soil. The Court of Justice held that member states were under a duty not only to eliminate all discrimination based on nationality but also all restrictions based on the free provision of services on the grounds that the provider is established in another member state. It also emphasized that all those national rules which apply to the providers of services permanently established in a member state will not necessarily automatically apply to those 'activities of a temporary character which are carried out by enterprises established in other member states'. It was held that the residence requirement was not justified.

The Court of Justice has moved further in the development of a rule which prevents the restriction of services from other member states but may still persist to limit activities of the home providers of services. In Case C-76/90 *Säger v Dennemeyer*, Dennemeyer wished to provide patent services in Germany, something requiring a license whose issue was restricted. His right to obtain a licence was challenged by a

German patent agent. D claimed breach of Article 59 (now 49). The rule was non-discriminatory in that it applied to all patent agents regardless of residence. The Court of Justice held that not just discriminatory rules are prohibited but any rules which are liable to prohibit or otherwise impede persons providing a service which they already lawfully do in the state of their establishment. Laws applying to the temporary provision of services must be:

(a) justified by imperative reason relating to the public interest; and

(b) the public interest is not already protected by the rules of the state of establishment; and

(c) the same result cannot be obtained by less restrictive means.

In Case C-55/94 *Gebhard*, a German lawyer had set up a second chamber in Milan was prevented from using the title Avvocato. No secondary law was held to apply to the situation. The issue was whether the Italian rules could be imposed on him. In principle and according to the general Treaty provision Article 43 (old 52), he was required to comply with national rules but the Court of Justice held that national measures which hinder or make less attractive the exercise of fundamental freedoms must fulfil four conditions. They must be:

(i) non-discriminatory in application;

(ii) justified by imperative reason relating to the public interest;

(iii) suitable to secure the objective sought; and

(iv) proportional.

In Case 340/89 *Vlassopoulou*, a Greek lawyer who had worked in Germany and gained some partial qualifications and experience in German law had her request for admission to the German bar rejected on that grounds that she did not have the necessary German qualifications. On reference to the Court of Justice, if was held that national authorities must take into account qualifications and experience which fall short of full qualification and undertake a comparison of the qualifications to see if they are the equivalent of the national requirements and not to dismiss them out of hand.

It is left to the national courts to determine whether qualifications are equivalent and here the danger is that some will and some will not. The consequence of these decisions is that establishment is now very close to services. Perhaps this is a fair result to achieve, i.e. that it does not matter where or how you practice, either on a temporary or permanent basis, provided qualifications are roughly equivalent. Rules which seek to prevent this must satisfy the criteria or be struck out, at least as far as non-national EC citizens, and eventually this might also lead to internal pressure in member states and thus the rules be abolished in respect of nationals also. Hence then as with goods, as with workers, the prohibited rules applying to the self-employed also include indirect discrimination and thus market access but similarly such rules may be objectively justified.

In Case C-384/93 *Alpine Investments*, a Dutch law which prevented financial services providers from making cold calling telephone calls either within or outside of Holland was challenged as breaching Article 49 (then 59) EC. The Court of Justice held that the rule was not to be equated with the selling arrangements rule established in case *Keck* and *Mithouard* for goods and thus outside the scope of EC law but held instead that because the rule affects access to other markets and thus is capable of hindering intra-Community trade in services it will breach the Treaty. Even still, such measures can be nevertheless objectively justified by imperative reasons of public interest which are necessary and proportionate. In the case itself it was decided that the Dutch Government's arguments of consumer protection and safeguarding the reputation of Dutch financial markets satisfied those criteria, therefore the prohibition did not offend Article 59 (now 49).

Even as a result of the early case law, the Commission realized that the harmonization approach was not the best solution to realize free movement and commenced work on a new approach to achieving free movement which was applicable to many professions across the board.

9.5.2 Legislative Developments

9.5.2.1 Mutual Recognition

With regards to establishment and the provision of services, a change of tactic was undertaken by the Commission to overcome the problems of tackling one profession at a time, which involved the enactment of the Mutual Recognition Directives to apply to many professions. Three reasons prompted new approach. First, the slow progress on specific professions, e.g. the architects Directive took 18 years. Also, following the case law, especially *Reyners* and *Van Binsbergen*, the Commission decided that it was not necessary to issue directives for each individual trade and profession and especially in the case of establishment and it was observed that the progress by the Court of Justice with regard to lawyers rights and others not subject to specific directives was minimal and uncertain. The Directives that had already been worked on and ones in the pipeline were not rendered redundant and were, in cases before the Court of Justice held to be amplifications or guidelines to the requirements of the Treaty Articles, although work on a number were abandoned.

The first general directive was the Mutual Recognition of Diplomas Directive

89/48[16] which applies to numerous professions, excepting those subject to specific Community Directives, who have completed a period, a minimum of three years, of post secondary education and professional training, and which are regulated under National law or subject to the requirement of a Diploma or other similar professional qualifications, the equivalent of a Diploma. It applies to a vast range of professions including, surveyors, chemists, town planners, chartered colourists, shipbrokers, foresters, accountants, and biologists, to name just a selection. It applies to professionally qualified persons as opposed to those who have only completed the university or college element of instruction and includes workers, not just the self-employed.

The basic principle contained in Article 3 denies the right of member state authorities to refuse the right of entry and practise of a profession on the grounds that the holder does not possess the appropriate national qualifications but where qualifications are insufficient or quite different, a period of adaptation or an aptitude test may be required.

The member states remain free under the terms of the Directive, to regulate the conduct and organization of the professions as they see fit. They would apply to nationals of all the member states who become members of a profession regardless of country of origin.

It does not allow the absolute freedom of those who have qualified in one member state to practise in any other member state but subjects this right to means, under Article 4(b), by which the member state can satisfy itself that the professional concerned is in fact qualified or experienced enough to operate in the host member state.

These means are in the form of requiring the would-be entrant to show evidence of experience and complete either a period of supervised training in the host state: An adaptation period; or an examination of his knowledge appropriate to that required: An aptitude test, Article 4(1)(a) and (b).

A clear distinction between the legal and other professions is made. The Directive requires that, for other than lawyers, the member states should offer the entrant a choice of either the adaptation period or the test. However, Article 4(1)(b) 'for professions whose practice requires precise knowledge of National law and in respect of which is an essential and constant aspect of the professional activity, the host member state may stipulate either an adaptation period or an aptitude test'. Thus the Directive inherently recognizes the necessarily distinct role played by lawyers as to other professions; because law, like language, is nationally distinct in concept.

Once the applicant has satisfied Article 4 and becomes established in the member state he/she is then entitled under Article 7(1) to use the professional title of the host state.

---

[16] OJ 1989 L19/16.

A second directive to capture many of the professions and activities not caught by the first was enacted in 1992. The second Directive on Mutual recognition 92/51[17] and more recently Directive 1999/42[18] further provide for recognition of vocational education and professional training, the details of which would not disturb most courses on EC law, so will not be considered here.

9.5.3 The Free Movement of Lawyers

Whilst not dealing with any other professions, as an exception in a book on EC law, it is appropriate to consider briefly the legislative provisions affecting the legal professions.

9.5.3.1 The Provision of Services by Lawyers

It was considered, against the trend of moving away from sectoral directives, to issue a directive to realize the freedom to provide services for lawyers. Directive 77/249[19] is limited to the recognition of practising lawyers from member states, who must be accepted on the basis that the training of lawyers in other members states is similarly strict as in the host state. Article 4(1) dispenses with residence and registration requirements for 'the representation of a client in legal proceedings.' Article 4(2) provides that lawyers providing services in judicial proceedings are required to observe both those sets of rules of professional conduct of the home and host states. Article 4(4) states that where justifiable the same rules apply to those providing services as nationals. Article 5 provides that:

for the pursuit of activities relating to the representation of a client in legal proceedings, a member state may require lawyers . . . to work in conjunction with a lawyer who practises before the judicial authority in question and who would, where necessary, be answerable to that authority . . .

The requirements of Directive 77/249 have been specifically considered in Case 427/85 *Commission v Germany* (Lawyers' Services). The Court of Justice held that local rules were acceptable but could not go beyond the strict requirements of Community law as to become a hindrance to free movement and the requirement to have local lawyers along side at all times, and also before courts where there was no compulsory representation and the requirement to live locally when only providing services was far too restrictive and therefore a breach of the Treaty. The rule that lawyers could only operate in strictly defined areas was not justified by Article 5 of the Directive and could not be applied to activities of a temporary nature carried out by lawyers

---

[17] OJ 1992 L209/29.   [18] OJ 1999 L201/77.   [19] OJ 1977 L78/17.

established in another member state, although they may still apply to national lawyers. This case is an example of reverse discrimination whereby the rule cannot be applied to Community lawyers from other member states but can still be applied to national lawyers. Germany has now repealed that rule.

9.5.3.2 Establishment by Lawyers (Practise under Home Title)

After a considerable period of discussion about the content but also whether such an establishment for lawyers directive was required, the Lawyers Home Title Directive[20] was enacted and which essentially provides under Article 2 that any lawyer shall be entitled to pursue on a permanent basis, in any other member state, under his home country professional title as an independent or salaried lawyer. To practise, lawyers need only register with the competent authority in the host state on the basis of their registration in the home member state (Art 3).

Article 5 provides that the host lawyer may give advice on the law of his home member state, on Community law, on International law, and on the law of the host member state. They must comply with the rules of procedure applicable in the national courts.

Article 5(3) provides that activities relating to the representation or defence of a client in legal proceedings may be reserved to lawyers practising under the professional title of that state, where the host state law provides for this. The state may require lawyers practising under their home country professional titles to work in conjunction with a lawyer who practices before the judicial authority in question and who would, where necessary, be answerable to that authority. In addition, access to supreme courts may be reserved to specialist lawyers.

Article 6 provides that in addition to the professional rules of the home state, a lawyer practising under his home country professional title shall be subject to the same rules of professional conduct as lawyers practising under the relevant professional title of the host member state in respect of all the activities he pursues in its territory.

Article 10 provides that a lawyer practising under his home country professional title who has effectively and regularly pursued for a period of at least three years an activity in the host member state in the law of that state including Community law shall, with a view to gaining admission to the profession of lawyer in the host member state, be exempted from the conditions set out in Article 4(1)(b) of Directive 89/48/EEC. There are detailed rules on providing the necessary proof of practise, training and qualifications.

---

[20] 98/5 OJ 1998 L77/36.

This so-called third approach provides an easier way of acquiring the professional title of the host member state and in effect circumvents the necessity under the Directive 89/48 to undertake the aptitude test to establish in another member state. The reason given for providing this is that it was primarily directed at experienced professionals, for whom an aptitude test would constitute an obstacle on account of the time that has elapsed since they obtained their qualifications but it is hard to see how it would not be used by lawyers of any length of service.

9.6 Derogations from the Free Movement Regimes

9.6.1 Restrictions on the Grounds of Public Policy, Security, and Health

Member states are able to restrict entry and deport EU nationals on the grounds set out under Article 39(3) which are public policy, security and health. Articles 46 and 55 (ex 56 and 66) EC subject establishment and provision of services to the same derogations as workers.

Closer definitions of what the member states could or could not do were introduced in Directive 64/221, which has now been replaced by Directive 2004/38 Article 27, which has consolidated both the previous statutory law and the case law of the Court of Justice. Article 27(2) requires that measures taken on grounds of public policy or public security shall comply with the principle of proportionality and shall be based exclusively on the personal conduct of the individual concerned and provides that previous criminal convictions shall not in themselves constitute grounds for taking such measures. It further provides that the personal conduct of the individual concerned must represent a genuine, present, and sufficiently serious threat affecting one of the fundamental interests of society. Justifications that are isolated from the particulars of the case or that rely on considerations of general prevention shall not be accepted. Personal conduct may not be considered a sufficiently serious threat unless the member state concerned takes serious enforcement measures against the same conduct on the part of its own nationals. Furthermore in Article 28, the member states are now required to take a number of factors into consideration, including how long the individuals concerned have resided within its territory, their age, state of health, family and economic situation, and social and cultural integration into the host member state, and the extent of the links with their country of origin, before taking the decision to remove an EU citizen or a member of his or her family. Removal decisions cannot be taken against Union citizens or family members, irrespective of nationality, who have the right of permanent residence within its territory or against family members who are minors.

Furthermore, any deportation orders which are taken must be subject to review for possible lifting under Directive 2004/38 Article 32 at least three years after being made.

The only case law, thus far, relates to the previous legislation.

Personal conduct was defined in Case 67/74 *Bonsignore v Köln*, in which an Italian national faced deportation as a general preventative nature, after conviction for fatally shooting his brother in a firearms accident. The Court of Justice held

that measures adopted on grounds of public policy and for the maintenance of public security against the nationals of member states of the Community cannot be justified on grounds extraneous to the individual case, and that only the personal conduct of those affected by the measures is to be regarded as determinative. As departures from the rules concerning the free movement of persons constitute exceptions which must be strictly construed, the concept of 'personal conduct' expresses the requirement that a deportation order may only be made for breaches of the peace and public security which might be committed by the individual affected.

In Cases 115–116/81 *Adoui and Cornaille*, French prostitutes facing expulsion from Belgium on public policy grounds could not be denied residence on the basis of their personal conduct when similar conduct on the part of nationals did not attract similar repressive measures to combat such behaviour.

In a somewhat less liberal judgment in Case 41/74 *Van Duyn v The Home Office*, the Court of Justice held that restrictions on the grounds of public policy must be interpreted very strictly and be subject to judicial review. In this case a Dutch woman obtained a position as secretary with the Church of Scientology in the UK but was refused entry by the Home Office on the grounds that public policy declared the Church to be socially harmful. Miss Van Duyn claimed that the refusal was not made on personal conduct but on the conduct of the group.

The Court of Justice held that personal conduct must be an act or omission to act on the part of the person concerned and must be voluntary. It need not, however, be illegal or criminal to offend public policy. The Court further held present association reflecting participation in the activities and identification with the aims of a group may be considered a voluntary act and could therefore come within the definition of conduct which hands back some of the discretion to the member states to determine whether an individuals' association in a group constitutes personal conduct.

Concerning previous criminal convictions, Case 30/77 *R v Bouchereau* involved a Frenchman who had been convicted in the UK on a number of occasions for drugs possession. The UK magistrate asked the Court of Justice whether he could be deported to stop him committing acts in the future. The Court of Justice held that it was not possible to look at past record to decide future conduct unless it constituted a present threat. Public policy measures could only be relied on where conduct and criminal convictions were a genuine and sufficiently serious threat affecting one of the fundamental interests of society. See also the case of *Antonisson*, considered above, whereby the lack of employment and the lack of any serious chance of obtaining one would justify expulsion.

In Case C-348/96 *Donatella Calfa*, a Greek rule of automatic life expulsion from Greek territory was applied following conviction of certain offences. As an exemption, the Court of Justice held that it must be interpreted restrictively and where a person has been convicted, expulsion could only be based on personal conduct outside of the conviction itself but in any event, a life ban was disproportionate and would now not conform with the requirement in Directive 2004/38 for a review of the expulsion after a minimum of three years (Art 32).

The public security proviso was specifically considered in Case C-100/01 *Otieza Olazabal* which involved the French imprisonment and ban on residence for activities undertaking for ETA, the Basque separatist movement. This was challenged but upheld by the Court of Justice as coming within the public security proviso.

Public health measures are given further definition in Article 29 and rather than listing particular diseases as was the previous practise, the directive now provides that

The only diseases justifying measures restricting freedom of movement shall be the diseases with epidemic potential as defined by the relevant instruments of the World Health Organization and other infectious diseases or contagious parasitic diseases if they are the subject of protection provisions applying to nationals of the host member state.

9.6.2 The Public Service Proviso

Article 39(4) exempts employment in the public service from the provisions of Article 39. The initial difficulty was that there is no Treaty definition of public service which can vary considerably from state to state and thus its understanding in different member states could vary considerably and could be claimed by the member states to apply to a vast range of workers employed by the state. Hence the Court of Justice has constantly stressed the need for a strict interpretation of this Article. It has been held to apply to entry and not to conditions of employment. In Case 152/73 *Sotgui v Deutsche Bundespost*, Mr. Sotgui, an Italian national was employed by the German Post Office but was not paid the same travel allowance as German nationals. This was held to be discrimination contrary to Article 39(1) and not excused by Article 39(4). In Case 149/79 *Commission v Belgium* (Public Employees), the Court of Justice held, public service derogation only applies to typical public service posts which exercise powers conferred by public law and which are there to safeguard the interests of state, regardless of the actual status in each of the member states. The Court of Justice has on this basis excluded from the scope of Article 39(4):

Case 307/84 *Commission v French Republic*; nurses
Case 66/85 *Lawrie-Blum v Land Baden-Würtemberg*; trainee secondary school teachers
Case C-4/91 *Bleis v Ministry of Education*; secondary school teachers
Case 33/88 *Alluè and Coonan v Università degli Studi di Venezia*; as above; foreign language lecturers.

In order to try to clarify the posts the member states claim to come within Article 39(4) the Commission has issued a notice, OJ 1988 C72/2, of those sectors which it thinks that positions would rarely be covered by the public service proviso. These include public health care, teaching in state educational establishments, non-military public research and public administration of commercial activities. Occasionally restrictions are accepted by the Court of Justice as in Case C-47/02 *Anker et al.* in which restricting the appointment of Ship's Masters to Germans was held to be acceptable in view of the public duties which had to be undertaken by the Masters of ships however the Court advised that such duties should not be a minor part of the activity of a Master only.

There is the equivalent of the public service exception for establishment in Article 45 (old 55)) but only on the more tightly defined ground of 'positions concerned with the exercise of official authority'. The Court held in the case of *Reyners* that the derogation was more concerned with the exercise of the prerogative power of the state rather than the preventing particular occupations from exercising rights under Community law.

Before moving on to consider how the scope of free movement rights are being widened, we will consider two developing sets of situations which demonstrate the boundary line of application between Community law and the member states' right to determine persons' rights.

9.7 The Wholly Internal Rule

The provision of the Community law free movement regime will not apply when a factual situation is regarded as being within the wholly internal legal competence of a member state and there is no personal fulfilment of the EC law rights to trigger any material rights under Community law. It has already been observed that EC law sometimes has the effect of producing reverse discrimination against nationals of member states when compared to EC nationals from other member states who have moved there and benefit from EC law. For example, where strict professional rules continue to apply to nationals established and providing services but which are held by the Court of Justice not to be suitable or appropriate to apply to EC lawyers providing services temporarily in the host state. See the restriction on areas of practise for lawyers in German in Case 427/85 *Commission v Germany* (Lawyers). The consequence of this judgment was that the German lawyers could still be restricted in the geographical areas in which they could practise because this was an entirely internal matter of the application of national rules to nationals. EC law in such a circumstance was not invoked in any way and the Court of Justice could not and would not interfere in a wholly internal matter. In Case 175/78 *R v Saunders*, a criminal sanction imposed a mobility restriction on Saunders which was applicable within the UK only. This was claimed by Saunders to be contrary to Article 48 (now 39). The Court of Justice held that there was no factor connecting the situation with Community law as there was no movement to or from another member state. Hence, the provisions on free movement of workers cannot be applied to situations which are wholly internal to a member state. The *Saunders* case can be compared with another to demonstrate the difference when Community law applies. In Case 36/75 *Rutili v France*, a restriction by France on the Italian national Rutili entering certain departments of France was regarded as contrary to both the Treaty and Community secondary legislation. The Court of Justice held that Article 48(3) (now 39) derogations may be imposed only in respect of the whole of the national territory.

Two further cases illustrate how the wholly internal rule appears to give rise to unfair and arbitrary results and thus discrimination because nationals or those lawfully resident in the member state in question are denied rights which EU nationals from other member states and family members from outside the EU are able to rely on.

In Case 35 and 36/82 *Morson and Jhanjan*, the applicants, both Surinamese nationals, claimed the right to stay in Holland with their Dutch national son and daughter working there. It was held by the Court of Justice that there was no application of Community law to the wholly internal situation where national workers had not worked in any other member state. There was no movement from one member state to another, therefore Community law did not apply and movement from a third country does not qualify. This was confirmed in Case 64 and 65/96 *Land Nordrhein-Westfalen v Uecker and Jacquet* concerning two third country nationals trying to rely on Community law as spouses of German nationals living in Germany. The case was deemed to be wholly internal and thus not within the scope of application of EC law. If in both cases, they were, for example, Spanish nationals moving to either Holland or Germany, they would be allowed to take TCN spouses or relatives with them. Of late, however, there appears to be some softening of the wholly internal rule. Some cases look wholly internal but because there was some prior movement is involved, Community law rights can be triggered against the home state. The amount of movement or degree of economic activity deemed necessary to take a situation out of being wholly internal to one where EC law applies, appears to be decreasing.

In Case C-370/90 *Surinder Singh*, an Indian spouse of a British national was able to use EC law to derive a right of residence in the UK on the basis that the spouse had previously exercised the right of free movement by providing services in another member state but who then re-established herself in the UK. In Case 419/92 *Scholz*, it was held, a frontier worker who continues to live in his or her home state and is just employed in another state but who crosses the border to work triggers Community rights which can be claimed within the home state.

In Case C-60/00 *Carpenter*, a Philippine national claimed a right of residence in the UK with her British spouse on the grounds that he provided services from time to time in other member states. The case is similar to *Singh* inasmuch as the fact that services had been provided in another member state before returning to the UK, except that Mrs Carpenter had not left UK soil whilst services were being provided by her husband both from the UK and travelling to other member states. The argument put forward by the applicants was that if Mrs Carpenter had also gone to another member state, both would have rights of residence and the right to work in the other host EU states. However, she chose to remain in the UK to look after the children and thus assist her husband in providing services in other member states. The EC Commission regarded the case as a wholly internal matter for the member state and thus just subject to its law. The Advocate General took the view that the matter was not wholly internal but that instead Mrs Carpenter was covered by Directive 73/148, which provides rights in similar terms to those provided for in Directive 68/360 for workers, for the self-employed and their spouses to move and reside in a host member state. However, the AG did not address the fact that there was no movement to reside in the host state by Mrs Carpenter, but looked instead for a connection with the member state which would then activate the application of Community law and in the case, Directive 73/148. The Court of Justice referred to Regulation 1612/68 which strictly, does not apply to the provision of services, but provides rules protecting of the family life of nationals of the member states in order to eliminate obstacles to the exercise of the fundamental freedoms guaranteed by the Treaty.

It is clear that the separation of Mr. and Mrs. Carpenter would be detrimental to their family life and, therefore, to the conditions under which Mr. Carpenter exercises a fundamental freedom. That freedom could not be fully effective if Mr. Carpenter were to be deterred from exercising it by obstacles raised in his country of origin to the entry and residence of his spouse. Para 39.

The Court of Justice noted that the marriage appeared genuine, there were no official complaints against her, and that she looked after the children while he was providing services. The Court held that Article 49 EC, read in the light of the fundamental right to respect for family life (ECHR Art 8), is to be interpreted as preventing a member state from refusing the third country national spouse of a provider of services established in that member state who provides services to recipients established in other member states, a right to reside in its territory.

In Case C-281/98 *Angonese*, an Italian citizen applied for a job in Italy but was refused entry to the selection process as he did not have the appropriate local authority certificate of bilingualism, despite being accepted by the local court as perfectly bilingual and possessing certificates of language study from the University of Vienna where he had studied. The Italian Government and defendant bank argued that the matter was wholly internal and had no connection with Community law. Whilst there was movement in this case in that Mr. Angonese had studied in Austria, the only economic activity was the receiving of educational services. The Court of Justice held that the previous movement for the purposes of study had triggered Community law rights.

The theme of connection to the state was taken up by AG Ruiz-Jarabo in Case C-138/02 *Collins and Secretary of State for Work and Pensions* as a way of pulling back from the arguably over-generous interpretation by the Court of Justice, which would seem to open up all benefits equally to all EU citizens. In 1998 Collins entered the UK on an Irish Passport to seek work. He claimed an income based jobseekers' allowance on the strength of ten months' part-time work from 1980 to 1981. The UK authorities refused the benefit as he was not habitually resident in the UK. Collins claimed that this was discrimination as nationals were advantaged by automatically satisfying the time period required whereas other Community nationals would have to fulfil this extra requirement. The intervening member states (UK and Germany) and the EC Commission agreed that Collins was lawfully resident (but under Art 39 EC and not Directive 68/360) and could stay for six months to find work. The AG considered he did not have the status any longer as a worker and was therefore not entitled to all the rights provided for in the secondary legislation. The AG then considered the case law on the Social Security Regulation 1408/71 to confirm the right of member states to require a period of habitual residence and was of the view that Collins had not demonstrated the required affinity with the UK. He thus distinguished Collins's situation from both *Sala* and *Grzelczyk*, considered below under the citizenship section, and gave the opinion that a required period of residence to show connection with a state was acceptable under Community law and that Collins had not fulfilled this so must fail in his claim to benefit. The Court of Justice followed this opinion by holding that it was permissible for member states to first require there be a genuine link between the work seeker and the state for the purposes of claming a work seeker's allowance. There was indirect discrimination in that nationals could far more easily establish this link but that for the reasons given by the UK, it was objectively justified as the job seekers' allowance was designed to reduce national unemployment for those living long term in the UK.

Case C-109/01 *Akrich* raised some important questions in respect of the scope of the *Singh* judgment, in particular whether a situation which would otherwise be wholly internal can be deliberately engineered to become one with a Community context. The case involves a Moroccan, who after both lawful and unlawful attempts to enter and remain in the UK, married a UK national and moved to Ireland for a short period expressly in order to take advantage of EC law rights and in particular the judgment in *Singh* to return to the UK. The Secretary of State considered that Mr. and Mrs. Akrich's move to Ireland was no more than a temporary absence deliberately designed to manufacture a right of residence for Mr. Akrich on his return to the United Kingdom and thereby to evade the provisions of the United Kingdom's national legislation, and that Mrs. Akrich had not been genuinely exercising rights under the EC Treaty as a worker in another member state. The Court of Justice was asked, amongst other questions, whether an engineered situation to evade national immigration laws was an abuse of Community law rights and if so whether the UK authorities could lawfully refuse entry. The Court of Justice held the motive for going to Ireland is not relevant to the status of a worker nor the decision to return to the home state but the Court of Justice did acknowledge that there would be an abuse if the facilities afforded by Community law in favour of migrant workers and their spouses were invoked in the context of marriages of convenience entered into in order to circumvent the provisions relating to entry and residence of nationals of non-member states. If, however genuinely married, Article 8 ECHR should be taken into regard in considering the unlawful residence status of the TCN. The Court of Justice held that Article 10 of Regulation 1612/68 applies to TCNs only if they are lawfully resident in a member state before they can move to another one to take advantage of the rights provided by the Regulation. It is not applicable where a marriage of convenience has been arranged to circumvent a member state's laws. So if the marriage is genuine, despite a lack of lawful residence, member states should pay regard to Article 8 ECHR. This judgment does not provide a full answer and the main question which is left to the member state is whether the marriage was genuine or not.

So, bearing in mind the developments so far, a factual circumstance, which on the face of it appears to be wholly internal, may nevertheless be subject to EC law, provided that there has been some previous movement into another member state or if services have been received in another member state. Thus, receiving rather than providing services, i.e. passively rather than actively engaging in an economic activity will trigger Community law rights. It is further arguable, that the movement can also be metaphysical, i.e. receiving services over the telephone or, more probable these days, over the internet. Such argument does, of course, raise the question, not yet decided by the Court of Justice and certainly not express in any legislative provision, whether receiving services in such a manner is within the concept of engaging in an economic activity? If the simple receipt of services, irrespective of the manner of delivery of these services, triggers the application of EC law, then it could be argued that potentially any receipt of services will do regardless of how minimal such as telephoning another country to get advice or other services or downloading advice packages from a computer server in another member state. This might be going too far and already the AGs in the *Carpenter, Angonese,* and *Collins* cases are suggesting a new test to determine whether EC law is triggered which relates specifically to the connection to the state of the person concerned. In other words, an economically determined level of activity could be set, below which EC rights would not be triggered for the reason that the services received were marginal.

9.8 The Treatment of Third Country Nationals (TCNs)

Nationals from third countries lawfully or unlawfully resident in a member state were not subject to EC law unless specifically catered for in some way such as family members of EU persons taking advantage of the free movement rules. Here we are only concerned with independent TCNs who obtain no rights under Community law to reside in the EU or move from country to country. Their rights were originally entirely a matter for national law regulation. TCNs, according to European Commission estimates comprise about 4 per cent of the population of the fifteen member states in 2000 which translates to roughly 13 million TCNs lawfully or unlawfully resident in the EU, a figure that no doubt will have risen significantly when the EU increases to twenty-five member states.

Whilst it might have been the case in the past that the treatment of TCNs was regarded as being below the standards of treatment to be expected from the European Community, more recently the Court of Justice has been addressing the rights of TCNs in the latest case law. A lot of attention has been directed to the immigration policies and the Schengen Agreement regarding the entry and visa regulation of TCNs, whereas less attention has been paid to the free movement rights of those already in the EU. Previously, the Court of Justice has held, for example, in Case 238/83 *Mr. and Mrs. Richard Meade,* that the Treaty articles on free movement of workers apply solely to EU nationals and not therefore to TCNs.

The first of the exceptions to this position is where TCNs have been provided with rights under the various association and cooperation agreements with countries such as Turkey, Algeria, and Morocco. Secondly, TCNs may form part of the workforce of workers of a company established in the EU which sends workers abroad to complete a contract in another member state. In Case C-43/93 *Van der Elst*, the court confirmed that nationals of third countries also have the right of free movement within the context of the right of free movement of companies which are established within the EU, providing that the non-EU nationals are part of the legal labour force of the company established in the home member state and where the employer provides services in another member state.

There has also now been legislative intervention in this area and further proposals have also been made. Regulation 1091/2001[21] was enacted which provides limited rights of free movement for those TCNs in the EU on a long stay visa. TCNs may also be helped by Directive 2000/43[22] to prohibit discrimination based on race, however, Article 3(2) states that it is without prejudice to the provisions and conditions relating to the entry and residence of TCNs and to any treatment which arises from the legal status of TCNs. So whilst it may prevent unequal treatment in the country of residence, it is unlikely to provide a right of free movement.

Specifically, addressing the situation of divided families with TCN family members, the Institutions have enacted Directive 2003/86[23] which provides that lawfully resident TCNs in member states may apply to have their family join them from a third country providing they are self-sufficient and has been in the member state for a year or more. Furthermore, Article 3 requires that they must have a reasonable prospect of remaining longer. The definition of family has been restrictively drawn and member states retain much discretion in deciding whether to grant an application. The directive does not apply to the UK, Ireland, and Denmark who have opted out of this section of the Treaty.[24]

A Directive has been enacted concerning the status of TCNs who are long-term residents in a Member State.[25] This Directive provides TCNs who have been lawfully resident in the EU for a minimum of five years to apply for and acquire a certain status which entitles them to long-term residence in the host state and limited rights of movement within the EU. These rights are subject to the public policy and security derogations, self-sufficiency, and sickness insurance requirements and quotas and restrictions on movements imposed by the other secondary states. The Directive extends to core family members as defined by the reunification Directive but these may not be admitted by a second EU state. Indeed whilst the Directive does provide new rights for TCNs, it only does so without prejudice to all the other legislative provisions already providing rights and is subject to interpretation by the member states which may dilute some of its provisions. It came into force on

---

[21] OJ 2001 L150/4. [22] OJ 2000 L180/22. [23] OJ (2003) L251/12.
[24] See the protocols attached to the Treaty of European Union and the amended EC Treaty.
[25] Directive 2003/109 OJ (2004) L16/44.

23 January 2006 and is nevertheless a welcome, if in the end, a somewhat modest improvement.

Finally, there is also Council Directive 2004/114[26] of 13 December 2004 on the conditions of admission of TCNs for the purposes of studies, pupil exchange, unremunerated training or voluntary service but which enters into force only in 2007.

Article 59 (now 49)(2) EC Treaty was amended by the SEA and now provides that the Council may, acting by a qualified majority on a proposal from the Commission, extend the provisions of the chapter to nationals of a third country who provide services and who are established within the Community. After many years of laying dormant, a proposal has finally been made under this Article.[27] However, there has been no further action on this since 8 May 2000 when an amended proposal was sent to the EP. This proposal, which does not go as far as to allow TCNs to establish in another member state, restricts the freedom to providing services, outside of transport services and does not include the freedom to move to receive services in other member states. They are required to be lawfully resident in the state where they must have been established and providing services for at least twelve months (see proposed Article 1) before being able to provide.

A further proposal has been made which concerns common conditions of entry and residence for TCNs who seek paid employment, or self-employment, within the EU (COM(2001) 386 final). Things therefore may be moving for TCNs in the future, but in the meantime there have been some case law developments.

In Case C-413/99 *Baumbast*, which actually covers under the same name two sets of factual circumstances and which essentially finds derived rights for TCNs. The case also involves a 'R', an American woman who, on the face of it, had no personal nor derived rights to remain in the EU but who nevertheless was held by the Court of Justice to have a right of residence under Community law enabling her to resist an attempt to deport her. R moved to the UK with her then French husband who had obtained work in the UK. Later they were divorced and in line with the jurisprudence of the *Diatta* and *Reed* cases, R lost her own legal right to remain in the host state under Regulation 1612/68, Article 10. R and her children nevertheless remained in the UK. Whilst the children were granted indefinite leave to remain, she was not. The UK authorities wanted to deport her and by necessity her children who, however, remained the children of a EU national but who was no longer working in the UK. The Court of Justice held that Regulation 1612/68

must be interpreted as entitling the parent who is the primary carer of those children,

---

[26] OJ (2004) L375/12.　　[27] Com(2000) 271 final (OJ 2000 C311/197.

irrespective of nationality, to reside with them in order to facilitate the exercise of that right notwithstanding the fact that the parents have meanwhile divorced. The fact that only one parent is a citizen of the Union and that parent has ceased to be a migrant worker in the host member state and that the children are not themselves citizens of the Union are irrelevant in this regard.

Hence then, there is an implied right within Article 12 of the Regulation, that the child of a migrant worker can pursue his education in the host member state and that that child has the right to be accompanied by the person who is his primary carer. Furthermore, that person is able to reside with him in that member state during his studies. According to the Court of Justice, to refuse to grant permission to remain to a parent who is the primary carer of the child exercising his right to pursue his studies in the host member state infringes that right (para 73). Obviously in that particular case there was still a connection with the host state which provided the right to remain but nevertheless it represents another slight widening of the scope of EC free movement law.

In Case 459/99 *MRAX*, the TCN spouses of Community nationals who did not possess a valid visa could not be refused entry to Belgium for this failure. The Court of Justice held that:

While Article 4(3) of Directive 68/360 and Article 6 of Directive 73/148 authorize the member states to demand, for the purpose of issue of a residence permit, production of the document with which the person concerned entered their territory, they do not lay down that that document must still be valid. (Para. 89)

This judgment may have been easier to understand if it had been put in the same terms as residence permit requirements in cases such as *Pieck*, whereby the permits themselves merely constitute evidence of a right and not the right itself. A response to not having a valid document or the correct document at all, which was the decision to expel a person not in possession of a valid residence permit would be disproportionate and thus contrary to Community law. The requirement to possess a valid visa could be viewed in the same light. The Court did however, follow the reasoning in Case C-376/89 *Giagounidis*, in which the Court of Justice held that member states are obliged to grant the right of residence within their territory to the workers referred to in Article 1 of Directive 68/360 who can produce either a valid identity card or a valid passport, regardless of the document with which they entered their territory. Consequently, the Court of Justice held,

a member state cannot make issue of a residence permit under Directives 68/360 and 73/148 conditional upon production of a valid visa. Furthermore, an order of expulsion from national territory on the sole ground that a visa has expired would constitute a sanction manifestly disproportionate to the gravity of the breach of the national provisions concerning the control of aliens. (Para. 90)

In Case C-109/01 *Akrich*, the position of a non-lawfully resident TCN who was married to a UK national was considered. In the case the Court of Justice held that the right to stay under Community law, was essentially to be determined on the basis of the member state's view on the genuineness of the TCN's marriage but there still had to be a derived right even if the marriage was genuine.

The statutory and case law developments represent some slight improvement in the position of lawfully resident TCNs in the EU. The EU legislature and the Court of Justice is having to be very careful in trying to provide rules for TCNs who have a good claim to reside and exercise rights of free movement without opening the door too widely so that unlawful residents gain a right to remain and obtain benefits, matters which are highly politically charged in the present day. Another way of regulating TCNs and simultaneously prompting further recognition of their rights in the EU is by the policies pursued, by the Schengen Agreement, which is not considered in this text.

Where TCNs are member of the family of a Union Citizen who has exercised his or her rights under Community law, then Directive 2004/38 certainly provides the most secure rights with, after five years, the right or permanent resident, even in the event of the death of the union citizen or divorce from the union citizen, see the noted in the text above.

9.9 The Further Widening of the Concept of Free Movement

Freedom of movement may exist for persons other than workers and the self-employed as this concept is widened to include those receiving services as opposed to providing services and further as rights to free movement are no longer anchored to an economic activity. This was initially addressed by three general directives, then by the introduction of a citizenship section into the EC Treaty and now by Directive 2004/38 which has replaced the three general rights of movement Directives. Whilst the receipt of services may and often is dealt with at the same time as the provision of services, it seems just as relevant in a section concerned with how Community rights of free movement have been expanded beyond those originally catered for by Community law, particularly in the light of developments to the meaning and worth of citizenship in the Community. In the following two sub-sections, therefore those receiving services and those having a right to move—not based on an economic activity—are considered.

9.9.1 Receiving Services

The concept of services has been expanded to those, who rather than actively pursue an economic activity instead passively receive services of an economic activity. Whilst there is nothing to confirm this category within the Treaty, it was expressly mentioned in Article 1 of Directive 64/221 but not in Directive 2004/38. Services can be received either by both movement to another member state or receiving services from another state in the home state. Initially, cases which confirmed this arose from the areas of educational provision and tourist travel.

In Case 286/82 *Luisi and Carbone v Ministero del Tesauro*, two Italian nationals were prosecuted under Italian Currency regulations for taking money out to pay for tourist and medical provisions abroad. These were held by the Court of Justice to be payments for services and thus coming under the provisions of the EEC Treaty, payments also being a fundamental freedom of the Community and the case was covered by Articles 59, 60, and 7 (now 49, 50, and 12).

In Case 293/83 *Gravier v City of Liège*, a decision to charge foreign students a fee for vocational training courses but not nationals was claimed to be contrary to Community law (Arts 12, 49, and 150 (ex 6, 59, and 128 EEC). This was upheld in the case and in two cases following, Case 24/86 *Blaizot v University of Liège* and Case 263/86 *Belgium v Humbel* which confirmed that university study was, for the most part, vocational training in EC law terms and that Community nationals have a right to equal access to receive that under equal conditions as nationals even where fees were financed by the host state. Note though that the judgments did not extend to establishing a right to scholarships and grants, although the *Grzelczyk* case, considered below, may have altered our view on this.

Case 186/87 *Cowan* confirms that tourists travelling and receiving services bring themselves within the protection of EC law not to be discriminated against even in areas, as in the case itself, such as participation in the French criminal injuries compensation scheme. In Case C-281/98 *Angonese*, it was the activity of receiving educational services which triggered other citizenship rights including under Article 12, the right not to be discriminated against.

Case C-109/92 *Wirth* involved a question from a German court of whether courses available in an institute of higher education had to classified as services under Article 50 (old 60). A German national was attempting to get a grant from German authorities to study in Holland. The Court of Justice held that courses given in a University or Institute of Higher Education which is financed essentially out of public funds do not constitute services within the meaning of Article 50 (old 60) of the EC Treaty, however, it noted many courses were financed by the students themselves paying fees with the aims that the course generate profit and could, in these circumstances, be regarded as coming within the concept of services. The conclusions from this case are therefore that member states remain able to determine their own system of grants and so discriminate against non-nationals but that access to institutions and tuition fees are subject to EC law. However, the citizenship case and in particular *Grzelczyk* may cause us to alter our conclusions on grants.

9.9.2 The General Free Movement Directives

The three general free movement directives (Directives 90/364, 90/365, and 93/96)[28] have now been replaced by Directive 2004/38 considered above and are only mentioned here in respect of the case law generated by them. Indeed, the Directives were soon overtaken by the introduction of the Citizenship rights and other developments in EC law, which are considered elsewhere in this chapter. The directives allowed for free movement not linked to an economic activity in the same way now provided by the new Directive 2004/38. In place of an economic activity, proof of self-sufficiency is instead required (Art 7b of Directive 2004/38). The Court of Justice has confirmed that member states may ask for evidence of self-sufficiency but cannot dictate what that evidence should consist of (Case C-424/98 *Commission v Italy*) and the Court of Justice held in Case C-184/99 *Grzelczyk*, that it may be possible to make a claim on the social funds of a member state provided that the burden on the state is not unreasonable. 'Unreasonable' was the qualifying word used in the preamble to the Directives rather than simply 'burden' which appeared in the article itself. In other words, a reasonable burden on the state, particularly if temporary in nature would be acceptable, which is a quite different matter and category. The decision leaves open who should define reasonableness in similar circumstances. Is it a matter for the Court of Justice or the member states? Presumably, in line with the Court of Justices' comments in *Grzelczyk*, this would be within the member states courts' discretion. The Court of Justice has also considered Directive 90/364 in *Baumbast* (C-413/99) and held, in view of the facts that Baumbast and family were not a burden on UK Social security and had German insurance cover, albeit not for emergency treatment, that the requirement for all risks insurance did not have to include emergency insurance which the Court noted that this was provided as a matter of course in the UK. The new Directive does not use 'unreasonable' in Article 7b but, as did the previous Directives, does include it in the preamble, thus presumably, the same Court of Justice qualification will apply.

---

28 OJ 1990 L180/26, OJ 1990 L180/28, and OJ 1993 L317/59.

9.9.3 The Treaty of European Union and European Citizenship

The Treaty of European Union signed at Maastricht introduced a small section on European citizenship to the EC Treaty.

Article 17 (old Article 8) provides that 'Citizenship of the Union is hereby established. Every person holding the nationality of a member state shall be a citizen of the Union. Citizenship of the Union shall complement and not replace national citizenship.' Furthermore, Article 18 provides that every citizen of the Union shall have the right to move and reside freely within the territory of the member states, subject to the limitations and conditions laid down in this treaty and by the measures adopted to give it effect.

The rights provided by the Treaty under citizenship remove the economic activity requirement of the previous free movement of persons regime, however, it was not immediately obvious as to its true scope and is only now becoming clearer as a result of Court of Justice judgments. It must also be noted that the right of residence under Article 18 is still subject to the limitations and conditions laid down in the Treaty and by the measures adopted to give it effect, in other words, limitations already in existence and those that might be contained in future implementing measures.

The first matter to be considered is a definition of European Union citizenship which Article 18 bases on the nationality of the member states, considered above in Section 9.3.1.1. Thus, there can be no Community definition of European Citizenship but that the concept can only be determined as the collective definitions of national citizenship from all of the member states. Thus if a person is a national of a member state, then Articles 17 and 18 apply.

The scope and restrictions of citizenship rights need then to be determined. Article 18 is subject to restrictions but it does not expressly state which restrictions apply to it. Arguably, although without judicial support for this view, it would appear that the public policy, security, and health provisos apply in which case Directive 2004/38 will also apply to the rights. These matters have already been subjected to the consideration of the Court of Justice in a number of cases coming before it.

9.9.4 Case Law on the Citizenship Articles

Citizenship was first raised in Case C-193/94 *Skanavi and Chyssanthakopoulos.* The Court of Justice, whilst considering Article 18, would not grant it primary status with other Articles granting free movement and residence in host states. Later, in Case C-274/96 *Criminal Proceedings v Bickel and Franz,* the self-standing status of Article 18 appeared to be increased, although not to an overriding Community law right but to one which could be pleaded in support of other rights, in this case to support the view that the refusal to allow Germans the use of German in the Italian South Tirol courts would be contrary to Article 12, where Italian citizens of Austrian extract in South Tirol were allowed to use German. They had lawfully entered Italy under Article 49 EC. In Case C-85/96 *María Martínez Sala v Freistaat Bayern*, Sala, a Spanish national who had worked in Germany for many years, lost her job but remained in Germany and had received social assistance from 1989. Her residence permit had expired but the German authorities supplied her with certificates stating she had applied for an extension to her permit. The authorities refused her a child allowance because she did not have a valid residence permit, which she claimed was contrary to Article 12 as German nationals were not subject to the same condition. Although in the case, her actual status as a worker was not determined, the Court of Justice held in any event, she was lawfully resident in Germany. Sala thus came within the personal scope of Treaty citizenship and that Article 8(2) (now 18) acted to attach other rights including the right to be protected against discrimination under Article 12 and that this in turn applied to a right within the material scope of the treaty such as the child allowance claimed in the case on an equal basis with nationals.

In Case C-378/87 *Criminal Proceedings v Florus Wijsenbeek*, a Dutch MEP refused to show his passport and state his nationality on entry to Holland and was prosecuted for that failure. He claimed that the rights under Articles 7a and 8a EC Treaty (now Articles 14 and 18) had direct effect and that he could rely on them. The Court of Justice held that even if they gave right of free movement, member states still had the right to carry out border checks, although did not state in clear terms that those articles were able to provide a direct right to free movement unattached to any other Community right to free movement.

In Case C-184/99 *Grzelczyk*, a French national who studied and worked on a part-time basis to help support himself for three years in Belgium applied at the beginning of his fourth and final year of study to the CPAS for payment of the *minimex*, a non-contributory minimum subsistence allowance. The CPAS granted Mr. Grzelczyk the *minimex* but then later denied this on the basis that he was not Belgium, hence clear discrimination on the grounds of nationality. This case did not determine a possible status as a worker but nevertheless held that the citizenship rights enable union citizens to be treated equally. The Court of Justice emphasized the new citizenship provisions and new competences, albeit limited, in education allowed it to hold that Articles 12 and 17 preclude discrimination as regards the grant of a non-contributory social benefit to union citizens where they are lawfully resident, even though not economically active.

In Case C-224/98 *D'Hoop*, a Belgium national had studied in France. She was refused a tide over allowance between study and work granted to nationals by the

Belgium authorities on the ground that she had studied in another member state. The Court of Justice had held that the tide-over allowance was a social advantage under Article 7(2) of Regulation 1612/68 but to take advantage of it the person must either have participated in the employment market or obtained a derived right in some way. She was not a worker and her parents had remained in Belgium, therefore she had no rights in her own right nor derived rights from the parents. The Court of Justice referred to the new contribution to education by the EC in encouraging mobility of students and teachers (Articles 3(1)(q) and 149(2) EC) and citing *Grzelczyk* paragraph 31, held that it would be incompatible with the right of freedom of movement if a citizen who had taken advantage of free movement then suffered discrimination as a consequence.

Such inequality of treatment is contrary to the principles which underpin the status of citizen of the Union, that is, the guarantee of the same treatment in law in the exercise of the citizen's freedom to move. The condition at issue could be justified only if it were based on objective considerations independent of the nationality of the persons concerned and were proportionate to the legitimate aim of the national provisions. (Paras. 35–6)

The Belgium authorities offered none, hence the limiting of places of education which qualify for the tide-over allowance, according to the Court of Justice, went beyond what is necessary to attain the objective pursued.

In Case C-413/99 *Baumbast*, Mr. Baumbast was self-employed in the UK, where he resided with his Colombian wife and two children, who were being educated in the UK. He was subsequently employed by a German company and worked outside the EU. His family remained in the UK. Their residence permits were not renewed, however, and Mrs. Baumbast and the children faced deportation. The case was referred to the Court of Justice, which emphasized the right of children of EU nationals under Regulation 1612/68 to continue their education even if the worker, from whom their rights derived, was no longer working. The Court of Justice further held the text of the Treaty does not permit the conclusion that citizens of the Union who have lawfully established themselves in another member state as an employed person are deprived, where that activity comes to an end, of the rights which are conferred on them by virtue of that citizenship. In the most important statement of the judgment, the Court of Justice held that his right to stay under Article 18(1) is conferred directly on every citizen of the Union by a clear and precise provision of the EC Treaty. Purely as a national of a member state, and consequently a citizen of the Union, Mr Baumbast therefore has the right to rely on Article 18(1) EC. It held,

The answer to the first part of the third question must therefore be that a citizen of the European Union who no longer enjoys a right of residence as a migrant worker in the host member state can, as a citizen of the Union, enjoy there a right of residence by direct application of Article 18 (1) EC. (Para. 94)

In summary, the citizenship law as developed through the cases by the Court of Justice would appear to be as follows. Article 18(1) has been declared to be directly effective and it can be activated in favour of EU citizens in a variety of ways: By exhausted free movement rights, i.e. those once enjoyed by a member state national and which gained him or her lawful entrance and residence in the host state when exercised but which no longer are or can be relied upon because of changed circumstances (as in the *Baumbast* case). By the movement to another member state to receive services (as in *D'Hoop*) which movement then serves as the economic activity to trigger the general rights of citizenship.

Whilst the right of residence under Article 18 continues, according to the Court of Justice, to be subject to the potential restrictions inherent in the Directives previously issued, Articles 17 and 18 appear, according to the Court of Justice, to ensure that providing union citizens are lawfully resident in a host state they cannot be discriminated against in social welfare benefits including non-contributory ones. Simple lawful residence will trigger citizenship rights, the most important of which are not the political rights contained in Article 19 but the general right to be treated without discrimination compared to nationals. Hence, for the moment it would seem that the right to any welfare benefit is dependant on being a lawfully resident EU citizen in the host state. However, a clear definition of what constitutes lawful residence is thus far missing in EC law with only the judgments of the Court of Justice in *Sala* and *Grzelczyk* to suggest that provided an EU citizen had a lawful right to enter the host state in the first place and has not done anything to endanger his or her residence subsequently, the right to remain continues. In *Grzelczyk*, the Court of Justice held that its judgment

does not, however, prevent a member state from taking the view that a student who has recourse to social assistance no longer fulfils the conditions of his right of residence or from taking measures, within the limits imposed by Community law, either to withdraw his residence permit or not to renew it. Nevertheless, in no case may such measures have the automatic consequence that a student who is a national of another member state requiring recourse to the host member state's social assistance system is required to leave as a matter of fact.

This would seem to suggest that if a member state does decide to withdraw the status of lawful residence, the member state would be entitled to deport them. Such a decision is subject to proportionality and the review of the Court of Justice. See for this review of the right of member states to determine whether EU citizens can or can not remain in the UK, Case 159/79 *R v Pieck* and Case C–292/89 *Antonissen*, in which respectively the Court of Justice held that deportation of Pieck would be disproportionate and thus contrary to EC law, whereas Antonissen could be deported. Hence, it would seem that previous cases law provides us with a workable model of how we decide lawful residence. A deportation that could be condoned by the Court of Justice would remove lawful residence.

9.10 The Extension of Citizenship Rights into Welfare and Family Rights

Recent Court of Justice judgments which have arisen under the citizenship provisions are not just concerned with the scope and meaning of the term 'citizenship' but evidence an assertive approach by which the Court of Justice has upheld welfare and family rights and not just through its interpretation of EC law but also by reference to the European Convention of Human Rights. It is worthwhile just to summarize these decisions here, most of which were considered above in various sections because the citizenship rights appear to go further than intended by the general free movement Directives by extending the welfare benefits rights of EU citizens who were not supposed to be a burden on the host member state. These developments appear to show that the Community is more concerned with the welfare rights of EU citizens and the sanctity of their family over any national concerns about the possible drain on national resources by the welfare claims by other member state EU citizens or the claim to a right of residence by TCNs.

In *Sala*, her right to rely on Treaty citizenship triggered other rights, including most importantly, Article 12, the right not to be discriminated against according to nationality. This, in consequence, included the right to receive, on equal terms, social welfare benefits including the non-contributory child allowance, the subject matter of the case. Similarly in *Grzelczyk*, the Court of Justice held that the new citizenship provisions and new competences, albeit limited, in education, allowed it to hold that Articles 12 and 17 preclude discrimination as regards the grant of a non-contributory social benefit to union citizens where they are lawfully resident, even though not economically active. In *D'Hoop*, the Court of Justice held that it would be incompatible with the right of freedom of movement if a citizen who had taken advantage of free movement but who then suffered discrimination with regard to a social benefit right as a consequence. It held:

Such inequality of treatment is contrary to the principles which underpin the status of citizen of the Union, that is, the guarantee of the same treatment in law in the exercise of the citizen's freedom to move. The condition at issue could be justified only if it were based on objective considerations independent of the nationality of the persons concerned and were proportionate to the legitimate aim of the national provisions.

Thus, as far as welfare rights' entitlement is concerned, it would seem now that the economic status of the person, i.e. whether worker or self-employed, is no longer an important factor. Providing there is movement in some way, even back to the home state or lawful residence in the host state, EU citizens will be entitled to be treated without discrimination compared to nationals in arguably, all matters.

The welfare rights cases considered here have dealt specifically with EU citizens thus far but could equally be extended, if and when cases arise which deal with members of the family of persons in a similar situation to the above cases, to non-EU nationals. The next cases are concerned for the most part with non-EU citizens. These cases, in which a greater respect for family life has emerged, are also a product of the move from regarding free movement rights in the EC legal order as wholly dependant on the pursuit of an economic activity to recognizing rights which are equally based on citizenship and fundamental freedoms.

In the *Carpenter* case, despite the views of the AG noted above, the Court of Justice was more concerned with family rights than arguments as to the basis for lawful residence of TCN members of the family! The Court of Justice referred to Article 49 EC and Regulation 1612/68, which read strictly does not apply to the provision of services. These provisions, according to the Court of Justice, provide rules protecting of the family life of nationals of the member states in order to eliminate obstacles to the exercise of the fundamental freedoms guaranteed by the Treaty. It held:

It is clear that the separation of Mr. and Mrs. Carpenter would be detrimental to their family life and, therefore, to the conditions under which Mr. Carpenter exercises a fundamental freedom. That freedom could not be fully effective if Mr. Carpenter were to be deterred from exercising it by obstacles raised in his country of origin to the entry and residence of his spouse. (Para 39)

The Court of Justice considered that the rights of residence could be subjected to objective restrictions, but which must comply with fundamental rights and that:

The decision to deport Mrs. Carpenter constitutes an interference with the exercise by Mr. Carpenter of his right to respect for his family life within the meaning of Article 8 of the Convention for the Protection of Human Rights and Fundamental Freedoms and does not strike a fair balance between the competing interests, that is, on the one hand, the right of Mr. Carpenter to respect for his family life, and, on the other hand, the maintenance of public order and public safety. (Paras. 42–3)

The Court of Justice noted that the marriage appeared genuine, there were no official complaints against her and that she looked after the children while he was providing services. The Court thus held that Article 49 EC, read in the light of the fundamental right to respect for family life, is to be interpreted as precluding a refusal, by the member state of origin of a provider of services established in that member state who provides services to recipients established in other member states, of the right to reside in its territory to that provider's spouse, who is a national of a third country.

Apart from promoting the protection of family life within the Community legal order, *Carpenter* also confirms that TCNs gain derivative rights from those providing services despite the absence in this area of law of an equivalent of Regulation 1612/68, although the proposed Directive, considered below, will remedy this.

Baumbast also highlights the support of the Court of Justice for family rights. It is settled law according to the Court in Cases 389 and 390/87 *Echternach* and *Moritz*, that rights enjoyed by members of a Community worker's family under Regulation 1612/68 can, in certain circumstances, continue to exist even after the employment relationship has ended.

The UK authorities wanted to deport R, but because the children had a right to remain and to pursue, under the best possible conditions, their education in the host member state, the Court of Justice reasoned that this necessarily implies that those children have the right to be accompanied by the person who is their primary carer and, accordingly, that that person is able to reside with them in that member state during their studies. To refuse to grant permission to remain to a parent who is the primary carer of the child exercising his right to pursue his studies in the host member state infringes that right. The Court of Justice held that Regulation 1612/68 interpreted in the light of Article 8 ECHR entitled

the parent who is the primary carer of those children, irrespective of nationality, to reside with them in order to facilitate the exercise of that right notwithstanding the fact that the parents have meanwhile divorced. The fact that only one parent is a citizen of the Union and that parent has ceased to be a migrant worker in the host member state and that the children are not themselves citizens of the Union are irrelevant in this regard.

This derived right stems this time not directly from the worker but from the children of the worker, who are themselves recipients of derived rights. This could be termed 'indirect derived rights'.

A further case which provides express support for family life is Case C-459/99 *MRAX* which involves the challenge by an interest group to the Belgium authorities application of Community law in respect of the visa requirements for TCN family members. Certainly, according to Article 3 of Directive 68/360, member states are entitled to demand a visa from the TCN family members. The Court of Justice reasoned that it is apparent, in particular from the Council regulations and directives on freedom of movement for employed and self-employed persons within the Community, that the Community legislature has recognized the importance of ensuring protection for the family life of nationals of the member states in order to eliminate obstacles to the exercise of the fundamental freedoms guaranteed by the

Treaty. (Para. 53) In this light, the Court of Justice considered that it is in any event disproportionate and, therefore, prohibited to send back a TCN married to a national of a member state not in possession of a valid visa where he is able to prove his identity and the conjugal ties and there is no evidence to establish that he represents a risk to the requirements of public policy, public security, or public health within the meaning of Article 10 of Directive 68/360 and Article 8 of Directive 73/148 para. 61. Hence then, the right to a family life protected by Article 8 ECHR has been instrumental in achieving a far reaching judgments on the rights of family members of Community citizens and clearly beyond any strict interpretation of Community law rights.

Case C-109/01 *Akrich*, also concerns Article 8 ECHR, which if the marriage in the case was determined to be genuine, should be taken into account when considering the importance of the unlawful residence of the TCN seeking to stay in the UK, although the Court of Justice attached no actual weight to the consideration which must be given.

9.11 Possible Effect of the Draft Constitutional

The Constitutional Treaty, if it ever comes into force, would seem only to have a limited effect on this area of law. However, it does establish rights within the Charter on Fundamental Rights, Article 15 which provides the right to seek employment, to work, to exercise the right of establishment and to provide services in any member state and also Article 15(3) which provides lawfully resident third country nationals with the right to work in a member state.

9.12 Concluding Remarks

The Community law provision for the free movement of persons has changed considerably from its inception. Whilst the Treaty articles themselves have hardly changed since 1957, the scope of the rights available now to individuals has expanded considerably due to expansion by both secondary legislation and judicial interpretation, and recently, most widely by the introduction of a section on European citizenship and the consideration of a number of cases considering wholly internal situations, the position of TCNs and family rights.

Thus far, we can tentatively say that if one is an EU citizen lawfully resident in another member state one does not have to be economically active to be entitled to equal treatment including for example, equal treatment in non-contributory welfare benefits on the same basis as nationals and one may nevertheless be a burden on the state, albeit a reasonable one only.

TCNs derive rights from their EU family members, including children and even where the children are non-EU nationals but who nevertheless have rights of their own to stay in the host state as in the case of R. EU nationals and TCN family members can derive rights in situations previously regarded as wholly internal or where the degree of movement or activity appears to be minimal or even, arguably according to the latest case of *Akrich*, where the movement is deliberately engineered.

Where citizenship rights are established through lawful residence, Article 12 EC applies.

With the present proposals in mind, it can be suggested that if you are a national having returned back to your home EU state after receiving services in another EU member state, you and members of your or your spouse's or partner's family, who are or who are not EU citizens will be entitled to reside with you and also obtain benefits on the same basis as nationals.

Given that the Court of Justice has already held that services include the provision of telephone services Case C-384/93 *Alpine Investments* and could easily therefore include provision of services over the internet and possibly the receipt of services over the internet as being a sufficiently strong cross border element to trigger EC law rights in the areas of family and welfare law. (E.g. would the receipt of advice from a professional in another member state over the internet be sufficient to help a TCN family member assert residence rights in any of the member states?)

Hence, the limit of the range of rights to EC law now applies is far from clear. Whether it should apply to rule out all discrimination against host EU citizens in comparison with nationals in all areas of law is the burning question left by the present development of the law. Docs, for example, an unemployed tourist on holiday receive services? If so, do these activate Article 18 citizenship rights? Again, if so, does this then trigger the general right of equal treatment, i.e. to get needed benefits on the same basis as nationals, if for the sake of argument he or she runs short of money whilst on holiday? These dangers of an over-expansive interpretation that EC law may now mean that EU citizens who have established lawful residence in a host state will have equal rights to the full spectrum of contributory and non-contributory social benefits and that as such the spectre of 'benefit tourism' has effectively been raised whereby EU nationals and their TCN family members can roam the member states in search of the 'good life'.

It would seem that EU citizens who do not move at any time to another member state to receive or provide services are the only ones unable to obtain these welfare and family rights unless provided for under National law. Particularly with regards to the rights of TCNs who are lawfully resident in the member states, Community law developments in free movement and citizenship appear to add even more pressure for legal reform to bring their rights into line.

Certainly, if the above suggestions were to be the legal effect of the rulings, the member states would understandably argue it was not something they had agreed to and that EC law was overriding National laws in the absence of an express agreement to that effect. Hence then there may be a possible backlash, resulting from the conclusion that the Court of Justice has gone too far and that the free movement and citizenship rights need to be qualified. There is evidence that this might be the case within the opinions of the Advocates General in the *Carpenter, Angonese*, and *Collins* cases, although in the first two cases, the opinions were not taken up by the Court of Justice. If this concern is real and made clear to the Court of Justice by the comments made by the member states amongst others, the Court of Justice may decide to continue to follow the opinion of the AG in *Collins* in any future cases raising similar issues. This would be a way of restricting or indeed preventing benefit tourism. An additional factor which may be lurking in the background and fuelling these concerns is the awareness of the present expansion of the number of member states. There was certainly sufficient concern that further demands would be placed on the existing member states following the ten new member states which joined in May 2004, that under the transitional arrangements permitted, thirteen of the fifteen member states closed access to their labour markets to the accession states workers, the exceptions being the UK and Sweden. These countries did not close their borders to workers from the ten new states to look for work and will treat them on an equal basis as any other EU national. These states will not, however, provide those coming without a job, any social benefits whilst looking for work.

It is clear that the legal regime regulating the free movement of persons has come a long way from the near empty and little used original Treaty provision for it. It is ironic then that at the present stage of the evolution of free movement rights, that the concern is whether those rights have now actually gone too far and encroached too much on areas of the member states' own national laws more than is universally acceptable. However, as is often the case with the very dynamic system of law that we have with Community law, the burning questions we are left with will only be answered by either the Court of Justice in future cases or by the intervention of the member states.

Further reading

Books

PIETER VAN DER MEI, A. *Free Movement of Persons within the European Community: Cross-border Access to Public Benefits*, Hart Publishing, Oxford 2003.

Articles

ACIERNO, S. 'The *Carpenter* judgment: fundamental rights and the limits of the Community legal order' (2003) 28 *EL Rev*, 398.

BARRETT, G. 'Family matters: European Community law and third-country family members' (2003) 40 *CML Rev*, 369.

DAVIES, G. 'The high water point of free movement of persons: ending benefit tourism and rescuing welfare' (2004) 26 *Journal of Social Welfare & Family Law*, 211–22.

FOSTER, N. 'Family and welfare rights in Europe: The impact of recent European Court of Justice decisions in the area of the free movement of persons' (2003) 25 *Journal of Social Welfare and Family Law*, 291–303.

ILIOPOULOU, A. and TONER, H. 'A new approach to discrimination against free movers? *D'Hoop v Office National de l'Emploi*' (2003) *EL Rev*, 389.

JACQUESON, C. 'Union citizenship and the Court of Justice: something new under the sun? Towards social citizenship' (2002) 27 *EL Rev*, 260.

PEERS, S. 'Implementing Equality? The Directive on Long Term Resident third country nationals' (2004) 29 *EL Rev*, 437–60.

REICH, N. and HARBACEVICA, S. 'Citizenship and Family on Trial: A Fairly Optimistic Overview of Recent Court Practice with regard to Free Movement of Persons' (2003) 40 *CML Rev*, 615.

SHUIBINE, N. 'Free Movement of persons and the wholly internal rule: time to move on?' (2003) 39 *CML Rev*, 731.

SPAVENTA, E. 'From Gebhard to Carpenter: Towards a (non-)economic European constitution' (2004) 41 *CML Rev*, 743.

WEATHERILL, S. 'Fair Play Please! Recent Developments in the Application of EC Law to Sport' (2003) 40(1) *CML Rev*, 51.

Web site addresses

Enlargement: http://europa.eu.int/comm/enlargement/negotiations/pdf/negotiations_report_to_ep.pdf.

2004 Accession Treaty: http://europa.eu.int/comm/enlargement/negotiations/treaty_of_accession_2003/index.htm

10

Social Policy: Equality Law

10.1 Introduction

As can be perceived from the title, this chapter is concerned not simply with sex discrimination law which is the classical or typical area of EC social law study dealing only with a single, albeit multi-faceted, example of discrimination, that being on the grounds of sex. Limiting ourselves to sex discrimination is too narrow a field of study in EC social law today. Therefore, the chapter will also include a study of other forms of laws to combat discrimination as a result of the expansion of what can be termed 'EC Equality law' or 'Equal Treatment law' in the Community legal order, e.g. race, age, or sexual orientation. In particular, Article 13 EC and the legislation enacted thereunder, will be considered.

10.2 A General Principle of Equality in EC Law?

Equality or non-discrimination has also been mentioned earlier in the book under general principles in Chapter 3. From the outset, it has to be stressed that whilst there is a debate as to whether the terms equal treatment, equality and non-discrimination are synonymous, they are used in this chapter and book as meaning the same thing, without spending time on the subtleties of the difference, if any.

There are a number of examples of express prohibitions of discrimination on different grounds within the Treaty but there is not as such, an express general principle of non-discrimination or equality in the Treaty. The specific prohibitions do however, support the emergence of a general principle in the Community legal order which is additionally supported by the judgments of the Court of Justice and academic commentary.

The Treaty articles which seek either to prohibit discrimination or promote equality are Articles 2 and 3 (equality between men and women), Article 12 (nationality),

Article 13 (general power to prohibit discrimination across a range of issues) Article 34 (2) (concerned with equality between producers and between consumers in the CAP), Articles 39, 43, and 50 (providing for equal treatment of workers and the self-employed), Article 86 (public undertakings), Article 90 (taxation), Article 137 (equality of men and women in the work environment) and, of course, Article 141 (equal pay), dealt with in depth following. Without going into details, all of these articles support the development of a general principle of equality by the establishment of a legal culture which does not tolerate the different treatment of like or the same treatment of unequals across a range of subject matters.

10.2.1 Article 12

Article 12, the prohibition of discrimination on the grounds of nationality, clearly stands out as already being close to a general principle itself because it has become a fundamental basis for integration, harmonization, and the removal of inequalities in the Community legal order through its application in various policy areas of the Community, most notably the free movement of persons and more recently citizenship considered in Chapter 9. The reason for this is that the Court of Justice has relied on Article 12 in many subject areas including those areas outside of those covered by specific equality articles noted above. As such then the Court of Justice has been able to fill any gaps in equality provision by resorting to Article 12 and a few examples will be cited here. Applied generally, equality as a principle, has been used to support judgments in staff Case 130/75 *Prais* concerned with the equal observance of religious holidays, Case C-13/94 *P v S & CCC* where discrimination could not be allowed as the consequence of a gender reassignment operation, in support of supremacy in Case 6/64 *Costa,* supporting equal rights in claiming welfare benefits in the cases of C-85/96 *Sala,* C-184/99 *Rudy Grzelczyk* and C-224/98 *Marie-Nathalie D'Hoop,* for the equal application of social security in Case C-44/65 *Hessische Knappschaft* and in the copyright Case C-92 and C-326/92 *Phil Collins* in requiring national intellectual property rights to be applied equally to UK and other EC nationals. Whilst its value as a distinct self-standing principle outside of the express applications is less clear to see, it nevertheless acts as the yardstick against which the pursuit of those specific policies by legislative enactments is measured.[1]

---

[1] See further reading at the end of the chapter for much more extensive treatments of this topic.

10.3 The Reasons for the Inclusion of Article 119 (now 141) in the Treaty

The prohibitions of discrimination in other articles of the Treaty can be quite readily understood because they all relate, more or less, to nationality and which therefore go to the very foundation of the establishment of the Community. That is the removal of national barriers to the establishment of the internal market. Nationality should not play a role in the free movement of goods, persons or capital. Non-discrimination on the grounds of sex though is less readily understandable in this context. On the face of it, it would appear to be essentially a socially based discrimination and not economic. It was, however, originally framed in the EC treaty as form of workplace based discrimination. Therefore, as was considered in the chapter on the free movement of persons, it is helpful and informative to go back to the drafting of the EEC Treaty to see why, what has clearly become a social law right, was included in the European Economic Community in the first place. Additionally, and viewed in the context of the initial more limited aims of the Communities to eliminate discrimination based on nationality, there is an odd feature to sex discrimination law, in that it does not require a cross state or community context. That is there needs to be no movement between member states, unlike the fundamentals freedoms: Goods, persons and capital which do. EC sex discrimination law is applicable in entirely or wholly internal situations! This begs the question of why were sex equality rights included? Given the original more economic nature of the Community, the EC would seem an unlikely source of women's equality rights. Fundamentally, it is first a vehicle to promote economic integration and development of the member states rather than provide equality between the sexes. That is arguably, really an internal matter for the member states, however, it is now generally accepted that the immediate reason for including Article 119 in the EEC Treaty was not for reasons of social justice, but out of economic considerations, i.e. the creation of level playing fields for industry in terms of the application of national social laws. The Article was alleged to have been included at the request of the French, whose law provided for equality of pay between male and female workers. It was feared that French industry would be at a disadvantage if equal pay were not enforced in the other member states. It is also rumoured this was aimed as much at Germany because although having the principle in law, in reality, French industry at the time had very few women workers whilst Germany in the post-war period relied on far more women workers to make up for the lack of male workers as many men of working age had been killed during the war. Pay equality enforced on member states would help to curb the resurgent German economic primacy. Regardless of the exact underlying motive, its inclusion would appear to be based on economic arguments which aim was to ensure that similar economic conditions apply in all the members states. There appears to be no social justification for its inclusion but one thing we know is that things never stay still in Community law and we do have the chance to see a Court of Justice view on the matter in Case 43/75 *Defrenne v Sabena (No. 2)*. The Court of Justice declared that

Article 119 also forms part of the social objectives of the Community, which is not merely an economic union, but is at the same time intended, by common action, to ensure social progress and seek the constant improvement of the living and working conditions of their peoples, as is emphasized by the preamble to the Treaty. . . . This double aim, which is at once economic and social, shows that the principle of equal pay forms part of the foundations of the community.

Hence, it was regarded in 1976 as one part of a double aim and was even promoted in subsequent judgments. In Case 149/77 *Defrenne v Sabena (No. 3)*, a couple of years later, the Court of Justice declared the elimination of discrimination based on sex as part of the fundamental rights within Community law. More recently, this has been confirmed in Case C-324 and 5/96 *Deutsche Telekom v Vick* by the Court of Justice that the social aims of Article 119 (now 141) prevail over those of the economic aims and subsequently confirmed in Case C-50/96 *Deutsche Telekom v Schröder*.

[I]t must be concluded that the economic aim pursued by Article 119 of the Treaty, namely the elimination of distortions of competition between undertakings established in different member states, is secondary to the social aim pursued by the same provision, which constitutes the expression of a fundamental human right.

Hence then, seemingly a complete turnaround in a thirty-year journey from an instrument of economic levelling or harmonization to an individual fundamental social right.

Sex equality law has developed much more slowly and much later than the central internal market areas of law, notably the free movements of goods and persons. This is argued to be because of the less extensive original provision for it in the Treaty but it is also clear that the delays by the member states in implementing the principle of equal pay and by the Commission in not introducing secondary legislation until prompted to do so by the Council of Ministers and not chasing the member states also played a significant part. Article 119 (now 141) was the sole original provision for the European Community to concern itself with sex discrimination. In contrast, there now exists a considerable body of Community law on the subject, in the form of Treaty additions, introduced notably by the Treaty of Amsterdam, a growing body of EC Directives and the very many progressive decisions of the Court of Justice.

10.4 **The Legislative Framework**

10.4.1 **Treaty Articles**

Article 141 (ex 119) (equal pay for equal work) originally provided the only specific mention of equal treatment in the EC Treaty but it has formed the basis upon which the principle of non-discriminatory treatment has been expanded into areas beyond equal pay. Now, following amendments by the Treaty of Amsterdam, EC Treaty references to the promotion of equality are more extensive. In addition to the main Treaty Article, which remains Article 141 (ex 119), the ToA introduced as one of the goals outlined in Article 2 'equality between men and women' and has added a new final sentence to Article 3 which reads: 'In all the activities referred to in this Article, the Community shall aim to eliminated inequalities, and to promote equality, between men and women.'

Equality between men and women in the working environment was also included in the 1989 Community Social Charter which has now been brought into Article 136 of the EC Treaty by the Treaty of Nice. The new and now amended Article 137, provides that, inter alia, the Community shall complement and support the activities of the member states in the field of equality between men and women with regard to labour market opportunities and treatment at work.

Article 141 has now been expanded beyond its simple original provision to ensure that men and women should get equal pay for equal work. The Treaty of Amsterdam has amended and added two sentences to Article 141 which locate within a Treaty base, the principles of equal pay for work of equal value and action to promote equality but which falls short of out and out positive discrimination. These rights were previously contained in Directives only which meant that they could not give rise to direct effects against other individuals.

Finally, as far as the treaty is concerned, a new enabling power has been introduced in Article 13 which provides that the Council, acting unanimously, and in consultation with the EP, may take appropriate action to combat discrimination based on sex or sexual orientation, amongst others. Article 13 will be considered later in the chapter along with the legislation which has now been enacted under it.

10.4.2 **Secondary Legislation**

It was only after the completion of the transition period for the common market in 1968 that the member states and Commission started to turn towards developing a social policy for the Community. The European Summit meetings, 1972–3 and in particular the Paris summit of 1972, requested the Commission to produce proposals for a Social Action Programme, as the first of what transpired to be a number of action programmes. The first report was published in 1974.[2] Amongst a number of measures dealing with redundancy and transfer of undertakings, three Directives concerned with equality between men and women were adopted, which will be considered as appropriate below: The Equal Pay Directive 75/117, the Equal Treatment Directive 76/207, and the Social Security Directive 79/7.[3]

A second social action programme was commenced in 1982[4] which led, as far as equality legislation is concerned to the enactment of Directive 86/378 on equal treatment in occupational pensions and Directive 86/613 on equal treatment of the self-employed and protection of self-employed women during pregnancy and motherhood.[5]

After the long period of stagnation of the Communities, the political will to complete the Single Market and at last allow for institutional reform of the Community brought in its wake a strengthening of social policies in the EC Treaty by the amendment by the SEA in 1986. This helped create the environment which led to the adoption of the Charter of Fundamental Social Rights of Workers (known as the Social Charter) in 1989 by eleven of the twelve (not the UK) member states. It provided, amongst other measures, under (g) the equal treatment of men and women. This in turn led to another action programme in 1989[6] and resulted in the enactment of the Pregnancy and Maternity Directive 92/85.[7]

The next step on this seemingly tortuous path to provide a comprehensive set of enactments covering equal treatment was the EC Treaty amendment by the Maastricht Treaty which attached an Agreement and Protocol on Social Policy (known as the Social Chapter) to the Treaty to which then fourteen from fifteen member states signed up (the UK having secured another opt-out from social legislation). This led to the enactment of further Directives including the Parental Leave Directive 96/34, the Burden of Proof in Sex discrimination cases Directive 97/80 and the Part-time workers Directive 97/81.[8] While this latter directive is not directly aimed to address sex discrimination, it will have this affect as it aims to reduce the inequality between full time workers and part-time workers, the majority of whom are women and thus likely to be indirectly discriminated against, a matter considered in this chapter.

Article 141 and the early legislation in particular have been subject to very liberal interpretation by the Court of Justice far beyond a literal reading of the provisions due, no doubt, in large part to the fact that for the first twenty years of the Communities

---

[2] OJ 1974 L14/10.   [3] OJ 1975 L 45/19, 1976 OJ L 39/40 and OJ 1979 L6/24.
[4] OJ 1982 C186/3.   [5] OJ 1986 L225/40 and OJ 1986 L359/86.   [6] COM(1989) 568).
[7] OJ 1992 L348/1.   [8] OJ 1996 L145/9, OJ 1998 L14/6 and OJ 1998 L14/9.

life, there was only Article 119 (now 141) to provide for equal treatment and that was confined to equal pay. During the subsequent ten years, this was supplemented by just the first three Directives dealing with equal treatment. The Court of Justice had to be inventive in order to make any progress. Whilst greater effort is being shown now by the Community institutions and the member states by the setting up of various fora to promote equality, in the beginning, action was more likely to be taken by individuals sometimes with the support of the national equality agencies, such as the Equal Opportunities Commission in the UK, rather than the Commission in enforcement actions. See, for example, the *Defrenne, Garland* and *Marshall* cases, considered below.

This chapter will concentrate on the core aspects of sex equality law in the EC, notably Article 119 (141), Directive 75/117, and the Equal Treatment Directive 76/207, which is now heavily amended by Directive 2002/73.[9] At the end of the chapter, other less prominent secondary legislation will be considered.

10.5 Article 141 and the Scope of the Principle of Equal Pay

Article 141 (ex 119) originally provided that 'member states shall ensure the application of the principle that men and women should receive equal pay for equal work'. Article 141 was amended by the Treaty of Amsterdam to refer to equal pay for work of equal value, a concept which was first introduced by Directive 75/117. Article 141(1) now reads: 'Each member state shall ensure that the principle of equal pay for male and female workers for equal work or work of equal value is applied' and secondly, attempts to define what equal pay actually means. Article 141(2) narrowly defines pay as 'the ordinary basic or minimum wage or salary or any other consideration, whether in cash or in kind, which the worker receives either directly or indirectly in respect of his employment from his employer'. Article 141(2) defines equal pay without discrimination to mean: (a) That pay for the same work at piece rates shall be calculated on the basis of the same unit of measurement; and (b) that pay for the same work at time rates shall be the same for the same job. Payment by piece rates is not so common now and basically means that a person is paid per each unit of a product that is made and was previously found in factory work or in home working such as the assembling of biro parts. The more assembled or made, the more that is paid. It took a long time, however, until this principle of equal pay was realized. Much of the

---

[9] OJ 2000 L269/15.

delay was due to a deliberate postponing of the application of the principle by the member states and it was only court action by individuals which allowed the Court of Justice to step in and at last provide for the application of the principle and simultaneously condemn the member states efforts not to provide for equal pay. The first significant case under Article 141 concerns an applicant who was previously unsuccessful in challenging a discriminatory pension system based on national legislation and thus held to be outside of Community law competence. However, she commenced a second action to challenge unequal pay. In Case 43/75 *Defrenne v Sabena (No. 2)*, a claim for compensation was made for the damage suffered from February 1963 until February 1966 because Gabrielle Defrenne was paid at a substantially lower rate than her male colleagues for the same work. The case was sympathetically received by the Court of Justice and Gabrielle Defrenne was successful. The Court of Justice held that the principle of equal pay was sufficiently clear and precise to have direct effects both vertically and horizontally. However, in response to the fears expressed by employers and the interventions of some member state, about the costs to industry if the judgment applied back to 1957 (i.e. all the back pay that would have to be paid) the Court of Justice declared the ruling to be prospective only from the date the original litigation by Defrenne commenced and any cases in the pipeline. This prospective only ruling is a type of ruling which is rare but repeated again in equality law in the *Barber* case considered below. With *Defrenne* having opened the gate, many more cases were referred to the Court of Justice which was then able to refine the definition of pay and thus the scope of Article 141.

10.5.1 The Meaning of Pay

Although previously, Case 80/70 *Defrenne v Belgium (No. 1)* seemed to rule out a wider definition of pay to exclude, as considered in the case, '. . . pension benefits in retirement', the term pay has been progressively defined. In Case 12/81 *Garland v British Rail Engineering*, Article 119 was held to include concessionary rail travel facilities for the family of an ex-employee. The Court of Justice held that the travel facilities in question were granted in kind by the employer to the retired male employee or his dependants directly or indirectly in relation to his employment, and could be regarded as an extension of travel facilities granted during employment. Pay as interpreted by the Court of Justice also includes rules by which seniority/loyalty payments are achieved in favour of full-time employees in Case C-184/89 *Nimz v Hamburg*; sick pay, even though part of a statutory scheme in Case 171/88 *Ingrid Rinner-Kuhn v FWW Spezial-Gebaudereiningung*; a severance grant in C-33/89 *Kowalska v Hamburg* and compensation for lost wages for attendance on training course for Works council members in Case C-360/90 *Arbeiterwohlfahrt der Stadt*

Berlin v Monika Botel. Unfair dismissal compensation and redundancy pay have also been confirmed to come within Article 141 in C-167/97 *Seymour-Smith & Perez.* Hence then pay is given a very wide meaning and any payments and benefits which arise from the employment relationship may be held to be pay under Article 141. One particular problem was the status of pensions because of the link that exists with retirement and the fact that EC secondary legislation appeared to retain this whole area within the competence of the member states and not the Community.

10.5.1.1 The Concept of Pay and its Relationship to Pensions

This topic has particular complications not just because the concept of pay is being stretched but because it straddles the very grey area of the boundary between the jurisdiction of the member states and that of the Community and Court of Justice. Directive 79/7 Article 7 stipulates that member states have the right to exclude from equal treatment the determination of pensionable age for the purposes of granting old age and retirement pensions and the possible consequences for other benefits. It was the meaning of the latter part of the article 'the possible consequences for other benefits' which caused the uncertainty due to its vagueness.

Case 152/84 *Marshall* had determined that the retirement age itself was not to be linked to the pension age and had to be equal for men and women. We had already learned though in the first *Defrenne* case that contributions into a statutory pensions or social security scheme were not to be considered as coming within the concept of pay under Article 141. It was widely assumed that this ruling was good for all forms of pensions schemes.

The reasons for the allowance in Community law for a difference in pensions ages are probably becoming lost in time. It was previously the case, and still is under transitional arrangements in many states, that men and women retired and gained pensions at different ages and women usually, five years early. This might seem odd, given that the life expectancy of women is on average greater than that of men and women might be expected to have to work longer in order to pay for this. However, historically it was precisely because of the greater life expectancy that women should gain their pension earlier for the following reasons. Pension ages and retirement ages in the eighteenth and nineteenth century were the same, but in those centuries, there was an average of three years age difference between men and women at marriage, men being the older. However, men tended to die first and if they died at any time up to 65 (which was the expected life expectancy of the working classes and many died before they got the chance to retire or soon thereafter) and their state pension entitlement died with them (which it did because it was personal and not transferable to the wife). Therefore, if pension ages were the same (which they were), the wife, aged on average between 60 and 63 would be without any means of support until she reached 65. So to protect women from being evicted from their homes and being thrown into the poor houses, the law was changed to enable them to get their state pension earlier. Being able to get their pension earlier, it soon followed that they would retire earlier—not a legal requirement but why carry on working when you could stop and get a pension? It then became the contractual standard for women to retire at 60, and thus it was generally considered that pensionable age also meant retirement age which in turn became lawfully enforceable as it became part of a standard contract of employment for women. Hence the reason for the Directive 79/7, Article 7 exception. Also it is the case that in the past, almost all pensions were state pensions with a few exceptions for high earners in private employment. However, pension schemes have been developing in both sophistication and complexity from the 1970s onwards and often involve a wholly or partly private or contractual element. Furthermore there has been an increasing privatization of pensions without any state involvement which only serves to further complicate this area! How are these now regarded by the Court of Justice?

In Case 69/80 *Worringham & Humphries v Lloyds Bank*, the Bank operated an arrangement whereby male workers under 25 were paid 5 per cent more than their female counterparts to enhance a pension. The reason for this was that part of the social and historical thinking up to that stage—and indeed factually according to the calculations of the actuaries, correct—was that males were more likely to be bread-winners and more likely to die before usually younger female spouses, so therefore it was regarded as not a bad idea to enhance the pension pay-ins of males at an early stage and thus increase the level of pension pay-outs later to the benefit of those surviving—i.e. the female spouses and offspring. The total enhanced payment package, however, formed the basis of calculation of other social advantages and welfare benefits. The defendant bank argued the enhancement was linked to pensions therefore they could lawfully discriminate. The Court of Justice ruled that such a contribution which determined other benefits linked to salary paid by employer is pay within the meaning of Article 119 (now 141), even if they were deducted at source and paid on behalf of the employee, i.e. the employee never sees them directly. This could include anything supplied by the employer to or on behalf of the employee on a pro rata basis such as annual bonuses. Thus as a result of this case, whilst it was not the pension itself that was considered to be pay, not all linked consequences were to be automatically excluded.

Case 170/84 *Bilka Kaufhaus v Karin Weber Van Hartz* concerned different access rules to a pensions scheme for full-time and part-time workers, the part-timers being mainly female. It was held that where supplements were made by the employer to the basic state pension under a contractual agreement and where the amount was linked to pay (i.e. as a proportion or percentage), it was pay for the purposes of Article 119.

Furthermore, if access to this scheme was discriminatory, as it was proved to be in the case, it also breached Article 119.

The next case was, like the second *Defrenne* case, highly significant in the Community legal order because of the impact it had on employers.

In Case C-262/88 *Barber v Guardian Royal Exchange Assurance Group*, Barber was made redundant by GRE at the age of 52. There was an agreed contracted out, i.e. private, pensions scheme. His redundancy package included a statutory redundancy payment, and an *ex gratia* payment (a top up), but entitlement to his occupational pension was deferred until the agreed pension age under the scheme of 62 for men and 57 for women. There was an agreement in the redundancy package was that if within ten years of the state pension ages, the pension could be obtained earlier. A redundant woman aged 52 would be entitled to immediate access to her pension as she was within ten years of the statutory pension age whereas Barber and other male employees were not (ten or more years adrift), which was the basis for the claim of unlawful discrimination. The defence claimed that there was a link to the pension age and the case therefore fell under the Directive 79/7 exemption, in which case it was lawful discrimination. The UK Government, intervening, claimed that the scheme, which replaced the state scheme should be regarded as coming within social security and not Article 119 (now 141). The Court of Justice concluded that the statutory redundancy pay and the benefits from his contracted out occupational pension (OP) scheme, i.e. the pension itself were 'pay' within Article 119. The deciding factor is whether the rules and thus payment of the specific scheme are a part of the employment contract or by voluntary inclusion of the employer. Only if entirely to do with the compulsory state pension does a case fall outside Article 141. The Court of Justice emphasized the importance of the fact that the OP scheme was funded without any contribution being made by the public authorities. (Para. 25)

The *Barber* decision gave rise to severe concern. It was not expected that pensions should be pay, indeed the first *Defrenne* case suggested that it was not. It would mean that there would be unlawful discrimination not previously thought to be the case, for which huge amounts of compensation, not previously contemplated, would be payable. This would not have been taken account of in the actuarial calculations and the pensions schemes would have had severe difficulties in making payments not previously foreseen. Hence then the Court of Justice declared Article 119 to be directly effective for pensions from date of judgment only, i.e. 17 May 1990 and for any cases in the pipeline. In other words, like the second *Defrenne* judgment on the direct effects of Article 119 before it, the judgment was prospective only applying from the date of judgment on and not validating any backdated claims for equal treatment which would cost industry severely. Indeed, the member states were so concerned about the judgment and possible future interpretations of it that they attached a specific Protocol (No. 2) to the Maastricht Treaty which states that the benefits arising from social security schemes shall not be considered as remuneration in respect of periods of employment prior to 17 May 1990 with the exception to those who had instigated proceedings prior to that date, i.e. only for benefits payable for service after 1990. This, like the judgment, was to overcome the economic effect on employers in the case of a retroactive application of the ruling. Thus, the period of earnings before the *Barber* judgment do not give rise to a claim. The protocol clarified the judgment and was expressly accepted by the Court of Justice in Case C-109/91 *Ten Oever*, which also extended the *Barber* ruling to pension benefits payable to the pension holder's survivors and further confirmed by the Court of Justice as coming within Article 141 in Case C-117/01 *K.B. v NHS Pensions.*

The *Barber* case, however, sparked off many more cases seeking to establish its exact meaning and consequences, only one or two of which are considered here. It also led to the extensive amendment of Directive 86/378 on Occupational Social Security Schemes.

In Case C-152/91 *Neath v Hugh Steeper*, it was held that inequality in employees' contributions arising from actuarial factors such as life expectancy, which differed according to sex would not be caught by Article 141 (ex 119). The case involved a conversion of a periodic payment to a lump sum pay-out. Whilst benefits and payments-out must be regarded as pay, this is not the case for the contributions which determine the size of the fund, as other factors other than a simple difference in sex are involved. The funding system to provide the amount of pension to be available does not come under Article 141 (ex 119). The amount needed for a pension is determined by actuaries who base their figures on the fact that women live longer after retirement and have a right to a pension at an earlier age thus they need more capital available to supply this. If they work the same time, they must pay more. This becomes quite clear when converted to a lump sum. Women will get more. In this case, the male applicant got less and claimed this was unlawful discrimination, however, according to the Court of Justice the difference in treatment was objectively justified as a result of the actuarial factors.

It has subsequently been established that the time limit in *Barber* and Protocol 2 do not apply to discrimination in relation to the right to join, i.e. access to an occupational pension scheme, which remains governed by the judgment in *Bilka Kaufhaus.* See, as confirmation Case C-57/93 *Vroege v NCIV Instituut.*

There are still very many cases arising from this very complex relationship between pay and pensions. It is complicated because there remains a lawful discrimination on the part of member states as to when females and males receive state pensions. Any difference which relates to the amount paid in or out to achieve a pension is in law entirely acceptable unless, according to *Barber*, it has become part of the contractual relationship by the intervention of an agreement between the employer and employee. It is then pay, it comes within Article 141 (ex 119) and the employer cannot lawfully discriminate.

10.5.2 The Equal Pay Directive (75/117)

The Equal Pay Directive added little to that interpreted for old Article 119 but did extend the principle of equal pay to 'work to which equal value is attributed' and extends to 'all aspects and conditions of remuneration', Article 1. This is now contained in the amended Article 141 and makes the situation much easier for claimants who work for a private employer, i.e. the vast majority of workers. It was with these concerns in mind, that many of the cases that were originally raised in respect of Directive 75/117 alone or in combination with Article 141 (ex 119), were decided upon by the Court of Justice with reference to Article 141 (ex 119) only. If the Court of Justice was not able to bring the case circumstances with the scope of Article 141, there would have been severe difficulties for many of the applicants because of the absence of horizontal direct effects in Directives.

10.5.3 The Basis of Comparison

In most situations where there is direct discrimination, it is usually clear and obvious that there is discrimination, e.g. it is easy to compare a man and woman who are doing the same job in the same work place for the same employer but are paid differently. There are however, many complications that could be added to this where the comparison is not so obvious, where the times of work differ, or the job differs slightly or the work place differs. It then becomes important that there is a valid comparator. In Case 129/79 *Macarthy's v Wendy Smith*, Smith was employed from March 1976 at a salary of £50 per week, and complained of discrimination because her predecessor, a man, had received a salary of £60 per week. The Court of Justice held that although the work actually performed by employees of different sex must be within the same establishment, the employees need not be employed at the same time. However, the Court of Justice was careful to point out that, 'It cannot be ruled out that the difference in pay between two workers occupying the same post but at different periods in time may be explained by the operation of factors which are unconnected with any discrimination on grounds of sex.' This is a question of fact for the national courts to decide. In this case the court therefore expressly left open the possibility of a genuine material factor defence. Hence, the scope of the concept of equal pay for equal work (same work) could not be restricted by a requirement by member states that the person whose work was being compared be contemporaneously employed.

Comparison can also be made with members of the other sex who do work of a lesser value to ensure that a women doing work of higher value cannot be paid less than the male comparator as was held in Case 157/86 *Mary Murphy An Bord Telecom Eireann*.

The Court of Justice had also expressed the view in the *Macarthy* case that it would not entertain a hypothetical comparator. However, in the light of the new statutory definitions of direct discrimination in the new equality directives (2000/43 and 2000/78) and introduced into Directive 76/207, it is quite possible that the Court of Justice could also now interpret into Directive 75/117 the same meaning, although the Directive itself has not been amended. Directive 2002/73 defines: '—Direct discrimination: Where one person is treated less favourably on grounds of sex than another is, has been or would be treated in a comparable situation.' It is thus arguable that 'would be' opens the door for even a hypothetical comparator to be sufficient. It may also encourage the Court of Justice to adopt a hypothetical comparator test in view of the disturbing consequences arising from some recent cases considering comparators.

10.5.4 Comparison Revisited

Comparison, or the lack of it, has become a crucial factor in two cases which have arisen from the contracting out of jobs to outside private companies under the compulsory competitive tendering schemes which were imposed on local authorities in the UK. In these schemes, some members of staff (predominantly women) have been removed from direct employment by the Local Authority and then re-employed by an independent employer. They are then returned to the same job but on less money than their (mainly) male counterparts doing the same job or work previously evaluated to be of equal value. In Case C-320/00 *Lawrence v Regent Office Care Ltd*, dinner ladies who were previously employed directly by the local authority had their contracts taken over by a private company. They continued to work in the same job but were paid less, also in comparison with male colleagues who were retained by the local authority but who had been rated to be doing work of equal value. The Court of Justice held that whilst Article 141 was not restricted to employees working for the same employer, Article 141 could not apply where there was no single overall authority responsible for deciding pay. Similarly, in Case C-256/01 *Allonby*, teachers who were mainly female had been made redundant by a college but taken on by an agency in a self-employed capacity and returned to work in the same college but were paid less than an alleged male comparator employed by the college. The Court of Justice held that as there was not a single source which led to the unequal pay, the work and the pay of those workers cannot therefore be compared on the basis of Article 141.

With the Court of Justice having held twice now that a comparison is not possible, the conclusion is that there can be no factual yet alone illegal discrimination, because there is no single body employer responsible to make the pay adjustment if inequality were found to be unlawful. These cases would appear to open up a very big loophole which allow the rolling back of the gains that have been made over the decades to ensure equal pay for women by condoning the hiving off of employment contracts according to sex in order to be able to pay unequally, thus either directly or indirectly discriminating against women under the ostensible reason given of delivering local authority services more economically and more efficiently. Although the compulsory competitive tendering scheme itself has now been abandoned, no doubt there will be a lot of cases following this particular development as other forms of outside contracting, agency contracting and various public private initiatives have been developed. These cases have also involved an issue which occurs a lot in discrimination law, that of indirect discrimination rather than direct and which will be considered next. In the UK, there is a Scottish case which was not referred to the Court of Justice but which was decided by the Scottish court itself, which allowed a comparison across local authorities from which the Court of Justice might take a leaf: see *South Ayrshire v Morton* [2002] IRLR 256.

10.5.5 Part-time Work and the Development of the Concept of Indirect Discrimination

It is in the area of part-time work that the concept of indirect discrimination has been most thoroughly explored by the Court of Justice. Whilst direct discrimination on the grounds of sex can arguably never be justified, either it is discriminatory and thus contrary to EC law or it is not, indirect discrimination can be justified. Article 141 and Directive 75/117 clearly outlaw direct discrimination, where a distinction is drawn between the rights of men and women overtly on the basis of sex. It is still factually possible to show that the discrimination was not based on sex but on some other factor. Indirect discrimination, which has already been encountered in free movement of persons, is more difficult to determine. In this area it covers cases where a class of persons is mainly or entirely constituted of one sex (usually women) and a difference is drawn between that class and another class which can consist of members of both sexes. In either class, no direct discrimination takes place, i.e. both genders are treated the same, but in comparison with the other class, a rule or measure operates in a discriminatory manner against the predominant sex, which can be either women or men. Whether the discrimination is actually unlawful is often dependent on the motives behind it and whether it can be justified objectively by those motives. As a result now of both the burden of Proof Directive 97/80 and the new Equal Treatment Directive 2002/73, there is a statutory definition of indirect discrimination as follows: Indirect discrimination: Where an apparently neutral provision, criterion or practice would put persons of one sex at a particular disadvantage compared with persons of the other sex, unless that provision, criterion or practice is objectively justified by a legitimate aim, and the means of achieving that aim are appropriate and necessary. Even with the statutory definition, it is nevertheless still instructive to see how this was developed by the Court of Justice which has considered indirect discrimination in a number of cases concerning pay differences between full time and part-time workers. These are also usually combined with objective justifications as elements of the cases.

In Case 96/80 *Jenkins v Kingsgate*, the employers paid full-time workers 10 per cent more per hour than part-time workers, in order, it was claimed, to discourage absenteeism and to achieve a more efficient use of their machinery. All but one of the part-time workers were women. The Court of Justice held

A difference in rates of remuneration between full and part-time employees did not offend against Article 119 (now 141) provided that the difference was attributable to factors which were objectively justified and did not relate directly or indirectly to discrimination based on sex.

and

If it is established that a considerably smaller percentage of women than men perform the number of hours necessary to be a full-timer, the inequality will contravene Article 119 (now 141) where, regard being had to the difficulties encountered by women in arranging to work the minimum number of hours per week, the pay policy of the undertaking cannot be explained by factors other than the discrimination based on sex.

In other words, it is more likely women will find it harder to work full-time and seek part-time work because of commitments to family and home but this does not make it lawful to discriminate against them.

10.5.5.1 Objective Justifications

The existence of an objective justification becomes crucial but in EC law we do not for the most part see this as this is usually a matter of factual consideration for the national court. For example, the justification given by an employer may be that the company needs to encourage the recruitment of full-time employees in which case, the national court could require evidence which demonstrates the relative number of full-time and part-time vacancies and applications for those posts to see whether the facts bear out the claim made by the company. Where there is no plausible explanation to account for the difference in pay, it is likely to be discrimination contrary to Article 141.

In Case 170/84 *Bilka Kaufhaus v Karin Weber Van Harz*, a store gave all full-time employees a non-contributory pension on retirement, whereas part-timers only qualified if they had been employed permanently for at least fifteen years. The undertaking claimed they needed to pay full-timers more to attract them in sufficient numbers. The Court of Justice ruled that Article 119 (now 141) is infringed where a company excludes part-time workers from its occupational pension scheme and where that exclusion affects a far greater number of women than men, unless the undertaking shows that the exclusion is based on objectively justified factors unconnected with discrimination based on sex. The Court of Justice went on to consider the question whether the undertaking could justify that disadvantage on the ground that its objective is to employ as few part-time workers as possible even though in the department store sector there are no reasons of commercial expediency which call for the pursuit of such a policy.

In order to show that the discrimination was objectively justified, the employer must show that the measures giving rise to the difference in treatment:

(a) correspond to a genuine need of the enterprise;

(b) are suitable for attaining the objective pursued by the enterprise; and

(c) are strictly necessary for that purpose, i.e. proportional.

The further requirement laid down by the Court of Justice that it was for the company to show that the discrimination was not based on sex rather than the complainant having to prove discrimination, was part of a move by the Court of Justice to shift the burden of proof to the company over a number of cases. In the particular case, the German court applying the ruling held that the difference was not objectively justified.

In Case C-167/97 *Seymour Smith and Perez*, for example, the Court of Justice held that national courts should look at both the numbers of men and women who can and cannot satisfy a particular requirement, e.g. full-time work, to determine whether there is a disproportionate affect on one sex, in which case discrimination will be assumed unless justified.

The next case considers the area of equal value claims but is also instructive in terms of the investigation the national court should undertake to assess the grounds for the indirect discrimination.

10.5.6 Work of Equal Value

Work of equal values claims cause further difficulties because it is not often clear that two jobs are of the same value and an appraisal has to be done, either by the national court or using formal a job evaluation scheme. Case C-127/92 *Enderby v Frenchay Health Authority* involved an equal value claim and the comparison of lower paid mainly women speech therapists with higher paid mainly men pharmacists and clinical psychologists. The Court of Justice held that is was for the national court to determine, if necessary by applying the principle of proportionality, whether and to what extent the shortage of candidates for a job and the need to attract them by paying higher pay constituted an objectively justified ground for the difference in pay between jobs of equal value. The Court of Justice held that it was up to the national court to decide whether the available statistics are representative enough to provide significant enough evidence to decide the justifications given. The difficulty with indirect discrimination is that higher demand for lower paid but flexible jobs especially where this demand is higher women, can be argued by the employer to constitute evidence that they need to pay less flexible and thus less attractive jobs, occupied mainly by men, at a premium or in effect the more flexible more sought jobs at a lower rate.

In Case 157/86 *Mary Murphy v An Bord Telecom Eireann*, an employee claimed equal pay for her work which was considered to be of even higher value than her comparator. The Court of Justice held Article 119 (now 141) of the EEC Treaty must be interpreted as covering the case where a worker who relies on that provision to obtain equal pay is engaged in work of higher value than that of the person with whom a comparison is to be made. The conclusion that has to be drawn from the case was that Article 119 (now 141) could also be applied to equal value claims, although not expressly stated in the Article at the time. Under the amended Article 141, it is expressly covered. The Court of Justice reasoned that whilst it was true that Article 119 (now Art 141) applies only in the case of equal work, nevertheless, if that principle forbids workers of one sex engaged in work of equal value to be paid a lower wage than the other sex, it prohibits much more strongly such a difference in pay where the lower paid category of workers is engaged in work of higher value. Interestingly in this case, the defendant was a public body and if the Court of Justice had wished, it could have resolved the case under Directive 75/117 as it would involve vertical direct effects but it chose instead to widen the scope of Article 119, which in the long run would assist more potential litigants than the Directive.

10.5.6.1 Job Evaluation Schemes and the Burden of Proof

In order to back up the principle of equal pay for work of equal value, Directive 75/117 provides under the second sentence of Article 1 that where a job classification scheme is used for determining pay, it must be drawn up so as to exclude discrimination based on sex. Furthermore, Article 2 requires member states to provide the legal means by which all employees who consider themselves discriminated against are able to pursue a claim. The UK was brought to task in Case 61/81 *Commission v UK* (Equal Pay for Equal Work) for failing to put in place a job classification system in the case where employers refused to make an assessment. This was then corrected by the Equal Pay (Equal Value Amendment) Regulations of 1983. In a number of cases the Court of Justice has ruled that any job evaluation schemes used must not be based on criteria which valued one sex only and had to be transparent, so that a claimant could see how particular wages were achieved. For example, in Case 237/85 *Rummler v Dato-Druck*, a job evaluation scheme which was based on muscular effort, fatigue, and physical hardship was held by the Court of Justice not to be in breach of Article 1 of Directive 75/117 as long as the following conditions were met: It must, in so far as the nature of the tasks carried out in the undertaking permits, take into account criteria for which workers of each sex show particular aptitude. The Court of Justice said that criteria based exclusively on the values of one sex contain a 'risk of discrimination'. Additionally, as was noted in the *Bilka* and *Enderby* cases, the Court of Justice has reversed the burden of proof so that the employer had to prove there was no discrimination, direct or indirect, rather than the employee having to show that there was discrimination, something that would be much harder for the employee, particularly in such cases as Case 109/88 *Handels-og Kontorfunktionaerernes Forbund i Danmark v Dansk Arbejds-giverforening* which involved a pay structure so complex that it was impossible for a women to identify the reasons which led to a difference in pay between her and a man doing the same job. The results of this case law has now been consolidated into Directive 97/80.[10]

10.5.7 Enforcement and Remedies

The member states are required under Article 6 of the Directive to take the necessary measures to ensure the principle of equal pay is applied and see that effective means are available to take care that the principle is observed.

10.6 The Equal Treatment Directive (76/207)

Directive 76/207 goes well beyond the original scope of Article 119 (now 141) which was concerned only with pay therefore the Directive had to be enacted under the general legislative power of Article 308 (ex 235). It extended the prohibition of discrimination on the grounds of sex into many facets of the employment relationship

---

[10]   OJ 1998 L14/6.

including inter alia access, appointment, dismissal, retirement, training, and working conditions. It has now been considerably amended by Directive 2002/73 but unfortunately in a rather complex manner. The amending Directive declares itself as entering into force on the day of publication but Article 2 also states that the member states had until 5 October 2005 to bring their laws into line. The reasons for this seemingly contradictory state of affairs is that because the Directive is a consolidation of much of the case law of the Court of Justice, much of the content is therefore argued to be valid law already. Secondly, by entering into force immediately, it is suggested that it prevents the member states from taking action contrary to its objectives whilst allowing time for the new measures to be accommodated into the national legal orders.

Article 1 refers to equal treatment for men and women which is required to be applied to working conditions, access to employment, including promotion, and to vocational training. Social security matters, covered by later directives, was expressly excluded from the ambit of this Directive. A new Article 1a sets out what is known as 'Gender Mainstreaming'. It requires member states to actively take into account the objective of equality between men and women when formulating and implementing laws, regulations, administrative provisions, policies, and activities in the areas referred to in paragraph 1.

10.6.1 The Concept of Equal Treatment/No Discrimination on the Grounds of Sex

The amended Article 2 introduces the concept of equal treatment which is immediately defined as no discrimination on the grounds of sex directly or indirectly by reference in particular to marital or family status. Furthermore it provides for a number of exceptions to the principle of equal treatment. The amended Article 2 has also introduced as a sub concept of discrimination that

Harassment and sexual harassment within the meaning of this Directive shall be deemed to be discrimination on the grounds of sex and therefore prohibited.

And then defines these terms:

—harassment: Where an unwanted conduct related to the sex of a person occurs with the purpose or effect of violating the dignity of a person, and of creating an intimidating, hostile, degrading, humiliating or offensive environment,—sexual harassment: Where any form of unwanted verbal, non-verbal or physical conduct of a sexual nature occurs, with the purpose or effect of violating the dignity of a person, in particular when creating an intimidating, hostile, degrading, humiliating or offensive environment.

Whilst, strictly, the new parts of the Directive will only have entered into force in 2005 and it will be thus only be after this date that it can be considered by the Court of

Justice, it would be no surprise if the Court of Justice was able to interpret harassment to be inherently covered by the existing provisions of the Directive in cases arising before that date.

As was discussed above, whilst the concepts of equal treatment and no discrimination are treated as being synonymous, in the context of this directive any distinction there may be takes on greater significance because of the much greater subject matter coverage of the Directive. Does equal treatment mean more than no discrimination? Case law has considered the scope of the protection provided for by these provisions in so far as what is meant by the right to equality within the framework agreed by the member states and interpreted by the Court of Justice. For example in Case C-13/94 *P v S and Cornwall County Council*, a male-to-female transsexual was dismissed from employment in an educational establishment after informing his employers he was going to undergo gender reassignment. The Court of Justice, in moving away from a simple interpretation of no discrimination on the grounds of sex simply to mean by a comparison of how each gender is treated, held that the dismissal was unlawful discrimination on the grounds of sex because it was 'based, essentially if not exclusively on the sex of the person concerned'. One of the difficulties in sex discrimination law is that the need to find a comparator is not always convenient or helpful in determining whether discrimination has been suffered, especially in relation to the pregnancy cases, considered below. In this case, if this is discrimination based on sex as the Court of Justice held, with whom can a comparison be made? There is no direct comparator as such, e.g. a female-to-male transsexual. The Court of Justice held that, where a person is dismissed on the ground that he or she intends to undergo, or has undergone, gender reassignment, he or she is treated unfavourably by comparison with persons of the sex to which he or she was deemed to belong before undergoing gender reassignment. This case engendered some debate that the Directive appeared not to be limited to discrimination on the grounds of sex, i.e. not just the difference between genders but to remove any discrimination where sex is a deciding/decisive factor. The question which was raised after this case was whether the concept of no discrimination on the grounds of sex had been transformed into no discrimination on the grounds of sexuality or even, no sexual orientation discrimination. The answer was soon forthcoming in a same sex female cohabitees case. In Case C-249/96 *Grant v South West Trains*, SW trains regulations specifically excluded benefits from same sex partnerships. Whereas opposite sex partners were included even where they were not married but provided a stable relationship was established, same sex partners did not. The Court of Justice held this was not discrimination based on sex as the rule would apply also using a direct comparison, to male same sex relationships. This was discrimination based on sexual orientation. The Court of Justice discussed a number of points in connection with this and found that in some member states such a relationship would, but only for a limited range of rights, be treated the same as an opposite sex relationship and in some states, such relationships were not recognized in any particular way. The Court of Justice referred to the then new Article 13 EC by which the member states in Council were empowered to take action to outlaw sexual orientation discrimination but stated that the, at that time, present state of law in the EC does not equate same sex relationships with opposite sex ones therefore the discrimination in respect of sexual orientation, although present was not contrary to Article 141 or the Directive. The Court of Justice confirmed this stance in Case 125/99P *D and Sweden v Council*. In both cases, the Court of Justice decided to leave the response to this form of discrimination to the legislative intervention of the member states who have now responded with Directive 2000/78 providing a framework for combating discrimination on grounds of sexual orientation, considered below. However, case C-117/01 *K B v NHS Pensions*, which although decided on the basis of Article 141 and not the Directive, is worthy of a brief note here because of the much more sympathetic judgment given by the Court of Justice in a case involving transsexual rights under existing Community legislation. The case concerned the inability to nominate as a pension beneficiary, a transsexual partner because national legislation required the partner to be an opposite sex spouse. National legislation would not allow the original sex of the partner to be altered to enable them to marry and thus satisfy the pension law requirement. The Court of Justice held that national legislation must be regarded as being, in principle, incompatible with the requirements of Article 141 on the grounds that it had already been found to be in breach of the ECHR, and prevented a couple such as *K B* and *R* from fulfilling the marriage requirement, necessary for one of them to be able to benefit from part of the pay of the other. However, the Court of Justice was not specific as to how exactly Article 141 might be offended apart from the fact that Article 141 would regard the benefit as pay. The Court of Justice acknowledged though that it was up to the member state to determine the conditions under which legal recognition is given to the change of gender of a person in R's situation and it would be up to the national court to decide whether KB can rely on Article 141. Equal treatment in this case then has been given a very wide scope to include the right to have a change in sex officially testified. Quite where a comparison fits in is difficult to see. Now that same sex civil partnerships have been given statutory recognition in the UK, this would no longer be a problem.

10.6.2 The Scope of the Directive

The scope of the prohibition within the Directive is spelled out in detail in an amended Article 3 which replaces the old Articles 3–5 and consolidates much of the previous case law in the process. It provides that the application of the principle of equal treatment means that there shall be no direct or indirect discrimination in the public or private sectors, including public bodies, in relation to:

(a) conditions for access to employment, to self-employment or to occupation, including selection criteria and recruitment conditions, whatever the branch of activity and at all levels of the professional hierarchy, including promotion;

(b) access to all types and to all levels of vocational guidance, vocational training, advanced vocational training, and retraining, including practical work experience;

(c) employment and working conditions, including dismissals, as well as pay as provided for in Directive 75/117/EEC;

(d) membership of, and involvement in, an organization of workers or employers, or any organization whose members carry on a particular profession, including the benefits provided for by such organizations.

Under paragraph 2 member states are required to take the necessary measures to ensure that:

(a) any laws, regulations and administrative provisions contrary to the principle of equal treatment are abolished;

(b) any provisions contrary to the principle of equal treatment which are included in contracts or collective agreements, internal rules of undertakings or rules governing the independent occupations and professions and workers' and employers' organizations shall be, or may be declared, null and void or are amended.'

Its very wide scope of application can be avoided for specific reasons given in the Directive only.

10.6.3 Equality with Regard to Employment Access, Working Conditions, Dismissal, and Retirement Ages

Article 3(1) of the amended directive, noted above, provides that there shall be no direct or indirect discrimination relating to all aspects of employment and notably access to jobs and conditions of employment. Cases which were previously considered under other provisions of the Directive, notably Article 5 which required equality of treatment in working conditions and conditions governing dismissal, are now covered also by the new Article 3(1). Most of the case law arising from the principle of equal treatment appears to have concerned retirement and pensions. There are one or two exceptions, as in the first case following. In Case C-177/88 *Dekker v VJM* Centram,

VJM (A Social Training Centre) refused to employ Mrs Dekker because she was pregnant and this would mean that insurance law, which did not recognize pregnancy as a reason for paying insurance money would not reimburse the employers during her maternity leave. As a social institution they argued that they could not afford to hire a replacement for her. The Court of Justice held that the employer was in direct contravention of Articles 2(1) and 3(1) of the Directive by their refusal to employ even though national rules economically forced this situation.

In Case C-312/86 *Commission v France* (Protection of Women), French legislation allowed certain privileges for women including extended maternity leave, reduction in working hours of women aged 59, bringing forward retirement age, time off for sick children, an extra day's holiday each year per child, a day off on the first day of a school term, and others. The Court of Justice considered that these special provisions only for women discriminated against men contrary to the Directive. They were not justified by Article 2(3) (now Art 2(7)) which protects women during pregnancy and maternity because the reasons given for the protection applied equally to male and female workers.

Turning to dismissal and retirement, we know from the section on equal pay above that member states can, under Article 7 of Directive 7/79, exclude the determination of pensionable age for the purposes of granting old age and retirement pensions and the possible consequences thereof for other benefits. It was thought and argued that this meant that any difference to do with either pensions entitlements or pensionable ages were excluded and thus, retirement and dismissal ages were also excluded. In Case 151/84 *Roberts v Tate and Lyle*, Mrs. Roberts was aged 53 and a redundancy scheme allowed access to a redundancy for both men and women at the age of 55. Roberts claimed unlawful discrimination because men could gain access ten years before their pensionable age but women only five. The Court of Justice held that access to a redundancy scheme was concerned with dismissal and therefore covered by Article 5 and not excluded by Article 7 of Directive 79/7. Access was not linked to the state security system. The Court of Justice held that Article 5(1) must be interpreted as meaning that a contractual provision which lays down a single age (55) for the dismissal of men and women under a mass redundancy involving the grant of an early retirement pension, whereas the normal retirement age is different for men and women, does not constitute discrimination on grounds of sex contrary to Community law.

In the leading case concerned with retirement, Case 152/84 *Marshall*, the compulsory earlier retirement of women was considered. National legislation allowed employers to retire women earlier than men. The Court of Justice though held that retirement also came within the scope of working conditions including dismissal and was thus covered by the Directive. When the Court of Justice came to consider whether the retirement age was linked to pensions, it decided relatively easily that the enforced earlier retirement for women than men did not fall within the justification of Article 7 of Directive 79/7 and was therefore direct discrimination. Directive 76/207 was held by the Court of Justice be directly effective but only vertically. Other means of enforcement must be pursued if a private employer is involved.

Case C-136/95 *Thibault* is notable for the clear statement from the Court of Justice about how Community law on equal treatment should be regarded and thus applied. Pay rises and promotion were assessed on the basis of the previous six months' work presence, which was argued to clearly discriminate against women on maternity absence who lost the chance to be assessed for pay increases or promotion. The Court of Justice held that this amounted to unlawful discrimination contrary to Articles 2(3) and 5(1) (as they were then). These provisions, in the view of the Court of Justice, required substantive and not just formal equality, i.e. real rights not just those on paper!

Finally, in this section, Case C-116/94 *Meyers* is worth noting because it extended the scope of the Directive to the social security benefit, Family Credit, something that quite reasonably might be considered to come under the Social Security Directive 79/7 and not 76/207. The credit was designed to supplement low paid workers in an attempt to persuade them to remain in work, thus satisfying the Court of Justice that it could be construed under the terms access to employment and working conditions, covered by Articles 3 and 5 (then) as it would both encourage employees to take up job offers and also be considered to be a condition of work. Working conditions thus applies to all aspects of the working relationship and not just those contained within the contract of employment.

Having regarded the widening scope of the principle of equal treatment, we now need to consider the derogations or exemptions which are provided under the Directive to exclude certain circumstances or situations from being subject to the principle of equal treatment. The first provision seeks to take out of the application of the principle of equal treatment, circumstances where factors other than sex allow discriminatory treatment, the second to take account of the unique circumstance of pregnancy and the third to allow for the possibility of promoting further equality for women.

10.6.4 The Power of Member States to Exempt Certain Occupations

Old Article 2(2) has been replaced by new Article 2(6) which provides the member states with the ability to exempt certain occupations from the application of the equal treatment principle where a characteristic not related to sex itself is a factor. The characteristic must constitute a genuine and determining occupational requirement in order not to constitute unlawful discrimination on the grounds of sex. Previously, cases showed that the member states were perhaps permitted a greater degree of discretion than under more recent cases, for example, in Case 165/82 *Commission v UK* (Equal Treatment for Men and Women), the restriction of access of males to midwifery was held to be acceptable but in such cases, member states are required to assess the restrictions periodically in order to decide, in the light of social develop-ments, whether there is justification for maintaining the exclusions concerned. They must notify the Commission of the results of this assessment under Article 9(2) of the Directive. Indeed, it is now the case that male midwives are accepted in the UK. In the same case, a blanket exemption from the provisions of the Directive which applied to all companies with less than six workers was held by the Court of Justice not to be sanctioned by the exemption and thus contrary to the Directive.

In Case 222/84 *Johnston v Chief Constable of the RUC*, the RUC did not renew the contracts of a number of female police officers and justified this under Article 2(2) because of a policy decision that women could not carry firearms. The Court of Justice held that the exception might apply to certain activities carried out by police officers, but not to police activities in general. The member states might therefore restrict such specific activities and the training for that activity, to men, provided that the situation was reviewed regularly to ensure that the restrictions remain justified, and that the restrictions complied with the principle of proportionality. The Court of Justice suggested the women could do other duties not involving use of firearms, rather than outright dismissal. Recent case law concerning employment in the armed forces, however, questions the restrictions permitted in *Johnston*. In Case C-273/97 *Angela Sirdar v The Army Board*, the Court of Justice said that although EC law can also apply to employment in the army, in the present case the exclusion of a women as a cook in the Royal Marines was acceptable because of the Marines' requirements of interoperability and front line duties, i.e. the unit's cook was expected to undertake all duties and also be involved in front line duties, therefore sex was a determining factor and the UK could therefore rely on the exemption. Sirdar, who was previously a cook for a Commando Regiment not having these same requirements, could not be a cook for the marines. In C-285/98 *Kreil v Germany*, a case which resembles *Johnston* but dealing with the army rather than the police force, the Court of Justice did not accept a general exclusion from military posts which meant that all armed units could remain exclusively male. The Court of Justice held that the national authorities contravened the principle of proportionality in taking the general position that the composition of all armed units in the Bundeswehr had to remain exclusively male. By rejecting the application out of hand by Ms Kreil to the weapons electronics maintenance service of the Federal German army, the German authorities had unlawfully discriminated against her. The armed forces are thus categorically included but with a discretion preserved for the member states to discriminate for particular circumstances as in *Sirdar*. Finally in the trio of army cases, is Case C-186/01 *Dory*, in which the compulsory military service for males only in Germany was challenged. The Court of Justice held 'that the Equal Treatment Directive applies to equality in the access to posts, it does not govern the member states choices of military organization for the defence of their territory or of their essential interests'. Germany's choice of compulsory male only military service, enshrined in their constitution was immune from Community law scrutiny. The Court of Justice was certainly showing an unusually high degree of respect for the German Constitution. The negative consequences for males as a result of their time spent in Military service such as a delay in comparisons to females in getting to the job market can, therefore only be remedied by the national authorities and courts, but see, however, *Schnorbus* below.

10.6.5 The Protection of Women Regarding Childbirth and Maternity

Article 2(3) of directive has now been replaced by a new Article 2(7) which provides: 'This Directive shall be without prejudice to provisions concerning the protection of women, particularly as regards pregnancy and maternity.' This is another derogation from the principle of equal treatment and a different legal regime can apply here, but this time specifically to protect women. However, these provisions should not be used to disguise discrimination. Directive Article 2(7) continues:

Woman on maternity leave shall be entitled, after the end of her period of maternity leave, to return to her job or to an equivalent post on terms and conditions which are no less favourable to her and to benefit from any improvement in working conditions to which she would be entitled during her absence. Less favourable treatment of a woman related to pregnancy or maternity leave within the meaning of Directive 92/85/EEC shall constitute discrimination within the meaning of this Directive.

Directive 92/85 concerns the protection of pregnant and breastfeeding workers. Its title comes across as somewhat inelegant but needs to be read alongside of Directive 76/207 to determine the rights women are entitled to when pregnant and on maternity leave. Article 10 in combination with Article 8 designates the period of special protection as from the beginning of pregnancy to the end of maternity leave (which must be a 14-week minimum continuous period of leave) in which women are protected from dismissal for any reasons connected to pregnancy. After the period has expired, the special protection is lost. Note that even during the period of special protection, they can be dismissed in the normal course of events where the reason for dismissal is not connected to pregnancy, e.g. for theft. In this particular area of law, the need to make a comparison is rejected in favour of allowing action which removes the substantive inequality suffered by reason of the pregnancy, which cannot be compared. Case law had, however, already expanded and clarified existing EC law ahead of Directive 92/85 coming into force.

In a case which predates the Parental Leave Directive, Case 184/83 *Hoffman v Barmer* Ersatzkasse, a father claimed that the refusal to grant six months paternity leave following the birth of his child while the mother went back to work was discrimination contrary to Articles 1, 2, and 5(1) of the Equal Treatment Directive. The Court of Justice held that the Directive was not designed to settle questions concerned with the organization of the family, or to alter the division of responsibility between parents and that parental leave may therefore be reserved to the mother by the member states by virtue of Article 2(3). The case makes it clear that Article 2(3) was an exception to the general principle of equal treatment established by the Directive exclusively in favour of women. Note now the protection against dismissal during a period of parental leave is extended to workers of both sexes by the Parental Leave Directive (96/34) but as this is not usually the subject of study in most EU/EC courses, it is not considered further here.

10.6.5.1 Dismissal During or After Pregnancy

A series of cases has now allowed us to see just how protective the Community regime of pregnant women is. The first case deals with a National law designed to protect pregnant women—albeit by excluding them from a certain type of work.

In C-421/92, *Habermann-Beltermann v Arbeiterwohlfahrt*, HB was employed on a permanent nights contract and was dismissed when discovered to be pregnant on the basis of a National law prohibiting the night time work of pregnant women. The employer argued that the prohibition of night work was allowed by the Directive and to that extent the Court of Justice agreed with the employer but not to justify dismissal. The Court of Justice held that neither national legislation nor employment contract rules could render void an employment contract by reason of the fact that the female worker was found to be pregnant. Dismissal was clearly disproportionate and the employer should, for example, find other work for her.

In Case C-32/93 *Webb v EMO Air Cargo (UK) Ltd*, a woman who was employed on an indefinite contract to replace her predecessor, who was on pregnancy and maternity leave, was dismissed when it was discovered that as a replacement she was also pregnant. The Court of Justice held that to be direct discrimination contrary to Articles 2(1) and 5(1) of Directive 76/207. This case arose before Directive 92/85 came into force and could not therefore be applied in the case which was therefore decided exclusively on Directive 76/207. The clear and forthright position taken by the Court of Justice in the case, was confirmed in Case C-207/98 *Mahlberg* in respect of the appointment of full time permanent employees. Dismissal because a woman is pregnant is a clear and direct breach of the Community law.

The next form of employment relationship which was considered by the Court of Justice to determine if they too are included with the scope of the Directive, were temporary employment contracts.

In Case C-438/99 *Melgar*, a woman was employed on a series of back to back fixed-term contracts. Her fourth one expired, allegedly according to the employee, without being renewed or extended, as in the past. Prior to that occurring, her employer learned of her pregnancy. However, the employers had offered a fifth contract but Melgar refused to sign it on the basis that her last contract had not expired and she had been dismissed unfairly. The national court did not determine as a matter of fact whether the case concerned a dismissal from an indefinite employment contract or a failure to employ on a new contract. The Court of Justice held that the failure to renew a fixed-term contract was not strictly a case of dismissal discrimination contrary to Article 10 of Directive 92/85, however, it considered that the non-renewal could be regarded as a refusal to employ based on pregnancy and thus directly discriminatory and contrary to Directive 76/207, Articles 2(1) and 3(1). The facts in the case, however, do not seem to support the view that there was a refusal to appoint, with the employers having offered a contract.

In a clearer fixed-term contract Case C-109/00 *Tele Danmark*, an interesting set of facts arose. A post was advertised as a six months only temporary contract. Training for the post, however, required two months before the person appointed could undertake full duties usefully. Ms Brandt-Nielsen was appointed as from 1 July 1995 but in mid August, she informed her employer that she was pregnant and due to give birth in early November. Under Danish law, she was entitled to paid maternity leave as from 11 September 1995, i.e. after two weeks useful work. She had not previously informed the employer she was pregnant and was dismissed with effect from 30 September 1995. She claimed unlawful dismissal. The Court of Justice held it was direct discrimination contrary to both Article 5(1) 76/207 and Article 10 of 92/85 and the fact that employment was fixed term was irrelevant, because the inability to work was due to pregnancy. The duration of employment was also not a factor which would influence the result. The Court of Justice held 'Had the Community legislature wished to exclude fixed-term contracts, which represent a substantial proportion of the employment relationships, from the scope of those directives, it would have done so expressly.' Not much later, was Case C-320/01 *Busch*, in which a woman who was on parental leave after the birth of her first child, became pregnant a second time and sought whilst pregnant to return early to work, and before the full amount of paid parental leave for the first pregnancy had expired. Her employer had a vacancy and she was permitted to return to work. She was seven months' pregnant when she did. She had not mentioned her pregnancy to her employer, nor had her employer asked whether this was so. On 9 April 2001 she started work and on 10 April 2001, she informed her employer she was seven months pregnant and was entitled to paid maternity commencing 23 May 2001 (i.e. after just 6 weeks of work). The employer rescinded the permission to return to work (not actually dismissal) on grounds of misrepresentation and mistake as to an essential characteristic. The reason given subsequently for returning to work early by Ms Busch was that the maternity leave allowance was higher than the parental leave allowance. The Court of Justice held that an employee is not under an obligation to inform her employee in seeking to return to work that because of certain legislative prohibitions, she is not able to carry out all of her duties. Furthermore, the Court of Justice held that an employer is not entitled to withdraw consent given to return to work because they were in error as to the employee being pregnant.

These last two cases may seem to be acting increasingly harshly on the employers, but there is not much doubt about the clear-cut support of the Court of Justice for the law as it presents itself and is helping provide substantive support for women in achieving equal treatment in circumstances where it is impossible to compare how a man might have been treated and where the Community has provided a special protective legal regime because of this. These laws may not have universal support from employers but the point is that as a society we have decided to correct an iniquitous situation, that pregnancy is an acceptable ground for dismissal or non-appointment.

10.6.5.2 Pregnancy and Illness

Cases which involve illness resulting from pregnancy are particularly difficult ones to resolve and have caused the Court of Justice to reach hard decisions on both sides of the line. In Case C-179/88 *Hertz v Aldi*, Mrs. Hertz was dismissed because of repeated absence due to illness which originated from her prior pregnancy. The Court of Justice held that although pregnancy related discrimination was a form of direct discrimination, the Directive did not apply to dismissals due to illness absence which took place outside of the maternity leave time granted. In such circumstances, it was necessary to look at national legislation to consider whether there was any direct or indirect discrimination in the grounds of dismissal. In this case, when the period of special protection has expired, it becomes possible again to make a comparison with men to see how they are treated if absent through illness over a long time.

The approach taken in *Hertz* was confirmed even after entry into force of Directive 92/85 in Case C-400/95 *Larsson v Dansk Handel & Service*. The directives thus do not prevent dismissals for absences due to illness attributable to pregnancy even where the illness arose during pregnancy and continued during and after the period of maternity leave. Dismissal is prohibited and thus unlawful during the period of protected maternity leave only. The dismissal after the leave period is not specifically catered for by EC law and the situation to determine unlawful discrimination reverts to comparing dismissal due to illness on a direct basis with the dismissal of a man for illness. Of course men are not usually dismissed for illness arising from pregnancy, although it is not inconceivable that mental illness and maybe even triggering physical illness could be caused by a pregnant partner's illness or even fact of the pregnancy itself! However, for the most part this is not the case. With these cases, the Court of Justice recognizes that certain disorders are specific to one sex or another, e.g. if a man was ill with prostate trouble or testicular cancer and took a lot of time off but was sympathetically treated by his boss and not dismissed, the comparison would have to be with a women who was ill for any reason. Similarly, a women dismissed for taking too much time off due to illness arising from pregnancy could be compared with a man suffering from any illness. So although pregnancy played its role as the source of the illness, outside of the protected period, it is the normal comparison which determines the legal position, something which is argued represents formal equality only and not the substantive pregnancy supposedly upheld by the Court of Justice.

Case C-394/96 *Brown v Rentokil* also concerned a dismissal which resulted from time taken off due to a illness originating during pregnancy but before maternity leave had commenced. The Court of Justice made it clear that the period or protection incorporated the entire pregnancy and the maternity leave. The *Larsson* case was corrected by the Court of Justice to the extent that any time taken off during pregnancy and maternity leave cannot now be taken into account in calculating the entire time taken off for the purpose of dismissal, i.e. time can only start to accrue for this purpose after the period of protection has ended. A woman would therefore be best advised to take her maternity leave as late as possible, if possible, to maximize the period of protection.

10.6.6 The Promotion of Equal Opportunity by Removing Existing Inequalities Affecting Opportunities

The statutory attempt to promote equal opportunity is often described in the term 'positive discrimination', although this is not an accurate description for what is allowed under the Community legal regime, as will be observed from the judgments of the Court of Justice. Both the Treaty and Directive 76/207 contain provision for some sort of action by the member states to try to promote equality. The Directive, which was first on the scene originally provided in Article 2(4) that the Directive shall be without prejudice to measures to promote equal opportunity for men and women, in particular by removing existing inequalities which affect women's opportunities in the areas covered by the Directive. A new Article 2(8) has replaced old Article 2(4) and provides: 'member states may maintain or adopt measures within the meaning of

Article 141(4) of the Treaty with a view to ensuring full equality in practice between men and women.' Hence, the Directive article now essentially backs up the Treaty provision of Article 141(4) but refers specifically to women whereas Article 141 mentions both men and women. Article 141 continues:

With a view to ensuring full equality in practice between men and women in working life, the principle of equal treatment shall not prevent any member state from maintaining or adopting measures providing for specific advantages in order to make it easier for the under-represented sex to pursue a vocational activity or to prevent or compensate for disadvantages in professional careers.

Whilst the measures concerned mostly contemplate women this is not exclusively the position, as can be observed in the case law. The extent to which the authorities of the member states can provide legislation or indeed private employers are able to discriminate positively in favour of women by, for example, shortlisting or interviewing only female candidates or if dismissals are required, dismissing males only, is a difficult question. The new Article 2(8) in Directive 76/207 would seem to allow more positive action than was previously the case by the use of the term 'equality in practice' i.e. not just on paper! As yet, no cases have arisen from the new Article. There are however, a number which have arisen under the old Directive Article and the Treaty amendment.

In Case 312/86 (Protection of Women) *Commission v France*, considered above, it can be seen that not all measures adopted by a member state to assist women will be considered to be fair by the Court of Justice. In contrast, in Case C-218/98 *Abdoulaye v Renault*, additional or guaranteed payments for females on maternity leave over and above those paid to males on paternity leave was recognized by the Court of Justice as acceptable due to the occupational disadvantages suffered by women during absence and was held not to be discriminatory.

There is a series of cases concerned with appointment procedures which have been adapted to introduce an element of rebalancing in favour of the under-represented sex. In Case C-450/93 *Kalanke*, the Court of Justice ruled that a national rule, which provided that where equally qualified men and women were candidates for a position with fewer women, women are automatically to be given priority, constituted direct discrimination on the grounds of sex contrary to the Directive. According to the Court of Justice, the rule had gone beyond promotion and had overstepped the exception provided for in Article 2(4). This decision was not taken kindly in some quarters as it seemed to undermine any possibility of providing affirmative action to improve the equality position of women, however, there was soon a refinement of the position both in the subtlety of approach by the member state authorities and the interpretation by the Court of Justice. Case C-409/95 *Marschall*, involved an application for a teaching post by a qualified man being rejected by the local authority according to a law which provided that women should be given priority in the event of equal suitability. However, in contrast to *Kalanke*, a 'saving clause' provided that if a particular male candidate has grounds which tilt the balance in his favour, women are not to be given priority. Thus the Court of Justice was able to conclude that the provision was one which could fall within the scope of Article 2(4) of the Directive and did not offend the prohibition of discrimination. There were, however, two safety mechanisms or which could otherwise be regarded as complications to the process, which should be set up. The first, to avoid discrimination against men and the second to stop the pendulum from swinging back against women. The Court of Justice considered such priority clauses are acceptable provided the candidates are objectively assessed to determine whether there are any factors tilting the balance in favour of a male candidate but that such criteria employed do not themselves discriminate against women. This is a somewhat convoluted judgment but probably gets there. Case C-158/97 *Badeck* confirms this last case that such laws are not in breach of EC law provided that the priority for women was not automatic and unconditional.

The new Article 141(4) backs up the ability of the Court of Justice to pursue the more liberal approach adopted in *Marschall*. Although the first case reaching it under the amended Treaty Article did not give the court an opportunity to be expansive. In Case C-407/98 *Abrahamsson*, a woman was appointed to a university chair in preference to a man on the basis of a positive discrimination regulation and despite a clear 5:3 vote in favour of the man, based on his qualifications and the overall higher ranking of male even after the positive discrimination factor had been taken into account. The university contended that the difference was not so great as to breach the objectivity requirement imposed by Community law in the light of the recent case law of the Court of Justice. The Court of Justice held that EC law, primary or secondary, does not support appointments based on automatic preference for the under-represented sex irrespective of whether the qualifications are better or worse and where no objective assessment of each candidate has taken place. It seems that only where women have equivalent or perceptibly near qualifications, that Community law will permit any affirmative action to be exercised.

A case involving female access only to child care facilities, save in emergency, was considered under Article 2(4) of the Directive. In Case C-476/99 *Lommers*, a Government Ministry restricted access to subsidized child care to women to address the lack of affordable facilities which caused many women to give up their jobs. Whilst this was held by the Court of Justice to be acceptable under Article 2(4) it could only be so, providing that the emergency rule that permitted single fathers to seek places was applied on the same conditions as for female workers. It seems there must always be a saving clause in the background to prevent positive being too positive and thus unlawfully discriminatory.

Finally, in this area, is Case C-79/99 *Julia Schnorbus v Land Hessen*, a decision addresses an imbalance disadvantaging men and the result is one way of addressing the army case conclusions reached by the Court of Justice in *Dory* above. In Germany, military or civilian service is compulsory but for males only. According to which service is performed this can take between 9 and 18 months and means that men wishing to go to university enter later, and all men enter the job market later. The Land Hessen provided rules in respect of entry to the second stage of German legal training which gave priority to men by deferring acceptance of applications by females by up to 12 months in comparison with males who applied at the same time. It argued, when challenged by a female applicant, that the rule was designed to counterbalance the disadvantage suffered by men. It was accepted by Court of Justice under Article 141 as being a proportionate response to the situation.

The measures found to be acceptable by the Court of Justice represent only modest steps in providing substantive and not just formal equality for men and women. However, as with all areas of Community law, it is an area which will certainly not stand still for long and therefore it is always wise in Community law to be looking out for new cases and the impact they have on the development of Community law.

10.6.7 Judicial Enforcement and Remedies

As with Directive 75/117, means to judicial enforcement and the possibility of a remedy for those damaged by breaches of the provisions was also provided in Directive 76/207 Article 6, which has now been amended by Directive 2002/73 to take account of the case law in the area, some of which is considered below. Article 6 now provides that not only must member states ensure that judicial and conciliation procedures are in place to enforce Community law obligations even after the employment relationship has ended but also that individuals can pursue claims for real and effective compensation without a fixed upper limit.

Up to 5 October 2005, Article 6 provided that member states must introduce into their own legal systems such measures as are necessary to enable all persons who consider themselves wronged to pursue their claims by judicial process. Case 14/83 *Von Colson and Kamann* concerned the reimbursement of their travel expenses as damages for discrimination. The Court of Justice ruled that full implementation of the Directive entails that sanctions must be such as to guarantee real and effective judicial protection and must therefore have a real deterrent effect on the employer. Where a member state chooses to penalize the breach of the prohibition of discrimination by the award of compensation, that compensation must be adequate in relation to the damage sustained and amount to more than purely nominal compensation. At the time, it held that Article 6 is not however itself directly effective, hence the development of the principle of indirect effect from this case. In Case C-271/91 *Marshall II*, it was held that damages means full compensation not restrictively limited by national statutory rules. At the time this ruling by the Court of Justice was very controversial and was one of the cases which prompted the UK government led by Major, to issue a discussion paper effectively advocating clipping the wings of the Court of Justice. Despite the Directive at the time providing that there be no limit to the damages, as the amended version also does, the Court of Justice confirmed the directive gave a right to full compensation from date of breach.

Other notable cases include C-180/95 *Draehmpaehl v Urania*. A job was advertised to females only, contrary to both Community and German law. In the consequent claim, damages were limited to a maximum of 3 months' salary but dependant on proving fault on the part of the employer. If more than one plaintiff sued, the aggregate compensation payable was limited to 6 months' salary. The Court of Justice held liability to compensate can not be made dependent on fault, compensation itself must guarantee real and effective judicial protection, have a real deterrent effect on the employer and be adequate in relation to the damage suffered. Limits such as three months salary are acceptable where the employer can prove that notwithstanding the discrimination a better qualified person was appointed and the complainant would not have been appointed in any event. However, an aggregate award ceiling regardless of the number discriminated against is not acceptable under Directive 76/207 as it might have the effect of dissuading applicants so harmed from asserting their rights.

These decisions are now reflected statutorily in the new Article 6, as is Case C-185/97 *Coote v Granada* in which Ms Coote settled a sex discrimination claim with Granada outside of court and the employment relationship was terminated by mutual consent. She found it difficult to obtain another job due to Granada's refusal to supply an employment agency with a reference. It was claimed this was contrary to Article 6 of Directive 76/207 (the Equal Treatment Directive) under which member states should take measures to achieve the aims of the directive and must ensure the rights can be enforced by individual before the national courts. The Court of Justice held that this right of recourse to the courts is a general principle of Community law reflected in the member states constitutions and Article 6 ECHR. The Court of Justice held that Article 6 of the Directive also covers measures an employer might take as a reaction against legal proceedings of a former employee outside of dismissal, because if employees found it difficult to get other jobs it might deter them from taking action where they considered they had been discriminated against on the grounds of sex. This extends the scope of EC protection beyond the protection against dismissal.

Article 7 requires member states to take the necessary measures to protect employees against dismissal by the employer as a reaction to a complaint within the undertaking or to any legal proceedings aimed at enforcing compliance with the principle of equal treatment. This has now been extended by Directive 2002/73 to protect employees' representatives who act in cases involving complaints against the employer.

Article 8 requires the member states to ensure that provisions of implementing laws are brought to the attention of employees by all appropriate means and new Articles 8a and 8b have been introduced for member states to set up bodies to promote equality and to engage in research and discussion to bring forward proposals for agreements and action to achieve equality.

10.7 Social Security Directive (79/7)

As the third instalment of the first wave of secondary legislative additions to Article 119 (now 141), Directive 79/7 was enacted to apply the principle of equal treatment to the field of social security and other elements of social protection. The scope of the directive is limited to statutory schemes, whereas private schemes and the increasing number of contracted out schemes were catered for later by Directive 86/378.

10.7.1 Personal and Material Scope

The Directive applies only to employment related schemes and not to social security schemes of a general nature or in favour of those who have not previously worked. This was considered in Cases 48, 106 and 107/88 *Achterberg et al*, concerning claims from three individuals who were unemployed on their own volition in order to look after children. The Court of Justice held that the Directive did not apply to those who were unemployed and who were not seeking work or suffering from one of the risks listed. Furthermore, in Case C-63–64/91 *Jackson and Cresswell v Chief Adjudication Officer*, the Court of Justice confirmed that the Directive applies only to the types of social security which replaced a worker's wage and not to general schemes to relieve poverty.

Article 2 provides that it applies to the working population which includes self-employed persons, workers, and self-employed persons whose activity is interrupted by illness, accident or involuntary unemployment, to persons seeking employment and to retired or invalided workers or self-employed persons. Part-time workers were confirmed as coming within the scope of the Directive by Case 102/88 *Ruzius-Wilbrink v Public Service Social Insurance Board (Holland)* and it was confirmed that its application is not limited by where only a few hours per week are worked, see Case C-317/93 *Nolte*.

Article 3 (1) provides that it applies to:

(a) statutory schemes which provide protection against the following risks: sickness, invalidity, old age, accidents at work and occupational diseases, unemployment; and

(b) social assistance, insofar as it is intended to supplement or replace the schemes referred to in (a).

Whilst Article 3 excluded its application to survivors' and family benefits, it was held in Case 150/85 *Drake v Chief Adjudication Officer* that Article 2 included persons who have been working but whose work had been interrupted by one of the risks referred to in Article 3 suffered not by themselves but by a family member. Mrs. Drake had given up her job to look after her mother but her application for a carer benefit was turned down as not available because she was married, although it would have been payable to a married man. The Court of Justice held first, that Article 3(1) must be interpreted as including any benefit which in a broad sense forms one of the statutory schemes referred to, or a social assistance scheme designed to supplement or replace such a scheme. The fact that the benefit which forms part of a statutory invalidity scheme is paid to a third party and not to the disabled person does not place it outside the scope of the Directive. It was held that Drake, as one of the working population, should be regarded as a recipient for the purposes of the directive and that the benefit should be paid without discrimination. However, in Case C-77/95 *Zuechner*, because Mrs. Zuechner had not been in work or looking for work when her husband was injured and required Mrs. Zuechner to care for him, she was denied the application of the Directive as she had not had an economic activity interrupted.

With regard to the material scope, this was interpreted quite restrictively by the Court of Justice in Case 243/90 *R v Secretary of State for Social Security ex Parte Smithson*, which involved a claim in respect of loss of housing benefit due to the operation of British Social Security rules. This was held by the Court of Justice not to be within the scope of Directive 79/7, which applied only to statutory schemes providing protection against certain named risks, including old age and illness if directly and effectively linked but not need of financial help with accommodation costs. This is regarded as a surprisingly restrictive interpretation of the provision. Also a child raising allowance was excluded in Cases C-245 and 312/94 *Hoever and Zachow* and a concessionary travel allowance in Case C-228/94 *Atkins and Wrekin* because they were not directly linked to the risks listed in Article 3.

However, despite family credit being an express exception in Article 3(2), it comes, in the view of the Court of Justice in Case C-116/94 *Meyer v Adjudication Officer*, within the scope of the Directive when it is paid as a means to enable, in the case, a single mother to go to work. Article 3 has also been held to include equality in being able to get relief from prescription charges. Previously in the UK, exemptions from prescription charges were linked to old age pensions and thus paid out at different ages for men and women. The Court of Justice held that they were part of a statutory scheme providing protection against sickness and were thus covered (see Case C-137/94 *R v Secretary of State for Health, ex parte Richardson*) despite the lack of a strict connection to work or to a national social security scheme. Winter fuel payments were also within its scope due to the link with old age risks in Case C-382/98 *R v Secretary of State for the Home Department, ex parte Taylor*.

10.7.2 Discrimination

Article 4 defines the principle of equal treatment as meaning:

—no discrimination whatsoever on grounds of sex either directly, or indirectly by reference in particular to marital or family status, in particular as concerns:

—the scope of the schemes and the conditions of access thereto;

—the obligation to contribute and the calculation of contributions;

—the calculation of benefits including increases due in respect of a spouse and for dependants and the conditions governing the duration and retention of entitlement of benefits.

Article 4(1) was held to be directly effective in Case 286/85 *McDermott v Minister for Social Welfare*, in which an Irish rule was held to be in breach of the Social Security Directive which granted social security supplements for dependants of married men without requiring them to prove that the persons in respect of whom they were claiming were in fact dependant on them, but in the case of married women required such proof. In *Drake* it was held the refusal of benefit for women on the basis that they were living with wage earning husbands constituted discrimination prohibited by the Directive as married men could have claimed the benefit.

In Case C-373/89 *Integrity v Rouvroy*, exemptions from social security payments were permitted for low wage earning women whereas, the male plaintiff who had earned very little in the past was not allowed the same exemption. This was held by the Court of Justice to be contrary to Article 4(1) of Directive 79/7 despite the argument that this was a measure intended to improve the position of women. Such direct positive discrimination was not acceptable under the Directive.

A case which echoes the concerns in the equal pay cases about indirect discrimination against part-time and thus predominantly women workers is Case 102/88 *Ruzius-Wilbrink v Public Service Social Insurance Board (Holland)*. A Dutch Law granted entitlement to a disability allowance to insured persons aged 17 or over who become incapable of working. The benefit was calculated on the basis of past earnings which discriminated against those being paid less than the minimum weekly wages, i.e. part-time workers. Official Statistics showed that 75 per cent of part-time workers were women and the plaintiff, who received a lower rate of benefit as an ex-part-time worker, claimed that the criteria were discriminatory on grounds of sex. The Court of Justice held that in circumstances like this where is effective discrimination against workers of one sex, the differentiation will be in breach of Article 4(1) of Directive 79/7 unless objectively justified. The fact that persons could now receive more in benefits then they had received in wages was not an objective justification in the eyes of the Court.

10.7.3 Maternity

Article 4(2) provides that the principle of equal treatment shall be without prejudice to the provisions relating to the protection of women on the grounds of maternity and the payment of maternity benefits, in other words special women only maternity benefits can be paid without constituting unlawful discrimination.

10.7.4 Remedies

Article 5 requires the member states to take the necessary measures to abolish any laws, regulations or administrative provisions which are contrary to the principle of equal treatment. Article 6 is the exact equivalent of Article 6 of the Equal Treatment Directive. It requires the member states to provide recourse to judicial process so that individuals may enforce the principle of equal treatment in the national courts. In Case C-66/95 *R v Secretary of State for Social Security, ex parte Eunice Sutton*, it was held that in contrast to the position taken in *Marshall (2)*, Article 6 of Directive 79/7, which is almost identical to Article 6 of Directive 76/207, does not oblige the member state to pay interest on the payment of benefits when the delay was the result of unlawful discrimination. The reason given was that the payments are made under social security benefits and not compensation for damage sustained. The Court of Justice did hold, however, that post *Francovich*, a member state must make good loss to an individual the result of a breach of Community law, but that it was up to the national courts to determine that.

10.7.5 Derogations

Article 7 empowers the member states to exclude from the scope of the Directive a number of reserved areas. These include most notably the determination of pensionable age for the purposes of granting old age and retirement pensions and the possible consequences thereof for other benefits, and the granting of old age or invalidity benefit by virtue of the derived entitlements of a wife.

The approach of the Court of Justice to the exception in Article 7(1)(a) has restricted it to statutory old age pensions but not to retirement itself, dismissal or their consequences as can be noted in Case 19/81 *Burton v British Railways Board*, Case 152/84 *Marshall v Southampton Area Health Authority*, considered above and in Case 262/84 *Beets-Proper v F. Van Lanschot Bankiers NV*. The judgment in Case C-262/88 *Barber* has had considerable consequences on the scope of this derogation as many of the pension schemes which might otherwise have been excluded from equal treatment are as a result of the *Barber* ruling now not within the scope of the derogation. Contracted out pension schemes were held to provide deferred pay and thus fall outside Article 7(1) of Directive 79/7. Further details of the *Barber* judgment and the follow up Protocol and case law are noted above.

It was held in Case C-9/91 *R v Secretary of State for Social Security, ex parte EOC*, that the different periods of contribution for men and women in the UK for retirement pensions was acceptable, because it was necessarily linked to the different pensionable ages allowed by Article 7. Reflecting the cases on pay above, the Court of Justice has held that the member states can continue to keep different pensionable ages for men and women and different periods of time of contribution to the schemes less for women who qualify for a pension earlier, see Cases C-377 to 384/96 *De Vriendt et al.* Payments which are reduced or removed once the pension age has been reached have been held to be those which are consequential to the pension age and thus within the scope of the exemption of Article 7(1), see Case C-196/98 *Hepple et al* which involved a disability allowance which ceased on reaching pensionable age, when a retirement allowance was paid instead.

10.8 Directive 92/85

The pregnant and breastfeeding workers Directive was enacted as a measure for the protection of workers under Article 118a (now 138) rather than a measure of equal treatment under Article 141 of the Treaty, which now allows general measures of equal treatment to be adopted rather than just pay as was the case prior to amendment. Directive 92/85 is essentially then a health and safety measure to protect pregnant and breastfeeding workers in the workplace including part-time workers. We have already considered Article 10 above in relation to the special period of protection in relation to dismissal for pregnant women from the beginning of pregnancy to the end of maternity leave. Dismissals therefore should now be considered under Directive 92/85. However, what constitutes a dismissal and what constitutes a refusal to take on an employee is not necessarily a clear cut point as was observed in Case C-438/99 *Melgar* because of the practice of employment on back-to-back or fixed-term contracts which is commonplace in industry and commerce. So, whilst strictly concerning, health and safety issues, the Directive is nevertheless important in providing a level of protection for women in a situation which is not comparable with men which without such protection might otherwise result in further inequality for women. For example, if paid time off to attend ante-natal clinics was not required by Article 9, not only might the time off not be paid but also the time taken off might be counted towards the amount of time absent from work for the purposes of dismissal. Hence then, it is worth taking a brief look at the provisions of this directive and some of the resulting case law to gain a better impression of the overall regime relating to equality.

10.8.1 Scope and Application

Articles 1–6 outline the purpose of the Directive, the definitions of those workers who are covered, the guidelines on the assessments which employers should make to identify tasks which carry a risk for pregnant and breastfeeding workers and the actions employers must take to eliminate the workers' exposure to the risks identified. In particular, Article 7 of the Directive provides that protected workers cannot be obliged to work nights but, as was observed in Case C-421/92, *Habermann-Beltermann* above, where national legislation actually prohibits night work by pregnant workers, this does not permit dismissal as the employer's reaction to a night worker employee's pregnancy.

Article 8 provides for a minimum 14-week maternity leave, Article 9 for paid time off to attend ante-natal examinations and Article 10, protection from dismissal from the beginning of pregnancy to the end of maternity leave. Article 11 provides that employment rights during the maternity leave must be secured including payments and allowances, at least the equivalent as those payable to workers on sick leave. This requirement was considered in Case C-342/93 *Gillespie*, which held that the level of pay must be such that it is not inadequate and thus undermines the protection intended and must take into account any pay increases awarded to other workers during the maternity absence.

In the ironic, but genuine Case C-411/96 *Boyle et al* v EOC, Articles 8, and 11 were considered in some detail. The Equal Opportunities Commission, set up to promote and defend equal rights, was accused of unlawful discrimination. Boyle and five colleagues raised a number of questions about the maternity scheme run by the EOC which reflected the UK civil service maternity scheme and thus applicable to many thousand more workers. It is this light the case should be seen. It had been agreed in the Industrial Tribunal and accepted by the Court of Justice that for the purposes of direct effects of the Directives, the EOC was an emanation of the state. The Court of Justice decided the various questions raised as follows:

A clause which required the repayment of additional maternity payments, which were made over and above the statutory minimum, if a women did not return to work following maternity leave when she had undertaken to return, was not contrary to the directive. Although, in comparison, there was no similar clause applying to those receiving higher rate sick leave payments, this was not discrimination against women according to the Court of Justice, as maternity leave under Directive 92/85 was a special provision not to be compared with that of a man or women on sick leave. Higher rate sick leave pay would apply to both women and men.

In answer to a question about the commencement of maternity leave, the Directive specified only the minimum number of weeks to be granted and left it to member states to lay down provision as to when it should commence.

A clause which prohibited women from taking sick leave during the minimum period of 14 weeks' maternity leave unless she elected to return to work and thus terminate her maternity leave, was held to be contrary to Article 8(1) of the Directive. However, a similar clause in respect of supplementary maternity leave was found to be compatible with Directives 76/207 and 92/85 because EC law does not apply to supplementary maternity leave paid out by the employer. A woman can be restricted to taking either maternity leave or sick leave.

Directive 92/85 Article 11(2)(a) requires maternity leave rights in the 14-week minimum period to be at least the same as minimum statutory rights when on sick leave. A clause which limited the period during which annual leave accrues to that 14-week period and not to any additional leave granted by the employer over and above the statutory 14-week period was held to be compatible with EC law. Outside of that period, no annual leave would accrue. There was no discrimination, direct or indirect, according to the Court of Justice, as all employees on unpaid leave accrued no annual leave entitlement. A right to obtain supplementary leave over and above the protection provided by the Directive, and which was available to women only, could not constitute less favourable treatment.

In contrast, in answer to the fifth question, a clause which restricted the accrual of pension rights to the 14-week period and denied it during the supplementary period of unpaid leave was held to be contrary to Directive 92/85. Although, under Article 11(4), entitlement to benefits could be made subject to the workers satisfying national legislation, this was not possible where the pension scheme was wholly occupational and governed by the employment contract. Therefore, the accrual of pensions rights was not dependant on receiving pay during the supplementary period. The case was a part success for the individual applicants but more importantly, the offending clauses could no longer be enforced either by the EOC or other employers with the same clauses.

Otherwise, Directive 92/85 has not featured in case law to any significant extent, so whilst it was originally assumed following its enactment that all cases concerned with dismissal during pregnancy or maternity will come under its provisions, the *Melgar* case shows that we still need to have an eye on Directive 76/207.

10.9 Related Secondary Legislation

10.9.1 Occupational Pensions Directive 86/378

This Directive extends the equal treatment principle to occupational as opposed to statutory pension schemes and applies similar rules to Directive 79/7. It did not come fully into effect until 1 January 1993. The wide definition given to pay in the *Barber* judgment meant much of this Directive was no longer relevant as some of the schemes concerned by it have been judged to constitute deferred pay and thus be covered by Article 141 EC. As a result, it has been amended extensively by Directive 96/97.[11] It applies to occupational security schemes which provide workers with benefits which either supplement or replace the statutory social security schemes. It covers the same range of persons and risks as Directive 79/7 but in contrast includes survivors' and family benefits where forming part of the consideration paid by the employer as a result of the contractual relationship (Arts 2–4). Article 6 as amended now provides a list of the provisions considered now to be within the scope of the Directive and thus prohibited where unequally applied to men and women such as in (f); fixing different retirement ages. Further analysis of this Directive would go beyond the depth of most undergraduate courses on EC law and for that reason is not undertaken here.

10.9.2 The Self-employed Equal Treatment Directive 86/613

This provides for the application of the equal treatment principle to the self-employed especially in respect of self-employed women during pregnancy and motherhood. It complements Directive 76/207 to the extent that the matter is not already covered by

---

[11] OJ 1997 L46/20.

Directives 76/207 and 79/7. It entered fully into force on 30 June 1991. It specifically includes farmers and the liberal professions and the spouses of the self-employed where they are not employed or (business) partners of the spouse but who nevertheless engage in the self-employed activities (Art 2). As with Directive 76/207 the principle of equal treatment does not prejudice any measures specifically taken to protect women during pregnancy and motherhood. As with Directive 86/378, further analysis here is beyond the scope of most undergraduate courses.

10.9.3 Parental Leave Directive 96/34[12]

This Directive, which was enacted under the Social Policy Agreement and extended to the UK by Directive 97/75[13] applies the principle of equal treatment to the right to parental leave. It provides that all workers can obtain parental leave of three months to care for a newly born or adopted child up to the age of 8 years. In seeking to claim leave and during leave itself, workers are protected from dismissal. The exact details of the application of the directive requirement are left to the authorities of the member states, including, most importantly, the basis on which the leave is granted and how the time is to be made up by the worker, if at all. There is no reference to pay, nor indeed also whether this individual, i.e. non-transferable right can be enjoyed by a couple at the same time, particularly where both parties work for the same employer. However, it is a welcome addition to the equality laws and to some degree, re-addresses the decision Case 184/83 *Hoffman v Barmer Ersatzkasse*, above, which denied parental leave to a father as a right under Directive 76/207. No further details will be considered here.

10.9.4 Part-time Workers Directive 97/81[14]

This Directive was also adopted under the Social Policy Agreement and was later extended to the UK by Directive 98/23.[15] Whilst not primarily aimed at addressing discrimination of women, the purpose of the Directive which is to remove the discrimination of part-time workers, will inevitably have the potential of helping more women than men simply because more women are in part-time work than men. The Directive also seeks to improve the quality of part-time work and develop part-time work opportunities in a manner which takes account of both employers and workers needs (Clause 1). Clause 4 provides that part-time workers should not be treated less favourably than full-timers unless objectively justified. In allows the principle of pro rata application of time qualifying rules to part-time workers with the clear

---

[12] OJ 1996 L145/9.   [13] OJ 1998 L10/24.   [14] OJ 1998 L14/9.   [15] OJ 1998 L131/10.

exception of pay which has been explored in detail above, e.g. where a full-time worker would take a three months to obtain a particular benefit, a part-timer working half the number of hours would be expected to take six months. Such rules would, however, have to satisfy the requirements of proportionality and not constitute indirect discrimination. The Directive would seem to make it easier for claimants in that any different treatment of part-timers to full-timers appears to be regarded as discriminatory unless justified by the employer.

10.9.5 **Fixed-Term Workers Directive 99/70**[16]

Also first adopted under the Social Policy agreement, this Directive applies much of the same considerations about part-time work to fixed-term work which is defined in Clause 3 as a contract of employment where the end is predetermined by the completion of a period of time or task or event. Under this Directive there should be no discrimination in comparison also with a full-time worker (Clause 4) unless objectively justified. Pro rata application of time based criteria can apply. Where there is no direct comparator, a comparison can be made against a relevant collective agreement or National laws or collective agreements or practice in general. Like the part-time Directive, it is also likely to be of benefit to women more than men because of their prevalence in this type of job and the inequitable pay and treatment they receive in such jobs. The Directive also attempts to tackle the problem of employment by the successive use of fixed-term contracts for the same employee undertaking the same tasks (Clause 5). Rather vaguely, the member states are required to introduce rules to tackle abuse in the issuing of fixed-term contracts after consultation with essentially all affected parties. The legal measures should deal with objective reasons for such contracts and the maximum duration and renewal of fixed-term contracts. The Directive also provides that information be provided to assist fixed-term workers to move into permanent contracts (Clause 6).

It can be seen that the EU is certainly tackling a number of inequitable situations with the array of secondary Community legislation above and to a greater degree than many of the member states. Some of these laws were enacted under the specific Treaty Article concerned with discrimination on the grounds of sex (Art 141), whilst others were enacted either under the general and vestigial law-making power under Article 308 because of the lack of a clear Community competence for them or under the Social Policy Agreement for similar reasons or under worker protection such as the Pregnancy Directive. This does not exactly assist in gaining an overall view of the state of the Community law equality regime. However, a Treaty amendment was made by

---

[16] OJ 1999 L175/43.

the Treaty of Amsterdam which should remove any difficulties with finding an appropriate Treaty base to tackle inequality. This is considered next.

10.10 Article 13 EC: The Expansion of EC Equality Law

The introduction of Article 13 by the Treaty of Amsterdam provided the EC Treaty with a new legal base for the enactment of legislation to tackle discrimination across a range is issues. Take note that the Article does not actually prohibit anything in its own right but empowers the Council to take action to combat discrimination based on sex, racial or ethnic origin, religion or belief, disability, age or sexual orientation. This also has to be tempered with the fact that the Article restricts the Community to acting within the scope of its competences and cannot therefore encroach on member state competences which bearing the mind the still economic basis of the EC and the type of legislation conceived means that any legislation enacted will always be close to the border line between the EU and the member states competences. Also, it is regrettable, that the law-making procedure chosen for Article 13 is the oldest one; the consultation procedure requiring unanimity on the part of the Council and consultation only of the EP. Clearly the member states wanted to avoid excessive EP influence on any matters to be considered under this Article. There are very few articles left requiring this undemocratic procedure. It is to be thankful that directives were issued without little delay under this Treaty Article and before a further ten member states came onboard which would have made it even more difficult to reach the unanimity required for measures under the Article. It can be said though, in contrast with the debate about the reasons for the inclusion of the original Article 119 in the first place, that there is no suggestion that Article 13 was included on economic grounds but instead it is a clear representation of the social concerns of the EU and to be welcomed for this reason. Legislation to combat discrimination has now been enacted under Article 13.

10.10.1 Secondary Legislation Enacted under Article 13

Two Directives were enacted in 2000, which between them and the 2002 amending Equal Treatment Directive, encompass all the matters identified in Article 13 where action was deemed necessary to combat discrimination. It may be concluded that they were enacted remarkably quickly following the Treaty addition of Article 13, however, the types of discrimination covered by them have been of increasing concern within the member states and the EU for many years with many reports and suggestions for action having been produced over the years. Perhaps what is more remarkable is that they were passed relatively quickly by the Council under the consultation procedure whereby Council unanimity is required, which might be argued was influenced by the entry into Austrian Government of the right wing party led by Joerg Haider.

As a consequence of the compromise required to enact them, there are the differences between the Directives in how equal treatment is to be achieved and the implementation periods and exceptions permitted the member states in their application.[17] There are, however, also similarities and both are noted below in this cursory introduction to the Directives which have considerably expanded equality law in the EU.

10.10.1.1 The Racial Equality Directive 2000/43[18]

This was the first directive to be adopted under the new Article 13 EC and seeks to apply the principle of equal treatment to persons regardless of racial or ethnic origin in matters of employment, social protection, education and access to public goods and services, including housing (Art 3(1)). An exception is provided which is similar to Article 2(6) (after amendment) of the Equal Treatment Directive, whereby differential treatment can be justified where a certain characteristic is a genuine and determining occupational requirement (Art 4(1)). The Directive requires the member states to establish a body to promote equal treatment in racial and ethnic and combat discrimination in these areas (Art 13). The Directive should have been implemented by the member states by 19 July 2003.

10.10.1.2 The Framework Employment Directive 2000/78[19]

This Directive, known as the 'Horizontal Framework Directive' because it applies across all sectors of employment, deals with all the other forms or discrimination identified by Article 13 with the exception of the matters covered by the Race Directive above and the Directives on equality between men and women. As part of the justification for the Directive it makes reference to the ECHR as referred to in Article 6 EC. It provides that there should be no discrimination direct or indirect on the grounds of religion or belief, disability, age, or sexual orientation. As with forms of indirect discrimination under previous directives it can be objectively justified providing it is proportionate (Art 4). An exception exists which is also similar to Article 2(6) (after amendment) of the Equal Treatment Directive, whereby different treatment can be justified by a certain characteristic which is a genuine and determining occupational requirement Article 4(1). There is also a special exemption for access to employment in religious organizations (Art 4(2)). There are also further exceptions

---

[17] See the article by Jones noted in further reading.   [18] OJ 2000 L180/22.
[19] OJ 2000 L303/16.

in respect of disability in Article 5 where measures to accommodate disabled persons would cause employers a disproportionate burden and numerous exceptions in respect of age in Article 6. The Directive should have been implemented by the member states by 2 December 2003 but Article 18 gave the member states three further years to implement the provisions on age and disability discrimination. There is not a requirement under this directive to establish a body to promote equality for the matters covered by this Directive in contrast to the Gender and Race Directives.

10.10.1.3 Common Characteristics

Both Directives share the definitions of equal treatment, as being no direct or indirect discrimination (Art 2(1), thus effectively removing any need for a prolonged debate as to whether these concepts are synonymous, similar, overlapping or different. They both then define, as does the amended equal treatment Directive, direct and indirect discrimination as well as harassment.

Neither of the Directives encroach on the existing prohibition on the ground of nationality (Art 12 EC) and do not apply in favour of third country nationals (Arts 3(2) in both Directives). Both contain the objective justification defence as first statutorily defined in Directive 97/80 (Art 4). Both also contain a provision to allow for positive action in support of achieving equality of treatment (Art 4 of 2002/43 and Art 7 of 2002/78). Remedies and enforcement considerations have been provided which are similar to those provided for in Directive 76/207 as amended (Arts 7–12 in 2002/43 and Arts 9–14 in 2002/78).

Whilst, there is quite a bit of overlap and common ground between the Directives, there are also differences, the details of which at this stage in their life would be too great to consider in this work. The Directives have already generated considerable academic comment, some of which is cited below in further reading—no doubt they will also generate considerable and interesting case law in due course.

10.11 The Draft Constitution and Equality Rights

Gender equality and equality generally were issues which was discussed during the drafting of the Constitutional Treaty. In particular, the burning question was not whether they should feature in the Constitution at all but where they should be placed within the Constitution. The Constitution as agreed by the member states on 29 October 2004, contains in the preamble, the equality of persons, as one of the European values, which is then repeated in Article I-2. Article I-4 provides that any discrimination on grounds of nationality shall be prohibited. Article I-9 provides that the community shall recognize the rights, freedoms and principles set out in the Community Charter on Fundamental Rights which is contained in Part II of the Constitution and that the Union shall accede to the ECHR which rights constitute general principles of Union law.

The Community Charter in Part II of the Constitution includes a third title dealing with equality rights in Articles 20–3.

Article II–20 Equality before the law.

Everyone is equal before the law.

Article II–21 Non-discrimination.

1. Any discrimination based on any ground such as sex, race, colour, ethnic or social origin, genetic features, language, religion or belief, political or any other opinion, membership of a national minority, property, birth, disability, age or sexual orientation shall be prohibited.

2. Within the scope of application of the Constitution and without prejudice to any of its specific provisions, any discrimination on grounds of nationality shall be prohibited.

Article II–22 Cultural, religious and linguistic diversity.

The Union shall respect cultural, religious and linguistic diversity.

Article II–23 Equality between men and women.

'Equality between men and women must be ensured in all areas, including employment, work and pay. The principle of equality shall not prevent the maintenance or adoption of measures providing for specific advantages in favour of the under-represented sex.'

Finally, in this review, in Part III of the draft Constitution, Article 108 essentially reproduces the present Article 141.

As set out, the rights provided would appear neither to disturb nor indeed add to the existing provision of equality law in the Community, with the possible exception of Article 20 which could be argued to apply to third country nationals, not presently covered by the Community equality regime.

10.12 Concluding Comments

Whatever the eventual position of equality between men and women in the new constitution and whether the preamble still counts as one of the fundamental European values, the equality of persons, it is certainly the case that from the original and quite limited Article 119, which strictly concerned equal pay for equal work only, EC equality law appears to have developed genuine and comprehensive legal instruments for the combating of discrimination in a range of areas. Quite whether we can yet identify a clear general principle of equality is less discernible. We have also as yet to see how the new directives issued under Article 13 will be used and how these new rights will be received by the courts of the member states and the Court of Justice. The fact remains, however, that they have been included in the Community legal order and that a general principle of Union equality law is now more of a reality than just an aspiration without substance.

Further reading

Books

SHAW, J. (ed.) *Social Law and Policy in an evolving European Union*, Hart Publishing, Oxford 2000.

TRIDIMAS, T. 'The Principle of Equality' in *The General Principles of EC Law*, OUP, Oxford 2000, chapter 2.

Articles

ANAGNOSTARAS, G. 'Sex equality and compulsory military service: the limits of national sovereignty over matters of Army Organisation' (2003) 28 *EL Rev*, 713–22.

BELL, M. and WADDINGTON, L. 'Reflecting on Inequalities in European Equality Law' (2003) 28(3), *EL Rev*, 349–69.

JONES, T. 'The Race Directive: Redefining Protection from Discrimination in EU Law' (2003) 5 *EHRLR*, 515–26.

PRECHAL, S. 'Equality of treatment, non-discrimination and social policy: achievements in three themes' (2004) 41 *CML Rev*, 533.

SCHIEK, D. 'A new framework on equal treatment of persons in EC Law?' (2002) 8 *ELJ*, 290–314.

TRYBUS, M. 'Sisters in Arms: European Community law and Sex Equality in the Armed Forces' (2003) 9 *ELJ*, 631–58.

WHITTLE, R. 'The framework directive for equal treatment in employment and occupation: an analysis from a disability rights perspective' (2002) 27 *EL Rev*, 303–26.

Index